OPEN SOCIETY INSTITUTE
EU ACCESSION MONITORING PROGRAM

Monitoring the EU Accession Process:

Minority Protection

Volume I

An Assessment of Selected Policies in Candidate States

COUNTRY REPORTS

BULGARIA
CZECH REPUBLIC
ESTONIA
HUNGARY
LATVIA
LITHUANIA
POLAND
ROMANIA
SLOVAKIA
SLOVENIA

2002

Published by

OPEN SOCIETY INSTITUTE

Október 6. u. 12.
H-1051 Budapest
Hungary

400 West 59th Street
New York, NY 10019
USA

© OSI/EU Accession Monitoring Program, 2002
All rights reserved.

⌀ TM and Copyright © 2002 Open Society Institute

EU ACCESSION MONITORING PROGRAM

Október 6. u. 12.
H-1051 Budapest
Hungary

Website
<www.eumap.org>

ISBN: 1-891385-26-7

Library of Congress Cataloging-in-Publication Data.
A CIP catalog record for this book is available upon request.

Copies of the book can be ordered from the EU Accession Monitoring Program
<euaccession@osi.hu>

Printed in Gyoma, Hungary, October 2002
Design & Layout by Q.E.D. Publishing

Table of Contents

Acknowledgements 5
Preface 9
Foreword 11
Overview 13
Minority Protection in **Bulgaria** 69
Minority Protection in the **Czech Republic** 123
Minority Protection in **Estonia** 189
Minority Protection in **Hungary** 245
Minority Protection in **Latvia** 297
Minority Protection in **Lithuania** 365
Minority Protection in **Poland** 419
Minority Protection in **Romania** 475
Minority Protection in **Slovakia** 527
Minority Protection in **Slovenia** 589

Acknowledgements

The EU Accession Monitoring Program of the Open Society Institute would like to acknowledge the primary role of the following individuals in researching and drafting these monitoring reports. Final responsibility for the content of the reports rests with the Program.

Bulgaria	Krassimir Kanev	*Bulgarian Helsinki Committee*
Czech Republic	Barbora Bukovská Pavla Boučková	*Counselling Centre for Citizenship, Civil and Human Rights*
Estonia	Klara Hallik	*Institute of International and Social Studies*
Hungary	Antal Örkény	*Eötvös Loránd University*
Latvia	Svetlana Diatchkova	*Latvian Centre for Human Rights and Ethnic Studies*
Lithuania	Eglė Kučinskaitė	*Roma Mission*
Poland	Beata Klimkiewicz	*Jagellonian University*
Romania	Florin Moisă	*Resource Center for Roma Communities*
Slovakia	Balázs Jarábik	*Center for Legal Analyses / Kalligram Foundation*
Slovenia	Darja Zaviršek	*University of Ljubljana*

Advisory Board Members: Minority Protection

Nicolae Gheorghe	*OSCE ODIHR*
Herbert Heuss	*PAKIV Germany*
José Antonio Moreno Díaz	*SOS Racismo*
Gábor Kardos	*Eötvös Loránd University*
Marko Knudsen	*Roma National Congress*
Aap Neljas	*Presidential Roundtable on National Minorities of Estonia*
Anton Niculescu	*Open Society Institute Romania*
Éva Orsós	*Hungarian Ministry of Health, Social and Family Affairs*
Dimitrina Petrova	*European Roma Rights Center*
Iveta Radičová	*Open Society Foundation Slovakia*
Ivan Veselý	*Dženo*
Antonina Zheljazkova	*International Center for Minority Studies and Intercultural Relations*

We would also like to thank the following individuals for their invaluable contribution to the reports by being available for interviews, providing information or research, or reviewing and critiquing draft reports: Judit Bari, Indra Dedze, Ilze Brands Kehre, Agnieszka Gabor, Dezideriu Gergely, James Goldston, Jean Goracel, Denisa Havrlová, Agnieszka Hess, Stephen Humphreys, Valeria Jakobson, Boris Koltchanov, Jana Krimpe, Tanel Matlik, Nils Muiznieks, Kalinka Nikolaeva, Artis Pabriks, Olga Pisarenko, Vadim Poleshchuk, Leonid Raihman, Janja Roser, Matěj Šarkozi, Aleksei Semjonov, Attila Szép, Josif Tyčina, Špela Urh and Timothy Waters.

OSI held roundtable meetings in many candidate countries to invite expert critique and commentary on the draft reports from representatives of the Governments, minority representatives, and civil society organisations and experts. We are grateful to the many participants at those meetings, who generously offered their time and expertise. Lists of the meeting participants are available from the EUMAP (euaccession@osi.hu).

THE EU ACCESSION MONITORING PROGRAM

Rachel Guglielmo	*Program Director*
Farimah Daftary	*Program Officer, Minority Protection*
Katy Negrin	*Program Officer, Minority Protection*
Andrea Gurubi Watterson	*Program Assistant*
Andrea Kiss	*Program Assistant*

Preface

The **EU Accession Monitoring Program (EUMAP)** was initiated in 2000 to support independent monitoring of the EU accession process. More specifically, and in keeping with the broader aims of the Open Society Institute, EUMAP has focused on governmental compliance with the political criteria for EU membership, as defined by the 1993 Copenhagen European Council:

> Membership requires that the candidate country has achieved stability of institutions guaranteeing democracy, human rights, the rule of law and respect for and protection of minorities.

EUMAP reports are elaborated by independent experts from the States being monitored. They are intended to promote responsible and sustainable enlargement by highlighting the significance of the political criteria and the key role of civil society in promoting governmental compliance with those criteria – up to and beyond accession.

In 2001, EUMAP published its first two volumes of monitoring reports, on minority protection and judicial independence in the ten candidate countries of Central and Eastern Europe. In 2002, new and more detailed minority reports (including reports on the five largest EU member States) have been produced, as well as reports on judicial capacity, corruption and – in cooperation with OSI's Network Women's Program/Open Society Foundation Romania – on equal opportunities for women and men in the CEE candidate States.

EUMAP 2002 reports on minority protection and the implementation of minority protection policies point to areas in which minorities appear to suffer disadvantages or discrimination, and assess the efficacy of governmental efforts to address those problems. The reports offer independent analysis and evaluation, policy assessment and recommendations.

EUMAP methodologies for monitoring minority protection in 2001 and 2002 (available at www.eumap.org) were developed by EUMAP with input from an international advisory board. The case study methodology used in five EU member States (France, Germany, Italy, Spain, and the United Kingdom) provides for a broad survey of the legislation and institutions for minority protection, drawing on existing research, statistical data, and surveys on minority issues in conjunction with interviews carried out by country reporters to assess the situation of one vulnerable minority group.

The policy assessment methodology used in the CEE candidate States provides for an evaluation of the special programmes these States have adopted to ensure protection of vulnerable minority groups and to promote their integration into society. The Reports assess the background to and process of developing these policies, as well as their content and the extent to which they have been implemented.

First drafts of each report were reviewed by members of the international advisory board and at national roundtables. These were organised in order to invite comments on the draft from Government officials, civil society organisations, minority representatives, and international organisations. The final reports reproduced in this volume underwent significant revision based on the comments and criticisms received during this process. EUMAP assumes full responsibility for their final content.

Foreword

Minority protection has been a concern of the Organization for Security and Co-operation in Europe (OSCE) since the conclusion of the historic Helsinki Accords in 1975. Since its inception, monitoring respect for the Accords and for the human and minority rights commitments undertaken by OSCE Member States in successive OSCE Documents has been key to its mission. OSCE ODIHR, including the Contact Point for Roma and Sinti Issues, has engaged in case by case monitoring across the OSCE region, combining fact-finding with practical advice in shaping governmental policies for Roma.

The adoption of the Copenhagen criteria by the EU in 1993, which included "respect for and protection of minority rights," *inter alia*, opened another chapter in minority rights protection in Europe. With the adoption of the Copenhagen criteria, the EU joined the OSCE, the Council of Europe, and other international organisations in the endeavour to articulate the content of minority rights, and to press States to respect those rights in practice.

Although the European Union is only one segment of the OSCE framework, it is nevertheless an extremely important segment, with capacity to influence the development of policies far beyond its political borders. Thus there is a critical need to streamline the EU's own standards and practices, and monitoring is an optimal tool to this end.

The monitoring activity initiated by EU Accession Monitoring Program (EUMAP) of the Open Society Institute in 2000 is implemented in the spirit of the Helsinki Final Act. It encourages independent monitoring of governmental efforts to comply with the human rights principles to which they have expressed their adherence. Like OSCE commitments, EU candidate State commitments cannot be "met" once and for all; they must be revisited time and time again, and the role of independent, non-governmental monitors in ensuring that Governments remain honest in revisiting their commitments is key to the health of all democracies. Among EUMAP's recommendations in its 2001 reports were the following:

- Make clear that the political criteria for membership in the European Union are applicable equally to candidates for EU accession and to EU member States.
- Undertake systematic monitoring of governmental policies and practices on a continuous basis throughout the EU and in the candidate States.

As revealed by EUMAP 2002 reports, which have taken up these recommendations by monitoring policies to protect Roma as well as the situation of Muslims and Roma in five EU member States, there are new challenges to minority protection in Europe. Roma in EU member States face similar issues to those that have been highlighted in candidate States; member States must also find ways to affirm their commitment to protection of Muslim minorities, in the context of widespread anti-Muslim public sentiment and Islamophobia.

EU enlargement has drawn one step closer with the Commission's recommendation for the admission of ten new members, yet it is increasingly clear that enlargement will not in itself provide instant or easy solutions to the problems that Roma currently face in both candidate and member States. Indeed, as the OSCE has affirmed throughout its existence, and as EUMAP underlines through its reports, ongoing monitoring is more important than ever. It is the means by which international organisations can press States to honour their human rights commitments, by which States can ensure that public goods and benefits flow to all members of society; and by which citizens can hold their Governments to the highest standard of performance. I particularly welcome EUMAP's attempt actively to involve Roma, Muslims, Russian-speakers, and other minorities in monitoring State minority rights commitments; this is the only way to ensure that these commitments are judged to have been met in practice.

I welcome the EUMAP reports as a contribution to our joint efforts better to define and implement minority rights standards, and to the development of a culture of monitoring in Europe.

Nicolae Gheorghe
Adviser on Sinti and Roma Issues
OSCE-ODIHR

OPEN SOCIETY INSTITUTE 2002

Monitoring the EU Accession Process: Minority Protection

Table of Contents

1. Introduction 16

2. Candidate States: Assessing Government Policies for Minority Protection and Integration 22
   - 2.1 Programme Content 23
   - 2.2 Programme Implementation – Problems of Coordination and Capacity ... 25
   - 2.3 Decentralisation: the Role of Local Government 28
   - 2.4 Evaluation and Assessment 29
   - 2.5 EU Funding to Support Implementation 30
   - 2.6 Minority Participation 32
   - 2.7 Minority Representation 34
   - 2.8 Public Support 35

3. Monitoring Minority Protection in EU Member States – the Situation of Muslims and Roma 37
   - 3.1 Public Attitudes 38
   - 3.2 Protection Against Discrimination 41
     - 3.2.1 Lack of data 43
     - 3.2.2 Discrimination against Roma 45
     - 3.2.3 Discrimination against Muslims 49

    3.3   Minority Rights 54
            3.3.1   Recognition 54
            3.3.2   Citizenship 55
            3.3.3   Minority rights issues for Roma 57
            3.3.4   Minority rights issues for Muslims .. 59

4. The Importance
of Monitoring and Evaluation 62
    4.1   Monitoring by International Organisations .. 62
    4.2   Governmental Monitoring............................ 64
    4.3   Civil Society 65

5. Recommendations 66

Monitoring the EU Accession Process: Minority Protection

1. Introduction

> *The European Union's one boundary is democracy and human rights. The Union is open only to countries which uphold basic values such as free elections, respect for minorities and respect for the rule of law.*[1]

This Overview and the accompanying country reports prepared by the EU Accession Monitoring Program (EUMAP) assess the state of minority protection in ten Central and Eastern European States seeking full membership in the European Union[2] and in five current member States.[3]

The geographical enlargement of the European Union has been accompanied by a parallel enlargement in the understanding of what the Union represents; from an essentially economic arrangement, the Union has evolved towards a political alliance based on common values. In the Community's foundational documents, there was little attention to fundamental rights or freedoms.[4] However, over time, and especially

---

[1] *The Future of the European Union – Laeken Declaration*, available at: <http://europa.eu.int/futurum/documents/offtext/doc151201_en.htm>, (accessed 19 September 2002).

[2] In these reports, the term "candidate States" refers to the ten States in which EUMAP has conducted monitoring – Bulgaria, the Czech Republic, Estonia, Hungary, Latvia, Lithuania, Poland, Romania, Slovakia, and Slovenia – and do not include consideration of Malta or Cyprus; nor does it include consideration of Turkey. References to the situation in specific candidate States in this Overview are generally made without citation; full citations are included in the accompanying country reports.

[3] The situation of Roma in Germany and Spain, and the situation of Muslims in France, Italy, and the United Kingdom.

[4] "The founding Treaties contained no specific provisions on fundamental rights. The credit for gradually developing a system of guarantees for fundamental rights throughout the European Union has to go to the Court of Justice." See <http://europa.eu.int/scadplus/leg/en/lvb/a10000.htm>, (accessed 5 October 2002).

in response to the demands of enlargement, the EU has increasingly articulated its aspiration to represent not only stability and prosperity, but also democratic values, culminating with the adoption of explicitly political criteria for membership at the Copenhagen Council in 1993, including "respect for and protection of minorities."

The immediate consequence of the Copenhagen declaration was that candidate States have been required to demonstrate that they ensure minority protection in order to gain admission to the EU. This has led to intense scrutiny of the situation of vulnerable minorities in candidate States, and triggered considerable activity by candidate State Governments,[5] each of which has adopted a programme to improve the situation of minorities or to promote their integration into society. It has also led to the realisation that the EU's own commitment to minority protection is insufficiently well-developed and inconsistently applied.

The accession process has thus done much to identify problems in thinking about the relationship of majorities to minorities, and to spur meaningful change. Yet the period of candidacy that marked the accession process is, for most States, coming to an end.

On the eve of enlargement, there is an urgent necessity to ensure that the momentum generated by the accession process is not lost. There are some indications that candidate State Governments have viewed their efforts to demonstrate compliance with the political criteria instrumentally, rather than as a genuine and permanent commitment. For example, a Bulgarian official recently observed that candidate State Governments "think in terms of closing chapters, not solving problems."[6] Such attitudes must be answered definitively, and prior to admission; it must be made clear that compliance with basic democratic standards is more than a condition for entry; it is a condition of membership. This will inevitably require a different approach that focuses on the EU's ability and willingness to maintain its focus on minority protection in the post-enlargement context.

---

[5] "The most important result of enlargement is how the parliaments of the new member states have worked day and night to change their legislations, to protect minorities, to [provide] local democracy. This is the most important job of Europe." Romani Prodi, speaking at the Council on Foreign Relations. R. McMahon, "EU: Membership Depends Primarily on Human Rights Criteria," RFE-RL Reports, 14 January 2002. Available at <www.rferl.org/nca/features/2002/01/14012002085048.asp>, (accessed 19 September 2002).

[6] OSI Roundtable Meeting, Sofia, May 2002. *Explanatory Note: OSI held roundtable meetings in each candidate and member State monitored to invite critique of its country reports in draft form. Experts present generally included representatives of the Government, minority groups, academic institutions, and non-governmental organisations.*

Minority protection as a continuing condition of EU membership

As EUMAP argued in its 2001 reports, a comprehensive approach to minority protection should consist of specialised legislation, institutions, and policies to ensure both protection from discrimination and promotion of minority identity.[7] In fact, such an approach has been reflected in the European Commission's Regular Reports on progress towards accession and in the statements of EU officials.[8] Moreover, EU institutions consistently underline the benefits of multiculturalism and diversity, values that imply a commitment to this approach.[9]

Yet even though this is clearly the EU's position, the standards for minority protection require clearer articulation. The Union has not matched the strength of its rhetorical commitment to democratic values and inclusiveness with a comprehensive clarification of the content of those values in policy and practice.

At a minimum, to make it clear that respect for and protection of minorities is a core EU value, the Copenhagen criteria – including "respect for and protection of minorities" – should be fully integrated into existing EU standards,[10] and stronger

---

[7] See EU Accession Monitoring Program, *Monitoring the EU Accession Process: Minority Protection*, Open Society Institute, Budapest, September 2001, available at <http://www.eumap.org> (hereafter, *Minority Protection 2001*).

[8] In addition to the clear EU non-discrimination standards, Commission officials have alluded to EU reliance on international minority rights standards elaborated by the UN, The Council of Europe, and the Organization for Security and Co-operation in Europe (OSCE). For example, when asked to spell out the Copenhagen criteria's description of "respect for minorities," a Commission representative answered that: "the Commission devotes particular attention to the respect for, and the implementation of, the various principles laid down in the Council of Europe Framework Convention for the Protection of National Minorities, including those related to the use of minority languages." Answer given by Mrs. Reding on behalf of the Commission to written parliamentary question by MEP Nelly Maes, 15 May 2001 OJ C 261 E, 18 September 2001, p. 162.

[9] For example, one Commission representative stated that "respect for cultural and linguistic diversity is one of the cornerstones of the Union, now enshrined in Article 21 of the Charter of Fundamental Rights." Written question E-3418/01 by Ionnis Marinos (PPE-DE) to the Commission 21 December 2001, C 147 E/174, Official Journal of the European Communities, 20 June 2002.

[10] The requirement to demonstrate "respect for and protection of minorities" is not matched in internal EU documents binding upon member States. Art. 6(1) of the Treaty on European Union (TEU) defines the principles "common to Member States" as "liberty, democracy, respect for human rights and fundamental freedoms, and the rule of law." Art. 49 TEU makes clear that only a European state "which respects the principles set out in Article 6(1) may apply to become a member of the Union." The EU Charter of Fundamental Rights and Freedoms does not mention minority rights explicitly.

mechanisms should be set in place to monitor compliance with human and minority rights standards by all EU member States.[11]

Beyond this, EUMAP member State reports reveal that the EU framework for minority protection is itself in need of reinforcement and review. First, despite its clear declaration at Copenhagen concerning the obligations on *new* candidates for membership, there is no consensus within the EU as to whether recognition of the existence of minorities is a *sine qua non* of membership,[12] nor any clear EU standard in the area of minority rights.[13] Even if they were applied clearly to candidate and member States, the Copenhagen criteria remain ill-defined, admitting of such broad and disparate interpretations as to render them of minimal utility in guiding States' actions.

Second, although the EU Race Equality and Employment Directives[14] provide clear benchmarks against which States' performance in the area of non-discrimination can be measured, they give primacy to race and ethnicity as indicators, with the result that religion has largely been missing from the discourse on minority protection. Discrimination on grounds of religious belief is covered only under the Employment Directive.

The Union, and its members, must do more to clarify the content of the common values it proclaims. This will not be an easy task. It seems clear that, in part, the EU has not given clear voice to the content of its professed values because of the difficulties in defining them, especially when 15 members with widely varying practices on minority protection – ranging from extensive protections to a denial that minorities legally exist – each have a legitimate stake in ensuring that any common definition is fair. Yet although the scope for choice in adopting particular policies may be very

---

[11] For a recent and forceful articulation of the need for such mechanisms, see J. Swiebel, "Draft Report on respect for human rights in the European Union, 2001, 2001/2014(INI), European Parliament, 27 August 2002.

[12] Member States France and Greece do not recognise the existence of minorities. Bulgaria has expressed some ambivalence on the question. See EU Accession Monitoring Program, *Monitoring the EU Accession Process: Minority Protection in Bulgaria*, Open Society Institute, Budapest, 2001, available at <http://www.eumap.org>.

[13] The European Court of Human Rights recently noted an "emerging international consensus… recognising the special needs of minorities and an obligation to protect their security, identity and lifestyle," but was "not persuaded that the consensus is sufficiently concrete for it to derive any guidance as to the conduct or standards which Contracting States consider desirable in any particular situation." *Chapman v. United Kingdom*, ECHR Judgement, 18 January 2001 (No. 27238/95), paras. 93–94.

[14] Council Directive 2000/43/EC of 29 June 2000 implementing the principle of equal treatment between persons irrespective of racial or ethnic origin, published in the Official Journal of the European Communities, 19 July 2000, L 180/22; Council Directive 2000/78/EC of 27 November 2000 establishing a general framework for equal treatment in employment and occupation, 27 November 2000, L 303/16.

broad, it is not infinite; to the degree that the Union and its members do wish to create a community of shared values, some measure of common standards should be identified that constitutes the minimum that membership requires.

The role of monitoring in defining standards

Equally importantly, the EU still has insufficient means of ensuring member States' compliance with the human rights commitments it is in the process of defining. While compliance with the *acquis communautaire* is subject to monitoring and compliance mechanisms, the fundamental political commitments expressed in the Copenhagen criteria are not considered part of the *acquis*; compliance with the Copenhagen criteria is monitored only in *candidate* States, and upon accession, this monitoring will end.

Yet such monitoring, if continued, would place no unwanted burdens on member States. The Union and its members decide for themselves what values they share in common, and to what degree they wish to bind themselves to a common political model. All Union-wide monitoring requires is that whatever the Union, through its members, agrees upon as constituting its shared values must have universal application. Monitoring may provide an impetus to the articulation of shared standards.

EUMAP's candidate State reports draw attention to the importance of devoting attention not only to the adoption of standards, but to their practical implementation, and to the role of civil society monitors in both prompting greater articulation of standards and in demanding that Governments comply with those standards, up to and beyond accession.

Monitoring is also an important instrument in ensuring that principles are translated into practice. Candidate State Governments have all adopted special programmes to improve the situation for vulnerable minority groups, or to encourage their integration into society more generally. The EU has allocated significant amounts of funding towards the implementation of these programmes. However, there has been little systematic evaluation of their impact and efficacy,[15] and insufficient involvement from minority representatives in their design, implementation and evaluation (see Section 2).

More regular and consistent monitoring is clearly necessary in member States as well, as demonstrated by the experience of Roma and Muslims (see Section 3). Yet existing

---

[15] The European Commission acknowledges that it has devoted insufficient attention to evaluation and monitoring, which it defines as "the continuous process of examining the delivery of programme outputs to intended beneficiaries, which is carried out during the execution of a programme with the intention of immediately correcting any deviation from operational objectives." See *Official Journal of the European Commission*, C 57/12, 22 February 2001.

EU monitoring mechanisms provide for little between silence and sanctions.[16] Regular evaluation – with participation from representatives of minority communities[17] – is vital to ensure that the standards are themselves subject to regular review, and that public policies are operating in fact to protect minorities from disadvantage and exclusion (see Section 4).[18]

Organisation of this Overview and the reports

The remainder of this Overview will examine, first, candidate States' implementation of their minority protection or integration programmes, and second, five member States' laws, institutions, and practices relating to minority protection of Roma or Muslims.

The choice of topic in the candidate States follows from EUMAP's 2001 finding that these programmes have been insufficiently reviewed and evaluated. Because EUMAP is monitoring member States for the first time in 2002, it has adopted the same methodology employed in 2001 for the candidate States, providing for a broad survey of the scope of minority protection in each country as a whole. This will allow for some measure of comparability between the two series of reports, since the present member State reports and last year's candidate State reports all survey the general state of minority protection according to similar criteria within a relatively narrow timeframe.

EUMAP has chosen to monitor the situation of one vulnerable minority group in each of the five largest EU member States to test the strength of their legislative and institutional frameworks for minority protection in general; the situation of Roma was monitored in Germany and Spain because Roma face serious problems of marginalisation and discrimination in both those countries, as in candidate States; Muslims in France, Italy and the United Kingdom constitute a particularly important group for testing States' commitment to minority protection, because of their great

---

[16] Art. 1(1) of the Treaty of Nice, Amending the Treaty on European Union, and treaties establishing the European Communities and certain related acts (2001/C 80/01), amends Article 7 of TEU as follows: "The Council […] may determine that there is a clear risk of a serious breach by a Member State of principles mentioned in Article 6(1) and address appropriate recommendations to that State […] The Council shall regularly verify that the grounds on which such a determination was made continue to apply."

[17] The majority of EUMAP country monitors or monitoring teams included one or more representatives of the minority group whose situation is being monitored.

[18] For more recommendations on the need to strengthen EU mechanisms for monitoring and evaluating the commitment and performance of EU member States with respect to human rights and common European values, see M. Ahtisaari, J. Frowein, M. Oreja, *Report on the Commitment of the Austrian Government to Common European Values*, 8 September 2000, para. 117. See also Comité des Sages, *Leading by Example: A Human Rights Agenda for the European Union for the Year 2000*, European University Institute, 1998, para. 19(e).

numbers, and because their perceived difference from the local majority and the relatively late arrival of their communities in western Europe have contributed to limited levels of assimilation and acceptance. A focus on Muslims also highlights the shortcomings with the Race Directive and with thinking about minorities more broadly, since discrimination against them tends to have a religious as well as an ethnic or racial aspect.

Monitoring such as that done by EUMAP could well address the situation of any discrete minority group, in any (or all) of the EU member States. No system of minority protection – whether at the State or Union level – is adequate if it protects only certain minorities, but not others, or only in certain places, but not universally; therefore monitoring the situation of a particular vulnerable group is a useful way of testing a system's effectiveness and commitment. One of the purposes of this limited project is to demonstrate that monitoring of minority protection on a broad scale is both feasible and necessary for the creation of a Union of common values. EUMAP supports the extension of monitoring to examine the situation of vulnerable minority groups throughout the EU.

2. Candidate States: Assessing Government Policies for Minority Protection and Integration

The Commission noted in its Enlargement Strategy Paper 2001 that "in all countries with sizeable Roma communities national action plans are now in place to tackle discrimination, which remains widespread, and to improve living conditions that continue to be extremely difficult."[19] Several countries with smaller Roma communities – Lithuania, Poland, and Slovenia – have also adopted such programmes, largely on their own initiative. In Estonia and Latvia, the adoption of programmes to promote the integration of large Russian-speaking minorities or non-citizens have been encouraged and praised by the Commission.[20] The very fact that all candidate States have adopted these programmes constitutes not only a response to the requirements of accession, but

---

[19] The full text of the Enlargement Strategy Paper is available at <http://europa.eu.int/comm/enlargement/report2001/index.htm>, (accessed 5 October 2002).

[20] See European Commission, *2001 Regular Report on Estonia's Progress Towards Accession*, Brussels, 2001, p. 24, available at <http:// http://europa.eu.int/comm/enlargement/report2001/ee_en.pdf>, (accessed 9 October 2002).

also a mark of Governments' willingness to take positive action to demonstrate their compliance with the political criteria.

Volume I of EUMAP's 2002 minority protection reports examines the degree to which these special policies and programmes have been implemented in practice. Although the reports focus on one programme in particular in each country, the findings are intended to have wider relevance for the development of more effective minority protection policies in general. Indeed, most Governments have taken initiatives and expend resources on minority communities outside the context of these programmes, although such activity falls beyond the scope of this study.[21]

As these programmes are relatively new, implementation is still at an early stage. Still, even at this point it is possible to evaluate the content of the programmes, their structures and mechanisms for implementation, and the initial results that have been achieved. Moreover, it is precisely at this early stage that it would be most useful to develop more effective ways of ensuring that monitoring and evaluation – both by the Government and the civil society organisations that often partner with the Government – are incorporated into the plan for programme implementation.

Although the programmes vary considerably, several reflect an insufficiently comprehensive approach to minority protection. Common issues affecting implementation are: ineffective coordination, lack of funding, lack of public support, and insufficient commitment of political will.

2.1 Programme Content

Several Government programmes – notably those of Bulgaria, the Czech Republic, Hungary and Romania – reflect a comprehensive approach to minority protection, clearly stating an intent to address discrimination as well as to promote minority identity. In Estonia and Latvia, where the principal target is Russian-speaking populations, Government programmes do not purport to guarantee comprehensive minority protection; instead, they promote societal integration through acquisition of proficiency in the State language.

---

[21] EUMAP reports do not evaluate Government policy towards minorities in its broadest sense, or over an unspecified period of time. Assessment is focused on the special programmes adopted by candidate State Governments in response to the accession process, and their record of implementation through August 2002. It does not attempt to either catalogue or assess all governmental funding that benefits minorities. Thus, for example, State social assistance benefits – to the extent they fall outside the realm of these programmes – also fall beyond the scope of EUMAP reports.

Direct EU influence is evident in the content of several programmes; expert input has been provided to support policy development or the drafting of legislation in Bulgaria, the Czech Republic, Romania, and Slovakia. However, condemnation of discrimination is still largely declarative. Legislative and policy initiatives to combat discrimination are still at an early stage; where they exist, they are still largely untested. Public officials as well as members of the legal profession have not received sufficient training on existing (or planned) anti-discrimination measures.[22] With EU encouragement, Bulgaria, the Czech Republic, Estonia, Hungary, Latvia and Slovakia are all engaged in reviewing their legislation with a view towards ensuring full compliance with the EU's Race Equality Directive. Romania has already adopted comprehensive anti-discrimination legislation and has taken steps towards establishing an institutional framework to guarantee implementation. Slovenia also has fairly comprehensive legislation in place.

Although the protection of Roma culture is a priority for many Roma civil society organisations, this dimension of minority policy is not fully elaborated in any of the Government programmes, though integration is often identified as an objective. In fact, the inclusion of "socialisation" elements in many programmes (Hungary, Lithuania, Poland, and Slovenia) suggests that Roma culture is still identified with poverty, deviance, and other negative characteristics, and is viewed as being at odds with majority society. For example, the Slovenian Employment Programme attributes the marginalisation and segregation of Roma to "different sets of living standards and moral values followed by the Roma…" The "Programme on the Integration of Roma into Lithuanian Society 2000–2004" attributes the persistent marginalisation of Roma to their "linguistic, cultural and ethnic features." The tendency to view Roma values as inherently inferior undermines the respect for cultural difference that is a foundation of multicultural society.

Both of the States with large Russian-speaking minorities prioritise linguistic integration instead of linguistic rights protection. The Estonian Integration Programme asserts that integration is a two-way process. However, its practical measures relate principally to the creation of a common linguistic sphere as a means of enhancing minority integration. Minority representatives have expressed concern that the exclusive emphasis on language does not take into account other barriers to integration in the legal and political spheres. The "Integration of Society in Latvia" Programme also declares support for minority integration and the need to protect minority rights, but does not address discrimination

---

[22] For a general review of judicial training as well as non-technical legal training on a wide range of legal issues, see EU Accession Monitoring Program, *Monitoring the EU Accession Process: Judicial Capacity*, Open Society Institute, Budapest, 2002 (forthcoming), available at <http://www.eumap.org>.

and proposes few measures to promote minority identities. In fact, Latvian officials state that minority protection is not the aim of the Integration Programme.

The ability to develop comprehensive policies is impaired in many candidate States by the absence of comprehensive statistics or other reliable data on the situation of minority groups. The lack of information is often justified by reference to legislation guaranteeing privacy and the protection of personal data. Yet in some cases it is apparent that police departments and other governmental agencies keep at least informal statistics on minority groups and their members, in apparent violation of data protection laws.

However, in many cases, legislation does not prohibit the collection of sensitive personal data *ab initio*; rather, it simply requires that protective mechanisms should be incorporated.[23] Some EU member States, such as the UK, have demonstrated that such data can be collected to good effect, allowing the development of more targeted, effective public policies to improve minority protection, and without violating personal privacy. Appropriate mechanisms should be devised to allow for the collection of ethnic and racial statistics necessary for the conduct of effective monitoring; these mechanisms should be developed and employed in cooperation with minority representatives to allay fears that such data could be abused.

2.2 Programme Implementation – Problems of Coordination and Capacity

Implementation of minority protection and integration programmes has not been comprehensive. In most cases, the bodies charged with responsibility for coordinating implementation are themselves marginalised, working within the constraints imposed by a lack of funding, staff and political support.

Governmental minority protection programmes are policy documents, rather than legislative acts; as such, in most cases the bodies primarily responsible for fully elaborating them and overseeing their implementation are specialised departments within Government ministries. However, these bodies seldom are authorised to do more than compile reports using information voluntarily supplied by participating ministries, and lack the mandate to coordinate the activities of other Government institutions efficiently and effectively.

---

[23] See *Ethnic Monitoring and Data Protection – the European Context,* Central European University Press – INDOK, Budapest, 2001.

In Bulgaria, the National Council on Ethnic and Demographic Issues (hereafter, NCEDI) has been given responsibility for coordinating minority policy generally, and for managing the Government's programmes for Roma.[24] However, the NCEDI has no authority to require implementation from other Government offices. It disposes of little funding.[25] As a result, though on paper the Framework Programme in particular is widely considered to be one of the more comprehensive in the region, implementation has been almost completely stalled. In Romania, the Joint Committee for Monitoring and Implementation has suffered not only from a weak mandate, but also has met only irregularly and often with the participation of lower-level staff not authorised to make decisions on behalf of their respective ministries. The Inter-Ministerial Committee in Hungary can propose that the Government address cases where ministries have failed to meet their obligations under the Government programme for Roma, but can only register its disagreement or disapproval by referring reports to the Government if appropriate action is not taken.

Although steps should be taken to guarantee coordinating mechanisms the support and authority they need to act effectively, the experience in Estonia, where the Integration Programme's Steering Committee appears to enjoy good cooperation from participating ministries, demonstrates that such bodies can be effective without being granted more coercive powers; where the importance of programme objectives are generally recognised at the Government level, administration is more functional and coordination more successful.

Without proper coordination, moreover, even otherwise successful projects run the risk of effecting only temporary relief to long-standing problems. The Czech "2000 Concept of Governmental Policy Towards Members of the Roma Community Supporting Their Integration into Society" is informed by a strong human and minority rights perspective, and offers a solid conceptual framework. However, effective central coordination and support is lacking, and practical implementation has consisted largely of *ad hoc* projects carried out by different ministries at their discretion, often with uncertain or time-limited funding; though some of these projects have posted positive results, their relationship to each other and to the Concept itself is ill-defined. Without coordinated measures to address systemic discrimination and to effect changes at the legal and institutional level, the implementation of such projects as a means of addressing deeply-rooted problems will have little long-term impact; without greater commitment of political will to the Concept, structural changes are

---

[24] The Framework Programme for Equal Integration of Roma in Bulgarian Society, and the "Integration of Minorities" section of the Government's comprehensive program "People are the Wealth of Bulgaria."

[25] Particularly low levels of funding have also been recorded in Lithuania, Poland, Romania, and Slovenia.

unlikely to occur, and bodies of national and local public administration will not take implementation seriously.

In Slovakia, despite recent attempts to enhance the administrative capacity to implement the Government Strategy, coordination of ministries' activity remains a weak point, as there is no mechanism to require their active involvement. Funding from the State budget has been insufficient.

In Latvia, most of the activities implemented under the Integration Programme to date had been initiated before it was adopted. Although mechanisms for administering and funding its implementation have begun functioning only recently, already the lack of effective coordination between various State and non-State actors involved and the lack of a clear implementation strategy are causing problems.

Slovenia's programmes for Roma also lack adequate central oversight mechanisms to ensure consistent funding. Under the general "Programme of Measures," adopted in 1995, the governmental Office for Nationalities is responsible for overall coordination of the Programme. In fact, no ministry or Government body has set aside dedicated funds for Roma programmes, as is the practice for other recognised minority groups. Municipal offices have also suggested that the Office for Nationalities should have more control over funding decisions than individual ministries, which are not as well informed about the situation of Roma, and should be responsible for allocating those funds to the local authorities.

The adoption of special programmes for minorities also raises certain risks. Namely, they may be used as a pretext for the State to divest itself of responsibility to provide minorities with the protection, benefits and services that are due to all. There has been little effort to promote awareness within the Roma community that all governmental policies should enable them to realise their fundamental rights to education, housing and healthcare, *inter alia*. While specialised programmes may be essential to address the specific needs of a minority community, care should be taken that these do not lead to the perception that Roma are not included in general programmes to alleviate poverty or improve education standards.

At the same time, special advisors or bodies to promote minority identity and culture should not be asked to take on social assistance functions. For example, minority self-government representatives in Hungary are sometimes asked to handle questions related to social assistance, though this is properly a responsibility of the local government. Czech and Slovak "Roma Advisors" – intended to facilitate the formulation of local policies and projects to improve the situation for Roma – instead have been placed in the role of social workers, a job for which they have received no training and are thus not qualified.

Though positive measures may be justified to ensure equal access in practice, they must not come to be seen as a replacement for essential State functions. Advisory positions should be clearly defined as such; programmes should always include guidelines for implementing officials and "communications components," which raise general public awareness of programme objectives and of the responsibilities of public officials.

2.3 Decentralisation: the Role of Local Government

In several countries, such as the Czech Republic, Hungary, Poland, Slovakia, and Slovenia the central bodies responsible for developing and implementing governmental minority protection policy lack the competence to influence local public administration effectively. Thus, efforts to enact reforms at the national level – particularly reforms which run counter to popular attitudes and perceptions resistant to giving minority groups "special treatment" may be undermined by local opposition and sometimes by contradictory local policies.

The Czech Republic, Poland, Romania and Slovakia have recognised the importance of integrating local public administrations in programme implementation by decentralising responsibilities and by appointing local and regional Roma experts or advisors. In some cases individuals occupying these offices have managed to raise the profile of governmental programmes, to facilitate better communications between Roma communities and local governmental structures, and to increase awareness of the needs of local Roma communities. However, most work with little institutional support, without clear definition of their competencies, and receive little or no specialised training for their positions. Moreover, following public administration reform in the Czech Republic, the central Government can no longer require the new regional bodies to employ Roma Advisors as it could under the former district system, and the future of this initiative is uncertain. In Slovakia, only a handful of Roma Advisors have been appointed thus far.

In Romania, for example, "Roma experts" were appointed in mayor's offices throughout the country. Many of these experts were selected and appointed on the basis of affiliation with a single Roma political party, through a particularly opaque and politicised process. Others are merely civil servants who have had the title "Roma expert" added to their existing responsibilities, without receiving training or support. A representative from a County Bureau for Roma noted that, "these civil servants do not have any knowledge and motivation to work for solving Roma problems; it is just another responsibility for them."[26] A large pool of qualified Roma candidates, many of whom have benefited from a successful tertiary-level affirmative action programme

---

[26] Interview with V. Gotu, Roma expert, County Office for Roma, Galaţi, 1 August 2002.

introduced by the Ministry of Education, as well as those with extensive experience in the NGO sector, could offer the expertise and initiative needed for these posts.

A decentralised approach to implementing both the 1995 "Programme of Measures for Helping Roma" and the Employment Programme in Slovenia has proven to be an effective means to address the varied and distinct problems of different Roma communities. However, there are several serious drawbacks to a system that devolves most of the programming decisions to local authorities. First, without counter-balancing coordination at the central level, there has been little opportunity to duplicate or build upon successful programmes; too, local officials have received little training or preparation for implementing projects for Roma. At the local level, there is little recognition of the role discrimination plays in compromising opportunities for Roma and many civil servants still express very negative attitudes, undermining constructive relations with Roma communities (and thus prospects for success) from the outset.

Though decentralisation can bring benefits in terms of encouraging local initiative and vesting responsibility in local decision-makers and communities, it should be balanced against the need for the expertise, capacity and authority of a Government-level body. Local officials assigned responsibilities to manage or oversee implementation of special projects to benefit Roma or other minorities should be provided with training to ensure that they are aware of programme goals and objectives; of higher-level political support for the programme; and of the culture and situation of the minority group(s) with whom they are being requested to work. Such training could be prepared and conducted in cooperation with local minority representatives.

2.4 Evaluation and Assessment

Candidate State Governments have evinced increasing support for the importance of regular assessment and evaluation of the minority protection programmes they have adopted.

Notably, while the Hungarian Government has not undertaken any formal evaluation of the present package of measures to improve the situation of Roma, the preparation of guidelines for the elaboration of a long-term strategy has involved substantial public discussion and comment. Moreover, the guidelines adopted indicate that some assumptions underlying the current policy have been challenged and the present programme may be modified following wider public debate and greater input from Roma representatives.

In several countries, lack of concrete progress on programme implementation has necessarily constrained monitoring activities. In Romania, the Government has demonstrated an early commitment to monitoring its own performance in implementation of its "Strategy to Improve the Situation for Roma" with the publication of an internal evaluation report in April 2002.[27] However, the comprehensiveness of the report is limited by a lack of available information on implementation – the report itself was released late due to difficulties gathering data from the relevant ministries.

For governmental monitoring reports to provide a basis for public scrutiny and a tool to increase public awareness of programme objectives and achievements, they must be publicly available. The annual media and general monitoring reports prepared by the Estonian Government are comprehensive, professionally presented, and widely available. In Slovenia, though reportedly some Government implementation reports have been prepared, they have not been made available to the public or to local officials. As a result, their utility for the purpose of improving existing projects and developing new projects on the basis of prior experience is limited.

The Czech 2000 Concept incorporates a requirement for an annual review and Update. This provides a valuable possibility for regular revision and amendment to integrate experience gained during implementation; though the quality of Updates has suffered to some extent from poor or incomplete information received from participating ministries and insufficient capacity to collect and compile the information, the idea of incorporating monitoring as an integral part of Concept implementation is sound. In Slovakia, too, annual evaluation reports are largely descriptive; there are no mechanisms for evaluating the effectiveness of the activities that have been realised on an ongoing basis.

In Lithuania, there is no overview available of the status of tasks being implemented under the Roma Integration Programme; in fact, there is some confusion over the extent to which various initiatives to improve the situation for Roma are related to the Programme.

2.5 EU Funding to Support Implementation

EU support has played a key role not only in prompting the adoption of minority protection and integration programmes, but in supporting their implementation. In some cases, such as Bulgaria, Lithuania, and Romania, implementation has been largely dependent on international funding; governmental funding has been minimal. Estonia, Hungary, Latvia and Slovakia have also received significant EU and other international

---

[27] Ministry of Public Information, "Report on the Status of Implementation," Bucharest, April 2002, p. 4.

funding, but have also committed significant Government co-funding to programme implementation.

In Bulgaria, the EU commended the adoption of the Framework Programme and has commented on implementation in its Regular Reports. However, EU funding for Roma-related projects has not consistently followed the strategies articulated in the Programme, and the observations in the Regular Reports have occasionally lacked the emphasis and specificity that would encourage better adherence to Programme goals. In Romania, however, the EU has backed up its praise for the Government Strategy's decentralised approach by allocating funding primarily to local initiatives and pilot projects fostering partnerships between local institutions and Roma groups. In the Czech Republic and Slovakia, though EU funding has supported implementation of many of the priority areas identified by the respective Governments, little funding has been allocated to address the serious issue of unemployment. EU funding should closely support the objectives that candidate State Governments have been at pains to elaborate.

Prior to the adoption of the Estonian Government's Integration Programme in 2000, the EU had contributed to funding Programme goals for several years. Like the Integration Programme itself, Phare funding has been focused primarily on Estonian language instruction. However, the 2001 Regular Report noted that proper attention and resources should be given to *all* elements of the integration programme, presumable alluding to the legal and political spheres, which have so far been accorded lower priority. As more than three-quarters of all Programme funding in 2000, including Phare funds, was allocated to measures related to language instruction, the EU's own funding priorities should emphasise measures to increase the rate of naturalisation' support for minority media, and other non-linguistic objectives.

In the Czech Republic and Slovakia, the share of Roma NGOs among implementing organisations in Phare projects appears to be particularly low, although the issue has been raised in a number of other countries as well, including by minority NGOs in Estonia. This may be due in part to extremely complicated application and reporting procedures. At the same time, often it is precisely the smaller or more local groups that have the greatest insight into the solutions most likely to improve the situation for Roma at the ground level.

The EU and other international donors should ensure that the selection process identifies proposals demonstrating authentic links to the intended beneficiaries and an understanding of their needs, and that local communities are involved in articulating their problems and addressing them. EU programmes should review their application and grants administration procedures with a view toward simplification and transparency; they should also accompany grants announcements with in-country training and assistants for potential applicants. Availability of this form of assistance is likely to increase in importance as levels of EU funding available to Central European and Baltic States increase.

2.6 Minority Participation

Minority participation in the development, implementation, and evaluation of programmes that are designed to benefit them has been called for by numerous international organisations,[28] including the EU. Minority participation is important not only for its own sake, but for the sake of programme effectiveness. Programmes which integrate minority perspectives and sensitivity to minority needs and concerns are more likely to be accepted by minority communities; projects which involve minorities actively in their development, implementation, and evaluation are more likely to be accepted by majority society and to facilitate integration than alternative measures such as the distribution of charity or social assistance.

Perceptions that Roma deliberately abuse the social welfare system are prevalent throughout the accession region. Programmes placing Roma in leading, management, decision-making roles are important to counter the popular misconception that Roma "prefer to remain on welfare;" "don't want anything better;" "aren't interested in school;" or "prefer to live together," which provide the justification for a whole range of discriminatory behaviours and policies.

In a number of countries initiatives to improve employment opportunities for Roma centre around public works projects. Public works projects constitute the primary source of government-sponsored employment for Roma in Slovenia. Despite the fact that such positions offer neither a steady income nor the opportunity to develop marketable skills, demand for such positions continues to outstrip availability. Public works programmes have been implemented in the Czech Republic and Slovakia as well, but their efficacy as a means of addressing long-term unemployment has been questioned. As most involve some form of manual labour, they tend to target men exclusively; there are especially few projects designed to increase women's capacity to enter the workforce.

Few projects implemented under Integration Programmes in Estonia and Latvia target employment inequalities; initiatives in this area generally focus on the linguistic dimension. Improving workers' language skills is intended to promote greater labour flexibility and mobility and increased employment opportunities. Adequate Latvian

---

[28] See e.g., Organization for Security and Co-operation in Europe, *The Situation of Roma and Sinti in the OSCE Area*, High Commissioner on National Minorities, 2001.

language proficiency is also a requirement for the assisstance of the State Employment Service, as well as for some jobs in the private sector.

In Slovenia, projects where consultation with Roma has taken place appear more successful and durable than those elaborated by local authorities alone, who may be more focused on meeting the needs of the municipality than the needs of the Roma community. Poorly targeted projects offer few obvious benefits to the target group and fail to encourage a long-term shift away from dependence on social welfare or other forms of State support. An evaluation of one project implemented under the EU's Partnership Fund for Roma in Romania also found that there were significant differences in the way in which local officials and Roma partners understood the project goals. The Roma saw the project as a source of direct assistance to participants, while the municipal representatives prioritised the interests of the municipality, seeing training as secondary. Consequently, the Roma participants were dissatisfied with their role, and the official assessment also concluded that the level of Roma participation should have been greater.[29]

In Hungary, little attention was given to minority input when the Government programme was first drafted. However, guidelines for the follow-up strategy place greater emphasis on the active participation of Roma, on encouraging independence, and increasing the future role of Roma-interest organisations in the process of European integration. In line with this shift in priorities, a new advisory body was formed in Summer 2002, directly under the Prime Minister's office; it will include a majority of Roma representatives from both the political and civil-society spheres.

The Estonian Integration Programme drew little input from minority organisations during drafting and there has been low participation during implementation (although there have been improvements. As a result, a clear divide between minority and majority perceptions of the goals and priorities of the integration process persists, and must be addressed in order to achieve mutually satisfactory results. Evaluations – though regular, comprehensive and publicly available – reportedly give little consideration as to how the Programme's shortcomings as perceived by the Russian-speaking community could better be addressed.

In Latvia, although the Integration Programme is based on a Framework Document that was debated widely and revised accordingly, including by minority consultants, direct minority participation as authors was low. Minority participation in implementation has also been low, although there have been recent efforts to involve minority NGOs and civil society to a greater extent.

---

[29] MEDE Evaluation Fiche, "The Establishment of the Ecological Guardians Corps in rural area of upper Timiş, Caraş-Severin county" (PFRO 322), Cluj Napoca, 2002.

Developing political and civil society movements within Roma and other minority communities promise to develop into an increasingly powerful lobby for minority interests; these can help to ensure that Government commitments to the Roma – both as minorities and as members of the broader society – are met. As one Bulgarian Roma leader has stated, "we have one document, the Framework Programme, which showed that we can unite for a common cause." It remains for Roma and other minority representatives to unite around efforts to press for more effective implementation of the minority protection programmes that have been articulated.

2.7 Minority Representation

Often, when Government have sought input from minority communities, they have done so through an official representative. This approach raises a number of difficulties. First, the designation or election of a single representative (or representative body) belies the diversity of minority populations. Second, it perpetuates dependency. Representative bodies are reliant on the Government for political and budgetary support, and are thus less likely to maintain a critical stance. Finally, making access open to only certain representatives, to the exclusion of others, engenders competition and mutual distrust within minority communities.

In some candidate States, mechanisms are in place to ensure minority representation at the Parliamentary or local levels. These measures constitute an important means of ensuring minority participation, but in several countries, Government policy has tended to distort or even co-opt this process, with negative implications for programme effectiveness.

In Hungary, a system of minority self-governments is established through the Minorities Act at both the national and local levels. This system has given rise to internal tensions among Roma groups, due to the fact that the Government has tended to rely upon the National Roma Self-Government as the sole "official" representative of the Roma nationally. The Government has negotiated principally with the National Roma Self-Government when preparing decisions affecting the Roma populations, although other organisations offer different perspectives and opinions. Relying exclusively on one organisation, which is itself dependent on the Government for funding and support, raises the risk that that organisation may be easily controlled. At the same time, an organisation which fails to make substantive or critical recommendations for fear of losing governmental support may quickly lose its legitimacy within the minority community. The Minorities Act should be reviewed to allow for amendments to encourage more diverse representation on national advisory bodies.

In Romania, the Roma Social Democrat Party (RSDP) holds the single parliamentary seat for Roma under provisions granting minorities representation where they fail to meet minimum electoral thresholds. However, in large part due to the Government's exclusive consultation with the RSDP, the organisation has come to be accepted as the sole representative for Roma at all levels, to the point where administrative hiring procedures are ignored in favour of simply accepting RSDP nominees for local civil service posts. According to some Romani activists, the Government's reliance on a single political organisation to represent the entire spectrum of Roma political and civil society organisations has had the effect of fragmenting the Roma NGO Community.

In Latvia, the lack of transparency in the selection process for nomination of NGO representatives (including minority NGOs) to the Council which supervises the work of the Society Integration Fund has been criticised by minority representatives.

Governments should work with minority communities to elaborate more sophisticated mechanisms for minority participation in public life, which would provide for the involvement of as broad a range of groups representing minority interests as possible and feasible. Where single official negotiating partner institutions are maintained for the purposes of facilitating communications between the Government and the minority community, alternative mechanisms for encouraging these institutions to engage in broad-based dialogue with other minority organisations should be devised.

Again, both Governments and minority communities stand to gain from enhanced minority participation in the refinement of policies, identification of best practices, and modification or elimination of under-performing projects.

2.8 Public Support

Policies perceived to have been adopted largely to satisfy EU requirements, regardless of whether they were adopted with good will and honest intentions, do not necessarily reflect a sea-change in public opinion: indeed, EU exhortations to improve the situation for minorities often have drawn resentment from majority populations and politicians as unwarranted and unwelcome external interference.

Broad public support is generally considered necessary for the implementation of any large-scale political programme, but the rapid pace of the accession process has meant that building public support for governmental policy often has been given short shrift in the wake of the broader accession imperative. Measures adopted to comply with economic requirements can be more easily justified by political leaders in terms of the economic benefits that Union membership is widely expected to produce. However, the case for the benefits and advantages to society as a whole of improving the situation for minorities has not been so persuasively made.

Indeed, resistance to the implementation of positive measures to improve the situation for Roma or to promote integration has constituted one of the principal obstacles to effective implementation. For example, in Slovenia, one local official reported that politicians deliberately do not prioritise Roma programmes because the local non-Roma inhabitants would react negatively;[30] similar observations have been noted in Bulgaria, the Czech Republic, Hungary, Lithuania, Poland, Romania and Slovakia. Allocating substantial sums of money to programmes to improve the situation of minority groups – particularly during periods of economic austerity, or when the minority group in question is held in low esteem – without corresponding efforts to build tolerance and understanding among the population as a whole will inevitably meet with resistance, placing such efforts at serious risk of failure.

Resistance to the adoption and implementation of minority protection programmes has emerged not only among the public, but among public officials as well. For example, Bulgarian officials have questioned why Roma have been singled out for support through a special programme, when other minority groups are also disadvantaged,[31] and the Ministry of Education recently cautioned against too-rapid integration of Roma and non-Roma schools, on the grounds that it could provoke a backlash against the minority population and even "lead to further exclusion of Roma living in segregated neighbourhoods."[32]

Public awareness of Government programmes for Roma is low in each of the candidate countries analysed. Few programmes incorporate provisions for promoting increased awareness, either among the target population or society as a whole; those that do have been insufficiently implemented. For example, the Czech 2000 Concept highlights the importance of public discussion, yet the necessary funds and human resources to launch a concerted public campaign to promote the Concept and related activities seem to be lacking. The Office responsible for coordination of Concept implementation has no public relations staff and efforts to publicise the Concept have not been systematic.[33]

Under the Estonian Integration Programme, quite extensive promotional efforts have been carried out, and regular monitoring of public opinion expressed through the media is also an important component of the Programme. These measures have been only partially successful in forging a common vision of integration, however; minority

---

[30] Interview with S. Ličen Tesari, Semič, 30 March 2002.

[31] OSI Roundtable Meeting, Sofia, May 2002.

[32] Ministry of Education and Science, "Organization and government of the activities of the schools of general education, professional and special schools," Sofia, 2002, p.156.

[33] OSI Roundtable Meeting, Prague, June 2002.

and majority society continue to hold quite different views as to the goals of integration and what its priorities should be.

Without sufficient public information, unscrupulous officials can misrepresent expenditures on minority programmes for political purposes. In Hungary, it has been observed that some public officials have emphasised expenditures for the benefit of Roma without underlining that these measures were undertaken to ensure equal access to opportunity in Hungarian society.[34] This approach can foster resentment, and may lead to a weakening of confidence and initiative among Roma communities.

Initiatives to improve minority participation in media organisations are particularly important for shaping more positive public perceptions of minority communities. In Hungary, non-governmental initiatives to promote Roma participation in and access to the media have proven successful. The Roma Press Centre produces news articles and other reportage for distribution to the mainstream media. It has also offered training to young Roma in collaboration with the Center for Independent Journalism, which has also supported the establishment of a similar agency in Bucharest.

Across the region, the lack of authentic political will to develop and carry out effective minority policies can be traced back to the lack of broader public sympathy and support for the common political values and principles underlying enlargement – and thus, perhaps, to insufficient efforts on the part of the EU successfully to underline the importance of these values and principles. EU structures and candidate State Governments must articulate and communicate more convincing arguments that minority protection is a fundamental component of the EU's common values.

3. MONITORING MINORITY PROTECTION IN EU MEMBER STATES – THE SITUATION OF MUSLIMS AND ROMA

More than ever, the European model rests on universal values: freedom, democracy, respect for human rights and fundamental freedoms, and the rule of law. For the most part, these ideals have essentially been achieved. Nonetheless, there is still some fighting to be done, even in our old democracies, to realise them to the full.[35]

---

[34] OSI Roundtable Meeting, Budapest, June 2002.

[35] Louis Michel, Preface to the European Parliament's Annual Report on Human Rights 2001, p. 7, available at <http://ue.eu.int/pesc/human_rights/en/HR2001EN/pdf>, (accessed 18 September 2002).

Volume II of EUMAP's 2002 reports focuses on the situation of a vulnerable minority group in each of the five largest EU member States.[36] These reports reveal some of the same problems evident in candidate States; Roma in Germany and Spain face prejudice, exclusion and discrimination in the same areas, including employment, education, housing, access to public goods and services, and the criminal justice system, as well as barriers to the full enjoyment of minority rights. Moreover, in contrast to candidate States, Germany has not adopted a special Government programme to address those issues.[37]

EUMAP member State reports also reveal a number of new and different issues. The emergence of large Muslim communities in France, Italy and the United Kingdom with different traditions and values – as well as the desire fully to participate in public life – poses challenges to the underlying assumptions of the European system for minority protection, which tends to view minority communities in terms of race and ethnic background, rather than religion.

3.1 Public Attitudes

Although there is great diversity within the population of Sinti and Roma in Germany and Roma/gitanos[38] in Spain, they are viewed as a single group by the majority society. Similarly, though "the Muslim community" is in fact composed of different national, ethnic and linguistic communities, Muslims are nonetheless often viewed as a monolithic group.[39]

In fact, disparate Muslim communities do share certain values and interests, and increasingly identify themselves as a group for the purpose of protesting discriminatory treatment and advocating for certain minority rights. This is also true for Romani communities. The fact that they do so should not undermine official efforts to encourage greater understanding of and appreciation for their internal diversity.

---

[36] EUMAP only examined the five largest EU member States, so this Overview refers primarily to minority protection in these five; obviously, the Program supports the extension of monitoring to cover all fifteen member States, to allow the conclusions drawn here to be expanded upon and refined further.

[37] Spain's "Roma Development Programme" was adopted in the 1980s, and, according to Roma representatives, is outdated and in need of revision.

[38] The terminology as recommended by the Romani Union of Spain: "Roma" as a general term, "Romani" for the singular feminine genitive form, meaning "of the Roma" or "characteristic of the Roma community" and "Roma/gitanos" or "Roma" when referring to the Spanish Roma.

[39] See European Monitoring Centre on Racism and Xenophobia (hereafter, "EUMC"), *Summary Report on Islamophobia in the EU after 11 September 2001*, Vienna, 2002, pp. 23–24.

Both Roma and Muslims are often perceived as foreigners in the countries in which they live[40] – even when they have resided there as citizens for generations, or even centuries, as is the case with Roma in Germany and Spain. As a result, minority policy is sometimes conflated with policies to fight xenophobia or provide social assistance to immigrants or foreigners. In Germany, for example, issues related to discrimination or violence against minorities[41] are referred to the "Commissions for Foreigners' Affairs;" there is no specialised body competent to deal with discrimination and violence against minority citizens or the promotion of minority identity at the Federal level.[42]

Though the majority of Muslims living in France are French citizens, segments of the public continue to consider Maghrebi Muslims – unlike immigrants from other countries such as Italy, Spain and Portugal – to be immigrants even after four generations in France. Perhaps due to the fact that Muslims are highly visible, Italians tend to overwhelmingly associate immigration with Islam, even though Muslims do not in fact constitute the majority of immigrants.[43] In the UK, there has been growing official acknowledgement of prejudice and discrimination against Muslim communities since the publication of a 1997 report of the Commission on British Muslims and Islamophobia.[44] However, Muslim community groups argue that the Government has been slow to translate the official acknowledgement of discrimination faced by Muslim communities into policy initiatives and legislative measures, claiming that the Government is "hot on rhetoric but slow on delivery."[45]

Both Roma and Muslims face prejudice from majority societies. The common perception of Romani communities in both Germany and Spain is negative and widely shared. A 1992 poll indicated that 64 percent of Germans had an unfavourable opinion of Roma, a higher percentage than for any other racial, ethnic or religious

---

[40] The EUMC has noted that "uncertainty about our identity, our belonging and our traditions has led to an increased fear of 'foreign' influences and to a corresponding resistance to anything that appears 'foreign' and different." Statement by Bob Purkiss, chair of the EUMC, and Beate Winkler, Director, on the occasion of the international day against racial discrimination, 21 March 2002, EUMC Newsletter Issue 11 March 2002, available at <http://eumc.eu.int>.

[41] Reference here is made to "visible" minorities, for example Sinti and Roma.

[42] In Italy as well, the situation of Roma and Sinti – the majority of whom (about 70 percent) are historically resident in Italy – has been dealt with by the Commission for Integration of Foreigners.

[43] Christians are the largest group, numbering about 800,000 (48 percent of the immigrant community).

[44] Commission on British Muslims and Islamophobia, *Islamophobia – a Challenge for Us All*, London: The Runnymede Trust, 1997.

[45] Interview with organisation G, London, 6 June 2002.

group,[46] and a 2001 survey revealed a pattern of continuing prejudice.[47] In Spain, Roma/gitanos are seen as resistant to integration, and relations with the rest of the Spanish population are marked by segregation in all areas of life – a "coexistence without togetherness."

A recent report of the European Monitoring Centre Against Racism and Xenophobia (EUMC) noted that media representations of Islam are frequently "based on stereotypical simplifications," and portrayed as a religion and ideology "completely extraneous and alternative to the enlightened secularity of the West."[48] Muslim leaders in France, Italy and the UK all assert that mainstream media tend to rely upon the same sources for information (allegedly, these are often radical or extremist sources that are not considered representative *within* Muslim communities), failing to represent a broad range of views and contributing to public stereotyping of Muslims as a threat to the values and culture of the societies in which they live.[49] According to one French Muslim organisation: "The media has used each incident … to feed Islamophobia and demonstrate that Islam is incompatible with the Republic."[50] Such media practices may contribute to growing Islamophobia and may have the unintended and unfortunate result of strengthening Muslim identity around a shared sense of vulnerability and exclusion from the majority society.

Public officials have a special responsibility to provide leadership in condemning discriminatory attitudes and acts and to counter prejudice. Yet while many have lived up to this responsibility, others have themselves made statements that fuel intolerance and undermine core European values. EU human rights monitoring bodies should assume a "watchdog" role, monitoring official discourse and media reports with an eye towards encouraging responsible discourse by public officials, condemning racist statements unequivocally, and expressing official disapproval when appropriate.

---

[46] 17 percent had an unfavourable opinion of Muslims; of Indians, 14 percent; of guest workers, 12 percent; of dark-skinned persons, 8 percent, and of Jews, 7 percent. Cited in G. Margalit, "Anti-Gypsyism in the Political Culture of the Federal Republic of Germany: A Parallel with Anti-Semitism?" See <http://sicsa.huji.ac.il/9gilad.htm>, (accessed 9 April 2002).

[47] This study was a part of a project, financed by the European Commission, to assess the situation of Sinti and Roma in select EU Member States (Germany, Italy and Spain) and to advise respective governments on policy. Interim report is on file with EU Accession Monitoring Program.

[48] European Monitoring Centre on Racism and Xenophobia, *Racism and Cultural Diversity in the Mass Media. An Overview for Research and Examples of Good Practice in the EU Member States, 1995-2000,* Vienna, February 2002, pp. 252, 262.

[49] See, e.g., E. Poole, "Framing Islam: An Analysis of Newspaper Coverage of Islam in the British Press," in K. Hafez, ed., *Islam and the West in the Mass Media,* New Jersey: Hampton Press, 2000, p. 162.

[50] Interview with the director of *Institut Formation Avenir,* 17 May 2002.

At present, however, negative attitudes and perceptions towards Muslims and Roma continue to colour behaviour towards them and form the context within which legislation is implemented and institutions operate.

3.2 Protection Against Discrimination

Not all EU member States have brought their legislation into compliance with EU standards in the area of non-discrimination, as set forth in the Race Equality and Employment Directives. Moreover, assessing the situation of Muslims living in Europe demonstrates that even these standards are not sufficiently comprehensive; discrimination on grounds of religious affiliation is covered only in the Employment Directive.

Neither Germany nor Spain has adopted comprehensive anti-discrimination legislation.[51] In both countries, efforts are underway to bring domestic legislation into compliance with the Race Directive, but little progress has been made. Even in those States that have already adopted comprehensive anti-discrimination legislation, there are still important gaps. For example, French anti-discrimination legislation recognises and sanctions discrimination on religious grounds, but does not offer a clear definition of indirect discrimination; according to one expert, doing so "would imply referring to [special] categories of the population (which is prohibited by the French Constitution)."[52]

The situation of Muslims reveals that the EU system itself is not comprehensive. The UK's legislative and institutional framework for guaranteeing protection against racial and ethnic discrimination largely complies with the Race Directive, yet there are indications it does not provide adequate protection to its Muslim citizens. Though some religious communities have won protection against discrimination by emphasising the extent to which they also constitute ethnic groups (i.e. Bangladeshis and Pakistanis), this option is not open to Muslims originating from countries in which Muslims do not constitute a majority. Outside of Northern Ireland, the governmental bodies for the promotion of equal treatment operate within the existing legislative framework addressing racial and ethnic inequality; they do not contemplate Muslims or other non-ethnic religious groups.

---

[51] For a detailed comparison of Spanish and German law and the minimum standards set by Council Directive 2000/43/EC, see "Anti-discrimination Legislation in EU Member States," chapters on Germany and Spain, European Centre for Monitoring Racism and Xenophobia, Vienna, 2002, available at <http://www.eumc.eu.int/publications/Article13/index.htm>, (accessed 10 October 2002).

[52] See D. Borillo, *Les instruments juridiques français et européens dans la mise en place du principe d'égalité et de non-discrimination*, (French and European legal tools in the implementation of the principle of equality and non-discrimination), note 3, p. 126.

Moreover, legislation is only a first, if necessary, step. Even in States which have relatively comprehensive anti-discrimination legislation, such as Italy and France, public awareness of the possibility of legal recourse is low and few cases have been advanced through the courts; awareness seems to be particularly low among immigrants and other vulnerable communities.[53] Public authorities in these countries have made some efforts to encourage more effective implementation of anti-discrimination legislation. For example, French courts have sought to facilitate discrimination cases by allowing the use of evidence gathered through "testing."[54] In Italy and Spain, a simplified procedure for filing complaints of discrimination is available.

In the UK, anti-discrimination legislation is complemented by an obligation on public bodies actively to encourage greater equality of opportunity between different ethnic and racial groups through policy development. To ensure non-discriminatory access to public services for Muslims, this obligation should be extended to cover religious belief.[55] As the UK Government itself has acknowledged, "modern local authorities are those in touch with all the people they serve, with an open decision-making structure and service delivery based on the needs of users rather than providers."[56]

Pan-European forums should be organised to encourage the development of a common baseline understanding and interpretation of the shape that national anti-discrimination legislation should take, in theory and in practice, to the extent permitted by differing legal and political traditions. Article 13 of the Treaty on the European Union provides for protection against discrimination on grounds of religion and belief as well as race and ethnic origin.[57] This paves the way for future initiatives to broaden the Race Equality Directive or to elaborate new directives covering other areas such as religion and language. The EU could also enhance its anti-discrimination framework by encouraging member States to sign Protocol 12 to the ECHR, which

---

[53] See I. Schincaglia, *Lo straniero quale vittima del reato (The Foreigner as a Victim of Crime)*, research report funded by CPII, DAS, Office of the President of the Council of Ministers, 1999.

[54] Court of Cassation, n. W 01-85.560 F-D. The technique of "testing," was pioneered by SOS Racisme to demonstrate the unjustified refusal of nightclubs and other public places to allow entry to persons of foreign or immigrant origin. SOS Racisme has argued that testing could be a useful tool for fighting against discrimination in other areas, such as employment and work. See <http://www.le114.com/actualites/fiche.php?Id_Actualite=68>, (accessed 26 September 2002).

[55] This is already the case under the Northern Ireland Act 1998 (NIA), which requires public authorities to give due regard to the need to promote equality of opportunity "between persons of different religious belief." NIA, s. 75(1).

[56] Local Government Association, *Faith and Community*, LGA Publications, London, 2002, p. 3.

[57] Protocol 12 to the European Convention for the Protection of Human Rights and Fundamental Freedoms (ECHR) contains a free-standing prohibition of discrimination.

contains a free-standing prohibition of discrimination, including on grounds of religious affiliation, and by acceding to the ECHR itself.[58]

Moreover, member States, through the EU, should formally embrace and act upon the principle that prohibition against discrimination must be accompanied by positive measures. State officials should be required to seek out ways of ensuring that public services are available on equal terms to all, with special consideration for vulnerable minority groups; opportunities for information-sharing among member States on positive practice in this area should be created. Until such time as States are in a position to adopt comprehensive legislation, they should issue guidelines or codes of practice to give practical assistance to public officials to prevent discrimination in the provision of State services.

3.2.1 Lack of data

The extent of discrimination against minority groups in many EU member States is obscured by the unavailability of comprehensive statistics or other reliable data. As in candidate States, lack of data is often justified by concerns for privacy and protection of personal data. At the same time, the absence of sufficient information presents a clear obstacle to the formulation of effective non-discrimination policy.

For example, there are no nation-wide, reliable statistics about the situation of Roma in either Spain or Germany, or about Muslims in France or Italy – a gap which specialised human rights bodies have encouraged the authorities to fill.[59] For example, CERD has highlighted that the lack of official socio-economic data on the Spanish Roma/gitano population may impair the effectiveness of policies to improve their situation.[60] The Race Directive also recommends the use of statistical evidence to establish instances of discrimination.

The Spanish and German Governments maintain that legal norms on gathering ethnically sensitive data make systematic data collection impossible. In fact, Spanish

---

[58] This recommendation has been supported by a wide range of human rights NGOs, including Amnesty International and Human Rights Watch, in a joint submission to the Convention on the Future of Europe.

[59] The UN Committee on the Elimination of Racial Discrimination (CERD), the UN Committee on Economic, Social and Cultural Rights (ECOSOC), the Advisory Committee on Implementation of the FCNM and the European Commission against Racism and Intolerance (ECRI) have all made recommendations regarding the importance of collecting statistics as a tool for establishing and combating discrimination.

[60] CERD, *Concluding Observations of the Committee on the Elimination of Racial Discrimination: Spain*, CERD/C/304/Add.8, 28 March 1996.

legislation does not prevent the collection of sensitive data, provided that respondents are properly informed and that legal provisions on the processing of data are respected.[61] The German Federal Constitutional Court stated that such data could be collected if the secrecy of the data could be assured.[62] The Government has argued elsewhere that collecting ethnic data on the situation of Sinti and Roma is impractical in any case, as it "could only be achieved with disproportionate investments of time and effort."[63]

Moreover, in some cases such data is already collected on a selective basis. For example, according to the Spanish Data Protection Agency as of 2000 there were 85 public and 60 legally registered private databases collecting and processing information related to the race/ethnicity of subjects,[64] and the laws on elaboration of statistics for community purposes contain few or no limitations on collecting racial or ethnic data.[65] This data is used to design policies for the benefit of recognised "peoples of Spain." Thus the lack of statistical data on Roma/gitanos appears to be due to lack of political will rather than legal obstacles, and constitutes a serious impediment to the development of targeted public policies to address the serious issues of discrimination and exclusion they face.

Ironically, some States have used the lack of reliable ethnic data as grounds for dismissing critiques of their record on providing adequate protection to minority groups against discrimination and violence. For example, Germany has rejected allegations that Romani children are disproportionately represented "special schools" by stating that there is "no reliable statistical evidence to suggest that this group has a lower rate of participation in education… [though] some Länder have reported that in *isolated cases* children of Sinti and Roma have a particularly high level of representation

---

[61] See, e.g., *Ethnic Monitoring and Data Protection – the European Context*, Central European University Press – INDOK, Budapest, 2001, pp. 200–227.

[62] However, it found that existing statistics legislation did not provide a sufficient guarantee. No steps have been taken since 1983 to amend the legislation to guarantee secrecy. See 1983 decision by the German Federal Constitutional Court, BVerfGE 65, 1ff.

[63] Comments of the Government of the Federal Republic of Germany to the Opinion of the Advisory Committee on the Report on Implementation of the FCNM in the Federal Republic of Germany, p. 9. See <http://www.humanrights.coe/int/Minorities/Eng/FrameworkConvention/AdvisoryCommittee/Comments.htm>, (accessed 10 October 2002).

[64] "Distribution of files containing sensitive data, registered in the General Register for Data Protection," *Catalogue of Files 2000*, CD-ROM issued by the Data Protection Agency.

[65] *Ethnic Monitoring and Data Protection – the European Context*, Central European University Press – INDOK, pp. 212–213.

in general remedial schools" [emphasis added].[66] Italy objected to ECRI findings that the number of racist acts in Italy was higher than the number of criminal proceedings before courts, on the grounds that this conclusion was "not enough supported by factual elements, or statistical data,"[67] though such data are not officially available.

In the UK, comprehensive ethnic statistics have proven an invaluable tool for the development of differentiated policies to improve the quality of public services offered to racial and ethnic minority groups. These statistics have revealed that in the areas of education, healthcare, social protection, housing, public service provision, employment, and criminal justice the Pakistani and Bangladeshi communities (which are overwhelmingly Muslim) experience particularly high levels of disadvantage, deprivation and discrimination even in comparison to other minority ethnic communities. On this basis, and on the basis of reports of discrimination from Muslim representatives, additional research and the compilation of statistical data on religious communities in the UK as well as in other member States seems justified. As decisions about how to categorise people reflect political decisions about which patterns are likely to be important, and which groups deserve protection, launching such research initiatives would send a strong signal that member States are committed to the protection of Muslim communities along with racial and ethnic minority communities.

Statistical information provide a solid basis for assessing the situation of minority groups, and for the development of effective public policies to address the disadvantages they may face, *before* they lead to alienation, disaffection and even conflict. The EU should devote resources toward researching, in close collaboration with minority representatives, acceptable methodologies for conducting research while ensuring respect for privacy and protection of personal data; it should also encourage member States to utilise these methodologies to compile more comprehensive research on the situation of vulnerable minority populations than is currently available.

3.2.2 Discrimination against Roma

Despite the almost complete lack of reliable data, EUMAP reports contain abundant anecdotal evidence that Romani communities in Germany and Spain face serious disadvantages in many areas; on the basis of this evidence, more comprehensive analytical and statistical research is warranted.

---

[66] Comments of the Government of the Federal Republic of Germany to the Opinion of the Advisory Committee on the Report on Implementation of the FCNM in the Federal Republic of Germany, p. 13.

[67] European Commission against Racism and Intolerance, Second report on Italy, adopted on 22 June 200 and made public on 23 April 2002, p. 30.

Like their counterparts in Central and Eastern Europe, Romani communities face crippling disadvantages in gaining equal access to **education**. These disadvantages stem in part from poor living conditions and poverty, but severe marginalisation and discrimination also play a role. In Germany, a disproportionate number of Sinti and Roma children are placed in "special schools" for mentally retarded or developmentally disabled children, regardless of their intellectual capacity; graduates of such schools have little prospect of attaining further education or gainful employment. Though levels of enrolment among Spanish Romani children have improved since 1980, high drop-out rates and absenteeism continue to pose serious problems, and few Roma/gitanos complete higher education. Spanish public schools are increasingly "ghettoised," and difficulties in accessing kindergartens and certain schools have been reported.

Both the German and Spanish Governments have acknowledged that inequalities in education need to be addressed. The Spanish Government has developed "compensatory" educational programmes to provide extra assistance for Roma/gitano children. However, some Roma leaders are concerned that these initiatives may reinforce – and at the very least do little to address – educational segregation. Moreover, a lack of central coordination has led to uneven implementation from one Autonomous Community to another.

The German Government has advanced "promoting schools" as a means of equalising opportunities for Sinti and Roma children. In the opinion of Sinti and Roma leaders, many of these "promotional opportunities" are imposed on Sinti and Roma children arbitrarily, and some school authorities acknowledge that "promoting schools" are merely "a new name for an old problem."[68] A number of German states provide support for NGO initiatives to overcome disadvantages faced by Sinti and Roma children in access to education. However, there has been no systematic evaluation of their effectiveness or assessment of "good practices" with a view towards sharing and exchanging these experiences, and no comprehensive policy to ensure that adequate and sustained financial support is committed to successful initiatives.

There are significant barriers to legal **employment** for Roma and Sinti. In addition to the disadvantage of generally low levels of education and training, they appear to face strong prejudices in hiring and at the workplace. Many Romani families are engaged in a combination of formal and informal employment, in jobs considered undesirable by the rest of the population, such as street-vending, solid waste collection, or seasonal work. Although there has been no systematic research on the subject, German and Spanish Romani leaders and human rights organisations concur that discrimination against Roma in the labour market is a daily reality. Employment offices in Spain report that many companies openly refuse to employ Romani applicants. According to

---

[68] OSI Roundtable Meeting, Hamburg, April 2002.

one representative of a special employment programme for Roma, "in five cases out of ten the employers tell me directly that they do not want Roma."[69] In neither Germany nor Spain are complaints of discrimination brought to court and there is little case-law in this area in either country.

Governmental response to employment issues affecting the Spanish Romani community have been framed in terms of clichés and generalisations about lack of skills and different cultural attitudes towards work among Roma/gitano communities; little consideration has been given to the role played by racial discrimination, and as a result few strategic policy responses to the reality of discrimination have been developed. One encouraging development is "Acceder," an EU-supported programme, which for the first time includes the Romani community as a special target group for the operative programmes of the European Social Fund.

Public authorities in some German states have made attempts to reduce high levels of unemployment among Sinti and Roma through various job-creation projects; however, the effectiveness of these projects has been limited. As in the area of education, there has not been any large-scale evaluation or assessment of successful job-creation projects with a view towards exchanging experiences to identify positive practices. Doing so could support the development of more systematic policy measures to alleviate the disadvantages faced by Sinti and Roma on the labour market.

The majority of Roma live in sub-standard **housing**, often in segregated shantytowns (in Spain) or settlements (in Germany) on the outskirts of urban centres, with minimal infrastructure, and often in conditions that pose serious **health** risks. Discrimination in access to public and private housing as well as other **goods and services** has been reported from both Germany and Spain. Advertisements for apartments to let that stipulate "no foreigners," "no Arabs," "no gitanos" or "no people from the East," are common in central Madrid and other big cities in Spain, and recent polls indicate persistent support for segregation: many non-Roma assert that that "[Roma] should live separately," "should not be allocated housing in our districts," or "should be expelled from the country."[70] In one 1994 survey, about 68 percent of Germans stated that they did not wish to have Sinti and Roma as neighbours.[71]

---

[69] Interview with a Romani woman who works in an employment office, anonymity requested, December 2001.

[70] T. C. Buezas, as cited by A. Piquero, "Received Worse than People from Maghreb," *G. El Comercio*, 10 April 2000.

[71] Cited in D. Strauss, "Anti-Gypsyism in German Society and Literature" in S. Tebbutt, ed., *Sinti and Roma: Gypsies in German-Speaking Society and Literature,* Berghahn Books, Oxford, 1998, p. 89.

The German Government has both acknowledged the need and confirmed the intention to improve the living conditions of Sinti and Roma and to promote their integration into society, and some *Länder* have initiated successful re-housing projects.[72] German Roma and Sinti representatives emphasise that most successful projects involve them directly in the decision-making process, and call for the integration of *ad hoc* projects into a broader and more comprehensive governmental housing policy to address widespread segregation.

In Spain, there were attempts in the 1980s and 1990s to eradicate segregated shantytowns by moving Roma/gitanos into "transitional" housing, consisting of basic (and sometimes sub-standard) buildings, often on the periphery of urban centres, as an interim step to full integration in mixed neighbourhoods. In the short term, though the policy did little to address patterns of marginalisation and segregation, the transfer of thousands of families from shanties to flats with water, electricity and sanitary facilities constituted an undeniable improvement.

However, the transfer was not conceived of or implemented as part of a long-term policy, and there is no central body to coordinate its implementation. Though this has granted local authorities great flexibility and discretion to design policies responsive to local conditions, and some have designed successful integration policies, it has also meant that there has been little or no coordinated exchange of positive and negative experiences among communities, and little evaluation or assessment. Solutions which were initially improvised to deal with crisis situations threaten to become permanent: as of August 2002, thousands of Roma are living in transitional housing, without any indication of when the transition period will end.

Like German Sinti and Roma, Spanish Romani leaders claim that the failure significantly to improve the housing situation is a direct result of State authorities' failure to secure their active participation in programme development and implementation. Moreover, there has been a tendency to displace responsibility for addressing housing problems to NGOs, which – particularly in the absence of a comprehensive State policy – lack the necessary authority and expertise to deal with problems of this scale systematically or effectively.

There are no national statistics or studies on the **health** situation of Romani communities in either Germany or Spain. However, data gathered at the regional or local level in Spain and abundant anecdotal evidence from both countries suggest that Roma suffer from lower life expectancy, a higher incidence of disease and illness, and

---

[72] See, P. Widmann, *An den Rändern der Städte. Sinti und Jenische in der deutschen Kommunalpolitik (On the Margins of Cities. Sinti and Jenishes in German Social Policy)*, Metropol, Berlin, 2001.

greater difficulty in accessing health services than the majority.[73] Roma in both Germany and Spain allege that healthcare personnel are often insensitive to their distinct cultural traditions and attitudes, which is a contributing factor to their under-utilisation of primary and preventive healthcare services and over-reliance on emergency services; in Germany, there is a legacy of mistrust for healthcare institutions dating back to the Nazi-era medical experimentation on Sinti and Roma.

The direct consequence of the almost complete lack of information in this area is that no specific Government programmes or policies exist in either country to address the serious health issues that Romani communities clearly confront. As a first step, there should be systematic attempts to confront widespread long-standing suspicion and mistrust toward healthcare providers among Roma communities. Health mediator projects implemented in a number of Central and East European countries, including Romania, might provide an example to be emulated. In Spain, State support for Romani health programmes focuses on AIDS, substance abuse or mental disorders – a selection that Romani leaders have criticised as inopportune and prejudiced.

The most troubling manifestation of discriminatory attitudes, of course, is **racially motivated violence,** which has been on the rise in both Germany and Spain. The effects of such violence are exacerbated by persistent and widespread allegations of discrimination in the **criminal justice system,** including ill-treatment and harassment by law enforcement officers. Despite the seriousness of these allegations, which have been made by several international monitoring organisations with regard to both countries, German legislation does not stipulate either enhanced sentencing for crimes committed with racial motivation, or specific sentencing enhancements for racially motivated crimes perpetrated by law enforcement officers. Moreover, the award of legal aid is based on the likelihood of a successful outcome. Though the Spanish Penal Code prohibits incitement to racially motivated discrimination, hatred, or violence, and stipulates sentencing enhancement for offences committed with a racial motivation, these provisions have been applied extremely rarely.

3.2.3 Discrimination against Muslims

As noted above, it is often difficult to substantiate the extent of discrimination against Muslims, as little data has been collected using religion as an indicator. However, the experience of Muslims in the UK may prove useful: many British Muslims arrived as immigrant workers several generations ago. It is only after several decades and the compilation of extensive ethnic and racial statistics indicating higher levels of

---

[73] See, e.g., J. F. Gamella, *The Roma Population in Andalucia*, Junta de Andalucia, Sevilla, 1996, p. 171.

disadvantage among predominantly Muslim Bangladeshi and Pakistani communities that awareness of religious discrimination and the need for targeted policies to address it has become increasingly apparent. Collecting differentiated data about the situation of Muslim communities in the UK as well as in other EU countries would allow policy-makers in those countries actively to develop effective two-way integration policies before problems emerge.

Patterns of segregation of Muslim children in **education** have been noted in some towns and cities in the UK, and are considered to have been one of the key contributing factors to serious rioting in Bradford, Burnley, and Oldham in the Summer of 2001.[74] The European Commission against Racism and Intolerance (ECRI) has raised concerns regarding the separation of foreign children or children or immigrant background in specialised education courses and certain districts and schools in France as well.[75]

There are still comparatively few immigrant children in the Italian education system, but patterns of lower than average attendance and achievement, and higher drop-out rates are already emerging, which the Government is seeking to address through the employment of "cultural and linguistic mediators" to assist and support teachers working with large numbers of foreign students.[76] The "linguistic mediator" is usually an adult of the same nationality as foreign students, who has the task of helping them adjust to school and easing relations between the school and the family. "Cultural mediators" assist teachers of publicly funded literacy and integration classes for foreign adults.[77]

However, no differentiated data are available to indicate the situation of Muslim children in particular in either France or Italy. In light of ethnic statistics in the UK, indicating that pupils from the Pakistani and Bangladeshi communities perform less well than other pupils at all stages of compulsory education, the collection of such data might be advisable in order to fashion effective education policy.

---

[74] Report of the Ministerial Group on Public Order and Community Cohesion, *Building Cohesive Communities*, London: Home Office, 2001; Report of the Independent Review Team chaired by Ted Cantle *Community Cohesion*, London: Home Office, 2001

[75] See European Commission against Racism and Intolerance, Second report on France, adopted on 10 December 1999 and made public on 27 June 2000, paras. 21–22; 44. The French Government acknowledged that "the phenomenon of disproportionate representation of disadvantaged categories of the population does exist," though it objected to ECRI's use of the term "separation."

[76] *Programmatic Document regarding state policy towards immigration and foreigners in the territory of the state,* on the basis of Art. 3 of Law 1998/40: 2001–2003, p. 50.

[77] These classes are offered at specially established *Centri Territoriali Permanenti* (Permanent Territorial Centres) for the education and training of adult immigrants. The Centres are established and receive state funding on the basis of O.M. 455/97.

British and French Muslims also report unfair treatment as a result of educational policies and practices that are insufficiently sensitive to their background and culture.[78] In France, for example, it is considered an important function of public educational institutions to impart Republic values, including *laïcité* (secularism). This has led to tensions when Muslim students have asserted their right to wear veils, revealing the difficulties inherent in balancing the requirements of *laïcité* and other Republic values – which largely accord with the values of the majority – against the cultural of Muslims; similar difficulties arise whenever the cultural assumptions of a minority group differ from those of the majority.

UK Home Office research shows that compared to other faith communities Muslims report the highest levels of unfair treatment in the area of **employment**.[79] Moreover, ethnic statistics show that lower rates of economic activity and employment and higher rates of unemployment are recorded among Pakistani and Bangladeshi Muslims than other ethnic minority groups.[80] Although no detailed statistics regarding discrimination against particular ethnic or religious groups is available in France, French temporary employment agencies report receiving specific requests from companies not to send Muslim workers, and in fact French Muslims report discrimination in hiring and at the workplace more frequently than in any other area, though few legal complaints are filed. There is no data to show that Muslims are particularly disadvantaged compared to other immigrants in Italy, most of whom work either in unskilled positions, seasonal occupations or illegal jobs, often with insufficient access to social protection.

The Employment Directive requires member States specifically and explicitly to prohibit direct and indirect religious discrimination in employment. It will thus require employers to monitor their employment decisions on the basis of religious affiliation in order to ensure that a policy, practice, provision or criterion does not have the unintended effect of disadvantaging Muslims or employees of any other faith. The Directive also requires measures to ensure effective implementation through dissemination of information, social dialogue, and dialogue with non-governmental organisations;[81] legislation will need to be complemented by practical guidelines to inform job-seekers, employers, and the broader public of their rights and responsibilities.

---

[78] P. Weller, A. Feldman, K. Purdam, *Religious Discrimination in England and Wales: Home Office Research Study 220*, Home Office, London, 2001, pp. 23–36.

[79] P. Weller, A. Feldman, K. Purdam, *Religious Discrimination in England and Wales: Home Office Research Study 220*, Home Office, London, 2001, pp. 37–50.

[80] Performance and Innovation Unit, *Improving labour market achievements for ethnic minorities in British Society*, Cabinet Office, London, 2001, p. 40.

[81] EU Framework Employment Directive, Arts. 12–14.

Immigrants in general appear to experience widespread discrimination in access to both public and private **housing** as well as other goods and services. Statistics collected on the basis of ethnicity in the UK reveal that particular disadvantage is experienced by the Muslim Pakistani and Bangladeshi communities. Though there has been little research on the situation of Muslims in particular, a number of studies in France have revealed that racial or ethnic discrimination is common in the process of screening and selecting applicants for subsidised public housing in particular,[82] as well as in the private housing market. In both France and Italy, there have been reports of public housing officials routinely allocating public housing on the basis of discriminatory evaluations of applicants presumed to be of foreign origin.[83] In Italy, this practice has been successfully challenged in court in at least one case, but awareness of legal provisions remains low among immigrant communities, and statistics from recent research demonstrate that the availability of public housing available to immigrants is very low compared to Italian and EU citizens.[84] Moreover, the housing which is made available of often of inferior quality.[85]

The failure of public service providers to take their needs into account in service delivery is a common and key concern expressed by many Muslim community groups in the UK. The lack of information and statistics about the experience of Muslims presents a significant obstacle to developing policies and ensuring service delivery appropriate to British, French and Italian Muslim communities.

Little research is available on the specific treatment of Muslim patients in the French public **healthcare** system, including in public hospitals, though anecdotal evidence suggests that Muslims commonly experience lack of comprehension and appreciation for distinct cultural and religious practices and requirements when accessing health services. Documented inequalities in **health** outcomes between different minority groups suggest that health service providers fail to reach Muslim communities or to meet their needs;[86] three-quarters of Muslim organisations in a Home Office study

---

[82] Note published by GELD on social housing, *Note 3*, 10 May 2001, "Les discriminations raciales et ethniques dans l'accès au logement social" (Racial and ethnic discriminations in the access to social housing") under the direction of Patrick Simon (hereafter GELD, *Note 3*). See <http://www.sos-racisme.org/presse/notegeld.htm>, (accessed 25 September 2002).

[83] Trib. Milano, 20 March 2002, Dr.ssa Paola Gandolfi, in the case *El Houssein, El Mouden, Zerai v. the Comune di Milano*, unpublished. On file with EUMAP.

[84] See Rete d'urgenza contro il razzismo, *Annual Report 2000*, pp. 16–21, at <http://www.unimondo.org/reteurg/ra00it.zip>, (accessed 18 September 2002).

[85] See Rete d'urgenza contro il razzismo, *Annual Report 2000*, pp. 8–36, at <http://www.unimondo.org/reteurg/ra00it.zip>, (accessed 18 September 2002).

[86] Social Exclusion Unit, *Minority Ethnic Issues in Social Exclusion and Neighbourhood Renewal*, London: Cabinet Office, 2000, para. 2.39, which cites the example of sexual health services that do not meet the needs of minority communities.

reported unfair treatment from social services staff and from practices in social services departments.[87]

Given the tendency among member State populations to associate Muslims with "foreign" elements in their societies and to view Islam as monolithic (see above), the events of 11 September 2001 provoked an increased association of Islam with terrorism and fundamentalism. There was a surge in harassment and **violence** directed at Muslims and those perceived to be Muslim after 11 September 2001 in many EU countries, including Italy and the UK.[88] While the number of racist acts in France actually decreased overall in 2001,[89] many of those that did take place were linked with 11 September.

According to British and French Muslim leaders there is a growing perception in Muslim communities that they are being stopped, questioned, and searched not on the basis of evidence and reasonable suspicion but on the basis of "looking Muslim." Studies of the **criminal justice system** in the UK also show differences in sentencing and imprisonment between black and white people.[90] There are also indications of inequalities in the justice system in France. For example, though systematic data has not been collected and it is impossible to isolate a religious motivation, there appears to be a pattern of discrimination in sentencing, with individuals whose ethnic origin (or supposed ethnic origin) is not French receiving longer sentences for similar crimes.[91] Law enforcement agencies should look to foster good relations with Muslim communities, as a way of decreasing mistrust and suspicion; doing so would also have the positive side-effect of providing police with assistance in fighting crime and gathering intelligence.

---

[87] P. Weller, A. Feldman, K. Purdam, *Religious Discrimination in England and Wales: Home Office Research Study 220,* Home Office, London, 2001, p. 72.

[88] C. Allen, J.S. Nielson, *Summary Report on Islamophobia in the EU after September 11 2001*, Vienna: European Centre on Racism and Xenophobia, May 2002, pp. 23, 28–29; Islamic Human Rights Commission, *UK Today: The Anti-Muslim Backlash in the Wake of 11th September 2001*, Islamic Human Rights Commission, London, 2001.

[89] Sixty-seven racist acts were recorded in 2001, compared to 146 in 2000. CNCDH Report 2001, published in March 2002.

[90] The Runnymede Trust Commission the Future of Multi-Ethnic Britain, *The Future of Multi-ethnic Britain – The Parekh Report*, Profile Books, London, 2000, p. 130.

[91] Discussion with Hanifa Chérifi, "Les musulmans victimes de discriminations. Une inégalité entre les religions" (Muslim victims of discrimination. Inequality between religions,) J-M. Blier, S. de Royer, *Discriminations raciales, pour en finir*, 2001, Paris, éditions Jacob-Duvernet, p. 62.

In response to post-September 11 violence, the UK has adopted legislation making religious motivation for some violent offences a separate offence,[92] and racial or religious motivation as an aggravating factor in sentencing for all offences.[93] In France and Italy, reports indicate that Arab, Muslim and immigrant communities appear to be subject to violence, it is difficult to isolate a religious motivation.[94] In France, however, racist violence clearly often has a religious dimension: places of worship (including both mosques and synagogues) are often the target of attacks, stone-throwing, and partial or total destruction. Training should be provided to law enforcement officials on policing issues arising from "religious" hate crimes, and monitoring of implementation and enforcement should be initiated in all member States.

3.3 Minority Rights

3.3.1 Recognition

Many member States have adopted restrictive definitions of "minority," creating a hierarchy of protection among different groups. In Italy, for example, a full range of minority rights is guaranteed to traditional national minority groups, such as the French, German and Slovenian minorities. Both Muslims and Roma – arguably two of the most vulnerable groups in the country – are excluded.[95] Roma/gitanos are not recognised as a *pueblo* (a constituent people of Spain), and therefore are treated less favourably than other minority groups in various spheres of economic, political and social life. In Germany, Sinti/Roma are a recognised minority group, along with Danes, Frisians, and Sorbs, but Muslims are not. In the UK, the Government has adopted an inclusive definition of national minority,[96] which however excludes Muslims and members of other faith communities from access to minority rights. The

---

[92] Crime and Disorder Act 1998, s. 28–32 as amended by the Anti-terrorism, Crime and Security Act 2001, s. 39.

[93] Powers of Criminal Courts (Sentencing) Act 2000, s. 153 as amended by the Anti-Terrorism, Crime and Security Act 2001, s. 39.

[94] See recent ECRI recommendation against attacks against Muslims in Europe after September 11 at
<http://www.coe.int/T/E/Communication_and_Research/Press/Themes_files/Combating_racism/e_ECRI_Rec5.asp#TopOfPage>, (accessed 18 September 2002).

[95] However, the almost complete lack of data in Italy makes it difficult to distinguish between disadvantages experienced by Muslims and disadvantages experienced by immigrants in general. See Section 3.2.1.

[96] See Advisory Committee on the Framework Convention for the Protection of National Minorities, *Opinion on the United Kingdom*, Strasbourg, 2001, para. 14.

concept of minority is not seen as relevant in France; the existence of minorities is seen as a threat to the Republican model, which aims to guarantee equal treatment for all. Though French Muslim representatives have not challenged this model, a consensus is emerging among them that they, as a group, are treated differently from other religious minorities.[97]

As a body which explicitly advances respect for and protection of minorities *vis-à-vis* third countries, and has set this as a requirement for new members, the demands of internal consistency require the EU to devote attention to working out a common definition of minority within the EU context and encouraging all member States to frame minority protection legislation and policies accordingly. This definition should be subject to regular review and evaluation, to account for and accommodate the emergence of new minority groups.

3.3.2 Citizenship issues

The majority of Muslims living in the UK are citizens, many of them second or third generation. By contrast, large numbers of Muslims living in France have become citizens only in the past decade or are non-citizens, and the majority of Muslims living in Italy have not obtained citizenship. Both "new minorities" and non-citizens have been excluded from minority rights regimes.

Non-citizens are particularly vulnerable in a number of important ways: they are prone to accept illegal work, without regulation or protection; they are often segregated in cheap, poor-quality housing districts and neighbourhoods; they face discrimination and violence; and with uncertain legal status and low awareness of their rights under the law, many fear rather than trust law enforcement authorities and other public officials. The rights and obligations of non-citizens generally fall under different legal regimes (i.e. outside of traditional regimes for minority protection), an in-depth examination of which falls beyond the scope of these reports.[98] However, it is generally acknowledged that basic human rights and protections must be accorded to all, regardless of citizenship status. Some States, such as Italy, have responded to the presence of large numbers of non-citizens by adopting special legislation to underline

---

[97] OSI Roundtable Meeting, Paris, July 2002.

[98] Though EUMAP reports have focused on the rights of Roma citizens in Germany and Spain, it should be noted that there are also large numbers of Roma refugees and asylum-seekers in these and other EU member States.

that protection against discrimination and violence is included among these basic rights and protections.[99]

There is increasing recognition that Muslim immigrants (including "temporary workers," asylum-seekers, and migrant workers) are in Europe to stay, and moreover that Europe's economies are increasingly reliant upon immigrant labour. Their different cultural and religious backgrounds, languages and values are already transforming the appearance and character of many EU member States, such as Italy and Spain, which were relatively homogeneous until quite recently.

Most member States have acknowledged that citizenship is a key step in the integration process, and have taken steps to facilitate naturalisation for immigrant workers and their families. Large numbers of French Muslims have obtained citizenship in the past decade, and a similar surge in the number of Muslim citizens can be expected in Italy. As more and more Muslims become citizens, the demand for traditional minority rights related to education, language, media, and particularly political participation is likely to grow.

The transformation of EU member States into multi-cultural and multi-faith societies raises new challenges to the existing legal regime for minority protection. Integration must be a two-way process, requiring not only the adaptation of new groups to European cultural and social environments, but also a guarantee of equal treatment and protection against discrimination as well as of respect for their distinct identities. Increasing sophistication in integration policy would benefit other marginalised groups, such as Sinti and Roma, whose culture, language and history has been undervalued and left on the side for centuries.[100]

Although it is clearly within a State's competence to determine which groups will receive recognition and when, the EU should encourage member States to adopt more expansive and inclusive definitions of "minority," thus extending minority rights to non-traditional groups. It should also work to articulate a minimum standard of equal treatment to those groups which do not fit within the definitions adopted. Member

---

[99] *Decreto legislativo 25 luglio 1998, n. 286 Testo unico delle disposizioni concernenti la disciplina dell'immigrazione e norme sulla condizione dello straniero* (Law on Immigration and the Legal Status of Foreigners), Chapter IV (hereafter, "Law 286/1998"). However, Law 286/1998 was amended on 11 July 2002, introducing a number of significant and controversial changes, including a provision requiring all immigrants who apply for a residence permit to be finger-printed (which has now been extended to citizens as well); reducing the validity of residency permits from three to two-year periods, tightening regulations on family reunification so as to exclude children over 18 years of age, and loss of one's job resulting in a loss of one's residency permit.

[100] For example, the legacy of past legislation (no longer in force) banning Roma/gitano customs, dress and language is that the Caló language has almost been lost.

States should also take steps to facilitate access to citizenship for non-citizen populations.

3.3.3 Minority rights issues for Roma

Romani communities in Germany and Spain have received very limited State support for the purpose of protecting and promoting their distinct cultural and linguistic identities; in some areas, State practice has actually discouraged the development of minority rights for Roma. Particularly when contrasted with generous treatment of certain other minority groups, less favourable treatment of Roma itself constitutes a form of discrimination.

For example, though the languages of numerous other minority groups are recognised and may be used extensively in the public sphere, Caló, the language of the Spanish Roma, is not legally recognised anywhere in Spain, nor is it recognised by the State as a protected language under the European Charter for Regional or Minority Languages (CRML).[101] Though very few Roma/gitanos speak Caló as a mother tongue, it plays an extraordinarily important role as a unifying ethnic symbol; in the political context, recognition of language is essential for recognition of minority identity, which is key to recognition of the political rights of a group.[102] Thus, the survival of Caló is of great importance to the Romani community, and Roma leaders have repeatedly requested Government assistance for promoting its study and use.[103] Especially in light of historical persecution of Romani communities for the use of Caló, *inter alia*,[104] it would seem appropriate for the State to acknowledge past injustice by supporting these requests.

As of August 2002, Hesse remains the only German state that has accepted all 35 points required for implementing Part III of the CRML, despite the fact that the Romani language "is spoken in most of the *Länder* of the Federal Republic of

---

[101] Council of Europe, *List of Declarations Made with Respect to Treaty no. 148, European Charter for Regional or Minority Languages,* Complete chronology on 18 May 2002. Spain recognised as regional or minority languages the official languages recognised as such in the Autonomy Statutes of the Basque Country, Catalonia, Balearic Islands, Galicia, Valencia and Navarra; other languages, which are protected by the Statutes of Autonomy in the territories where they are traditionally spoken, are also considered regional or minority languages.

[102] I. Álvarez Dorronsoro, "Interview with Teresa San Román: Change and Continuity of the Romani identity," *Revista Hika* 111, <http://www.hika.net/revista/zenb111/Ha_a_Teresa.html>, (accessed 20 August 2002).

[103] "Manifesto for the Constitution of Platform for the Statute of the Roma Nation – Romipen," Toledo, 12 February 2000, para. 14, see <http://www.cenfor.com/romipen/manifiesto.htm>, (accessed 20 August 2002).

[104] See A. G. Alfaro, *The Great Gypsy Roundup*, Editorial Presencia Gitana, 1995.

Germany."[105] With regard to the right to use Romanes with public officials, the Government has asserted that since Sinti and Roma "grow up as bilingual speakers of Romany and German and, as a rule, have a command of both languages, no actual requirement for using Romany in relations with administrative authorities has been observed."[106] Sinti and Roma leaders have expressed concern about the lack of protection afforded in practice to Romanes.[107]

In both Germany and Spain, the dominant approach to teaching Roma is compensatory or "promotional" education classes (see Section 3.1.2);[108] within this framework, Roma identity and culture is often perceived by teachers as a problem to be overcome rather than an advantage to be cultivated. Though Spanish teachers' associations and Roma NGOs have repeatedly requested the inclusion of specialised courses on the history and culture of Spanish ethnic groups and intercultural communication and teaching into university curricula for teachers, psychologists, magistrates, and social workers, these recommendations have not been taken up. Some information of this nature has been published and distributed in a number of German states, but Sinti and Roma leaders maintain that school curricula do not as yet provide adequate information about their history and culture, or about their victimisation during the Holocaust.

Competence for most educational and cultural issues rests with individual German states. With the exception of Hamburg, no German state presently provides for instruction in Romanes within the public school system, on the grounds that such instruction is "not wanted by German Sinti parents."[109] The Government has also asserted that the majority of Sinti and Roma[110] oppose the development of a written

---

[105] Report submitted by the German Government to the Advisory Committee on Implementation of the Framework Convention on National Minorities, 1999, pp. 10–11 (hereafter, "German State FCNM Report"). Several other states have accepted Part II of the CRML.

[106] German State FCNM Report, p. 79.

[107] "Sorge um Sprache: Sinti und Roma fordern Schutz des 'Romanes'" ("Concerns about the Language: Sinti and Roma Promote Protection of Romanes"), *Wiesbadener Tagblatt*, 28 July 2001.

[108] J. D. Santiago, intervention published in Working Documents 43, "Debate on Romani People," p. 69.

[109] German State FCNM Report, p. 112.

[110] The German FCNM Report acknowledges that some Roma organisations take a different view, and "argue in favour of the inclusion of Romany in school education and wish to support measures, like those taken in European neighbouring countries, for the development of a written form of this language," but indicates that the Government chooses to respect the will of the majority of Sinti, who reportedly insist on "cultivat(ing) their language exclusively within the family and family clans." German State FCNM Report, p. 96.

form of Romanes, and object to outsiders learning and providing instruction in it.[111] However, this assertion is not based on a broad assessment of the opinions of Sinti and Roma communities throughout Germany, but on the views expressed by the organisation recognised by the Government as the official representative of the Sinti and Roma community.[112]

In both Germany and Spain, Roma are poorly represented both in public administration and in governmental bodies to protect or promote minority rights. In both countries, diverse Romani communities are represented officially by one or more organisations which receive most of their funding from the Government. Though this approach provides Governments with a ready interlocutor and reliable partner in implementing various projects, it does not tend to promote the development of independent Romani views and critiques, and has fuelled conflict rather than cooperation among different Romani organisations.[113] In Spain, it has meant that the State's principal national policy to improve the situation for Roma has taken on the character of a social assistance programme rather than a strategic plan to protect and promote the rights and identity of the Roma minority.

Governments should develop more inclusive mechanisms to ensure that Sinti and Roma are afforded equivalent opportunities with other recognised minority groups, including the right to cultivate and study their language. They should also develop more sophisticated mechanisms for ensuring them the opportunity to participate fully in public life, including through active participation in the development of policies and programmes to benefit them, and in leading implementation and evaluation of those policies and programmes.

3.3.4 Minority rights issues for Muslims

By definition, Muslims are largely excluded from consideration under existing minority protection regimes in France, Italy and the UK (see Section 3.3.1). Majority

---

[111] German State FCNM Report, p. 86.

[112] The OSCE High Commissioner on National Minorities has noted, with regard to State-funded NGOs (in Spain), that NGO representatives "cannot be expected to dispense fully disinterested advice" when this is likely to affect their own funding. OSCE High Commissioner on National Minorities *Report on the Situation of Roma and Sinti in the OSCE Area*, 2001, p. 145.

[113] At the same time, the lack of unity among Romani organisations if often seen as a primary cause for the limited success of State efforts to improve their situation. See, e.g. "The State and the Gypsies," interim report on the policy research project of the European Migration Centre, Berlin, November 2001; on file with EUMAP.

institutions, even when they are formally neutral or secular, often implicitly (and sometimes explicitly) favour the culture and religion of the majority. For example, Christmas and Easter are recognised as public holidays; religious symbols and rituals are often used during official State ceremonies; and school curricula are informed by Christian traditions and history (even in schools with few, if any, Christians).[114] Still, all three Governments formally embrace the value of multiculturalism and diversity, and have made efforts to address the religious and cultural needs of Muslim communities within the context of existing legal and institutional frameworks.

There are significant differences in the relationship of all three States with different faiths. The Church of England is the Established Church in England[115] and a Concordat regulates relations between the State and the majority religion (Roman-Catholicism) in Italy.[116] Only religions represented by an officially-recognised church institution are legally entitled to certain benefits (such as tax exemptions on religious buildings) in France[117] and Italy, producing inequalities in treatment among different forms of worship;[118] in neither country have Muslims succeeded in concluding an agreement with the State, and thus their exercise of religious rights is limited in practice.

To address these inequalities, State authorities have encouraged Muslims in France and Italy to designate a single representative to facilitate the negotiation of a State agreement. However, the process has proven difficult. In Italy, for example, it seems likely that the designation of one organisation as "representative" might result in the alienation of others, and the State has concluded that it is too early for an agreement. In France, several Muslim associations have participated in a consultation process that has produced a draft agreement on a methodology for electing a representative body,

---

[114] In both Italy and the UK, public schools must provide religious education for all registered pupils, including in daily collective Christian worship, although parents can choose to withdraw their children.

[115] The Church of Scotland is the national church of Scotland; there is no established church in Wales or Northern Ireland.

[116] The concordat was ratified by Law 121/ 25 of March 1985, Ratification and execution of the Accord, with additional protocol, signed in Rome, 18 February 1984, with modifications to the Lutheran Concordat of 11 February 1929 between the Republic of Italy and the Holy See.

[117] Lutheran and Reform Protestantism, Judaism and Catholicism are all legally recognised forms of worship under the Combes Law of 1905.

[118] In Italy, for example, groups that have not signed a State agreement cannot allocate a quote of the personal income tax to their community, deduct donations to the community from taxes, delegate teachers to public schools to provide religious instruction, legitimately abstain from work on religious holidays, *inter alia*.

but other groups did not participate, and some association leaders feel that they have been excluded.

Until such agreements are negotiated, Muslims living in France and Italy will not enjoy legally-guaranteed access to important religious rights. Though some local authorities have taken steps to accommodate the needs of Muslim communities, they do so on a discretionary basis, and sometimes run up against resistance from their electorate; in both France and Italy, local communities have often opposed the construction of Islamic places of worship.

In important ways, existing frameworks for dealing with minority religious communities are not well-suited to the realities and demands of large and diverse Muslim populations. This is not surprising, as they were originally developed under much different conditions than presently pertain, in response to the needs of indigenous religious communities. Some Muslims (and non-Muslims) have criticised the State's approach as "post-colonial," intended to control Muslim communities rather than facilitate their participation. States should re-examine frameworks for regulating religious community life to determine the extent to which they serve the needs and interests of religious minority groups; where appropriate, these frameworks should be amended to make them more responsive to present-day realities.

The diversity of the Muslim communities in France, Italy, and the UK means that they have no single "minority language." Therefore, requests for minority language use and education in a minority language are not relevant for the Muslim community as a whole, though they may be relevant for particular linguistic groups. Though Muslim communities in France and the UK in particular recognise the need to learn the majority language, they also place importance on learning Arabic and on the degree to which schools promote awareness of Islam and the contribution of Muslims on an equal footing with other faiths. British Muslims have emphasised the importance of providing public school teachers with basic knowledge of Islam to allow them to operate more effectively in a multi-faith environment. Recognising the Islamic dimension of Muslim students' identity and working with Muslim community bodies may be important in developing innovative policies that work to improve standards in schools.

At present, most Arabic-language teaching and religious education in Islam takes place either at home or in the mosque sector, after school hours. With limited time and resources at their disposal, mosques are often able to impart only basic knowledge of Arabic and Islam. The younger generations of Muslims therefore lack opportunities to engage fully with their religion and to acquire adequate knowledge of the history and traditions of Islam. Without adequate education and knowledge, young Muslims are ill-equipped to engage in debate and dialogue with organisations that offer differing and perhaps more radical interpretations of Islam.

Providing Arabic classes in the context of modern language classes in State schools would create an opportunity to develop the interests and skills of Muslim pupils and parents and a chance to integrate learning about Arabic-speaking communities and cultures into the curriculum. Where there is demand, schools should consider offering Arabic as a modern language option alongside modern European languages.

As noted above, public awareness of the traditions and history of Islam is extremely low and intolerance towards Muslims is a problem, which is exacerbated by reliance on oversimplified and stereotyped images of Islam in the mainstream media. Muslim response to media stereotyping appears to be limited; media regulatory bodies could usefully provide targeted public information about complaints mechanisms to Muslim communities. Governments and media bodies should also consider supporting projects to encourage more active participation of Muslims within media organisations; where some such projects have already posted notable successes, there should be a concerted effort to identity and promote examples of positive practice.

4. THE IMPORTANCE OF MONITORING AND EVALUATION

Although only a few may originate a policy, we are all able to judge it.[119]

4.1 Monitoring by International Organisations

It is well established as a principle in international law that certain fundamental human rights and freedoms are not derogable, and monitoring mechanisms have been established to ensure that signatories to international human rights treaties and conventions comply with those principles in practice. In the past decade the EU, too, has made respect for human rights a touchstone for its policies; the EU has included human rights clauses in its trade association agreements with other States and, of course, it has required candidate States to demonstrate respect for human and minority rights as a condition for membership.

At the same time, many EU member States have not been receptive to criticism or monitoring from international bodies, and some have fallen behind in reporting to international bodies on their own human rights records. Within its own sphere, the EU has not yet devoted sufficient attention to articulating clearly its human rights

---

[119] Pericles of Athens, about 430 BC, cited in K.R. Popper, *The Open Society and its Enemies, Volume I*, London: Routledge, 1945, p. 7.

requirements, and has not set in place robust mechanisms for internal monitoring of member States' compliance with human rights norms.[120] Existing monitoring mechanisms are excessively dependent on member State cooperation, and should be supported and strengthened.[121]

Some member States have reacted defensively to the human rights critiques offered by international monitoring bodies. For example, Greece reacted to the 2000 report of the European Commission for Monitoring Racism and Intolerance (ECRI) by stating that:

> Generalisations and conclusions abound in the text but in most cases no facts are adduced to support them. In other instances such conclusions are clearly based on isolated incidents, which are improperly (and unfairly) treated as the norm and not as the exception, indeed the aberration, that they actually are.[122]

The German government asserted that ECRI's conclusions regarding problems of racism were "much too sweeping and do not reflect the actual situation in Germany,"[123] and judged its critique that measures to promote integration had been insufficient as "inadmissible."[124] The French government expressed dissatisfaction with ECRI's apparent questioning of "the French Republican model…which stem[s] from a legal tradition dating back two hundred years," and ruled out "any 'reconsideration' of the egalitarian approach, on which our Republic is founded."[125]

The Danish Centre for Human Rights has noted that criticisms by international bodies regarding growing racism and xenophobia in Denmark "were rejected out of hand almost in unison by politicians and the press," and that:

---

[120] For a comprehensive discussion of the lack of mechanisms for monitoring human rights performance within the EU, see P. Alston and J.H.H. Weiler, "An 'Ever Closer Union' in Need of a Human Rights Policy: The European Union and Human Rights," in Alston (eds.), *The EU and Human Rights,* Oxford University Press, 1999.

[121] The EU's European Monitoring Centre on Racism and Xenophobia was established in 1997 to monitor public and media attitudes towards racial and ethnic minorities in EU member States. It has produced useful reports on a wide range of topics. However, the organisations upon which the EUMC relies for information are often funded by member State Governments; member States must also approve the EUMC's annual reports prior to publication. These factors clearly undermine the EUMC's independence and capacity to publish criticisms.

[122] Observations provided by the authorities of Greece concerning ECRI's Report on Greece, 2001, p. 24.

[123] Observations provided by the German authorities concerning ECRI's Second Report on Germany, 2000, p. 27.

[124] ECRI Country by Country Approach: Second Report on Germany, 2000, p. 27.

[125] Observations provided by the French authorities concerning ECRI's Report on France, 2000, p. 24

A great majority of politicians and the press never reflected on the message, but chose instead to shoot at the messengers – a group of foreign observers. Rather than discussing the contents, the criticism was rejected as being unscientific and sloppy. Thereby, they avoided having to relate critically to the question of whether the image drawn of Denmark's attitude to refugees and immigrants in the report reflects the reality of Danish society.[126]

EU candidate States have proven equally sensitive to external critique. Following the release of the EU's 2001 Regular Reports, former Hungarian Prime Minister Viktor Orbán stated that Hungary "must grit its teeth and suffer [as] other assess its performance in reports if it wants to join the EU. We do not write country reports and therefore it is not entirely clear to us why others have an insurmountable yearning to make reports on us."[127] The EU should make it clear to aspiring members that assessment of basic human and minority rights will continue after accession; the best way to convey the seriousness of this message is to initiate genuine and thorough assessment of all member States.

International monitoring bodies – including the EU – should certainly strive to offer balanced and well-informed critiques, in which Governments could assist by collecting and providing comprehensive information on their efforts to comply with human rights obligations. However, defensive reactions to critique belie a lack of commitment to monitoring as a tool for self-improvement; they bespeak an unwillingness to acknowledge that compliance with human rights norms is not something that States achieve definitively, but something for which they must strive continuously. The fifteen current member States now vested with the authority to determine the future size and form of the European Union have a special responsibility to set an example by the way in which they accept and make constructive use of critique.

4.2 Governmental Monitoring

Appreciation for the role and importance of monitoring is also revealed by the extent to which Governments prove themselves willing to scrutinise their own performance. Monitoring provides information crucial to the provision of public goods and services in an effective manner. To the extent that it provides public officials with information about ways in which services are not reaching certain groups, monitoring may also be viewed as an important tool for conflict prevention.

With respect to minority protection in particular, monitoring is the best way for service providers to ensure that their policies do not indirectly discriminate and that they are

---

[126] The Danish Centre for Human Rights, "Human Rights in Denmark, Status 2001, p. 10.
[127] Radio Free Europe/Radio Liberty Newsline, vol. 5, no. 217, part II, 15 November 2001.

providing an equal service to all. Without monitoring, it would be difficult to identify indirect, often unintended, ways in which policies disadvantage communities or to see whether policies aimed at reducing inequality are succeeding. To monitor effectively, Governments must identify the different communities that legislation is intended to protect, institutions serve, and public services reach.

Government can play a crucial role in supporting local and regional governmental structures that have fallen short in their efforts to reach minority communities, including through practical guidelines for improvement. The Beacon Council Scheme for monitoring service delivery in the UK may be a model that could be taken up in other member States as well as by EU structures. The scheme identifies centres of excellence in local government in different areas of service delivery; councils awarded Beacon status are given grants to support the dissemination of good practice to other local governments. This technique could be used to identify the extent to which different religious, linguistic, ethnic or other communities are benefiting from State policies in practice.

4.3 Civil Society

Naturally, however, the willingness and ability of Governments to critique themselves inevitably will be limited in important ways; it is to be expected that Governments will seek optimal evaluations of their own performance. Important critical input can be gained by soliciting the opinions of those to whom protections and benefits are supposed to be provided, taking steps to ensure that critical opinions are welcomed, and ensuring that negative consequences do not flow from having offered them.

Yet where civil society efforts to provide constructive critique are limited by lack of capacity, lack of funding, or an intolerant environment, governmental performance will tend to become more insular and less responsive to social needs. Thus, it is in society's interest not only to have a Government that welcomes critique, but one that supports the development of civil society organisations' capability to articulate and offer constructive analysis. This is perhaps particularly true for policy affecting minority groups, which are sometimes at a disadvantage in accessing opportunities for education and training.

Monitoring of governmental human and minority rights policies by civil society organisations also carries other benefits. First, it has the potential to increase awareness of governmental objectives and initiatives among a broader audience. This is important, as lack of public support is often a critical impediment to the success of many of the minority protection programmes that have been adopted (see Section 2). More broadly, however, monitoring encourages an active and engaged attitude on the part of civil society – a "culture of critique," which encourages members of society, including minorities, to become more involved in shaping and taking responsibility for the legislation, institutions and policies that are meant to benefit them. And the individual's full enjoyment of the right to formulate and advance critiques – particularly of Government policy – is the hallmark of an open society.

5. RECOMMENDATIONS

Recommendations directed to individual States are included in the country reports. Here, only generally applicable recommendations and recommendations to the EU are noted.

To candidate and member States

- Where such policies do not exist, consider the development and adoption of a special Government programme (or programmes) to address the situation of vulnerable minority populations.

- Undertake regular review of the content of existing minority protection or integration programmes, in cooperation with minority representatives, to ensure that they are comprehensive in their approach, and reflect the developing needs and interests of minority communities as fully as possible.

- Base programme reviews on comprehensive research on the situation of minorities. Where such information is lacking, develop appropriate mechanisms for compiling data, consistent with the legitimate requirements for the protection of personal data.

- Review legislation to ensure full compliance with the Race Equality and Employment Directives.

- To the fullest extent possible, provide in law for the creation of a positive duty for public authorities to eliminate unlawful discrimination on any grounds in relation to their function and to promote equality of opportunity and good relations between persons of different ethnicities, cultures, languages, and religious beliefs.

- Take steps to communicate the goals and objectives of minority protection or integration programmes to the broader public, emphasising the link to common EU values.

- Ensure that political support for minority protection programmes is clearly expressed by vesting central coordinating bodies with sufficient authority and human and financial resources to coordinate implementation effectively.

- Provide specialised training on programme objectives to local and regional public officials overseeing implementation of Government policy towards minorities; such training should emphasise public officials' positive duty to guarantee equal access to quality services.

- Re-examine frameworks for regulating religious communities to determine the extent to which they serve the needs and interests of religious minority groups; where appropriate, amend these frameworks to make them more responsive to present-day realities.

- Take steps to facilitate access to citizenship for non-citizen populations; promote understanding of integration as a two-way process.

- Develop and give preference to projects that involve minority representatives in an active, decision-making capacity rather than as the passive recipients of Government assistance.

- Support efforts to facilitate good relations between law enforcement agencies and minority communities, as a way of decreasing mutual mistrust and suspicion.

- Extend support for capacity-building activities to encourage the formulation of well-grounded, well-formulated, and constructive critiques of Government policy. Maintain an open attitude toward critique offered by inter-governmental bodies as well as by independent, non-governmental monitors, as an impulse toward improving governmental effectiveness and efficiency.

To the European Union

- Emphasise that respect for and protection of minorities is a core value common to the Union and a continuing obligation of EU membership, including through the adoption of explicit legal provisions to this effect at the level of European institutions.

- Stress that a comprehensive approach to minority protection – incorporating both prevention of discrimination and advancement of minority rights – is an essential aspect of the continuing obligations of EU membership.

- Ensure full compliance by all member States with the Race Equality and Employment Directives; consider broadening the Race Equality Directive to account for discrimination against religious minorities and support the elaboration of new Directives as necessary to ensure that basic human rights are ensured to groups which, for various reasons, have not been accorded recognition.

- Encourage dialogue among member States toward developing a common baseline understanding of terms such as "minority," "minority protection" and "integration," encouraging definitions which are as expansive and inclusive as possible; articulate minimum standards to guarantee equal treatment for groups that do not fit within the definitions adopted.

- Assist States in developing effective public policies based on a comprehensive approach to minority protection; create a positive duty to eliminate all forms of discrimination in the provision of services and to promote equality of opportunity and good relations among persons of different race, ethnicity and religious belief.

- Strengthen and support EU-level mechanisms for identifying and sharing good practice in the implementation of minority protection policies.

- Devote resources toward developing acceptable methodologies for the collection of data based on ethnic and religious affiliation, while ensuring respect for privacy and protection of personal data; encourage member States to utilise these methodologies to compile comprehensive research on the situation of vulnerable minority populations.

- Strengthen existing monitoring mechanisms, such as the European Centre for Monitoring Racism and Xenophobia (EUMC) and the emerging "Network of Human Rights Experts," and develop new mechanisms to ensure that attention is maintained on efforts to ensure respect for the full range of human rights.

- Provide support for capacity-building in minority organisations, so that they will be able to play an active role in monitoring the effectiveness of policies designed to benefit them.

- Counter anti-minority sentiment by openly and vigorously condemning racist expressions by member State politicians and by developing mechanisms to encourage responsible public discourse, including by supporting programmes to improve levels of minority participation in media organisations.

- Review procedures for NGOs to apply for and administer Phare and other funding programmes, with a view toward maximising simplicity and transparency; provide in-country training and assistance to potential applicants.

- Improve the quantity and quality of information available to the public on the allocation and use of EU funding to support minority protection programmes.

Minority Protection in Bulgaria

AN ASSESSMENT OF THE FRAMEWORK PROGRAMME
FOR EQUAL INTEGRATION OF ROMA IN BULGARIAN SOCIETY
AND THE "INTEGRATION OF MINORITIES" COMPONENT
OF THE PROGRAMME PEOPLE ARE THE WEALTH OF BULGARIA.

Table of Contents

1. Executive Summary 72
2. The Government Programmes – Background 75
   2.1 Background to Present Programmes 76
   2.2 The Programme – Process 77
      2.2.1 The Framework Programme 77
      2.2.2 The Integration of Minorities Programme 79
   2.3 The Programme – Content 80
      2.3.1 The Framework Programme 80
      2.3.2 Integration of Minorities Programme 81
   2.4 The Programme – Administration/ Implementation/Evaluation 82
   2.5 The Programmes and the Public 83
      2.5.1 The Framework Programme 83
      2.5.2 The Integration of Minorities Programme 84
   2.6 The Programmes and the EU 84
3. Government Programmes – Implementation 87
   3.1 Stated Objectives of the Programmes 87
   3.2 Government Programmes and Discrimination 88
      3.2.1 Education 92
      3.2.2 Employment 97
      3.2.3 Housing and other goods and services 100

		3.2.4	Healthcare and other forms of social protection 104

- 3.2.4 Healthcare and other forms of social protection 104
- 3.2.5 The criminal justice system 107
- 3.3 Protection from Racially Motivated Violence 108
- 3.4 Promotion of Minority Rights 111
  - 3.4.1 Education 112
  - 3.4.2 Language 113
  - 3.4.3 Participation in public life 114
  - 3.4.4 Media 116
  - 3.4.5 Culture 117
4. Evaluation 118
5. Recommendations 120

1. Executive Summary

The Bulgarian Government's approach to the situation of Roma is at present framed by two documents: the Framework Programme for Equal Integration of Roma in Bulgarian Society, and the "Integration of Minorities" section of the comprehensive Government programme "People are the Wealth of Bulgaria."

The Framework Programme is generally a well-constructed strategy: it includes measures both to prevent discrimination and to promote minority rights. It largely reflects the input of Roma organisations solicited during the drafting process, although the Government deleted important provisions addressing police misconduct from the final version. The Integration of Minorities programme takes a more general approach, and gives less attention to anti-discrimination measures, suggesting that the Government lacks the resolve to confront discrimination directly.

Unfortunately, implementation of the two programmes has until very recently been at a standstill. Little or no funding was allocated from the Government's budget to realise programme goals. Moreover, certain projects that have been carried out, including some supported with Phare funds, appear poorly tailored to the specific circumstances of the target population and the goals of the Framework Programme. The structures responsible for overseeing implementation have failed to ensure Programme commitments are met, due to a lack of authority, resources, and political will.

The Bulgarian Roma community has given its support to the Framework Programme, and while some sections of the text should be revised to reflect developments since 1999, it is generally agreed that full implementation of the measures provided by the Programme is the best course forward.

Background

The history of the Framework Programme highlights the Government's ambivalence towards both minority issues and civil society organisations. While considerable input was solicited from Roma and NGO representatives in drafting the Framework Programme, the Government scaled back the version finally adopted in April 1999. The 2001 Integration of Minorities Programme is the result of a purely political process and was adopted without any pretence of consultation with minority NGOs and without being discussed publicly. It is narrower in scope and weaker in measures proposed than the Framework Programme.

The relationship between the two programmes is not altogether clear, although the Integration of Minorities Programme states its intent to both "change and supplement" and "monitor" the implementation of the Framework Programme. There has been little attempt to introduce and explain either Programme to the general public.

Administration

A Government office, the National Council for Ethnic and Demographic Issues (NCEDI) is charged with coordinating implementation of the Framework Programme.[1] Although the involvement of other Government institutions is indispensable to the success of the two Programmes, the NCEDI does not have the authority to require implementation from other Government offices, nor to require regular and transparent evaluation and reporting on Programme-related activities. There have been calls for the Council to be raised to the level of an executive agency, if not a ministry in its own right.[2] The Integration of Minorities Programme recognises that more robust powers are called for to oversee effective implementation of minority policy, yet it fails to set forth a clear vision as to what form an enhanced agency could take, or what its authority might be.

Each of the bodies responsible for implementing projects under the Framework Programme submits its annual budget to Parliament for approval, and subsequently has the authority to determine how it will distribute the allocated sum, including how much will be allocated to NGOs involved in implementation. In addition, the ministries are responsible for submitting project proposals to the Ministry of Foreign Affairs for inclusion each year in Bulgaria's Phare funding proposal to the EU.

EU Support

The EU has been supportive of the Government's efforts to improve the situation of Roma, commending the adoption of the Framework Programme, and monitoring its implementation in the Regular Reports. However, EU funding for Roma-related projects has not consistently followed the strategies articulated in the Framework Programme, and the observations related in the Regular Reports have occasionally lacked the emphasis and specificity that would encourage better adherence to Programme goals.

Content and Implementation

Overall, the implementation of both programmes' specific measures remains low. The EU remains the primary source of funding for Roma-related projects, although in 2000 no Phare funds were allocated for integration projects as the Government did not submit any proposals for Roma programmes that year.

---

[1] *Rules and regulations for the structure and organisation of the National Council on Ethnic and Demographic Issues,* State Gazette 118, 10 December 1997, Article 2.

[2] OSI Roundtable, Sofia, May 2002. *Explanatory note: the Open Society Institute held a roundtable meeting in Sofia in May 2002 to invite critique of a draft version of this report. Experts present included representatives of the Government, Roma groups, and non-governmental organisations.*

The Framework Programme acknowledges that discrimination is an important factor contributing to inequalities in Bulgarian society, while the Integration of Minorities Programme places greater emphasis on the promotion of minority identity. Comprehensive anti-discrimination legislation is being drafted, as the current legal framework does not meet international standards. While discrimination is specifically addressed in the Framework Programme, and measures are set out to combat inequalities in the spheres of education, employment, and housing, there have been few Government-sponsored projects to realise these commitments. First steps towards addressing segregation in the school system were taken only in Autumn 2002. The Framework Programme does not adequately address discrimination in health care or in the criminal justice system, and acute problems in these areas remain.

Promotion of minority rights remains underdeveloped in the Framework Programme and the Integration of Minorities Programme. Mother-tongue education in Romanes is theoretically available but no classes have been organised. Neither programme specifically addresses the use of minority languages in the public sphere, and there is no consensus in the Roma community on the need to advocate for change in this regard. Roma representation in public and political life is very low, and structures that would increase representation have not been developed. Roma experts have been appointed to a number of ministries, but these posts often have no defined responsibilities or mandate, and some experts feel that their positions and responsibilities are largely nominal.[3]

Conclusion

The Framework Programme's approach to integration of Roma is quite comprehensive. It deals with a wide range of problems and offers a variety of solutions. It was widely accepted by the Roma community. Nevertheless, there are areas needing improvement, notably in the areas of criminal justice and healthcare.

At the same time, the Bulgarian Government has demonstrated a lack of political will to systematically implement the Programme, and has apparently retreated from some of its objectives, as seen in the Integration of Minorities Programme. The relationship between the two programmes is in urgent need of clarification. There has not been sufficient effort to build support for the programmes among the general public, which contributes to politicians' reluctance to follow through on their commitments.

The main problem with the Framework Programme is that full implementation has not started yet, three years after its adoption. There is no effective mechanism for Programme administration, which has led to difficulties in ensuring appropriate allocation of funds, reporting, and evaluation. Government funding has been minimal,

---

[3] OSI Roundtable, Sofia, May 2002.

and implementation has been limited in scope and content to support provided by NGOs or international organisations. A detailed and specific action plan should be drawn up, with designated responsibilities and deadlines in each sphere addressed by the Programmes, and funding allocated accordingly.

2. THE GOVERNMENT PROGRAMMES – BACKGROUND

At present the Bulgarian Government's approach to minorities is framed by two programme documents – The Framework Programme for Equal Integration of Roma in Bulgarian Society and the "Integration of Minorities" section of the comprehensive Government programme "People are the Wealth of Bulgaria." In addition, there are 12 district Government programmes dealing with minorities, differing both in quality and in the degree of association with the Government programmes. None of the district government programmes has allocated a budget for implementation, and only five provide for the implementation of concrete measures.

The Framework Programme for Equal Integration of Roma in Bulgarian Society was adopted on 22 April 1999 by the Government of the United Democratic Forces (UtDF).[4] The present coalition Government is comprised of the National Movement Simeon the Second (NMSS), which won the June 2001 parliamentary elections, and the Movement for Rights and Freedoms (MRF), a political party representing mostly Bulgarian Turks and also supported by some Roma and Bulgarian-speaking Muslims.[5] The coalition adopted the programme "People are the Wealth of Bulgaria" in October 2001. This programme recognises some continuity with the Framework Programme but deals with a more limited number of issues and intends to both "monitor" and "change and supplement" the Framework Programme, rather than to replace it.[6]

---

[4] The text of the Framework Programme has never been published officially. This report uses the version supplied by the National Council on Ethnic and Demographic Issues (NCEDI, also available at the BHC web site, see <http://www.bghelsinki.org>, (accessed 19 September 2002).

[5] The text of the Government programme "People are the Wealth of Bulgaria" is available at the Bulgarian Government's official web site: <http://www.Government.bg>, (accessed for the Bulgarian-language text on 23 February 2002). The same web site also hosts a very concise English-language version of only the "key priorities." This version however does not summarise the main ideas of the "Integration of Minorities" part.

[6] A comparison of the themes and priorities in the Framework Programme and the Integration of Minorities Programme is discussed in detail below.

2.1 Background to present programmes

Bulgaria has a history of both long-term and short-term programmes attempting to support, regulate, and intervene in different aspects of the minority situation. The communist Government had a number of programmes dealing with issues such as access to education, housing, and medical care for Roma, their forced settlement, and other restrictions of minority rights. All these programmes were undertaken at the central or local levels through acts of different Government institutions, but were always sanctioned by the top Communist Party leadership. After the beginning of the transition to democracy in 1989, several consecutive Governments passed acts and drafted programmes aiming to restore minority rights that had been suppressed under the communist regime. These measures included restoring names changed in previous coercive assimilation campaigns, restitution of individuals' property confiscated or lost during the exodus of Bulgarian Turks in 1989, restitution of religious communities' property confiscated during the communist regime, amnesties and compensation for imprisonment and for other coercive measures that had been taken by the communist authorities.[7]

The first programme after 1989 that explicitly addressed the situation of the Roma was adopted by the socialist Government on 30 January 1997 and had the ambitious name "Programme for Resolution of Problems of Roma in the Republic of Bulgaria."[8] The overall approach of this programme was to view Roma as a socially disadvantaged population, rather than as an ethnic group facing discrimination. Consequently, the areas addressed and the measures proposed totally disregarded the prevention of discrimination; as they were general in nature they would have given only an indirect benefit to Roma.[9] Although the programme dealt with the protection of minority identity, it did so within a very limited scope. This programme proposed measures in six areas, including employment, social welfare, housing, health care, and access to education. The programme was to be financed by the State budget and through international sources (UN, EU, International Monetary Fund and the Council of Europe) on the basis of joint projects.

---

[7] See, for more details on the history of the legislation and policy towards minorities in Bulgaria, K. Kanev, "Law and Politics on Ethnic and Religious Minorities in Bulgaria," in A. Krasteva (ed.), *Communities and Identities in Bulgaria*, Ravenna, Longo Editore, 1998, pp. 55–93.

[8] See the English-language version in Ministry of Foreign Affairs of the Republic of Bulgaria, *Situation of Roma in Bulgaria*, Sofia, February 1997, pp. 13–23.

[9] See Section 3.2 on the difficulties in developing special ethnically based measures to ensure full and effective equality steaming from the 1992 interpretation by the Constitutional Court of the anti-discrimination provisions of the Bulgarian Constitution.

The "Programme for Resolution of Problems of Roma in the Republic of Bulgaria" did not see even the beginning of its implementation, however. Five days after its adoption, the socialist Government resigned following mass protests throughout the country against its economic policies. As the programme was not adopted in consultation with all Roma groups, most of them learned about it months after the fall of the Government or not at all.[10]

2.2 The Process of Adoption of the Present Programmes

2.2.1 The Framework Programme

The history of the Framework Programme highlights the Government's ambivalence both towards minority issues, especially discrimination, and civil society organisations. A team of Roma and non-Roma NGO experts drafted a first version of the programme in the late autumn of 1997. Throughout the period between the winter of 1997–1998 and March 1999 the Human Rights Project (HRP), the Roma rights NGO coordinating the preparation of and advocacy activities related to the Framework Programme, initiated consultation with the most active Roma NGOs.

The Government has downplayed the extent of discrimination in Bulgaria. In its 1996 report to the UN Committee on the Elimination of Racial Discrimination, it recognised the existence of racially motivated assaults by private parties, but not by public officials.[11] As the larger part of the Framework Programme involves the recognition and effective prevention of discrimination, it was met with hostility by a number of governmental institutions from the earliest stages of drafting.[12] Furthermore, in January 1998, the Legislative Council of the Ministry of Justice issued an opinion that the establishment of a State body to combat discrimination was unconstitutional.[13]

Roma NGOs on their part actively endorsed the Framework Programme both in the media and at specially organised public forums, as well as in their meetings with Government officials. One such event was the roundtable organised by the HRP on 3

---

[10] Interviews with: Stela Kostova, President of the Roma Youth Organisation, Sofia, 14 March 2002; Hristo Kiuchukov, President of "Diversity" Foundation, Sofia, 6 March 2002; Vassil Chaprazov, President of the United Roma Union, 6 March 2002; Toma Tomov, MP from "Coalition for Bulgaria" in the 39th National Assembly, 13 March, 2002; Simeon Blagoev, Roma expert in the Ministry of Culture, 8 March 2002.

[11] See CERD/C/229/Add.7, §§ 41-42.

[12] See more on the content of the Framework Programme below.

[13] *Opinion of the Legislative Council of the Ministry of Justice and Legal Euro-Integration* from 19 January 1998 (in Bulgarian).

October 1998. There the Government, represented by the then Deputy Prime Minister, agreed that the Government programme would be developed by the joint efforts of Government institutions and Roma NGOs.

However, the newly-created Government office on minorities, the National Council on Ethnic and Demographic Issues (hereafter, NCEDI), soon started its own efforts to develop a programme. These efforts involved consultation with only one Roma NGO (the Social Council "Kupate") and were based on principles different from the ones embedded in the Framework Programme. The Government drafts did not discuss discrimination or measures to combat it. These drafts were apparently unknown even within the various Government institutions. At a number of meetings between Roma NGOs and Government officials, Roma representatives voiced objections to the different versions of the Government draft. When the Government realised that it had lost the support of the Roma organisations, it ultimately abandoned its drafts.[14]

At a National Roundtable on 7 April 1999, co-organised by the HRP and the NCEDI, the Government and 75 mostly Roma NGOs co-signed a protocol stating that the Government would adopt the preliminary version of the Framework Programme, entitled "Programme for Equal Participation of Roma in Public Life of Bulgaria" after "editorial changes" by a joint commission.[15]

The editing process resulted in a significantly weaker document than the one agreed to at the National Roundtable. Government officials diluted the anti-discrimination provisions of the Framework Programme that had been supported by Roma groups. For example, the draft programme envisaged the creation of two Governmental bodies with effective powers to combat discrimination – one general and one special, dealing exclusively with complaints of citizens against illegal actions of police. However, in the final version of the Framework Programme the creation of a special body is not envisaged.[16] The draft programme did not prescribe the rules of procedure and for presentation of evidence to be used in establishing and prescribing sanctions against ethnic discrimination. The final version of the Framework Programme explicitly states that the procedural and evidentiary rules set out in the Law on the Administrative Offences and Punishments should be used. These rules provide that the burden of proof lies with the prosecution rather than requiring the defence to affirmatively

---

[14] For more details on the process of adoption of the Framework Programme see OSCE High Commissioner on National Minorities, *Report on the Situation of Roma and Sinti in the OSCE Area*, 2000, pp. 146–147.

[15] This draft version was published by the HRP in both English and Bulgarian, with the names of all organisations that signed it: See Human Rights Project, *Programme "For Equal Participation of Roma in Public Life of Bulgaria,"* Sofia, 1999, (hereafter, "Framework Programme").

[16] See Section 3.2.

demonstrate there has not been discrimination.[17] The draft programme also recommended that the entire Government anti-discrimination body be elected by the Parliament following proposals from minority organisations, but no such requirement was included in the final version of the Framework Programme.

2.2.2 The Integration of Minorities Programme

Unlike the Framework Programme, the Integration of Minorities Programme is a result of a purely political process and was adopted without consultation with minority NGOs and without being discussed publicly.[18] It originated from two different streams of pre-election political action – that of the NMSS and that of the MRF, which converged after the June 2001 parliamentary elections to form a coalition Government.

In one of the few statements on minority politics in its election platform, the NMSS stated that it would pursue "preservation and encouragement of the culture of **different ethnic groups and religions.**"[19] In a key pre-election address however, on 5 June 2001, the leader of the movement stated: "My goal is to raise the standard of living of all Bulgarian citizens without regard to their ethnic origin. Urgent measures are needed to solve the acute problems of the Roma in Bulgaria. For this purpose I will propose the establishment of a Governmental structure, dealing with the problems of the Roma minority. It ought to be headed by a representative of the Roma themselves."[20]

The election programme of the Movement for Rights and Freedoms had a special section on minorities. There the movement formulates three goals of its practical minority policy: full restoration of the rights suppressed under previous assimilatory and discriminatory policies; and creation of conditions for the expression, preservation, and development of the ethnic, cultural, linguistic and religious identity of national

---

[17] See Framework Programme, Part Two, Section I.2 and the Law on the Administrative Offences and Punishments, Art. 7, Para.1, Art. 24, Para.1 and Art. 84. See alternatively: *EU Council Directive 2000/43/EC of 29 June 2000 implementing the principle of equal treatment between persons irrespective of racial or ethnic origin*, Art. 8.1: "Member States shall take such measures as are necessary, in accordance with their national judicial systems, to ensure that, when persons who consider themselves wronged because the principle of equal treatment has not been applied to them establish, before a court or other competent authority, facts from which it may be presumed that there has been direct or indirect discrimination, it shall be for the respondent to prove that there has been no breach of the principle of equal treatment."

[18] Interview with Mihail Ivanov, Secretary of the NCEDI, Sofia, 26 February 2002.

[19] *Bulgaria – Hospitable Home for its Citizens*: pre-election programme of the "National Movement Simeon the Second," emphasis in the original.

[20] Address of Simeon Saxe Coburg-Gotha from 5 June 2001.

minorities. The programme further calls for undertaking appropriate measures to raise the educational, cultural and socio-economic status of minorities with the aim of achieving full and effective equality between them and the majority population. In addition, the election programme provides for the adoption of an anti-discrimination law with an effective enforcement body, desegregation of Roma education, and transformation of the National Council on Ethnic and Demographic Issues into "a body of the executive power of a sufficiently high rank and capacity."[21]

Several months after its formation, on 26 October 2001, the coalition cabinet of the NMSS and MRF proposed its programme "People are the Wealth of Bulgaria" with a special chapter on "Integration of Minorities" to the Parliament. This was the first Governmental programme after 1989 to contain a chapter on minorities. In a short press conference on 24 October, the Chairman of the National Council of Ethnic and Demographic Issues and its new Secretary outlined the content of the Integration of Minorities Programme and expressed the Government's readiness to implement the Framework Programme in addition to the Integration of Minorities Programme.[22]

2.3 Content of the Programmes

2.3.1 The Framework Programme

The prevailing theme of the Framework Programme is the elimination of discrimination against Roma. Discrimination is recognised in the introduction, and the "elimination of discrimination against Roma" is characterised as "one of the main political priorities of the Bulgarian State."[23] The Government is expected to undertake this task with some input from Roma groups.[24] The Framework Programme sets out concrete measures in eight spheres of social life:

- Anti-discrimination legislation
- Employment and economic development
- Healthcare and sanitation
- Housing and neighbourhood regulation

---

[21] *Bulgaria-Europe: A non-standard way of development*, election platform of the Movement for Rights and Freedoms.
[22] Government press statement from 24 October 2001.
[23] Framework Programme, Part I.
[24] See Section 2.4.

- Education
- Protection of Roma culture
- Developing the Roma presence in the national media
- Elimination of discrimination against Roma women

2.3.2 Integration of Minorities Programme

As stated in its introduction, the Integration of Minorities Programme seeks to preserve and develop minority identity and to encourage "multi-ethnicity." It also aims to reinforce anti-discrimination legislation. The programme has three parts: a statement of goals, the formulation of tasks and development of an action plan in three phases – up to the end of 2001, up to the end of 2002, and up to the end of the present Government's mandate. However, it is rather vague in formulating its goals and activities, most of which are stated in very general terms. It includes a reference to establishing "an adequate institutional mechanism to include all levels of different authorities with clearly defined responsibilities and powers."[25] It does not envisage any input from minority groups during implementation.

In comparison with the Framework Programme, the Integration of Minorities Programme is narrower in scope and weaker in measures proposed. Some of the provisions of the Framework Programme are in fact diluted by the Integration of Minorities Programme. This is the case with anti-discrimination legislation: while the Framework Programme envisages enacting a special anti-discrimination law dealing with discrimination on racial and ethnic grounds, the Integration of Minorities Programme discusses anti-discrimination legislation generally, without defining whether it would address discrimination on the basis of ethnicity, gender, or other grounds. Although the Integration of Minorities Programme regrets the lack of progress in realising the Framework Programme and seeks to monitor its implementation,[26] there are no concrete deadlines envisaged for any actions related to some of its main objectives, such as the desegregation of Roma schools, or housing and neighbourhood regulation.

---

[25] Goals include "political, socio-economic and cultural integration of minorities in Bulgarian society," Integration of Minorities Programme: Goals, see <http://www.government.bg/English/Government/Program/137.html>, (accessed on 19 September 2002), (hereafter, "Integration of Minorities Programme").

[26] Integration of Minorities Programme: State.

The Integration of Minorities Programme foresees the adoption of an anti-discrimination law by the end of 2002. This is also the deadline for the fulfilment of its other main objective, the creation of a State agency on minorities. The programme also calls for the creation of structures dealing with minorities at the central and local levels; ratification of Protocol 12 of the ECHR by the end of 2002; submission of a national report under the FCNM by the end of 2001 (already overdue as of October 2002) and the adoption of a strategy for development of underdeveloped regions with high populations of minorities by the end of the current Government mandate.

2.4 Administration and Implementation of the Programmes

The Integration of Minorities Programme explicitly states that all issues related to the implementation of the Framework Programme are to be handled by the National Council on Ethnic and Demographic Issues.[27] Indeed, according to its rules and regulations, the Council's powers encompass a broad range of coordination activities at the domestic and international levels.[28] Given the wide scope and multidisciplinary nature of most of the issues it deals with, the involvement of other Government institutions is indispensable to the work of the NCEDI, in particular the various ministries and other State institutions such as Parliament and municipal Governments. However, the Council does not have powers to require implementation from other Government offices nor to require regular and transparent evaluation and reporting.

The Integration of Minorities Programme observes that, "concrete mechanisms and instruments for the realisation of the basic principles of the Framework Programme… are lacking,"[29] apparently suggesting that the NCEDI or a future coordinating body should have a more robust mandate. However, there is no clear vision set out as to what form a future agency will take, or what its powers might be. NGOs have called for the Council to be raised to the level of an executive agency, if not a ministry in its own right.[30]

Funding of any project follows the same general rules for budget formation and implementation. General budget items are subject to annual approval by the Parliament. Each institution then has the power to determine how it will distribute the

---

[27] Integration of Minorities Programme: State.
[28] *Rules and regulations for the structure and organisation of the National Council on Ethnic and Demographic Issues,* State Gazette 118, 10 December 1997, Article 2.
[29] Integration of Minorities Programme: State.
[30] OSI Roundtable, Sofia, May 2002.

allocated sum of money. It also determines how much money it can allocate to NGOs participating in implementation. The procedures by which responsibilities for implementation are divided among international, Government and non-governmental actors involved in the process are described in detail in individual project contracts, as are the procedures for overseeing and reporting on expenditures. There has been no project specifically implementing the Framework Programme since its adoption in April 1999, and therefore no official reports on implementation and evaluation have been issued to date.

The Framework Programme provides for input from Roma communities in a number of ways: it provides that the anti-discrimination body should inform the community of its activities, and it provides that minority organisations should participate in the working group on the draft anti-discrimination law. It calls for the recruitment of Roma into the governing body of the State fund for support to businesses employing minorities, and it envisages a number of ways to empower Roma organisations in implementing measures to protect Roma culture. As comprehensive implementation of the Framework Programme has not yet started, no mechanism has been put in place to coordinate collaboration between Governmental bodies and non-governmental organisations in implementation and evaluation.

2.5 The Programmes and the Public

2.5.1 The Framework Programme

The general public knows of the Framework Programme, and the Roma community in particular became aware of the Programme through the extensive negotiations undertaken prior to the Programme's adoption. Awareness has been raised primarily through the efforts of NGOs rather than through Government initiatives, however. Public knowledge is at a basic level; people generally know only that a programme to "do some good" for the Roma exists. Very few details of the programme are familiar to the public or discussed publicly, probably due to the fact that implementation has not yet started and therefore has not affected the well-being and interests of any group, ethnic Bulgarians or Roma.

Reporting on the Framework Programme has not been on the agenda of any media; it has been mentioned only as part of interviews with acting or former State officials or in articles written by them,[31] in the statements of NGO activists[32] or tangentially, in

---

[31] *Dnevnik*, 17 October 2001, *Demokraciia*, 8 August 2001.

[32] *Sega*, 23 March 2001.

reporting on events not directly related to the Programme.[33] No media outlet in Bulgaria has analysed the content of the Framework Programme in depth or has made financial and social cost estimates for its implementation since its adoption in 1999. When discussing topics that are a part of the Framework Programme, such as desegregation of Roma schools, media do not make any connection with Government policy.[34]

2.5.2 The Integration of Minorities Programme

The Integration of Minorities programme is not as well known to the public or to its intended beneficiaries as the Framework Programme, perhaps because it was not adopted in consultation with minority organisations. A number of minority leaders and activists have expressed disagreement with its content and resentment against the way it was adopted and publicised. Some are not even aware of its existence.[35] Others have claimed that it is too general or vague.[36] The only Roma leader who has indicated publicly his support for the Integration of Minorities Programme is an MP from the ruling majority coalition.[37]

2.6 The Programmes and the EU

The EU has been supportive of the Government's efforts to improve the situation of Roma, commending the adoption of the Framework Programme, and monitoring its implementation in the Regular Reports. However, EU funding for Roma-related projects has not consistently followed the strategies articulated in the Framework Programme, and the observations in the Regular Reports have occasionally lacked the emphasis and specificity that would encourage better adherence to Programme goals.

The EU accepted the Framework Programme without any criticism of its content from the beginning. The European Commission's 1999 Regular Report describes the main aspects of the Programme in brief, stating that its very adoption "reflect[s] the political

---

[33] *Sega* from 6 August 2001.

[34] *Trud*, 14 September 2001; *Demokraciia*, 8 March 2001; *Demokraciia*, 20 September 2001; *Demokraciia*, 20 October 2001; *Sega*, 27 December 2001; *Republika*, 30 July 2001.

[35] Interviews with: Hristo Kiuchukov, President of "Diversity" Foundation, Sofia, 6 March 2002; Petar Georgiev, President of the Roma Confederation "Europe," 6 March 2002.

[36] Interviews with: Vassil Chaprazov, President of the United Roma Union, 6 March 2002; Toma Tomov, MP from "Coalition for Bulgaria" in the 39th National Assembly, 13 March, 2002; Svetlana Vassileva, former Secretary of the NCEDI, 5 March 2002.

[37] Interview with Alexander Filipov, MP from the NMSS, 21 March 2002.

commitment of the Bulgarian Government towards improving the situation of Roma."[38] The sole concern expressed in the 1999 report regarded the lack of funding to implement the programme.

The 2000 Regular Report is somewhat imprecise and superficial in evaluating progress in implementing the Framework Programme. It recognised that "the administrative capacity of the NCEDI to implement the programme remains low,"[39] but also noted that "some progress has been made." According to the report, this progress included the appointment of 24 experts on ethnic and demographic issues in the districts, six experts in two of the ministries and recruiting of 50 young Roma into the police.[40] However, these measures were not foreseen by the Framework Programme.

The analysis of the minority situation is more concrete and precise in the 2001 Report, however.[41] For the first time, the European Commission took notice of measures to desegregate Roma schools in a favourable light, noting "It is a positive step that the process of desegregation of Roma schools has started, with some NGO projects testing different methodologies."[42] The Report goes on to observe that "[desegregation] has to become Government policy, and the methodology and the approach have to be broadly discussed and accepted by the Roma community."[43]

The 2001 Regular Report acknowledges that "very little progress has been made on implementation" of the Framework Programme,[44] apparently referring to the appointment of Roma experts in the public administration. As the Framework Programme does not provide for the appointment of Roma to administrative bodies *per se*, and there were not in fact any further Roma appointments after the release of the 2000 Regular Report, the basis of the Commission's observation is not clear.

Within the framework of the annual Phare Bulgaria National Programmes, the EU provides funding for most of the activities undertaken in implementation of the Framework Programme. Annually, each Ministry is responsible for submitting project proposals to the Ministry of Foreign Affairs for inclusion in Bulgaria's overall proposal

---

[38] European Commission *1999 Regular Report on Bulgaria's Progress Towards Accession*, (hereafter, "1999 Regular Report") p. 14.

[39] European Commission *2000 Regular Report on Bulgaria's Progress Towards Accession*, (hereafter, "2000 Regular Report") p. 22.

[40] 2000 Regular Report, p. 22.

[41] The report cites data on the share of the illegally built housing in the Roma community and the estimates of unemployment, for example.

[42] European Commission *2001 Regular Report on Bulgaria's Progress Towards Accession*, (hereafter, "2001 Regular Report") p. 23.

[43] 2001 Regular Report, p. 23.

[44] 2001 Regular Report, p. 23.

to the EU. While the integration of Roma is one of priorities of the 1999/2000 and 2001 Accession Partnerships,[45] projects to implement the Framework Programme have not consistently been included in Bulgaria's Phare National Programme budget.

Phare support constitutes a vital source of funding for Roma-related projects. However, not all EU-funded projects clearly correspond to the objectives articulated in the Government programmes. The Government itself has not done enough to take advantage of the opportunities afforded by the EU accession process: as one official has stated, "the Government thinks in terms of closing chapters, rather than solving problems."[46] However, Phare procedures have also been criticised as too unwieldy and often a large percentage of funding has been devoted to paying for European expert consultants.[47]

For 1999 there was only one project affecting Roma within the Phare framework, "Promoting the Integration of Roma,"[48] for a total of €500,000, a rather moderate sum both in relation to the scope of the project and in relation to other elements in the 1999 Phare National Programme. The project had two components: education and urbanisation. The educational component provided for training of teacher assistants, preparing Roma secondary school graduates to apply for universities, training for Roma working in police units and a number of seminars and publications, all only loosely connected to the objectives set out in the Framework Programme. The urbanisation component envisages incorporation of one neighbourhood in Stara Zagora within the municipal boundaries, and the construction of several houses in Pazardzhik. These activities fall within the scope of the Framework Programme's goals in principle, although implementation is on a very small scale. Realisation of the 1999 project started only in the Autumn of 2001. It is not yet completed and consequently no official evaluation has been made to date.

For the year 2000 the Government did not include any project for the integration of Roma in its proposal to the EU, and accordingly no Phare funding was allocated to implementation of the Programme in 2000. However, the Phare 2001 National Programme allocates a total of €8,288,000 divided into three large-scale projects:

---

[45] See *Accession Partnership 1999*, p. 4, and *Proposal for a Council Decision on the principles, priorities, intermediate objectives and conditions contained in the Accession Partnership with Bulgaria 2001*, p. 6.

[46] OSI Roundtable, Sofia, May 2002.

[47] OSI Roundtable, Sofia, May 2002.

[48] Project BG 9907.01. A short financial memorandum of the project is available at <http://www.evropa.bg>, (accessed 20 March 2002). This and the other EU projects are discussed in more detail under Section 3.

- *Roma Population Integration* with two main components: improving school attendance and assistance in the preparation of an anti-discrimination law;
- *Social Inclusion* with several components, including development of cultural centres, job creation and entrepreneurial promotion, among others. This project includes also a small amount of money for integration of the disabled;
- *Healthcare* with two components: improved access to health in 15 towns and a healthcare awareness campaign.[49]

The Phare 2001 project is also better integrated with the Framework Programme. Still, some aspects, especially those related to education, have raised concerns within the NGO community.[50] At present, all 2001 Phare projects are at the pre-contracting preparatory stage. No implementation activities have started for any of them.

3. Government Programmes – Implementation

3.1 Stated Objectives of the Programmes

The Framework Programme's underlying assumption is stated in its introduction: "Discrimination against Roma in social life pre-determines the problems of the community in socio-economic and cultural-educational aspects."[51] The Programme takes into account the need both to prevent future discrimination and to address existing inequalities. Accordingly, the Framework Programme proposes the establishment of a general mechanism for the prevention of ethnic discrimination in all spheres of social life, and measures to ensure full and effective equality in particular fields such as education, employment, housing, health care, and social protection.[52] In addition to its strong focus on discrimination, the Framework Programme sets out measures for the promotion of Roma ethnic identity in the spheres of education, culture and media.

---

[49] The fiches for the projects are available at <http://www.evropa.bg>, (accessed 20 March 2002).
[50] See Section 3.2.1.
[51] Framework Programme, Chapter I.
[52] The establishment of a general mechanism for the prevention of ethnic discrimination through an administrative body with effective powers to investigate and punish discrimination, suggested by the Framework Programme, should protect against discrimination in all spheres outlined below, in addition to the specific measures envisaged in each one of them.

The Integration of Minorities Programme is not as explicit or unequivocal in recognising discrimination. It is more focused on measures for the protection of ethnic minority identity. As it states in its introduction, "preservation and development of the minority identity is a priority in the Government's politics." Nonetheless, it does prescribe measures to combat discrimination, acknowledging that "anti-discrimination legislation and the mechanisms of its enforcement are not effective enough."[53] It also regrets that the Framework Programme has not been fulfilled and proposes to establish a monitoring mechanism to promote its implementation.

3.2 Government Programmes and Discrimination

Discrimination is highlighted as a problem both in the Framework Programme, and by civil society. Nevertheless, the legal framework to combat discrimination remains very weak. General anti-discrimination provisions exist in the Constitution and in a number of laws, but these have never been enforced.[54] Anti-discrimination measures have been implemented inconsistently, particularly in the spheres of education and housing. The Government programmes have not set up a mechanism that is strong enough to overcome the lack of political will within the bodies tasked with carrying out activities to address inequalities.

In its decision from 10 November 1992 the Constitutional Court prohibited the State's adoption and enforcement of "special measures" to promote full and effective equality on the grounds explicitly mentioned in the Constitution's anti-discrimination provision, Art. 6(2). These grounds include race, ethnicity and sex among others.[55] Such measures, according to the Court's ruling, would be privileges that would constitute a breach of the principle of equality.[56] However, the Court did not exclude the possibility of affirmative action that would indirectly benefit disadvantaged minorities by ruling that the State not only can but is also obliged to take measures aiming at "elimination of the existing inequalities for the purposes of achieving the

---

[53] Integration of Minorities Programme: State.

[54] See EU Accession Monitoring Program, *Monitoring the EU Accession Process: Minority Protection*, Budapest, CEU Press, 2001, p. 84, (hereafter, *"Minority Protection 2001"*). See also M. Ilieva, *Legal Analysis of National And European Anti-Discrimination Legislation: A Comparison of The EU Racial Equality Directive & Protocol N° 12 With Anti-Discrimination Legislation in Bulgaria*, European Roma Rights Center; Interights; Migration Policy Group, September 2001 pp. 5–6, (hereafter, *"Legal Analysis, Bulgaria"*).

[55] Article 6 (2) states: "There shall be no restrictions of rights or privileges based on race, national origin, ethnic appurtenance, sex, descent, religion, education, beliefs, political affiliation, personal and social status, or property status."

[56] Constitutional Court Decision No.14/10 November 1992.

stipulated equality." Such measures cannot be based on any of the 11 grounds listed in Article 6(2). Thus, some special measures envisaged in the Framework Programme, if adopted on a purely ethnic basis, would contravene current Constitutional Court jurisprudence.[57]

The Framework Programme is the only Government document or programme that recognises or discusses discrimination. Moreover, both before and after the adoption of the Framework Programme the Government continued to deny the existence of discrimination at domestic and international forums. In its 1999 reply to the UN Committee on Economic, Social and Cultural Rights regarding Bulgaria's third periodic report under the ICESCR, the Government rejected the conclusion of the Committee that Roma are subject to discrimination in receiving land as well as in receiving social assistance.[58] Previously, in its report to the Committee on the Elimination of Racial Discrimination from 26 June 1996 the Government recognised the existence of discrimination by private parties, but not by public officials.[59]

Bulgaria is obliged to incorporate the European Council Directive Implementing the Principle of Equal Treatment Between Persons Irrespective of Racial and Ethnic Origin, the "Race Equality Directive," as part of the *acquis communautaire*. At present, the existing framework lacks required comprehensive anti-discrimination legislation, and sets standards lower than those required under the Directive.[60]

Under the Phare 2001 Bulgaria National Programme a separate "Twinning Light" component of the Roma Population Integration Project[61] has been approved to assist the Bulgarian Government in adopting an anti-discrimination law. A total of €150,000 is allocated to solicit the expertise of one medium-term and one short-term expert from EU member States, who are to work with Bulgarian experts to draft a bill establishing a body for the promotion of equal treatment without discrimination on the basis of racial or ethnic origin, and for the training of law enforcement officials.

As of June 2002, a working group established to draw up anti-discrimination legislation had prepared an initial draft and submitted it to the Council of Ministers.

---

[57] The EU Race Equality Directive allows, but does not oblige states to take action to "prevent or compensate for disadvantages linked to racial origin" (Council Directive 2000/43/EC of 29 June 2000 implementing the principle of equal treatment between persons irrespective of racial or ethnic origin, (OJ L 180, 19/07/2000) Art. 5).

[58] See replies by the Government of Bulgaria to the List of Issues: Bulgaria. 09/07/99. (CESCR), §§ 4.1 and 4.6.

[59] See CERD/C/229/Add.7, §§ 41 and 42.

[60] See M. Ilieva, *Legal Analysis, Bulgaria*, p. 7.

[61] Phare Project BG 0104.01, fiche available at <http://www.evropa.bg>, (accessed 20 March 2002).

The working group is comprised of Government and NGO representatives. Two EU experts, one from the UK and the other from Austria, also assisted with the drafting process, although the Twinning project did not officially begin until the Autumn. These experts will remain as consultants during the parliamentary discussion of the law expected later in the year.

Racial discrimination is identified as a problem by different sectors of civil society, although to varying degrees. The Bulgarian Helsinki Committee surveyed 19 ethnic minority newspapers published between May 1999 and May 2000 to analyse the extent to which these periodicals addressed themes of racism, xenophobia, and ethnically motivated violence.[62] The survey found that these issues comprised a substantial share of the content in Turkish and Roma publications, 22.4 and 19.4 percent respectively in the two largest newspapers.[63] Recent publications in the minority press have described cases of employment discrimination when Roma apply for jobs,[64] called attention to discriminatory legal provisions in the Constitution and in laws regulating the use of minority languages, teaching of religion and provision of social welfare,[65] and discussed discrimination in Macedonians' exercise of their basic rights and freedoms.[66]

Human rights NGOs also highlight ethnic discrimination in their publications and through other activities. According to the survey above, discrimination, racism, xenophobia, and racially motivated violence together comprise 47.1 percent of the content of the Roma-language publication *Romano Obektivo* of the Bulgarian Helsinki Committee and 44.4 percent of the content of *Roma Rights in Focus*, the periodical of the Human Rights Project. In its September 2001 memorandum to the new Government the Bulgarian Helsinki Committee emphasised the necessity of enacting an effective anti-discrimination law that would be in conformity with the Race Equality Directive and the need to improve the existing legal procedures to combat ethnic discrimination.[67]

Trade unions have not taken an active role in identifying and combating discrimination against minorities. According to information supplied by the largest trade union in Bulgaria, the Confederation of Independent Trade Unions (hereafter,

---

[62] See *The Ethnic Press in Bulgaria*, Sofia, BHC, 2000 (in Bulgarian).

[63] See *The Ethnic Press in Bulgaria*, Sofia, BHC, 2000, pp. 126–136.

[64] *Drom Dromendar*, "There is hidden discrimination," from February 2002 (in Bulgarian).

[65] *Kaynak*, July–August, 2001 (in Turkish).

[66] "The election of a president of Bulgaria and the problem with our rights and freedoms," *Narodna volia*, December, 2001 (in Bulgarian).

[67] Memorandum of the Bulgarian Helsinki Committee to the Government of Bulgaria, 10 September 2001, see <http://www.bghelsinki.org>, (accessed 5 March 2002).

CITU), the union has been involved with Roma mostly through expert consultations in job-creation projects. Recently, CITU has organised festivals and assemblies with ethnic groups in order "to decrease the impression of discrimination formed in the representatives of different communities."[68]

The mainstream media generally do not discuss minority issues in light of racism, discrimination and xenophobia. Between June 2000 and June 2001 the Bulgarian Helsinki Committee undertook a survey of ethnic publications in the mainstream press and some regional periodicals. The survey showed significantly lower levels of discussion of discrimination, racism, xenophobia, and racially motivated violence in the mainstream press compared to the levels of discussion in the minority press. In the two biggest newspapers the share of these themes in the pool of all minority publications (generally, a tiny share of all publications) is negligible (2.3 percent in the biggest daily *Trud* and 3 percent in *24 chasa*). The situation in other periodicals is similar, with slightly better coverage in the two left-wing dailies *Duma* (13.1 percent) and *Sega* (9.6 percent).[69]

Minority leaders and activists are unanimous in their opinion that discrimination against Roma is a serious problem in Bulgarian society. They all use almost the same words to characterise its scope and effect – it is referred to as "flagrant," penetrating "all spheres of social life," and a "serious problem for society" that has brought "tragic results" for the Roma community.[70]

---

[68] Letter of the Chairman of CITU, Dr. Zheliazko Hristov, to BHC from 5 April 2002, available in the BHC archive.

[69] *Ethnic Minorities in the Press*, BHC, Sofia, 2002 (in Bulgarian). Once again, the percentages in the minority press reflect shares from all publications while those in the mainstream press reflect shares from the minority publications only.

[70] Interviews with: Stela Kostova, President of the Roma Youth Organisation, Sofia, 14 March 2002; Hristo Kiuchukov, President of "Diversity" Foundation, Sofia, 6 March 2002; Vassil Chaprazov, President of the United Roma Union, 6 March 2002; Toma Tomov, MP from "Coalition for Bulgaria" in the 39th National Assembly, 13 March, 2002; Simeon Blagoev, Roma expert in the Ministry of Culture, 8 March 2002; Zlatko Mladenov, President of Roma Social Council "Kupate," 8 March 2002; Petar Georgiev, President of the Roma Confederation "Europe," 6 March 2002; Svetlana Vassileva, former Secretary of the NCEDI, 5 March 2002; Alexander Filipov, MP from the NMSS, 21 March 2002.

3.2.1 Education

Discrimination in education has been widely documented by both Bulgarian and international human rights groups.[71] Schools in exclusively Roma neighbourhoods give rise to *de facto* segregation, exacerbated by the lack of resources supplied to such schools; Roma children are also over-represented in the system of "special schools" for the developmentally disabled and for juvenile delinquents. According to census data supplied by the NCEDI, between 1992 and 2001 the illiteracy rate among Roma (excluding those younger than seven) rose from 11.2 percent to 14.9 percent, and the share of Roma holding a university degree decreased from 0.3 percent in 1992 to 0.16 percent in 2001.[72]

Discrimination in education specifically is a concern of both Roma leaders and activists and civil society groups. Some Roma leaders and activists mention educational discrimination as a specific problem.[73] Others consider the very existence of schools in which only Roma are enrolled as discrimination.[74] National and international human rights and other civil society organisations also identify educational discrimination as a serious problem affecting the Roma community.[75]

The Framework Programme addresses education at length, identifying six specific problem areas, most arising from past or present discrimination. It envisages specific measures to achieve full and effective equality in educational opportunities between Roma and non-Roma, and to ensure the promotion of minority rights. The Integration of Minorities Programme incorporates the objectives of the Framework Programme, but does not set deadlines for implementation of its objectives.

According to the Framework Programme, the key to equalisation of educational opportunities for Roma is desegregation. Segregation of Roma in the educational system became widespread during communism when rapid urbanisation led to the establishment of extensive Roma ghettos in almost every large Bulgarian city. Schools

---

[71] See, e.g. D. Denkov, E. Stanoeva, V. Vidinski, *Roma Schools: Bulgaria 2001*, Sofia, OSF, 2000; J. Tanaka, "Parallel worlds: Romani and non-Romani schools in Bulgaria," *Roma Rights*, No.3, 2000; *Minority Protection 2001*, pp. 86–90.

[72] Interview with Ilona Tomova, NCEDI Expert, Sofia, 21 May 2002.

[73] Interviews with: Hristo Kiuchukov, President of "Diversity" Foundation, Sofia, 6 March 2002; Vassil Chaprazov, President of the United Roma Union, 6 March 2002; Zlatko Mladenov, President of Roma Social Council "Kupate," 8 March 2002; Svetlana Vassileva, former Secretary of the NCEDI, 5 March 2002.

[74] Interview with Stela Kostova, President of the Roma Youth Organisation, Sofia, 14 March 2002.

[75] See J. Tanaka, "Parallel Worlds," K. Kanev "Why is Desegregation Necessary," in *Obektiv*, November 2001 – January 2002.

were established in the midst of these neighbourhoods, giving rise to *de facto* segregation. Altogether about 70 percent of school-age Roma are enrolled in such schools.[76] According to a 2001 survey, schools that enrol between 50 and 100 percent Roma students included 60 elementary, 350 primary and nine secondary schools.[77]

In the mid-1960s the Government established special educational programmes in these schools, focusing on training for manual labour. These programmes existed for almost three decades and were abolished only in the 1990s.[78] The professional community of educators considered these schools the least prestigious, and as a consequence the teachers appointed there were often the least competent and motivated. One recent comprehensive survey of Roma schools in Bulgaria describes their quality of education in the following terms:

- Five percent of the students in these schools have a "slim chance" of graduating from secondary school;
- It is not uncommon for a fourth grader to be illiterate;
- Some schools lack basic educational tools such as blackboards and chalk;
- Only 0.3 percent of Roma students take an interest in national exams for admission to elite schools after the seventh and eighth grades;
- In more than 50 percent of Roma schools windows are covered by cardboard instead of glass.[79]

The Framework Programme calls for the development of a "long-term strategy towards full abolition of segregated schools in Roma neighbourhoods," ensuring the free access of Roma children to "normal" schools and prohibiting the enrolment of Roma in segregated classes.[80] In addition to desegregation, the Framework Programme envisages pre-school education in Bulgarian for Roma children who speak it as a second language, abolition of early professional education in Roma schools, dismissal of unqualified teachers, recruitment of Roma "teacher assistants," and material and logistical support for Roma families.

The second objective of the Framework Programme in the field of education is to reduce the overrepresentation of Roma children in special schools for the

---

[76] Report from the conference "The Desegregation of Romani Schools – A Condition for Equal Start for Roma," Sofia, Bulgaria, 27 April 2001, p. 6.

[77] See D. Denkov, E. Stanoeva, V. Vidinski, *Roma Schools: Bulgaria 2001*, Sofia, OSF, 2000, p. 10.

[78] See for more details: *Minority Protection 2001*, p. 87.

[79] D. Denkov et al., *Roma Schools: Bulgaria 2001*, pp. 10–11.

[80] Framework Programme, Part V.

developmentally disabled. The Bulgarian educational system is unable to take into account cultural specifics and to deal with the effects of poverty and neglect on Roma families: placement tests are in the Bulgarian language, are not culturally sensitive and are often very formal.[81] As a result, a substantial number of Roma children are placed in special schools for purely social reasons. According to a recent survey of academic abilities in three special school classes conducted by Step by Step – Bulgaria, 46 percent of the students were performing up to a standard that would allow their integration into mainstream schools.[82]

The third educational objective of the Framework Programme is the introduction of measures to combat racism in the classroom, including educational measures targeting teachers, parents and students, as well as effective sanctions against racist behaviour. All are envisaged in the context of desegregation. The Programme also aims to support university education for Roma by organising preparatory courses for application to university, and by disseminating information among Roma regarding the availability of stipends for university education. Finally, adult education and re-qualification courses are envisioned under the Programme.

Until very recently no action was taken to implement most of the Framework Programme's objectives in the field of education. In September 2002, the Ministry of Education issued its annual instructions on the organisation and regulation of school activities, including a new annex entitled "Guidelines for the Integration of Children and Students from Minorities."[83] These instructions direct municipalities to create their own programmes for the gradual integration of Roma with their peers from schools outside segregated settlements. The closure of Roma schools is not advised until local communities have been adequately prepared for integration.[84]

Moreover, in August 2002, the Ministry of Education issued Ordinance No. 6, on the education of children with special educational needs or disabilities.[85] This ordinance defines the conditions of acceptance in special kindergartens and schools for children with all levels of developmental disabilities, not only for mild retardation, as had

---

[81] J. Tanaka, "Parallel worlds", p. 39.

[82] *School Success for Roma Children: Step by Step Special Schools Initiative,* Interim Report, Budapest, OSI, December 2001, p. 32.

[83] Ministry of Education and Science, *Organization and government of the activities of the schools of general education, professional and special schools,* Sofia, 2002, Annex 10, (hereafter, "Ministry of Education, 2002 Guidelines"). See also, Human Rights Project, *Bulgaria: Three and Half Years After the Adoption of the 'Framework Programme for Equal Integration of the Roma in Bulgarian Society' at Last the First Important Steps were Done,* Sofia, 13 September 2002.

[84] Ministry of Education, 2002 Guidelines, Annex 10.

[85] SG No. 83, 2002, 19 August 2002.

previously been the practice. The Ordinance states that special education programmes may only accept "children and students for whom all other possibilities for education have been exhausted."[86] The Ministry guidelines further direct that "the existing practice to track normally developed children in schools for the mentally retarded should be stopped."[87] The Ministry has also pledged to pass an ordinance providing for the participation of an interpreter during evaluations for placement in special education programmes.[88] At the time the guidelines were released, however, the evaluation commissions continued to work without an interpreter and most of them had already completed their assessments for the 2002–2003 school year; most classes had already been determined, as the process begins as early as April or May of each year.

These promising developments can in the meantime create a favourable atmosphere for desegregation projects already being implemented by NGOs. However, they represent only the beginning of the process, and appear to offer minimal concrete support to local authorities in the actual process of desegregation. A more detailed strategy, including resources and assistance for building greater support for desegregation in local communities, should be considered as a necessary complement to the Ministry's instructions.

The Phare 1999 Bulgaria National Programme has a specific education component. It included several activities, not all of which are related to each other. The principal measures include:

- Preparation of a curriculum for 50 Roma teacher assistants to be trained for one month within a university department. Teacher assistants are then expected to be employed to help Bulgarian teachers (more than 90 percent of the teachers in the Roma neighbourhoods) maintain contacts with the community;

- Publication of a guide on Roma culture and history, to be used for teaching in mainstream elementary schools;

- Two training courses for two weeks for 50 Roma high school graduates to prepare them to apply to university faculties, including the police academy;

- Training for 50 Roma working in the police.

None of these activities is related to desegregation of the Roma educational system, a Framework Programme priority. Training of "teacher assistants" is envisaged in the Framework Programme as such, but in the context of desegregation. The preparation of "teacher assistants" within the current educational system runs the risk of

---

[86] SG No. 83, Art. 2 (3).
[87] Ministry of Education, 2002 Guidelines, p. 157.
[88] Ministry of Education, 2002 Guidelines, p. 157.

perpetuating segregation rather than abolishing it, as the presence of Roma assistants will be seen only as "helpers" for the ethnic Bulgarian teachers, and will discourage the systemic reform that is necessary. Training Roma to apply for universities is envisaged in the Framework Programme but training of police officers is not. Nevertheless, for the latter the 1999 project allocates the largest share of funds (€67,000 of the total €179,000).

The Phare 2001 Bulgaria National Programme includes a large educational component under the Roma Population Integration project.[89] It has three sub-components, which comprise:

- delivery of basic primary school packages, such as food, materials and clothes; support of educational activities to teach the Bulgarian language to Roma children; support of the schools' boards of trustees; publication of inter-cultural materials and training activities for Roma children and adults.

- Identification of areas with high dropout rates of Roma students for the implementation of a pilot project to address this problem; training for 300 teachers' assistants, and publication of a textbook.

- Curriculum development in teacher training institutions, and launching an information campaign on the revised curricula.

This is the largest of the Bulgarian Phare 2001 projects related to Roma (€1,750,000) and the least clearly related to the Framework Programme. Although the Framework Programme is noted in the project documents, the need to desegregate Roma schools is not even mentioned.[90] No activity is planned in that regard, and the teacher-assistant training is completely detached from the objective of desegregation.

Beginning in the 2000–2001 school year desegregation projects organised by Roma NGOs started operating in several Bulgarian cities. The first and the most successful of these is in Vidin, operated by Drom Association. In the 2001–2002 school year, similar projects started in five other cities, all operated by local NGOs. The attitudes of local authorities towards these projects have ranged from active support to open hostility.[91] EU representatives have also expressed ambivalence regarding the need for desegregation, and at no point was the Bulgarian Government involved in supporting any of the projects financially, in spite of the Roma communities' clear commitment to the process.

---

[89] Phare Project BG 0104.01, see <http://www.evropa.bg>, (accessed 20 March 2002).

[90] Phare Project BG 0104.01.

[91] K. Nikolaeva, "Problems and Challenges before the Programme 'Desegregation of the Roma Schools in Bulgaria'," in *Roma Rights in Focus*, No. 20, 2001.

Given the importance that most domestic and international organisations place on improving the educational situation for Roma, and the scope of the problems involved, there have been some suggestions that the Framework Programme should be revised and amended, and that a specific action plan on education should be elaborated to accelerate the realisation of activities.[92]

3.2.2 Employment

Racial discrimination played a specific role in isolating the Roma community from access to employment during the first wave of job cuts in 1990–1993. Local and international human rights monitors documented flagrant cases of dismissals based on ethnicity.[93] However, the Government does not collect data on unemployment by ethnicity, and no case of discrimination on any ground has been sanctioned by the courts since the promulgation of the Labour Code. A recent survey indicated that some 71 percent of working-age Roma are unemployed.[94] While unemployment correlates with the lower levels of education among Roma (also the result of discrimination, in part), there is evidence that direct discrimination in dismissals from and hiring for jobs also plays an important role.[95]

For some discrimination in unemployment is the most frequent form of discrimination experienced by Roma.[96] Roma have expressed concerns about employment discrimination at public forums and before media. At a rally against discrimination in Sofia's biggest Roma neighbourhood, "Fakulteta," speakers reported that, "when employers understand that some candidate is of Roma origin, they don't accept him."[97] According to another Rom from Sofia interviewed by a Sofia daily: "There are lots of ads in the newspapers for work. When I go there however and they see that I am a

---

[92] OSI Roundtable, Sofia, May 2002.

[93] See D. Petrova, *Violations of the Rights of Gypsies in Bulgaria*, Report of the Human Rights Project, Sofia 1994; Helsinki Watch, *Destroying Ethnic Identity: The Gypsies of Bulgaria*, New York, June 1991.

[94] Anti Poverty Information Center, "Social integration of the Roma population in Bulgaria," report prepared for the United Nations Department for Economic and Social Affairs, Sofia, October 2000, p. 32, (hereafter, "*APIC/UNDESA survey*").

[95] ECRI, *Second Report on Bulgaria*, 18 June 1999, §43, see <http://www.coe.int/T/E/human_rights/Ecri>, (accessed 16 March 2002). Interviews with: Stela Kostova, President of the Roma Youth Organization, Sofia, 14 March 2002; Vassil Chaprazov, President of the United Roma Union, 6 March 2002.

[96] Interview with Simeon Blagoev, Roma expert in the Ministry of Culture, 8 March 2002.

[97] "'Fakulteta' protests against discrimination," *Trud*, 15 October 2001.

Gypsy, they wouldn't offer anything. For a Bulgarian however they would."[98] Bulgarian Turks also complain of ethnic discrimination. In an interview for one of the daily newspapers, an MP stated that, "Our voters often complain that when they apply for jobs, directors would tell them: 'Change your name and you will get the job.'"[99]

Furthermore, the redistribution of land as a result of restitution disenfranchised Roma who were engaged in agricultural work under communism. The land was restored to its pre-collectivisation owners and their heirs, very few of whom were Roma. As a result, Roma have been excluded from all forms of land cultivation since 1989, making the employment situation of Roma villagers even more desperate than that of Roma living in cities.

The Framework Programme deals with employment discrimination and with measures to promote full and effective equality. In Chapter I it provides for the creation of a special Government body to combat discrimination in all spheres of social life, including employment. In Chapter II, "urgent measures" are set forth to create employment opportunities for Roma. These measures include:

- Development of programmes for employment qualification and re-qualification, adapted to both the demands of the market and to traditional skills among Roma;

- Creation of a special Government fund, which would offer loans under the condition that they are used to create job opportunities for Roma; the fund is to be overseen jointly by governmental experts and Roma representatives;

- Creation of an effective information network to facilitate employment counselling for Roma;

- Simplification of the land appropriation procedure and legal reform to enable Roma to acquire land and to gain acceptance into existing agricultural cooperatives.[100]

The Integration of Minorities Programme is more general in its approach to employment and proposes different measures to decrease unemployment among minorities. There is no explicit recognition of the existence discrimination in employment (or in other areas), though, as mentioned above, the adoption of anti-discrimination legislation is foreseen. Rather, it calls for the "creation of socio-economic and cultural conditions for effective integration of minorities." In the long-term perspective, by the end of the present Government's mandate, the Integration of Minorities Programme proposes the adoption of a strategy for the development of

---

[98] "Gypsy time," *Dnevnik*, 8 March 2001.

[99] "There is discrimination towards the Turkish population," *Monitor*, 7 August 2001.

[100] Framework Programme, Chapter II.

underdeveloped regions with compactly settled minority populations (generally referring to ethnic Turks and Bulgarian-speaking Muslims) No concrete measures are envisaged that would specifically benefit Roma.

Most of the objectives of the Framework Programme in the field of employment discrimination have not been realised. The adoption of anti-discrimination legislation is still pending; no Government fund to promote Roma employment has been created; and no changes in the Land Law facilitating access to land have been made.

In its Progress Report 2000[101] on the legislative and policy measures taken to implement EU recommendations for accession, the Government mentioned several initiatives to improve employment prospects for Roma, including several at the regional level, which aim to provide "the Roma community adequate possibilities for work realisation and vocational training." In contrast with its position in the Framework Programme, in the Progress Report the Government does not characterise racial discrimination as a cause of the high unemployment among Roma, emphasising rather that "the predominant part of the Roma is without education or vocational qualification, with low working discipline."[102]

While some of the regional programmes highlighted in the Progress Report will undoubtedly benefit Roma because they are over-represented among the unemployed, they do not target Roma specifically. For example, the two-tier training programme "From Education to Employment" of the District of Pernik, envisages a training scheme and subsequent employment placement for unemployed persons in general; it does not target Roma specifically.[103] The programme "Socially Useful Activities" in Omurtag municipality, proposes general training and temporary employment through public works; neither it nor a similar programme in the municipality of Antonovo specifically targets Roma.[104] The programme "Improvement of Living Conditions in the Municipality of Turgovishte" offers temporary employment for the long-term unemployed.[105] Another project cited in the Progress Report, "job placement of Roma people in gathering and processing plastic waste products," allegedly "financed with

---

[101] See <http://www.mfa.Government.bg/eiweb>, (accessed 17 March 2002).

[102] *Progress Report 2000*, Ch.13, see <http://www.mfa.Government.bg/eiweb>.

[103] Interview with Ekaterina Markova, Director of the Bureau of Labour, Pernik, 20 March, 2002.

[104] Interview with Stanimira Todorova, Director of Municipal Industrial and Budgetary Activities, Omurtag, 26 March, 2002 and Mr. Lazarov, Secretary of the Municipality, Antonovo, 28 March 2002.

[105] Interview with Snezhina Slavcheva, Officer at the Administrative Control, Regional Development and State Property, Turgovishte, 26 March 2002.

priority" was cancelled by the Regional Initiative Fund in the autumn of 2001 because of financial irregularities.[106]

The "Social Inclusion" project, part of the Phare 2001 Bulgarian National Programme, envisages several job creation activities for Roma and entrepreneurial promotion for Roma and the disabled.[107] The job creation component foresees the development of six job creation programmes, including four specifically targeting Roma. These programmes are designed to provide funding to organisations capable of delivering job-creation initiatives. The other component plans to provide entrepreneurial training, consulting and business support to individuals seeking to become self-employed or to develop an existing enterprise. In this case as well, delivery of services is planned on the basis of proposals coming from organisations at the local level. In both the job creation and the entrepreneurial promotion components, the Government provides one-third of the funding as co-financing. The activities planned in the Phare 2001 Social Inclusion project are all drawn from Chapter II of the Framework Programme. However, the participation of minorities in the governing bodies of these funds, as provided for in the Framework Programme, is not ensured in the project design and it remains to be seen how this will affect implementation.

Employment discrimination has long been a concern for Roma and other minority and human rights organisations, Roma leaders and activists, and ordinary Roma. Roma NGOs report that qualified Roma are not hired for jobs as soon as prospective employers see an address indicating a Roma neighbourhood.[108] In March 2000 the regional coordinator of the Movement for Rights and Freedoms in Lovech stated that employers refuse to hire minorities, which has compelled some people to change their Muslim names to Bulgarian ones.[109]

3.2.3 Housing and other goods and services

Housing has been another cause of serious concern for Roma and for domestic and international observers. According to a survey conducted in 2000 by the Bulgarian Helsinki Committee based on information from district and municipal Government offices, 70 percent of the houses in Bulgaria's Roma neighbourhoods are built "illegally,"

---

[106] Interview with Mihail Ivanov, Secretary of the NCEDI, Sofia, 26 February 2002.

[107] Phare Project BG 0102.06, fiche available at <http://www.evropa.bg>, (accessed 21 March 2002).

[108] "There is hidden discrimination," interview with Leonchia Ivanova, coordinator of "Partners-Bulgaria," *Drom Dromendar*, February 2002.

[109] Bulgarian Helsinki Committee, *Human Rights in Bulgaria in 2000*, *Obektiv*, March 2001, see also the BHC web site, <http://www.bghelsinki.org>.

either outside municipal boundaries or without appropriate authorisation documents. In some neighbourhoods this proportion reaches 85–90 percent of the houses,[110] some of which are seriously sub-standard. As these settlements are not formally included in municipal plans, they do not receive services such as garbage collection, public transport and electricity at all, or to a much lesser extent than other areas.[111] The law permits State seizure of illegal buildings under certain circumstances.[112] Indeed, in some cases illegal buildings become easy targets for demolition, especially when lucrative interests are at stake for municipalities and private companies.[113] In others, the existence of unregulated Roma properties after the restitution of the agricultural land on which they were built heightened tensions between Roma and ethnic Bulgarians.[114] The conditions in these neighbourhoods worsened after 1989 with growing impoverishment and with the flight of the ethnic Bulgarian residents. In a number of towns, Roma access to commercial enterprises, such as bars, discos, restaurants, and swimming pools is restricted on racial grounds.[115]

The Framework Programme deals with the prevention of discrimination and the improvement of housing conditions for Roma in two interrelated sections: Prevention of Discrimination and Territorial Planning of Roma Neighbourhoods. Establishment of a framework for the effective prevention of discrimination is also intended to address housing and the provision of goods and services. The chapter on the territorial planning of Roma neighbourhoods provides for:

- Amendments to the Law on the Regulation of Territories and Settlements, in order to simplify the complicated bureaucratic procedure for legalisation of housing;

- Legalisation of Roma housing based on the principle of minimal interference in the existing state of affairs, so that Roma occupants may become owners as quickly as possible;

---

[110] See *Minority Protection 2001*, pp. 93–94.

[111] See I. Zoon, *On the Margins: Roma and Public Services in Romania, Bulgaria, and Macedonia*, Open Society Institute, New York, 2001, pp.138–143.

[112] See Mihail Gheorgiev, "Fighting for Fakulteta: advocating Roma housing rights in Bulgaria," *Roma Rights*, No. 2, 2000.

[113] For the demolition by Sofia municipality of the Roma neighborhood "Asanova Mahala," see Bulgarian Helsinki Committee, *Human Rights in 2001, Obektiv*, Special Issue, March, 2002, <http://www.bghelsinki.org>, (accessed 22 October 2002). See also the Human Rights Project's letter to the Mayor of Sofia in *Obektiv*, March 2001 (in Bulgarian).

[114] Report of the Human Rights Project on the implementation of the Framework programme on Equal Integration of Roma in Bulgarian Society, in *Andral*, No. 6, 1999, p. 6 (in Bulgarian).

[115] Human Rights Project, *Annual Report*, 1999, p. 15.

- Improvement of the existing housing fund through access to credit, materials and land;

- Procurement of Governmental subsidies to improve infrastructure in Roma neighbourhoods;

- Adapting municipal housing programmes to allow for the resettlement of Roma to offer enhanced opportunities to improve their living environment.

The Integration of Minorities Programme notes that the objectives of the Framework Programme have not been achieved, including those related to the territorial planning of Roma neighbourhoods. However it does not envisage any specific activities to address these shortcomings.

In December 2000 the Parliament passed the Law on the Regulation of Territory, superseding the old Law on the Regulation of Territories and Settlements. The new law however, does not address the concerns of the Framework Programme in any way. It does not simplify the regulation and legalisation procedure and does not oblige the municipalities to deal with illegally built houses.

The second component of the Phare 1999 Bulgaria National Programme is urbanisation. This project has been under implementation since Autumn of 2001 under the management of the Bulgarian "Habitat for All" Foundation. It operates in two Bulgarian cities – Stara Zagora and Pazardzhik. According to the project's terms of reference, in both cities it aims to amend the general town-planning scheme in order to include Roma settlements within the city boundaries and to construct several Roma houses. Because of the scarce funds (a total of €270,000), the latter activity was ultimately restricted only to the city of Pazardzhik.[116] Thus, the only Governmental activity related to the Framework Programme's territorial planning component is a small-scale operation with little effect on the Roma community as a whole. Concerns have also been raised that as demand for the new housing (14 houses in all) far outstrips supply, arriving at a fair and equitable means of allocating the housing will be extremely difficult.[117] An alternative, and possibly more effective use of funds could be the provision of legal advice and support for Roma to regularise their property, which could potentially assist a much larger number of beneficiaries.[118]

The Phare 2001 Bulgaria National Programme includes the development of Roma information and cultural centres ("*chitalishte*") to enhance the relationship between

---

[116] Interview with Mariana Barouh, Executive Director of "Habitat for All" Foundation, Sofia, 15 March 2002.

[117] OSI Roundtable, Sofia, May 2002.

[118] OSI Roundtable, Sofia, May 2002.

Roma communities and "statutory authorities, for example national and local labour offices, regional educational inspectorates, drop-out centres and vocational training centres, employers and their organisation."[119] This project has four components:

- Provision of literacy and mathematical training. The expectation is that at least 4,500 Roma will receive such training under 300 programmes;

- Extension of mediation services with authorities to address language difficulties and develop better communications with Romani communities;

- Awareness training for public authorities to make them more sensitive to Roma needs;

- Extension of information services identifying potential employers and disseminating this information within the Romani community.

The Framework Programme includes the objective to advance adult literacy and qualification.[120] Promotion of information services also can be considered to be in line with the Framework Programme's provisions designed to improve access to the labour market for Roma.[121] The other two components are not directly related to any Government programme.

Discrimination in housing and in the provision of public goods and services has long been a serious concern for the Roma community.[122] Roma report that they are barred from access to bars and cafes,[123] excluded from kindergartens,[124] offered a lower standard of service for public utilities and other municipal services in Roma neighbourhoods,[125] and subject to *de facto* curfews due to lack of public transport.[126]

Discrimination in the provision of publicly organised goods and services has not been addressed through any targeted governmental activity, nor is not addressed in the Phare

---

[119] Social Inclusion Project BG 0102.06, see fiche at <http://www.evropa.bg>.

[120] Framework Programme, Chapter V Section 6.

[121] Framework Programme, Chapter II Section 2.

[122] According to the President of the Roma Youth Organisation, the very existence of ghettos is discrimination, Interview, Sofia, 14 March 2002.

[123] See e.g. K. Anguelova, "Teteven café forcefully closed for serving representatives of minorities," *Obektiv*, November 2000 – January 2001, also: Human Rights Project, *Annual Report*, 1999.

[124] "Minority children – no man's land of today," *Obektiv*, November 2000 – January 2001.

[125] I. Zoon, *On the Margins*, pp. 138–142.

[126] I. Zoon, *On the Margins*, pp. 140–141.

Bulgaria National Programmes, except in a general manner, through efforts to draft an anti-discrimination law.[127]

3.2.4 Healthcare and other forms of social protection

Due to poverty and exclusion the majority of Roma are heavily and in many cases exclusively dependent on social welfare.[128] In 1999 Bulgaria introduced universal health insurance as part of a reform of the national healthcare system. Although in theory the system was supposed to improve access to healthcare for all, in practice it has had serious negative consequences for both employed and unemployed Roma. Due to high levels of unemployment (this itself due in part to discriminatory practices in education and employment) and their exclusion from the social welfare system, many Roma have found themselves without health insurance and consequently without any access to healthcare.[129] According to a recent survey, almost 30 percent of Roma do not have a general practitioner (GP), the primary health care provider, a much higher share than among the population as a whole.[130]

Even those who do have a GP are often unable to pay for transportation to the hospital, to pay doctors' fees or to buy prescribed medications.[131] 31.2 percent of Roma participating in a survey conducted by "Fakt Marketing" in December 2001 had never visited their personal GP, while 35.4 percent reported that they cannot pay the user tax of one Lev (approximately €0.50[132]) for an examination even if they have a GP.[133] Discriminatory treatment by health care practitioners, including physical and verbal abuse, segregation of Roma women in maternity wards, and negligence in examinations, also work to alienate Roma from the healthcare system.[134]

The Framework Programme envisages two measures in the area of healthcare: improving sanitary conditions in Roma neighbourhoods, and increasing health education programmes, as well as stimulating Roma participation in these programmes. The

---

[127] See Section 3.2.

[128] According to a recent survey, 63.5 percent of Roma depend on social welfare for their survival. *APIC/UNDESA survey*, p. 27.

[129] I. Zoon, *On the Margins*, pp. 91–94.

[130] *APIC/UNDESA survey*, pp. 27–28.

[131] I. Turnev, O. Kamenov, M. Popov, L. Makaveeva, V. Alexandrova, *Common health problems among Roma – nature, consequences and possible solutions*, Sofia, OSF-Bulgaria, January 2002, p. 3.

[132] The exchange is calculated at BGL 1.95 = €1.

[133] Interview with Ilona Tomova, NCEDI Expert, 21 May 2002.

[134] I. Turnev et. al, *Common Health Problems Among the Roma*, pp. 6 and 10.

Integration of Minorities Programme does not address healthcare and social protection at all. It states only that the main objectives of the Framework Programme, including those relating to healthcare, have not been achieved, without specifying any measures to remedy this situation.

The Framework Programme was developed before the introduction of the national healthcare reform. The Programme's measures to address social protection and healthcare are thus in need of revision. With regard to social protection, the Programme requires that an amendment be made in the law to differentiate a subgroup of "vulnerable ethnic minorities" within the general category of the "socially weak," so that the special measures undertaken directly address their specific situation. An obstacle to implementing this measure became evident when the Framework Programme was adopted, in view of the Constitutional Court's prohibition against taking special measures on an ethnic basis.[135] The Framework Programme further requires that monitoring of the social welfare system should be strengthened through the involvement of Roma NGOs, although the precise nature of this collaboration has not been articulated.

Since the adoption of the Framework Programme, legislative and policy developments generally have had a negative impact with regard to Roma access to healthcare and social protection. The introduction of universal health insurance excluded many Roma from access to health care. A number of factors built into the existing social welfare legislation contributed to the further exclusion of Roma from monthly benefit payments. These factors include the exclusion of those sanctioned for not reporting their income,[136] and for travelling abroad,[137] and an increase in the number of poor people who must be supported by their relatives under the law.[138] The extremely bureaucratic application procedure is another factor discouraging potential applicants.

The Regulations for the Application of the Social Assistance Act have been amended several times since the adoption of the Framework Programme, including by the present Government. Some of these amendments did have a positive impact on Roma access to welfare. In November 2001, the provision imposing a three-year limit on the

---

[135] See Section 3.2.

[136] Sanction envisaged in the Regulations for the Application of the Social Assistance Act, Art.11.5.

[137] Sanction envisaged in the Regulations for the Application of the Social Assistance Act, Art.11.7. E.g. some Roma who travelled to Norway in the summer 2001 were prohibited from claiming monthly welfare benefits for a period of one year (See Bulgarian Helsinki Committee, Human Rights in Bulgaria in 2001, *Obektiv*, Special Issue, March 2002, see <http://www.bghelsinki.org>, (accessed 22 October 2002).

[138] They are to be excluded from monthly payments under the Regulations for the Application of the Social Assistance Act, Art.11.2.

payment of monthly social welfare assistance to working-age unemployed people was abolished. However, another provision, providing that those who have refused the offer of agricultural land can be excluded from monthly welfare payments, was not.[139] Those affected are mostly Roma, who have been compelled to decline land offers as they have no money to buy equipment and grain.[140]

The Phare 2001 Bulgaria National Programme includes the project, "Ensuring Minority Access to Health Care," aiming at "ensuring justice and equality of social opportunities in health access for Roma."[141] The total budget for the project is €1,100,000, of which €100,000 is provided by the Government. The project has two components: improving access to healthcare in 15 towns, and health issues awareness campaigns directed at Roma communities. The first sub-project includes three related activities:

- Delivery of healthcare equipment for GPs practising among Roma, in 15 towns including those with the largest Roma communities. Rehabilitation of buildings in which these practices are based is also envisaged;

- Training of GPs and nurses serving the Roma population to work with the new healthcare equipment and to promote health in the Roma community;

- Training of 50 Roma leaders to act as mediators between health authorities and Roma.

The second sub-project envisages information campaigns in target areas to address health risks and to disseminate healthcare information through NGOs and churches working with Roma. The project will be managed by the Ministry of Health and will be overseen by a committee composed of Government officials, Roma and NGOs. In addition, 15 local working groups including Roma NGOs will be established in the areas where the project is to be implemented.

If implemented as planned, the project will benefit those Roma who have registered with GPs. However, the project will not address the more fundamental problem of complete lack of access to the healthcare system for people who have dropped out of the social assistance system altogether. The overall approach of the project is to seek ways to adapt Roma to the system without also modifying the system to meet Roma needs.

---

[139] Regulations for the Application of the Social Assistance Act, Art.11.6.

[140] See the statement of the then Mayor of Russe and now Minister for State Administration, Dimitar Kalchev, in: Rositza Stoykova, "Non-payment of social benefits as part of the budget," *Obektiv*, November 2000 – January 2001.

[141] Ensuring Minority Access to Health Care Project BG 0104.02.

Part of the Phare 2001 Social Inclusion Project[142] aims to extend mediation services to facilitate communications between Roma and public authorities, including the social welfare administration. This should eventually improve access for Roma and will increase the sensitivity of the administration staff to the Roma situation. At present very few Roma work within the social welfare administration; increasing the number of Roma employees in social services would also improve communications with and services for Roma communities.

3.2.5 The criminal justice system

A number of serious problems have been noted in the Bulgarian criminal justice system including unfair pre-trial and trial proceedings, excessive use of physical force by law-enforcement officers, and corruption and selective targeting of the poor and disenfranchised. These problems affect all people who come into contact with the criminal justice system. Very few Roma leaders and activists express concerns with discrimination against Roma in the criminal justice system. Only one of those interviewed mentioned the existence of discrimination in the work of the police and in the judiciary.[143]

Nonetheless, some legal provisions are discriminatory on their face. For example, the police are not obliged to inform those arrested of the reasons for the arrest or of the charges brought them in a language that they understand. In addition to being discriminatory, this directly contradicts Art. 5(2) of the European Convention of Human Rights and Art. 10(3) of the Framework Convention for the Protection of National Minorities.

Moreover, there is a growing body of evidence that criminal defendants belonging to a minority group (especially Roma and Turks) are discriminated against in all phases of criminal proceedings. According to a number of surveys conducted by the Bulgarian Helsinki Committee since 1999, minorities are more likely to be physically abused during detention, less likely to be represented by a lawyer at all stages of criminal proceedings, more likely to be charged with serious crimes, and more likely to be

---

[142] See Section 3.2.3.
[143] Interview with Petar Georgiev, President of the Roma Confederation "Europe," 6 March 2002.

sentenced to effective imprisonment.[144] According to the most recent surveys conducted by the Bulgarian Helsinki Committee in 2001 and 2002, the probability of being represented by a lawyer during trial clearly depends on a defendant's ethnicity; all other conditions being equal, the probability of being represented by a lawyer during trial decreases by between four and six percent if the defendant is not an ethnic Bulgarian.[145]

The final version of the Framework Programme does not deal with discrimination within the criminal justice system specifically. The proposed legislation to combat ethnic discrimination generally is intended to protect against ethnic discrimination within the criminal justice system as well. An earlier draft of the Framework Programme provided for a mechanism to investigate complaints against illegal police actions, but this was omitted from the final version.[146] The Integration of Minorities Programme does not deal with discrimination in the criminal justice system. No other Government initiatives or policies to combat discrimination in this sphere exist beyond the two programmes. No EU or other international programmes address this issue.

3.3 Protection from Racially-Motivated Violence

Racially motivated violence, and particularly police brutality against Roma, have long been serious issues.[147] Racist attitudes continue to be common even in the official

---

[144] See Legal Defence of Defendants in the Criminal Process and its Effect, at <http://www.bghelsinki.org>, (accessed 22 March 2002); K. Kanev, "The access to justice of indigent criminal defendants did not improve," in *Obektiv*, November 2000/January 2001; Bulgarian Helsinki Committee, *Human Rights in Bulgaria in 2001*, *Obektiv*, Special Issue, March 2002, see <http://www.bghelsinki.org>, (accessed 22 October 2002). See also *Minority Protection 2001*, pp. 97–99.

[145] The survey involved examination of 1,891 criminal files and interviewing 1,001 prisoners, *Access to Legal Defense in the Criminal Justice System of Bulgaria*, see <http://www.bghelsinki.org>, (accessed 7 April 2002).

[146] See Section 3.3.

[147] Some of the more recent reports with evidence of racially-motivated violence include: "The case of Blago Atanasov from Gelemenovo," *Roma Rights in Focus*, January–July, 1999, pp.3-4; "The case from Sotiria," in *Roma Rights in Focus* January–July, 1999, p.4; "Bulgarian police violence against Roma," *Roma Rights*, No. 4, 2000. See also BHC annual reports on human rights in Bulgaria for 1992–2001, at <http://www.bghelsinki.org>, (accessed 25 March 2002); *Racial Discrimination and Violence against Roma in Europe*, ERRC submission to the 57th Session of CERD, August 2000; and Helsinki Watch, *Destroying Ethnic Identity: The Gypsies of Bulgaria*, p. 47.

discourse of senior police officers.[148] Such attitudes can mute the official response to racially motivated violence by private groups.[149] Three recent surveys of the use of force during arrest and in custody by law enforcement officials conducted by the Bulgarian Helsinki Committee in 1999, 2001 and 2002 have established that Roma are more likely than the other defendants to be physically abused during arrest and inside the police station.[150]

Roma leaders and activists have widely varying views on the existence and the role of racially motivated violence against Roma. Some identify it as a serious and frequent problem.[151] Others believe that it exists as both private and institutional behaviour but is not a serious problem on the level of nationalist principles, or that it only expresses itself from time to time.[152] Still others believe that it is hidden or that it exists only at

---

[148] A characteristic example from a letter of P. Purvanova, Director of the International Cooperation Directorate of the Ministry of Interior, to E. Poptodorova, Director of the Human Rights Directorate, Ministry of Foreign Affairs, for preparation of the initial report due under the Framework Convention for the Protection of National Minorities, from 14 December 2001, (hereafter, "letter of P. Purvanova") : "Socio-economic factors, demographic and ethno-cultural characteristics of the Roma population explain the relatively high crime rate among it. Because of the low professional qualification of the majority of Roma, they were dismissed from work during the structural adjustments of the enterprises. As a consequence, the Gypsy criminality is "justified" as a form of social resistance." In the same letter legitimate protest actions, such as public rallies against electricity cuts and delays in the payment of social welfare money are called "anti-social behaviour."

[149] Another example from the letter of the Director of the International Cooperation Directorate of the Ministry of Interior: "Despite society's traditional tolerance towards minorities, some isolated accidents of intolerance can be observed, motivated by the perception of the representatives of Roma community as potential criminals. Such negative attitudes find expression in the actions of youth groups, imitating the "Skinheads" movement." Letter of P. Purvanova.

[150] K. Kanev, "The access to justice of indigent criminal defendants did not improve," in *Obektiv*, November 2000/January 2001; Bulgarian Helsinki Committee, *Human Rights in Bulgaria in 2001*, *Obektiv*, Special Issue, March 2002, see <http://www.bghelsinki.org>.

[151] Interviews with: Stela Kostova, President of the Roma Youth Organisation, Sofia, 14 March 2002; Svetlana Vassileva, former Secretary of the NCEDI, 5 March 2002.

[152] Interviews with: Vassil Chaprazov, President of the United Roma Union, 6 March 2002; Zlatko Mladenov, President of Roma Social Council "Kupate," 8 March 2002.

the level of private groups.[153] There are also Roma leaders and activists who believe that it would be an exaggeration to refer to racially motivated violence.[154]

The Government has been reluctant to recognise the problem of racially motivated violence, especially when Government agents are responsible. The version of the Framework Programme signed by the Government and Roma NGOs on 8 April 1999 included a section providing for the creation of a special governmental body for investigating complaints of citizens against illegal actions by police. However, as a result of the "editing" which took place after the agreement on the Programme had already been signed, no such bodies are envisaged in the final version of the Framework Programme.

Illegal use of force and firearms by law enforcement officials was referred to in the 8 April Programme as "one of the most serious manifestations of ethnic discrimination against Roma." Accordingly, the draft programme agreed to on 8 April 1999 provided for the establishment of committees at the central and local levels to review complaints against law enforcement officers. These committees, in which ethnic minorities were to be proportionally represented, would have been authorised to refer cases to the prosecutor's office and to take part in criminal investigations, to give recommendations for compensating victims, and to sanction administrative offences. The final Framework Programme envisages only the introduction of changes to the Penal Code that would provide for heavier penalties if racial animus is proven as a motive for the commission of a given crime. The Integration of Minorities Programme does not deal with racially motivated violence at all.

Racially motivated violence is also not addressed adequately by the Government outside the scope of the Framework Programme. On 15 August 2000 a Specialised Commission on Human Rights was created within the police, which was assigned the task of planning activities to sensitise the police force to human rights. According to information submitted by the Ministry of the Interior, as of November 2001 the Ministry of Interior had realised six projects relating to human rights and police work:

- The publication of teaching materials on human rights and translation of the video "Police and Human Rights – Let's be More Careful," sponsored by the Council of Europe;

---

[153] Interviews with: Hristo Kiuchukov, President of "Diversity" Foundation, Sofia, 6 March 2002; Simeon Blagoev, Roma expert in the Ministry of Culture, 8 March 2002.

[154] Interviews with: Toma Tomov, MP from "Coalition for Bulgaria" in the 39th National Assembly, 13 March, 2002; Petar Georgiev, President of the Roma Confederation "Europe," 6 March 2002.

- Six seminars on police violence and procedures for filing complaints, as well as on the internal relationships within police structures for 180 police officers, sponsored by the World Organisation against Torture;

- Seminars on human rights and policing for senior police chiefs, sponsored by the Office of Technical Assistance of the US Treasury Department;

- Training seminar for the regional coordinators of the human rights commission sponsored by the ADACS;

- Experts' working meeting on police ethics to discuss the Code of Conduct of National Police Officers sponsored by the Council of Europe.

- A training project on policing in a multiethnic environment in the Roma neighbourhood of Plovdiv sponsored by the UK Know-How Fund.[155]

Human rights NGOs took part in some of these projects and discussed police violence against minorities but no programme addressed racially motivated violence as such as its topic. None of these projects appears to have been effective in combating racially motivated violence, which has remained at a consistently high level, particularly with regard to police violence during arrest and in custody.[156] Civil society organisations have assisted victims in filing cases before domestic courts and international tribunals, and the European Court of Human Rights has issued three decisions against Bulgaria on cases of ill treatment/torture of Roma by law enforcement officers, finding that the State had failed to adequately investigate allegations of police misconduct.[157]

3.4 Promotion of Minority Rights

The overall legal framework for the protection of minority rights is weak and in some cases at variance with international standards.[158] Enforcement of existing laws has been both restrictive and discriminatory and has further curtailed those rights provided for under the Constitution and in separate legislation.

---

[155] Letter of P. Purvanova,, 14 December 2001.

[156] K. Kanev, "The access to justice of indigent criminal defendants did not improve," in *Obektiv*, November 2000/January 2001; Bulgarian Helsinki Committee, *Human Rights in Bulgaria in 2001*, *Obektiv*, Special Issue, March 2002, see <http://www.bghelsinki.org>.

[157] *Assenov and Others v. Bulgaria*, ECHR Appl. No. 24760/94, Judgment from 28 October 1998; *Velikova v. Bulgaria*, ECHR Appl. No. 41488/98, Judgment from 18 May 2000; *Anguelova v. Bulgaria*, ECHR Appl. No. 38361/97, Judgement from 13 June 2002.

[158] For example, the Constitution prohibits the formation of political parties on an ethnic or religious basis. Bulgarian Constitution, Art. 11 (4).

Both the Framework Programme and the Integration of Minorities Programme provide for the promotion of some minority rights, though neither programme sets forth a comprehensive plan covering the entire spectrum of minority rights. Nevertheless, some Governmental activities directed at protecting minority identity and culture have taken place outside the scope of the Government programme.

3.4.1 Education

Most Roma leaders and activists believe that Romanes should be studied in public schools, as an extension of existing programmes for the study of other minorities' native languages. Opinions as to how this should best be implemented vary, and there are also Roma leaders and activists who think that there is no need to study Romanes in the schools or have no opinion on the matter.[159] In 1994–1995, some 4,000 Roma students received Romanes mother-tongue education. Since then, however, the number of students has declined, and at present there are no students studying in Romanes.[160]

At the time the Framework Programme was created, mother-tongue education was organised for all minorities as an elective subject, which could be taught as a supplement to the regular school curriculum, and for which students did not earn a grade. The Framework Programme envisages introduction of Romanes as an obligatory elective subject in public schools. In addition, the programme calls for the training of teachers of minority languages in the pedagogical universities and institutes, including Sofia University. As part of its objective to combat racism in the classroom,[161] the Framework Programme provides that the Ministry of Education should develop programmes for teaching tolerance to teachers and introduce anti-racist education in schools. In the section on the protection of ethnic identity and culture of Roma the Programme requires the introduction of themes related to Roma history and culture "into the textbooks for the elementary, primary and secondary education, in the general context of the Bulgarian history and culture."[162]

The Integration of Minorities Programme does not envisage concrete measures related to mother-tongue education or to any other educational activities, but reiterates the Government's commitment to the implementation of the Framework Programme and the FCNM. By the end of the mandate of the present Government it pledges to

---

[159] Interviews with: Toma Tomov, MP from "Coalition for Bulgaria" in the 39th National Assembly, 13 March, 2002; Simeon Blagoev, Roma expert in the Ministry of Culture, 8 March 2002; Zlatko Mladenov, President of Roma Social Council "Kupate," 8 March 2002.

[160] See *Minority Protection 2001*, pp. 106–107.

[161] See Section 3.2.1.

[162] Framework Programme, Part VI.

"ensure full and effective enforcement of the FCNM by undertaking concrete measures of legislative and other character."[163]

In 1999 the legislative framework for mother-tongue education was changed, and it became an obligatory elective subject. Consequently, all minority students (Turkish, Armenian, Jewish, and others) who previously studied their mother tongue as a free elective subject started studying it on an obligatory elective basis. This change did not affect Roma however, as no mother tongue education was organised for them on any basis. There have been no efforts to train teachers qualified to teach Romanes at public schools and no Government-sponsored programmes have been introduced within the county's pedagogical institutes.

One of the activities envisaged in the Roma Population Integration project as part of the Phare 2001 Bulgaria National Programme[164] proposes the introduction of a nation-wide multicultural content-revised curriculum in order to provide students with a greater understanding of Roma culture. These activities are to be supported by an information campaign targeted at school management and civil society organisations and by supporting training needs and cost assessment for the planned in-service training of teachers. As with the other Phare 2001 projects, implementation has not yet begun.

Several NGOs have organised training activities for teachers in multicultural education, with the permission of the Ministry of Education. They have also published teaching materials on minority history and culture. The scope of these activities has been very limited, however.

3.4.2 Language

Roma leaders and activists are not unanimous in their opinions as to the need to enable Roma to expand the use of Romanes in communications with public authorities. Some believe that Romanes could or should be used;[165] others believe that such measures would not meet with broad societal acceptance, or that they are not necessary.[166] Roma

---

[163] Integration of Minorities Programme, Activities.

[164] See Part 3.2.1.

[165] Interviews with: Stela Kostova, President of the Roma Youth Organization, Sofia, 14 March 2002; Hristo Kiuchukov, President of "Diversity" Foundation, Sofia, 6 March 2002.

[166] Interviews with: Simeon Blagoev, Roma expert in the Ministry of Culture, 8 March 2002; Toma Tomov, MP from "Coalition for Bulgaria" in the 39th National Assembly, 13 March, 2002; Alexander Filipov, MP from the NMSS, 21 March 2002; Svetlana Vassileva, former Secretary of the NCEDI, 5 March 2002 Vassil Chaprazov, President of the United Roma Union, 6 March 2002 Zlatko Mladenov, President of Roma Social Council "Kupate," 8 March 2002.

leaders and activists are similarly divided regarding the use of Romanes on public signs; some endorse the idea[167] while others do not accept it.[168]

Neither the Framework Programme nor the Integration Programme envisages measures to encourage the use of Romanes with public authorities, including in judicial proceedings, on public signs, and in their names and surnames.

The Government has not implemented any measures to ensure the expansion of the public use of Romanes or other minority languages.

3.4.3 Participation in public life

Roma are grossly underrepresented at all levels of decision-making and in the public employment sector.[169] During the municipal elections in 1999 two *de facto* Roma parties, "Free Bulgaria" and "Future for All" won 102 and four seats respectively in municipal councils or as mayors. At present there are only two Roma in the Parliament, both elected on the tickets of mainstream parties, the NMSS and the Coalition for Bulgaria.

Roma leaders and activists unanimously voice concern about the inadequate representation of Roma in governmental institutions, although they advance different models to improve the situation. The majority believes that Roma should have their own political party through which they should take part in elections at both central and local level.[170] Some prefer participation through the mainstream political parties.[171] Others consider that participation through single-constituency candidates would be

---

[167] Interviews with: Stela Kostova, President of the Roma Youth Organization, Sofia, 14 March 2002; Hristo Kiuchukov, President of "Diversity" Foundation, Sofia, 6 March 2002; Vassil Chaprazov, President of the United Roma Union, 6 March 2002; Zlatko Mladenov, President of Roma Social Council "Kupate," 8 March 2002.

[168] Interviews with: Simeon Blagoev, Roma expert in the Ministry of Culture, 8 March 2002; Petar Georgiev, President of the Roma Confederation "Europe," 6 March 2002; Svetlana Vassileva, former Secretary of the NCEDI, 5 March 2002.

[169] See *Minority Protection 2001*, p. 110.

[170] Interviews with: Stela Kostova, President of the Roma Youth Organisation, Sofia, 14 March 2002; Vassil Chaprazov, President of the United Roma Union, 6 March 2002; Toma Tomov, MP from "Coalition for Bulgaria" in the 39th National Assembly, 13 March, 2002; Simeon Blagoev, Roma expert in the Ministry of Culture, 8 March 2002; Zlatko Mladenov, President of Roma Social Council "Kupate," 8 March 2002. The Constitution (Art. 11.4) however prohibits political parties organised along ethnic or religious lines.

[171] Interview with Petar Georgiev, President of the Roma Confederation "Europe," 6 March 2002.

most effective,[172] and still others believe that Roma should participate in decision-making predominantly as experts.[173]

In its introduction, the Framework Programme states that: "Roma should not be only a passive object of influence but an active subject in the public sphere."[174] In its conclusion it reiterates: "The active position of Roma at all levels of state institutions, which are responsible for the realisation of this programme, is a condition for its successful implementation."[175] The Framework Programme mandates the participation of Roma in some of the governing bodies it proposes to establish, such as the special governmental fund to create employment opportunities for Roma.[176] In the draft version of the Framework Programme, the proposed anti-discrimination body was to be elected by the Parliament with its composition at both central and local level "proposed by minority organisations and correspond[ing] to the relative share of the respective ethnic group."[177] However, this provision was eliminated when the Programme was "edited," and is not included in the final text.

The Integration of Minorities Programme provides that the realisation of the programme's priorities is to be achieved "through the direct participation of the minorities in the development and the realisation of politics."[178] It further envisages among its short-term activities the "creation of structures dealing with the problems of minorities in the central, district and municipal administrations."[179]

Since the adoption of the Framework Programme, representation of Roma in public life improved somewhat but still remains unsatisfactory. Several Roma work on minority issues in different Governmental agencies, including the Ministry of Education, the Ministry of Culture, the NCEDI, and the State Agency of Youth and Sports. A few Roma work in these agencies as ordinary employees at positions unrelated to minorities. The employees from both groups occupy some of the lowest levels of the administrative hierarchy.

A number of Roma work as experts on ethnic and demographic issues at the district and municipal government level. These posts often have no defined responsibilities or

---

[172] Interview with Alexander Filipov, MP from the NMSS, 21 March 2002.
[173] Interview with Svetlana Vassileva, former Secretary of the NCEDI, 5 March 2002.
[174] Framework Programme, Introduction.
[175] Framework Programme, Conclusion.
[176] See Section 3.2.2.
[177] Programme "For Equal Participation of Roma in the Public Life of Bulgaria," Section 1.1.
[178] Integration of Minorities Programme, Priorities.
[179] Integration of Minorities Programme, Activities.

mandate, and some experts feel that their positions and responsibilities are largely nominal.[180]

According to information from the Ministry of Interior, by the end of 2000 only 92 Roma worked in the National Police, 88 of whom were sergeants.[181] Thus, the participation of Roma in the implementation of the Framework Programme at different levels of state institutions, as the programme itself requires, is negligible at present.

3.4.4 Media

Roma leaders and activists are almost unanimous in identifying a need for newspapers, radio and TV broadcasts in Romanes. Some believe that such broadcasts should be organised on all channels and that there should also be a special Roma channel.[182] Others think that the Government should provide financial and legal support for the organisation of such broadcasts.[183] There are also Roma leaders and activists who do not see a need for media in Romanes as their existence would "encapsulate" the community and isolate it from majority Bulgarian society.[184]

The Framework Programme is critical of the representation of Roma in the media. It states that Roma are "deprived of the possibility of equal access to national media," which, given their stereotyped portrayal of Roma, "leaves the development of negative social attitudes without an alternative."[185] The Programme envisages State support for Roma participation in the Bulgarian National Television and National Radio through the inclusion of Roma broadcasts and of Roma journalists. The Framework Programme also envisages State support for Roma print publications.

The Integration of Minorities Programme does not envisage any measures to improve minority representation in the national media, nor does it stipulate support for minority publications.

Since the adoption of the Framework Programme, stereotyped representation of Roma in the media has continued unchanged, and Roma voices continue to be absent from both the electronic and print media. The only relevant broadcast on Bulgarian

---

[180] OSI Roundtable, Sofia, May 2002.

[181] Letter of P. Purvanova, 14 December 2001.

[182] Interview with Alexander Filipov, MP from the NMSS, 21 March 2002.

[183] Interview with Toma Tomov, MP from "Coalition for Bulgaria" in the 39th National Assembly, 13 March, 2002.

[184] Interview with Svetlana Vassileva, former Secretary of the NCEDI, 5 March 2002.

[185] Framework Programme, Part VII.

National TV at present is a one-hour programme on Channel 1 dedicated to Roma problems, which is broadcast in Bulgarian.[186] Some private radio and TV stations air programmes for Roma without any support from the Government. Several Roma periodicals are published, most of them irregularly, and some receive modest financial support from the Government. In 2001 the NCEDI supported the publication of the largest Roma newspaper *Drom dromendar* for a total of BGL 3,300 (approximately €1,692), allocated BGL 5,983 (approximately €3,069) to a Roma association in Brusartsi for a media campaign, and BGL 600 (approximately €308) to the studio "Roma" in the Mizia regional radio centre in Pleven.[187]

3.4.5 Culture

The Framework Programme has a special section on the protection of Roma culture in which it plans support for the "development of the Roma culture as a specific ethnic culture and at the same time as a part of the Bulgarian national culture."[188] The Framework Programme envisages a series of measures to achieve this goal:

- To restore information and cultural centres in Roma neighbourhoods;

- To encourage Roma participation in national and regional folk festivals;

- Protection of authentic Roma folklore through support for Roma music festivals, through the publication and distribution of audio and video products and by ensuring access to national media for Roma;

- Restoration of the Roma national theatre.

The Integration of Minorities Programme does not envisage specific objectives for the protection of Roma culture in addition to those stated in the Framework Programme, though it states a general goal of "preservation and encouragement of the culture of different minorities."

Some State funding is available annually to support the organisation of Roma cultural activities, including folk festivals and the celebration of holidays. In 2001 the National Council on Ethnic and Democratic Issues contributed a total of BGL 7,500 (approximately €3,847) for Roma cultural events and festivals. Another BGL 47,880 (approximately €24,557) was allocated to support Roma Information and Cultural

---

[186] See *Minority Protection 2001*, p. 108.
[187] Information on Funds from the NCEDI budget for projects – 2001, offered by the NCEDI.
[188] Framework Programme, Part VI.

Centres, whose activities include the organisation of cultural events.[189] The Ministry of Culture allocated an additional BGL 14,500 (approximately €7,437) to Roma cultural activities in 2001.[190]

Phare 2001 Bulgaria National Programme's Social Inclusion Project envisages development of Roma *chitalishte*. They are expected to retain their existing role as centres of Roma cultural events (see Section 3.2.3). In addition, the project envisages strengthening their role as mediators between the Roma community and authorities in the provision of literacy, information services for job creation, and awareness training for public officials.

4. EVALUATION

The Framework Programme for Equal Integration of Roma in Bulgarian Society was developed and accepted with enthusiasm across the Roma community. Both domestic and international organisations considered it to address the most serious problems affecting the Roma community. The Bulgarian Government benefited internationally from the adoption of the Framework Programme, receiving praise for its active attempt to facilitate the integration of minorities.

The Framework Programme's approach to integration of Roma is quite comprehensive. It deals with a wide range of problems and offers a variety of solutions. Nevertheless, a close reading of its provisions reveals some gaps, including:

- *Racial discrimination in the criminal justice system.* The Framework Programme does not deal adequately with discrimination in the criminal justice system and does not offer solutions. No other governmental or international effort exists to address these problems.

- *Protection from racially motivated violence.* Racially motivated violence continues to be a taboo subject when governmental agents are implicated. The Framework Programme does not develop any specific objectives and no other national or international programme has addressed the issue either.

---

[189] Information on Funds from the NCEDI budget for projects – 2001, offered by the NCEDI.

[190] 2,000 Leva for the celebration of "Bangu Vassil"; 3,000 Leva for the 8 April nation-wide celebration; 4,000 Leva for the celebration of 8 April in Montana; 4,000 Leva for the Festival of Roma Song in Stara Zagora; 1,500 Leva for the Roma Spring Musical Days in Stara Zagora.

- *Discrimination in health care.* The Framework Programme's approach to Roma healthcare is minimal, as it was adopted before the introduction of universal health insurance, which has produced widespread discriminatory effects within Roma communities.

- *Use of minority language publicly and before administrative authorities.* The Framework Programme does not address the issue of use of Romanes as a minority language. This is an area in which there is no apparent consensus within the Roma community.

- *Problems relating to the internal consistency of some of the approaches of the Framework Programme.* The relationship between different approaches and objectives in the Framework Programme is not always clear. For example, not enough consideration was given to harmonising desegregation with training for teachers' assistants The Programme would benefit from formal review and evaluation and adjustment as necessary.

The anti-discrimination provisions of the Framework Programme also require further development to bring them into conformity with the EU Race Equality Directive.

The main problem with the Framework Programme, however, is that its comprehensive implementation has not yet begun, three years after its adoption; only some of the measures envisioned have been implemented, and in a poorly-coordinated manner. There is still no effective programme administration, with appropriate allocation of funds, reporting, and evaluation procedures. As the Council of Europe's Commissioner on Human Rights observed in his 2002 Report, "although the framework programme is the result of a formal agreement with the Government and answers the expectations of both the Roma/Gypsy community and the authorities, it has so far come to nothing."[191]

Although the Framework Programme represents a minimalist, rather than maximal approach in light of the scale of the problems faced by Roma, it appears to be viewed as a burden that politicians and society as a whole is not prepared to accept; there has been a marked lack of will to undertake systematic implementation of its measures, and little attempt to clarify the relationship between the Integration of Minorities Programme and the Framework Programme. While the Integration Programme formally states that the Framework Programme continues to form the basis for activities to promote the integration of Roma, the Government has failed to take the necessary next step of developing concrete objectives for its comprehensive implementation. The Government's views on key issues, such as desegregation of

---

[191] Commissioner for Human Rights, *Second Annual Report April 2001 to December 2001, to the Committee of Ministers and the Parliamentary Assembly,* Strasbourg, 2002, p. 84.

Roma schools and the involvement of minorities in the prevention of racial discrimination, remain unclear.

For its part, the EU has not demonstrated that it expects concrete and comprehensive implementation of the Framework Programme's provisions. Although the European Commission praised the adoption of the Framework Programme, it has only expressed regret at the lack of implementation since. Moreover, there appears to be no clear relationship between EU funding to support the integration of minorities and the Framework Programme. In some cases, such as the educational component of the 2001 Phare Roma Population Integration project, EU funding may impede rather than encourage further implementation of the Framework Programme.

The implementation of the Framework Programme so far is a model case of a failed attempt to bring about improvements in the area of minority protection. Nevertheless, the adoption of the Programme with the support of a broad range of civil society organisations and the Roma community remains a significant achievement. The Framework Programme is well known both among Roma and internationally, and has raised expectations about the possibility for making significant improvements to the situation of Roma. As one Roma leader has stated, "we have one document, the Framework Programme, which showed that we can unite for a common cause."[192] Therefore, its implementation is likely to remain on the political agenda of both the Government and the Roma community.

5. RECOMMENDATIONS

In order to initiate systematic and comprehensive integration of Roma in Bulgarian society the Government of Bulgaria should:

- Reconfirm its commitment to implement the Framework Programme for Equal Integration of Roma in Bulgarian Society at the highest governmental level;

- Plan and implement measures with the involvement of top political and governmental leadership on a non-partisan basis to educate the public on the need to integrate Roma into Bulgarian society;

- Clarify the relationship between the Integration of Minorities Programme and the Framework Programme, and develop a unified strategy for implementation;

---

[192] Interview with Petar Georgiev, President of the Roma Confederation "Europe," 6 March 2002.

- Supplement the Framework Programme with objectives in areas where the Framework Programme does not set out concrete measures, such as the criminal justice system, protection from racially motivated violence, health care, public use of minority language and religious freedom;

- Start developing an action plan for implementation with concrete objectives in all areas covered by the Framework Programme;

- Allocate funds for implementation, and establish adequate reporting and evaluation procedures in all spheres covered by the Framework Programme;

- Involve civil society and especially Roma organisations at all stages of planning, implementation and evaluation;

- Address EU and other international donors for financial support only on the basis of a comprehensive plan to implement the Framework Programme.

The European Union should encourage and help Bulgaria to implement the Framework Programme by:

- Making the Framework Programme and its implementation the yardstick for monitoring the Government's efforts to ensure human rights and minority protection;

- Targeting all its funding in line with the objectives set forth in the Framework Programme;

- Ensure that civil society and especially Roma organisations are involved in all activities directed toward the integration of Roma through both the EU-Bulgaria twinning programmes and civil society programmes.

OPEN SOCIETY INSTITUTE 2002

Minority Protection in the Czech Republic

AN ASSESSMENT OF THE CONCEPT OF GOVERNMENTAL POLICY TOWARDS
MEMBERS OF THE ROMA COMMUNITY SUPPORTING
THEIR INTEGRATION INTO SOCIETY.

Table of Contents

1. Executive Summary 126

2. The Government Programme – Background 130
   - 2.1 Background to Present Programme 130
   - 2.2 The Programme – Process 132
   - 2.3 The Programme – Content 133
   - 2.4 The Programme – Administration/Implementation/Evaluation 135
   - 2.5 The Programme and the Public 142
   - 2.6 The Programme and the EU 143

3. The Government Programme – Implementation 144
   - 3.1 Stated Objectives of the Programme 144
   - 3.2 Government Programme and Discrimination 145
     - 3.2.1 Education 148
     - 3.2.2 Employment 154
     - 3.2.3 Housing and other goods and services 158
     - 3.2.4 Healthcare and other forms of social protection 164
     - 3.2.5 The criminal justice system 167

3.3	Protection from Racially Motivated Violence		167
3.4	Promotion of Minority Rights		171
	3.4.1	Education	174
	3.4.2	Language	177
	3.4.3	Participation in public life	178
	3.4.4	Media	179
	3.4.5	Culture	181

4. Evaluation 182

5. Recommendations 185

1. Executive Summary

In the post-independence period, the Czech Government has developed a succession of documents intended to form the conceptual framework for the implementation of measures to promote the integration of individuals belonging to the Roma community.

The "Concept" adopted in 2000 lays out a promising trajectory for achieving meaningful improvements in the situation of Czech Roma. However, the measures implemented have not gone far enough to address the root causes of discrimination or to enact structural changes through accompanying legal reform, and their impact has been minimal to date. Implementation has been hampered by the lack of adequate comprehensive anti-discrimination legislation, lack of an evaluation mechanism, and the inability of central governmental bodies to effectively influence local policies.

Background

The Czech Republic has in recent years taken numerous steps to improve the situation of Roma. The 1997 "Bratinka Report" outlined the problems faced by Roma and has formed the basis for subsequent governmental policies.

The Concept of Governmental Policy Towards Members of the Roma Community Supporting Their Integration into Society, adopted on 14 June 2000 (hereafter, "2000 Concept"),[1] provides the framework for governmental efforts in this area. The Concept is to be updated annually to reflect new developments and experience gained from implementation.

Some efforts have been made to consult with Roma representatives, NGOs and human rights activists in developing and implementing the 2000 Concept, though there is room for improvement in this area.

Administration

The Government has developed a complex mechanism for administering and monitoring implementation of governmental policy towards Roma at the national level. Roma and civil society organisations participate in an advisory capacity at the national level, but no mechanisms to ensure their participation at the local level has been developed. There are also no legally-prescribed mechanisms for evaluation and assessment or for effectively influencing local policy.

---

[1] *Koncepce politiky vlády vůči příslušníkům romské kommunity, napomáhající jejich integraci do společnosti* (Concept of Governmental Policy Towards Members of the Roma Community Supporting Their Integration into Society), adopted by Government Decree No. 599 (14 June 2000), <http://www.vlada.cz/1250/vrk/vrk.htm>, (accessed 22 August 2002) (in Czech only).

The Government's approach integrates the human rights, minority rights and social rights perspectives. Three different institutions oversee activities in these areas: the Council for Human Rights (chaired by the Commissioner for Human Rights), the Council for National Minorities, and the Council for Roma Community Issues (CRCI). The Vice Chair of the Government and Head of the Legislative Council, who also chairs the CRCI and the Council for National Minorities, bears overall responsibility for administration and implementation of the 2000 Concept. An important role in implementation at the local level is also assigned to "Roma Advisors" and their assistants.

The 2000 Concept itself does not contain specific tasks; rather, it provides a set of guiding principles as well as an overall framework within which to coordinate related activities. The implementation of specific tasks is assigned to ministries and other actors, either by the decree by which the 2000 Concept was adopted, or through separate decrees. The main actors – individual ministries – decide independently how much money to allocate for the activities within their competene.

Although the Concept incorporates a built-in mechanism for regular review of activities being implemented, the capacity to assess and evaluate their impact comprehensively and systematically is lacking. A descriptive report is compiled annually by the Vice Chair of the Government together with the Commissioner for Human Rights based on the information submitted by individual ministries. Each year an Updated Concept is prepared as a complement to (not a replacement for) the 2000 Concept.[2] The Commissioner for Human Rights has also prepared a short report on implementation of programmes in which the CRCI administered in 2000 and 2001.

There is no mechanism for ensuring the active involvement of the ministries and other actors involved in implementation, or for exercising effective influence over local policy. While the CRCI is entitled to request information on implementation, it has no authority to require compliance; this is the exclusive competence of the Government.

EU Support

The EU has supported the Government's initiatives through the Phare Programme. Increasing amounts of funding have been allocated to several of the Concept's most important components, including: education, media campaigns to promote tolerance, and training for Roma advisors and their assistants. The EU has also supported efforts to develop the legal and institutional framework for combating racial and ethnic

---

[2] *Koncepce romské integrace* (Concept of Roma Integration), adopted by Government Decree No. 87 (23 January 2002), <http://www.vlada.cz/1250/vrk/vrk.htm>, (accessed 22 August 2002) (in Czech only). The Concept is to be next updated by 28 February 2003.

discrimination. No EU funding has been allocated to improve the employment or housing situation, although the 2001 Regular Report noted that further measures are needed in these areas.[3] However, the EU plans to support small-scale re-qualification and job creation activities, as well as NGO capacity building, an area which has not received sufficient attention to date.

Content and Implementation

The 2000 Concept is a comprehensive document, reflecting the principal concerns of the Roma community. However, there has been little accompanying legal reform, and measures have been implemented on an *ad hoc* basis. Thus, there has been little structural change, without which there can be little long-term impact.

The 2000 Concept is divided into twelve chapters outlining the main issues and directions for action, including racial discrimination, employment, housing, Romani language and culture, education (including multicultural education), and civil society, *inter alia*.

Combating discrimination against Roma and the promotion of tolerance are among the Concept's primary objectives. Efforts in this area have been hampered by the lack of effective anti-discrimination legislation, including legislation which would allow for the implementation of positive measures to overcome deeply-rooted disadvantages in many areas. The proposal for comprehensive anti-discrimination legislation that is expected by the end of 2002 will represented an important step forward.

Despite several initiatives in the area of education, the segregation of Roma children persists, and their educational situation has not improved as a result of Concept implementation. Structural changes to the educational system are urgently needed. Preparatory classes and Roma teacher's assistants have been successful, although additional funding is needed to expand their reach. Some support has been provided to Roma secondary school students, but no measures have been proposed at the university level.

Little has been done to address discrimination in the area of employment. Efforts to date have targeted long-term unemployment among "persons difficult to place on the labour market." The idea of an Office for Ethnic Equality has been abandoned, at least temporarily, and the 2000 Concept's remaining measures, for example re-qualification courses and "public benefit works," are widely regarded as having been minimally effective.

In the area of housing, the focus has been on the short-term solution of providing additional cheap housing rather than on addressing the root causes of segregation and

---

[3] European Commission, *2001 Regular Report on the Czech Republic's Progress Towards Accession*, 13 November 2001, pp. 26–27, (hereafter, *"2001 Regular Report"*).

poor housing conditions. The 2000 Concept does not address problems of racial discrimination with regard to the privatisation of flats, State-guaranteed loans to purchase housing, or access to rented housing – problems that are as much causes of the current Roma housing crisis as affordability. The Czech Trade Inspection (CTI) has attempted to monitor equal access to goods and services, including for Roma. However, though Roma consumers claim that they frequently meet with discrimination in this area, there have been few cases in which discriminatory practices by service providers have been sanctioned.

The 2000 Concept stipulates few health-related initiatives, and the issue of equal access to healthcare is not addressed. A comprehensive study on low-category flats commissioned by the Government detailed the serious health risks for inhabitants and offered a number of recommendations in the area of healthcare, including one for State construction and hygienic authorities to exercise a more vigorous control with regard to conditions in low category flats. These have not been utilised.

Discrimination in the criminal justice system is not addressed in the 2000 Concept. The Government commissioned an analysis of judicial files concerning racially motivated crime; however, the study did not indicate the percentage of minority individuals in the surveyed group. Racially motivated violence continues to be a serious concern, and implementation of existing legislation has been minimal, though there are some signs of improvement. Efforts to evaluate the effectiveness of the criminal justice system in processing cases of racially motivated violence should be continued and extended. Substantial efforts have already been undertaken, despite limited funds, to train the police and to monitor extremism.

The 2000 Concept states the need to protect and promote the Romani language and culture, primarily through research, education and publication activities. State policy regarding minority protection is based on a new Minority Law.[4] However, as minority groups must constitute ten percent of the population of a municipality to benefit, most Roma communities will be excluded from its provisions in practice.

Neither the 2000 Concept nor any other governmental policy establishes specific tasks to promote the participation of Roma in public life – a shortcoming which Roma representatives have criticised. Roma participate mostly in an advisory capacity through a consultative body to the Government at the national level, while the district and regional Roma Advisors are not necessarily Roma.

---

[4] Law No. 273/2001 Coll. on the Rights of Members of National Minorities (entered into force 2 August 2001).

Conclusion

Despite the strong conceptual framework offered by the 2000 Concept, implementation has not been effected in a coordinated, coherent manner. Without measures to address institutional discrimination and to effect changes at the legal and structural level, the implementation of *ad hoc* projects to address deeply-rooted problems will touch only the tip of the iceberg, and will have little long-term impact. Without greater commitment of political will to the Concept, systemic changes are unlikely to occur, and bodies of national and local public administration will continue to fail to take Concept implementation seriously.

2. THE GOVERNMENT PROGRAMME – BACKGROUND

2.1 Background to Present Programme

The Czech Government has developed a succession of conceptual documents in the post-independence period, intended as strategies to promote the integration of Roma. Four such documents have been adopted since 1997 (in 1997, 1999, 2000, and 2002). Prior to these, there had been a number of partial attempts to address the integration of Roma and to develop some measures in response.[5]

The first document summarising the critical situation of the Roma community and putting forward certain proposals to address it was the so-called "Bratinka Report" from 1997.[6] Though it presented well-known facts, the Report's principal innovation was in its comprehensive presentation. It did not propose a coordinated governmental programme to remedy the situation. However, one concrete measure taken as a result

---

[5] See the Overview of the Decrees of the Government of the Czech Republic on the Issues of Roma, Discussions of the Council of National Minorities of the Government of the Czech Republic concerning the Roma Community and Measures of Individual Departments concerning the Roma (since 1992), <http://vlada.cz/vrk/rady/rnr/cinnost/romove/zprava/cast1/priloha2/il2.htm>, (accessed 23 May 2002). A list of prior governmental measures concerning the Roma is also contained in Annex 2 of the 1997 "Bratinka Report" (see below).

[6] "Report on the Situation of the Roma Community in the Czech Republic and Governmental Measures Assisting its Integration into Society," presented to the Government by Minister without Portfolio Pavel Bratinka and taken into consideration through Government Decree No. 686 (29 October 1997), <http://www.vlada.cz/1250/vrk/komise/krp/krp.htm>, (accessed 22 August 2002).

of the Bratinka Report was the establishment of an Inter-Ministerial Commission for Roma Community Affairs (IMC).[7]

On 7 April 1999, the Government approved the Concept of Governmental Policy Towards Members of the Roma Community Supporting Their Integration into Society (hereafter, "1999 Concept Proposal").[8] It was developed by an expert group consisting of specialists from different fields (academics, Roma activists, and the State administration, *inter alia*).[9]

The 1999 Concept Proposal consisted of a brief and compact political programme aimed principally at supporting the emancipation of Roma, based on respect for their traditions and culture.[10] It proposed that governmental policy should be focused on the "restoration of mistakes and injustice caused by centuries of discrimination and wrong policies of previous governments."[11] The 1999 Concept Proposal's overriding emphasis on emancipation meant that many important issues, particularly housing, segregation and other social issues, were addressed only marginally.[12]

Nonetheless, Roma leaders have expressed appreciation for some of the measures undertaken by the Government, particularly the establishment of Roma Advisors at district offices and Roma Coordinators at the regional level, the organisation of pre-school preparatory classes and employment training for police work. However, they have emphasised that inadequate attention has been devoted to the need for improved

---

[7] The IMC was established on 17 September 1997 by Government Decree No. 581 and its statutory rules were adopted by Government Decree No. 640 (15 October 1997). It had 12 Roma and 12 non-Roma members, and was chaired by the Commissioner for Human Rights. See also Decree No. 686 (29 October 1997), Sections III and IV, as well as its Annex 1 which contains the IMC's statute.

[8] Approved by Government Decree No. 279 (7 April 1999).

[9] The list of all the persons who contributed is contained in Annex A of the 1999 Concept Proposal. They contributed either orally, through working meetings, or in written form to the IMC Office.

[10] 1999 Concept Proposal, Part 1.4.

[11] 1999 Concept Proposal, Part 1.6.

[12] See A. Baršová, *Problémy bydlení etnických menšin a trendy k rezidenční segregaci v České republice* (Problems of Housing of Ethnic Minorities and Residential Segregation Trends in the Czech Republic), LGI, Open Society Institute, Budapest/Prague, 2001.

legislation to fight racially motivated violence and racial discrimination, particularly regarding access to goods and services.[13]

2.2 The Programme – Process

This report shall focus on the Concept of Governmental Policy Towards Members of the Roma Community Supporting Their Integration into Society – adopted on 14 June 2000 (hereafter, "2000 Concept"),[14] together with the 2002 Updated Concept – adopted on 23 January 2002,[15] highlighting new proposals where relevant. It will analyse not only the implementation of tasks assigned under the Concept,[16] but also tasks assigned by additional decrees based on the directions for action established by the 2000 Concept or earlier documents, such as the 1997 Bratinka Report and the 1999 Concept Proposal.[17]

The 2000 Concept was elaborated on the basis of the 1999 Concept Proposal,[18] with the participation of some of the same experts.[19] Relevant ministries were also consulted.

---

[13] These opinions regarding governmental policy towards the Roma generally were collected from the Roma members of the Council for National Minorities and presented in: Secretariat of the Council for National Minorities, *Report on the Situation of National Minorities in the Czech Republic in 2001*, Report No. 731/02, May 2002, approved by Government Decree No. 600 (12 June 2002), p. 72, <http://wtd.vlada.cz/files/rvk/rnm/zprava_mensiny_2001.pdf>, (accessed 22 August 2002) (in Czech).

[14] *Koncepce politiky vlády vůči příslušníkům romské kommunity, napomáhající jejich integraci do společnosti* (Concept of Governmental Policy Towards Members of the Roma Community Supporting Their Integration into Society), adopted by Government Decree No. 599 (14 June 2000), <http://www.vlada.cz/1250/vrk/vrk.htm>, (accessed 22 August 2002) (in Czech only) (hereafter, "2000 Concept").

[15] *Koncepce romské integrace* (Concept of Roma Integration), adopted by Government Decree No. 87 (23 January 2002), <http://www.vlada.cz/1250/vrk/vrk.htm>, (accessed 22 August 2002) (in Czech only) (hereafter, "2000 Updated Concept").

[16] Tasks were assigned to various actors by Decree No. 599 (14 June 2000) by which the 2000 Concept was adopted.

[17] As its name suggests, the 2000 Concept itself does not establish concrete tasks but rather seeks to provide a framework for the strategy of the Government.

[18] See the task of the Commissioner for Human Rights and Chairman of the IMC (a position occupied by the same person at the time), assigned by Government Decree No. 279 (7 April 1999), Parts II.1.a and II.1.b.

[19] See e.g. Introductory Report to the 1999 Concept Proposal, Appendix II to the proposal of the Vice Chair and Head of the Legislative Council of the Government, No. 3533/00 LRV (24 May 2000).

A draft was presented to the Government in December 1999, together with the main objections of the Ministry of Interior concerning the proposal to establish an Office for Ethnic Equality. The 2000 Concept was finally adopted on 14 June 2000, after several working versions had been circulated.

The contribution of Roma representatives and civil society to the development of the 2000 Concept was ensured through consultations with the members of the above-mentioned expert group (nearly half of whom were Roma). However, some Roma leaders believe that the Government's approach to consultation – soliciting written comments on the draft versions – was not effective in assuring broad participation from the Roma community, and that the organisation of one or more consultative roundtables would have been preferable.[20]

The 2000 Concept, which covers the period 2001–2020, incorporates a requirement for annual updates to reflect new developments and the experience gained from implementation.[21] The regularly updated Concept thus serves as the basis for the further development of the Government's strategy concerning Roma.

2.3 The Programme – Content

The overall aim of the 2000 Concept is "to achieve the non-conflictual co-existence of Roma communities with the rest of society."[22] Integration is presented as the primary means of achieving this objective.[23] While recognising the right of Roma to be integrated into society, the Government also states that it will support the strengthening of Roma identity, traditions and culture, as the basis for its policies.[24]

---

[20] Others have suggested that there was insufficient time and money to organise a roundtable. OSI Roundtable, Prague, June 2002. *Explanatory note: OSI held a roundtable meeting in the Czech Republic in June 2002 to invite critique of the present report in draft form. Experts present included representatives of the Government, Roma representatives and non-governmental organisations.*

[21] 2000 Concept, Part 12.3.

[22] 2000 Concept, Part 1.7.

[23] "Integration" is defined as "the full incorporation of Roma into society while preserving the majority of the cultural specifics and differences that characterise Roma and which they wish to preserve, unless these differences are in contradiction with the laws of the Czech Republic." 2000 Concept, Part 1.5.

[24] 2000 Concept, Parts 1.4, 1.9.

The 2002 Updated Concept reflects a coherent and comprehensive approach, covering both protection from discrimination and promotion of minority rights, within the context of three distinct perspectives:[25]

- A *human rights perspective*, aiming to enable all citizens, including Roma, to enjoy fully and without any discrimination all individual human rights;

- A *national (ethnic) perspective*, relying on the specific rights of members of national minorities;

- A *broader socio-cultural perspective*, based on the concept of "Roma community" which only partially overlaps with the concept of "Roma national minority,"[26] and problems faced by this socially disadvantaged group.

The 2000 Concept acknowledges the existence of frequent discrimination against Roma in employment, housing, the provision of services, and other areas. The Government also expresses its will to "remedy the injustice of centuries of discrimination and damages caused before 1989 by the policy of forced assimilation."[27] The minority rights dimension receives somewhat more attention in the 2002 Updated Concept than in the 2000 Concept as it is given equal weight as the human rights and socio-cultural perspectives. However, perhaps the Concept's most significant gap lies in its lack of concrete measures to promote the effective participation of Roma in public life.[28]

The 2000 Concept principally provides a set of guiding principles for the integration of Roma as well as an overall framework for the coordination of various activities conducted in pursuit of this aim. It consists of twelve chapters:

- Basic Premises
- Racial Discrimination
- Institutions
- Compensatory Measures – Employment, "Re-qualification" (Training) and Housing
- Romani Language and Culture
- Schools (Education)
- Multicultural Education

---

[25] 2002 Updated Concept, Part 1.1.
[26] See Section 3.4 of this report.
[27] 2002 Updated Concept, Part 1.10.
[28] Some observers have suggested that a section on Roma participation and democratic representation should be added. OSI Roundtable, Prague, June 2002.

- Increasing the Security of Roma
- Research on the Co-existence of Various Ethnic Groups
- Civic Counselling Centres
- NGOs
- Conclusions

The 2002 Updated Concept consolidates the issue areas identified in the 2000 Concept into eight chapters.[29]

There have also been complementary governmental initiatives to ensure minority protection more broadly. A Minority Law was adopted in 2001 (see Section 3.4); a proposal for comprehensive anti-discrimination legislation is expected by the end of 2002 (see Section 3.2).

2.4 The Programme – Administration/Implementation/Evaluation

The Government has developed a complex mechanism for administering and monitoring implementation of the 2000 Concept and governmental policy towards Roma in general, with several bodies involved in coordinating policies at the national level. Mechanisms to ensure the broad participation of Roma and civil society in an advisory capacity are also in place at the national and, to a certain extent, at the regional and local levels.

The flexibility of this system can be considered positive in some respects. Individual ministries decide independently how much money to allocate for the implementation of those aspects of the Concept within their competence. On the other hand, there are no legally-prescribed mechanisms to ensure evaluation and assessment or to require active participation from ministries. Moreover, there are few tools by which local actors can be induced to implement the policies developed and agreed upon centrally.

---

[29] The 2002 Updated Concept deals with mostly the same issues as the 2000 Concept in eight chapters: Basic Premises; Institutional Support for Roma Integration; Anti-discrimination Measures; Compensatory Measures; Support for the Development of the Romani Language and Culture; Influencing the Majority Society; Ensuring the Security of Roma; and Conclusions. While there is no separate chapter on education, issues of equal access to education are dealt with under "Compensatory Measures," multicultural education is covered in the section on "Influencing the Majority Society."

The Vice Chair of the Government and Head of the Legislative Council, who also chairs the Council for Roma Community Issues (CRCI) and the Council for National Minorities, bears overall responsibility for the administration and implementation of the 2000 Concept. Three national bodies are involved in coordinating governmental efforts in three main policy areas (human rights, minority rights, and more general socio-economic issues).

The Council for Human Rights (CHR)[30] deals with the implementation of the human rights component of the 2000 Concept. The CHR has established several specialised committees,[31] including the Committee against Racism, and the Committee for Economic, Social and Cultural Rights. These committees are involved in the preparation of periodic reports for the monitoring mechanisms of international human rights treaties.

The Council for National Minorities[32] advises the Government concerning the rights of all national minority groups, including Roma. It is responsible for evaluating the effectiveness of the Minority Law as well as relevant international instruments.

The CRCI (which replaced the IMC on 19 December 2001) is an advisory body to the Government on Roma issues generally with the aim to promote the integration of Roma into society. It manages the development and implementation of governmental policy towards Roma; half of its 28 members are Roma representatives (one for each

---

[30] The Council for Human Rights is an advisory body to the Government tasked with monitoring the compliance of domestic legislation with ratified international human rights treaties. It was established by Government Decree No. 809 (9 December 1998). It has 20 members consisting of the Chairman (the Commissioner for Human Rights), seven deputy ministers (Ministry of Foreign Affairs, Ministry of Justice, Ministry of Interior, Ministry of Labour and Social Affairs, Ministry of Culture, Ministry of Health, and Ministry for Regional Development), as well as the Head Inspector for Human Rights Protection of the Ministry of Defence, the Chairman of the Institute for Public Information Systems, and experts, including one Roma representative. The number of members of State administration representatives roughly equals the number of expert public representatives in the CHR. For the CHR's Statute, see the Appendix to Government Decree No. 132 (17 February 1999). See also EU Accession Monitoring Program, *Monitoring the EU Accession Process: Minority Protection*, Open Society Institute, Budapest, September 2001, p. 167, (hereafter, "*Minority Protection 2001*").

[31] Committee members consist of equal numbers of State administration representatives and NGO representatives and human rights activists, including Roma representatives.

[32] Also known as the Council for Nationalities. The current Council was created in accordance with the Minority Law, Art. 6(3). The Roma minority, like the Slovak and Polish minorities, has three representatives. The Council for National Minorities is the only body discussed in this report whose existence is based on law rather than on a decree. This means that, contrary to the CRCI or the CHR, the existence of the Council (in case of a change of government) is more stable.

region).[33] Its activities are supported by an Office within the Human Rights Department.[34] The CRCI's competencies include: preparing conceptual materials for governmental decisions, presenting opinions on relevant proposals by other bodies, evaluating the implementation of relevant governmental decrees, proposing the distribution of funding for supplementary governmental programmes in support of Roma integration, cooperating with non-governmental and international organisations, and ensuring the implementation of public campaigns.

Again, the 2000 Concept itself does not set forth specific tasks; rather, it outlines the main issues and possible solutions. Concrete tasks are assigned to various actors – mainly ministries – in an annex to Government Decree No. 599 (14 June 2000) by which the 2000 Concept was adopted, with an indication of the deadline for completion where appropriate.[35] Further tasks concerning the integration of Roma are assigned to ministries through additional governmental decrees on the basis of the 2000 Concept or earlier documents (e.g. the Bratinka Report or the 1999 Concept Proposal). Ministries have not always taken up the tasks assigned to them willingly and there is no mechanism for requiring or even encouraging them to do so.

An important role in implementing the Concept at the local level is played by the "Roma Advisors" and "Roma Assistants" who have been appointed in the district

---

[33] See the Statute of the Council for Roma Community Issues, adopted by Government Decree No. 1371 (19 December 2001), Art. 3., at <http://wtd.vlada.cz/scripts/detail.php?id=471>, (accessed 7 May 2002) (in Czech). The CRCI has 28 members, including a Chairman and two Vice-Chairmen. The other 14 members are deputy ministers from the following ministries: Ministry of Education, Ministry of Finance, Ministry of Culture, Ministry for Regional Development, Ministry of Defence, Ministry of Trade and Industry, Ministry of Justice, Ministry of Labour and Social Affairs, Ministry of Interior, Ministry of Foreign Affairs and Ministry of Agriculture. The CRCI is chaired by the Vice Chair of the Government and Chair of the Legislative Council; the First Vice Chairman is the Deputy of the Government for Human Rights; the Second Vice Chairman is a Roma representative. The composition of the CRCI, is at <http://www.vlada.cz/1250/vrk/komise/krp/krp.htm>, (accessed 22 August 2002).

[34] 2002 Updated Concept, Part 2.2.3. The costs of the CRCI are covered from the budget of the Office of the Government (Art. 10). Members of the CRCI are not salaried employees; however, travel and other costs are reimbursed.

[35] Tasks for the Implementation of the Concept on Governmental Policy Towards Members of the Roma Community Supporting Their Integration into Society. Annex to Government Decree No. 599 (14 June 2000). Tasks were assigned to the Ministries of Justice, Interior, Labour and Social Affairs; Regional Development (five tasks); Education, Youth and Sports; Foreign Affairs; Defence (one task); Culture (one task); and to the Commissioner for Human Rights (five tasks). The Heads of District Offices are also assigned a couple of tasks. The Ministry of Health is not mentioned.

offices.[36] Roma Advisors are employees of the State administration. Advisors were meant to be employed at the Office of the Head of District; usually, however, they are employed within the social or health departments.[37] By 1 January 1999, the position of Roma Advisor had been filled in all 81 districts. Only about half, however, were of Roma origin (this is not a condition for the job). Furthermore, as these positions are mostly filled on the basis of fixed-term contracts, the total number of Roma Advisors and Assistants employed at any given time varies. According to the CRCI Secretary, there were 73 Roma Advisors as of April 2002; only about 15 were employed within the office of the Head of District.[38]

The Roma Advisor coordinates the work of Roma Assistants, whose task is to engage in community social work, collection of information and "educational activities" between the majority and minority communities. Roma Assistants are also employed by the District Offices; there is supposed to be one Roma Assistant for every 1,500 Roma in a given district on average.[39] While Roma Advisors have played an important role in facilitating communication with the local Roma communities, it has been pointed out that in practice they have acted as social workers, a task for which they have received no training and are thus not qualified.[40] Moreover, their future is uncertain due to the ongoing reform of State administration[41] according to which districts – and therefore the position of Roma Advisor at the District Office level – will be eliminated by 1 January 2003, and responsibility for Roma Advisors will be transferred to the new regional self-governments.[42] It will be up to regional self-governments to decide whether to employ Roma Advisors or not; the central Government cannot compel them to do so (as it could at the district level).[43] However, the position of Coordinator of Roma Advisors at the regional level has been introduced under the 2002 Updated Concept,[44] and five have been appointed thus far.[45]

Several specialised bodies have been established within certain ministries to facilitate the implementation of policies targeting minorities, including the Roma minority.

---

[36] This position was established by Government Decree No. 686 (29 October 1997).

[37] See 2000 Concept, Part 3.1 on "Roma Advisors;" see also 2002 Updated Concept, Part 2.5.1.

[38] České noviny, 28 April 2002.

[39] The Roma assistant employed at the District Office is different from the Roma "teacher's assistant."

[40] OSI Roundtable, Prague, June 2002.

[41] See Law No. 128/2000 Coll., on Municipalities, and Law No. 129/2000 Coll., on Regions.

[42] Government Decree No. 781 (25 July 2001).

[43] A decree, unlike a law, is not binding on local self-governments.

[44] See 2002 Updated Concept, Part 2.5.3.

[45] Report on the Situation of National Minorities, p. 72.

These include a Commission of the Ministry of Labour and Social Affairs,[46] the Consultative Committee for Minority Culture Issues (Ministry of Culture),[47] and the Consultative Group on Minority Education Issues (Ministry of Education).[48]

Funding

Each ministry decides independently how much money to allocate for the implementation of the Concept within its competencies.

In order to fund the implementation of assigned tasks, individual ministries:

- Fund activities related to Roma as a part of their broader activities or policies, within their spheres of competence; there is no special chapter on Roma issues within the budget of each ministry;

- Administer the funding awarded by the CRCI (and allocated to the CRCI from the State budget) to individual grantees, as the CRCI itself is not equipped to administer grants.[49] The funding is distributed by public tender to NGOs, municipalities, and public universities, *inter alia*.[50] Grants are awarded by decision of special committees consisting of members of the CRCI (including its Roma members), financial experts and a representative from each of the relevant ministries. No Roma organisations are known to have participated in or won these tenders.

The Council for National Minorities oversees the distribution of funding for minority cultural activities[51] according to a procedure by which, following consultations with the

---

[46] The "Commission of the Ministry of Labour and Social Affairs on the Implementation of Measures to Support the Employment of Persons with Difficult Placement on the Labour Market with Regard to Members of the Roma Community" was created by Order of the Minister No. 4/1998. This is a consultative body which implements the tasks outlined in the National Plan on Employment, adopted by Government Decree No. 640 (23 June 1999), and other decrees on this issue. 2002 Updated Concept, Part 2.4.2. Information on whether it includes any Roma representatives is not available.

[47] The Consultative Committee for Minority Culture Issues oversees the cultural activities of national minorities. It is tasked, *inter alia*, with the selection process for financial support for projects of national minorities. It is composed of representatives of national minorities, including Roma. 2002 Updated Concept, Part 2.4.2.

[48] The Consultative Group on Minority Education Issues also includes Roma representatives. 2002 Updated Concept, Part 2.4.2.

[49] Government Decree No. 98/2002 determines the conditions for providing funding from the State budget for activities of members of the Roma community.

[50] Interview with the CRCI Secretary, Prague, 15 April 2002.

[51] See "Orders of the Government on providing financial support from the state budget for activities of members of national minorities," approved by Government Decree No. 98/2002.

Council, individual ministries propose activities to support minority cultural activities from within their annual budget. Grants are distributed through a competitive procedure after a second round of discussions with the Council concerning the main fields of distribution.

A list of programmes administered by the CRCI gives some indication of ministry priorities. In 2000, the CRCI took part in five programmes: (1) local social/integration projects; (2) education for Roma children and youth; (3) research on co-existence between the Roma minority and the majority society; (4) support for field social workers; and (5) support for Roma students in secondary schools.[52] In 2001, in addition to four of the above-mentioned programmes (excluding the research programme), the CRCI was also involved in a programme of research on low-income housing and in efforts to promote Roma participation in the 2001 Census.

Monitoring and evaluation

The Concept incorporates a mechanism to ensure that it is reviewed and updated on an annual basis, in cooperation with ministry representatives, district and municipal officials from areas where large numbers of Roma live, and Roma activists and experts. Thus, every year, the Vice Chair of the Government and the Commissioner for Human Rights must jointly present a report to the Government on the status of implementation of all governmental decrees concerning the integration of Roma. This report is compiled on the basis of the information supplied by the relevant ministries. Reports submitted to date have been mainly descriptive, with little assessment or analysis other than whether tasks were "fulfilled," "in the process of being fulfilled" or "implementation cannot be assessed;" and whether deadlines were respected. The annual report is supplemented by an update to the Concept, incorporating changes and amendments considered necessary on the basis of new research, the experience of the previous years' implementation or the situation in the country.[53] The most recent information on implementation, together with the 2002 Updated Concept, was

---

[52] Report of the Commissioner for Human Rights on the Programmes Implemented with the Participation of the CRCI on the Realisation of Roma Integration in 2000 and 2001, <http://www.vlada.cz/1250/vrk/komise/krp/krp.htm>, (accessed 22 August 2002), (hereafter, "*Commissioner's Report 2000–2001*"). This report is annexed to Government Decree No. 87 (23 January 2002) (Section IV, Annex 1).

[53] 2000 Concept, Part 12.2.

approved by Government Decree in January 2002.[54] This report examines the status of implementation of tasks concerning Roma integration assigned by 11 decrees adopted between October 1997 and November 2001. The Concept is to be updated again by 28 February 2003.[55]

The Commissioner for Human Rights has also prepared a separate report on the programmes for Roma integration implemented with the involvement of the CRCI in 2000 and 2001.[56] The report provides a brief description of the programmes and an overview of expenditures, along with a short evaluation.

Individual ministries must present an expenditure report to the CRCI by the end of March every year.[57] In 2001, the Government allocated CZK 21 million (€690,108) to the CRCI to administer projects; this amount was increased in 2002 to CZK 25 million (€821,558).[58] NGOs which have received grants must also report on project implementation and expenditures. However, neither the CRCI nor the ministries have established any special mechanisms to monitor the effectiveness of implementation; according to one CRCI representative, this is due to a lack of sufficient staff and resources.[59]

The CRCI (as well as its expert committees and working groups) is also entitled to request relevant information from other State administration authorities, from organisations and institutions subordinated to the State administration and, if necessary, from municipal authorities.[60] However, the CRCI has no legal authority to request compliance from the various entities involved in implementation, such as the ministries; its role is limited to summarising and evaluating the information provided.

---

[54] "Information on the Implementation of Government Decrees Concerning the Integration of Roma Communities and the Active Approach of State Administration in the Realisation of Measures Adopted Through These Decrees, as of 31 December 2001", (hereafter, *"Information on the Implementation of Government Decrees as of 31 December 2001"*). This report is annexed to Government Decree No. 87 (23 January 2002) (Section III), <http://www.vlada.cz/1250/vrk/komise/krp/krp.htm>, (accessed 22 August 2002) (in Czech). Reports were also presented to the Government in September 1998, January 1999, November 1999, May 2000 and December 2000.

[55] Government Decree No. 87 (23 January 2002).

[56] *Commissioner's Report 2000–2001*.

[57] See the latest report: Overview of State Financial Resources Allocated for the Implementation of the Concept of Governmental Policy Towards Members of the Roma Community Supporting Their Integration into Society), Government Decree No. 87 (23 January 2002), Section III, Annex 2 (in Czech).

[58] The exchange rate is calculated at CZK 30.43 (Czech Koruna) = €1.

[59] Interview with the CRCI Secretary, Prague, 15 April 2002.

[60] Statute of the CRCI, Art. 2(3).

The participation of NGO and Roma representatives in implementation and evaluation is secured through their membership as independent experts (rather than representatives of particular organisations) in the above-mentioned consultative bodies. About half of the Roma Advisors currently employed are of Roma origin; however, they work as State employees, not as representatives of the Roma community. There has been no independent evaluation of implementation of the Concept conducted by an NGO.

2.5 The Programme and the Public

The 2000 Concept highlights the importance of public discussion,[61] yet the necessary funds and human resources to launch a concerted public campaign to promote the Concept and related activities seem to be lacking. The Office of the CRCI has no public relations staff and efforts to publicise the 2000 Concept have not been systematic.[62]

The adoption of the 2000 Concept was announced in the media; however, the media has given it little attention. This may be due to a perceived lack of interest among the public in minority issues. Rather, media coverage tends to focus on concrete areas of governmental policy, such as the programme for field social workers, community housing, tolerance campaigns, and educational and vocational activities.[63] Over the past two years, the Government has used media campaigns as an opportunity to generate public support for its goals and to foster tolerance towards minorities, including Roma. These efforts should be continued.

The 2000 Concept is well known by those Roma representatives who are directly participating in its implementation as well as by Roma community leaders.[64] However, while individual elements of the Concept, such as ongoing activities in the area of education or social policies, seem to be well known among their beneficiaries, overall awareness of the existence of a comprehensive Government programme is low.

---

[61] 2000 Concept, Chapter 12.

[62] OSI Roundtable, Prague, June 2002.

[63] A survey of the press since 1997, conducted by the Counselling Centre for Citizenship and Human Rights (Prague), found articles on specific components of the Concept, but no articles on the Concept itself.

[64] OSI Roundtable, Prague, June 2002.

2.6 The Programme and the EU

The EU has supported governmental policy regarding Roma by allocating increasing amounts of funding through the Phare Programme.[65] In 1998, the amount allocated to such activities through the Phare National programme was €900,000; by 2001, it had increased to €3,000,000. Funds are not allocated specifically in support of implementation of the Concept but rather to projects aimed at promoting the integration of Roma and important issues identified in the Concept, such as education, media campaigns to promote tolerance, and training of Roma Advisors and Assistants.

The EU has also supported efforts to develop the legal and institutional framework to combat racial and ethnic discrimination and to promote equality through a Twinning Project with the United Kingdom (Phare 2000).

No funding had been allocated under Phare to support efforts to improve the situation with regard to employment or housing, although the 2001 Regular Report noted that further measures are needed in these areas.[66] However, the 2001 Phare Programme will include support for small-scale re-qualification and job creation activities. Extensive support will also be granted to NGO capacity building and promoting Roma participation, an issue that has been largely neglected to date.

The Phare 2001 Programme focuses on civil society organisations (Phare allocation of €3,000,000).[67] The aim is to support the creation of better opportunities for the participation of Roma in consultative and elected positions, as well as small scale re-qualification and job creation activities.

Additional Phare funding is allocated to Roma-related projects through two specialised funds: the Civil Society Development Foundation (NROS) – which supports projects in the areas of human rights, minorities, and sustainability of civil society

---

[65] For complete information on all Phare-funded programmes for the Roma in the Czech Republic, see: DG Enlargement Information Unit, *EU Support for Roma Communities in Central and Eastern Europe*, May 2002, <http://europa.eu.int/comm/enlargement/docs/pdf/brochure_roma_may2002.pdf>, (accessed 22 August 2002).

[66] European Commission, *2001 Regular Report on the Czech Republic's Progress Towards Accession*, 13 November 2001, pp. 26–27. <http://europa.eu.int/comm/enlargement/report2001/cz_en.pdf>, (accessed 22 August 2002), (hereafter, "2001 Regular Report").

[67] DG Enlargement Information Unit, *EU Support for Roma Communities in Central Eastern Europe*, p. 21.

organisations,[68] and the European Initiative for Democracy and Human Rights (EIDHR) – which supports projects in the area of human rights and democracy.[69]

Phare funding has provided essential support to activities and initiatives to improve the situation for Roma in a wide range of areas. However, monitoring and evaluation of the efficacy and impact of these projects has been minimal. Internal evaluation reports prepared by the EU Delegation in Prague simply state project objectives and whether the goals were met; there appears to be little information available on the amount of Government co-financing. No detailed assessment of the impact of each project has been conducted, nor has there been independent evaluation of EU expenditures.

Phare funding is therefore not used as efficiently as it could be to support the implementation of a coordinated governmental policy to promote the integration of Roma. Increasing the degree of harmonisation between EU funding and Concept objectives would improve the effectiveness of both EU and Government efforts. Civil society – and especially Roma representatives – should be involved to a greater degree in the implementation and evaluation of Phare-funded projects.

3. The Government Programme – Implementation

3.1 Stated Objectives of the Programme

The overall aim of the 2000 Concept is the "attainment of the non-conflictual co-existence between the Roma communities and the rest of society."[70] It sets seven priority objectives:[71]

a) Ensuring the security of Roma and Roma communities;

---

[68] The Phare Civil Society Development Foundation aims to strengthen democracy and civil society in the Czech Republic and supports specific NGO projects. Under the various schemes administered by the NROS, grants have been awarded to over 1,400 projects since its establishment in April 1993, totalling €6.8 million. Over €3 million will be available in the course of 2002.

[69] This initiative brings together the budget lines for promoting human rights, democracy, and conflict prevention in countries outside the EU. The aim of the EIDHR is to promote political, civil, economic, social, and cultural rights. The total amount of the fund is €300,000.

[70] 2000 Concept, Part 1.7.

[71] 2000 Concept, Part 1.7., reiterated in the 2002 Updated Concept, Part 1.10, with the exception that the 2000 Concept objective on the emancipation of Roma (e) is not listed in the 2002 Updated Concept.

b) Eliminating "external obstacles," primarily all forms of discrimination against individuals or groups defined by race, skin colour, nationality, language, or membership in a nation or ethnic group;

c) Eliminating "internal obstacles," such as disadvantages in education;

d) Reducing of unemployment and improving housing and health conditions;

e) Enhancing participation for Roma in decision-making in matters concerning Roma communities;

f) Ensuring the development of the Roma culture and Romani language;

g) Creating a tolerant environment in which membership in a group defined by race, skin colour, nationality (ethnicity), language, or membership in a nation does not provide the basis for discriminatory attitudes.

3.2 Government Programme and Discrimination

The Government has acknowledged the problem of discrimination and prejudice against Roma in various spheres of life.[72] The 2000 Concept explicitly sets forth the aim to combat discrimination,[73] and devotes two chapters to outlining the framework for comprehensive anti-discrimination legislation (Chapter 2), and for the adoption of positive measures to overcome discrimination in various areas (Chapter 4).

These measures are necessary. The provisions of the EU Race Equality Directive[74] have not yet been fully incorporated into Czech legislation, though some important steps have already been taken.[75] For example, the reversal of the burden of proof will apply in cases of alleged racial discrimination from 1 January 2003.[76] There is no definition

---

[72] See 2002 Updated For example, the 2002 Updated Concept states: "the Government considers that it is undeniable that Roma are very often the object of discriminatory behaviour. Discrimination against Roma in access to employment, housing, services and in other areas of life continues. At the same time, it is evident that only a small share of this discrimination is effectively penalised." 2002 Updated Concept, Part 3.2.

[73] See especially 2000 Concept, 1.7, (b) and (g); 2002 Updated Concept, 1.10. (a) and (e).

[74] Council Directive 2000/43/EC of 29 June 2000 implementing the principle of equal treatment between persons irrespective of race or ethnic origin.

[75] However, several laws focusing on the partial implementation of EU directives on equal opportunities have been adopted. See EU Accession Monitoring Program, *Monitoring the EU Accession Process: Equal Opportunities for Women and Men*, Open Society Institute, Budapest, 2002 (forthcoming).

[76] Law No.151/2002 Coll. (amendment to the Civil Procedure Code).

of direct or indirect discrimination in Czech legislation and no provision in the Czech legal system to provide victims of racial discrimination in employment or other areas with the possibility to demand that discrimination be stopped, its consequences removed and corrective action be taken, and to claim monetary compensation for other than the material losses suffered.

The Office of the Public Defender of Rights (Ombudsman) began operating in December 2000,[77] but no data is available on the number of complaints submitted by Roma as the collection of ethnic data is prohibited by law. The 2000 Concept proposed the establishment of an Office for Ethnic Equality within the framework of the Minority Law,[78] but the proposal met with opposition and was abandoned. Acknowledging that this gap needs to be filled, the 2002 Updated Concept called for the strengthening of the CRCI as the main institution to support integration for Roma.[79]

The Vice Chair of the Government presented a report recommending measures to combat racial discrimination, especially in the area of economic, social and cultural rights,[80] at the beginning of 2002, and has been tasked,[81] together with selected Ministers and the Commissioner for Human Rights, with presenting a draft of a comprehensive anti-discrimination law by 31 December 2002. This effort has been supporting by an EU-supported Twinning Project with the United Kingdom.[82]

According to various reports published by domestic and international NGOs, widespread problems of racism and discrimination against Roma in the fields of

---

[77] The competencies of the Ombudsman are regulated by Law No. 349/1999 Coll., on the Public Defender of Rights which came into force on 28 February 2000.

[78] The 2000 Concept had proposed establishing an "Office for the Rights of National Minorities (for Ethnic Equality and Integration)." 2000 Concept, Chapter 2; see also Part 3.2. It is expected to be taken up again within the context of the comprehensive anti-discrimination legislation being prepared.

[79] 2002 Updated Concept, Part 2.2.6.

[80] Report on Options for Combating Discrimination, approved by Government Decree No. 170 (20 February 2002).

[81] Government Decree No. 170 (20 February 2002) assigned to the Vice Chair of the Government, in cooperation with the Commissioner for Human Rights and selected Ministers, to present to the Government draft legislation on protection against discrimination, implementing EU Directives 2000/43/EC (EU Race Equality Directive) and 76/207/EHS.

[82] Consultative roundtable discussions between Government officials, opinion makers, civil society and Roma representatives, were organised on the topics of policing, health, education, training, employment, civic participation and access to housing, also as a means of disseminating information on government policy. The project was implemented from April 2001 to June 2002 by the Human Rights Department of the Office of the Government and the UK Home Office Race Equality Unit. Its proposals were presented to the Government as part of the Report on Options for Combating Discrimination.

education, employment, housing, provision of healthcare and other services, and the criminal justice system persist.[83] According to a recent survey carried out by the Centre for Research on Public Opinion (CVVM), one third of Czechs do not "always" tolerate foreigners; and half are intolerant of people with a different skin colour.[84] Compared to findings for 2000, tolerance had grown towards all groups except Roma.

A principal objective of the 2000 Concept is to promote tolerance. Accordingly, several campaigns have been implemented with governmental support since December 1999, including a State-sponsored anti-racism campaign in 1999–2000,[85] which supported activities for teachers and high school students, *inter alia*. According to an evaluation conducted by the Sofres-Factum Agency, two-thirds of the population were aware of the campaign, though estimations of its usefulness were mixed.[86]

The follow-on campaign planned for 2001 was never implemented due to problems during the tendering process.[87] However, the Government did support a two-month campaign entitled "Be kind to your local Nazi" (see Section 3.3).

---

[83] See e.g. *Shall we Take Discrimination Seriously?*, Project report, Counselling Centre for Citizenship, Civil and Human Rights, Prague, 2001; see also, *Minority Protection 2001*, pp. 133–151.

[84] Cited by ČTK on 29 May 2002, in "One Czech in Three Intolerant of Foreigners," RFE/RL *Newsline*, 30 May 2002.

[85] The "Tolerance Project," which received a Government allocation of CZK ten million (€328,623) and €1,643 from Phare. Some elements of the campaign, provoked strong reactions, such as billboards with a photograph of a human foetus, accompanied by the inscription: "Do you recognise its colour?" See "The Tolerance project has caused controversial reactions," *Mladá Fronta Dnes*, 17 July 2000.

[86] 36 percent of respondents expressed the view that such campaigns can help eliminate racist attitudes, while 40 percent held the opposite view. The political opposition criticised the huge amount of funds allocated to media agencies. For more, see e.g. "The governmental Tolerance project points to the negative impact of racism and xenophobia," *Slovo*, 8 February 2000; "Rychetský appreciated the campaign against racism, Mlynář did not," *Zemské noviny*, 2 August 2000. The considerable amount of funding allocated to media agencies was criticised by the political opposition, but Previa Agency, the sub-contractor for the campaign, denied this by referring to the fact that only eight of the CZK ten million allocated were available for the campaign after tax deductions, and that only one third of this amount was actually used for the media campaign. Furthermore, the director of Previa Agency emphasised that the real value of the media campaign was CZK 30 million. See "The Tolerance Project has caused controversial reactions," *Mladá Fronta Dnes*, 17 July 2000.

[87] Two participants excluded from the public tender obstructed the final commissioning until November 2001 when their appeal was rejected by the Institute for the Protection of Economic Competition. The whole tender was ultimately cancelled because of the short time remaining until the end of the year (funds may not be transferred to following financial year).

3.2.1 Education

The 2000 Concept embodies a two-way approach to integration, proposing to adapt the school system to the needs of Roma children rather than seeking to adapt Roma children to the school system.[88] However, the 2000 Concept does not propose a comprehensive plan for achieving its objectives, and many observers believe that the *ad hoc* measures it does propose are not sufficient to bring about the transformation the school system necessary to overcome such deeply-rooted problems as the systematic segregation of Roma children.

The 2002 Updated Concept states the need to abolish special schools within the context of the proposed Law on Schools;[89] however, it emphasises that positive measures are also necessary in order to overcome socio-cultural handicaps. The measures it proposes include special preparatory classes and the employment of teacher's assistants.[90]

The following general measures are proposed in the 2000 Concept to overcome disadvantages faced by Roma children in the educational system:[91]

- Ensuring the possibility of transfer from "special schools" *(zvláštní školy)*[92] to regular primary schools and vice versa;[93]

- Transformation of "special schools" into ordinary primary schools and the gradual transfer of pupils from special schools to primary schools;

- Establishment of a network of preparatory classes; education and employment of Roma assistants in schools, in consultation with parents;

- Training for teachers;

- Development of a legislative framework for positive action.

---

[88] 2000 Concept, Part 6.1.

[89] 2000 Concept, Part 6.11.

[90] 2002 Updated Concept, Part 4.4.1.

[91] See Chapters 4 and 6 of the 2000 Concept.

[92] According to § 28 of the Schools Law (Law No. 29/1984 Coll.), "special schools" *(speciální školy)* provide education for mentally-, sensually- or physically-disabled pupils, pupils with multiple disabilities, pupils with educational disorders, and pupils who are ill or weak. Within the category of special schools, there are also "specific schools" *(zvláštní školy)*. These provide education to pupils with such mental deficiencies *(rozumové nedostatky)* that they cannot be educated in primary schools nor in special primary schools. However, the term "special school" shall be used in this report in reference to the *zvláštní školy* (literally "specific schools").

[93] See Task 5.a for the Ministry of Education in the Appendix to Government Decree No. 599 (14 June 2000), to be implemented with the assistance of the Commissioner for Human Rights.

Accordingly, the following tasks were assigned to the Ministry of Education and were evaluated in the 2002 Updated Concept, *inter alia*:[94]

- Extension of the network of preparatory classes;[95]
- Support for the employment of teacher's assistants, including at the level of secondary vocational education;[96]
- Review of testing procedures to prevent placement of Roma children into special schools without accurate determination of their intellectual and educational abilities;[97]
- Ensuring the possibility of transfer of successful pupils from special schools to primary schools, as part of the process of transforming the educational system;[98]
- Development of full-day educational programmes in five pilot schools;[99]
- Laying the legislative foundations for positive action measures.[100]

It is estimated that only two percent of Roma have completed university-level education, and 13 percent have completed high school or vocational education.[101] However, the 2000 Concept does not propose any measures to support university attendance for Roma, and the Law on Academic Institutions lacks provisions which would allow for the establishment of quotas.[102]

---

[94] These tasks are assigned by Decree No. 599 (14 June 2000) as well as by additional decrees (see below). In some cases, the 2000 Concept further specifies tasks assigned by earlier decrees.

[95] These tasks coincide with the Ministry of Education's "Strategy to Improve the General Situation of Education of Roma Children, with Action plan" (approved on 14 December 2000).

[96] Government Decree No. 686 (29 October 1997); Government Decree No. 599 (14 June 2000), Annex, Task 5.b.; Government Decree No. 1145 (7 November 2001) – a long-term task, not evaluated in the 2002 Updated Concept.

[97] Government Decree No. 686 (29 October 1997).

[98] Government Decree No. 599 (14 June 2000), Task 5.a see also 2000 Concept, Part 6.15.

[99] Government Decree No. 1145 (7 November 2001) – a long-term task, not evaluated in the 2002 Updated Concept. Full-day educational programmes include after-school activities. The five schools are to be selected in cooperation with the CRCI and the project is due to be started in the 2002/2003 school year.

[100] Government Decree No. 686 (29 October 1997), to be fulfilled by 2020. The Ministry of Education did not provide information on its implementation for the 2002 Updated Concept.

[101] *Report on the Situation of National Minorities*, p. 71.

[102] Law No. 111/1998 Coll. which also vested self-governing authority to universities.

Transformation of the educational system

The 2000 Concept's proposal to transform special schools and the tasks assigned to the Ministry of Education by Decree No. 599[103] are meant to be realised within the context of a broader transformation of the school system based upon the so-called "White Book."[104] The White Book explicitly rejects the "segregated education of children with special needs"[105] However, the course of action it proposes will do little to overcome the segregation of Roma children in practice:[106] it proposes the establishment of classes offering the regular primary school curriculum *within* special schools, and measures to promote the gradual transfer of capable children to these classes. In other words, children who have not been accepted into mainstream primary schools will continue to be taught together with mentally-handicapped children in special schools;[107] there are no measures to promote the integration of disadvantaged children into the mainstream educational system.

These measures are on hold at present as the Government's proposal for a new School Law was rejected by Parliament, and the proposals outlined in the White Book will depend on implementation of Programme Declarations of the new Government formed after the June 2002 elections.[108]

"Positive action": preparatory classes, teacher's assistants, adult education

The Government has stated its preference for positive action measures, or "focussed assistance," rather than quotas.[109] However, as schools are managed by local governments, the ability of the Ministry of Education to promote the implementation of positive action measures is limited.

Preparatory classes for children from socially disadvantaged families have constituted one of the most important forms of focused assistance to date.

---

[103] See 2000 Concept, Parts 6.11, 6.12 and 6.15; see also Government Decree No. 599 (14 June 2000), Annex, Task 5.a.

[104] The National Programme of Educational Development in the Czech Republic (the so-called "White Book"), was approved by Government Decree No. 113 (7 February 2001). See the website of the Ministry of Education, <www.msmt.cz>, (accessed 11 March 2002).

[105] *White Book*, p. 24.

[106] See e.g. *Minority Protection 2001*, pp. 136–139.

[107] *White Book*, p. 25.

[108] Programme Declarations of the Government, August 2002, <http://www.vlada.cz/1250/vlada/vlada_progrprohl.htm>, (accessed 19 September 2002).

[109] See Part 4.2 in both the 2000 Concept and the 2002 Updated Concept. A quota system would also be difficult to implement due to the difficulty of obtaining exact data on the ethnic origin.

Funding for preparatory classes at various levels has been provided through the State budget, as well as through the Ministry of Education, municipalities, and private sources, benefiting a total of 1,364 children.[110] However, the Ministry of Education has acknowledged that the need for preparatory classes is considerably higher.[111]

A further form of focussed assistance is the employment of Roma as teacher's assistants in primary schools and pre-schools, with the responsibility of providing additional assistance to teachers, helping children prepare for school, and acting as mediators between the school, the family and the community. Following a trial period, during which the training and placement of Roma teacher's assistants (as well as preparatory classes) was tested starting in September 1997 by the NGO *Nová škola* (New School) and the Association of Roma in Moravia, the Ministry of Education endorsed them.[112]

The 2002 Update Concept states that preparatory classes and teacher's assistants should be made available to all Roma children who would benefit from them;[113] it also proposes that teacher's assistants be employed in secondary and vocational schools as well.[114] However, it acknowledges that the need for these measures outstrips available resources, even though the number of preparatory classes and teacher's assistants has increased.[115] Though Phare and other EU sources have provided some support for the training of teacher's assistants,[116] funds are still lacking.[117]

---

[110] According to data provided by the Ministry of Education, in the 2000/2001 school year, preparatory classes were established in 63 primary schools and seven pre-school establishments; another 40 preparatory classes were established in special schools (36 percent of the total number of preparatory classes).

[111] Government Decree No. 87 (23 January 2002), Section III, Annex 2, "Overview of the Financial Sources Allocated by the State for the Implementation of the Concept," <http://www.dzeno.cz/czech/dokumenty/finance.doc>, (accessed 22 August 2002).

[112] See Guideline No. 25484/200-22 of the Ministry of Education.

[113] 2002 Updated Concept, Part 4.4.2.

[114] 2002 Updated Concept, Part 4.4.2.

[115] According to the 2002 Updated Concept, there are now about 230 teacher's assistants. Part 4.4.2, footnote 13.

[116] Teacher's assistants were also trained in 2001 with Phare 1999 funds by the People in Need Foundation (under the "*Varianty*" project), in cooperation with the NGO *Nová škola*. The project was commissioned and supervised by the CRCI. The Ministry of Education is considering contributing financially to a follow-up with Phare 2000 support. See <http://www.varianty.cz/novinka.asp?novinka=45>, (accessed 17 September 2002).

[117] OSI Roundtable, Prague, June 2002.

The Ministry of Education has suggested that the failure to implement these measures widely is also due to a lack of information about the possibility and lack of interest from school directors, who make the ultimate decision as to whether they will be applied in their schools,[118] and the Ministry can only issue recommendations that they do so. In fact, the Ministry is planning to issue recommendations in this area to Regional Offices.[119] The Government has tasked the Ministry of Education with continuously intensifying its support for preparatory classes and teacher's assistants.[120] The 2002 Concept proposes that the Ministry use direct financial incentives to encourage school directors' participation.

The Ministry of Education has also provided support for the organisation of adult education classes for Roma who completed special schools.[121] However, some charge a fee as high as CZK 4,000 (€131),[122] making them inaccessible to many of those they are designed to benefit. The Ministry of Education does not have any figures on the number of adults who have graduated from these courses, and Roma have expressed little interest, except when the courses are organised in tandem with re-qualification classes offered by employment agencies.[123] Measures to reduce or eliminate fees are under consideration, and the Ministry is reportedly developing a set of recommendations for the administration of adult education courses for Regional Offices.[124]

Placement tests

In order to meet the special needs of children from different backgrounds, a new and improved basis for testing their educational abilities has been developed by the Ministry of Education. These tests are also to be administered to pupils who are candidates for transfer from a special school to a primary school.[125] The new tests, which are administered at pedagogic-psychological testing centres throughout the country, were approved only in 2001, and neither the Ministry

---

[118] 2002 Updated Concept, Part 4.4.3.

[119] Information provided by the Coordinator and Officer for the issues of education of Roma children, Ministry of Education, Prague, 17 July 2002.

[120] Decree No. 1145 (7 November 2001).

[121] 2000 Concept, Part 6.14.

[122] The minimum monthly wage in the Czech Republic amounts to some 5,000 CZK (€164).

[123] Information provided by the Coordinator and Officer for the issues of education of Roma children, Ministry of Education, Prague, 17 July 2002.

[124] Information provided by the Coordinator and Officer for the issues of education of Roma children, Ministry of Education, Prague, 17 July 2002.

[125] The Ministry of Education has also issued a guideline on "Methodical instructions for the transfer of successful pupils from special to primary schools" (Guideline No. 28 498/99-24).

of Education nor the Institute of Pedagogic-Psychological Counselling, which developed the test, has evaluated their effectiveness to date.

Programme of Support to Roma Students in Secondary Schools

Finally, the Ministry of Education is providing financial support to Roma students in vocational secondary schools.[126] Although implementation has been hampered to some degree by territorial reform in 2001 and change of individual school directors, this measure has been particularly well-received by the Roma community and by others; many observers stress that supporting the emergence of a Roma middle class is key to improving communications between Roma communities and the majority society.[127]

Approximately 900 students were supported in 2000, and 1,531 students in 2001.[128] Due to the programme's success, the IMC recommended that levels of funding should be increased in 2002.[129] In a positive example of coordinating the implementation of special measures to improve the situation for Roma with other governmental policies, the Government has tasked the Ministry of Labour and Social Affairs with taking measures to ensure that assistance provided to Roma pupils in secondary schools is not considered as a source of income when assessing families' entitlement to social benefits.[130]

Additional training for special school graduates

Graduates of special schools are at a disadvantage in applying to secondary schools compared to students have completed regular schools. The Government has supported the organisation of special courses to assist special school

---

[126] Funding is provided to schools to cover students' school fees, per diem, accommodation and school supplies.

[127] "*Organizace, zaměřené na romskou problematiku, jsou leckdy odtrženy od reality*" (Organisations focusing on Roma issues are sometimes disconnected from reality), *Deník chomutovska*, 5 September 2001.

[128] A total of CZK 2,925,000 (€96,122) was allocated by the Ministry of Education in 2000 and CZK 6,837,000 (€224,680) in 2001. 2002 Updated Concept, Part 4.4.10; see also *Commissioner's Report 2000–2001*, Parts I.5 and II.3.

[129] CZK 10 million (€328,623) were allocated in 2002. *Commissioner's Report 2000–2001*, Part II.3. See also "Information on the Programme of Support to Roma Pupils in Secondary Schools," <http://www.vlada.cz/1250/vrk/vrk.htm>, (accessed 16 July 2002) (in Czech).

[130] *Commissioner's Report 2000–2001*, Part II.3.

graduates in preparing for admission tests to secondary schools.[131] This measure does little to address the deeper problem of segregation of Roma into special schools but the experience could be used more broadly in Roma education projects.

The overall impact of the various initiatives taken in the area of education to date has been minimal and the segregation of Roma children persists. Some successful measures, such as preparatory classes and Roma teacher's assistants, have been expanded and the programme to support Roma students in vocational high schools has also been well-received. However, more systematic and comprehensive measures are necessary to address structural flaws in the education system, and to increase the number of Roma students entering secondary school and university.

3.2.2 Employment

Government measures in the area of employment have focused primarily on addressing long-term unemployment among "persons difficult to place on the labour market;" little has been done to address the problem of discrimination against Roma. As noted above, the Concept's original proposal to establish an Office for Ethnic Equality was abandoned, and without the central coordination this Office would provide, other Concept measures, such as re-qualification courses and public benefit jobs, lack cohesion and have had minimal impact. Draft anti-discrimination legislation is expected to revive the proposal to establish the Office, which could bring rapid and significant improvements to Concept implementation in this area.

The following employment-related tasks have been assigned to the Ministry of Labour and Social Affairs (and others), *inter alia*:

- Create the conditions for combating discrimination in employment, including through legislative changes;[132]

- Provide the legal grounds for positive action in order to eliminate disadvantages experienced by members of the Roma community;[133]

---

[131] Originally, a project funded under the Phare 1997 Programme sought to help Roma students pass the one year qualification course that was required for entrance to secondary school for special school graduates. After an amendment to the School Law eliminated this requirement, the project was refocused on preparing Roma special school graduates for secondary school entrance exams.

[132] Government Decree No. 279 (7 April 1999), Task 2.a.

[133] Government Decree No. 279 (7 April 1999), Task 2.b.

- Establish guidelines for Roma Advisors and Assistants at district offices, including through vocational training;[134]
- Examine the possibility of hiring Roma Assistants in Counselling Centres, in cooperation with the Association of Citizens' Advisory Bureaux (CAB).[135]

The positive measures proposed by the 2000 Concept[136] seek to combat long-term unemployment, including through:

- Providing opportunities for Roma to obtain additional education and professional qualifications (See Section 3.2.1);
- Offering qualification and re-qualification courses, in conjunction with established labour market needs to ensure that Roma who complete these courses can find employment;
- Developing incentives for employers to hire persons "difficult to place on the labour market;"[137]
- Creating a system of preferences in public tenders for so-called "Roma companies."[138]

Combating racial discrimination in employment, including through legislative measures

The proposed Office for Ethnic Equality was to have ensured protection against all forms of racial discrimination, including discrimination in access to employment and in the workplace.[139] As the Office has not been established, the Ministry of Labour and Social Affairs has assumed responsibility for implementing this component of the Concept. However, until comprehensive anti-discrimination legislation is adopted and the Office is operational, efforts to ensure effective

---

[134] Government Decree No. 599 (14 June 2000), Annex, Task 3.a – a task of the Vice Chair of the Government and the Ministry of Labour and Social Affairs, together with the Ministry of Interior and the Commissioner for Human Rights.

[135] Citizens Advisory Bureaux are NGOs which have not received State funding to date. Decree No. 599 (14 June 2000), Annex, Task 3.d.

[136] See Chapter 4 on Compensatory Measures, 2000 Concept.

[137] According to the guidelines established by the Ministry of Labour and Social Affairs (see below).

[138] A "Roma company" is defined as a company employing more than 60 percent of either Roma or "persons difficult to place on the labour market." 2000 Concept, Part 4.19.

[139] 2000 Concept, Section IV; see also *Commissioner's Report 2000–2001*, Parts II.1.5 and II.1.6.

protection against discrimination in employment (and in other areas) will be limited due to the fragmented legislative framework in this area.[140]

The Ministry of Labour and Social Affairs and the Labour Offices jointly exercise the competence to monitor compliance with existing employment laws and guidelines; however, their ability to impose sanctions in cases of violation is limited;[141] under existing legislation, it is extremely difficult to prove discrimination or even to establish negligent fault.[142]

Establishing the legislative grounds for positive action

The Ministry of Labour and Social Affairs has been tasked with drafting legislative amendments to establish the basis for positive action in the field of employment.[143] The 2002 Concept Update noted that this task had not been fulfilled as the Ministry did not propose any new amendments, and simply made reference to already-existing general non-discrimination clauses in the Law on Employment.[144] Thus, there is still no basis in domestic law for positive measures in employment.[145]

---

[140] For a detailed analysis of existing legislation to provide protection against discrimination in employment and other areas, see B. Bukovská and L. Taylor, *Legal analysis of national and European anti-discrimination legislation. A comparison of the EU Racial Equality Directive & Protocol No. 12 with anti-discrimination legislation in Czech Republic*, European Roma Rights Center/Interights/Minority Policy Group, Budapest/London/Brussels, September 2001, <http://www.migpolgroup.com/uploadstore/Czech%20Republic%20electronic.pdf>, (accessed 26 september 2002)

[141] Fines of up to CZK 250,000 (€8,216) can be levied on employers for an intentional violation of their duties, and up to CZK one million (€32,862) for persistent violators. Law No. 1/1991 Coll. on employment, § 9.

[142] However, the definition of a misdemeanour introduced by the amendment of Law No. 200/1990 Coll., on Misdemeanours (273/2001 Coll.) should be applicable in this context. It adds the definition of a misdemeanour committed by anyone who restricts or denies the execution of the right of a minority member, and anyone who causes another person injury, *inter alia* because of membership in a national minority or due to ethnic origin, race, etc. (see Section 3.4 of this report).

[143] Government Decree No. 279 (7 April 1999).

[144] Law No. 1/1991 Coll., Amendment No.167/1999.

[145] However, several international treaties to which the Czech Republic is a party explicitly provide for positive action, such as ICERD, Art. 1.4.

Measures to support the employment of "persons difficult to place on the labour market" [146]

The objective of this initiative is to develop a more unified approach to the problem of long-term unemployment, which affects mainly Roma, by coordinating the efforts of State agencies, municipalities and trade unions.

The Ministry of Labour and Social Affairs has developed a programme for the employment of "persons difficult to place on the labour market." The programme provides for financial incentives to employers who offer "public benefit jobs;"[147] these jobs are established by the employer on the basis of a written contract with the Labour Office or municipality. Public benefit jobs are offered on a short-term basis, not exceeding twelve months. The programme also provides support for re-qualification projects, and financial incentives for the establishment of new jobs.[148] These activities are regularly evaluated by the Labour Offices. In 2001, the Ministry also established a special Commission to evaluate the programmes being implemented within this framework.[149]

However, as of yet, no agreement has been reached among the relevant ministries on the Concept's proposed measure to provide financial incentives to companies employing Roma; disagreements have focused on the appropriate method for delivering these benefits: through tax incentives or as a direct allocation to employers.[150]

---

[146] These persons are defined as: (1) long-term unemployed persons or persons with characteristics of prospective long-term unemployment; (2) persons with low or no qualifications, which might be connected with a disability; and (3) persons of low social standing following from a different socio-cultural background. These measures were approved by Government Decree No. 640 (23 June 1999). See also Government Decree No. 599 (14 June 2000), Annex, Task 3.c.

[147] The legal basis for these measures is provided by the Law on Employment and Competency of Czech Authorities in the Area of Employment (Law No. 9/1991 Coll.). Public benefit jobs are new jobs established by the employer on the basis of a written contract with the Labour Office (see § 5 of Law No. 9/1991 Coll.). Public benefit jobs can also be created by municipalities. Job seekers are employed in a public benefit job on a rather short-term basis, not exceeding twelve months. Employers' expenses in providing these jobs are covered to a certain extent (up to the level of the provided salaries, taxes and insurance connected with the salary) by the Ministry of Labour or by the Labour Office.

[148] Information on the Implementation of Government Decrees as of 31 December 2001, Part 2.1.3.

[149] Established by Ministerial Order No. 11/2001. See also the Report on Options for Combating Discrimination.

[150] 2002 Updated Concept, Part 4.5.3.

Evaluation of the impact of the above initiatives is difficult, as there are no official statistics on unemployment among Roma, and the collection of such statistics is prohibited.[151] However, they are widely regarded as having been minimally effective, and the appropriateness of public benefit jobs as a measure to combat long-term employment has been questioned. Furthermore, the limited efficacy of these policies sometimes has been used to support claims that Roma are unwilling to work, and some have claimed that they are discriminatory against members of the majority.[152]

In a recent document evaluating efforts to date and setting guidelines for future action to improve the situation for Roma in the sphere of employment, the Ministry of Labour and Social Affairs called for greater attention to supporting the capacity, qualification and motivation of individual job-seekers.[153] It pointed to the need for research on minimum wage requirements. The 2002 Updated Concept called for priority to be given to the development of focussed programmes to address unemployment among Roma and for the next Update to lay the foundations for more extensive measures to be taken in this area.

3.2.3 Housing and other goods and services

Housing

The Concept acknowledges that segregation and exclusion of Roma communities is a key problem and proposes the provision of low-income housing as the principal solution.[154] However, this approach seems to reflect a view that these problems are due exclusively to poverty and lack of income; it fails to recognise and address the role played by discrimination.

---

[151] General statistics on unemployment as of August 2002 are at <http://www.mpsv.cz/scripts/nezamestanost/info.asp?lg=1>, (accessed 17 July 2002).

[152] See e.g. "*Romové většinou pracovat moc dlouho nevydrží*" (Roma are usually unable to work too long), *Večerník Praha*, 28 December 2001; "*Foros – město i práce*" (Foros – town and work), *Deník Jablonecka*, 29 January 2002; "*Město přestane vyplácet Romům příspěvek k platu*" (The city will stop paying Roma supplements to their salary), *Deník Litoměřicka*, 12 July 2001.

[153] Priorities of Employment Policy, updated on 23 March 2002, <http://www.mpsv.cz/scripts/clanek.asp?lg=1&id=2544>, (accessed 17 July 2002).

[154] 2000 Concept, Part 4.23.

Moreover, many Roma debtors are already living in low-rental housing, in constant threat of eviction,[155] and a programme to offer even lower rents is hardly a realistic option.

Because of profound changes in the structure of the housing market, the analysis provided by the 1997 Bratinka Report is now outdated.[156] The 2002 Updated Concept notes the results of some initial Government-sponsored research on housing issues,[157] but given deteriorating conditions in this area more comprehensive research is necessary as the basis for formulating broader-ranging policy solutions.

The 2000 Concept proposes only *ad hoc* solutions. Specifically, the Ministry for Regional Development was tasked with:

- Elaborating a concept for the provision of low-income housing to disadvantaged families;[158]
- Supporting housing development programmes involving unemployed Roma and flat occupants in the construction work;[159]
- Conducting and evaluating research on the housing available to socially disadvantaged members of the Roma community in all districts.[160]

---

[155] Some landlords use indebtedness as a reason for evicting Roma tenants in order to renovate and rent out flats for so-called "economic" rents which can be 20 times higher. See e.g. "*Kolem neplatičů nájemného se zřejmě stahuje smyčka*" (A noose is tying itself around the neck of rent defaulters) *Večerník Praha*, 25 January 2002.

[156] The rate of private ownership of houses and flats has risen dramatically over the past decade due to restitution, privatisation and the availability of state-subsidised loans and home mortgages. See the results of the 2001 Census, <http://www.czso.cz:8005/sldbr-win/owa/gt11?xjazyk=CZ&xuzemi=1&xtyp=1>, (accessed 18 July 2002). *Note: Following flooding in Summer 2002, the website was redone and this information is no longer available.* See: <http://www.czso.cz/cz/sldb/index.htm>, (accessed 5 October 2002).

[157] Government Decree No. 599 (14 June 2000), Annex, Tasks 4.b and 4.e; see also *Information on the Implementation of Government Decrees as of 31 December 2001*, Part 10.4.5; and *Report on the results of research on the issue of 'holobyty' in relation to the Roma community*, annex to Government Decree No. 87 (23 January 2002).

[158] 2000 Concept, Annex 4

[159] 2000 Concept, Annex 4. This task was also assigned by Government Decree No. 686 (29 October 1997); see also the projects of community housing assigned by Government Decree No. 978 (22 September 1999) and Government Decree No. 387 (19 April 2000).

[160] 2000 Concept, Annex 4.

Research study on low-quality flats

Within the framework of the Concept, the Government commissioned a research study on low-quality flats (so-called *"holobyty"*).[161] The study assesses the situation with regard to housing segregation and offers proposals to promote integration. It underlines the need for comprehensive anti-discrimination legislation effectively to combat segregationist policies by local governments. While its recommendations are rather general, this study represents an important step towards developing a comprehensive policy to address segregation.

However, the study was limited in scope; it did not examine other areas in which discrimination has been a problem, such as in the privatisation of flats and in access to State-supported housing loans and rental housing. These problems are particularly evident at the municipal level, where local government are authorised to issue by-laws and other measures to guide municipal housing policies.[162] For example, often flats in areas where Roma live are not offered for sale to tenants, as is the case in areas inhabited by non-Roma; rather, entire buildings are sold off to other owners. Some municipalities have removed Roma from neighbourhoods by purchasing houses in the countryside and moving them there. The introduction of anti-discrimination legislation will provide an essential tool to challenge such policies; at present, discriminatory procedures in housing by-laws are not explicitly prohibited.

The current system of rent control based on regulated lump-sum rents rather than targeted rent control should also be examined, as it tends to impede access to housing other than that provided by municipalities. In many cases, Roma families who are evicted from rent-controlled flats cannot afford alternative housing;[163] over time they have been moved into ghettos and second-class

---

[161] The Ministry for Regional Development allocated CZK 500,000 (€16,431) for this study. See Socioklub, "Report on the Results of Research on the Issue of *'holobyty'* in relation to the Roma Community," Realised for the Ministry for Regional Development, Annex to Government Decree No. 87 (23 January 2002), Section IV, Annex 2.

[162] See e.g. I. Tomeš, *Sociální soudržnost, vyloučenost a tvorba sociální politiky kraje a obce* (Social cohesion, exclusion and developing regional policy), 18 April 2002, <http://www.mpsv.cz/scripts/clanek.asp?id=11&lg=1>, (accessed 17 July 2002); see also B. Bukovská, *Difference and Indifference: Bringing Czech Roma Ghettoes to Europe's Court*, <http://www.eumap.org/articles/content/70/703>, (accessed 17 September 2002).

[163] For rent regulation, the date of the contract is decisive rather than social need, and the option of unlimited contractual rent has driven rents to unacceptably high levels.

accommodations.[164] The practice of usury has impoverished entire settlements.[165]

More comprehensive research would facilitate the articulation of a more comprehensive approach to housing issues, with guidelines for the adoption of effective policies at the central and local levels.[166] It would be particularly important to identify means of tackling the discriminatory practices emanating from municipal by-laws and regulations.

Construction of cheap housing

The Construction Programme of Rented Housing (completed in 2002) financed the construction of cheap housing (though not explicitly for Roma). However, the Ministry for Regional Development was unable to influence selection criteria for tenants; these were set by the municipalities.[167] Recently, the Ministry has developed a second complementary housing programme,[168] but it is not yet functioning due to lack of funding.

Two community housing projects in Ostrava-Muglinov and Brno received State funding for the building and renovation of apartment buildings respectively, with the participation of Roma residents.[169] The preliminary results of the two projects were provided in the 2002 Updated Concept. In the case of the Brno project, for example,[170] the renovations are expected to be finalised in mid-2002;

---

[164] Recently, the Ombudsman submitted a complaint to the Constitutional Court claiming, *inter alia*, that current price regulations were a violation of the State obligation to ensure equal access to housing according to Art. 11 of the International Covenant on Economic, Social and Cultural Rights. See <www.ochrance.cz>, (accessed 22 March 2002). The Ombudsman concluded that current pricing regulations are discriminatory with regard to tenants who signed a rental contract after the decisive date, and who are therefore excluded from rent regulations without regard to their level of income. This has also caused inequality in access to housing.

[165] For more, see the website of the People in Need Foundation, <www.pinf.cz>, (accessed 23 May 2002).

[166] Some comprehensive research – including useful policy recommendations – is already available from non-governmental sources. See A. Baršová, *Problems of Housing of Ethnic Minorities and Residential Segregation Trends in the Czech Republic*.

[167] *Information on the Implementation of Government Decrees as of 31 December 2001*, Part 10.1.1.

[168] *Information on the Implementation of Government Decrees as of 31 December 2001*, Part 10.4.1.

[169] Decrees No. 978 (22 September 1999) and No. 387 (19 April 2000) respectively.

[170] *Information on the Implementation of Government Decrees as of 31 December 2001*, Part 10.3.1 and Section III, Annex 1, "Interim Report on the Development Programme of Community Housing of Inhabitants of Roma Ethnicity in Brno and the Improvement of Inter-Ethnic Relations in Society."

the original 2001 deadline having been extended due to the unexpectedly poor state of the buildings and the need for additional funding. In the final post-construction phase of the project, a self-government body will be established to ensure that Roma families remain involved in the long-term management of the buildings.

Critics have pointed out that these projects do little to promote integration; in fact, they reinforce existing patterns of segregation, as the great majority of the inhabitants of the renovated buildings are Roma. Moreover, the projects were very expensive,[171] and provide assistance to relatively few families compared to the level of need.

In order to be effective, governmental policy should aim to address discrimination in housing in a comprehensive manner, targeting not only socially disadvantaged members of the Roma community but discrimination in all types of housing. Furthermore, instead of creating ethnically homogenous enclaves, residents should have the possibility to move from social housing to other types of housing when their economic situation allows.

Other goods and services

The 2000 Concept proposed that the Office for Ethnic Equality would provide protection against racial discrimination in access to goods and services.[172] Since the idea to create such an institution was abandoned, activities in this area remain

---

[171] Even with voluntary labour from Roma inhabitants of the apartments, costs of the Brno project were estimated at about CZK 65.5 million (€2,152,481) in 2000. *"Romové absolvovali v rámci komunitního bydlení školení"* (Roma have completed training within the framework of community housing), Radio Praha, 25 April 2000 and at CZK 63 million (€2,070,325) in Ostrava. *"Stavba osady vázne na penězích"* (The construction of settlements stagnates because of money), *Mladá Fronta Dnes*, 25 September 2001, p. 2. The Secretary of the CRCI has stated that such projects are too expensive and will therefore not be continued.

[172] Discrimination against consumers is defined as an offence in the Law on Consumer Protection (Law No. 634/1992 Coll.). However, no definition of consumer discrimination is given, and there are no separate provisions providing protection against discrimination consisting of a denial of services or goods in the court procedure. For victims of racial discrimination, there is no provision constituting their right to seek protection by the court, to demand that the discriminatory behaviour be stopped, its consequences removed and reasonable satisfaction and monetary compensation awarded. In theory, however, it is possible for a victim of discrimination to seek protection under the Civil Code, § 11 and below, governing the general protection of the personal rights of an individual. However, only the protection of portraits, pictorial images, visual and sound recordings, and expressions of a personal nature is explicitly mentioned in the Code. See also *Minority Protection 2001*, pp. 146–148.

restricted to the regular reporting of the Czech Trade Inspection (CTI), under the supervision of the Ministry of Industry and Trade.[173] The CTI provides the CRCI with the number of checks and the number of ascertained violations. An overview of CTI inspection findings on racial discrimination shows the extremely low success rate of checks performed in response to consumer protests in 1996–2001.[174] The actual experience of Roma consumers with racial discrimination, however, is quite frequent.[175] Since the efficiency of the CTI in fighting discrimination is apparently very low,[176] Roma usually do not report cases of discrimination to the CTI but rather to the police or stop going to the establishment which discriminated against them entirely.

---

[173] According to Law no. 634/1992 Coll., on Consumer Protection, the Czech Trade Inspection is responsible for controlling discrimination against consumers. Decree No. 686 (29 October 1997) tasked the Ministry of Industry and Trade to control the observance of § 6 of the Law on Consumer Protection, imposing penalties on businesses which refuse to provide services because of a consumer's racial or ethnic origin. *Information on the Implementation of Government Decrees as of 31 December 2001*, Part 5.1.1.

[174] The numbers were provided for the 2002 Updated Concept. Over a six-year period, CTI was able to prove discrimination in only eight of the 89 inspections conducted following consumer protest. A total of 485 checks were carried out by two Roma inspectors in 2001. CTI currently employs only one Roma inspector in Ostrava and one in Ústí nad Labem. It is questionable whether such a practice is effective as the two inspectors might be well known to the personnel of many establishments.

[175] E.g. see "*Romské studentky si nezatančily*" (Roma students did not dance), *Plzeňský deník*, 3 August 2001. For two students of the 12th International Summer Language School in Plzeň, a visit to the Music Club ended with a charge lodged by them with the police for having been denied entry. A similar case of discrimination against two other Roma students had taken place the previous year in the same club. "We are shocked by the personnel's behaviour even more since, at that time, we were assured that the strategy of this enterprise is to fully respect equality of entry of guests." International Language School Director Dagmar Jangl-Janoušková has instructed the students not to go to the club. See also *Minority Protection 2001*, pp. 146–148.

[176] The low efficiency of CTI is caused by factors of a rather legislative character as CTI is responsible for controls within the limits set by the Law on Consumer Protection, including violations of the non-discrimination clause. It can initiate an administrative proceeding only if it finds problems during a check but not on the basis of a report. Discrimination against an inspector or conducted in his/her presence can be sanctioned with a fine of up to CZK one million (€32,862), and a double penalty imposed for persistent violations.

3.2.4 Healthcare and other forms of social protection

Healthcare

Decree No. 279 (7 April 1999) by which the 1999 Concept Proposal was adopted tasked the Ministry of Health with:

- Creating the conditions preventing racial (and eventually other forms of) discrimination (in the area of health) and, if needed, to present to the Government proposals for legislative amendments;

- Including into the amendments of laws provisions providing a legal basis for positive action in order to remove possible disadvantages for members of the Roma community (in the area of health);

- Conducting research regarding the state of health of the Roma population.[177]

The 2000 Concept highlights the health risks connected to housing in connection with efforts to combat segregated housing.[178] However, the impact of hygiene conditions on emerging health hazards for the Roma community is not addressed. The 2000 Concept did not contain any specific tasks for the Ministry of Health; nor did it recommend developing comprehensive programmes to address difficulties in the area of health protection and equal access to medical care. It did, however, discuss some aspects related to access to healthcare, such as poor health resulting from poor housing conditions,[179] as well as the need for complex studies and analysis.[180]

In its reporting for the 2002 Updated Concept, the Ministry of Health reported that it had supported research on the state of health of the Roma population.[181] The results of this project, "Determinants of Health of the Roma Population in the Czech Republic," are expected to be publicly available in mid-2002. Initiatives to inform the Roma community of health risks and to raise health awareness were also implemented in 2001 within the framework of the national health programme.

---

[177] Decree No. 279 (7 April 1999), Section II, Parts 2.1.a, 2.1.b.

[178] 2000 Concept, Part 4.28; 2002 Updated Concept, Part 4.6.3. Hygiene conditions are very closely connected to housing as they depend on access to clean and safe drinking water, infrastructure providing power for cooking, heating and lighting, and functioning waste and sanitary facilities, as well as the condition of buildings.

[179] *Commissioner's Report 2000–2001*, Part 3.12.

[180] *Information on the Implementation of Government Decrees as of 31 December 2001*, Part 4.28.

[181] *Information on the Implementation of Government Decrees as of 31 December 2001*, Part 12.3.

The 2002 Updated Concept has recommended establishing the position of health assistant for the Roma community at the regional level.[182] However, what is really needed is a complex analysis of all relevant factors in order to elaborate a detailed proposal, include a proposal for an appropriate legislative framework, policies at the central and local level, as well as a framework for positive measures and means of influencing local policies.

Social protection

The extremely high level of unemployment among Roma, itself a result of factors such as low levels of education and poor health, exacerbates the negative effects of dependence on social benefits.[183] The salary for unqualified labour – often the only work that unskilled Roma are able to secure – is only slightly higher than social benefits, further reducing motivation. High levels of dependence on social benefits further reinforce prejudice and resentment towards Roma among the majority population.[184]

The 2000 Concept proposes the following measures in the area of social protection:[185]

- Minimise the negative impact of the current system of social benefits and supporting programmes on socially disadvantaged families;
- Establish a functioning network of field social workers in excluded communities.

Neither the 2000 Concept nor other governmental documents identify specific means of overcoming the de-motivating effect of long-term unemployment and dependence on social benefits. By contrast, the more specific measure to establish a network of "field social workers" who interact directly with Roma communities, has brought positive results.

Programme of "Field Social Workers"

Started in 2000 as a pilot programme, 22 "field social workers" received training and were employed in fifteen districts.[186] In 2001, funding was increased to employ a total of 54 field social workers covering 35 districts.[187]

---

[182] 2002 Updated Concept, Part 4.6.3.

[183] Comments from a Roma District Advisor and Vice Chair of the CRCI.

[184] OSI Roundtable, Prague, June 2002.

[185] See 2000 Concept, especially Parts 4.29, 4.30, 4.32, and 4.33.

[186] CZK 2,800,000 (€92,014) was allocated by the Government to municipalities, districts and regions employing field social workers. *Commissioner's Report 2000–2001*, Part I.4.

[187] CZK 6,060,000 (€199,146) was allocated in 2001. *Commissioner's Report 2000–2001*, Part II.4.

On the basis of this pilot programme, the Ministry of Labour and Social Affairs elaborated a project to support the establishment of a network of social workers in excluded Roma communities.[188] The aim of the project is to research the situation of these communities, with a view to promoting their integration through social work.[189] Initial assessments of the programme by the Government and by civil society organisations is quite positive. Working directly "on the ground" with communities has allowed social workers to develop a more sophisticated understanding of the causes of conflictual situations, and thus to identify concrete solutions to the practical problems they encounter.[190] The Ministry of Labour and Social Affairs has highlighted work in socially excluded Roma communities as a priority for the 2003 funding round for the NGO sector.[191]

Some problems in the relationship between the social workers and State administration have been identified. According to a top official of the social prevention department of Teplice District Office, "[i]n some places, Roma field workers have infringed upon the competencies of State administration officials."[192] Formal articulation of the competencies of field social workers would reduce the potential for conflicts of this nature.

Despite the success of this programme, an urgent need remains for a comprehensive analysis of the root factors causing dependence on social benefits. This would allow for the development of comprehensive policies to reduce disadvantage and dependency. *Ad hoc* proposals cannot be expected to produce more than isolated and short-term positive effects.[193]

---

[188] Decree No. 1145 (7 November 2001). On 22 November 2001, the IMC recommended increasing funding in 2002 to CZK 10 million (€328,623). *Information on the Implementation of Government Decrees as of 31 December 2001*, Part 2.5; see also 2002 Updated Concept, Part 4.6.1.

[189] Information provided by a Representative of the People in Need Foundation. See Programme of support for field social work in Roma socially excluded communities, <http://www.vlada.cz/1250/vrk/vrk.htm>, (accessed 17 July 2002).

[190] J. Černý, "*Drobná práce na velkých změnách*" (Minute work on big changes), *Respekt*, 4 December 2000, p. 7.

[191] See the website of the Ministry of Labour and Social Affairs, <http://www.mpsv.cz/scripts/clanek.asp?lg=1&id=2780>, (accessed 5 October 2002).

[192] "*Romští terénní pracovníci již znají své kompetence*" (Roma field workers already know their competencies), *Deník Směr*, 12 April 2002.

[193] For example, partial amendments to the Law on Social Benefits, so that placing a child for a maximum of five days per month into pre-school education no longer causes the termination of the entitlement to parental benefits, are not sufficient for raising the motivation of families.

3.2.5 The criminal justice system

Discrimination in the criminal justice system is not addressed in the 2000 Concept. At the same time, anecdotal evidence suggests that Roma have little trust in the criminal justice system,[194] and a number of independent studies have indicated that further research in this area is warranted.[195] The 2002 Updated Concept acknowledges that: "[…] stereotyping Roma as (potential) perpetrators and not victims, their underestimation as witnesses and persons submitting complaints and the overall different approach to Roma is still a relatively common phenomenon in the work of police, investigators, public prosecutors and judges."[196]

3.3 Protection from Racially Motivated Violence

The 2000 Concept asserts that ensuring the security of Roma is one of its priorities.[197] The level of protection offered by legislation is sufficient,[198] though there are problems with implementation, and the high incidence of racially motivated violence continues to raise serious concerns for Roma.[199]

The 2002 Updated Concept notes that a majority of asylum seekers list fear of racially motivated violence and insufficient protection in their applications.[200] It further recognises that downplaying the racial on motivation for crimes is a common phenomenon; "there is no doubt that underestimating the information provided by

---

[194] According to one Roma representative, "[…] Roma do not believe in the police, State prosecutor and courts." OSI Roundtable, Prague, June 2002.

[195] See e.g. Socioklub, *"Romové v České republice"* (Roma in the Czech Republic), Prague, 1999.

[196] 2002 Updated Concept, Part 7.1.

[197] 2000 Concept, Chapter 1 and Chapter 8 "Enhancing the Security of Roma" (Chapters 1 and 7 respectively of the 2002 Updated Concept).

[198] Law No. 134/2002 Coll., which amended Law No. 140/1961 Coll., (Criminal Code), inserted new provisions on racially motivated crimes, further extending criminal offences to crimes against the life and health of persons. The anti-discrimination legislation being developed (see Section 3.2 of this report) will not address the issue of racially motivated violence.

[199] According to a spokesperson for a local Roma association in Most (Northern Bohemia), renewed skinhead attacks, along with high unemployment, are prompting Roma to emigrate. "Czech Roma Say Renewed Skinhead Attacks Force Them Into Emigration," RFE/RL *Newsline*, 29 March 2002.

[200] 2002 Updated Concept, Part 7.1.

Roma is a result of the fact that many policemen – along with a large part of society – consider Roma as a criminal subculture whose members are a priori untrustworthy."[201]

In 2001, 302 racially motivated crimes were registered,[202] compared to 364 in 2000,[203] and 316 in 1999.[204] A total of 402 such crimes were investigated by the police in 2001, compared to 311 in 2000.[205] According to the Commissioner for Human Rights, the Czech legal system deals "benevolently" with attacks committed by right-wing extremists, citing prejudice against Roma as a possible reason.[206] However, more recently there have been a number of cases in which racial motivation was recognised and a heavier sentence imposed accordingly.[207]

The campaign "Be kind to your local Nazi," implemented by the People in Need Foundation with Government support,[208] had the focused objective of seeking to decrease the appeal of skinheads among young people. According to an impact evaluation, it reached one-third of the national population, including almost half of all persons under 24,

---

[201] 2002 Updated Concept, Part 7.1.

[202] Statistics of the Courts and State Attorney Offices, provided by the Ministry of Justice, Department of Organisation and Supervision, 2002.

[203] Statistics of the Ministry of Interior. There might be slight discrepancies in the numbers registered by the Ministry of Interior and the Ministry of Justice, as the former registers cases investigated by the police while the latter only registers cases decided by the Courts upon final judgement (convictions).

[204] Ministry of Interior, *Report on the Situation in the Area of Public Order and Inner Security on the Territory of the Czech Republic*, 1999, Appendix 2, para. 2.

[205] An Interior Ministry spokeswoman cited in the daily *Pravo*, in "Racially Motivated Crime on the Rise in the Czech Republic," RFE/RL *Newsline*, 12 March 2002.

[206] Statement of the Commissioner for Human Rights, Jan Jařab, to *Mladá Fronta Dnes* on 25 July 2001; cited in "Czech Courts Lax on Racist Crime?," RFE/RL *Newsline*, 25 July 2001.

[207] For example, V. P., a skinhead who stabbed a Roma man to death in July 2001, was sentenced on 29 March 2002 to a thirteen-year sentence by a court in Hradec Králové which found him guilty of having committed a racially motivated crime. He had previously received a very light sentence for another crime. "Czech Skinhead receives heavy prison sentence for killing Rom," RFE/RL *Newsline*, 2 April 2002.

[208] The Government provided CZK two million (€65,725) to the People in Need Foundation for the campaign. Phare 1999 support was also provided. See <http://www.varianty.cz/default.asp?mn=7&pa=med>, (accessed 17 July 2002); see also 2002 Updated Concept, Parts 6.2.2 and 6.3.

among whom it appears to have had a particularly positive impact.[209] Reducing levels of skinhead activity would be likely to reduce the incidence of racially-motivated violence towards Roma.

A series of steps have been undertaken by the Ministry of Interior and the Ministry of Justice to address the issue of racially motivated violence against Roma as a result of measures proposed by the 2000 Concept as well as earlier decrees. These consist mostly of police training and monitoring and, as they are considered by the Government to have been successful, no additional measures have been proposed.

Analysis of current criminal legislation

The Ministry of Justice was tasked with carrying out an analysis of current criminal legislation protecting persons from racially motivated crimes and racial discrimination of all forms (including penal offences).[210] According to a report commissioned by the Ministry,[211] Czech criminal law basically fulfils the International Convention on the Elimination of All Forms of Racial Discrimination (ICERD), though there are gaps: for example, the establishment of a racially intolerant organisation is not a specific crime. The report also concluded that problems result not from inadequate provisions but rather from the fact that "giving proof and especially proof of national, racial, ethnic or similar motives is difficult. Usually, there is no admission of the perpetrator that could serve as the only direct proof [...]."

In addition, the Ministry of Interior was tasked, *inter alia*, with developing methodologies to facilitate establishing proof of racially motivated crimes as well as measures to facilitate the dissolution of civil associations which aim to suppress the civil rights and freedoms of persons on the basis of ethnic origin or

---

[209] While the population as a whole had some reservations regarding the campaign, young people evaluated it positively. 65 percent of young people who had seen the campaign held a negative position towards skinheads, compared to 40 percent of respondents who had not seen it. Conducted by AISA, for the People in Need Foundation, <http://www.varianty.cz/default.asp?mn=7&pa=med>, (accessed 17 July 2002).

[210] Government Decree No. 599 (14 June 2000).

[211] Institute for Criminology and Social Prevention, *Ethnic Minorities, their Protection against Racial Discrimination and Possible Integration into Society* (unpublished report). The results of the research were also published in: M. Štěchová, *Právní ochrana etnických menšin v ČR* (Legal Protection of Ethnic Minorities in the Czech Republic), Institute for Criminology and Social Prevention, Prague, 2002.

and race.[212] This task was realised by introducing new regulations to better fight extremism and racially motivated crimes.[213]

Training of the police

Police have received training on identifying racially motivated crimes in order to reduce the risk that racial motivation will be ignored.[214] However, the 2000 Concept noted that efforts in this area have been limited by lack of funding.[215]

In 2000, the Ministry of Interior prepared a report entitled "Information on Concrete Educational Activities of the Police Focusing on the Elimination of their Racist and Xenophobic prejudices."[216] The Ministry of Interior has also reported that the topics of racism and xenophobia are covered in the curricula of police schools, and that the training of the police force includes the identification of racial motivations as well as basic information on the Roma culture and cultural differences. It has proposed creating a State-funded "Centre for Human Rights Education" at the Secondary Vocational Police School in Prague for further human rights training.

In 2000–2001, the Ministry of Interior, in cooperation with the UK, conducted several seminars on police work with national minorities. In 2001, the Ministry of Interior, in cooperation with the British Home Office, began developing a "Strategy for Police Work in the Area of National Minorities."[217] The Strategy stresses the need for the police to establish a partnership with communities of different ethnic backgrounds, for efforts to eliminate discrimination by the police. Strategy activities are expected to produce greater respect for the police force as well as increased involvement in policing by national minorities.

Monitoring

Efforts have been made to monitor the problem of racially motivated violence and to produce relevant statistics. Every year, the Ministry of Interior must prepare a "Report on Extremism" on the basis of which it tasks the relevant ministries with

---

[212] Government Decree No. 789 (28 July 1999).

[213] *Information on the Implementation of Government Decrees as of 31 December 2001*, Part 3.3.1.

[214] See e.g. a task assigned to the Ministry of Interior by Government Decree No. 789 (28 July 1999) to ensure through hiring policies and seminars that the police are able to determine racially motivated crimes in order to reduce the risk of disparagement. Roma have also been hired in the police (see Section 3.4.3 of this report).

[215] See the 2000 Concept, Part 8.4; see also the 2002 Updated Concept, Part 7.2.

[216] Government Decree No. 672/00.

[217] *Information on the Implementation of Government Decrees as of 31 December 2001*, Part 3.3.2.

obligations.[218] Moreover, the President of the Security and Information Services and the Ministry of Interior are tasked with presenting detailed information about these organisations in an appendix to the Report. Finally, the Report on Extremism in the Czech Republic for 2000 provides an important source of information which can be used to develop policies to fight extremism.[219]

The 2002 Updated Concept approved of the measures undertaken by the Ministry of Interior. It supported the dissolution in 2000 of the National Party (established by neo-Nazi activists) and the refusal to register several extremist political parties in 2001.[220] It also noted significant progress concerning measures taken by the police and commended the quality of the reports on extremism. The 2002 Updated Concept therefore did not propose any new measures in this area.[221] However, it referred to a pilot project to re-socialise perpetrators of less serious racially motivated crimes as a measure which could usefully be followed up.[222]

3.4 Promotion of Minority Rights

Chapter 5 of the 2000 Concept deals with measures for the protection and promotion of the Romani language and culture.[223] The tasks outlined in Chapter 7 on "Multicultural Education" also include the teaching of the history, culture and literature of national

---

[218] This is a task established by Government Decree No. 684 (12 July 2000). The Decree focuses on civil associations, political parties and movements and other organisations registered by the Ministry of Interior which display extremist attitudes or violate the law.

[219] The document was prepared by the Ministry of Interior, in cooperation with the Ministry of Justice. The Report goes beyond the scope of racially motivated crimes, covering all aspects of extremism, and points to the difficulty of fighting the activities of extremist groups which are familiar with the law and try to proceed legally. For example, in 2000 more than in 1999, extremists used the platform of civil associations and also tried to establish themselves as political parties.

[220] The procedure is based on Art. 12(3) of Law No. 83/1990 Coll., on Citizens' Assemblies. It was applied to the National Social Alliance, the National Party, the Communist Movement of Czechoslovakia, and also the association Republican Youth with regard to their publication of the document "Programme of the Republican Youth."

[221] 2002 Updated Concept, Part 7.4. As stated in Decree No. 87 (23 January 2002) by which the 2002 Updated Concept was adopted, all ministries are tasked with the adoption of "suitable measures for implementation of the tasks concerning the integration of Roma communities listed in the Concept that have not been fulfilled or those whose implementation is continuous or to undertake measures supporting the implementation of those measures.

[222] See the 2002 Updated Concept, Part 7.3.

[223] See also 2002 Updated Concept, Part 5.

minorities in general school curricula as well as the production of information materials on national minorities.[224]

The preliminary results of the 2001 Census, if taken at face value, indicate that the Roma minority is the second smallest minority in the Czech Republic. The number of persons identifying themselves as Roma dropped to 11,716, significantly less than the number recorded by the previous Census in 1991.[225] By contrast, the Government estimates a Roma population of between 150,000 and 300,000 persons.[226]

This development occurred despite State efforts to encourage Roma participation in the Census.[227] A number of explanations have been offered, including that respondents simply chose not to answer the question on ethnic origin, as it was optional; that a process of homogenisation of the population set in after the split of Czechoslovakia; that respondents may have been afraid to list an ethnic origin other than Czech; and that assimilation or integration processes have advanced in the past ten years.[228]

Government policy based on the Concept seeks to connect the two imperatives of overcoming social exclusion and preserving the Roma cultural identity.[229] As an argument against positive action on behalf of the Roma minority, it has often been emphasised that, without data on the actual size of the Roma minority, it is impossible to determine whether Roma are under-represented or disadvantaged in various areas.

The introduction of the term "Roma communities" by the Bratinka report has helped overcome resistance to the collection of ethnic data, on the basis that this information is of a private character.[230] Indeed, a distinction has been introduced between the terms "Roma national minority" and "Roma community" and the latter, broader, term is being increasingly used in governmental documents. The difference between the two terms is explained in the 2002 Updated Concept as follows:

---

[224] See also 2002 Updated Concept, Part 6.2.

[225] For preliminary results of the 2001 Census from 5 March 2002, see: <http://www.czso.cz/eng/figures/4/41/410101/data/tab41.pdf>, (accessed 4 June 2002). In the 1991 Census, 32,903 persons claimed Roma national origin.

[226] *Report on the situation of National Minorities*, p. 69; for further estimates, see K. Kalibová, *"Romové z pohledu statistiky demografie"* (Roma from the Point of View of Demographic Statistics), in: *Romové v České republice* (Roma in the Czech Republic), p. 107.

[227] The Czech Statistical Office allocated CZK 536,000 (€17,614) for the participation of Roma as census takers. *Commissioner's Report 2000–2001*, Part II.6.

[228] *Report on the Situation of National Minorities*, p. 3.

[229] 2002 Updated Concept, Part 1.5.

[230] According to the Charter, Art. 3(2), and special laws, data regarding membership in a national minority are of a private character and cannot be subjected to statistical evidence, unless special laws expressly state so.

> The term 'Roma community' only partly overlaps with the term 'Roma national minority'. While the defining characteristic of a member of the Roma national minority is 'the active will to be regarded as a member of a minority and, together with other members, to develop the language and culture, a member of the Roma community is de facto anyone identified as such by the majority as a member of this socially and ethnically defined group.[231]

State policy regarding national minorities is now based on the Law on the Rights of Members of National Minorities (hereafter, "Minority Law"),[232] which elaborates on the rights contained in the Charter of Fundamental Rights and Freedoms (hereafter, "Charter").[233] However, the benefit to the Roma minority is minimal as the application of many of the rights guaranteed under the Minority Law requires that a given minority constitute at least ten percent of the population of a municipality, Roma are effectively excluded in most municipalities. Moreover, the provisions of the Minority Law are rather general and declaratory in nature, mostly paraphrasing the declarations of the Charter[234] and referring to provisions of special laws. Finally, the Minority Law restricts enjoyment of the rights it stipulates to Czech citizens, meaning that in some cases it offers less protection than some of the special provisions in other legislation to which it refers.[235]

An amendment to the Law on Misdemeanours[236] defined a misdemeanour committed by anyone who restricts or denies the execution of minority rights, and by anyone who

---

[231] 2002 Updated Concept, Part 1.4.

[232] Law No. 273/2001 Coll.

[233] Minority rights are also guaranteed in the Constitution (Art. 6) (Law No. 1/1993) and the provisions of the 1991 Charter of Fundamental Rights and Freedoms (Arts. 3, 24 and 25). The Czech Republic is also a party to the Framework Convention for the Protection of National Minorities (FCNM) (entered into force 1 April 1998). It has signed but not yet ratified the European Charter for Regional or Minority Languages (signed on 9 November 2000). On the general situation of minorities in the Czech Republic, see the *Report on the Situation of National Minorities*; see also the *Report Submitted by the Czech Republic Pursuant to Article 25, Paragraph 1 of the Framework Convention for the Protection of National Minorities*, received on 1 April 1999, <http://www.riga.lv/minelres/reports/czech/czech.htm>, (accessed 4 June 2002); and the Resolution of the Council of Ministers of the Council of Europe, *Resolution ResCMN (2002)2 on the implementation of the Framework Convention for the Protection of National Minorities by the Czech Republic*, adopted on 6 February 2002, <http://cm.coe.int/stat/E/Public/2002/adopted_texts/resCMN/2002xn2.htm>, (accessed 22 August 2002).

[234] Charter, Arts. 24, 25.

[235] For example, the Law on Civil Court Procedure acknowledges the right to use the mother tongue before courts to every party in a judicial procedure, not only to citizens.

[236] Law No. 200/1990 Coll. on Misdemeanours.

causes another person injury because of, inter alia, membership in a national minority or due to ethnic origin or race.[237] As the Minority Law only recently entered into force (2 August 2001), it is not yet possible to evaluate the effectiveness of this provision. However, prosecution of this misdemeanour falls within the competence of municipal misdemeanour commissions, whose members do not always have the necessary expertise or legal training, greatly reducing the likelihood of effective implementation.

3.4.1 Education

The 2000 Concept emphasises the importance of promoting the Romani language and culture, as well as the need to develop a multicultural education system, and proposes a series of measures to achieve these aims. In practice, however, action in this area has been insufficient.

More specifically, the Concept promises State support for "private, church or foundation schools and classes for Roma children with the Romani language as the language of instruction or even Czech, provided that their curricula focus on Roma cultural emancipation and on the integration of Roma into society."[238] The Chapter on "Multicultural Education" advocates the development of a multicultural educational system to promote greater tolerance of cultural differences. Measures proposed include: courses on the history, culture and literature of national minorities in general school curricula; courses on tolerance; the training of teachers in conflict prevention; and the education of teachers on the history, language and culture of the Roma and other minorities.

The 2002 Updated Concept calls for the development of new, multicultural educational programmes for all types of schools as well as the inclusion of a component on multiculturalism into teacher-training courses at all levels.[239] It also proposes to further support Roma Studies departments at Charles University and other universities.[240]

Though Czech law provides for State funding to minority schools,[241] there is currently no network of State-funded schools providing education in the Romani language. However, it must be acknowledged that this question is not generally considered as

---

[237] See Law on Misdemeanours, Art. 49(1.e), and the Minority Law, Art. 14(1).

[238] 2000 Concept, Part 6.23.

[239] 2002 Updated Concept, Part 6.2.2.

[240] 2002 Updated Concept, Parts 5.2, 5.3, 5.4.

[241] See the Minority Law, Art. 11. There is no minimum threshold of minority children necessary to establish a class in the minority language. See also Law No. 76/1978 Coll., on Schools as subsequently amended.

pressing as the need to integrate Roma children into mainstream schools.[242] Still, despite the fact that Roma children are often concentrated into separate classes and schools, this has generally served as a pretext for providing lower quality "special" education, rather than an opportunity to provide positive reinforcement of the Romani language and culture.

The Report on the Situation of National Minorities in the Czech Republic in 2001 further elaborates on the lack of recognition for Romani in schools – and the impact this has had on the status of the Romani language, both at school and within Roma communities:

> Because of a badly functioning school system, not capable of working with minorities, children of refugees, etc., very often the Romani language was used to justify placing Roma children in special schools (allegedly, the children cannot speak Czech well, this is caused by the Romani language). Therefore, Roma themselves started to regard their language as lacking prospects, to be forgotten or used only passively. Many Roma today say quite honestly, and they also believe it, that they do not teach their children and will not, because then they have problems at school. They do not understand that it is not about not speaking with their children in Romani, but rather about not talking to them, in addition, in WRONG [emphasis in original] Czech. After 1989, the situation regarding the use of the Romani language in Roma families did not improve, but it certainly improved with regard to the area of publication and media […].[243]

There have been some efforts to present the Roma culture and history in schools, though the Government has acknowledged that there is significant room for

---

[242] The Advisory Committee on the FCNM has recommended that the Government examine to what extent the current situation meets the demands of the Roma community and establish, in consultation with those concerned, whether further measures are needed. Advisory Committee on the Framework Convention for the Protection of National Minorities, *Opinion on the Czech Republic*, adopted on 6 April 2001, made public on 25 January 2002, Art. 14, para. 66.
<http://www.humanrights.coe.int/Minorities/Eng/FrameworkConvention/AdvisoryCommittee/Opinions/Czech percent20Republic.htm>, (accessed 4 June 2002). See also the *Comments of the Government of the Czech Republic on the Opinion of the Advisory Committee on the Implementation of the Framework Convention for the Protection of National Minorities in the Czech Republic*, 15 October 2001, published on 25 January 2002,
<http://www.humanrights.coe.int/minorities/Eng/FrameworkConvention/AdvisoryCommittee/Opinions/Czech.Comments.htm>, (accessed 4 June 2002).

[243] *Report on the Situation of National Minorities*, p. 70.

improvement in this area.[244] and multicultural educational curricula are under development by the Ministry of Education.[245] Roma representatives and others have called for more attention to minority issues in teacher-training courses.[246]

The function of Coordinator for Multicultural Education, an Advisory Group of the Minister for National Minority Schools as well as an advisory group for minority education have been established.[247] Both groups include representatives of minorities (including Roma). The Ministry of Education requires that educational materials incorporate information on the situation of ethnic and national minorities in order to receive ministerial approval. The Ministry has also approved a plan for the distribution of funding to civic associations under the Programme of Education in the Languages of National Minorities in 2002. The funding allocated for activities of national minorities is monitored in the budget of the Ministry of Education. The share of funding allocated for initiatives concerning the Roma is not known.

The *"Varianty"* project realised in 2001 by the People in Need Foundation included a component on multicultural education, which consisted of developing a proposal for multidisciplinary school curricula by a team of experts. It is currently being tested in pilot schools. However, its incorporation into official school curricula depends on the future level of cooperation with the Ministry of Education.[248] Although the Ministry

---

[244] In its Report on implementation of the FCNM, the Government acknowledges that "[e]ducation of the majority population about the culture, history, language and religion of national minorities has traditionally been neglected. In spite of a certain progress made during the last ten years, Czech instruction books remain largely textbooks of the Czech ethnic nation, its history, its culture, its fight for ethnic autonomy and later state sovereignty, always in contrary to the German element. It is as though the Czech Lands have not traditionally been the home of various ethnic, cultural and religious communities, especially the German and Jewish national minorities, and also the perpetually disregarded Romanies." *Report Submitted by the Czech Republic*, Art. 12.

[245] Government Decree No. 279 (7 April 1999) tasked the Ministry of Education, *inter alia*, with ensuring that primary and secondary school curricula reflect the history of the Roma, including the Holocaust. No information was provided by the Ministry in the *Information on the Implementation of Government Decrees as of 31 December 2001*. Government Decree No. 789 (28 July 1999) also assigned the task of ensuring that the training of teachers include the topic of multicultural education, tolerance and racism. In 2000, the Ministry of Education recommended to the relevant institutions that such topics be included and attached guidelines.

[246] OSI Roundtable, Prague, June 2002.

[247] Established by Order of the Minister of Education No. 20/1999.

[248] An important component of educational section of the "*Varianty*" project is a multicultural handbook for high school teachers, see <http://varianty.rebex.cz/default.asp?mn=3&pa=ss_vys#Manuál interkulturní výchovy>, (accessed 17 July 2002).

has apparently expressed interest in the curricula, it is not expected that they will be ready for use before the start of the 2002/2003 school year.

In 1998, a private Roma Secondary Social School was opened in Kolín.[249] It is fully funded by the Ministry of Education. The Romani language is taught two hours a week in each grade. The curriculum also includes information on the Roma history, culture and language in order to prepare graduates for work with the Roma community.

3.4.2 Language

In the 1991 Census, 24,224 individuals claimed Romanes as their mother tongue (half of those who claimed Roma ethnic origin).[250] According to the preliminary results of the 2001 Census, 12,967 respondents indicated a combination of Czech and Romanes as their mother tongues. Of these, 9,086 were born between 1941 and 1985, but only 3,462 – between 1986 and 2001. The actual number of speakers of Romanes is believed to be much higher.

Under the Charter, minorities are guaranteed the right to communicate, receive and disseminate information in their own languages, and the right to use their languages in official contacts. The Minority Law provides for the implementation of these rights; however, the requirements that at least ten percent of a municipality's population has registered as a member of a given minority effectively excludes most Roma. This applies to the right to use bilingual signs, to use of names and surnames, and to use of the minority language in administrative proceedings and before courts, *inter alia*.

The Civil Procedure Code established that the court must provide an interpreter if needed to enable persons to communicate in court in their mother tongue.[251] The Criminal Procedure Code also states that anyone who declares that he does not understand Czech is entitled to use his/her mother tongue in contacts with law enforcement authorities and in court.[252] There have been reports of shortages of interpreters for Romanes speakers in criminal proceedings.[253]

---

[249] <http://www.osf.cz/djuric/KOLINCZ.htm>, (accessed 4 June 2002).

[250] Results of the 1991 Census, cited in the *Report submitted by the Czech Republic*, Section I, footnote 8.

[251] §18 of Law No. 99/1963 Coll.

[252] §2 Art. 14 of Law No. 141/1961 Coll.

[253] Advisory Committee on the FCNM, *Opinion on the Czech Republic*, Art. 10, para. 57.

3.4.3 Participation in public life

One of the main objectives of the 2000 Concept is to enhance Roma participation in decision-making on matters concerning their communities. It also supports the emergence of increased political representation for Roma.[254] However, the Concept fails to propose specific measures to achieve these goals. Moreover, there is no research to ascertain the degree to which Roma are in fact under-represented, and no research is proposed in the Concept. However, the inclusion of Roma representatives in consultative bodies to the Government and within certain ministries, such as the CRCI, the Council for National Minorities and the CHR, can be considered to advance increased Roma participation of Roma.[255]

The 2000 Concept presents the initiative to employ Roma Advisors at District (and now Regional) Offices as a measure to support the emancipation and integration of Roma,[256] and they have contributed to improving communication between the State administration and Roma communities.[257] However, in practice, the position of Roma Advisor as well as the new position of Roma Advisors Coordinator at the regional level cannot be considered as a mechanism for promoting Roma participation, since these positions are filled by State administration officials who are not minority representatives *strictu senso*. Moreover, Roma Advisor positions are not necessarily filled by Roma.

The 2002 Updated Concept is missing the objective to support increased participation for Roma. This may be due to the fact that the newly-adopted Minority Law guarantees members of national minorities the right to active participation in cultural, social and economic life, especially with regard to matters concerning national minorities at the municipal, regional and national levels (Art. 6.1), a right which is to be executed through the Council for National Minorities and Committees for National Minorities. However, the right applies to minorities which meet the ten percent threshold in a given municipality or region.[258]

---

[254] 2000 Concept, Parts 1.7.e., 1.10.

[255] See also *Minority Protection 2001*, pp. 161–164.

[256] 2000 Concept, Part 3.1.2.

[257] The *2001 Regular Report* notes that these Roma advisors have become contact points for the Roma communities and that they liase with the IMC (in which some are members), *2001 Regular Report*, p. 25.

[258] The Minority Law reduced the threshold from 15 to 10 percent in the case of districts, from 10 to 5 percent for regions, and from 15 to 5 percent for the city of Prague. See also Law No 129/2000 Coll., on Regions, Law No. 131/2000 Coll., on the Capital City of Prague, and Law No. 128/2000 Coll., on Municipalities.

Committees for National Minorities have been established in 32 municipalities, four regions and in the cities of Brno and Liberec.[259] When a minority group constitutes less than ten percent of the population, as in the case of Roma, self-governing bodies may decide to establish commissions for the purpose of ensuring their representation. For example, the Municipal Council in Prague has established a Commission for National Minorities whose members are representatives of all of the minority organisations in Prague. It is too early to determine whether these committees/commissions will include Roma representatives or whether their work will have a significant impact on the situation of the Roma minority.

According to Government estimates, there are currently ten Roma representatives elected to local governments as deputies of mainstream Czech political parties or independently.[260] The Roma Civic Initiative (ROI), the only registered Roma political party, obtained only 0.01 percent in the latest parliamentary elections (June 2002). According to one Roma leader, the lack of political representation for Roma has effectively prevented their involvement in decision-making. There is currently no democratically-elected representative to articulate the needs and concerns of Roma.[261]

The Advisory Committee on the FCNM has encouraged the Government to devise and implement measures to enhance the representation of minority views during the decision-making process, especially when these decisions affect them.[262] It has also called for greater participation of Roma women in the implementation of the 2000 Concept.[263]

3.4.4 Media

The 2000 Concept does not address the issue of support for minority media.

The creation and transmission of radio and television programmes on members of national minorities is governed by two laws: the Law on Czech Television[264] and the

---

[259] *Report on the Situation of National Minorities*, p. 13.

[260] *Report on the Situation of National Minorities*, p. 13.

[261] OSI Roundtable, Prague, June 2002.

[262] Advisory Committee on the FCNM, *Opinion on the Czech Republic*, Art. 15, para. 70.

[263] Advisory Committee on the FCNM, *Opinion on the Czech Republic*, Art. 4, para. 30.

[264] The Law on Czech Television states that one of the main goals of Czech Television is the creation and transmission of programmes and providing a balanced offer of programmes for all sections of the population with regard to their, *inter alia*, ethnic or national origin and national identity and the development of the cultural identity of the Czech population, including members of national or ethnic minorities. Law No. 483/1991 of the Coll. on Czech Television, as amended.

Law on Czech Radio.[265] The Minority Law guarantees the right to cultural development and to the dissemination of information in the minority language (in radio and television broadcasting).[266] In general, it can be stated that both on Czech State Television and Radio, limited attention and time is devoted to broadcasting programmes in minority languages or to programmes about national minorities.[267]

The Council for National Minorities monitors broadcasting related to minorities. Efforts have also been made to improve cooperation between Czech Television (the State broadcaster) and national minorities. According to an employee of the Research Department of Czech Television, the overall interest in programmes on Roma issues is low in general; the motivation to devote time to this issue on television is therefore also low.[268] The lack of rules providing for obligations of media in the area of minority broadcasting has been criticised by Roma representatives.[269]

The involvement of Roma minority members in the media is more active in the area of radio broadcasting, with independent minority departments including Roma staff. However, national minority representatives are not involved in the programme planning of Czech Television or in the televised broadcasts of minority programmes. The Council for National Minorities will initiate an advisory group in Czech Television.[270]

---

[265] Law No. 484/1991 Coll., on Czech Radio, as amended. Similar provisions for Czech Television are lacking.

[266] Minority Law, Art. 13.

[267] The is a weekly one-hour programme on Czech Radio *"O Roma vakheren"* (The Roma speak). Czech Television does not currently broadcast any programme in Romanes. An earlier programme in Romanes (*Romale*, broadcast twice a month) has been replaced by a multicultural programme "Velký vůz." The current level of presentation of the life and culture of national minorities on Czech State Television is evaluated very negatively by representatives of national minorities. See e.g. in the *Report on the Situation of National Minorities*; see also J. Balážová, *Konec Romale* (The end of Romale), <http://www.dzeno.cz/Amarogendalos/1-2-00/2425.htm>, (accessed 22 August 2002).

[268] "What does it mean to be Roma?" Czech Television, 12 November 2001.

[269] These opinions were collected from the Roma members of the Council for National Minorities. *Report on the Situation of National Minorities*, p. 72.

[270] *Report on the Situation of National Minorities*, p. 16.

Funding in support of periodicals of minorities is approved by the Council for National Minorities, which also recommends the amounts to be allocated to individual periodicals. Funding is provided by the Ministry of Finance.[271]

3.4.5 Culture

Measures to support the Roma culture are supported within the context of the broader Programme of Support for the Cultural Activities of National Minorities.[272] Since 1993, the Ministry of Culture has announced annual competitions for projects supporting the cultural activities of members of national minorities, including the Roma minority.

In 2001, CZK 7 million (€230,036) was allocated from the State budget to the Programme of Support of Activities of National and Ethnic Minorities.[273] This amount was increased to CZK 8,200,000 (€269,471) in 2002, of which CZK 3,808,000 (€125,140) was granted to projects related to the Roma culture and identity. Support for the Roma culture includes support to the Museum of Roma Culture in Brno.[274]

There are also small local projects administered by districts and municipalities which focus predominantly on Roma cultural life and on activities in support of societal

---

[271] The following Roma minority periodicals were supported by the Ministry: *Amaro Gendalos* (CZK 1,940,000) (€63,753); *Kereka* (CZK 1,620,000) (€53,237); *Romano hangos* (CZK 1,420,000) (€46,664); *Romano kurko* (CZK 1,400,000) (€46,007). These comparatively high levels of funding are due to the fact that the periodicals are mostly distributed for free or at a reduced price.

[272] Approved by Government Decree No. 40 (10 January 2001). Decree No. 40 updated the Concept of Cultural Policy in the Czech Republic – Strategy of Improved State Support to Culture, approved by Government Decree No. 401 (28 April 1999). See also Government Decree No. 260 (15 March 2001), Annex 1 "Main areas of State grant policy towards non-governmental non-profit organisations for the year 2001."

[273] 96 organisations with 152 projects had sought support for a total amount exceeding CZK 34 million (€1,117,318). Communication with an official from the Ministry of Culture, Minority Culture Department, Prague, July 2002.

[274] The Museum of Roma Culture received CZK 1,600,000 (€52,580) in 2001. It also received a further CZK 7 million (€230,036) for remodelling and the creation of a permanent exhibition. *Information on the Implementation of Government Decrees as of 31 December 2001*, Part 4.1.2.

integration.[275] Projects for Roma children and youth have also been funded under the "Socio-educational Programme."[276] Altogether, 376 projects were supported through these two programmes of the CRCI in 2001 with funds from the State budget.

Finally, the Government will support the establishment of a House of Nationalities;[277] this is part of the project "House of Nationalities – Multicultural Centre in Prague" elaborated by the Commission of the Council of the Capital City of Prague.[278]

4. EVALUATION

Current governmental policy towards Roma aims to promote integration and to improve the relationship between Roma communities and the majority society. While an increasing amount of Government attention and resources has been devoted to achieving these aims, and while certain initiatives have posted positive results, the overall impact to date has been minimal.

The 2000 Concept is comprehensive in its approach; it is informed by a strong human and minority rights perspective, and thus offers a solid conceptual framework for the implementation of governmental policies towards Roma. It addresses the majority of the concerns that Roma leaders have articulated, with the significant exception that it does not stipulate measures to promote effective participation in public life. A number of other important issues, such as equal access to higher education, healthcare, the criminal justice system and the media are not addressed.

The Concept is innovative in the sense that it incorporates centralised mechanisms for coordination, monitoring and evaluation. However, the bodies within which these mechanisms reside do not operate on the basis of a strong legal grounding and lack

---

[275] In 2000, CZK 8 million (€262,898) was allocated through the IMC/CRCI to district offices and municipalities for 365 projects for Roma, mostly in the sphere of culture, under the "Social Integration Programme (Local Projects)." Due to new budgetary regulations, in 2001, the CZK 6,530,000 (€214,591) allocated through the IMC/CRCI was managed by various ministries (Culture, Education and Labour and Social Affairs, Health). The IMC has decided not to continue administering this programme due to the bureaucracy involved. *Commissioner's Report 2000–2001*, Parts I.1 and II.1.

[276] CZK 4 million (€131,449) was allocated in 2000 and CZK 4,300,000 (€141,308) in 2001. *Commissioner's Report 2000–2001*, Parts I.2 and II.2.

[277] Government Decree No. 173 (19 February 2001).

[278] State participation of at least 50 percent is foreseen. *Report on the Situation of National Minorities*, p. 39.

political support, and their effectiveness in coordinating implementation has been limited. Steps should be taken to equip them with the authority they need to require quality involvement and input from ministries and other institutional partners.

Further, the central bodies responsible for developing and implementing the Concept lack the competence to influence local public administration. Thus, efforts to enact policy at the national level may be undermined by local practice. This is an even greater issue of concern due to territorial reform, which devolves greater competencies to the newly-created regions. Though this may bring benefits in terms of encouraging local initiative and vesting responsibility in local decision-makers and communities, it should be balanced against the need for the expertise, capacity, and authority of a central body.

Annual Updates provide a valuable possibility for the Concept to be revised and further developed on the basis of experience gained during implementation. Though the quality of Updates has suffered to some extent from poor or incomplete information received from participating ministries, the idea of incorporating monitoring and evaluation into Concept implementation is sound, and should be supported.

A number of the initiatives taken under the Concept have proven successful, notably measures to boost school attendance through expanding pre-school education and employing Roma teacher's assistants. Programmes to support Roma students in vocational schools and to train field social workers have also been received positively. Roma Advisors and regional Coordinators of Roma Advisor have facilitated more positive communication between Roma communities and various State institutions in some areas. A common element of many of these initiatives supported by NGOs has been the involvement of the Roma themselves in resolving issues which they face on a daily basis. The participation of the Roma in these programmes is key to their sustainability.

However, wide-ranging legal and institutional reforms and measures to address systemic discrimination – a persistent problem in many areas – are needed. In this light, the expected adoption of comprehensive anti-discrimination and establishment of a State body to monitor discrimination and promote equal treatment will represent a particularly positive step. The Minority Law, though it provides for a wide range of minority rights, effectively excludes most Roma, as few Roma communities meet the ten percent threshold it stipulates. Alternative mechanisms should be developed to ensure that Roma, too, have access to the rights and benefits deriving from the new Law. Without complementary legal and institutional reform, *ad hoc* programmes in education, employment, housing and social protection, though many are positive in themselves, do not address the root causes of the problems faced by Roma in these areas, and cannot be expected to have long-term impact.

There are encouraging signs that policy development is increasingly based on in-depth assessment of the needs of the Roma community. However, there is still a lack of comprehensive research in many areas. Without ethnic data, it is difficult to ascertain the extent to which Roma are under-represented or suffer disadvantage. Such research is vital to the development of a differentiated yet systematic approach, on the basis of which comprehensive solutions can be developed. As restrictions on the collection of ethnic data constitute an impediment to research at present, there is an urgent need for the development of data-collection methodologies which would not violate the right to privacy and protection of personal data. This should be done in partnership with Roma communities.

The Government has sought to engage in dialogue with Roma representatives on Concept implementation. However, at present, Roma participate mainly in an advisory capacity and there is little opportunity for developing Roma leadership through broad and active involvement in decision-making, implementation, and evaluation.

Without greater commitment of political will to implementation of the Concept, systemic changes are unlikely to occur, and bodies of national and local public administration will continue to fail to take Concept implementation seriously. With greater institutional and budgetary support, the Office of the CRCI could do much to promote broader understanding and support for the objectives of the Concept across governmental institutions.

Broader public support is also vital to Concept implementation. Surveys indicate that, despite considerable amounts invested in tolerance campaigns, results are slow to come; discrimination and racially motivated violence continue to give cause for serious concern. The positive potential of the media to generate enhanced understanding for initiatives to improve the situation for Roma should be explored, both by State implementing bodies and by Roma communities themselves.

5. Recommendations

To the Government

- Strengthen the legislative basis of the various bodies tasked with coordinating and implementing governmental programmes for Roma.

- Develop mechanisms vesting coordinating bodies with sufficient authority to encourage the active involvement of various governmental ministries and other bodies tasked with responsibilities under the Concept more effectively.

- Consider elaborating mechanisms allowing central coordinating bodies to influence the development and implementation of policies at the local level in various areas touched upon under the Concept.

- Enhance existing mechanisms for regularly and systematically evaluating the impact of governmental initiatives in the various areas covered by the 2000 Concept.

- Enact comprehensive anti-discrimination legislation to provide protection for victims of racial discrimination in employment, education, housing, access to goods and services and social protection; establish an appropriate institutional framework, including an Office for Ethnic Equality.

- Devise means of collecting ethnic data without violating the privacy of individuals for the purpose of developing more comprehensive policies, including positive measures.

- Ensure a greater degree of involvement at the decision-making level of Roma representatives in the implementation and evaluation of overall governmental policy as well as of specific initiatives; develop more effective means of soliciting and incorporating the opinions of project beneficiaries.

- Develop a public relations strategy to promote the objectives of the Concept and of governmental policy concerning the Roma, including by providing necessary human and financial resources to the CRCI.

- Support targeted media campaigns on the basis of research and feedback on previous initiatives to identify the most effective means of generating increased public support for activities implemented under the Concept.

In the area of education

- Develop and implement a comprehensive strategy for improving the education of Roma taking into account all levels of education, following an assessment of the success of measures implemented to date and taking into account the opinions of experts, beneficiaries and civil society representatives, especially Roma.

- Expand the scope of the Concept to include higher levels of education (secondary and university education) and develop a programme to compensate for inequalities at these levels.

- Develop incentives, including financial incentives, to encourage school directors and other key local actors to implement national policies.

In the area of employment

- Design a programme to compensate for disadvantages faced by Roma in access to employment; conduct research and implement pilot programmes to ensure that employment projects both raise motivation and build marketable skills.

- Devise targeted means of addressing inequalities in other aspects of employment, such as equal remuneration and pay and working conditions.

- Develop an effective incentive system for companies employing Roma.

In the area of housing

- Support more in-depth research to analyse access for Roma to the entire range of housing opportunities; expand the scope of the Concept to cover areas identified by this research, including through the development of positive measures.

In the area of healthcare and social protection

- Cover both medical and preventive hygiene aspects of healthcare, conduct research and analysis of the current state of protection, and of the negative impacts of the current system of social protection; develop recommendations.

- Develop long-term strategies, including the material conditions and human resources strategies for field social work.

Criminal justice/racially motivated violence

- Support research on the treatment of Roma in the criminal justice system.

- Comprehensively monitor the phenomenon of racially motivated violence, including by law-enforcement authorities, and make this information available to the public.

- Bolster efforts to hire minorities in the police force and expand such efforts to other related sectors such as court and prison administrations.

Minority rights

- Implement new multicultural curricula promoting tolerance and the culture and history of minority groups, including the Roma.

- Continue to support Roma cultural activities and Roma media.

- Evaluate the degree to which the new Minority Law meets the needs of the Roma national minority, and further develop alternative mechanisms to ensure that communities which do not meet the ten percent threshold nonetheless enjoy access to minority rights.

- Offer the option of Romani language classes within integrated schools.

To the European Commission

- Provide support for the further development of the institutional capacity to implement and evaluate the Concept and related measures.

- Target assistance to encourage coordinated initiatives, aimed at developing comprehensive policies in the areas of education, employment and housing.

- Continue to support capacity building for civil society organisations; provide training to NGOs – particularly minority NGOs – in navigating Phare funding application procedures and grant administration.

Minority Protection in Estonia

An Assessment of the Programme Integration
in Estonian Society 2000–2007.

Table of Contents

1. Executive Summary 192

2. The Government Programme –
   Background 195
   2.1 Background to the Present Programme 195
   2.2 The Programme – Process 196
   2.3 The Programme – Content 200
   2.4 The Programme – Administration/
       Implementation/Evaluation 203
   2.5 The Programme and the Public 205
   2.6 The Programme and the EU 207

3. The Government Programme –
   Implementation.. 209
   3.1 Stated Objectives of the Programme 209
   3.2 The Government Programme
       and Discrimination 210
       3.2.1 Education 215
       3.2.2 Employment 219
       3.2.3 Housing and other goods
             and services 223
       3.2.4 Healthcare and other forms
             of social protection 223
       3.2.5 The criminal justice system 224

3.3	Protection from Racially Motivated Violence		225
3.4	Promotion of Minority Rights		226
	3.4.1	Education	229
	3.4.2	Language	231
	3.4.3	Participation in public life	233
	3.4.4	Media	236
	3.4.5	Culture	238
4.	Evaluation		240
5.	Recommendations		244

1. Executive Summary

The current Government programme, "Integration in Estonian Society 2000–2007" (hereafter, "Integration Programme") is the first to address the integration of the large population of Russians and Russian-speakers who settled in Estonia during the Soviet Era.

The Integration Programme provides for a two-way process, promoting the integration of minorities while protecting their distinct identity. The chosen tool for promoting greater inclusion is the Estonian language, and an overwhelming majority of projects funded and carried out under the Programme are accordingly related to language instruction. By its own measures, the Programme is proceeding successfully in the spheres that it identifies as priorities; minority representatives, however, express concern that too little has been accomplished in the legal and political spheres. A clear divide between minority and majority perceptions of the goals and priorities of the integration process exists, which must be addressed in order to achieve mutually satisfactory results.

Background

The process of developing the Programme included substantial political debate, although less time was allowed for non-governmental and minority groups to comment on earlier drafts of the Programme. A commission appointed by the Minister for Population and Ethnic Affairs in 1997 produced a draft integration policy concept by the end of that year. Between the Government's adoption of the commission's policy concept and the promulgation of the final Integration Programme more than two years later, the draft documents were circulated among members of Parliament, Government bodies, and local governments, eliciting significant response. Following this period of discussion, the present version of the Integration Programme was adopted on 14 March 2000.

Administration

Coordination and administration of the Programme is generally effective and efficient. The Minister for Population and Ethnic affairs is responsible for its overall coordination and a ten-member Steering Committee oversees implementation, and may make any necessary modifications to its content. The Minister for Population and Ethnic Affairs chairs the Steering Committee, whose members are representatives of six ministries,[1] the Integration Foundation and the Institute of International and Social Studies. The Integration Programme assigns responsibility for implementing its four sub-programmes to corresponding Government bodies. Less attention has been focused on achieving the

---

[1] The Ministries of Education, Culture, Internal Affairs, Social Affairs, Agriculture, Defence and Finance.

Programme's goals through local or regional governments, which could be important partners in improving cooperation with minority communities.

EU Support

The EU has supported language-based integration projects since the mid-nineties, and has praised the Integration Programme in its Regular Reports. Although cautioning that more remains to be done with regard to the integration of non-citizens in particular, the EU appears to support the language-centred approach adopted by the Programme. The Commission has noted the need to address all aspects of integration, and EU funding has been allocated to regional development projects that could serve to broaden the scope of the integration process, though the focus on developing the legal and political dimensions of integration could be sharpened.

Content and Implementation

The Integration Programme reflects a view of integration as a two-way process. It envisions allowing minorities to retain their distinct identity, while increasing their participation in and loyalty to the Estonian State, mainly through the medium of Estonian language instruction; a common linguistic sphere is viewed as both a means to enhance inclusion of minorities, and to reduce inequalities or tensions that may exist. Minority representatives have expressed concern that the emphasis on language does not take into account other barriers to integration, which the Integration Programme suggests should be addressed through complementary programmes.

Discrimination is not addressed by the Integration Programme; however, the Programme does include strong components to increase societal understanding and tolerance. This approach seeks to prevent future discrimination, but does not address existing inequalities. Generally, discrimination has not been widely recognised in Estonian society or Government policy; at present, however, a draft Equality Act is under development.

The Integration Programme recognises the preservation of separate ethnic identities as one of the overarching principles of integration, and elaborates a number of measures in several spheres to enhance this principle. Issues in these spheres are a high priority for the Russian-speaking community, but have been accorded lower priority – and less funding – in implementation. State-funded primary education is widely available in Russian, but smaller minorities have struggled to find the means to support mother-tongue instruction. Concerns have also arisen over the continued availability of Russian-language education at the secondary level. The Programme addresses obstacles to the acquisition of citizenship, implementation of the National Minorities Cultural Autonomy Act, and other barriers to participation in public life, but funding for such measures remains low and the legal reforms in these areas called for by some minority representatives are explicitly beyond the scope of the Programme.[2]

Conclusions

The Integration Programme has defined three main spheres for the integration of Estonia's Russian-speaking minority: linguistic-communicative, legal-political and socio-economic. In practice, however, only the linguistic-communicative sphere has been fully developed in the Integration Programme's action plans, and measures in the education and language sectors receive three-quarters of all funding allocated to Programme integration.[3] This approach is in accord with the priorities defined in the Integration Programme, but rests on the assumption that relevant measures in the fields of legal-political and socio-economic integration should be taken up within the framework of other Government programmes. As few other Government programmes have included such measures, only selected dimensions of integration have been carried out in practice.[4]

The common position among all representatives of minority and civil society organisations is that the elaboration and implementation of the Integration Programme itself is a significant achievement.[5] It has taken strides towards changing attitudes in both Estonian and non-Estonian-speaking communities, towards a more positive understanding of inter-ethnic relations, and greater acceptance of the need for societal integration. The text of the Programme and the formal statements of the Government reflect the affirmative and preventative approach of the strategy, promoting tolerance, cultural plurality, and the preservation of ethnic differences. In implementation, however, concerns remain that the heavy emphasis on the unification of society through the Estonian language will result in a more one-sided process than that promised by the Programme text.

---

[2] See Government of Estonia, *State Programme. Integration in Estonian Society 2000–2007*, Tallinn, 2000, p. 16. See <www.riik.ee/saks/ikomisjon>, (accessed 15 April 2002), (hereafter, Integration Programme).

[3] See Government of Estonia, *Action Plans for Sub-Programmes of State Integration Programme for the years 2000–2003*, Tallinn, 2001. See <www.riik.ee/saks/ikomisjon>, (accessed 15 April 2002).

[4] For example, a detailed action plan for the National Employment Plan for Ida-Viru Region (approved by the Government in 2001) is to be drafted in 2002.

[5] Interviews with: A. Semjonov, Director of the Legal Information Centre for Human Rights, Tallinn, 27 March 2002; A. Laius, Director of the Jaan Tõnisson Institute, Tallinn, 9 April 2002; Jaak Prozes, the President of the Union of National Minorities of Estonia, Tallinn, 3 April 2002.

2. The Government Programme – Background

2.1 Background to the Present Programme

The 2000 Government programme, "Integration in Estonian Society 2000–2007" (hereafter, the "Integration Programme") is the first to directly address the issue of integrating national minorities into Estonian society.[6] In the period following Estonia's reassertion of independence from the Soviet Union in 1991, the large population of Russians and Russian-speakers who had settled in Estonia during the Soviet period was regarded as a foreign community. Its members were required to obtain residency permits or to go through a naturalisation procedure to become citizens of the re-established State. Until 1998, Estonian Government policy towards this population was centred on changing the ethnic balance, particularly through encouraging re-emigration to Russia.[7]

The official change in approach towards the Russian-speaking minority was prompted by several factors: studies within the academic community, pressure from international organisations, activities of minority organisations, and political initiative within the Estonian Government itself. First, several prominent sociologists who came to be known as the "Vera" group coordinated a series of workshops during the course of 1996, bringing together over two dozen Estonian researchers for discussion of integration and minority issues. The Ministry of Education funded this project and the results of its research and analysis were published in three volumes between 1997 and 1998.[8] The conclusions recommended opening public debate on State policy and

---

[6] The terms "ethnic minorities," "Russian-speakers," and "non-Estonians" in this report refer to the many inhabitants of Estonia who are not ethnically Estonian, most of whom speak Russian as their first language.

[7] As the leader of the Fatherland Union Party and the former prime minister (1992–1994, 1999–2002) Mart Laar recently declared in his article that all Estonian Governments had "supported the re-migration of colonised people back to their homeland." See M. Laar, *"Eesti lapsed või sisseränne Venemaalt"* (Estonian children or migration from Russia), *Eesti Päevaleht*, 22 March 2002. See <http://www.epl.ee/leht/artikkel.php?ID=199381>, (accessed 15 April 2002).

[8] P. Järve (ed), *Vene noored Eestis: sotsioloogiline mosaiik* (Russian adolescents in Estonia: a social mosaic). *Projekti Mitte-eesti noorte integratsioon Eesti ühiskonnas väljaanne.* VERA I. (Publication of the project The integration of non-Estonian adolescents in Estonian society. VERA I). TÜ Kirjastus, Tartu, 1997; M. Heidmets (ed), *Vene küsimus ja Eesti valikud* (The Russian question and Estonia's choices). TPÜ Kirjastus, Tallinn, 1998; M. Lauristin (ed), *Mitmekultuuriline Eesti: väljakutse haridusele* (Multicultural Estonia: challenge to education). *Projekti Mitte-eesti noorte integratsioon Eesti ühiskonnas väljaanne.* VERA II. (Publication of the project The integration of non-Estonian adolescents in Estonian society. VERA II). TÜ Kirjastus, Tartu, 1998.

minority issues, and that specific strategies to resolve the problems of minority citizenship and education should be formulated.[9]

Intergovernmental organisations such as the OSCE, the Council of Europe, and the European Union also exerted their influence to encourage greater attention to the situation of minorities. In June and July 1993, the Aliens Law drew criticism from the international community, as did changes to the laws on language use and citizenship in 1995.[10] Accordingly, Phare and the UNDP each funded an expert group to draft strategies for integration and language instruction in 1997.

A new Government was formed in May 1997, and the cabinet included a post of minister without portfolio responsible for population and minority issues. The new minister proceeded to appoint a commission to draft general policy principles for integration, the first versions of the strategy that ultimately evolved into the Integration Programme.

2.2 The Programme – Process

In the process of developing the draft integration strategy, the Government took steps to solicit comments on the initial version of the programme. While there was considerable discussion at the highest political levels, some concerns have been raised regarding the degree to which the public, and in particular civil society organisations, were able to take part in the drafting process. A key aspect of the initial draft was nevertheless modified in the final version of the programme, shifting the text's language away from a strategy integrating minorities into Estonian society towards a more reciprocal vision of integration that calls upon both the majority and minorities to take part in the integration process.

The commission appointed by the Minister for Population and Ethnic Affairs in 1997 produced a draft integration policy concept by the end of that year. The Government approved this document on 10 February 1998, and on 10 June Parliament gave its assent. Between the Government's adoption of the commission's policy concept and

---

[9] M. Heidmets, *"Mitte-eesti noorte integratsioon Eesti ühiskonda: arengurajad"* (Integration of non-Estonian youth into Estonian society: path of development), in P. Järve (ed). *Vene noored Eestis: sotsioloogiline mosaiik* (Russian adolescents in Estonia: a social mosaic). *Projekti Mitte-eesti noorte integratsioon Eesti ühiskonnas väljaanne.* VERA I. (Publication of the project The integration of non-Estonian adolescents in Estonian society. VERA I). TÜ Kirjastus, Tartu, 1997, pp. 345–347.

[10] V. Poleshchuk, *Advice Not Welcomed. Recommendations of the OSCE High Commissioner to Estonia and Latvia and the response.* Lit VERLAG Münster-Hamburg-Berlin-London, 2001 pp. 42–43, 53–54, 56, 67, (hereafter, *"Advice not Welcomed"*).

the promulgation of the final Integration Programme more than two years later, the draft documents were circulated among members of Parliament, Government bodies, and local governments. On 2 March 1999, the Government adopted the Action Plan, which defined the schedule for compiling the Integration Programme; the text of the present Integration Programme was adopted on 14 March 2000.

There was significant response to the draft Integration Programme when it was circulated in 1999. The Government's commission for elaboration of the Integration Programme received more than 100 written responses, overwhelmingly welcoming its introduction.[11] However, these responses reflected widely disparate views as to how and on what basis integration should be achieved. The draft was modified following this debate, although a solution fully satisfying all viewpoints could not be achieved given the diversity of opinions.

The Centre Party faction of Parliament welcomed the idea of adopting an integration programme while rejecting the draft's proposal to introduce Estonian language instruction in Russian-language secondary education. They criticised what they considered to be an assimilative approach, indicating that the Integration Programme did not adequately address the role of ethnic Estonians in the integration process.[12] Two Russian-speaking members of the expert commission withdrew, accusing the authors of the Programme of striving for assimilation, and attempting to close down all Russian education facilities at the secondary and tertiary levels.[13] The MP heading the Estonian United People's Party (EUPP), which also represents Russian-speakers, argued that the Integration Programme was excessively language-centred and did not address the real obstacles to the integration of non-Estonians: lack of citizenship and under-representation in the labour market and in State administration.[14] The MP emphasised that a programme of this significance, implicating such broad social issues, would require

---

[11] The Government of Estonia, *Report on the implementation of the State Programme "Integration in Estonian society 2000–2007" in 2000*, Tallinn, 2001, p. 3, (hereafter, "Government Report 2000"). See <www.riik.ee/saks/ikomisjon>, (accessed 15 April 2002).

[12] *Riigikogu Keskfraktsiooni kiri minister Katrin Saksale* (Letter of the Centre faction of Parliament to Minister Katrin Saks), No 87/3–8, 27 January 2000.

[13] *Novosti, Strana i stranniki* (News, Country and countrymen), *Molodjezh Estonii*, 11 January 2000. See <http://www.moles.ee/00/Jan/11/news.html>, (accessed 15 April 2002).

[14] *Riigikogu Eestimaa Ühendatud Rahvapartei kiri minister Katrin Saksale* (Letter of the Estonian United People's Party of the Parliament to Minister Katrin Saks), No 4–10/112, 31 January 2000.

building a wider consensus among the population. Therefore, the EUPP drafted a conception for an alternative approach, which was presented to the Government.[15]

The members of the predominantly Russian-speaking Narva City Council called for the Integration Programme to ensure the effectiveness of State language training and to develop amendments to the Citizenship Act to simplify naturalisation procedures.[16] An MP wrote that the draft Integration Programme "…does not consider opinions of both the Estonian and Russian communities." He emphasised that the first priority should not be linguistic, but legal and political integration, and that the Integration Programme should provide for legislation recognising the multiethnic nature of Estonian society.[17]

Taking the opposite view, the leading faction of the Government, the Fatherland Union, expressed acute dissatisfaction with the multicultural approach of the Integration Programme: "[a]ccording to the Constitution, Estonia is not a multicultural state but a nation-state, and legislators have never decided to accept multicultural ideology as a development model for Estonia."[18] The coalition also rejected recognising the inclusion of non-citizens as minorities.

On a conceptual level, the main change resulting from these discussions related to the understanding of integration. Initial concepts of the programme drew critical comments from minority groups, which read the concept as suggesting that within a multicultural Estonia, the Estonian language and culture should have a privileged status.[19] This approach was modified in the final version of the text, fundamentally shifting the Programme's conceptual basis. While the 1999 integration policy concept

---

[15] *Riigikogu Eestimaa Ühendatud Rahvapartei fraktsiooni kiri peaminister Mart Laarile* (Letter of the Estonian United People's Party faction of the Parliament to Prime Minister Mart Laar), No 3–6/224, 8 March 2000.

[16] *Narva Linnavolikogu kiri minister Katrin Saksale* (Letter of the Narva City Council to Minister Katrin Saks), No. 33–1.20, 4 February 2000.

[17] *Riigikogu liikme Sergei Ivanovi kiri minister Katrin Saksale* (Letter of Sergei Ivanov, the MP, to Minister Katrin Saks), 31 January 2000.

[18] Riigikogu Isamaaliidu esimehe T. Sinisaare kiri *Isamaaliidu saadikurühma seisukoht riikliku programmi "Integratsioon Eesti ühiskonnas 2000–2007" suhtes* (Letter of T. Sinissaar, the chairman of the Fatherland Union Party faction of the Parliament Position of the Fatherland Union faction of the Parliament in regard to the State Programme "Integration in Estonian society 2000–2007"), 31 January 2000.

[19] A. Semjonov, "Estonia: Nation Building and Integration – Political and Legal Aspects," in Paul Kolstoe (ed.) *Nation Building – Integration and Ethnic Conflict in Estonia and Moldova*. USA: Rowman and Littlefield, 2002. See <http://www.copri.dk/publications/WP/WP%202000/8-2000.doc>, (accessed 29 September 2002).

approached the issue as integration of ethnic minorities *into* Estonia society, the Integration Programme is based on the concept of integration *within* Estonian society, where both Estonians and ethnic minorities must take steps to achieve the main goals.

The President's Roundtable on Minorities and unions of ethnic minority organisations[20] was an important venue for the discussion and development of the Integration Programme. According to the minutes of the Government Commission for the elaboration of the Integration Programme, the initial version of the Integration Programme did not include a separate sub-programme for the protection and development of minority identities. This section was included only after the Roundtable submitted several proposals to the Government Commission.[21]

Some representatives of civil society organisations expressed concern that only a few consultations with NGOs were held during the elaboration process.[22] The Programme was presented to the public and NGOs only in late December 1999, three months before it was approved by the Government. At the time, minority representatives called for more extensive discussions before a final text was adopted.[23] According to another view presented by some civil society and minority organisations, NGOs were consulted but had only limited possibilities to influence the drafting process in any meaningful way.[24] Although the European Commission was not formally consulted during the elaboration process, the development of integration-related EU Phare programmes reflect the input of EU experts.

---

[20] The Roundtable was established in 1993 as an institution within the Office of the President. According to its statute, it is a standing conference whose function is to discuss matters of political and public life, including societal, ethnic, economic and social-political issues with representatives of minority groups and stateless persons. See <http://www.president.ee/eng/institutsioonid/?gid=11437>, (accessed 29 September 2002); see also Open Society Institute, *Monitoring the EU Accession Process: Minority Protection*, Budapest, 2001, pp. 208–209, (hereafter, "*Minority Protection 2001*").

[21] *Etniliste vähemuste Eesti ühiskonda integreerumise küsimustega tegeleva asjatunjdate komijsoni istungi protokollid* (Minutes of the Expert Commission dealing with issues of integration of ethnic minorities into Estonian society), meetings No. 2, 27 August 1999; No. 3, 14 October 1999; No. 4, 1 November 1999.

[22] Interview with A. Semjonov, Director of the Legal Information Centre for Human Rights, Tallinn, 27 March 2002.

[23] See J. Tolstikov, *Molodjezh Estonii*, 2 March 2000; Leivi Sher, *Molodjezh Estonii*, 4 April 2000; Mati Hint, *Den za Dnem*, 10 March 2000.

[24] Interviews with: A. Laius, Director of the Jaan Tõnisson Institute, Tallinn, 9 April 2002; Jaak Prozes, the President of the Union of National Minorities of Estonia, Tallinn, 3 April 2002.

2.3 The Programme – Content

The Integration Programme envisions a process that will allow minorities to retain their distinct identity, while increasing participation in and loyalty to the Estonian State. The main tool it identifies for achieving integration is Estonian language instruction, as a common linguistic sphere is viewed as a means to enhance the inclusion of minorities; this process may also have the effect of reducing existing inequalities or tensions. Minority representatives have expressed concern that the emphasis on language does not take into account other barriers to integration or aspects of minority protection such as prevention of discrimination. The Integration Programme suggests that these issues should be addressed through complementary programmes.

The stated goals of the Integration Programme are to offer ethnic minorities the opportunity to preserve their distinctive cultural and ethnic characteristics and also to develop common or shared characteristics between the minority and majority elements of society.[25] The Integration Programme identifies "common core" characteristics as democratic values, a shared information sphere and Estonian language environment, and common Government institutions, and calls upon both Estonians and non-Estonians to take part in the "bilateral process" of integration.[26]

The Programme targets only certain sectors: "in order to avoid the potential duplication of activities, the Integration Programme has primarily concentrated on measures in the areas of education, culture, the media, and legislation."[27] The first and highest priority is the linguistic integration of minorities in specific spheres. The underlying assumption of the Programme is that Estonian language instruction is the gateway to integration: its goals, planned activities, and financial support are predicated on this assumption. The education and adult language instruction sub-programmes are explicitly dedicated to language training, while the "social competence" sub-programme also incorporates language instruction into its design. Promotion of minority rights is addressed primarily through the "education and culture of minorities" sub-programme. Some aspects of the "social competence" sub-programme also relate to the promotion of minority rights,

---

[25] Government of Estonia, *State Programme. Integration in Estonian Society 2000–2007*, Tallinn, 2000, p. 15. See <www.riik.ee/saks/ikomisjon>, (accessed 15 April 2002), (hereafter, "Integration Programme").

[26] Integration Programme, p. 15.

[27] Integration Programme, p. 11.

providing for projects to increase tolerance, and to provide greater opportunities for minorities to participate in public life.[28]

The language-centred approach has not met with universal acceptance, however. By following a coalition agreement reached in March 1999, neither the Parliament nor the Government took into account proposals offering alternative approaches to citizenship and language policies when the Integration Programme was being drafted.[29]

The naturalisation procedure, which can be difficult and burdensome,[30] is an important dimension of the integration process from the minority perspective, but is not addressed in detail by the Programme. This issue is especially relevant as ethnic or national minorities are defined under Estonian law as "citizens of Estonia who reside on the territory of Estonia; maintain long-standing, firm and lasting ties with Estonia; possess ethnic, cultural, religious or linguistic characteristics differing from those of Estonians; and demonstrate a sense of solidarity directed towards preserving their culture, traditions, religion, or language." [31] The Estonian Government asserts that this definition conforms to international standards,[32] but it has been criticised for failing to adequately reflect the actual situation of minorities in Estonia,[33] as a large proportion

---

[28] See missions I.4, IV.1-IV.6, in Government of Estonia, *Action Plans for Sub-Programmes of State Integration Programme for the years 2000–2003*, Tallinn, 2001. See <www.riik.ee/saks/ikomisjon>, (accessed 15 April 2002).

[29] Coalition Agreement of the Reform Party, Fatherland Union and the Moderates, 17 March 1999. Interview with Katrin Saks, the former Minister for Population and Ethnic Affairs, head of the Government Commission responsible for the elaboration of the Integration Programme from 1999–2000, Tallinn, 1 April 2002.

[30] FCNM Advisory Committee *2001 Opinion on Estonia*, para. 69; see also, *Minority Protection 2001*, pp. 180–182.

[31] Cultural Autonomy for National Minorities Act, State Gazette I, 1993/71/1001, Article 1. Unofficial translation in English, see <http://www.minelres.lv/NationalLegislation/Estonia/Estonia_KultAut_English.htm>, (accessed 30 September 2002).

[32] See *Comments of the Estonian Government on the Opinion of the Advisory Committee on the Implementation of the Framework Convention for the Protection of National Minorities in Estonia*, Tallinn, 2002, p. 4, available at <http://spunk.mfa.ee/eesti/oigusloome/Konventsioonid/rahv.vahem.kommentaarid.pdf>, (hereafter, "Government Comments on FCNM Advisory Committee 2001 Opinion").

[33] See Advisory Committee on the Framework Convention for the Protection of National Minorities, *Opinion on Estonia, adopted on 14 September 2001*, at para. 17. Available at <http://spunk.mfa.ee/eesti/oigusloome/Konventsioonid/2001cm159.pdf>, (accessed 15 April 2002), (hereafter, "FCNM Advisory Committee *2001 Opinion on Estonia*").

of non-Estonian inhabitants are without Estonian citizenship and consequently are not officially recognised by the State as minorities.[34]

The Integration Programme does not directly address the question of discrimination on the basis of ethnicity. Discrimination has emerged as a topic of discussion only recently, and there is little existing legislation to define or address the issue.[35] It has been observed that little data has been collected regarding the relative situation of minorities across various spheres of social life, limiting the degree to which problems can be identified and addressed.[36]

No other large-scale programmes for minority protection exist outside the scope of the Integration Programme. However, there are several regional development projects and programmes supported by local governments,[37] embassies,[38] and foundations.[39] In particular, the Foundation for Vocational Education and Training Reform is currently implementing a Phare project to support human resources development in Ida-Viru county and southern Estonia, through vocational education and training and

---

[34] FCNM Advisory Committee *2001 Opinion on Estonia*, para. 18. The Integration Programme distinguishes between long-standing national minorities and minorities that migrated to Estonia after World War II. The term "ethnic minority" is used in the text as a common term referring to both groups. See Integration Programme, p. 37.

[35] Analysis Regarding the Compliance of Estonia with the Framework Convention for the Protection of National Minorities'. The Working Group Evaluation, adopted by Presidential Roundtable on National Minorities, Tallinn, 19 February 1999.

[36] European Commission Against Racism and Intolerance, *Second Report on Estonia*, 22 June 2001, pp. 17–18, (hereafter, "ECRI *Second Report on Estonia*").

[37] The Ida-Viru County Government has elaborated and implemented the regional development plan for the Ida-Viru County for the years 1998–2003, see Ida-Viru County Government, *Principal lines of the Regional Developmental Plan of Ida-Viru County for the years 1989–2003*, Jõhvi, 1998. See <http://www.ivmv.ee/arengukava/Ak_ik.pdf>, (accessed 15 April 2002). It includes, *inter alia*, measures to improve the teaching quality at the Russian-language schools in northeastern Estonia.

[38] The main foreign funding institution has been the European Commission, see Ida-Viru County Government, *EL välisvahendid Ida-Viru maakonnas* (external assistance resources of the EC in Ida-Viru County), in Ida-Viru County Government, *Principal lines of the Regional Developmental Plan of Ida-Viru County for the years 1989–2003*, Jõhvi, 1998. See <http://www.ivmv.ee/arengukava/el1999.html>, (accessed 15 April 2002). In addition, various embassies have supported projects.

[39] Among foundations, the Open Estonia Foundation has been a significant contributor to the integration-related projects in the past. See Open Estonia Foundation Yearbooks 1994–1999. See <http://www.oef.org.ee/english/publications/>, (accessed 15 April 2002).

improving cooperation between social partners in these regions to enhance effectiveness in solving problems in the labour market.[40]

2.4 The Programme – Administration/Implementation/Evaluation

Administration of the Integration Programme has been quite efficient. A Steering Committee manages overall budget and reporting activities, while individual ministries are responsible for budgeting and carrying out specific activities under each sub-programme. There is regular and comprehensive monitoring of Programme implementation, and the resulting reports are made available to the public. While coordination among the Government structures involved in implementing the Programme appears to function well, few steps have been taken to enhance the participation of NGOs and minority groups in the implementation process.

The Minister for Population and Ethnic Affairs is responsible for overall coordination of the Integration Programme, and chairs the ten-member Steering Committee that oversees its implementation and may modify its content as necessary. The Steering Committee's members are representatives of the Ministries of Education, Culture, Internal Affairs, Social Affairs, Agriculture, Defence and Finance, the Integration Foundation, and the Institute of International and Social Studies. On 14 May 2002, the Government revised the membership of the Steering Committee to reflect recent changes in the Government and within ministries.

The Steering Committee plans the overall budget for the Integration Programme each year. The Programme assigns responsibility for implementing its four sub-programmes to corresponding Government bodies; each ministry designates specific sums for the implementation of the Programme in its annual budget, based on the costs projected in the "Action Plan 2000–2003" and recommendations from the Steering Committee. The allocations are then subject to the standard procedures regulating annual budget formation, provided for in the State Budget Act.[41]

The Steering Committee is charged with presenting an annual implementation report to the Government, and may request that State and local government agencies provide necessary documents for this purpose. On 15 May 2001, the Government examined the first such report *The implementation of the State Programme "Integration in Estonian society 2000–2007" in 2000*, submitted by the Minister for Population and Ethnic

---

[40] See <http://www.sekr.ee/www/phare/en/phare_projects.html>, (accessed 2 July 2002).
[41] State Budget Act, State Gazette, RT 1999/55/584.

Affairs.[42] The Report analyses society's attitudes towards integration, surveys significant developments and legislation adopted, and presents extensive statistics for each sub-programme. Drawing upon academic research, media monitoring, and reports from the participating ministries, the Report concludes that the Programme is performing successfully, although noting there is room for improvement with regard to changing attitudes and increasing tolerance in society.[43]

This comprehensive report demonstrates the Government's impressive commitment to carrying out internal monitoring of the Programme and its implementation; however, the evaluation gives little attention to the Programme's shortcomings as perceived by the Russian-speaking community. While recognising the need to increase naturalisation rates and other factors related to the legal and political dimensions of integration, the Report does not indicate that there will be any shift in priorities to allocate more resources to projects outside the linguistic sphere.

It has been observed that mechanisms to involve local government in implementation of the Programme have been neglected.[44] While the Integration Programme provides for local authorities to elaborate their own programmes to promote integration, only in Tallinn has such a programme been developed, and has still not been implemented due to political discord.[45] Regional disparities argue for greater attention to local initiatives, as the situation in the less-developed Northeast where the majority of the population is Russian-speaking, is distinct from that in Tallin, which is both more diverse and more prosperous.

The Integration Programme also provides for an expert group within the Steering Committee to ensure that the Integration Programme continues to reflect the actual processes of integration taking place, as a form of management feedback. The expert group should include representatives of non-governmental organisations performing general and media monitoring as prescribed by the Integration Programme, and representatives of scientific institutions involved in integration-related research.[46] However, this expert group has not yet been formed. Otherwise, NGO involvement is not addressed in detail in the Programme. The Council of Europe's Advisory Committee on the Framework Convention for the Protection of National Minorities

---

[42] Available from the Office of the Minister for Population and Ethnic Affairs (on paper and CD-ROM), the Integration Foundation, and on the Internet at <www.riik.ee/saks/ikomisjon>, (accessed 22 October 2002).

[43] See Government Report 2000, p. 96.

[44] Comments from the Estonian Association for Human Rights on a draft of the present report, on file with the EU Accession Monitoring Program, (hereafter, "EAHR Comments").

[45] EAHR Comments.

[46] Integration Programme, p. 19.

has also weighed in on the need for broad consultations in its Opinion on Estonia's measures to implement the Convention:

> [L]egislation does not provide for consultative bodies with an official status representing national minorities in Estonia. Bearing in mind the importance of involving national minorities in decision-making processes, the Advisory Committee is of the opinion that Estonia should consider the establishment of such structures of consultation, which would also include numerically small minorities such as Roma.[47]

The establishment of such a structure could build trust between the Government and minority communities by offering information about the Integration Programme's activities and results from a direct source. Also, this body would be a channel through which minorities could articulate their problems and intentions to the Government. So far such an exchange of information has been taking place mainly at various seminars and conferences, as well as through meetings of the President's Roundtable on Minorities.

2.5 The Programme and the Public

While several widespread campaigns promoting the Integration Programme have raised awareness of the Programme's existence and general goals, public knowledge of the actual text of the Programme remains low.[48] The adoption of the Integration Programme was generally welcomed as a necessary measure, although majority and minority views as to how integration should be achieved remain divided.

The Government, NGOs, and public policy institutes have introduced the Integration Program in various public seminars and conferences in Estonia and abroad. Extensive materials on the Programme, its implementation and evaluations have been produced for the international audience. The text of the Integration Programme and other materials, including the 2000 report on implementation, are unofficially available on the internet at the web site of the Office of the Minister for Population and Ethnic Affairs.[49]

In 1999, the Media Monitoring project set up under the Integration Programme (see Section 3.2) observed that more frequent discussion of ethnic and integration issues in

---

[47] See FCNM Advisory Committee, *2001 Opinion on Estonia,* para. 58.

[48] It has been observed that this is a common problem with all government policy documents. OSI Roundtable, Tallinn, 6 June 2002. *Explanatory Note: OSI held a roundtable meeting in Estonia in June 2002 to invite critique of the present report in draft form. Experts present included representatives of the government, minority groups, and non-governmental organisations.*

[49] See <www.riik.ee/saks/ikomisjon>, (accessed 22 October 2002).

both Estonian and Russian-language mass media had been achieved in that year. The increase in coverage of inter-ethnic topics was brought about by various factors, including changes to several laws,[50] Russian-speaking youngsters' protests against NATO, as well as the planned reform of Russian-language secondary schools and projects under the Integration Programme itself.[51] Estonian-language print media referred to the Integration Programme in ten percent of all Estonian-language integration-related publications in 2000, and Russian-language print media in 24 percent.[52] Similar figures were reported in 2001.[53]

According to the data of one sociological study (Tallinn 2001) at least half of the population in Tallinn is aware of the Integration Programme. About one-third of ethnic Estonians and one-fifth of non-Estonians evaluate it positively, and about half in each national group see both positive and negative aspects. At the same time, only three percent of both Estonian and Russian-speaking respondents were familiar with the text of the Integration Programme,[54] although this is not disproportionate to the level of familiarity with other Government documents.

It is widely accepted that the adoption and implementation of the Integration Programme alone was a significant achievement. The Government only began to publicly discuss the

---

[50] These laws include the Amendment to the Citizenship Act in 1998 on simplifying the conditions for applying for and acquiring Estonian citizenship by the underage children of stateless parents, the Government's implementing regulation in August 1999 resulting from the Language Act, which defines the language proficiency required mainly from the employees in the public sector.

[51] See T. Vihalemm, "The informative and identity-building significance of media: the case of Estonian Russophones", in M. Lauristin and R. Vetik (eds), *Integration in Estonian society: monitoring 2000*, IISS, Tallinn, 2000, p. 48. See
<http://www.meis.ee/eng/monitoring/Triin.rtf>, (accessed 15 April 2002), and
P. Tammpuu, "The Treatment of Events, Subjects and Institutions Related to Integration in the Estonian and the Russian-speaking Press", in M. Lauristin and R. Vetik (eds), *Integration in Estonian society: monitoring 2000*, IISS, Tallinn, 2000, p. 56. See <http://www.meis.ee/eng/monitoring/Piia1.rtf>, (accessed 15 April 2002).

[52] R. Kõuts (ed), *Integratsiooniprotsesside kajastumine Eesti ajakirjanduses aastal 2000. Projekti "Integratsiooni meediamonitooring" aruanne* (Coverage of integration processes in the press in Estonia in 2000. Report of the project "Media Monitoring of Integration), BAMR, Tartu, 2001, (hereafter, "*Media Monitoring 2001*").

[53] R. Kõuts, *Integratsiooniprotsesside kajastumine Eesti ajakirjanduses aastal 2001. Projekti "Integratsiooni meediamonitooring" aruanne* (Coverage of integration processes in the press in Estonia in 2001. Report of the project "Media Monitoring of Integration), BAMR, Tartu, 2002, p. 11, See <http://www.meis.ee/trykised/meediamonitooring01.rtf>, (accessed 15 April 2002), (hereafter, "*Media Monitoring 2002*").

[54] A. Semjonov (ed), *Integratsioon Tallinnas 2001* (Integration in Tallinn 2001), LICHR, Tallinn, 2002, pp. 76–77.

need to promote the integration process in the year 2000, identifying the need to accelerate the pace of naturalisation, increase the level of tolerance and awareness of society's cultural pluralism, and to improve cooperation between Estonian and non-Estonian-speaking communities. The existence of the Programme appears to have encouraged a more positive reception of integration themes.

Estonians and non-Estonians nevertheless continue to have conflicting views on the underlying assumptions of the process and its goals. The majority of Estonians see the purpose of integration as the transformation of non-Estonians into loyal citizens, and the appropriate demonstration of this loyalty as mastery of the Estonian language. In this view, learning the State language is primarily a personal obligation. For the majority of non-Estonians, integration should begin with the transformation of current laws and norms to moderate citizenship and language requirements, which would allow minorities to be loyal Estonian citizens while retaining their distinct ethnic and cultural identity.[55]

Representatives of civil society and ethnic minority organisations frequently express concern about the low level of inclusion of ethnic minorities and NGOs in general in the coordination of Integration Programme implementation. This is one dimension of the more general complaint that the Government has not given sufficient attention to building the capacity of the NGO sector.[56]

2.6 The Programme and the EU

The EU has supported language-based integration projects since the mid-nineties, and has praised the Integration Programme in its Regular Reports. Although cautioning that more remains to be done with regard to the integration of non-citizens in particular, the EU appears to support the language-centred approach adopted by the Programme. The Commission has noted the need to address all aspects of integration, and EU funding has been allocated to regional development projects that could serve to broaden the scope of the integration process, though the focus on developing legal and political dimensions of integration could be sharpened.

---

[55] J. Kruusvall, "Understanding integration in Estonian society," in M. Lauristin and R. Vetik (eds), *Integration in Estonian society: monitoring 2000*, IISS, Tallinn, 2000, pp. 19, 21. See <http://www.meis.ee/eng/monitoring/Juri.rtf>, (accessed 15 April 2002). See also, A. Semjonov (ed), *Integratsioon Tallinnas 2001* (Integration in Tallinn 2001), LICHR, Tallinn, 2002, pp. 76–77.

[56] Interviews with: A. Laius, Director of the Jaan Tõnisson Institute, Tallinn, 9 April 2002; Jaak Prozes, the President of the Union of National Minorities of Estonia, Tallinn, 3 April 2002.

Through the Phare Programme, the European Commission has supported integration-related projects since 1996, mainly in Estonian language instruction. Among the projects completed prior to the adoption of the Integration Programme was "Language Training 1996–1997," which drafted a 10 to 15 year plan for Estonian language instruction for the non-Estonian population. The strategy was elaborated and approved by the Government in April 1998. Another component of the project was to coordinate various language training programmes and projects, including efforts to attract foreign assistance for these projects. The activity culminated in 1998 with the adoption of large-scale and multi-donor programmes coordinated by Ministry of Education and UNDP that replaced a number of smaller projects that had been supported between 1993 and 1997. A further €1.4 million was allocated to the project "Estonian Language Training Programme 1998–2000," and Phare has also budgeted €3.1 million for the ongoing project "Estonian Social Integration and Language Training Programme for Ethnic Minorities in Estonia 2001–2003."

These projects were elaborated by Ministry of Education; the Integration Foundation then selected implementing partners through a competition process. The Phare programme's steering committee oversees the use of funds through its approval of activity and budget plans.[57]

In Spring 2000, the UNDP commissioned an intermediary evaluation from an international assessment committee for the EU Phare *Estonian Language Training Programme* 1998–2000.[58] The main conclusions in respect to the Phare projects are positive, noting that the coordinating role of the UNDP and the work of the Integration Foundation itself have both contributed to overall efficacy.[59] While reporting that language camps and similar programmes were extremely popular with young people and ought to be expanded, the assessment noted that adult language instruction projects were less successful, and greater focus on economic and socio-cultural projects for the older minority population should be incorporated.[60] For the future, the evaluation noted that it should be ensured that language-related activities could be merged into other, more general initiatives related to integration.

On several points the evaluation noted that there had been little opportunity for beneficiaries or "programme target groups" to offer input to the programme, and

---

[57] The Committee is comprised of representatives of the Ministries of Education, Ethnic Affairs, Finance, and Parliament, academic and research institutions, and minority organisations.

[58] See M. Hopkins, T. Elenurm, G. Feldman, *Mid-term evaluation of social integration projects in Estonia*, Tallinn, May 2000. See <http://www.meis.ee/eng/hinnang-eng.rtf>, (accessed 15 April 2002), (hereafter, *"Mid-term evaluation of social integration projects in Estonia"*).

[59] *Mid-term evaluation of social integration projects in Estonia*, p. 4.

[60] *Mid-term evaluation of social integration projects in Estonia*, p. 6

recommended that the project's steering committee incorporate an additional member whose role it would be to advocate the needs of non-Estonians.[61]

In its Progress Report 2000, the European Commission welcomed the Government's adoption of the Integration Programme. In the 2001 Regular Report, the EC described the implementation scheme of the Integration Programme, and the cost of activities provided for in the Action Plans (EEK 225 million, Estonian Kroons, approximately €14.4 million[62] for the period 2000–2003). Regarding the next steps for implementation, the Report stated:

> It is necessary for the Estonian Government to continue to devote adequate resources and give proper attention to the implementation of all elements of the integration programme. This includes, in particular, the need to ensure a high level of awareness and involvement in integration process across all sections of the Estonian population.[63]

3. THE GOVERNMENT PROGRAMME – IMPLEMENTATION

3.1 Stated Objectives of the Programme

The Integration Programme is planned to extend over the period between 2000 and 2007. In addition to the objectives to be achieved within this time frame, some of its goals are characterised as "long term" – to be accomplished only after 2007. These aims include: the creation of a "common sphere of information in the Estonian language environment, under conditions of cultural diversity and tolerance"; legal and political integration; forming a loyal population and reducing the number of non-citizens and stateless persons; increased economic competitiveness and social mobility for all members of Estonian society.

The main objectives of the Programme are considered short-term, to be achieved by 2007. They are classified into four sub-programmes, with projected goals as follows:

- Education: Elementary school graduates are knowledgeable about the Estonian State and culture, and able to participate in the larger Estonian society; have medium-level knowledge of the Estonian language; secondary school graduates

---

[61] *Mid-term evaluation of social integration projects in Estonia*, p. 7.
[62] The exchange rate is calculated at EEK 15.64 = €1
[63] European Commission, *Progress Report Estonia*, Brussels, 2000, p. 23.

have the Estonian language knowledge necessary for everyday life and work and are capable of continuing their studies in Estonian.

- Education and Culture of Ethnic Minorities: Ethnic minorities possess opportunities to acquire education in their mother tongue and to preserve their culture.

- Adult Estonian Language Instruction: Opportunities have been created for non-Estonian adults to improve their knowledge of Estonian and to enhance their social and cultural participation.

- Social Participation: Individuals participate actively in the development of civil society; attitudes of Estonians and non-Estonians are favourable to the achievement of the main aims of the State Programme; individuals with special social needs have increased opportunities for integration.[64]

3.2 The Government Programme and Discrimination

Discrimination is not addressed by the Integration Programme, and even incidental inequalities are not addressed in any detail. The Programme does have strong components to increase the level of understanding and tolerance in society, which do not address existing inequalities but aim to reduce the incidence of future discrimination. Generally, discrimination has not been widely recognised in Estonian society or Government policy; however, a draft Equality Act is under development.

The Integration Programme acknowledges that there are barriers that hinder many non-Estonians from participating fully in society, although it does not mention discrimination among these;[65] lack of Estonian citizenship and poor knowledge of the State language, as well as an attitude that "non-Estonians are the problem" that dominates among Estonians are identified as the principal obstacles to minority participation. The Integration Programme asserts that these barriers can be removed by increasing language proficiency and increasing Estonian citizenship among ethnic minorities,[66] but does not provide any description of measures for the amendment of relevant legal provisions regulating language requirements.

---

[64] Integration Programme, p. 16.
[65] Integration Programme, p. 12.
[66] Integration Programme, p. 14.

Anti-discrimination law and practice

Estonia's Constitution contains provisions prohibiting discrimination on the basis of race or nationality.[67] Anti-discrimination provisions are also set forth in the Criminal Code, as well as in the Law on Employment Contracts.

There is no unanimous view on the existence of discrimination as a problem in any sector of society. Whereas some representatives of minorities do not see discrimination as a problem for minorities,[68] integration-related surveys show that a large number of minorities identify discriminatory treatment on the basis of ethnicity as a factor, primarily based on language usage. The Legal Information Centre for Human Rights has drafted a list of provisions giving rise to unequal treatment, primarily related to language.[69]

In response to observations by the Advisory Committee on the FCNM, in September 2001 the Estonian Government indicated that a draft Equality Act is currently under preparation by the Ministry of Justice.[70] The draft Act will address both direct and indirect forms of discrimination, and covers employment, education, work conditions, membership in professional organisations, social security and healthcare, and access to public services.[71] This significant step is expected to bring Estonia's legislation into line with the "Race Equality Directive," which Estonia must transpose into national law as part of the *acquis communautaire*.[72] The oversight institution required by the Directive has already been established in the Office of the Ombudsman, which is authorised to receive complaints of discrimination, and is charged both with putting a prompt stop

---

[67] *Eesti Vabariigi Põhiseadus* RT, 1992, 26, 349, (Constitution of the Republic of Estonia, hereafter, "Constitution"), Art. 9: "the rights, freedoms and duties of each and every person, as set out in the Constitution, shall be equal for Estonian citizens and for citizens of foreign states and stateless persons in Estonia;" Art.12: "No one shall be discriminated against on the bases of nationality, race, colour, sex, language, origin, religion, political or other opinion, property or social status, or on other grounds"

[68] Interview with Jaak Prozes, the President of the Union of National Minorities of Estonia, Tallinn, 3 April 2002.

[69] See Legal Information Centre for Human Rights, "LICHR Recommendations to the participants in the seminar "Recent amendments to the Estonian legislation in the light of the international standards on minority rights," in *Problems and trends in the integration process of Estonian society. Workshop, 12. 05. 2000. Collection of presentations and materials,* Tallinn, 2000. In 2000, LICHR registered complaints and requests for help from 473 persons belonging to ethnic Russian community in Estonia. See *Minority Protection 2001*, p. 189.

[70] *Government Comments on FCNM Advisory Committee 2001 Opinion*, p. 5.

[71] Ministry of Justice, *Võrdõiguslikkuse ja võrdse kohtlemise seadus*. Eelnõu 24.04.02. (Draft Equality and Equal Treatment Act).

[72] European Council Directive Implementing The Principle Of Equal Treatment Between Persons Irrespective Of Racial And Ethnic Origin (OJ L 180, 19/07/2000).

to any ongoing discrimination and with protecting the rights of those discriminated against.[73] The Ministry of Justice has invited some NGOs with expertise in minority protection to comment on the draft Act.

The Government and the Parliament have acted to amend some of the laws that had been viewed as having a discriminatory and exclusionary effect on Russian-speakers. For example, the amendment to the Law on National Elections and the Law on Local Elections passed by the Parliament on 21 November 2001 abolished language requirements for candidates in national and local elections, thus bringing the law into line with international norms and standards, particularly Article 25 of the United Nations International Covenant on Civil and Political Rights.[74] However, as the requirement to use Estonian as the working language even in local council meetings remains fairly strict, withdrawing the language requirements for candidates may do little to improve access in practice.[75]

The question of language proficiency certificates raised concerns among the non-Estonian community in the past year, but pending legislation promises to settle the issue at least for the time being. A new certification system was introduced in 1999, and although no expiration date was specified on previously issued proficiency certificates, the 1999 Act Amending the Language Act and State Fees Act provided that the old certificates would expire in July 2002;[76] holders of older certificates would thus be required to take an examination again. This provision of the amendments was strongly criticised by many representatives of the Russian-speaking community, as well as by international experts.[77] Parties representing Russian-speakers favoured a

---

[73] *Government Comments on FCNM Advisory Committee 2001 Opinion*, p. 5.

[74] Serious concern about the Estonian language proficiency requirements was expressed also by the Advisory Committee on the FCNM in its opinion on Estonia, adopted on 14 September 2001 The Committee stated that "these requirements have a negative impact on the effective participation of persons belonging to national minorities and that they are not compatible with Article 15 of the Framework Convention." See FCNM Advisory Committee *2001 Opinion on Estonia*, at para. 54.

[75] *See* Report Submitted by Under Article 9 of the International Convention on the Elimination of All Forms of Racial Discrimination, Estonia, February 2002, p. 27. *See* <http://www.unhchr.ch/tbs/doc.nsf/(Symbol)/fa6627fccbb3a493c1256bf900484c42?Opendocument>, (accessed 6 August 2002).

[76] See Act Amending the Language Act and State Fees Act, State Gazette RT I 1999, 16, 275.

[77] The Advisory Committee on the Framework Convention for the Protection of National Minorities stated in its opinion on Estonia that "the recent amendments pertaining to the required language levels must be implemented without causing any undue burden to those individuals who have already passed the required language tests and obtained certificates in accordance with the previously applicable rules." See FCNM Advisory Committee *2001 Opinion on Estonia* at para. 60.

modification to allow for certificates to be renewed without an additional exam, while some ethnic Estonian representatives opposed automatic renewals.[78] In April 2002, the Government submitted the Draft of the Act Amending the Language Act and Deleting Section 6 of the Act Amending the Language Act and State Fees Act for Parliament's approval. The Draft provides for the expiration date for the older certificates to be postponed to 1 January 2004.

Estonia's citizenship requirements have also come under sharp criticism both internationally and by local minority representatives.[79] Since the adoption of the Integration Programme, naturalisation rates have in fact declined, a fact acknowledged in the Government's *Report on Implementation* of the Programme in 2000.[80] While some measures have been taken to moderate the requirements for citizenship, the fact that the number of successful applicants is decreasing while the number of stateless persons remains high suggests that the Government should re-examine both the legal procedures and the incentives for naturalisation. Recently, one political party proposed that long-term residents should be able to acquire citizenship if they complete civics courses, a proposal dismissed as pre-election posturing by other parties.[81]

The perception of discrimination and inequality among non-Estonians is especially relevant in the context of the Integration Programme. Although given only passing mention in the text of the Integration Programme, perceptions of discrimination have been monitored by civil society organisations. According to one survey conducted in Tallinn in 2001, 15 percent of ethnic Estonians and 37 percent of non-Estonians have had personal experience or heard about discrimination experienced by others in the past two years.[82] According to the respondents' evaluations, Estonians' rights are most often violated in labour relations and in contacts with State officials, while minorities additionally allege discriminatory practices in the process of acquiring residency permits and citizenship. According to the survey data, over 40 percent of non-Estonians believed that ethnic discrimination occurs, while 46 percent reported experiencing unequal treatment from State officials due to their insufficient fluency in Estonian. Survey responses indicate that discrimination on the basis of language and

---

[78] See K. Kalamees, "*Selgub keeletunnistuste kehtivusaja pikendamine*" (The issue of extending language certificates will be clarified), *Eesti Päevaleht*, 2 April 2002. See <http://www.epl.ee/leht/artikkel.php?ID=200321>, (accessed 15 April 2002).

[79] See, e.g, ECRI, *Second Report on Estonia*, p. 8; V. Poleshchuk, *Advice Not Welcomed*, pp. 51–65.

[80] *The Implementation of the State Programme "Integration in Estonian society 2000–2007" in 2000*, p. 66.

[81] See RFE/RL *Newsline*, 15 July 2002, "Estonia's Res Publica Proposes Easier Citizenship for Russians."

[82] A. Semjonov (ed), *Integratsioon Tallinnas 2001* (Integration in Tallinn 2001), LICHR, Tallinn, 2002, pp. 53, 54, 88.

ethnicity also takes place in the workplace, but not so often as in the official or administrative spheres.[83] According to this survey the most vulnerable group are stateless people, who perceive that they are discriminated against more severely both in the workplace and the public sphere.

At the same time, integration studies show that the majority of Estonians do not consider the position of ethnic minorities to be worse than their own, and do not recognise that minorities are subject to unequal treatment.[84] In this context, the goal of the Integration Programme "to increase awareness about multiculturalism, and to support [adaptation to a] multicultural Estonia"[85] should target ethnic Estonians in the first place to increase their awareness in this sphere.

Tolerance promotion

The approach adopted by the Integration Programme does not address discrimination, but does provide for measures to promote greater tolerance in society and to reduce negative ethnic stereotypes in society and in the media. This dimension of the integration process is intended to target both minority and majority groups to facilitate the "two-way" integration mentioned in the Programme text. Nevertheless, some minority advocates have suggested that the Programme still requires more accommodation by non-Estonians than by the Estonian State or majority society, and that the promise of a two-way process has not been fulfilled.

Analysis of the results of the Media Monitoring programme established under the Integration Programme[86] suggests that a certain common sphere has started to emerge in the Russian and Estonian language press, as both have increased content related to various national groups and mutually-relevant information. Perspectives on these issues as presented in the Estonian and minority-language media have also grown more similar. As journalists and editors have become increasingly aware of stereotyping and negative characterisations, the language and content of journalism have become more neutral, an improvement from the previous period when studies showed negative

---

[83] A. Semjonov, *Integration in Tallinn 2001*, pp. 53, 54, 88.

[84] J. Kruusvall. "Understanding integration in Estonian society," in M. Lauristin and R. Vetik (eds), *Integration in Estonian society: monitoring 2000*, IISS, Tallinn, 2000, pp. 18, 27. See <http://www.meis.ee/eng/monitoring/Juri.rtf>, (accessed 15 April 2002).

[85] Integration Programme, p. 41.

[86] The Integration Programme provides for a media-monitoring component to take note of the regularity and content of journalism relating to integration, national relations, citizenship and language issues, and national minorities' culture and political issues. The program has reviewed all Russian and Estonian-language newspapers since the project was initiated in 1999, and from 2000 onwards, television broadcasts, and in 2001, monitoring of the Russian language public radio service.

stereotypes prevailing in both Estonian and Russian-language media.[87] The Integration Foundation also financed new television programmes with the aim of increasing Russian-speaking viewers' interest in locally-oriented programming.[88]

Two large-scale tolerance promotion campaigns were launched under the Integration Programme, and numerous publicity efforts for other projects such as adult language education were also produced. Campaigns promoting diversity – "Lots of Great People" in 1999 and "Friendship Starts with a Smile" in 2000 – received €41,935 and €76,774 respectively. Citizenship promotion efforts and language learning promotions, including the "Untie!" campaign to promote adult language instruction received a total of €174,052 from 1999 to 2001.[89]

Social advertising was not previously used extensively in Estonia, and the response to this new approach has been mixed. Criticism most often centred on the utility of these campaigns, with suggestions that funding could be put to better and more practical use.[90] Minority representatives in particular have called for more concrete measures in the political, legal, and social spheres represented in the Integration Programme to complement the ongoing projects in the language and education sectors.

3.2.1 Education

The Integration Programme acknowledges that some opportunities are foreclosed to ethnic minorities due to their lack of proficiency in the Estonian language,[91] but does not explicitly address discrimination in the sphere of education. Concerns relating to minority access to education generally involve the quality and availability of instruction

---

[87] R. Vetik, *Interethnic Relations in Estonia 1988–1998. Doctoral dissertation*, University of Tampere, Tampere, 1999. See also M. Raudsepp, "Rahvusküsimus ajakirjanduse peeglis" (National question in media mirror), in M. Hidmets (ed), *Vene küsimus ja Eesti valikud* (The Russian question and Estonia's choices). TPÜ Kirjastus, Tallinn, 1998, p. 113-135.

[88] Public Communication Programme Integrating Estonia, *Final Report*, Hill and Knowlton, p. 13.

[89] Integration Foundation, *Final Report of the Project "Support to the State Programme for Integration of non-Estonians into Estonian Society,"* Tallinn, 2001; Integration Foundation, *Integration Foundation Yearbook 2000,* Tallinn, 2001, <http://www.meis.ee/eng/aastaraamat>, (accessed 15 April 2002); Integration Foundation, *Integration Foundation Yearbook 2001,* Tallinn, 2002, manuscript.

[90] O. Peresild, *"Sotsiaalreklaam integreeruva ühiskonna kontekstis"* (Social Advertising in Social Integration Context), in R. Kõuts (ed), *Integratsiooniprotsesside kajastumine Eesti ajakirjanduses aastal 2001. Projekti "Integratsiooni meediamonitooring" aruanne* (Coverage of integration processes in the press in Estonia in 2001. Report of the project "Media Monitoring of Integration"), BAMR, Tartu, 2002.

[91] Integration Programme, p. 12.

in the mother tongue (see Section 3.3.1), which affect access to employment, social security, and social and political participation.

This focus on Estonian language teaching at Russian-language schools, and especially the planned transformation of Russian-language schools to Estonian-language instruction after 2007, has caused concern among some representatives of the Russian-speaking community. The Advisory Committee on the FCNM has also expressed reservations regarding these plans, stating that it "considers it essential that the voluntary nature of participation in [language immersion programmes] is fully maintained and that the decision to allocate substantial resources to these programmes does not hamper the availability or quality of minority language education in the areas concerned."[92]

The Integration Programme's Education sub-programme emphasises the role of Estonian language proficiency as a key factor for integration in all spheres. Specific education projects are included under both the "education" and "Estonian language training for adults" sub-programmes; together, these components received over 75 percent of all Programme funding in 2000.[93] In the same year, two projects addressed language training, which can enhance opportunities in spheres beyond education, particularly employment.

Language camps and family exchange projects

Language camps provided Russian-speaking youngsters an opportunity for intensive study of the Estonian language in a recreational setting. In the family exchange programme, Russian-speaking children stayed with Estonian-speaking host families for a month, allowing for a greater depth of cultural exchange.

The Integration Foundation was responsible for preparing the project competitions. After activities were completed, they were evaluated by the Estonian Language Camp and Family Study Council, made up of representatives from donor programmes, the Ministry of Education, the Language Inspection Board, the Camp Managers Board, an Estonian language teacher from a Russian-language school, and a non-Estonian university student. Project beneficiaries were asked to give their opinions on the activities in order to help organise future camps and language study options.

Between 2000 and 2001, 72 projects were implemented, consisting of 45 language camp projects and 27 family exchange projects. 3,500 young people took part in these

---

[92] See FCNM Advisory Committee *2001 Opinion on Estonia* at para. 54
[93] *Government Report*, p. 86.

activities, including approximately 2,700 minorities.[94] The high interest level among beneficiaries is borne out by the number of young people taking part, and Russian-speaking participants have reported favourably particularly on their experiences in the family exchange projects. There was no corresponding opportunity for ethnic Estonian children to live with Russian families, although the Integration Programme does anticipate a two-way exchange.

According to the Media Monitoring report, language camps and family exchange projects were the most frequently mentioned activities in the Estonian and Russian-language mass media in Estonia in 2001.[95] Both Russian and Estonian language media reflected positively on these projects, although the Russian language media valued the family exchange projects more highly than their Estonian-language counterparts.[96] There was an effort to raise awareness of the projects using press releases, and the Integration Foundation's web site provided some basic information about the projects, although mainly in Estonian.[97]

An international evaluation team made both a mid-term and final assessment of the project. The team noted that greater attention to monitoring the host family exchange programme could ensure that the goals of integration are met.[98] In the first evaluation, the team did not include a minority representative, but one of three members of the final evaluation team belonged to a minority. This change may perhaps reflect the mid-term evaluators' own recommendation that greater input from the intended beneficiaries should be incorporated into project design.[99]

---

[94] The budget for these projects was provided by the Ministry of Agriculture (EEK 238,159), and various funds from the Integration Foundation (EEK 2,493,280 from the Nordic/UK/UNDP; EEK 2,125,888 from the Phare Estonian Language Training Programme), for a total of EEK 5,857,327 (€374,350). See G. Feldman, M. Kuldjärv, O. Vares, *Report of the Final Evaluation of the Nordic/UK/UNDP Project "Support to the State Integration Programme,"* Tallinn, October 2001 pp. 18–19, (hereafter, *Final Evaluation of the Nordic/UK/UNDP Project*).

[95] R. Kõuts, *Media Monitoring 2002*, p. 11.

[96] R. Kõuts, *Media Monitoring 2002*, p. 11.

[97] The Foundation's web site has some information in English and Russian at <http://www.meis.ee/eng/index.html>, (accessed 22 October 2002).

[98] *Final Evaluation of the Nordic/UK/UNDP Project*, p. 18.

[99] *Mid-term evaluation of social integration projects in Estonia*, p. 19.

Adult Language Instruction Project InterEst

The project, designed to encourage adults to learn the Estonian language, was initiated in 1999, before the Integration Programme was adopted.[100] In its first stages, the project was confined to the predominantly Russian-speaking regions in the Northeast and in Tallinn, but has since expanded to involve all regions of Estonia. Adults who successfully complete the instruction courses are eligible to have their costs partially reimbursed by the State.

The companies offering language instruction are given training to keep them current with the language exam requirements. Some 120 teachers took part in the training courses in 2000, and also received methodology texts, test handbooks, and exercise booklets published with the support of the Phare Estonian Language Training Programme. 4,800 non-Estonian students had completed the language courses by the end of 2000, of which nearly one-third passed the competence exam and were reimbursed for part of the costs of the course.

The expert group responsible for developing the language instruction reimbursement system included representatives of minority groups, as well as state and local government officials, language training firms, and NGOs.

According to a survey carried out in March 2000,[101] approximately 79 percent of Russian-speaking respondents were aware of the campaign to introduce the *InterEst* project to the public. Only approximately 11 percent of respondents indicated that they did not need additional Estonian language training. At the same time, the percentage of those who planned to improve their language knowledge was not very high – some 33 percent of all respondents. 48 percent of respondents reported that they did not plan to go to language courses; by regions, the percentage giving this response was the highest in predominantly Russian-speaking Narva, which reflects the reality that many Russian-speakers still function in a monolingual environment. The Council of Europe's Commission against Racism and Intolerance (ECRI) has recommended that language-teaching efforts need to be redoubled in areas where daily exposure to Estonian is still quite low.[102]

The Estonian-language media reported more favourably on the *InterEst* project than did the Russian-language media, according to Media Monitoring 2001.[103] As with the

---

[100] The total budget for the project is EEK 3,106,307 (€198,528), drawn from the State budget resources (EEK 171,307) and external assistance funds (EEK 2,935,000) from the Integration Foundation.

[101] OÜ SaarPoll, *Interest kampaania mõju uuring* (Feedback survey on campaign Interest), Tallinn, 2000.

[102] ECRI, *Second Report on Estonia*, p. 9.

[103] *Media Monitoring 2002*, pp. 100, 105.

language camps and family exchange projects, the results of each project have been publicised through press releases, and there is information about the reimbursement scheme available on the Integration Foundation web site.[104]

Again, the project was subject to both mid-term and final evaluation by international teams under the Nordic/UK/UNDP programme.

Advertising campaigns promoting language studies were quite successful, as the number of people enrolling in language training courses sharply increased during the campaign and immediately after.[105] The last such campaign, "Untie," was intended to have a "shock effect," featuring pictures of people with gagged mouths. Managed and carried out by an entirely Russian-speaking team, the campaign exceeded expectations and brought 6,500 students to language courses within seven months (although the surge in participation may also have been linked to the expiration of language certificates[106]). An Integration Foundation staff officer voiced a typical response to the campaign: "the posters are disgusting and personally I hate them, but they turned out to be extremely effective, so as a coordinator I am totally satisfied with the results."[107]

3.2.2 Employment

As in education, discrimination in the employment sector is not identified as a cause of inequalities between Estonians and non-Estonians in the Integration Programme. Estonian language proficiency is a prerequisite for access to employment in certain sectors, both public and private, and indirectly related to access to employment in areas outside regions where the Russian language predominates. The Programme again focuses on Estonian language training as a means to increase access, although some legal provisions in turn restrict opportunities for those without fluency in Estonian.

The unequal position of non-Estonians in the labour market is a consequence of several factors, including structural changes to move the Estonian labour market away from Soviet-style production, inequality of regional development, which has especially affected Northeast Estonia, lack of Estonian citizenship among minorities, and insufficient proficiency in the State language. It is therefore difficult to establish that inequalities in levels of employment are caused by discrimination, which is officially

---

[104] <http://www.meis.ee/eng/index.html>.
[105] Interview with H. Hinsberg, Integration Foundation expert, Tallinn, 28 March 2002.
[106] OSI Roundtable, Tallinn, June 2002.
[107] Interview with H. Hinsberg, Integration Foundation expert, Tallinn, 28 March 2002.

prohibited on any grounds by the Employment Contract Act of 1992.[108] There have been no reports of cases related to employment discrimination in the Estonian Labour Disputes Resolution Commission, nor has the National Labour Inspectorate made any findings of discrimination in the workplace.[109]

The Language Law requires proficiency in the Estonian language for certain private-sector professions, on the basis of "justified public interest."[110] ECRI's 2001 Report on Estonia notes that the categories are rather vague and implementation of this provision may lead to discrimination as "employers may in some cases prefer to hire Estonian mother-tongue speakers or even to dismiss non-Estonian speaking employees to avoid difficulties in respect of the law."[111] Domestic observers have raised similar concerns.[112] Draft amendments to the Language Law currently under development by the Ministries of Education and Justice include provisions intended to ensure that the level of language ability required for each profession corresponds to the real demand in practice.[113]

Few projects implemented under the Integration Programme have an impact on employment inequalities, and these initiatives generally focus on the linguistic dimension. Improving workers' language skills is intended to promote greater labour flexibility and mobility among minorities, giving Russian-speakers more opportunities to work outside the specific industries in which they have traditionally been employed.

A representative of the Confederation of Estonian Trade Unions (hereafter, EAKL) acknowledged the unequal position of Russian-speakers in the labour market, but attributed these inequalities not to ethnic discrimination, but to a decline in the economic activities in which most Russian-speakers were employed during the Soviet period.[114] Thus, trade unions do not consider it necessary to emphasise the ethnic

---

[108] The Employment Contract Act, State Gazette 1992, 15/16/241, Article 10. See <http://www.legaltext.ee/et/andmebaas/tekst.asp?dok=X1056K5&keel=en>, (accessed 15 April 2002).

[109] V. Poleshchuk, *Legal Analysis of National and European Anti-Discrimination Legislation: Estonia.* European Roma Rights Centre; Interights; Migration Policy Group, Brussels, 2002, p. 18.

[110] Law on Language, Amendment published RT I 2000, 51, 326. Art. 2. The definition relates to jobs involving public order, healthcare, protection of consumers' rights, and workplace safety, *inter alia*.

[111] ECRI *Second Report on Estonia,* p. 9.

[112] See European Centre for Minority Issues, *Social Dimension of Integration in Estonia and Minority Education in Latvia,* December 2001, p. 5.

[113] Interview with Mailis Rand, Minister of Education, Tallinn, 4 April 2002.

[114] Interview with Harry Taliga, Social Secretary of Confederation of Estonian Trade Unions (EAKL), Tallinn, 9 April 2002.

dimension of unemployment. Where larger enterprises have remained in operation after denationalisation, Russian-speaking workers still predominate and their trade union organisations are much stronger than these of ethnic Estonian workers: on average, trade unions unite 12 to 15 percent of employees nation-wide, while Russian-speaking workers from Ida-Viru county alone make up one-quarter of EAKL members. A Union representative also acknowledged that some plants owned by foreign (Western) companies often use unlawful temporary contracts to hire employees, which leave them without any social guarantees in case of the enterprise's restructuring or closure.[115] Once again Russian-speakers, especially women, are at a disadvantage. Despite the fact that Estonian labour policies have come under considerable scrutiny as a result of the EU accession process, Estonia has not ratified those ILO conventions (especially Convention 111) that would increase the implementation of the principle of equal opportunities on the Estonian labour market.[116]

Data on the 2000 labour force released by the Statistical Office bear out several conclusions regarding minority employment. Non-Estonians do participate in all economic spheres, although their role is especially important in several economic sectors. Minorities are underrepresented at the highest levels of public and private industry, especially in public administration and defence, as well as in the social security administration.[117]

The ethnic division of labour includes significant elements of social inequality; in view of this, some policy-makers have noted that it is necessary to shift the focus of the Integration Programme to concentrate more precisely on the social aspect of integration in planning future integration measures.[118] The Advisory Committee on the FCNM noted in its Proposal for conclusions and recommendations by the Committee of Ministers "that there remain shortcomings as concerns the effective participation of persons belonging to national minorities in economic life, in particular with respect to their access to the labour market," and "recommends that Estonia pursue decisively its efforts to alleviate such shortcomings."[119] Language instruction, while an important element in promoting employment opportunities, is only one

---

[115] Interview with Harry Taliga, Tallinn, 9 April 2002.

[116] See *Monitoring the EU Accession Process: Equal Opportunities for Women and Men in Estonia*, Open Society Institute, Budapest, 2002 (forthcoming).

[117] 2.6% of total employed ethnic Russians are employed in these sectors, as compared with 7.7 percent of ethnic Estonians or 14.4 percent of the total group. Employers among ethnic Estonians constitute 3.3 percent (with 7.7 percent self-employed), and among non-Estonians, 2.5 percent (self-employed 2.8 percent). Statistical Office of Estonia, *Labour Force 2000*, Tallinn, 2001, pp. 163, 165, 167.

[118] Interviews with: Katrin Saks, former Minister for Population and Ethnic Affairs, Tallinn, 1 April 2002; Tiit Sepp, Deputy Chancellor of the Ministry of Interior, Tallinn, 1 April 2002.

[119] FCNM Advisory Committee, *2001 Opinion on Estonia*, p. 24.

dimension of unequal employment opportunities. Coupling Estonian language instruction with additional measures, such as job retraining, could increase the efficacy of the Programme as a whole, particularly among older non-Estonians for whom existing integration measures have been less attractive.[120]

Projects implemented under the Integration Programme in the employment sphere have included:

Labour Force Exchange

Several two to three-week labour force mobility projects was carried out in Spring 2000.[121] Police officials from Ida-Viru County, medical staff from Kohtla-Järve and library staff from Sillamäe were assigned to positions in different regions of Estonia (Saare, Lääne, Võru, Põlva and Viljandi counties). The project participants lived with ethnic Estonian families and conducted their everyday work in an Estonian-language environment. The project was intended to facilitate language acquisition for non-Estonians, and to promote cultural exchange between ethnic groups. These goals, in turn, were intended to promote greater work-force mobility for minorities.

For the project efficiency assessment, an expert group comprised of representatives of minorities, NGOs, and state and local government officials examined reports and spoke with project participants and employers. A three-member evaluation team, including one minority representative, prepared the final evaluation report.

The projects received some modest media attention, which was generally favourable in both the Estonian and Russian-language media. Efforts to publicise the project were made through press releases and the Integration Foundation web site.

Over 60 persons have received language teaching and specialised practical training through the exchange project. According to the evaluation team, the project was well-organised and efficiently administered. However, the assessors pointed out that the major challenge to the project's effectiveness was the lack of a formal mechanism for participants to retain and improve their Estonian after they return to a predominantly Russian-language environment.[122] It is also unclear if a sufficient number of job opportunities outside of Ida-Viru County will indeed become available for those who have taken part in the project and whether those individuals would be willing and able to take advantage of such opportunities.[123] Therefore, either the goal or the method of

---

[120] See *Mid-term evaluation of social integration projects in Estonia*, p. 15.

[121] The total cost of the project was EEK 744,000 (approximately €47,550), supplied by the external assistance funds of the Integration Foundation.

[122] *Final Evaluation of the Nordic/UK/UNDP Project*, p. 26.

[123] *Final Evaluation of the Nordic/UK/UNDP Project*, p. 26.

stimulating large-scale employee mobility throughout Estonia with this activity should perhaps be reconsidered as scant evidence exists to suggest that this will actually occur.

Training Officials from Ida-Viru County

Public sector officials from the predominantly Russian-speaking area of Ida-Viru received a two-day course on conflict management, as part of a capacity-building initiative for the region.[124] An evaluation found that the trainers "did not seem to possess a balanced view of the working circumstances of the trainees," and had unrealistic expectations of their skills, and the project was therefore not as useful as expected.[125]

3.2.3 Housing and other goods and services

Some social factors that are often closely correlated to ethnicity, such as income or employment, have an impact on inequalities in the housing sector. Following denationalisation reforms, over 90 percent of housing is privately owned. However, research indicates that the high number of minorities without Estonian citizenship may have had limited their possibilities to influence the privatisation process, placing them in a disadvantaged position in obtaining housing.[126]

The Integration Programme only briefly refers to housing problems, as an objective to be addressed within the sub-programme "Social Competence."[127] However, no measures have been taken in regard to the issue.

3.2.4 Healthcare and other forms of social protection

The system of social protection is based on the principle that State support is given to all legal residents regardless of citizenship status. The increasing cost of healthcare services, lack of human resources and an increasing proportion of services operated by the private sector are problems for society at large. Again, minorities are often disproportionately affected by these factors due to their over-representation in vulnerable groups, such as residents of depressed regions, the unemployed, and the

---

[124] *Final Evaluation of the Nordic/UK/UNDP Project*, p. 25.

[125] *Final Evaluation of the Nordic/UK/UNDP Project*, p. 25.

[126] See *Minority Protection 2001*, p. 203.

[127] Integration Programme, p. 59.

poor.[128] Those people who have not acquired a residency permit since Estonia regained its independence in 1991 are at a special disadvantage.

In the "social competence" sub-programme, the Integration Programme refers to the problems of groups at social risk among ethnic minorities.[129] Among the goals of the sub-programme are the guarantee of care and a favourable environment for the abandoned children of minority individuals, family counselling, and the guarantee of social services to handicapped non-Estonians. However, few measures have been taken to implement these goals. Youth at risk have been especially targeted by some of the language camp and family exchange projects, and counselling and after-school activities are available.[130]

3.2.5 The criminal justice system

The Integration Programme does not address the criminal justice system. Discrimination in this sphere is not widely reported by NGOs or minority groups. Non-Estonians are disproportionately represented among prison populations, while ethnic Estonians are twice as likely to be sentenced to parole compared with ethnic minorities.[131]

There are no countrywide statistics for representation of minorities in the police, and the Police Department could only provide data on Tallinn and Narva for the beginning of 2001. In Tallinn, approximately 50 percent and in Narva 94 percent of the police officers graduated from Russian-language schools or universities, although the vast majority of these officers (91 percent) are fluent in Estonian.[132] ECRI has noted that measures exist to ensure minority applicants for the police force are not at a disadvantage due to the fact they speak Estonian as a second language.[133]

---

[128] ECRI, *Second Report on Estonia*, p. 19.

[129] Integration Programme, p. 59.

[130] *Government Report 2000*, p. 19

[131] V. Poleshchuk, *Social Dimension of Integration in Estonia and Minority Education in Latvia*, European Centre for Minority Issues, December 2001, p. 9.

[132] Interview with N. Veber, Police Department press secretary, Tallinn, 7 April 2002.

[133] ECRI, *Second Report on Estonia*, p. 18.

3.3 Protection from Racially Motivated Violence

The Integration Programme does not analyse or make recommendations concerning racially motivated violence, although it does identify the possibility of interethnic conflict:

> It is important to recognise that integration does not rule out contradictions and conflicts, since the social harmonisation of society and the preservation of differences are often conflicting processes. In this sense openness and tolerance towards differences is one of the principal challenges for Estonian society as a whole.[134]

The overall approach of the Integration Programme is therefore focused on promoting tolerance rather than providing specific measures against racially motivated violence. (See Section 3.2)

Racially motivated violence is addressed by several legal instruments, including the Constitution. In recent years, several cases of violence have occurred that appeared to have an inter-ethnic dimension, including a conflict in Paldiski between members of the Estonian Defence Forces and local people on 23–24 August 2001,[135] and in the regions of Tallinn (Lasnamäe, Õismäe) and Ida-Viru County between Estonian and Russian-speaking schoolchildren during October-November 2001.[136] The Government publicly condemned all these events; in Tallinn an official investigation was carried out. There are still disagreements over whether these were conflicts occurred on the basis of inter-ethnic tensions or due to other, unrelated factors.

There is no unanimous view on the impact of racially motivated violence among the population. On the one hand, the results of the Integration Programmes' General Monitoring 2000[137] indicated that only seven percent of ethnic Estonian and non-Estonian-speaking respondents had personally been involved in even non-violent conflicts on ethnic grounds. Yet more than one-third of Estonian-speaking respondents and nearly half of non-Estonian-speaking respondents reported witnessing conflict on ethnic grounds quite frequently.[138]

---

[134] Integration Programme, p. 14.

[135] See *Media Monitoring 2002*, p. 29.

[136] See *Media Monitoring 2002*, pp. 79–80.

[137] General Monitoring was commissioned by the Integration Foundation to analyse the impact of the Integration Programme in society.

[138] I. Pettai, "Tolerance of Estonians and non-Estonians," in M. Lauristin and R. Vetik (eds), *Integration in Estonian society: monitoring 2000*, IISS, Tallinn, 2000, p. 8. See <http://www.meis.ee/eng/monitoring/Iris.rtf>, (accessed 15 April 2002), (hereafter, "Tolerance of Estonians and non-Estonians").

For both Estonians and non-Estonians, confrontations are most likely to occur in public places and in the media. Ethnic Estonians cited the street and shops as the scene of most ethnic confrontation, while for non-Estonians, conflicts are also perceived to occur in contacts with governmental institutions.[139] However, the conflicts or harassment mentioned both by Estonians and non-Estonians relate to verbal insults. As both ethnic Estonians and minorities noted only isolated instances of ethnic conflict, one author has concluded that there is no general perception that hostility or discriminatory attitudes are pervasive in society.[140]

Given the generally peaceful relations among ethnic groups, several minority organisations have expressed concern in relation to the recent more violent events mentioned above. A comprehensive analysis of different approaches was carried out by the Media Monitoring project in 2001.[141] In the Paldiski case, the events were described similarly in both Estonian and Russian-language media. However, opinions as to the cause of the event were quite different. To a greater extent than in the Russian media, the Estonian-language print media characterised the event primarily as the result of drunken and unruly behaviour. Both Estonian and Russian-language media accused the Estonian Defence Forces of failing to enforce strict rules of behaviour in the armed forces. On the general level, moreover, both Estonian and Russian-language media also observed the inefficiency and lack of detail in the Integration Programme as a negative factor that had contributed to the conditions in which such events might take place.[142]

3.4 Promotion of Minority Rights

The Integration Programme recognises the preservation of a separate ethnic identity as one of the overarching principles of integration, and elaborates a number of measures in several spheres to enhance this principle. Issues in these spheres are a high priority for the Russian-speaking community, but have been accorded lower priority in actual implementation. State-funded primary education is widely available in Russian, but smaller minorities have struggled to find the means for mother-tongue instruction. Concerns have also arisen over the continued availability of Russian-language education at the secondary level. Obstacles to the acquisition of citizenship, implementation of the National Minorities Cultural Autonomy Act, and other barriers to participation in public life are addressed by the text of the Programme, but funding for such measures remains

---

[139] I. Pettai, "Tolerance of Estonians and non-Estonians," p. 8.
[140] I. Pettai, "Tolerance of Estonians and non-Estonians," p. 8.
[141] See *Media Monitoring 2002*, pp. 29–40.
[142] See *Media Monitoring 2002*, p. 39.

low. The legal reforms called for by some minority representatives are explicitly beyond the scope of the Programme and have not been addressed systematically outside the Programme's framework, but rather on an *ad hoc* basis.

A main principle of the Integration Programme is the recognition of the cultural rights of ethnic minorities. The Program calls for "enabling of the preservation of ethnic differences" by establishing the societal conditions in which individuals who are interested in preserving and cultivating their ethnic identity may do so.[143] This objective is primarily addressed through the sub-programme "the education and culture of ethnic minorities," which has three components:

- increasing awareness among the population of cultural plurality and tolerance;
- increasing cooperation between the Estonian State and ethnic minority organisations;
- promoting and protecting ethnic minority identity through language, education, and cultural development.[144]

The sub-programme was only introduced as the result of proposals from the President's Roundtable on Minorities;[145] the relevance of this dimension of integration has been consistently highlighted by minority organisations. However, State investment in these sub-programmes has been far lower than for linguistic projects. In 2000, spending on sub-programme I, "Education," totalled more than EEK 36 million (approximately €2.3 million); for sub-programme II, "the Education and Culture of Ethnic Minorities" the total was just over EEK 3.5 million (approximately €226,000).[146] The number of projects elaborated in the Education and Adult Language Education components is also significantly higher. Most funds allocated under the "education and culture of ethnic minorities" sub-programme have gone to support ethnic minority cultural organisations, including Sunday schools.

Estonia has a diverse population, with a reported 142 nationalities and 109 mother tongues.[147] However, 97 percent of the population speaks either Russian or Estonian as a mother tongue, with only two percent naming one of the other 107 as their first language. Russian is the first language of 29.7 percent of the population.

---

[143] Integration Programme, p. 15.
[144] Integration Programme, pp. 37–42.
[145] See Section 2.2.
[146] *Government Report 2000*, pp. 21–41.
[147] Statistical Office of Estonia 2000. *Population and Housing Census II*, pp.13–14, Tallinn, 2001.

Table 1 Distribution of minority population of Estonia by mother tongue

Nationality	Total population	*Percentage speaking as mother tongue*		
		Native language	Estonian	Russian
Russians	351,178	98.2	1.4	
Ukrainians	29,012	41.1	0.2	56.8
Byelorussians	17,241	28.7	0.0	69.7
Finns	11,837	38.5	31.3	29.8
Tatars	2,582	47.6	0.0	50.1
Latvians	2,330	53.3	8.9	36.9
Poles	2,193	24.6	6.1	61.0
Jews	2,145	5.8	11.6	80.6
Lithuanians	2,116	54.2	0.9	40.1
Others	19,199	25.8	6.2	30.6

Source: 2000 Population and Housing Census II, 2001: 151.

A long-standing concern has been the National Minorities Cultural Autonomy Act, which was adopted by Parliament in 1993 as a mechanism for national minorities to protect and promote their ethnic identities.[148] According to the Act, Germans, Russians, Swedes, Jews and other minority groups with over 3,000 members living in Estonia are guaranteed the right to form cultural self-governments, which can act to preserve their mother tongue, ethnic affiliation, cultural traditions, and religion.[149]

However, the Act has yet to be implemented, due to concerns of both majority and minority groups. Minority representatives have charged that the approach could lead to the "privatisation" of minority life, whereby responsibilities for mother-tongue education and cultural activities would be shifted away from the State to minority organisations. Also, some observers have noted that this strategy of authorising parallel institutions could potentially give rise to the territorial autonomy of Northeast Estonia and the

---

[148] Available at
<http://www.minelres.lv/NationalLegislation/Estonia/Estonia_KultAut_English.htm>, (accessed 2 October 2002).

[149] National Cultural Autonomy Act of 1993, Art. 5 (1). The main functions of cultural self-governments are the organisation and administration of funds for mother tongue instruction; forming minority cultural institutions and the organisation of their activities; the organisation of ethnic cultural events; and the creation and allocation of funds for the advancement of the culture and education of minorities.

federalisation of the country. In fact, only Russians, Ukrainians, Byelorussians, and Finns are numerous enough to meet the current population threshold requirement. Some observers have suggested that the Act should also apply to non-citizens.[150] Furthermore, the Act specifies no commitment from the State with regard to funding for these bodies. Efforts have been made to revise the Act to address some of these perceived shortcomings, but no resolution proposed so far has found consensus.[151]

The Integration Programme recognises the need to review the Act with a view towards adapting it to the needs of minorities interested in the promotion of their cultural identity, and to reduce bureaucratic barriers hindering groups from establishing cultural self-governments.[152] The lack of a coordinating body[153] to take the initiative to re-draft the Act may have contributed to the present inactivity. The Advisory Committee on the FCNM has also recommended that the Government should pursue some revision of the Cultural Autonomy Act.[154] Greater attention to this element of the Integration Programme could demonstrate the Government's willingness to address the minority population's outstanding concerns, and help to build confidence in the Programme.

3.4.1 Education

Formal State-funded education is available from primary to high-school level in Estonian and Russian languages. As the number of speakers of each of the other minority languages is very small (see Table above), extra-curricular Sunday schools have been the main medium for the development of teaching these minority languages and cultures.

It has been observed that even though pre-school is not obligatory and is fee-based,[155] the right to Estonian-language pre-school education is guaranteed by law, while no such provision exists for students whose mother tongue is not Estonian.[156] In the

---

[150] See CERD, *Concluding observations of the Committee on the Elimination of Racial Discrimination*. 19 April 2000. See <http://www.unhchr.ch/tbs/doc.nsf/(Symbol)/CERD.C.304.Add.98.En?Opendocument>, (accessed 15 April 2002).

[151] ECRI, *Second Report on Estonia*, p. 10.

[152] Integration Programme, p. 40.

[153] Possibly the Ministry of Culture or the Minister for Population and Ethnic Affairs.

[154] FCNM Advisory Committee, *2001 Opinion on Estonia*, p. 20.

[155] ECRI, *Second Report on Estonia*, p. 17.

[156] See *Minority Protection 2001*, pp. 196–197.

2000/2001 school year, there were 100 Russian-language comprehensive schools and 19 schools with mixed languages of instruction (mainly Russian).

On 26 March 2002, the Parliament approved amendments to Sections 3 and 9 of the Basic Schools and Upper Secondary Schools Act permitting the continuation of Russian-language instruction in the Russian-language general secondary schools ("gymnasiums") owned by a local government after the year 2007. This was the result of a long debate regarding the reform of Russian-language gymnasiums owned by state or local governments.[157] In particular, the President's Roundtable on Minorities discussed this issue in several meetings in 2001 and 2002. The amendment will mainly concern Russian-language gymnasiums in Tallinn and Northeast Estonia.[158] However, there are reports that the availability of Russian-language instruction continues to decline, especially in areas with more mixed populations where the numbers of Russian-speaking students are decreasing.[159]

For numerically smaller minorities, mother-tongue education has been confined primarily to programmes outside of school, although there have been efforts to open private schools with mixed success due to the low numbers of students and lack of funding.[160] There has been continuous discussion among minorities regarding the need to improve the quality of teaching and facilities in Sunday schools, many of which are reportedly limiting their activities due to a lack of resources.[161]

Currently the Ministry of Education and the State-level associations of ethnic minorities are developing a new model for extra-curricular language instruction in minority languages. In addition to this, the Ministry of Education has proposed the

---

[157] The issue of reduction of Russian as a language of instruction at schools concerned also the Committee on the Elimination of Racial Discrimination (CERD). See CERD, *Concluding observations of the Committee on the Elimination of Racial Discrimination.* 19 April 2000.

[158] MP Mihhail Stalnuhhin estimated that it would concern approximately 30 gymnasiums in the North-East of Estonia. See ETA uudis, *"Gümnaasiumides säilivad venekeelsed klassid"* (ETA news, Russian-language classes will remain in gymnasiums), Internet portal *Delfi*, 26 March 2002. See <http://www.delfi.ee/archive/article.php?id=3342594&ndate=1017093600&categoryID=120>, (accessed 15 April 2002).

[159] For example, the local authorities decided to not continue Russian-language instruction in the secondary school in Räpina, *Molodjezh Estonii*, 12 June 2002.

[160] The first ethnic comprehensive school to be re-opened was the Tallinn Jewish School opened in 1990 in Tallinn, which in 1999 was attended by 260 pupils in 12 forms. A Ukrainian class also temporarily operated at the Tallinn 48th Secondary School. See Government of Estonia, *Report "Integrating Estonia 1997–2000,"* Tallinn, 2001. See: <http://www.meis.ee/eng/rtf/report_integrating_estonia.rtf>, (accessed 15 April 2002).

[161] OSI Round Table, Tallinn, June 2002.

possibility of developing mother tongue education in the form of "hobby schools" (private extra-curricular institutions).

The second on-going development concerns Section 2 of the Basic Schools and Upper Secondary Schools Act, according to which conditions shall be created for the study of the mother tongue for minority students at Estonian-language schools, with the aim of preserving their ethnic identity. The initial draft of this regulation was introduced at the President's Roundtable on Minorities on 2 April 2002.[162] The proposed amendment would permit schools to apply for an extension of the transition period to Estonian-language instruction, first to the local authorities and later to the Government. This approach may not offer a stable institutional framework for continued Russian-language instruction in gymnasiums, however, as extensions are contingent upon the authorities' good will rather than a legal guarantee.

Although the Integration Programme expresses the intent to develop awareness of Estonia as a multicultural state,[163] there have been concerns that this approach has not been adequately reflected in mainstream curricula. Minority organisation have emphasised the importance of changing the curriculum at higher educational institutions to take into account Estonia's cultural plurality, and to improve the quality of translation from Estonian to Russian and *vice versa*, especially in textbooks.[164]

3.4.2 Language

The Integration Programme does not identify priorities or objectives related to the use of minority languages with public authorities, on public signs, in names and surnames, and during judicial proceedings, although these issues have been especially contentious. The 1995 Language Law regulates the use of languages other than Estonian in the public sphere; the Law has been amended in response to domestic and international criticism, but concerns remain that its measures are excessive in relation to its goals.

---

[162] The current version of the draft is supported by the Estonian Union of National Minorities. Interview with Jaak Prozes, the President of the Union of National Minorities of Estonia, Tallinn, 3 April 2002. On the other hand, it has been criticised by the Estonian Federation of Associations of Ethnic Cultural Societies "Lüüra."

[163] Integration Programme, p. 12.

[164] *Eesti ühiskonna integratsiooniprogrammi põhiseisukohad. Lisa Riigikogu Eestimaa Ühendatud Rahvapartei kirjale peaminister Mart Laarile* (Basic principles of the Estonian integration programme. Annex to the letter of the Estonian United People's Party of the Parliament to Prime Minister Mart Laar), No 3–6/224, 8 March 2000, (hereafter, "Annex to EUPP letter to Prime Minister Laar").

Some of the restrictions in the Law have sparked public controversy. For example, in Autumn 2001 the local government in Narva submitted an open letter opposing the planned closure of the local OSCE Mission, citing restrictions on the use of Russian in local government meetings as its main arguments. As cited in the official response to this complaint, the Language Law only permits minority languages to be used in local government meetings where more than half the local population belongs to an ethnic minority and use of the State language is also guaranteed. The Language Inspection Board asserts that the second requirement has not yet been met in Narva.[165]

According to the Government, the Language Law was amended in early 2002 to allow persons unable to communicate with authorities in Estonian to use a "foreign language familiar to those officers or employees by agreement of the parties."[166] This amendment, reportedly introduced to reflect a process already informally accepted, permits all State and local government bodies to accept written or oral communications in languages other than Estonian, not only those in regions where minorities comprise at least a half of population.[167]

The second issue is related to the requirement in Article 23 of the Language Law that provides that public signs, signposts, announcements, notices, and advertisements shall be in Estonian. In their proposal to the Prime Minister, the Estonian United People's Party proposed that the use of languages of national minorities should be permitted for public information in regions where non-Estonians comprise at least 25 percent of the local population.[168] The Advisory Committee on the FCNM has also noted that,

> [Article 23] is so wide in its scope that it hinders the implementation of the rights of persons belonging to national minorities, especially since the term "public" appears in this context to encompass also a range of information provided by private actors and since the obligation to use Estonian is largely interpreted as excluding the additional use of a minority language.[169]

The Government has maintained that its restrictions on the use of languages other than Estonian have been within the acceptable parameters of public security, public order, public administration, public health, health protection, consumer protection and occupational safety since amendments were adopted in 2000.[170]

---

[165] "Linguistic competence and communicative capabilities of Russians in Estonia," p. 37.
[166] *Government Comments on FCNM Advisory Committee 2001 Opinion*, p. 11.
[167] Language Law, Art. 8, pp. 1, 2, 4.
[168] Annex to EUPP letter to Prime Minister Laar.
[169] FCNM Advisory Committee 2001 *Opinon on Estonia*, para. 43, p. 12.
[170] *Government Comments on FCNM Advisory Committee 2001 Opinion*, pp. 11–12.

3.4.3 Participation in public life

A primary goal of the Integration Programme is to develop a greater sense of citizenship and loyalty to Estonia among minorities. Achievement of this goal has been limited by the fact that many Russian-speakers still lack residency permits or citizenship. Obstacles to the regularisation of residency status have restricted the degree to which the Russian-speaking population can take part in public life, particularly beyond the local level. In addition, linguistic requirements for public office restricted the number of Russian speakers eligible for candidacy until these requirements were abolished in early 2002.[171]

The Integration Programme provides only a description of problems and objectives regarding cooperation between the State and minorities in the sphere of promotion of ethnic identity. The issues of participation in elections and in decision-making bodies on local, regional and national governmental levels and representation in public service have not been analysed to a large extent.

Considering their percentage of the voting population, non-Estonians are underrepresented at both the Parliamentary and local government level.[172] For the first time after 1992, in 2002 one non-Estonian was included in the cabinet. Nevertheless, in 2001 Russian-speakers made up only nine percent of all judges, six percent of officers within the Ministry of Internal Affairs;[173] there were no Russian-speakers working as officials in the Ministries of Justice or Education.[174]

The participation level of non-citizens in Estonian public and political life has dropped steadily: the rate of non-citizens participating in the local elections has changed as follows: 52.6 percent in 1993, 85 percent in 1996, 43 percent in 1999. This change

---

[171] See Section 3.2.

[172] See BNS Valimised (BNS Elections) at <http://valimised.bns.ee/>. Local representation was calculated on the basis of the data of web-site *Kohaliku omavalitsuse volikogude valimine* (Results of the Municipal Elections 1999 by Counties) of the Estonian National Electoral Committee. See <http://www.vvk.ee/k99/tulemus.stm>, (accessed 15 April 2002).

[173] Calculated on the basis of the web-site *Ametnike haridus* (Educational level of officials) of the Ministry of Internal Affairs, see
<http://www.sisemin.gov.ee/ministeerium/ametnike_haridus.htp>, (accessed 15 April 2002). Confirmed in interview with Maia Burlaka, Domestic Affairs Ministry press-secretary, Tallinn, 24 March 2002.

[174] Calculated on the basis of the web-site of the Ministry of Justice. See <http://www.just.ee>, (accessed 15 April 2002) and <http://www.hm.ee>, (accessed 24 May 2002).

partly reflects a broader trend in electoral behaviour: the participation rate of citizens has also decreased from 60 percent in 1993 to 49 percent in 1999.[175]

Two projects have components intended to increase minorities' level of participation in public life.

Citizenship and Migration Board Assessment and Activity

As only citizens have full access to political participation at all levels, projects enhancing the work of offices handing citizenship issues have an important role in improving minority access to public participation. One such project was undertaken from November 1998 to November 2001, with a total budget of €39,383, provided by the Nordic/UK/UNDP project. It was coordinated entirely by ethnic Estonians and included the following activities:

- *Analysis of Citizenship and Migration Board (CMB) activities*: Two Estonian sociologists monitored the opinions and complaints of the CMB, revealing that there were serious problems with internal service and client information.[176]

- *Training sessions:* 250 civil servants were trained in customer service, Russian as a foreign language, the development of managerial skills, and the integration process. Training for another 250 civil servants was financed by the CMB itself. The evaluation suggested that the training courses benefited from well-designed feedback mechanisms that solicited input from participants, giving a clear understanding of which topics to include in future training courses.[177]

- *Russian Language Citizenship Information:* 10,000 copies of bilingual leaflets providing an overview of various CMB departments and activities were printed in February 2000. Another 10,000 leaflets explaining to ex-Soviet military officers how to apply for a residency permit extension were printed in February 2001. Additionally, another nine information leaflets were published in August-September 2001, outlining the rules for acquiring various necessary identification documents.

- *Legalising Residential Status*: The CMB carried out the project "Informing and legalising recipients of social benefits or pensions who are illegally residing in the Republic of Estonia." 3,024 people were targeted during the project, of whom 81 percent now possess the necessary documents, while the others are being processed.

---

[175] Estonian National Electoral Committee, *Valimised ja referendumid Eestis 1989–1999* (Elections and Referendums in Estonia 1989–1999). See <http://www.vvk.ee/english/overview.html#lgce99>, (accessed 15 April 2002).

[176] *Mid-term evaluation of social integration projects in Estonia*, pp. 36–37.

[177] *Final Evaluation of the Nordic/UK/UNDP Project*, p. 28.

Coverage of these initiatives in the media was limited to reporting that the projects were carried out. There was positive public feedback on the bilingual leaflets. Regular evaluation reports noted that friendly, client-oriented service was essential since the CMB was often the main point of contact in the integration process, for ethnic Estonians and non-Estonians alike.[178] Informally, many non-Estonians agree that the CMB staff has become much more polite and professional than in the first part of the 1990s: clients wait less, the period for issuing documents is shorter, and there is more information available in CMB offices.

Financial support for President's Roundtable on National Minorities

This body, formed in 1993, provides a forum for consultations between different Estonian minority groups and the President of Estonia on issues and initiatives that will have an impact on minorities. The budget of the sub-project for October 1999 – November 2001 was €13,811, provided by the Nordic/UK/UNDP project. The draft Integration Programme was discussed at the Roundtable, and some changes were introduced in response to the proposals of minority representatives. The Roundtable has also allowed for the timely presentation of information on competitions for Integration Programme funding[179]

The results of the work of the Roundtable have been widely discussed in the media and generally received favourably, especially the minority rights legislative initiatives that have emerged from this forum. However, it has been noted that as the Roundtable serves only in an advisory capacity, its influence goes only as far as executive offices choose to defer to its recommendations.[180]

The Roundtable has its own web site (<http://www.president.ee/eng/institutsioonid>), where the majority of international reports on minority rights in Estonia are available. The Nordic/UK/UNDP Final Evaluation Report notes that the Roundtable has

> effectively built bridges between Russian-speaking leaders and Estonian leaders in the legislative and executive offices in the Estonian Government… In addition to making legislative and policy proposals and organising conferences, the Roundtable adds legitimacy to integration since it guarantees an advocate for various Russian-speaking interests at the highest levels of government.[181]

---

[178] *Mid-term evaluation of social integration projects in Estonia*, p. 37.

[179] Integration Foundation, Final report of the project *"Support to the State Programme for Integration of non-Estonians into Estonian Society,"* Tallinn, 2001, p. 27.

[180] ECRI *Second Report on Estonia*, p. 12.

[181] *Final Evaluation of the Nordic/UK/UNDP Project*, p. 29.

The FCNM Advisory Committee recently urged the Estonian Government to increase the Roundtable's influence, noting, "[t]he effectiveness of the Roundtable could [...] be improved if the relevant authorities would consult the said body more consistently when addressing issues falling within its competence."[182]

The results of projects to enhance public participation are analysed in regular evaluation reports, including the annual Integration Foundation report, prepared by ethnically mixed evaluation teams. However, these analysts must rely heavily on the documentation prepared by the Integration Foundation staff, which includes no representatives of minorities.

According to the Integration Foundation Director, the projects planned have been successful overall. The Director attributes projects' success to the Foundation's careful selection process, on the basis of open competition. Nevertheless, he recognised that the respective coordinators predictably evaluate themselves slightly higher than the Integration Foundation administration.[183]

In general it is expected that activities directed to increase public participation of non-Estonians will continue in 2002-2003. €16,125 is earmarked for the CMB in 2002, for use in preparing teaching materials for Russian-language schools, where young people can take a combined Estonian language and citizenship exam.[184] Support to the Presidential Roundtable is also anticipated, but the use of this funding will depend mainly upon the Roundtable's own programme.

3.4.4 Media

The Integration Programme attempts to reach its goal of developing a common cultural domain through the media, *inter alia*. As part of its sub-programme on "social competence," the Programme sets itself the more specific tasks of facilitating integration by using the media to raise public awareness, to ensure the availability of information related to integration to the public at large, and to facilitate the creation of innovative approaches to integration.

In 2002 the Russian-language media included 12 newspapers, a selection of leisure and entertainment periodicals, a public service radio station that also provides monthly transmissions in other minority languages, four private regional stations, several cable television channels with regional coverage, and assorted broadcasts on otherwise

---

[182] FCNM Advisory Committee *2001 Opinion on Estonia*, para. 57, p. 15.
[183] Interview with M. Luik, director of the Integration Foundation, Tallinn, 08 April 2002.
[184] Interview with M. Luik, director of the Integration Foundation, Tallinn, 08 April 2002.

Estonian-language public and private television channels.[185] One of the most popular web-portals, where national issues are discussed, functions in two languages.[186] Some 56 percent of Russian-speakers read some local Russian-language newspapers at least once a week, while 88 percent report listening to local Russian-language radio stations regularly. More than 80 percent watch Russian Federation television channels daily.[187]

Media projects developed under the Integration Programme fall into four broad categories: the media monitoring project, television and radio broadcasts, social tolerance advertising campaigns, and training of journalists. The first two categories are addressed in Section 3.2 of this report; two projects aimed at promoting minority media are described below.[188]

Training of Journalists

One component of the sub-programme "social competence" sets out objectives to improve public awareness of integration issues, and to decrease the use of ethnic stereotypes in the media. Projects intended to improve the capacity and professionalism of the Russian-speaking media were carried out under this heading.

A series of seminars were held in 1999 to 2001, organised and led mainly by experienced Russian-speaking journalists. There were five sessions in 1999 (three of which were held in Northeast Estonia); systematic training for Estonian Television's Russian Studio in 1999-2000; and five more seminars in 2001. 15 to 20 journalists participated in each event, with a total number of participants of 50 to 60 journalists.[189] The seminars were conducted by the Integration Foundation and Russian-speaking editors from Estonian public television, private Channel 2, Tartu University's Narva College, and the Tallinn Pedagogical University. Journalists were

---

[185] Baltic Media Book, *Tallinn–Riga–Vilnius: Baltic Media Facts*, 1999. See also T. Vihalemm "The Informative and Identity Building Significance of Media: the Case of Estonian Russophones," in Lauristin M., Vetik R. (Eds.): *Integration of Estonian Society. Monitoring 2000*, Institute of International and Social Studies, Tallinn, 2000, pp. 44–48.

[186] DELFI, available at <http://www.delfi.ee>, (accessed 22 October 2002).

[187] Integration Foundation, Final report of the project *"Support to the State Programme for Integration of non-Estonians into Estonian Society,"* Tallinn, 2001, p. 40.

[188] Three main sources provided funds to media projects: the Nordic/UK/UNDP project, which contributed approximately €270,000 between 1998 and 2001, Phare, which invested €209,870 in 1999–2001, and Estonian State support, which contributed some €115,000 in 2000. See Integration Foundation, *Integration Foundation Yearbook 2000*, Tallinn, 2001, <http://www.meis.ee/eng/aastaraamat>, (accessed 15 April 2002).

[189] €18,477 from the Nordic/UK/UNDP project grant was allocated for this project between 1998–2001. Integration Foundation, *Final Report of the Project "Support to the State Programme for Integration of non-Estonians into Estonian Society,"* Tallinn, 2001.

expected to gain exposure to a wider range of Estonia-related issues, and a better understanding of professional techniques.

An evaluation commission concluded that the project was "strategically important in regard to the State Programme's goal of redirecting the attention of Russian-speakers away from the media of the Russian Federation and toward that of Estonia" and "helpful in encouraging cooperation across ethnic lines within the media profession throughout Estonia."[190]

Support to Newspapers

Also with the support of the Nordic/UK/UNDP fund, a monthly Russian-language supplement was included with the Estonian-language newspaper for teachers, *Õpetajate Leht*. The Russian articles included translations of school-related legislation, and other items from the Estonian paper related to schools and education. The rest of the supplement is dedicated to issues specific to Russian-language schools.[191]

The Government has been critical of its own efforts in the media sphere. In its report on implementation in 2000, the Government observed that "the potential of the Russian-language media in the area of [...] integration [...] remains largely unused, due to the low viewership of programmes. The reason for this is the lack of financing for Russian-language television and isolation from its viewership."[192] It remains to be seen whether additional financing for such projects can help to realise the media's potential.

3.4.5 Culture

The Integration Programme clearly states that Estonia is a multicultural society, albeit one in which Estonian culture has a special status in relation to the State.[193] While the Programme provides for minorities' cultural development opportunities, funding has been dramatically lower for the sub-programme on "education and culture of minorities" than for the education and adult Estonian language education sub-programmes.[194] The Integration Programme points out that,

> in the case of the education and cultural life of ethnic minorities, the initiative and responsibility lie with the ethnic minority itself through the

---

[190] *Report of the Final Evaluation of the Nordic/UK/UNDP Project*, p. 32.

[191] *Report of the Final Evaluation of the Nordic/UK/UNDP Project*, p. 31.

[192] *Government Report*, p. 64.

[193] Integration Programme, p. 15.

[194] *Government Report 2000*, pp. 21–41.

activities of the cultural self-government, and the role of the state is above all one of creating and supporting corresponding opportunities.[195]

However, as implementation of the Cultural Autonomy Act has not begun, the Government continues to oversee allocation of funds for minorities' cultural activities.

From the Ministry of Culture's budget, 89 projects in total were supported in 2000, including 43 from ethnic Russian societies and art groups, eight from ethnic Ukrainian societies, six from ethnic Byelorussian societies, and 32 from other ethnic minorities.[196] 24 projects received support from the Integration Foundation's State budget funds, and another 27 projects received support from external assistance funds.[197]

According to Media Monitoring 2001, projects initiated by cultural societies were of equal interest to the Estonian and Russian-language media. The main recommendation of the evaluation teams was that it is necessary to take measures to ensure the participation of smaller and less experienced national minority organisations that either fail to receive funding or are under the patronage of umbrella groups.[198]

Several minority groups, civil society organisations, and Russian political parties have repeatedly expressed their interest in protecting and developing their unique cultural identity. Among them, the Estonian Union of National Minorities expressed its concern about cultural issues in its proposal to the Minister for Population and Ethnic Affairs, highlighting:

- technical-administrative issues related to lack of funds to pay the rent for rooms or buildings, electricity and other expenses necessary for minority societies to organise events and activities;

- a lack of necessary resources, such as computers and internet access, to introduce their culture and language to the members of their own communities and to the wider community;

- a lack of funds for the development of Sunday schools and establishment of minority (summer) schools;

---

[195] Integration Programme, p. 40.

[196] See Government of Estonia, *Action Plans for Sub-Programmes of State Integration Programme for the years 2000–2003,* Tallinn, 2001.

[197] A total of EEK 2,748,300 (€175,648) was allocated to the programme, including EEK 1,540,000 from the Ministry of Culture, EEK 663,300 from the Integration Foundation state budget funds, and EEK 545,00 from the Integration Foundation external assistance funds (Nordic/UK/UNDP project "Support to the State Integration Programme").

[198] *Final Evaluation Report of the Nordic/UK/UNDP Project,* p. 23.

- a lack of funds for the development of newspapers, televison and radio broadcasts in the mother tongue.[199]

The Estonian United People's Party submitted a proposal for the elaboration of an "alternative" Integration Programme to the Prime Minister on 8 March 2000, to address the perceived low level of societal recognition for ethnic minority cultures. The proposal argued that it is necessary to increase the number of officials working on cultural projects, and to finance the development of ethnic minority cultures. The proposal further suggested that the heritage of ethnic minority cultures should be supported through films, archives, and cultural events of ethnic minorities.[200] However, this proposal did not receive significant public attention and was not discussed further.

Some minority representatives have raised concerns about the level of cooperation between the Estonian State and ethnic minorities, including the low level of inclusion of minorities in implementation schemes at ministries and in the Integration Foundation. Minority representatives have also claimed that the State has demonstrated little interest in developing institutions to facilitate everyday communication with minority organisations.[201]

4. EVALUATION

The Integration Programme has defined three main spheres for the integration of Estonia's Russian-speaking minority: linguistic-communicative, legal-political and socio-economic. In practice, however, only the linguistic-communicative sphere has been fully developed in the Integration Programme's action plans; measures in the education and language sectors receive three-quarters of all funding allocated to Programme integration.[202] This approach follows the priorities defined in the Integration Programme, but rests on the assumption that relevant measures in the fields of legal-political and socio-economic integration should be taken up in the framework of other Government programmes and development plans. Currently only

---

[199] See *Eestimaa Rahvuste Ühenduse presidendi J.Prozese kiri minister Katrin Saksale* (Letter of J. Prozes, the President of the Estonian Union of National Minorities to Minister Katrin Saks), 19 January 2001, No 708.

[200] Annex to EUPP letter to Prime Minister Laar.

[201] Interview with Jaak Prozes, the President of the Union of National Minorities of Estonia, Tallinn, 3 April 2002.

[202] See Government of Estonia, *Action Plans for Sub-Programmes of State Integration Programme for the years 2000–2003,* Tallinn, 2001.

the Foundation Enterprise Estonia is supporting concrete projects aimed at improving the economic situation in Northeast Estonia through the Estonian Regional Development Agency.[203] No other strategies and development plans have included a specific action plan for such supplementary measures, and thus only selected dimensions of integration have been carried out in practice.[204]

The common position among all representatives of minority and civil society organisations is that the elaboration and implementation of the Integration Programme itself is a significant achievement.[205] It has taken strides towards changing attitudes in both Estonian and non-Estonian-speaking communities, developing a more positive understanding of inter-ethnic relations, and greater acceptance of the need for societal integration. The text of the Programme and the formal statements of the Government reflect the affirmative and preventative approach of the strategy, promoting tolerance, cultural plurality, and the preservation of ethnic differences. In implementation, however, concerns remain that the heavy emphasis on the unification of society through the Estonian language will result in a more one-sided process than that promised by the Programme text.

The minority community has identified a number of issues that have been overlooked in implementation of the Integration Programme. These include supporting the education of smaller ethnic minorities in their mother tongue and improving the social status of vulnerable groups such as the unemployed and youth at risk among minority groups. A revised approach for supporting the use of minority languages in the public sphere, accelerating the naturalisation process, and the improvement of the socio-economic situation in predominantly Russian-speaking regions of Estonia have also been called for.[206]

The Government has taken steps to address the legislative issues of greatest concern to minorities: a number of amendments to the Language Law, Aliens Act, and Citizenship Act have been adopted by the Parliament, and several Government regulations in the

---

[203] See the web site of the Estonian Regional Development Agency *Tööstuspiirkondade toetatud projektid 2001* (Supported projects in industrial areas). See <http://www.erda.ee/toostuspiirkondade_toetatud_projektid2001.doc>, (accessed 14 October 2002).

[204] In the case of the National Employment Plan for Ida-Viru Region (approved by the Government in 2001), the relevant action plan is to be elaborated in 2002.

[205] Interviews with A. Semjonov, Director of the Legal Information Centre for Human Rights, Tallinn, 27 March 2002; A. Laius, Director of the Jaan Tõnisson Institute, Tallinn, 9 April 2002; Jaak Prozes, the President of the Union of National Minorities of Estonia, Tallinn, 3 April 2002.

[206] *Riigikogu Eestimaa Ühendatud Rahvapartei kiri peaminister Mart Laarile* (Letter of the Estonian United People's Party of the Parliament to Prime Minister Mart Laar), No 3–6/224, 8 March 2000.

relevant fields have been promulgated in recent years. Although these reforms are essential to the realisation of the Integration Programme's goals, the Programme explicitly rules out the inclusion of a detailed legislative action plan as part of its approach.[207] The process of elaborating these amendments has thus been undertaken by various ministries on an *ad hoc* basis, and in the absence of any coordination or comprehensive plan.[208] Therefore, further progress on the sub-programmes and projects outlined in the Integration Programme is contingent upon good will rather than on a well-planned and coordinated strategy. The highly politicised climate surrounding the legislation in question[209] has prevented the preparation of a more comprehensive strategy for further development. Given these circumstances, a truly comprehensive approach to integration issues, in a manner incorporating measures in all three spheres, has not yet been achieved.

More efforts are needed to develop general public consensus on the basic understanding of the integration process, as minority and majority society retain quite different views on integration and how it should be achieved. Whereas there are no basic disagreements regarding the Integration Programme's main aims, views are more diverse relating to the objectives and measures of its sub-programmes. On the one hand, there are critics who state that all sub-programmes should deal exclusively with the teaching of Estonian to non-Estonian speaking children, youth, and adults, and the improvement of civics education at non-Estonian schools. This approach advocates eliminating existing support for the protection and promotion of minorities' ethnic identity, which in this view should instead be carried out by ethnic minorities themselves, through Government measures outside the Integration Programme.[210] On the other hand, minority representatives have criticised the Integration Programme for concentrating too much on teaching the Estonian language and omitting other aspects of integration.

---

[207] Integration Programme, p. 16.

[208] As an example, there was an attempt to combine the state civics exam for graduates of basic and high schools with an exam required for citizenship, which would make citizenship more accessible to youth. This proposal of the Minister for Population and Ethnic Affairs and Decision of the Government (11 December1999) was not accepted by the Ministry of the Interior and the Ministry of Education, and the relevant exam has not yet been introduced. Interview with Katrin Saks, former Minister for Population and Ethnic Affairs, 1 April 2002.

[209] The Citizenship Act, Language Act, and Aliens Act.

[210] *Riigikogu Isamaaliidu esimehe T. Sinisaare kiri, Isamaaliidu saadikurühma seisukoht riikliku programmi "Integratsioon Eesti ühiskonnas 2000–2007"* suhtes (Letter of T. Sinissaar, the chariman of the Fatherland Union Party faction of the Parliament Position of the Fatherland Union faction of the Parliament in respect of the State Programme "Integration in Estonian society 2000–2007"), 31 January 2000.

Administration and coordination of the Programme function well at the Government level. None of the published reports and evaluations of the Integration Programme has identified any serious problems in efficient and transparent fund management; on the contrary, the work of project staff has been evaluated highly. However, some evaluations have noted that there is insufficient staff to implement complex projects and programmes.[211] Several representatives of minority and civil society organisations have claimed that there is a lack of information available regarding upcoming tenders and the results of project competitions.[212] Moreover, it has been noted that few local programmes have been elaborated as provided for in the Programme; the centralised approach could be balanced by greater attention to regional initiatives.[213]

The Government report on the Integration Programme's implementation in 2000 was published on the Internet and on CD-ROM in June 2001; while examining various aspects of implementation in some detail, the report is apparently not intended to offer proposals for refining or improving future implementation efforts. There has not been any overall evaluation of the Integration Programme since its launch in March 2000. The Integration Programme itself prescribes that evaluations on its effectiveness and efficiency should be commissioned, but so far there have been only evaluations by several external assistance projects.

The Government did not organise a large-scale discussion of the Integration Programme's aims and objectives during its elaboration, as both the minority and majority community expressed a preference for the rapid introduction of concrete projects and their corresponding benefits to individuals over a potentially long and abstract process of debates among scholars and experts. However, the persistent lack of a shared concept of integration policy may also be traced back to the absence of any substantive public debate in the drafting phase. A public discussion of the Integration Programme, moderated by the authorities would be an effective way to achieve consensus among the population in its understanding of the term "integration."[214]

---

[211] M. Hopkins, T. Elenurm, G. Feldman, *Mid-term evaluation of social integration projects in Estonia*, Tallinn, May 2000, p. 4.

[212] *Mid-term evaluation of social integration projects in Estonia*, p. 4.

[213] EAHR Comments.

[214] See J. Kruusvall, "Understanding integration in Estonian society," in M. Lauristin and R. Vetik (eds), *Integration in Estonian society: monitoring 2000*, IISS, Tallinn, 2000, pp. 19–21.

5. RECOMMENDATIONS

General recommendation to all integration-related institutions

- Promote integration projects at the local level, to stimulate the elaboration of regional and municipal sub-programmes in order to help minority groups find their niche in society at the local and community level.

Recommendations to the Government

- Streamline legislative and administrative mechanisms to decrease the number of non-citizens and make naturalisation more accessible for stateless people.

- Elaborate a more comprehensive set of measures to stimulate the inclusion of non-Estonians into public life, and to develop partnership relations between State and local authorities and minorities.

- Reviewing the Cultural Autonomy Act with a view to making amendments to enhance implementation.

Recommendations to State institutions responsible for implementation of the Integration Programme and to the Integration Foundation

- Develop public awareness of racially and ethnically motivated discrimination and violence, and take measures accordingly to prevent and eliminate these phenomena.

- Consider the establishment of a joint general body for governmental and non-governmental institutions to enhance cooperation in the implementation and evaluation of the Integration Programme.

Minority Protection in Hungary

AN ASSESSMENT OF THE MEDIUM-TERM PACKAGE
OF MEASURES TO IMPROVE THE LIVING CONDITIONS
AND SOCIAL POSITION OF THE ROMA IN HUNGARY.

Table of Contents

1. Executive Summary 248
2. The Government Programme – Background 251
   2.1 Background to the Present Programme 251
   2.2 The Programme – Process 253
   2.3 The Programme – Content 254
   2.4 Administration/Implementation/Evaluation 256
   2.5 The Programme and the Public 261
   2.6 The Programme and the EU 262
3. The Government Programme – Implementation 264
   3.1 Stated Objectives of the Programme 264
   3.2 Government Programme and Discrimination 264
       3.2.1 Education 268
       3.2.2 Employment 273
       3.2.3 Housing and other goods and services 276
       3.2.4 Healthcare and other goods and services 278
       3.2.5 The criminal justice system 281
   3.3 Protection from Racially Motivated Violence 281

3.4 Promotion of Minority Rights 283
    3.4.1 Language 283
    3.4.2 Education 284
    3.4.3 Participation in public life 287
    3.4.4 Media 289
    3.4.5 Culture 293

4. Evaluation 293

5. Recommendations 295

1. EXECUTIVE SUMMARY

Current policy towards Roma is based on the 1999 Government programme known as the "Medium-Term Package of Measures to improve the living conditions and social position of the Roma in Hungary" (hereafter, "Medium-Term Package"). Guidelines for a long-term strategy have been prepared, and their adoption in Parliament is expected in 2002.

The Medium-Term Package takes a multi-dimensional approach to improving the situation of the Roma: it acknowledges the importance of preventing discrimination and addressing inequalities, and incorporates measures to enhance the protection of minority rights. However, the coherence of the programme as a whole has been questioned, and uneven implementation has led to concerns regarding the effectiveness of its coordinating bodies. The Government should ensure that policies are developed with the input of both Roma political organisations and civil society groups. While the Government has produced a number of impressive reports and presentations for the international audience, less attention has been devoted to raising awareness of the programme domestically, particularly among relevant local and regional authorities. By continuing to refine and communicate its approach, lasting gains for the Roma community can be achieved, to the mutual benefit of Roma and society at large.

Background

After the change of regime in 1989, several years passed before Government policy began to address the situation of Roma with due emphasis. In 1997 the Government adopted the first Medium-term Package of Measures for improving the situation of Roma.

This package was substantially revised in 1999 to form the current action plan for Government efforts in this area. The updated 1999 Medium-Term Package also highlights the importance of developing a long-term strategy for Roma policy in the future, and guidelines were accordingly drafted, with an emphasis on regional input from public discussions.[1] In May 2001, the Government adopted a decision establishing the guidelines for a long-term programme.[2]

Administration

The Inter-ministerial Committee for Roma Affairs coordinates implementation of the Medium-Term Package. Until Summer 2002, when the Committee was placed under

---

[1] Conferences were held in Békéscsaba, Debrecen, Miskolc, Győr, Szolnok, Pécs, Nagykanizsa and Budapest.

[2] See <http://www.meh.hu/nekh/Angol/guiding.htm>, (accessed 19 September 2002).

the Prime Minister's Office, the Minister of Justice served as Committee president. The Office for National and Ethnic Minorities performs the secretarial duties of the Inter-ministerial Committee and oversees coordination among the bodies concerned.

Individual ministries are responsible for implementing different elements of the programme. Ministries are required to prepare annual action plans and allocate resources from their own budgets accordingly: each ministry must set funding levels for programme activities in its own annual budget, in accordance with its specific responsibilities. However, mechanisms for implementation are not regulated in any further detail, and thus coherent monitoring and reporting processes are neither formalised nor standardised.

Reports made by the ministries are discussed by the Inter-ministerial Committee, which also oversees their performance and evaluates their achievements. Concerns have been raised over the capacity of the Inter-Ministerial Committee to effectively coordinate implementation of the Package, given the failure of most ministries to meet many of the deadlines even for reporting on implementation.[3] It has been suggested that the body charged with coordinating the programme should be placed at the level of a ministry,[4] and vested with authority sufficient to enforce implementation.

EU Support

The EU has emphasised the importance of addressing the situation of the Roma through the Accession Partnership and its Regular Reports. EU funding has been made available for Roma-related projects, especially in the education sector. However, there have been difficulties in utilising funding by specified deadlines, particularly at the local level. Moreover, Roma groups have indicated that the complex application process for Phare support has made it difficult for their organisations to gain access to Phare funding. The process of selecting proposals for funding does not always appear effectively to identify those organisations with a genuine knowledge of or connection with the Roma communities they purport to serve.

Content and Implementation

The terms of the Medium-Term Package are fairly detailed, but in many cases elaborate no specific projects to actively redress existing inequalities or to promote

---

[3] Open Society Institute EU Accession Monitoring Program, *Monitoring the EU Accession Process: Minority Protection*, Budapest 2001, p. 217, (hereafter, *"Minority Protection 2001"*).

[4] OSI Roundtable, Budapest, June 2002. *Explanatory Note: The Open Society Institute held a roundtable meeting in Hungary in June 2002 to invite critique of the present report in draft form. Experts present included representatives of the Government, Roma representatives, and non-governmental organisations.*

minority identity. Its provisions instead call for preliminary research and development of additional, more focused measures.

Hungarian law provides some protection against discrimination, but the system lacks consistency and enforcement has been ineffective. In late 2001, the Government established a new legal aid network to offer counsel and representation to individuals with claims of discrimination. However, civil society representatives have questioned whether the network is in fact structured in such a way as to provide accurate information about discrimination claims, as the Ministry of Justice has asserted. The Medium Term Package acknowledges that discrimination is a problem in many areas of life, but concrete measures to address inequalities are still few, and their approach is sometimes short-sighted, doing little to address such systemic issues as over-reliance on State support and social marginalisation. Implementation has fallen behind schedule, particularly in the health and housing spheres.

Minority rights are recognised in the Medium-Term Package in several spheres, most notably education and public participation. However, implementation of measures in these areas has raised concerns, particularly with respect to the approach of local authorities. Indeed, Roma groups have raised concerns that flaws in the systems for Roma minority education and the formation of the Roma self-government have actually perpetuated inequalities and worked to exclude groups other than the official representatives of the Roma community.

Conclusions

Since 1997, the Government has sought to continuously develop and update its policy towards Roma. The Medium Term Package of Measures adopted in 1999 is a detailed strategy covering a broad range of issues related to improving the situation of Roma. However, its provisions often call only for further research and elaboration of specific measures – and even these commitments have not been met on schedule consistently.

The Medium-Term Package is both centralised and compartmentalised. The State has not yet succeeded in fully integrating minority self-governments or the NGO sphere into the implementation process, and has done little to seek wider social acceptance for programme objectives. Ministries make their own planning and programming decisions based on their individual resources and competencies, which also limits the opportunity to foster a more integrated overall approach. Greater attention to projects' links with Roma communities and the needs that they articulate should be incorporated into the funding selection process. Roma themselves must press for the realisation of their basic rights not only through the promulgation of specific Roma policy, but as an integral dimension of all Government programmes.

The Government's approach toward dialogue and negotiation with Roma organisations and the NGO sphere has come in for particular criticism from civil society representatives. Activists point out that official policy discourse directed by the Government has remained isolated from the discussions and discourse among NGOs and in the media.[5] The lack of attention to the way in which the Package and its implementation have been presented to the public has allowed an important opportunity to build support to evaporate. The media were not mobilised in order to present programme objectives, and the programme has had little success in reducing general prejudice or strengthening social solidarity.

The Government's willingness to continue refining its policies towards Roma is impressive, and the long-term policy guidelines promise to build upon the experience of ongoing initiatives. However, the importance of maintaining consultations and gathering data should not impede the realisation of practical projects.

2. THE GOVERNMENT PROGRAMME – BACKGROUND

2.1 Background to the Present Programme

After the transition to democracy in 1989, several years passed before Government policy began to address the situation of Roma with due emphasis. From 1990 to 1995, the Government began reviewing and transforming the entire legal and institutional background with regard to Roma and other minority groups.

By the second half of the 1990s, it became apparent that Government-level intervention was needed to address the dramatic deterioration of the position of the Roma population, manifested in an increase in unemployment, resurgent social prejudice, and entrenched discrimination. The first Government programmes to improve the situation of Roma appeared in 1995. Government Resolution 1120/1995 (December 1995) was the first significant Government strategy that sought a definite resolution to the increasingly dire situation of the Roma, and particularly the inequalities of opportunity faced by Roma in several spheres. The Public Foundation for Gypsies in Hungary, and the Coordination Council for Roma Affairs, the first body

---

[5] OSI Roundtable, Budapest, June 2002. *Explanatory Note: The Open Society Institute held a roundtable meeting in Hungary in June 2002 to invite critique of the present report in draft form. Experts present included representatives of the Government, Roma representatives, and non-governmental organisations.*

with comprehensive authority to coordinate different programmes related to Roma, were established at the same time.[6]

However, the strategy fell short in several areas. It failed to clearly establish responsibilities at the Government and local levels, and training for officials implementing the policy was either not available or not appropriate. It did not provide for consistent or adequate levels of funding.[7]

In July 1997, the socialist-liberal Government then in office adopted the first Medium-Term Package of Measures for improving the situation of Roma.[8] This programme was the first such strategy based on the understanding that improving the position of Roma requires a longer-term approach, and that due to the depth and complexity of the situation, only a broad set of measures would be effective. The package accordingly included 63 measures, addressing geographical and social inequalities, calling for cooperation with Roma groups, and reducing social prejudices. This programme focused on reducing inequalities in education, employment, and access to social benefits, while seeking to counteract discrimination and enhance the role of Roma in the public sphere. It was also the first attempt to establish close cooperation among the ministries involved with respect to Roma-related issues.

The 1997 strategy relied on successful, functioning Government programmes and existing institutions, and assigned greater responsibilities to local authorities, especially encouraging the involvement and activity of local Roma communities. The 1997 programme recognised the need to eliminate and sanction discrimination by State and local authorities, especially in police proceedings.

The programme provided that funding allocations must be established annually and implementation evaluated each year. Although the programme provided for the development of public awareness activities to inform the public about governmental efforts to improve the situation of a Roma and a programme was prepared, no resources were allocated and it was never carried out.[9] Diversity training courses and programmes for reducing prejudice were not effective in preparing teachers, social workers, government officials, judges, and journalists working with Roma.[10] The State did not establish adequate anti-discrimination measures or legal aid mechanisms.

---

[6] Established under Government Resolution 1121/1995.

[7] Éva Orsós, *Az EU delegáció felkérésére készített szakértői anyag* (An expert paper requested by and prepared for the EU delegation), manuscript, Budapest, 1998, (hereafter, É. Orsós, *"EU Expert Paper"*).

[8] Government Resolution 1093/1997.

[9] 1997 Medium-Term Package of Measures for Improving the Situation of Roma, Chapter I, Section 6.2.

[10] É. Orsós, *EU Expert Paper*.

Moreover, no funding requirements were established and programme implementation suffered from a chronic lack of funding. The emergent NGO sphere and non-profit sector was not able to counterbalance these deficiencies.[11]

The original Government programme adopted by the centre-right FIDESZ–FKGP coalition, which was elected in 1998,[12] generally addressed the interests of majority society.[13] The chapter covering minorities pledged that the Government would support minority groups in strengthening their identity, while making efforts to raise awareness of "common values from the past and a common responsibility for the future."[14] The programme provided for a coordinated series of governmental measures to bring the existing system of minority self-governments closer to a form of cultural autonomy.[15] The specific situation of the Roma minority was not addressed in the Government programme, which did not outline any measures to be taken against ethnic discrimination or social prejudice. However, the programme stated that it would make efforts to stop the further exclusion of Roma through focused assistance, primarily in the spheres of education, child protection, and youth policy.

2.2 The programme – Process

An essential shift in policy occurred in May 1999, when the Government revised the Medium-Term Package of Measures to Improve the Living Standards and Social Position of Roma with Government Resolution 1047/1999 (hereafter, "Medium-Term Package").[16] The revised package sets out to define specific, practical, and collaborative steps in order to create equal opportunities and decrease social prejudices against Roma.[17]

The 1999 Government Resolution enhanced the basic principles of the earlier Government Resolution, but at the same time, priorities such as education, child

---

[11] É. Orsós, *EU Expert Paper*.

[12] The coalition was made up of the Hungarian Civic Party, the Independent Smallholders' Party, and the Hungarian Democratic Forum.

[13] *Az ország jövője a polgárok jövője* (The Country's Future is the Future of the Citizens – A Programme by the Government of the Hungarian Republic), at <http://www.htmh.hu/kormanyprogram.htm>, (accessed 19 September 2002).

[14] See <http://www.htmh.hu/kormanyprogram.htm>.

[15] See <http://www.htmh.hu/kormanyprogram.htm>.

[16] See <http://www.meh.hu/nekh/Angol/6-1999-1047.htm>, (accessed 19 September 2002).

[17] Medium Term Package of Measures to improve the living standards and social position of Roma, Government Resolution 1047/1999, 5 May 1999, (hereafter, "Medium-Term Package").

protection, social benefits such as provision of textbooks and meals for Roma students, and the importance of eliminating segregation at school all lost momentum.

The Medium-Term Package also highlights the importance of developing a future long-term strategy for Roma policy. The responsibility for developing guidelines for a long-term strategy was assigned to the Office for National and Ethnic Minorities; an international expert panel commission comprised of representatives from the Council of Europe, the Hungarian Academy of Sciences, researchers, politicians, and representatives of national and local minority self-governments also took part in the drafting process. Widely publicised regional workshops where the major objectives of the strategy were discussed had an important role in guiding the paper's development.[18]

In May 2001, the Government adopted a decision on the guidelines for a long-term programme. The decision foresees that the Hungarian National Assembly will pass a resolution on new measures for a programme in continuity with the Medium-Term Package.[19] The long-term strategy envisages implementation over a period of 20 years, in two ten-year phases. If the programme is accepted by Parliament, which strategy developers anticipate by the end of 2002, the exact logistics of implementation, a detailed breakdown of tasks, and a system of monitoring and evaluation will need to be developed.

2.3 The programme – Content

The Medium Term Package takes a comprehensive approach, covering many spheres of social policy. Its measures are often outlined in broad strokes, and many lack detail and specificity. Both anti-discrimination provisions and measures to promote minority rights are to be implemented through centralised mechanisms. By contrast, the guidelines for the long-term strategy advocate a multicultural approach, to be realised through a decentralised structure.

The Medium-Term Package proposes measures in six areas:

- Equalising opportunities in education and training
- Decreasing unemployment among Roma
- Maintaining and enhancing Roma cultural identity

---

[18] Conferences were held in Békéscsaba, Debrecen, Miskolc, Győr, Szolnok, Pécs, Nagykanizsa and Budapest.

[19] See Discussion Paper, *Guiding Principles of the long-term Roma social and minority policy strategy*, Budapest 2001, p. 26, (hereafter, "Guiding Principles of the long-term Roma strategy").

- Improving access to healthcare and housing opportunities
- Improving official responses to cases of discrimination against Roma
- Improving perceptions of the Roma among the general public

The Package places the main responsibility for implementation of the programme on State or Government bodies and the National Roma Self-Government.[20] It highlights the importance of regional and area development projects, but does not elaborate a framework for integrating such projects into the national Package.

The Package gives relatively little attention to social, health, and housing problems, and provides that discrimination against Roma shall be reduced through existing statutes that prohibit negative discrimination and require correct police behaviour. It does not include any plan to broaden the legal background to create a comprehensive anti-discrimination framework.

The study "Hungary's national development in the framework of EU accession and the globalised world,"[21] prepared for the Prime Minister's Office and published in its yearbook in 2001, sets out certain premises that provide the context for the Medium-Term Package. This study characterises the basic dilemma of Roma social integration as "whether the state should support the assimilation of Gypsies or the emergence of 'another society' should be facilitated."[22] Set against this background, the Medium-Term Package is fundamentally an assimilation strategy. It aims to moderate existing inequalities, but only for those who are willing to accept the basic cultural and moral principles of majority society; those who are not able or willing to do so will not benefit from State-supported assistance. It also implies that the State does not have an active role to play in counteracting discrimination and racism or in strengthening ethnic identity, and accordingly the Package provides only limited measures in these spheres.

Guidelines for the Long Term Strategy

The Government adopted long-term strategy guidelines in May 2001 to "strengthen and stabilise medium- and short-term Roma-oriented schemes promoted by governments and the tasks involved in the acceptance, modification and implementation of their programmes."[23]

---

[20] The National Roma Self-Government was established under the 1993 Minorities Act. See Section 3.4.2.

[21] L. Práger, "Hungary's national development in the framework of EU accession and the globalised world."

[22] L. Práger, "Hungary's national development in the framework of EU accession and the globalised world."

[23] Guiding Principles of the long-term Roma strategy, p. 26.

The guidelines' priorities place greater emphasis on the active participation of Roma and on encouraging independence, focusing on improving families' self-sufficiency, strengthening social cohesion, and increasing the future role of Roma-interest organisations in the process of European integration. The political philosophy of the long-term programme is fundamentally democratic and consensual, building on active and broad social initiative rather than centralised Government control.

The guidelines also suggest that the critical social problems faced by the Roma must be addressed through general social policy frameworks, in order to ensure that questions of social policy and questions of minority policy are clearly differentiated. The document observes that mingling minority policy with social measures frequently leads to the isolation and segregation of the Roma and the "ethnicisation" of their social problems.[24]

The strategy adopts a multicultural approach, rejecting all forms of political, legal, or social discrimination that violate the rights of individuals or groups to freely choose their identity. The guidelines accept ethnic diversity as a positive social value, and approach the issue of equal opportunities for Roma in the social and political spheres. In this way, the philosophy of the long-term strategy fundamentally differs from that of the Medium-Term Package.

Both the means of preparation and the content of the long-term strategy have been well received by representatives of the Roma community and civil society organisations.[25] However, experts have noted that the strategy contains few specific elements.[26] Implementation of the programme is a continuous process; a new Government took office in Spring 2002,[27] and early initiatives and appointments suggest that the new administration is committed to carrying through the goals of the long-term strategy by further specifying mechanisms and programmes for its practical implementation.

2.4 Administration/Implementation/Evaluation

The main responsibilities for financing and implementing the Medium-Term Package fall to Government ministries. The Inter-ministerial Committee for Roma Affairs is responsible for coordinating the work of the ministries, overseeing reporting and evaluating achievements. However, the Committee is dependent upon the ministries to submit accurate and timely information and has no authority to compel cooperation

---

[24] See <http://www.meh.hu/nekh/Angol/guiding.htm>, (accessed 19 September 2002).
[25] OSI Roundtable, Budapest, June 2002.
[26] OSI Roundtable, Budapest, June 2002.
[27] The Hungarian Socialist Party.

where efforts fall short, as has often been the case. Mechanisms should be established to enhance the efficiency of the coordinating body and make it more effective; granting the Committee ministry-level authority is one possible solution.

Resolution 1048/1999 established the Inter-ministerial Committee for Roma Affairs to implement the Medium-Term Package and coordinate the relevant activities of ministries and national-level organisations under the Package. This institution not only replaced the Coordinating Council of Roma Affairs formed under the 1995 Government programme, but also has much greater potential power and a broader institutional background than its predecessor.

In June 2002, the Government reorganised the structures addressing minority affairs, and Roma issues in particular. A new State Secretariat for Roma integration policy was established, and the President of the National Alliance of Roma Organisations appointed as its first head.[28] The Office for National and Ethnic Minorities has also been placed under the supervision of a second State Secretariat, and will continue to oversee aspects of minority policy related to the protection and promotion of minority identity, including Roma.[29]

Prior to the 2002 restructuring, the Inter-Ministerial Committee worked under the presidency of the Minister of Justice; now the Committee falls directly under the Prime Minister's Office.[30] As before, the chairman of the Office for National and Ethnic Minorities serves as its vice-president, and deputy State Secretaries of the ten ministries involved are standing members.[31] The members of the Inter-ministerial Committee also include the president of the National Roma Self-Government, chairs of the boards of trustees for the Public Foundation for Gypsies in Hungary and the Gandhi Public Foundation.[32] The Office for National and Ethnic Minorities performs the secretarial

---

[28] Office for National and Ethnic Minorities, *Selected News on the Integration of the Roma in Hungary*, July–August 2002, p. 1, (hereafter, "Selected News on Roma July–August 2002").

[29] *Selected News on Roma July–August 2002*, p. 2.

[30] Interview with staff of NEKH, Budapest, 29 August 2002.

[31] The Parliamentary Commissioner for the Rights of National and Ethnic Minorities also has a standing invitation to the Inter-ministerial Committee.

[32] The Gandhi Foundation was established in Pécs in 1994 as part of an initiative to provide secondary level minority education to the Roma community in South-western Hungary. See OSCE Office for the High Commissioner for National Minorities, *Report on the Situation of Roma and Sinti in the OSCE Area*, The Hague, 2000, p. 86, (hereafter, "OSCE Report on the Situation of Roma"). The Foundation has submitted several proposals in relation to counteracting discrimination and increasing equal opportunities since the establishment of the Inter-ministerial Committee. Although these proposals were not adopted during the implementation of the Medium-Term Package, they were ultimately incorporated into the basic principles of the long-term programme.

duties of the Inter-ministerial Committee and oversees coordination among the bodies concerned. In 2001 the Inter-ministerial Committee for Roma Affairs held four meetings and three sub-committee discussions; as of April 2002 it had adopted 86 resolutions and 52 reports since its establishment.[33]

Individual ministries are responsible for implementing different elements of the programme. These ministries are required to prepare annual action plans and allocate resources from their own budgets accordingly. However, mechanisms for implementation are not regulated in any further detail, and thus coherent monitoring and reporting processes are neither formalised nor standardised. Each ministry must set funding levels for programme activities in its own annual budget, in accordance with its specific responsibilities. Moreover, when implementing specific items from the Package, the ministries must exercise care to balance the needs of Roma with attention to other groups in order to avoid public charges of unfairly privileging one minority.

Reports made by the ministries are discussed by the Inter-ministerial Committee, which also oversees the performance of tasks by ministries and evaluates their achievements. Concerns have been raised over the capacity of the Inter-Ministerial Committee to effectively coordinate implementation of the Package, given the ministries' failure to meet many of the deadlines even for reporting on implementation.[34] While the Committee oversees the work of the ministries, it can only voice its disagreement, or if it does not accept a given report, it can propose that the Government should address the case. However, its authority does not extend beyond this point. It has been suggested that the body that is charged with coordinating the programme should placed at the level of a ministry, with sufficient authority to enforce implementation.[35] As the Committee's statute will be redrawn to reflect its transfer out of the Ministry of Justice's portfolio, a more thorough review of the Committee's powers and structure should also be considered.

The Deputy President of the Office for National and Ethnic Minorities has acknowledged the need to increase the authority of the oversight Committee, suggesting that independent financial resources should be established for direct disbursement by the Committee.[36] In June/July 2001, the Government authorised the

---

[33] *Jelentés a kormány részére "A cigányság életkörülményeinek és társadalmi helyezetének javítására irányuló középtávú intézkedéscsomagról szóló … kormányhatározat" 2001 évi végrehajtásáról* (A Report on the 2001 implementation of Government Resolution on the medium-term measures to improve the living standards and social position of the Roma population). Budapest, Inter-ministerial Committee for Roma Affairs, April, 2002, (hereafter, "Report on 2001 Implementation").

[34] See *Minority Protection 2001*, p. 217.

[35] OSI Roundtable, Budapest, June 2002.

[36] Office for National and Ethnic Minorities, *Roma Policy in Hungary: International Conference 26 January 2002*, Budapest, 2002, p. 49.

Ministry of Justice to "examine the appropriateness and the possibility of establishing a system monitoring the implementation, the coordination and the communication of the related government tasks" of the Medium Term Package.[37] In May 2002, the Government adopted a resolution that calls for establishing a unified monitoring mechanism for the evaluation of projects carried out under the auspices of the Medium-Term Package.[38]

In 2000 the Roma-related budgetary expenditure specified in the State budget was HUF 7.2 billion (Hungarian Forints, approximately €29.6 million[39]). From this sum, projects were funded as follows:

- HUF 1.7 billion for implementation of training and education for Roma;
- HUF 100 million for grants to gifted Roma students living in poverty;
- HUF 529.5 million for compensatory training for permanently unemployed Roma;
- Over HUF 1.5 million for encouraging the participation of Roma in public work and public utility work programmes;
- HUF 85.5 million for the social land distribution programme.
- Approximately HUF 500 million for Roma applications submitted to public foundations;
- HUF 148.9 million as annual budgetary aid for the National Roma Self-Government;
- More than HUF 431 million for local Roma minority self-governments.[40]

Through its Phare programme, the EU contributed an additional HUF 2.5 billion (approximately €10.3 million) to Government projects for the integration of younger Roma in 2000, to be distributed over two years.

---

[37] Government Resolution No. 1057/2001. See Office for National and Ethnic Minorities, *Selection of News on the integration of the Roma*, June and July 2001.

[38] Government Resolution 1051/2002 (14 May 2002). A database will be established with Phare support, to centralise collection of regional data on the efficacy of different projects. See *Selected News on Roma, July–August 2002*, p. 1.

[39] The exchange is calculated at HUF 243.212 = €1.

[40] Data as of 14 August 2000 provided by political State Secretary Dr. Csaba Hende.

In 2001 and 2002 the following central Government resources were allocated for the programme (in million Forints):[41]

Central budget resources	2001	2002
	9.364	12.095
Ministry of Economic Affairs	2.300	2.500
Ministry of Social and Family Affairs	1.660	2.713
Ministry of Justice	400	*650
Ministry of Agriculture and Regional Development	353	588
Ministry of Education	142	290
Ministry of Health	136	236
Public Foundation for Gypsies in Hungary	350	550
Gandhi Gymnasium	236	404
Support for Roma minority self-governments	455	470
Support for the National Roma Self-Government	171	188
Support for minority education	2.395	2.800

Note: * Of which HUF 400 million were allocated as educational grants for young Roma.

In the initial period of implementation after the Package was adopted in 1999, no resources were set aside specifically for project implementation from the central budget. However, funds were allocated beginning in 2000, and in 2001 the Government increased its allocation by 30 percent. The more than HUF 9 billion (€37 million) available in 2001 came from three different budgetary sources: €23 million targeting Roma directly; from funding for all national and ethnic minorities; and from support to economically disadvantaged groups without respect to ethnicity. However, the impact of these allocations on Roma communities can be satisfactorily assessed only for the funding targeting Roma directly.

Inconsistencies in the Package's financial reporting process have led to problems in adequately tracking expenditures. The relevant bodies report their expenditures to the Office for National and Ethnic Minorities, each according to its own internal accounting regulations, making it difficult for the Office to process this data. The Deputy President of the Office for National and Ethnic Minorities noted in an interview that it is much more difficult to manage funds which are not specifically allocated for Roma issues, but

---

[41] Information provided by the Inter-Ministerial Committee, published in the 16 March 2002 issue of the *HVG*. Total allocations in 2001 were approximately €38,500; in 2002 €49,730.

nevertheless spent on Roma affairs.[42] The Office is not able to track the movement of such funds or to calculate the precise number of beneficiaries.

The non-governmental sphere has also contributed to the development of Roma-related projects, although the level of funds available from the NGO sector has been declining in recent years (due in turn to a decrease in funding from international donors). Some civil society representatives have claimed that a certain level of mistrust has limited the effectiveness of collaboration between NGOs and the Government in the past.[43]

2.5 The Programme and the Public

While the Government has made substantial efforts to present the programme to the international audience, producing a range of materials on the Medium-Term Package and the guidelines for the long-term strategy in English, less attention has gone to promoting the Medium-Term Package to the Hungarian public and to the Roma community. Reportedly, governmental efforts to publicise the Medium-Term Package domestically have distorted perceptions of the programme, emphasising expenditures on Roma without placing the programme into its context of realising fundamental rights.[44]

The Office for National and Ethnic Minorities published materials related to implementation of the Package in January and May 2002, in connection with a conference that was attended by international representatives, as well as Hungarian organisations and activists.[45]

Awareness of the Medium-Term Package is also very low among Roma, including those serving as members of local minority self-governments. Moreover, there has been little effort on the part of the Government, or from Roma representatives themselves, to promote awareness within the Roma community that all governmental policy should enable them to realise their fundamental rights to education, housing, and healthcare, *inter alia*. While specialised programmes may be essential to address the specific needs of a minority community, creating a discrete Roma policy can paradoxically lead to perceptions that Roma are not included in general programmes such as those to alleviate poverty or improve education standards. Again, Roma

---

[42] Interview with the Deputy President of the Office for National and Ethnic Minorities, Budapest, 14 April 2002.
[43] OSI Roundtable, Budapest, June 2002.
[44] See *Minority Protection 2001*, p. 256.
[45] See Office for National and Ethnic Minorities, *Roma Policy in Hungary: International Conference 26 January 2002*, Budapest, 2002.

representatives and NGOs can have a crucial role in changing these perceptions among authorities, the Roma community, and the general public.

In drafting the long-term programme guidelines, the Office of National and Ethnic Minorities has taken steps to discuss the current programme with the public, and especially the Roma community. Regional conferences were organised to discuss the major objectives of the strategy and were an important dimension of the drafting process.

2.6 The Programme and the EU

The EU has emphasised the importance of addressing the situation of the Roma through the Accession Partnership and its Regular Reports. EU funding has been made available for Roma-related projects, especially in the education sector. However, there have been difficulties in utilising funding by specified deadlines, especially at the local level. Moreover, Roma groups have indicated that the complex application process for Phare support has made it difficult for their organisations to gain access to Phare funding. The process of selecting proposals for funding does not always appear effectively to identify those organisations with a genuine knowledge of and connections with the Roma communities they purport to serve.

The Accession Partnership agreement, signed in 1999 and updated in 2001, requires Hungary, as a priority, to

> improve the integration of the Roma minority […] through more efficient implementation and impact assessment of the medium-term Roma action programme, with particular emphasis on promoting access to mainstream education, fighting discrimination in society (including within the police services), fostering employment, and improving the housing situation[46]

According to the annual Regular Reports of the European Commission,[47] Hungary meets the political criteria defined in Copenhagen. However, the chapters on minority rights and the protection of minorities in these reports continuously emphasise that despite the Government's achievements, Roma struggle with serious problems. The 1999 Progress Report observes that, despite the measures taken, the situation of Roma remains very difficult, and "[f]urther attention needs to be paid to fighting the

---

[46] European Council, *Proposal for a Council Decision on the principles, priorities, intermediate objectives and conditions contained in the Accession Partnership with Hungary*, Brussels, 2001, p. 6.

[47] See European Commission, *2001 Regular Report on Hungary's Progress Towards Accession*, Brussels, 2001, available at <http://europa.eu.int/comm/enlargement/report2001/hu_en.pdf>, (accessed 19 September 2002; hereafter, "2001 Regular Report").

prejudices of the majority of the population."[48] The 2001 Regular Report commends the progress made in the education and housing spheres, but suggests that the Hungarian authorities create appropriate structures and institutions required to successfully implement Roma integration policies, to closely involve local authorities in implementation, and to increase Roma participation in processes of forming these policies.[49] These continue to be valid concerns; however, EU financial support appears not always to have been allocated according to these same principles, especially regarding Roma participation.

EU-provided funding

The European Union contributes to improving the situation in relation to the Roma issue mainly through funds from the Phare programme. In the 1999 Country Programme, a joint application from the Hungarian Ministry of Education and Ministry of Social and Family Affairs received financial assistance to advance the social integration of disadvantaged youth, including Roma. In 2000 the Programme for the Social Integration of Roma prepared by the Office for National and Ethnic Minorities received support. As a continuation of the 1999 Phare-funded programme, a second phase of support for Roma education was approved as part of the 2001 Phare National Programme; the Ministry of Education and the EU will each contribute half of the total budget of €10 million.[50]

Projects related to Roma rights were also given support through other European Union programmes, including the "Leonardo da Vinci" programme.[51] The National Development Programme, which focuses on underdeveloped regions where Roma are a large minority, also receives money from the EU.

Roma organisations have expressed concern that the application process for Phare funding is excessively burdensome and can be too complex for smaller organisations to navigate successfully. Often it is these smaller or more localised groups that have the greatest insight into the solutions most likely to improve the situation for Roma. The EU and other international donors should ensure that the selection process identifies

---

[48] European Commission, *1999 Regular Report from the Commission on Hungary's Progress Towards Accession,* Brussels, 1999, p. 16.

[49] 2001 Regular Report, pp. 22–23.

[50] Office for National and Ethnic Minorities, *Roma Policy in Hungary: International Conference 26 January 2002,* Budapest, 2002, p. 42.

[51] Support was allocated to an anti-discrimination project in higher education that began in 1998, with English, Finnish, Dutch and German partners. Three organisations from Hungary – the Office for National and Ethnic Minorities, and one organisation of the higher education and non-governmental sectors, respectively – participated in implementation. This programme was completed in 2001.

proposals demonstrating authentic links to the intended beneficiaries and an understanding of their needs, and that local communities are involved in articulating their problems and addressing them. Greater support from the EU itself, especially through an office in Hungary, would serve to increase Roma groups' access to these important funding opportunities.[52]

Concerns have also been raised about the slow disbursement of Phare funds in some cases. In the 1999 Phare Programme, none of the funds due to be spent by September 2001 had yet been disbursed by May of that year.[53] In a speech given in January 2002, the Deputy President of the Office for National and Ethnic Minorities observed that "local utilisation of EU supports is generally delayed, and there is a feeling of disappointment during programme implementation."[54]

3. THE GOVERNMENT PROGRAMME – IMPLEMENTATION

3.1 Stated Objectives of the Programme

The Medium-Term Package defines a set of tasks in the fields of education, culture, employment, agriculture, regional development, housing, healthcare, social welfare, anti-discrimination, and communication. According to the Office for National and Ethnic Minorities,

> the tasks defined in the ... package are intended to promote the social integration of the Roma without reinforcing segregation processes. One purpose of the government measures is to increase chances for equal opportunity and to prevent or reduce prejudice and discrimination, while the other is to reinforce the identity and culture of the Roma communities.[55]

3.2 Government Programme and Discrimination

Hungarian law provides some protection against discrimination, but the system lacks consistency and enforcement has been ineffective. In late 2001, the Government

---

[52] OSI Roundtable, Budapest, June 2002.

[53] See *Minority Protection 2001*, p. 230.

[54] Office for National and Ethnic Minorities, *Roma Policy in Hungary: International Conference 26 January 2002*, Budapest, 2002, p. 49.

[55] Office for National and Ethnic Minorities, Government Measures to Improve the Living Conditions of the Roma in Hungary 2000–2001, Budapest, 2002, p. 1.

established a new legal aid network to offer counsel and representation to individuals with claims of discrimination. However, civil society representatives have questioned whether it can provide accurate information about discrimination claims as the Ministry of Justice has asserted. The Medium Term Package acknowledges that discrimination is a problem in many areas of life, but concrete measures to address inequalities are still few and their approach is sometimes short-sighted, doing little to address such systemic issues as over-reliance on State support, and marginalisation. Implementation has fallen behind schedule, particularly in the health and housing spheres.

The Medium-Term Package states that,

> in accordance with Article 45 of Act XI of 1987 on Legislation, the practical implementation of legal provisions containing the ban on negative discrimination shall be examined continuously. [...] Based on the results of the examination, the necessary amendments shall be made. The possibility that future legislation would guarantee or promote the assertion of non-discriminative practices shall be created.[56]

At present, this rather vaguely formulated legal norm should serve as the basis for the reform of Hungarian anti-discrimination legislation.[57]

Human rights groups have criticised the present system of Hungarian anti-discrimination legislation as being rather incoherent.[58] Its starting point is the general anti-discrimination clause in Article 70(a) of the Constitution. Scattered anti-discrimination provisions are then set forth in laws regulating different spheres such as labour and education. Most anti-discrimination provisions are of a declarative nature, and no adequate system of sanctions is attached to them – the exception being the Labour Law, which is augmented by a number of sanctions that may be applied against employers violating the requirement of non-discrimination.[59]

The Media Act provides that the activities of programme providers must not incite hatred against national, ethnic and linguistic minorities, and broadcasting may not aim, openly or covertly, at insulting or excluding any minority. No sanctions have been imposed based on this provision of the Media Act, although the National Radio and

---

[56] Medium Term Package, Point 5.1.

[57] An extensive analysis of Hungary's anti-discrimination legislation has been prepared within the framework of a joint project by European Roma Rights Centre, Interights and the Migration Policy Group. See A. Kádár, L. Farkas, M. Pardavi, *Legal Analysis of National and European Anti-Discrimination Legislation: Hungary*, Brussels, 2002. Available at: <http://www.migpolgroup.com/uploadstore/Hungary%20electronic.pdf>, (accessed 19 September, 2002; hereafter, *"Anti-Discrimination Legislation Analysis"*).

[58] *Anti-Discrimination Legislation Analysis*, p. 7.

[59] *Anti-Discrimination Legislation Analysis*, p. 22.

Television Board (hereafter, ORTT) has itself found radio programmes to be in violation of this clause. Thus, even where broadcasts were found to have committed violations and the Act stipulates possible penalties, the findings have had no practical consequences.[60]

Current Hungarian anti-discrimination legislation is not in line with the EU's Race Equality Directive, which must be transposed into national law as part of the *acquis communautaire*. To reach the level required by the Directive, Hungarian legislation must overcome its lack of basic definitions and the incoherent nature of regulation; certain fields presently lack anti-discrimination provisions altogether. There is no consistent system of sanctions or an institutional framework to enforce anti-discrimination provisions and apply sanctions. Nor is there is any provision for organisations to initiate court proceedings in the form of a class action.[61] The restricted and inconsistent application of the reversed burden of proof standard also does not reach the level required by the Directive.[62]

While the Government did not take action to address existing weaknesses in anti-discrimination legislation,[63] the office of the Minorities Ombudsman developed a draft anti-discrimination act in 2000, largely based on the Race Equality Directive and international best practices.[64] However, the draft was ultimately rejected in Parliamentary committee.

In March 2001 a Government commission was established to consider various different approaches to anti-discrimination legislation. The commission concluded that the "sectoral approach," comprised of provisions in different laws currently in force should stand, with continuous review to ensure that all spheres are adequately covered.[65] In mid-2002, however, the Government announced that it would begin

---

[60] According to an article on Pannon Rádió (published in *Magyar Hírlap*, 25 October, 2001, *Visszavonás fenyegeti a Pannon Rádió műsorszolgáltatói engedélyét*) before 2000 the ORTT had never pursued sanctions in court even if broadcasts were found to have committed violations.

[61] OSI Roundtable, Budapest, June 2002.

[62] See generally, *Anti-Discrimination Legislation Analysis*.

[63] The Ministry of Justice explicitly stated no such initiative would be taken. See *Minority Protection 2001*, p. 223.

[64] See in *Beszámoló a Nemzeti és Etnikai Kisebbségi Jogok Országgyűlési Biztosának tevékenységéről, 2000. január 1. – december 31.* (Report on the Activities of the Parliamentary Commissioner for the Rights of National and Ethnic Minorities, 1 January – 31 December 2000) *(Ombudsman Report 2000)*, Budapest: *Országgyűlési Biztosok Hivatala*, 2001, pp. 155–178.

[65] Office for National and Ethnic Minorities, *Roma Policy in Hungary: International Conference 26 January 2002*, Budapest, 2002, p. 56. The Constitutional Court had previously found that the lack of a unitary anti-discrimination law was not unconstitutional. See Decision 45/2000 of the Constitutional Court, 21 August 2000.

drafting a comprehensive anti-discrimination act, and undertake to amend other legislation to improve provisions against hate speech.[66]

At present there is no body specifically vested with the right and duty to promote equal treatment in Hungary. Some experts urge the establishment of an independent anti-discrimination office (supervised by either the legislature or the executive branch), which would be authorised to establish the occurrence of discriminatory acts and to impose different sanctions, including warnings, fines, or publication of the name of the discriminating entity.[67]

In October 2001 the Ministry of Interior, the Office for National and Ethnic Minorities and the National Roma Self-Government established the Client Service Network for Anti-Discrimination.[68] The primary role of lawyers within the Network is to give information to clients, but they may also draft documents and provide representation in legal proceedings. As of January 2002, the Network had received 196 requests for assistance, of which 22 percent were related to property, 16 percent to criminal law, 13 percent to social benefits, some 13 percent to labour issues, and eight percent to allegations of discrimination.[69] Twenty-two court cases had been initiated as a result.[70]

The Ministry of Justice has publicised the Network's free services, but does not call attention to one significant *caveat*. While initiating a lawsuit through the Network is free of charge, plaintiffs who do not prevail must cover the court costs, which the Network does not underwrite. The risk of incurring such costs deters many Roma clients from taking legal action against discrimination, and undermines the Ministry of Justice's objective of gathering data and experiences to reveal deficiencies in the present system.

While agreeing that legal aid is needed, NGOs have questioned the Government's choice to support the Network's services exclusively, and expressed concern that existing expertise has not been effectively utilised.[71] For example, the Legal Defence Bureau for National and Ethnic Minorities (NEKI), an NGO run by the Foundation for Otherness and the Foundation for Roma Civil Liberties both handle a high volume

---

[66] *Selected News on Roma, July–August 2002,* p. 4.

[67] Balázs Tóth, *"Impossibilium nulla obligatio est,"* in *A hátrányos megkülönböztetés tilalmától a pozitív diszkriminációig* (From the ban on negative discrimination to affirmative action), Budapest: AduPrint – INDOK, 1998, pp. 95–96.

[68] With an annual budget of approximately HUF 30 million (approximately €123,350). Press Conference, by Csaba Hende of the Ministry of Justice, Budapest, 12 October 2001.

[69] Office for National and Ethnic Minorities, *Roma Policy in Hungary: International Conference 26 January 2002,* Budapest, 2002, p. 62.

[70] Office for National and Ethnic Minorities, *Roma Policy in Hungary: International Conference 26 January 2002,* Budapest, 2002, p. 62.

[71] OSI Roundtable, Budapest, June 2002.

of discrimination claims. NEKI publishes an annual report detailing its findings.[72] These established, experienced organisations can offer valuable insight to the Government as well as services to the minority population, and their expertise should be better utilised.

3.2.1 Education

Although the Medium-Term Package does not explicitly address discrimination in education, reducing inequalities in this sphere has been identified as a priority by the Government. While individual Roma have benefited from the grant scheme provided for under the Package, the quality of education available for the broader Roma community remains a concern. Programmes targeting Roma do not appear to be integrated with ongoing efforts to improve school standards generally. The persistence of negative and prejudiced attitudes in the classroom has not yet been decisively addressed, including discrimination in the processes by which children are evaluated before entering school or for placement in programmes for the developmentally disabled.

The Medium-Term Package identifies regular school attendance as key to improving education levels among Roma, from the pre-school to secondary levels. The Package delegates additional responsibilities for development of concrete programmes to the Ministry of Education, which has existing obligations under a separate Act and Decree on Minority Schooling (See Section 3.4.2).[73]

The Medium-Term Package does not set out the activities to be undertaken in the sphere of education in detail. Its general objectives under this heading do set the stage for a range of projects to increase Roma access to education, and to improve the quality of education available. These include:

Student Grants

Point 1.4 of the Medium-Term Package provides for a system of grants to facilitate the successful on-going studies of young Roma. In the period 1999–2001, a total expenditure of HUF 232 million (approximately €928,000) was allocated directly to the beneficiaries of this programme. Altogether, 7,580 Roma received support through such grants.

---

[72] The *Fehér füzet,* or White Booklet.

[73] Act on Public Education No. LXXIX./1993 and amendments of the relating legal provisions, according to Decree No. 32/1997. (XI. 5.) MKM on Issuing the Directives of the Nursery and School Education of National and Ethnic minorities.

The grants aim to give young Roma who meet application requirements the financial means to attend educational institutions. In the first quarter of 2000, the Office for National and Ethnic Minorities held a discussion with the participation of representatives from the Ministries of Justice, Education, the National Roma Self-Government, the Public Foundation for Minorities, and the Public Foundation for Gypsies in order to establish procedures for allocating grants. Invitations for grant applications available in the academic year 2000–2001 were announced on the basis of agreed-upon target groups and criteria.[74]

All parties agree that the student grants programme provides an important resource for Roma students, and this programme represents the most substantial governmental expenditure in the education sphere. However, many individual grants are too small to be considered more than token support.[75] Moreover, the programme is not structured to address broader factors discouraging Roma school attendance, such as discrimination, language, and cultural issues. The grant-making approach supports students who have already overcome these first obstacles to education and have achieved good academic standing; marginalised students – those in greatest danger of dropping out – do not benefit.

Vocational Training Programme

The Medium-Term Package does not specifically identify vocational training as part of its approach to education, but does provide for supporting "the obtaining of qualifications and employment by – particularly Roma – youngsters and young adults."[76] In this context, the National Fund for Vocational Training was established with support from Phare. Two-thirds of the total sum of almost HUF 1 billion (approximately €4.1 million) is provided by the State. This is unusual for Phare programmes, for which the EU generally contributes the greater proportion.

Beneficiaries participate in vocational training programmes in 70 professions.[77] Additionally, 14 vocational schools received HUF 62.5 million (approximately

---

[74] Funding has been offered by the Public Foundation for Minorities to 673 students in secondary and tertiary education (HUF 50.5 million or approximately €202,000) in 1999–2000; the Public Foundation for Gypsies, to 6505 students in 1999–2001 (HUF 85 million or €340,000); and the Ministry of Justice to 2,448 secondary through tertiary students in 2000–2001.

[75] See *Minority Protection 2001*, p. 231.

[76] Medium-Term Package, Point 1.3.

[77] 2,400 young Roma are to be involved in related programmes. In a sub-project for young people without vocational qualifications, the disadvantaged and those who did not complete primary school, 25 applications were accepted and 163 training programmes already have been launched.

€250,000) under the fund for workshop development. Training usually lasts for two years and participants also receive grants to cover their costs.

The reliance on traditional vocational courses does not take advantage of the possibility to develop alternative forms and methods of training outside the structured school environment. Moreover, pairing the system of adult education with small business start-up grants could allow Roma to acquire valuable vocational qualifications and practical experience. Training programmes currently available have been criticised for offering qualifications in unmarketable professions.[78] More attention to the continuing education of Roma women who left school to start a family is also needed.

Dormitories for Socially Disadvantaged Students

Point 1.2 of the Medium-Term Package provides for expanding the accommodation available for Roma students attending secondary school. In 1999, the construction of two institutions for education and training, similar to the Gandhi Gymnasium, were planned with Phare support.

This plan has since been reduced to the construction of two dormitories for disadvantaged students, especially Roma, in Szolnok and Ózd, with support from Phare and the Ministry of Education. According to the Office for National and Ethnic Minorities, the dormitories will serve as a regional centre and will accommodate an additional 40 students.[79] Agreements with a further three student hostels will provide accommodation for 50 Roma, who will take part in preparatory courses for higher education.[80]

While offering accommodation for Roma students who might not otherwise have the means to attend school can improve access to education, it is unclear whether Roma were consulted when the project was scaled back from its original goals. Such research should be conducted to assess the Roma communities' response to the project and whether it meets their needs.

Placement in "Special schools"

The proportion or Roma among children attending special schools for the developmentally disabled is 60 percent nationally, but it exceeds 80 percent in some parts of Eastern Hungary. Experience shows that these special-curriculum institutions generally do not facilitate reintegration into mainstream education, but increase existing educational differences. It is estimated that more than 150 schools have special

---

[78] OSI Roundtable, Budapest, June 2002.

[79] Office for National and Ethnic Minorities, Selection of News on the integration of the Roma, August and September 2001.

[80] Office for National and Ethnic Minorities, Selection of News on the integration of the Roma, August and September 2001.

Roma classes. In recent years legislation concerning the transfer of children into special classes defined stricter criteria for transfers, and the "special status" of the pupil can now be revised at any time.[81]

However, in practice "special status" is rarely re-examined and children are seldom transferred out of these programmes. The lack of precise definitions of discrimination and corresponding sanctions inhibits legal action in such situations. As a preventative measure, the relationship between the committees assessing children's abilities and Roma parents should be improved as part of the school enrolment process. The pre-school evaluation test should be tailored to help as many pre-school-age children as possible begin their studies within the normal, integrated school system; compensatory programmes should be made available only where demonstrably necessary.

Funding Issues

In the central budget for the 2000–2001 school year, funds were set aside for all socially disadvantaged children, including Roma. Prior to reforms in 2000, structural flaws in the current system of funding perversely offered an incentive for schools to channel Roma students to "catch-up" classes.[82] Schools are entitled to receive subsidies both for remedial classes for Roma, and for minority education.[83] While schools no longer receive higher subsidies for remedial programmes than for minority education, they may still receive State support to organise "catch-up classes" instead of minority education for Roma students,[84] and many continue to do so.

Moreover, unlike standard funding, funding for special education programmes is allocated by tender, although little research has been conducted to identify effective programmes, and there are no criteria or standards for awarding tenders or for quality assurance and evaluation of projects.[85] Experts argue that focused and continuous

---

[81] *A nemzeti és etnikai kisebbségi jogok országgyűlési biztosának éves jelentése, 2002* (Annual Report by the Parliamentary Commissioner for the Rights of National and Ethnic Minorities, 2002).

[82] See OSCE Report on the Situation of Roma, pp. 74–75; Human Rights Watch, *Rights Denied: The Roma of Hungary*, 1996, pp. 69–72; *Minority Protection 2001*, pp. 226–228.

[83] According to Act CXXXIII of 2000 on the state budget of the Republic of Hungary for years 2001 and 2002, an additional contribution of HUF 29,000 in 2001 and HUF 33,000 in 2002 is available after every child who participates in a programme within Roma minority education. The budgetary law defines that an additional contribution of HUF 15,000 per capita in 2001 and HUF 17,000 per capita in 2002 can be spent on day care activities at primary schools and compensatory education for disadvantaged students. This contribution shall not be available if the student participates in special education for the Roma minority.

[84] Interview with staff of NEKH, Budapest, 29 August 2002.

[85] P. Radó, in *Jelentés a magyar közoktatásról 2000* (A Report on Hungarian Public Education 2000), Chapters 9 and 10, (hereafter, "Report on Hungarian Public Education 2000").

support should be available for these programmes, which the tender system cannot ensure.[86] Politics also adversely affects programme continuity: projects that have been running for years can be terminated, others programmes are transformed with each change of Government, and entirely new and unrelated projects are launched in each political cycle, all factors operating to weaken their effectiveness.

Research in recent years points to evidence that enhancing the quality of education is the most decisive factor in ensuring educational success for children with different social backgrounds.[87] The importance of quality assurance standards for public education has been increasingly recognised in the education system, but these standards are not applied to education for Roma, for which no evaluation and assessment system appears to have been developed. The processes of improving standards generally and improving opportunities for Roma in particular appear to be disconnected; a more integrated approach could benefit all students.

The Medium-Term Package does not address fundamental problems such as discrimination in educational institutions or the lack of support for increasing teachers' awareness of and sensitivity to Roma needs. In November 2001 the Minorities Ombudsman presented the findings of a survey showing that 38.5 percent of students to graduate that year from teacher-training colleges are "slightly prejudiced" towards the Roma minority, while 14 percent (roughly every seventh student) are "decidedly prejudiced."[88] An earlier survey among students at technical and teacher-training colleges revealed that more than 80 percent of would-be mid-level technical associates and teachers would not be willing to work with a colleague of Roma origin.[89]

Discrimination has been recognised and addressed to some extent by the Ministerial Commissioner for Educational Rights. The Commissioner has found cause to intervene on a number of occasions, by taking measures against segregated education, initiating an investigation in relation to textbooks with racist overtones, and voicing his opinion on the eviction of families with children, *inter alia*. The Minorities Ombudsman also handles complaints about the school system; the Ombudsman's

---

[86] OSI Roundtable, Budapest, June 2002.

[87] Report on Hungarian Public Education 2000, Chapters 9 and 10.

[88] *Magyar Hírlap*, 28 November 2001.

[89] Á. Horváth, B. Marián and I. Szabó, *Főiskolások állampolgári kultúrája. Empirikus vizsgálat két kecskeméti főiskola hallgatói körében* (The citizen culture of college students. An empirical survey among the students of two colleges in Kecskemét). MTA PTI Etnoregionális Kutatóközpont, 1997. Munkafüzetek 14., p. 1–40.

2002 report concludes that the educational disadvantages of Roma children and the number of related discrimination cases has not been decreasing.[90]

The need to overcome prejudice in the teaching profession is recognised in the preparatory documents for the long-term strategy, where it is noted that teacher training must include information "about the content and form of discriminatory practices, about what can be done to remedy such practices, how to recognise prejudice and the methods by which is can be avoided."[91] The expected elaboration of concrete measures to implement this objective will constitute a positive development.

3.2.2 Employment

To date, despite provisions calling for the recruitment of Roma to work in employment centres and the adoption of measures to facilitate ownership of farmland, the Medium-Term Package has approached the problem of high unemployment among Roma primarily through public works projects. These have offered jobs for some Roma, but have provoked criticism as they fail to offer any viable long-term employment prospects or to address systemic and institutional factors affecting unemployment among Roma. Land law reform that would allow distribution of farmland to Roma has also slowed the realisation of agricultural programmes.

Section 3 of the Medium-Term Package states the aim of increasing opportunities for the disadvantaged population, including Roma, in employment and the labour market. The Package provides for "emergency measures" to counterbalance enormous job losses among Roma, such as ensuring public works projects, social land programmes, regional development programmes and other programmes to decrease persistent unemployment. The Package highlights the need for regional and area development activities without clarifying their actual content. The Ministers of Economic Affairs and Social and Family Affairs were given responsibility for implementation, with the deadline of 31 December 1999.

Discrimination in employment is not explicitly addressed by any of the measures provided under the Package. Though it mentions the importance of positive discrimination at the workplace and in facilitating Roma employment, it does not elaborate the processes by which this will be achieved, and no specific measures have been promulgated to date. The Labour Law was amended in July 2001 to broaden the scope of its anti-discrimination provisions to include practices or instructions preceding

---

[90] *A nemzeti és etnikai kisebbségi jogok országgyűlési biztosának éves jelentése, 2002* (Annual Report by the Parliamentary Commissioner for the Rights of National and Ethnic Minorities, 2002).

[91] Guiding Principles of the long-term Roma strategy, p. 15.

or promoting the establishment of an employment relationship, thereby extending protection to recruitment procedures.[92] However, establishing employment discrimination of any kind, never easily proven, is further impaired by the prohibition against maintaining records or statistics including ethnic data.

Publication of an information booklet summarising the experiences of functional employment programmes is provided for under Point 3.1.2 of the Package. Intended to assist the replication of successful initiatives, the booklet has not yet been prepared.

Public Works Projects

A significant aspect of implementation falls under Point 3.1.6, which provides for public work projects at the local level. A number of public work programmes have been organised in accordance with regional development programmes, to improve employment opportunities for the long-term unemployed.

The Government provided HUF 2 billion (approximately €8.1 million) in 1999 and 2000 for public works programmes. Based on estimated data, 40 percent of the participants in public works programmes are Roma. County labour organisations also allocated HUF 7.7 billion (approximately €31 million) for prioritised funding of public works programmes, financed from the Employment Fund within the Labour Market Fund, which accounts for 30 percent of funds available. In practice, an estimated ten percent of beneficiaries were Roma.[93]

Prioritised aid is also available for public works projects organised by municipalities or minority self-governments and Roma NGOs. In 2000, the Labour Market Fund transferred approximately HUF 6.8 billion (€27.2 million) to municipalities to create further opportunities within the ambit of provisional public employment for people receiving benefits.

Regional centres for labour force development have focused on continuing training related to public work programmes. Training centres can build strong contacts with local and regional Roma organisations, and with representatives of county and national minority self-governments. HUF 106.3 million (approximately €430,000) disbursed in 1999 enabled four to five thousand unemployed people to participate in training programmes; an estimated 30 percent of participants were Roma. A programme of similar scale was launched in 2000. According to a follow-up questionnaire on the training, the subsequent job placement proportion was 80 percent.[94] Roma received approximately 40 percent of available resources in public works programmes launched

---

[92] *Anti-Discrimination Legislation Analysis*, p. 21.

[93] Report on 2001 implementation, pp. 17–19.

[94] Report on 2001 implementation, pp. 17–19.

by the Ministry of Social and Family Affairs. According to the Package, these programmes should be subject to annual evaluation, involving the local Roma Self-government and other representative organisations.[95]

Since resources available to finance public works are scarce, the availability of such employment constantly fluctuates. Ongoing public works projects – with appropriate State funding – could be provided by either local authorities or NGOs, but Roma could also be involved in State investments such as motorway construction and similar large-scale projects. Attention should focus on more stable sources of employment, particularly those that would be less likely to foster passive dependence on Government assistance than public works programmes.[96] The State could also grant tax allowances for family income generation and self-sustenance programmes, and a successful pilot small enterprise "incubator" project could also be extended to Roma communities.[97]

The long-term strategy discussion paper emphasises the continued importance of public works projects as a source of income for the unskilled and those with lower levels of education. However, the need to create incentives for the employment of Roma in other sectors is also highlighted in the discussion paper, where financial preferences for employers and trainers, as well as interest-free refundable subsidies to Roma enterprises are mentioned as possible means to achieve higher employment in a range of industries.[98]

Point 3.1.1 of the Medium-Term Package calls for local agreements between county labour offices and Roma self-governments to specify measures for increasing employment among Roma, and suggests that additional posts for Roma may be created in employment centres. The Ministry of Social and Family Affairs reports that such cooperation agreements with Roma organisations and minority self-governments have become standard in labour centres. In programmes under these agreements, assistants for community development and labour organisation as well as social workers have been trained. In several counties, these agreements have also facilitated the development of training programmes organised by labour organisations for church-sponsored nurses and social workers, and for Roma entrepreneurs..

The Medium-Term Package also sets forth various measures to encourage Roma to take part in agricultural activities.[99] The Ministry of Agriculture and Rural Development, the Ministry of Social and Family Affairs and the Prime Minister's Office were assigned

---

[95] Medium-Term Package, Point 3.1.3.
[96] OSI Roundtable, Budapest, June 2002.
[97] OSI Roundtable, Budapest, June 2002.
[98] Guiding Principles of the long-term Roma strategy, pp. 17–18.
[99] Medium-Term Package, Point 3.2.

responsibility for a social land programme under Point 3.2.1. These Ministries were to develop criteria for including State-owned cultivable areas into a social land fund that later could be transferred to local governments for rental to Roma families. However, the development of the social land programme was dependent on adoption of the Law on Land, which was passed only in late 2001, and thus implementation has been delayed. In 2001, HUF 260 million (over €1 million) was spent on the social land programme, 40 to 50 percent of which went to Roma beneficiaries.

Although programmes providing employment for people who live in disadvantaged regions are ongoing, as provided for in Point 3.1.6 of the Package, they affect relatively few families or settlements. These programmes are usually limited to raising livestock and crops for the "independent family farm" or household. The Public Foundation for Gypsies also funds the programme, mainly supporting farming activities.

In addition to the Medium-Term Package, the Government has implemented employment programmes through the National Public Foundation for Employment, which have benefited Roma as well as non-Roma. The National Public Foundation for Employment is a Government body that develops and enhances models and programmes of employment policy and implements programmes originating from various regions.[100] Its primary long-term objective is to reduce unemployment and to improve the employment potential among the unemployed, while increasing the number of jobs available. Its main target group includes Roma who do not have adequate qualifications or higher-level training.

The Foundation's activities generally have a Roma participation rate of between 30 and 40 percent. Programmes focus on integrating the unemployed through training and community enterprise projects. In particular, its Roma employment project has given support to between 300 and 320 Roma entrepreneurs through community organisations.[101]

3.2.3 Housing and other goods and services

The Medium-Term Package does not address housing or accommodation in any detail; its focus is on health and sanitation problems arising from poor housing and infrastructure. In terms of concrete objectives, the Package provides for an assessment to establish the scope of the problem, according to which "a programme shall be developed along with a feasibility study and a detailed financing schedule" to improve

---

[100] In addition to facilitating Roma employment, its responsibilities include reducing unemployment in general with different programmes and policies.

[101] Interview with István Nemoda of the National Public Foundation for Employment, Budapest.

the conditions in slums and "to develop their infrastructure as well as to offer a technical solution for the problems of drinking water supply."[102] The assessment was scheduled be completed in late 1999 but no action had been taken as of August 2002.

The Inter-ministerial Committee has not evaluated the social housing support programme launched by the National Roma Self-Government and the Foundation for Welfare Service in 1996, similar to that called for under point 4.4 of the Medium Term Package. The public utility corporation (Szociális Építő Kft.) founded by the National Roma Self-Government received HUF 40 million (approximately €163,000) in two instalments from the State to be disbursed among 250 families for construction of housing. The deadline for ending the programme was modified several times thereafter, but the flats were still not completed on schedule. Reliable information regarding the number of houses actually completed has not been released.

Nevertheless in January 2001 the Government extended this flat construction programme, allocating €1.1 million for the purpose of including more Roma beneficiaries. Thereafter, in May 2001, the National Roma Self-Government signed a cooperation agreement with the Ministry of Economic Affairs on implementing the project.[103] Under the terms of the agreement, the municipality provides land and utility connections; poor Roma families contribute labour, and the Roma Self-Government provides assistance in the selection of beneficiaries.[104] A condition of eligibility for Roma families is that their children must attend school, and at least one of the parents should have a job or participate in a communal or work service programme. This second condition excludes those Roma families most in need of housing.[105] Moreover, implementation of the programme has been delayed, as the Ministry and National Roma Self-Government did not succeed in spending the HUF 300 million (approximately €1.2 million) allocated in 2001.

The Minorities Ombudsman has reported that those complaining of housing problems are usually unable to build their own homes without State subsidies and often find it very hard to maintain their flats due to lack of income.[106] The problem is exacerbated

---

[102] Medium-Term Package, Point 4.3. The Ministers of Agriculture and Rural Development, Interior, Health, Economic Affairs, Traffic, Communication and Water Conservancy and the President of the Office for National and Ethnic Minorities are responsible for these measures, involving local authorities and minority governments and NGOs.

[103] Office for National and Ethnic Minorities, *Roma Policy in Hungary: International Conference 26 January 2002*, Budapest, 2002, p. 36.

[104] Office for National and Ethnic Minorities, *Roma Policy in Hungary: International Conference 26 January 2002*, Budapest, 2002, p. 36.

[105] See *Népszabadság*, 26 January 2002.

[106] *A nemzeti és etnikai kisebbségi jogok országgyűlési biztosának éves jelentése, 2002* (Annual Report by the Parliamentary Commissioner for the Rights of National and Ethnic Minorities, 2002).

by the diminishing stock of affordable housing in recent years and the fact that few, if any, new flats have been built. According to an estimate made by the Ministry of Agriculture and Rural Development, 13 thousand new flats would be required to satisfy the demands of all the families living in ghettos.[107] Roma rights advocates and NGOs have observed that current housing policy provides for benefits on paper but has shown no actual results.[108] A fully elaborated anti-poverty policy would be an important first step towards addressing the housing crisis, particularly for Roma who are disproportionately affected.

Evictions remain at a high level, following amendments to prevent illegal occupancy in May 2000.[109] These amendments were enacted *after* the Medium-Term Package committed to continue programmes that "support the solution of the housing problems of the socially disadvantaged classes, including the Roma."[110] A simple modification in the housing laws could regularise the situation of those occupants who do not have a rental contract but have been paying apartment fees to the local authorities for 20 years, which would reduce the number of evictions. Prohibiting the eviction of families with children would also avoid highly publicised incidents such as those which took place in Budapest in November 2001[111] and May 2002.[112]

The first judgement against a private proprietor for refusing to serve Roma was handed down in June 2002, against a bar owner in northern Hungary. The owner was fined HUF 100,000 (approximately €400).[113]

3.2.4 Healthcare and other goods and services

The section addressing public health in the Medium-Term Package sets out little in the way of concrete measures to be implemented. While Roma health indicators fall below those of the rest of the Hungarian population, there is insufficient data to conclude whether inequalities stem from general flaws in the system or from ethnic discrimination. Programmes recently introduced or currently in development plan to target the Roma

---

[107] OSI Roundtable, Budapest, June 2002.

[108] OSI Roundtable, Budapest, June 2002.

[109] See *Minority Protection 2001*, p. 234.

[110] Medium-Term Package, Point 4.4.

[111] *Népszava*, 14 November, 2001.

[112] Roma Press Centre news, 13 June 2002.

[113] See RFE/RL *Newsline*, 3 July 2002, "Bar Owner In Hungary Fined for Refusing to Serve Roma."

population particularly through preventative care, in line with the Package's Point 4.2, calling for the expansion of screening programmes and other prophylactic measures.

The Package calls for additional research "exploring the indicators of the health of the Roma population, and the relationship between the institutions providing medical services and the residents affected,"[114] and a detailed strategy is to be developed on this basis. Accordingly, the Ministry of Health drew on the findings of a general survey from 2000–2001 with the voluntary participation of 1,200 families, including many Roma.[115] As the data was collected only once, however, only limited conclusions could be drawn. A tracking procedure, following respondents over time, is needed both to assess health conditions currently and to test how modifications in the healthcare system improve the situation for Roma.[116]

Additional healthcare measures

The Package does not detail any further specific measures or activities to improve the health status of Roma. However, the Ministry of Health has developed a number of initiatives and is incorporating the needs of Roma communities into its general public health programme.

In-service training courses are currently available for all healthcare workers, but are especially recommended for those working in settlements with disadvantaged populations.[117] 2,700 visiting nurses from all counties participated in the first stage of an in-service training programme which focused on raising awareness of the specific problems faced by disadvantaged population groups, including negative attitudes and prejudice. During these training sessions, local Roma leaders gave lectures and led discussions, and successful programmes from other regions were presented. Twenty healthcare workers participated in a pilot training in Sárospatak, as preparation for work with Roma in settlements with particularly poor healthcare conditions.

The job title "assistant activist" (engaged in healthcare or social work) will also be officially registered in the National Training Register. These activists are to be employed by the local authorities, with the support of labour centres. Assistant activists are expected to play an important role both in improving the quality of healthcare and social services for Roma and ensuring a better understanding of the situation among public service professionals.

---

[114] Medium-Term Package, Point 4.1.
[115] The Ministry of Health plans to publish the results of the survey in the future.
[116] Interview with the staff at the Ministry of Health, Budapest, 22 April 2002.
[117] Ministry of Health, *For a Healthy Nation*, Chapter 7, Action 4.

A network of health centres is also planned, building on existing pilot facilities such as the one that has been established in Köröm. The intention is that these health centres will disseminate information on health, hygiene and cooking through training sessions on these and other related topics.[118]

The development of a long-term strategy for improving health conditions among Roma communities is currently under way: social and regional discussions have been held, and the Office for National and Ethnic Minorities is responsible for preparing a final report. The strategy was developed in coordination with a number of ministries, in an effort to build a consensus around specific long-term priorities. In particular, the discussion identified the importance of enabling Roma to benefit from regular healthcare check-ups. It has been proposed that family counsellors and social workers should be engaged to improve awareness of available resources among Roma communities. The implementation of local programmes is expected to centre around general practitioners; visiting nurses will also play an important role.

At the local level, funds will be distributed through tenders to programmes developed by local organisations and institutions in accordance with the various sub-chapters of the public health programme. Moreover, a monitoring and statistical system and a tender system are under development, and the Inter-Ministerial Committee is looking for ways to assist organisations in the preparation of tender proposals.

The National Public Health and Medical Officers' Service deals with Roma in a separate sub-programme, which is still in a preparatory phase. The associates of this programme collected data in selected Roma settlements, on the basis of questionnaires that included almost 90 items focused on hygiene and lifestyle issues.[119]

The 2000 EU Regular Report assessed the health status of Hungarian Roma quite critically,[120] and Phare funding was made available to initiate pilot programmes for developing infrastructure in isolated Roma settlements in 2000.[121] However, no information was available regarding the results of and lessons learned on the basis of implementation of these programmes

Discrimination in access to social benefits

Some cases of discrimination have been reported in the sphere of social benefits, for example when local authorities arbitrarily cut off benefits, or unreasonably delay their

---

[118] Ministry of Health, *For a Healthy Nation*, Chapter 7, Action 6.

[119] From the Hungarian Internet portal site *Origo*, 20 November 2001.

[120] European Commission, *2000 Regular Report on Hungary's Progress Towards Accession*.

[121] DG Enlargement Information Unit, *EU Support for Roma Communities in Central and Eastern Europe*, May 2002, p. 10.

response. Legal defence advocates find that there are few checks on local authorities and limited remedies against their abuse. Neither the Medium-Term Package nor the preliminary materials for the long-term strategy addresses these issues.

3.2.5 The criminal justice system

The Medium-Term Package devotes little attention to issues of discrimination in the criminal justice system, although discrimination has been detected in the adjudication of criminal offences: Roma often receive more severe sentences than non-Roma for the same offence.[122]

Several local conflict-management offices and programmes have been established under the auspices of the Ministry of the Interior, and the Ministry of Justice provides free legal advice to Roma. A sub-project of the Phare Programme for the Social Integration of Roma launched by the Office for National and Ethnic Minorities, will provide support to the legal protection bureaux specifically for Roma, support regional anti-discrimination training programmes, and will provide resources to promote the quality of professional activities in these bureaux (see Section 3.2).

The National Roma Self-Government has concluded agreements with the Ministry of the Interior and the National Police Headquarters; as provided by these agreements, components on Roma culture have been introduced into police training, and a programme to encourage young Roma to join the police force is planned.[123] Nevertheless, as of yet no solution has been reached that would appropriately prepare and train policemen to interact with Roma in a correct, lawful, and unbiased manner.

3.3 Protection from Racially Motivated Violence

Neither the Medium-Term Package nor the preliminary materials for the long-term strategy addresses racially motivated violence. Nevertheless, there is ample evidence to suggest that racially motivated violence is a serious problem.

The Medium-Term Package does address the issue of police misconduct; point 5.2 notes, "the lawfulness of the police behaviour in connection with the members of the

---

[122] *Magyar Hírlap*, 9 April, *"Ellentmondó adatok a rendőri brutalitásról"* (Contradictory data about police brutality).

[123] Office for National and Ethnic Minorities, *Roma Policy in Hungary: International Conference 26 January 2002*, Budapest, 2002, p. 35.

Roma minority shall be continuously followed with attention."[124] The Inter-Departmental Committee on Roma Affairs is obliged to prepare an annual report on the issue, and to draft an action plan concerning the solutions. No action plan has been prepared as of August 2002, nor have annual reports been issued.

Police violence against Roma has been well documented. The overall number of complaints regarding unjustified police measures lodged at the Offices of the Ombudsman for National and Ethnic Minorities and for Civil Rights increased in 2000. Of the complaints brought, only around 30 percent resulted in court cases while in 70 percent no investigation occurred.[125] Many cases are still pending.

According to a survey carried out among policemen in 1997, ten percent of the officers could be labelled as racist, as manifested in extreme rejection, hostility and intolerance.[126] Less intense hostility prevailed among another 27 percent of the police that could be labelled as prejudiced. Point 5.2 of the Medium-Term Package provides that "in the education of undergraduates and graduates working in the bodies of law enforcement – in the interest of a discrimination-free, human service supply – knowledge of social history, culture, sociology etc. regarding the Roma shall be taught on the level of practical use." Police officers have received special training on Roma culture in order to decrease the number of cases of mistreatment and efforts are underway to promote the recruitment of Roma officers. According to the National Program for the Adoption of the *Acquis* prepared by the Ministry of Foreign Affairs, "the training material … gives priority to the historical development and state of the minority and ethnic issue in Hungary, including the historical roots, traditions, current social welfare and social situation of the Roma population as well as the efforts of the government to overcome multiply disadvantageous situations and promote social integration."[127]

The number of cases of abuse made public nevertheless has been on the rise. The EU's 2001 Regular Report observed that police officers are often suspected of corruption and accused of frequent use of excessive force.[128] In particular, international human rights organisations reported cases of unjustified and harsh police action against Roma.

---

[124] Medium-Term Package, Section 5.2.

[125] See in *Beszámoló a Nemzeti és Etnikai Kisebbségi Jogok Országgyűlési Biztosának tevékenységéről,* 2000 (Report on the Work of the Ombudsman for National and Ethnic Minorities, 2000).

[126] Csepeli György, Örkény Antal, Székelyi Mária (1997): 'Szertelen Módszerek' (The Borders and Limits of Non-Discriminatory Behavior), in *Szöveggyűjtemény a kisebbségi ügyek rendőrségi kezelésének tanulmányozásához,* (Textbook for Analysing Minority Issues in Police Practice), Budapest: COLPI, pp. 130–172.

[127] Ministry of Foreign Affairs, Department for European Integration, *National Program for Adoption of the Acquis, Hungary,* Revised version 2001, Volume II, p. 82.

[128] 2001 Regular Report.

A significant example took place in February 2002. After a police raid on the Roma settlement of Bag (Pest county), dozens of people made claims at the county prosecutor's investigation department, charging that more than 20 uniformed men burst into their homes and brutally beat them.. Despite the fact that thirteen police officers were interrogated as suspects by the investigating authority, the case was dismissed due to lack of evidence.[129]

3.4 Promotion of Minority Rights

The Medium-Term Package identifies "maintaining and enhancing Roma cultural identity" among its primary objectives, and sets forth specific measures with regard to education and public participation. However, implementation of these provisions at the local level has not consistently met expectations, partly due to poor financial oversight. Roma groups have also called attention to flaws in the systems for Roma minority education and the formation of the Roma Self-Government, claiming that, unreformed, these structures may actually perpetuate inequalities and contribute to the marginalisation of groups other than the official representatives of the Roma community.

3.4.1 Language

The Medium-Term Package delegates the development of educational and cultural opportunities in the Roma mother tongue and the assessment of financing opportunities for this purpose to the Ministry of National and Cultural Heritage and the Education Minister.

Language issues are not otherwise addressed in the Medium-Term Package, and have not generally been identified as a problem outside the education sphere. The Minorities Act provides generally that "everybody may freely use his/her mother tongue wherever and whenever he/she wishes to do so."[130]

Hungary has ratified the European Charter for Regional or Minority Languages. However, the Roma languages of Beas and Romanes are explicitly excluded in spite of the large number of Hungarian Roma who speak some dialect of the Romanes

---

[129] See <http://www.frisshirek.hu/article/id=3164/s>, (accessed 19 September 2002).
[130] Minorities Act, Art. 51 (1). See also, *Minority Protection 2001*, p. 247.

language.[131] The Committee examining compliance with the Charter found that no provisions exist that promote the teaching of minority languages to non-speakers of the language living inside the areas where it is primarily used.[132] The organisation of such learning groups or classes is permitted on private initiative.

Roma activists and experts have indicated that educational, cultural and administrative institutions should be made aware of their responsibilities and obligations with respect to preserving the Romani languages and enlarging the circle of individuals who can speak these languages. The Roma community has called for the establishment of institutions to facilitate use of Romanes, such as theatres, educational opportunities, television and radio programmes, and research.[133]

3.4.2 Education

Based on Act 68 Section (2) of the Constitution, Hungary ensures education in the mother tongue for members of national or ethnic minorities. The Act on Public Education entitles parents to decide if their children should participate in minority- or Hungarian-language education, and the parent or custodian cannot be limited in exercising this right.[134] Point 1.5 of the Medium-Term Package requires the Ministry of Education to prepare textbooks and teaching materials for Roma minority education. This has been carried out and approved by the National Minority Committee,[135] and these materials will be ready for use in the relevant institutions beginning in the 2002–2003 school year. Point 2.2 of the Medium-Term Package calls for mother-tongue educational material to be available, in line with an assessment of the actual demand and financial resources available.[136]

---

[131] The Government maintains that the area where these languages are spoken cannot be geographically defined and therefore cannot be formally recognised. See *Minority Protection 2001*, p. 246. The committee examining compliance with the European Charter for Regional or Minority Languages has observed that only some 20 percent of people of Roma origin can still speak Romanes in Hungary, and an additional ten percent still use Beas. See <http://www.meh.hu/nekh/Angol/4-1.htm>.

[132] See <http://www.meh.hu/nekh/Angol/4-1.htm>, (accessed 19 September 2002).

[133] OSI Roundtable, Budapest, June 2002.

[134] Act 43 Section (2) of Act LXXVII of 1993.

[135] The National Minority Committee is a body established under the Minorities Act, comprised of representatives of each recognised national minority. The Committee is consulted on measures related to minority rights; members can veto proposed measures, but cannot impose modifications or changes.

[136] Medium-Term Package, Point 2.2.

Task forces have prepared working papers on the standardisation and use of Beas and Romanes. In 2001, broad professional discussions were held in two cycles, and the working papers are undergoing further elaboration as a result. It was concluded that these languages could be standardised only on the basis of a broad professional consensus, which is likely to require a lengthy consultation process.

In the discussion paper drafted in preparation of the long-term strategy, the Government reiterates the importance of native language education for Roma. The paper notes that while the legal framework for such instruction exists, "further efforts are required in the 'standardisation' of these languages, as well as in the area of the training of pre-school instructors and teachers speaking the Roma languages."[137]

The Medium-Term Package repeatedly refers to "Roma minority education" without defining what in fact constitutes minority education.[138] As noted above, existing State-funded "Roma minority programmes" have been criticised for perpetuating ethnic inequalities in education,[139] and in practice have often served more as a means of misappropriating funds for general purposes than for offering Roma an educational option.[140] One recent study of 71 schools in southern Hungary revealed that though 28 schools were currently receiving funding for Roma minority programmes, they were all implementing remedial programmes rather than minority education programmes.[141] Just 40 percent of the schools were in contact with local minority self-government regarding these programmes.[142]

All education laws affecting minority education have been drafted in consultation with national minority self-governments, and public foundations are required to include Roma in decision-making. While the Minorities Act stipulates that minority self-governments are entitled to monitor the implementation of minority education programmes, oversight of the local use of funding is weak, since measures in 1999 removed restrictions on how State support for minority education should be spent.[143] While the local Roma Self Government has the legal authority to monitor the use of these funds, they are often unaware of or unable to exercise their rights in this area.[144] The Act prescribes that minority self-governments may retain experts to audit schools.

---

[137] Guiding Principles of the long-term Roma strategy, p. 13.

[138] Medium-Term Package, Point 1.5.1–1.5.9.

[139] See, e.g. Human Rights Watch, *Rights Denied: the Roma of Hungary*, 1996, pp. 67–72; *Minority Protection 2001*, pp. 226–227.

[140] Interview with staff of the Ministry of Education, Budapest, 11 April 2002.

[141] Diplomadolgozat, Orsós Ferenc, Pécsi Tudományegyetem, Pécs 2002, pp. 16–20.

[142] Diplomadolgozat, Orsós Ferenc, Pécsi Tudományegyetem, Pécs 2002, pp. 16–20.

[143] Interview with staff of NEKH, 29 August 2002.

[144] Interview with staff of NEKH, 29 August 2002.

However, as there are no resources set aside for this purpose, minority self-governments wishing to investigate the uses of funding for minority education must apply to the local authorities for the means to do so – often the same authorities that administer the school funding in the first place.

There have been calls for the system in place prior to 1999 to be reinstated, re-imposing greater specifications on how such funding should be spent.[145] In any case, minority self-governments should be involved in a continuous audit and review process to ensure that funding allocated for minority education programmes is actually used for that purpose.

Although restructuring of the minority education system is provided for in national legislation under the Guidelines for Pre-School and Instruction and School Education of National and Ethnic Minorities and referred to in the Medium-Term Package,[146] little progress has been made towards this end. No comprehensive system of Roma education institutions has been developed at the primary school level, and there are few institutions providing training on the basis of pedagogical programmes for the Roma minority at the secondary level, such as the Gandhi Gymnasium and its dormitory in Pécs. Through the "Arany János" programme, schools may apply to the Ministry of Education for scholarships and housing allowances for talented Roma students. As of September 2002, three schools had applied under this programme, which doubles the standard *per capita* allowance for the students selected.[147] This and other measures can help to ensure that there is sufficient institutional infrastructure to meet the demand for minority education among Roma.

Based on an investigation carried out by the Ombudsman and warnings from the National Roma Self-Government, the Education Minister initiated a national survey on Roma minority education and "special education" programs in 2001. The Minister requested that approximately 900 municipalities confirm their fulfilment of and compliance with the applicable regulations on minority education. School supervisors sent their summary reports to both the administrative offices concerned and to the National Centre for Public Education Assessment and Examination.[148] According to the Ministry the evaluation process of the reports had not yet been completed as of August 2002. Results should be made available to the public, and should be used to initiate a broad discussion on the need for additional institutions to ensure the level of support, training, and resources necessary for high-quality education for Roma.

---

[145] Interview with staff of NEKH, 29 August 2002.
[146] Decree No. 32/1997, 5 November 1997.
[147] Interview with staff of NEKH, 29 August 2002.
[148] *Az Oktatási Minisztérium 2001 évi jelentése a CTB felé*, 2001 (2001 report by the Ministry of Education to the Inter-ministerial Committee for Roma Affairs, 2001).

Civil Society Initiatives

Civil society initiatives have addressed some gaps in Roma education programmes. For example, the Roma School Success Program works with Roma university students and activists to offer presentations on Roma language, history, and culture. In the 2000–2001 school year some 1,800 students were reached through the programme. Textbook and curricula were also developed for lessons on Roma history and culture.[149] The Roma School Success Program also promotes Roma non-governmental organisations' efforts to develop effective and appropriate education for Roma children.

3.4.3 Participation in public life

There are no specific measures for enhancing Roma participation in public life in the Medium-Term Package. The Package does call for increased cooperation with the existing Roma National Self-Government in several areas.

Following the election of minority self-governments in 1998 on the basis of the Minorities Act, municipal-level Roma minority self-governments were established. As of Autumn 2002, 724 self-governments are functional, giving more than 3,000 Roma the opportunity to participate in public life. Local minority self-governments and representatives have also formed county associations that ensure mid-level interest representation in several counties. However, this system has also given rise to internal tension, due to the fact that the Government considers the National Roma Self-Government to be the sole "official" representative of the Roma nationally. The Government negotiates only with the National Roma Self-Government when preparing decisions affecting the Roma population, although several organisations claim and compete for the right of Roma political representation.

In his 2002 report, the Minorities Ombudsman concluded on the basis of complaints received by his Office that in many places local authorities and minority self-governments are not aware of their respective rights and responsibilities under the law. Some municipalities do not see minority self-governments as partners of equal rank, and do not wish to cooperate with them.[150] Civil society and Roma groups have repeatedly called for amendments to the Minorities Act, to clarify the content of "consultative rights" and to replace the short-list electoral system with a mixed system for selecting candidates. The minority self-government structure has the potential to play a significant role in political

---

[149] See the American Friends Service Committee web site, <http://www.afsc.org/intl/europe/rssp.htm>, (accessed 19 September 2002).

[150] Annual Report by the Parliamentary Commissioner for the Rights of National and Ethnic Minorities, 2002.

life, if its measures are fully realised. However, electoral reform proposals have elicited fierce opposition from entrenched political parties.[151]

Concerns have been raised that the National Roma Self-Government is easily controlled by the Government, does not exercise real authority and has failed to make specific recommendations when the opportunity arises. During the periods of programme development and implementation, most proposals originated with the Office for National and Ethnic Minorities and were submitted to the Self-Government for assessment. The Self-Government produced few proposals itself, and ultimately accepted those initiatives submitted by the Office for National and Ethnic Minorities, presenting them as its own.

For the first time since the early 1990s, four Roma were elected to Parliament in 2002, all on mainstream party tickets. Much publicity was given to the pre-election agreement between FIDESZ and Lungo Drom, a Roma political organisation; opinion within the Roma community was divided on the issue, some welcoming it as a significant advance, others suggesting that Lungo Drom had become an "extension" of the centre-right party.[152]

The guidelines for the long-term strategy include an expanded section on participation in public life. The discussion paper calls for various measures for training representatives and funding minority self-governments, on the grounds that all projects for improving the situation of Roma can be successful if Roma communities are involved in all aspects of drafting and implementation. "That is why it is a priority to increase Roma participation in social processes and in relevant local, county, and national decision-making."[153]

Since assuming office in June 2002, the State Secretary responsible for Roma integration policy issues has taken several initiatives to increase the representation of Roma at the Government level. First, a Council on Roma Affairs has been established under the chairmanship of the Prime Minister.[154] This body is to be comprised of 21 members from both the political and civil society spheres, including a majority of Roma representatives.[155] The Council is to act in an advisory capacity, as a forum for broader consultation at a high political level. In addition, Roma Commissioners will be

---

[151] OSI Roundtable, Budapest, June 2002.

[152] See OSCE Office for Democratic Institutions and Human Rights, *Republic of Hungary Parliamentary Elections Observation Report,* Warsaw, 6 June 2002, Section V. See <http://www.osce.org/odihr/documents/reports/election_reports/hu/hu_pe_april2002_efr.php3>, (accessed 19 September 2002).

[153] Guiding Principles of the long-term Roma strategy, p. 23.

[154] Government Resolution No. 1140/2002, 12 August 2002.

[155] Interview with staff of NEKH, 29 August 2002.

appointed in six ministries to facilitate coordination within and among ministries and to act as focal points on Roma issues. The first such commissioner, a Romani activist previously working in the civil society sphere, was appointed to the Education Ministry in July 2002.[156] In ministries where a commissioner is not appointed, Roma departments will be established or desk officers named to coordinate Roma-related issues in their respective spheres.[157] These initiatives promise to ensure higher visibility of Roma issues at the Government level, and should prove useful complements to the structures established under the Medium-Term Package. Structures specifically tasked to address the problems confronting the Roma community should also ensure these issues are integrated into general governmental policy and not treated as marginal issues.

3.4.4 Media

A system of support for minority media predates the Medium-Term Package, and Point 6.1 provides only that "the harmonisation of the activities of funds, public foundations and institutions that support the Roma minority's media shall be initiated with the purpose of continuous cooperation and the effective use of the sources."[158] This reflects the existing system of support for minority media, which obliges State-owned public-service television and radio to broadcast programmes prepared by or for minority communities, and provides funding for the publication of minority papers. However, this system remains poorly coordinated and there is no sign of the harmonisation called for in the Medium-Term Package.

Two laws, the Minorities Act[159] and the Media Act,[160] regulate the relationship between the media and minorities. According to the Minorities Act, "public service television and radio stations will ensure that national and ethnic minority programmes are produced and broadcast on a regular basis."[161] The Media Act regulates the non-public service, non-profit segment of the media market through incentives, making allowances to encourage minority interests. This is achieved through the process of frequency allocation among the different applicants: those who can prove that their programme would represent any minority interest are given an advantage. Nevertheless, in practice almost

---

[156] See RFE/RL *Newsline*, 25 July 2002, "Hungarian Education Ministry Appoints Romany Official."

[157] See Office for National and Ethnic Minorities, Selected News on the Social Integration of the Roma in Hungary, July–August 2002, p. 2.

[158] Medium-Term Package Point 6.1.

[159] Act LXXVII of 1993 on the Rights of National and Ethnic Minorities.

[160] Act I on Radio and Television Broadcasting, 1996.

[161] Act LXXVII of 1993 on the Rights of National and Ethnic Minorities.

all applicants declare their intention to represent a specific minority interest, and no real benefits to any community are achieved. The National Radio and Television Board (ORTT) can set a certain degree of national and ethnic minority-oriented programming as a requirement for application, but in practice only loosely controls compliance with these conditions and does not sanction violations.

Applicants who produce minority programmes have a head start in applications for local frequencies, but most local media have not launched such programmes despite promises to do so. However, there are some positive examples: several regional television and radio stations broadcast Roma programmes.

The Hungarian system has been criticised as confining minority communities to specific, minority-oriented broadcasts that are easily marginalised, rather than affording opportunities to appear across the full range of mainstream programming. Public-service television can meet its formal legal obligation by broadcasting a separate weekly 25-minute minority programme, but this is insufficient time to meet the real needs of minority groups. Media experts simply call Roma programmes "ghetto programmes," referring to the fact that neither minority interests nor minority actors are presented anywhere within the State-owned public-service media beyond the fulfilment of public-service quotas. Programming as a whole consequently has a rather ethnocentric quality. Despite the continued efforts of those working in the minority media, they have been unable to win better or longer time slots, or to improve technical and personal conditions for minority programmes; the number of people aware of minority programming remains low.

In recent years the only significant development in this field was the establishment of Rádió ©, a Budapest regional Roma radio station. The establishment of Rádió © is by all accounts a significant development: staffed by Roma, it has the potential to become a workshop for Roma pursuing a career in broadcasting as well as being the first medium in the Hungarian market in which the production of Roma programmes is produced independently of the State and State support. The chief editor and managing director has observed that the frequency was granted to a group of Roma working in radio, rather than to a more politically influential organisation. All representatives of Roma public life have recognised the importance of this decision.

Following a one-month pilot period, broadcasting began in the Autumn of 2001. Most associates – all announcers, and most of the music editors – are Roma, while non-Roma dominate only in the news editing staff. The selection of associates began during the pilot period, which also served as a kind of casting call. Youths selected during the screening participated in a few months' training accredited by the BBC. The target audience of the station is the Roma community living in Budapest and environs, although some programmes were developed to appeal to young non-Roma intellectuals. However, the radio staff considers it important that the station does not aim to win over a prejudiced *Gadzo* (non-Roma) audience but speaks to Roma from a Roma perspective.

In terms of print media, minority newspapers are maintained by the Public Foundation for National and Ethnic Minorities, and all struggle with financial and distribution difficulties. Motivation to solve these problems is low, however, as support from the Foundation is not dependent on the number of readers but based on an *ad hoc* decision of the board members.

Only a few Roma papers are published more or less regularly: the *Lungo Drom* and *Amaro Drom* have been stable for years, while other papers are published irregularly or have already gone out of circulation. *Világunk*, which has become the paper of the National Roma Self-Government, is relatively new in the market. Few people know of or read these papers, according to both circulation data provided by their editors and a survey on Roma media consumption carried out in 2000. The latter showed that only 20 of 458 respondents knew of and nine more or less regularly read *Lungo Drom*, six knew of *Amaro Drom*, and proportions were even lower for other papers.[162]

Under the Phare 1999 National Programme, implementation of a project to establish internet access in Budapest and seven regional community centres for Roma is underway. This three-year project has a budget of approximately €500,000.[163]

Two NGO initiatives have made significant contributions to the Roma presence in the media:

The Roma Press Centre

The Roma Press Centre (RPC) was established in 1995 by a group of anti-discrimination activists to focus greater attention on the Roma minority and to provide more credible information about events and news concerning Roma. The RPC is supported by a number of Hungarian and international institutions.[164] It functions as a news agency, offering information about events relevant to Roma through its national network of correspondents, who prepare news items that are published by the mainstream press. Most news items from the RPC appear in at least one, but often several, daily papers, and a significant part of Roma-related reports published in the

---

[162] Bernáth and Messing, *Fehér keretben* (In a White Frame), Budapest, Új Mandátum, publication forthcoming.

[163] Interview with staff of NEKH, 29 August 2002.

[164] The Soros Foundation, the Autonomy Foundation, the Office for National and Ethnic Minorities, consulates, the Council of Europe, the British Know-How Fund, and others.

Hungarian mainstream press originates from this organisation.[165] Therefore, the news agency significantly influences the picture formed about Roma in the mainstream press by introducing new topics and offering a different perspective on many events.

The RPC also has sponsored training for Roma journalists. In 1996 the RPC launched its programme for media interns in order to fill a gap caused by the lack of Roma journalists in Hungarian media. Each year 20 to 25 young Roma secondary-school graduates have the opportunity to learn the profession in a mainstream medium (television, radio or a print medium) or with the RPC. The programme provides practical training sessions, which are completed with ten-month theoretical courses provided by the Center for Independent Journalism (see below). Many of the 25 students who first completed the programme currently work as journalists or editors in a mainstream medium, and an increasing number of interns are entering the field, offering fresh perspectives on the problems faced by Roma communities. Otherwise, Roma youths are excluded from mainstream training opportunities for journalists, as very few Roma reach higher education, and most journalism training relies on tuition fees which Roma cannot often afford. The RPC therefore offers a vital service to both the Roma and majority communities. The RPC also disseminates Roma-oriented news to the international media, to raise the profile of Roma issues in Eastern Europe to the widest possible audience.

In 1998 the RPC expanded its activities, establishing a staff to prepare materials such as reports, interviews, background materials, and news for radio stations in addition to the institution targeting the printed press. The materials prepared for radio are broadcast by Magyar Rádió and its regional studios, and by local radio stations. These radio programmes put great emphasis on informing the Roma audience.

The Center for Independent Journalism

Another important initiative in this field is the Center for Independent Journalism (CIJ), which cooperates with the RPC on several projects. The CIJ was founded by the Independent Journalism Foundation (based in New York) in four regional capitals: Budapest, Bucharest, Bratislava, and Prague. The main goal of the CIJ is to establish independent, impartial and ethical reporting, particularly "reporting diversity," through the dissemination of news about ethnic and other minorities.

The CIJ holds training sessions for mainstream journalists and editors, among others, on producing news for and about minorities. It is also engaged in a programme to train members of minority organisations (including local minority self-governments,

---

[165] Only one relevant figure is available: according to a study analysing how the flight of Roma from Zámoly was presented in the media, more than one-tenth of articles covering this topic originated from the RPC.

political, and cultural organisations in identifying means by which they can build contacts with and "handle" mainstream media. This programme is run in cooperation with the RPC.

3.4.5 Culture

In advancing its objectives in the area of minority rights, the Medium-Term Package focuses mainly on culture. It provides that the infrastructure for Roma public cultural institutions and other specialised institutions should be developed by the Ministry of National and Cultural Heritage, under Point 2.1. In cooperation with the National Roma Information and Cultural Centre, the Ministry was required to prepare a detailed draft programme of developing the system of Roma institutions by the end of 1999, but this draft had not been completed as of August 2002.

Tasks identified under the Package include support for cultural events, the organisation of camp activities and for the establishment of "houses of culture." Since receiving information on such opportunities in a timely manner is a serious problem for small settlements, the Ministry plans to set up county offices of the National Roma Information and Cultural Centre in order to facilitate information flow However, no information was available on the status of implementation of these measures.

4. EVALUATION

Since 1997, the Hungarian Government has been engaged in a continuous process of developing and refining its policy towards Roma. The Medium Term Package of Measures adopted in 1999 is a detailed strategy covering a broad range of issues related to improving the situation of Roma.

The Medium-Term Package recognises both prevention of discrimination and promotion of minority culture as objectives. While taking a comprehensive and coordinated approach, the Package is weak in several areas. No measures are stipulated to broaden the legal framework to provide protection against discrimination, and a draft anti-discrimination law prepared by the Minorities Ombudsman has not been adopted by Parliament. Health and housing issues are not given sufficient attention, and racially motivated violence is not addressed at all.

Few specific strategies for improvement are elaborated in the Package; rather, it often calls for research, assessment, and evaluation of the situation in each sphere, and for more detailed programmes to be developed in line with findings in each area.

However, implementation of research projects has fallen behind schedule in many areas. With even this initial phase yet to be completed, the more relevant practical activities to address identified problems are even farther from realisation.

The Package's coordinating body, the Inter-Ministerial Committee for Roma Affairs, has been unable to take measures to improve levels of implementation. The Committee cannot compel the various ministries to complete activities on schedule, and has not even been able to ensure reporting to meet initial deadlines. The Office for National and Ethnic Minorities, charged with overseeing expenditures on Roma-related projects, must decipher the accounting systems of separate submissions by the different ministries, which inhibits precise record-keeping on overall expenditures and number of beneficiaries. There is no system of independent, external monitoring, and the flow of funds is often obscure. Apparently, impact analyses have not been prepared for any programme.

Those projects that have been initiated share a common approach: providing assistance to those who demonstrate their willingness to take part in the system. This approach, while helping motivated individuals to achieve their goals and offering incentives for participation, tends to neglect the large population of Roma who are effectively excluded from education, employment, and social services at the most basic level. Improving access at this level has been a secondary objective in the funding of projects under the Medium-Term Package. The most vulnerable are those who fall outside these support systems, and the Package fails to provide concrete measures for greater inclusion as an initial step.

The Medium-Term Package is both centralised and compartmentalised. The State has not integrated local authorities, minority self-governments or the NGO sphere into the implementation process, and has done little to seek wider social acceptance for programme objectives. Implementation is also characterised by discrete decision-making and *ad hoc* activities by the individual ministries, limiting the opportunity to foster the development and implementation of integrated programmes.

The process of negotiation with Roma organisations and the NGO sphere has come in for particular criticism from civil society representatives. Activists point out that official policy discourse as articulated by many Government officials remains isolated from the discussions and discourse among NGOs and in the media.[166] The lack of attention to the way in which the Package has been presented to the public has allowed an important opportunity to build broader support for implementation to evaporate. The media were not mobilised in order to present programme objectives, and the programme has had little success in reducing general prejudices or strengthening social solidarity.

---

[166] OSI Roundtable, Budapest, June 2002.

While the Medium-Term Package has represented the working agenda for the Government since its adoption, preparation of a long-term programme began almost immediately after it was adopted. The Government's approach to drafting guidelines for the long-term strategy demonstrates an increased commitment to including the perspectives of Roma themselves in the process, and towards building greater consensus in the population. The Medium-Term Package maintains centralised control of policies through the Inter-ministerial Committee for Roma Affairs, while the long-term guidelines support the delegation of greater responsibilities to local authorities.

The Government's willingness to continue refining its policies towards Roma is impressive; however, the importance of maintaining consultations and gathering data should not impede the realisation of practical projects. The 2002 elections have brought a new Government into office, whose early initiatives have focused on creating new structures to raise the level of coordination and to enhance the input of civil society actors. The Medium-Term Package presents a strong basis from which to work, yet redoubled efforts are required to bring about positive, sustainable change in the situation of Roma.

5. Recommendations

In addition to the recommendations elaborated in the Overview Report, the following measures could contribute to more effective Government policy towards Roma:

- Bring Hungarian law into conformity with the requirements of the EU Race Equality Directive, and adopt comprehensive anti-discrimination legislation, ensuring that the implementing body mandated by the Directive is fully independent and adequately staffed and financed.

- Establish a stable funding structure for implementation of the Medium-Term Package. Mechanisms for reporting funding allocations and expenditures should be harmonised and regular evaluations of Government spending on Roma issues should be prepared, presented, and made available to the public.

- Ensure the implementation of the Medium-Term Package's objectives by investing a coordinating body with sufficient authority to compel the competent structures to carry out their respective responsibilities and to enhance inter-ministerial collaboration.

- Modify the electoral system for minority self-government as necessary to encourage broader representation of different Roma groups and interests in the political sphere; provide training in the system's provisions for minority self-government representatives and local government officials to raise awareness of these rights.

- Continue to revise school-funding schemes to create incentives for authentic Roma minority education at the local level; provide guidelines and develop materials in cooperation with Roma NGOs and activists to help schools and teachers develop genuine minority education programmes for Roma.

- Develop a quality measurement programme for education, to evaluate the progress of all students according to recognised standards.

- Develop programmes to reduce discrimination and increase awareness of Roma culture in the teaching profession.

- Decrease the emphasis on passive subsistence employment projects such as public works schemes, and develop more active income-generating activities for Roma.

- Provide guidelines to public employment office staff on the prevention of discrimination and reiterate the positive duty to provide service to all clients without discrimination.

- Develop means for collecting data to facilitate the implementation of legal measures offering protection against discrimination in employment.

- Continue dialogue with a range of Roma representatives and organisations to foster both diversity and cooperation in the development and implementation of policy as well as in the identification of issues of common concern and the best means of addressing those issues.

- Integrate Roma policy into general development policy, and enhance public awareness of the basis and need for Roma programmes, not only the costs.

OPEN SOCIETY INSTITUTE 2002

Minority Protection in Latvia

An Assessment of the National Programme
"The Integration of Society in Latvia."

MONITORING THE EU ACCESSION PROCESS: MINORITY PROTECTION

Table of Contents

1. Executive Summary 300

2. The Government Programme –
   Background 304
   - 2.1 Background to Present Programme 304
   - 2.2 The Programme – Process 305
   - 2.3 The Programme – Content 308
   - 2.4 The Programme – Administration/
     Implementation/Evaluation 311
   - 2.5 The Programme and the Public 317
   - 2.6 The Programme and the EU 319

3. The Government Programme –
   Implementation 321
   - 3.1 Stated Objectives of the Programme 321
   - 3.2 Government Programme
     and Discrimination 322
     - 3.2.1 Education 324
     - 3.2.2 Employment 333
     - 3.2.3 Housing and
       other goods and services 338
     - 3.2.4 Healthcare and other forms
       of social protection 338
     - 3.2.5 The criminal justice system 338

        3.3   Protection from Racially
              Motivated Violence 339
        3.4   Promotion of Minority Rights 340
              3.4.1   Education 340
              3.4.2   Language 344
              3.4.3   Participation in public life 346
              3.4.4   Media 355
              3.4.5   Culture 357

4. Evaluation 359

5. Recommendations 362

1. Executive Summary

The adoption of the National Programme "The Integration of Society in Latvia" (hereafter, "Integration Programme")[1] in February 2001 is an achievement in itself, as it is the result of a broad public debate on integration and on the country's future ethnic policy. Its aim is to enhance the integration of Latvian society as a whole. Thus, while it deals with several aspects of minority integration and states in general terms the need to protect minority rights, it does not address discrimination and proposes few measures to promote the minority identity.[2]

As implementation and funding mechanisms were established only recently, most activities realised to date are those which were begun by various actors before the adoption of the Integration Programme. Already, however, it is clear that the lack of coordination between various authorities and the lack of a coherent implementation strategy are likely to hinder successful implementation unless these problems are addressed. Moreover, implementation of the Integration Programme has often lacked transparency. Much will depend on the capacity of the Society Integration Foundation (SIF)[3] to take up responsibility for administering EU funds as well as on greater financial commitment from the State. A more effective participation of minorities in implementation is also needed.

A monitoring system is now being elaborated, on the basis of which the new priorities of the Integration Programme will be defined. More should also be done to promote

---

[1] *Valsts programma "Sabiedrības integrācija Latvijā"* (National Programme "The Integration of Society in Latvia"), Riga, February 2001, <www.np.gov.lv>, (accessed 23 August 2002) (in Latvian and in English). All citations of the Integration Programme in this report are based on the official English translation.

[2] The Integration Programme often refers to the term "minority" (for which there is no official definition in Latvia) as well to "non-Latvians." In this report, the term "minority" will be used in reference to non-ethnic Latvians. As of 1 July 2002, ethnic Latvians constituted 58.3 percent of the total population of 2.3 million. Russians represented 29.1 percent, Belarussians – 4.0 percent, Ukrainians – 2.6 percent, Poles – 2.5 percent, Lithuanians – 1.4 percent, Jews – 0.4 percent, Estonians – 0.1 percent, and others – 1.6 percent. 76 percent of residents were citizens of Latvia, 22 percent were non-citizens (stateless persons), and 1 percent were aliens. Data of the Board for Citizenship and Migration Affairs, <http://www.np.gov.lv/fakti/index.htm>, (accessed 23 August 2002). The term "minority" or "non-ethnic Latvian" does not coincide with the term "Russian-speaking population" as 36 percent of all residents aged 7 and over, including 3 percent of ethnic Latvians, consider Russian as their mother tongue. Central Statistical Office, Provisional Results of the 2000 Population Census, *Statistical biļetens* (*Statistical Bulletin*), Riga, 2001, pp. 40–41.

[3] This is the main body responsible for allocating funding from the State and other sources for projects under the Integration Programme.

further discussion within society, with a view to reaching a consensus on minority-related policies. Finally, there is a need for further improvements to legislation to ensure minority protection, including protection against discrimination.

Background

The Integration Programme was adopted in February 2001, on the initiative of a number of civil society organisations and the Naturalisation Board, after a three-year elaboration and adoption process. Although it is based on a considerably debated and revised Framework Document (December 1999) to which minorities also contributed, direct minority participation as authors of these two documents was low.

While it is the first comprehensive governmental programme of its kind, the Integration Programme was preceded by several initiatives which also sought to promote integration. The majority of these, which were funded primarily by foreign sources (with some State contribution), have been incorporated into the Integration Programme.[4] In addition to these prior "A projects," the document lists projects to be implemented as soon as funding is received ("B projects"), as well as possible future projects ("C projects").

Administration

The Society Integration Department (SID) at the Ministry of Justice, and the SIF are the principal mechanisms for administering and funding implementation of the Integration Programme. However, as they have begun functioning only recently, it is too early to draw conclusions about their efficiency. However, the lack of effective coordination between various authorities and the lack of a clear implementation strategy are likely to hinder effective implementation. The participation of minorities in implementation has been low, although efforts have been made recently to involve minority NGOs and civil society.

Most of the activities implemented to date had been initiated before the adoption of the Programme. However, the SIF has sought to initiate increased participation by civil society organisations and to involve municipalities by allocating State funding for projects and providing training for the potential tender applicants, including NGOs. A first group of projects was approved in a closed process in November 2001 without the involvement of SIF expert commissions; it was strongly criticised by civil society organisations due to its lack of transparency and the very limited opportunities for NGO participation. By August 2002, the SIF had announced two public tenders for

---

[4] These include namely the activities of State actors, such as the National Programme for Latvian Language Training (NPLLT), the Naturalisation Board and ministries, and non-State actors such as the Soros Foundation–Latvia (SFL).

State funding. While these were more transparent as they were organised according to newly-adopted SIF guidelines, a relatively small amount of funding was allocated. A tender for EU Phare-funded pilot projects has also been announced.

Few projects by minority NGOs are listed in the Integration Programme and few had received funding from the SIF as of Summer 2002. Minority representation in the SIF Council, which supervises the work of the SIF,[5] is also viewed as insufficient.

There is a need to coordinate monitoring by various actors. The SID has begun to elaborate a general monitoring and evaluation system to review the Programme's priorities each year. However, there is a need to revise priorities for 2003 before the system is completed. Also, according to the SIF, the impact of SIF-funded projects cannot be evaluated until 2004.

EU Support

In its Regular Reports, the European Commission has recommended implementing activities to promote the integration of minorities and has positively evaluated any developments in this field, including the adoption of the Integration Programme.[6] Through the Phare Programme, the EU has strongly supported efforts to promote integration since 1996, allocating significant funds for Latvian language training and has supported activities of the National Programme for Latvian Language Training (NPLLT) and the Naturalisation Board, in line with the priorities established in Latvia's 1999 Accession Partnership.[7] At the same time, it has sought to encourage the Government to allocate more funds for Latvian language training.[8]

The EU has not made a link between the possible impact of the Integration Programme on the protection and promotion of minority rights, beyond viewing it as a means of supporting primarily the integration of non-citizens. It has, however, drawn attention to problems with the transition of minority schools to bilingual education within the context of educational reform, without, however, assessing the level of

---

[5] The SIF Council consists of a representative of the President, five ministers, five municipal representatives, and five NGO representatives, two of which are representatives of minority NGOs.

[6] European Commission, *2001 Regular Report on Latvia's Progress Towards Accession*, Brussels, 13 November 2001, p. 24, (hereafter, *"2001 Regular Report"*).

[7] DG Enlargement, *Latvia: 1999 Accession Partnership*, <http://europa.eu.int/comm/enlargement/dwn/ap_02_00/en/ap_lv_99.pdf>, (accessed 26 September 2002).

[8] *2001 Regular Report*, p. 25.

public support for this controversial reform.[9] It has not explicitly evaluated NPLLT or Phare expenditures.

Recently, Phare support has focused on improving the capacity of the SIF with a view to designating it the implementing agency of Phare national projects and the ACCESS Programme. The SIF will also administer funding for Phare pilot projects.

Content and Implementation

The Integration Programme addresses the following aspects of integration: Civic Participation and Political Integration; Social and Regional Integration; Education, Language and Culture; and Information. It seeks to address issues of concern to the general population with the aim to "form a democratic, consolidated civil society founded on shared basic values."[10] One argument for developing the Programme was the need to promote overall social cohesion because of the presence of a large number of Soviet era immigrants, many of whom are not proficient in the Latvian language and feel alienated from the State and from Latvian culture.[11]

While it addresses several aspects of minority integration, such as the promotion of naturalisation, bilingual education, Latvian language training, and support for minority culture, it does not identify and address issues of discrimination against members of minority communities.

At the same time, while the protection and promotion of minority rights is not its primary aim, it does recognise the right of minorities to preserve and develop their identity and notes in general terms the need to protect minority rights. Therefore, investigating whether and to what extent the Integration Programme has elicited minority participation, sought to address discrimination, and promoted minority identity is a legitimate exercise.

While it has encouraged a broad social dialogue on ethnic policy and facilitated integration activities at the local level, a broad consensus within civil society on the content of the Integration Programme has not been achieved. A principal obstacle to this is the fact that it is based on the existing legislative framework and governmental policies which many minority representatives have criticised, especially in the area of education. The Integration Programme, and governmental policy in general, do not pay sufficient attention to concerns of civil society and minorities in the area of minority rights, such as the need for greater access to education and the electronic media in the mother tongue, greater promotion of minority languages, the need for dialogue between minorities and the State, and the effective participation of minorities in public life.

---

[9] *2001 Regular Report,* p. 25.
[10] Integration Programme, p. 8.
[11] Integration Programme, pp. 8–13.

Given the absence of a comprehensive legal framework for the prevention of discrimination and the protection and promotion of minority rights, the lack of references to international standards and documents on human rights, minority rights and non-discrimination in the Integration Programme is a gap which should be remedied in the future.

2. THE GOVERNMENT PROGRAMME – BACKGROUND

2.1 Background to Present Programme

The National Programme "The Integration of Society in Latvia" (hereafter, "Integration Programme")[12] adopted in February 2001 is the first comprehensive governmental programme of its kind. However, it incorporates several programmes and projects implemented by various State and non-State actors which are also considered to promote the general aim of integration.[13] These prior initiatives are included in the list of projects of the Integration Programme, even though they are supported primarily by foreign sources and were started before and during its elaboration.[14] Their impact will also be considered in this report, together with that of projects resulting directly from implementation of the Integration Programme with State funding.

---

[12] *Valsts programma "Sabiedrības integrācija Latvijā"* (National Programme "The Integration of Society in Latvia"), Riga, February 2001, <www.np.gov.lv>, (accessed 23 August 2002) (in Latvian and in English).

[13] There is no shared opinion among the institutions and experts involved about the status and significance of these projects. However, some experts believe that one possible motivation for referring to these projects was the Government's desire to demonstrate to the international community and to Latvian society that it had made efforts in the field of integration. Interview with the Director of the Latvian Centre for Human Rights and Ethnic Studies (LCHRES), Riga, 4 April 2002.

[14] E.g. the National Programme for Latvian Language Training (NPLLT) (1996–2006), a State non-profit organisation established with the help of the United Nations Development Programme (UNDP) in late 1995 and funded primarily from foreign sources, with an increasing share of State funding. Various ministries (e.g. the Ministry of Education and Science) and NGOs (e.g. SFL) have also realised projects in the field of bilingual education. At the local level, initiatives supporting social integration were started in 1999 by municipalities and by the Naturalisation Board – a State body established in 1994 to implement the Law on Citizenship (1994). For more on these projects and their results, see Section 3.

2.2 The Programme – Process

The Integration Programme, an initiative of civil society and the Naturalisation Board, was adopted in February 2001, after a three-year elaboration and adoption process.[15] Indeed, its development took place in a complex political environment; certain influential nationalist politicians did not support the idea of integration.[16] Although it is based on a considerably debated and revised Framework Document (December 1999) to which minorities also contributed, direct minority participation as authors of these documents was low.

The need for integration of Latvian society was articulated by Latvian social scientists in the mid-1990s. The grounds for the Government's ethnic policy were laid by a research project entitled "Towards a Civil Society" initiated in 1997 by the Soros Foundation–Latvia (SFL), the National Human Rights Office (NHRO) and the Naturalisation Board.[17] A main argument for the elaboration of an integration programme was the large number of non-citizens and their slow rate of naturalisation.[18] The decision of Government officials to initiate its elaboration was also to a great degree influenced by the recommendations of international organisations, above all those of the OSCE and

---

[15] For more on the process, see the Integration Programme, pp. 5–7.

[16] Some feared that naturalisation would undermine their electoral base. Moreover, integration ran counter to their stated goal of preventing naturalisation and promoting the voluntary repatriation of non-citizens as it would result in an increased number of citizens of non-ethnic Latvian origin. Interview with the Director of the LCHRES, Riga, 4 April 2002. See e.g. the goals stated in the 1997 programme of one of the leading factions at the time in the Saeima (Parliament) "For Fatherland and Freedom" (LNIM) (Latvia's National Independence Movement) and a member of the ruling Government coalition, at <http://www.tb.lv/download/programma.doc>, (accessed 23 August 2002).

[17] Baltic Data House, *Ceļā uz pilsonisku sabiedrību* (Towards a Civil Society), Results of the First and Second Stage, 1997/1998, <www.policy.lv>, (accessed 25 September 2002) (in Latvian), (hereafter, *"Towards a Civil Society 1997/1998"*).

[18] 687,486 persons (28 percent of residents) did not have Latvian citizenship in 1997. More than 98 percent of non-citizens were ethnic non-Latvians, predominantly Russians, Ukrainians and Belarussians. Around two thirds of non-citizens were born outside Latvia. Only 4 percent of non-citizens who had the right to apply for Latvian citizenship (5,000 out of around 124,000) applied and were naturalised between 1995 and mid-1997. UNDP, *Latvia Human Development Report 1997*, Riga, 1997, pp. 52–56, <http://ano.deac.lv/html_e/index_09_01.htm>, (accessed 23 August 2002). The survey *Towards a Civil Society* showed that 90 percent of non-citizens had decided to live in Latvia. The inability to pass the Latvian language and history exam, lack of information as well as the high naturalisation fee were stated as the main obstacles for naturalisation. *Towards a Civil Society 1997/1998*, pp. 38–39.

the European Union, which stressed the need to facilitate the naturalisation and integration of Russian-speaking non-citizens to strengthen domestic political stability.[19]

In Autumn 1998, a draft Framework Document was prepared by a group of experts, headed by the Advisor to the President on Nationality Issues and consisting of representatives of State institutions, academic establishments and NGOs (but no minority NGOs). In 1999, a Steering Committee,[20] headed by the Director of the Naturalisation Board, was established with the overall task of organising public debates and coordinating the further elaboration of the Integration Programme. Accordingly, the draft Framework Document was made public and debated from March to May 1999, and a broad social dialogue on ethnic policy ensued.[21] It should be noted that this debate was largely initiated and managed by the SFL, with UNDP funding.[22] The representatives of the European Commission were also consulted during the elaboration of the Integration Programme.[23]

The Framework Document was significantly revised to incorporate the results of the public debate and was adopted by the Cabinet of Ministers on 7 December 1999.[24]

---

[19] See the recommendations of the OSCE High Commissioner on National Minorities, at <http://www.riga.lv/minelres/count/latvia.htm>, (accessed 23 August); see also the Opinion on Latvia's Application for Membership (July 1997) and the Regular Reports of the European Commission, at <http://europa.eu.int/comm/enlargement/latvia/index.htm>, (accessed 23 August 2002).

[20] Decree No. 46 of the Prime Minister on the Steering Committee for the Elaboration of the National Programme "The Integration of Society in Latvia," *Latvijas Vēstnesis* (*Official Gazette*), 18 February 1999, p. 2. The Steering Committee consisted of representatives of the Government, ministries and other state institutions.

[21] Materials were also published and distributed. *Final Report. Public Discussion of the Conceptual Framework Document of the National Integration Programme*, Materials of the Information Centre of the Naturalisation Board.

[22] A large number of minority representatives, NGOs and municipalities, *inter alia*, took part in the seminars organised by the SFL throughout the country. A. Pabriks, *Public debates organised by the Steering Committee on the Integration of Society and the UNDP, Report on the Debates, March through May 1999*, SFL, Riga, p. 1, <http://www.sfl.lv/seminari/seminari14.htm>, (accessed 23 August 2002) (in Latvian). The NPLLT, the Naturalisation Board, the Ministry of Education and Science and others also organised public debates.

[23] OSI Roundtable, Riga, June 2002. *Explanatory Note: OSI held a roundtable meeting in Latvia in June 2002 to invite critique of the present report in draft form. Experts present included representatives of the Government, the Commission Delegation, representatives of minorities, and non-governmental organisations.*

[24] Framework Document "The Integration of Society in Latvia," Riga, 2001, <www.np.gov.lv>, (accessed 25 September 2002) (in Latvian and in English), (hereafter, "Framework Document").

The final version of the Integration Programme was not adopted until 6 February 2001, after governmental bodies, municipalities and NGOs had been invited to submit project proposals for inclusion in the document. This last stage was managed by the Steering Committee and the authors on the basis of the revised Framework Document.[25]

While representatives of minority NGOs were consulted during the finalisation of the Framework Document, none served on the Steering Committee, and only few were involved in the drafting of the Framework Document as authors.[26] Three persons with opposing views, including one minority representative, worked together to elaborate the language chapter of the Framework Document, eventually achieving a compromise.[27] On the other hand, the level of cooperation between minority representatives and representatives of the Ministry of Education and Science who drafted the chapter on education – the Programme's most controversial component – has been evaluated by some as insufficient.[28]

The establishment of the principal administering and funding mechanisms – the Society Integration Department (SID) (November 2000) and the Society Integration Foundation (SIF) (October 2001) – was also delayed by protracted political debates.

---

[25] The Integration Programme itself was not discussed in public fora; however, the stated objectives and directions of action in the two documents are similar. The main difference is that the Integration Programme contains lists of projects.

[26] A few minority representatives were invited as contributors during the finalisation of the Framework Document. Several representatives of minority NGOs, academia, media and Members of Parliament were also recruited as "consultants" on the Framework Document (around 14 out of 53 persons involved). *Composition of the Expert Group for the Elaboration of the National Programme "The Integration of Society in Latvia" after the Public Debate*, Materials of the Information Centre of the Naturalisation Board. Some representatives of minority NGOs were also involved in an Advisory Council established in November 2000 at the Ministry of Justice which discussed, *inter alia*, the Integration Programme and normative acts concerning implementation mechanisms. Its 11 members were representatives of State institutions and experts, including three representatives of minority NGOs. See the composition of the Advisory Council at <http://www.integracija.gov.lv/doc_upl/min_kon.doc>, (accessed 23 August 2002).

[27] OSI Roundtable, Riga, June 2002.

[28] OSI Roundtable, Riga, June 2002. No major changes were made to the education chapter, despite sharp criticism during the public debate. However, provisions for minority participation in the elaboration of education programmes were included. Interview with the Director of the Association for the Support of Russian-Language Schools in Latvia (LASHOR), Riga, 28 March 2002. See also Section 2.3.

2.3 The Programme – Content

The Integration Programme addresses the following aspects of integration of society:

- Civic Participation and Political Integration
- Social and Regional Integration of Society
- Education, Language and Culture
- Information[29]

Each chapter consists of stated goals, main directions for action, a list of projects which had already been launched but for which funding in 2002 has been requested ("A projects"), as well as planned projects ("B projects") to be implemented as soon as funding is available. A list of possible future projects ("C projects") is provided in an annex to the Programme.

The main arguments for the Integration Programme are: mistrust towards State institutions and alienation between different segments of society and the State.[30] More specifically, the Programme notes that "Latvia has inherited more than half a million Soviet era immigrants and their descendants, many of whom have not yet become integrated into the Latvian cultural and linguistic environment,[31] and thus do not feel connected to the Latvian state." It also notes that a lack of connection with the State exists to some degree also among Latvian citizens.[32] Integration is therefore considered

---

[29] A final chapter is devoted to implementation mechanisms.

[30] See the Integration Programme, pp. 8-12. Also, Government officials stressed the need to prevent the development of two separate communities of citizens and non-citizens, "with their own language, celebrations and socio-psychological tendencies." A. Čepanis, "*Latvijas sabiedrības integrācija – relitāte vai iespējas*" (The Integration of Latvian Society – Reality or Possibility), *Lauku Avīze* (*Rural Newspaper*), 21 May 1998, p. 4.

[31] Russian is still more widely spoken than Latvian. According to a recent survey, only 40 percent of the non-ethnic Latvian population possessed the medium or highest level of Latvian language proficiency. A majority of minorities (60 percent) still have poor or no Latvian language skills, while only 12 percent of non-ethnic Latvians claim that they do not speak any Latvian. In eight years, the number of Latvian speakers has grown by ten percent, although the data for the last three to four years has not changed. In comparison, around 83 percent of ethnic Latvians possess the medium or highest level of Russian language proficiency. The Baltic Institute of Social Sciences and the NPLLT, *Language. A sociological survey*, November 2001 – January 2002.

[32] Integration Programme, p. 8.

as a process by which "[…] diverse groups within the society must reach understanding among them and learn to work together in one single country."[33]

The choice to focus the Programme on society as a whole rather than on ethnic integration issues explicitly was largely influenced by the public debate, during which many participants, including minority representatives, suggested that more attention should be paid to social, regional and other problems concerning the entire population.[34]

The position of the Integration Programme on the issue of discrimination against minorities is contradictory. The authors of the document claim that addressing discrimination was not a primary aim and, according to Government officials and representatives of State institutions, discrimination issues and the promotion of minority rights should be dealt with outside the Integration Programme, on the grounds that its target group is Latvian society in its entirety, not minorities exclusively.[35] The Integration Programme therefore does not directly address issues of discrimination against members of minority communities; in fact, it does not mention discrimination at all.

It does, however, state that the protection of minority rights is one of its overall objectives,[36] and that "[i]ntegration is also based on a willingness to accept Latvian as the state language, and respect for Latvian as well as minority languages and cultures."[37] It is expected that "Latvians also will develop an attitude of 'receptiveness' toward non-Latvians."[38] It also emphasises that integration does not mean forced assimilation.[39] Yet, few measures are proposed to promote minority ethnic and cultural identities. Given the emphasis on the Latvian language and culture as necessary for the integration of

---

[33] It goes on to say that "[t]he foundation for integration of society is loyalty to the state and awareness that each individual's future and personal well being are closely tied to the future stability and security of the State of Latvia." Integration Programme, p. 8.

[34] Some observers, however, claim that the chapter on Social and Regional Integration was included in order to accommodate many ethnic Latvian participants who did not support integration as a minority-oriented effort only, and that its inclusion is in contradiction with the original concept of integration focussing primarily on ethnic issues. Interviews with: an Associate Professor at Vidzeme University, Riga, 5 April 2002; the Director of the LCHRES, Riga, 4 April 2002; and a Representative of the Latvian Human Rights Committee, Riga, 2 August 2002.

[35] OSI Roundtable, Riga, June 2002.

[36] "In order to foster democracy, secure the rule of law and facilitate the balanced performance of civil rights institutions and protect the rights of minorities, the government should facilitate the formation of integrated society." Integration Programme, p. 5.

[37] Integration Programme, p. 8.

[38] Integration Programme, p. 12.

[39] Integration Programme, p. 10.

minorities, many representatives of minority NGOs are concerned with the lack of corresponding measures to protect and promote minority rights and to promote the emergence of a multicultural society – in the Integration Programme and in general. This criticism is primarily connected to the Government's education policy, which is perceived as posing a threat to the ethnic identity of Russians and the quality of their education.[40] Some minority NGOs have asserted that the minority rights approach should be incorporated into further implementation of the Integration Programme.[41]

Even though a large number of minorities were consulted during the drafting process, several of them have claimed that the Integration Programme does not adequately reflect their opinions and concerns.[42] One reason is that it is based on the existing legislative framework and governmental policies which many minority activists have criticised, especially in the area of education.[43] Nationalist politicians and Government officials also strongly criticised the draft Framework Document.[44] As a result of these criticisms, recommendations to ratify the Framework Convention for the Protection of National Minorities (FCNM) and to adopt national legislation on minority rights, for example,

---

[40] Interview with the Director of the LASHOR, Riga, 28 March 2002; see also *More NGOs on integration of the society in Latvia*, 22 April 1999, <http://racoon.riga.lv/minelres/archive//04221999-22:13:11-25909.html>, (accessed 23 August 2002); Y. Pliner, "What form should the integration of society take?," *Panorama Latvii*, 5 April 2002, p. 2 (in Russian); and *Minority Issues in Latvia*, No. 25, 25 February 2001, p. 3, <http://racoon.riga.lv/minelres/archive//02272001-06:16:11-23883.html>, (accessed 23 August 2002).

[41] OSI Roundtable, Riga, June 2002. Interviews with: a Representative of the Latvian Human Rights Committee, Riga, 3 August 2002; and the Director of the Latvian Association of the Teachers of Russian Language and Literature, Riga, 30 July 2002.

[42] OSI Roundtable, Riga, June 2002. See also Section 2.3.

[43] The main criticisms by minority NGOs regarding the education chapter concerned the provisions on discontinuing State financing for secondary, professional and higher education in minority languages, and the use of bilingual education as a tool for transition to Latvian as the language of instruction in minority secondary schools. These provisions, as well as the emphasis on the need to use the Latvian language and the lack of measures to promote the minority identity have been perceived as assimilatory in intent. See *More NGOs on integration of the society in Latvia*, 22 April 1999.

[44] 34 amendments were submitted by the ministers of the (ethnic Latvian) party "For Fatherland and Freedom." *Minority Issues in Latvia*, No. 10, p. 1, <http://racoon.riga.lv/minelres/archive//11271999-18:57:30-21424.html>, (accessed 23 August 2002).

were not included in the final version of the Framework Document.[45] Given the absence of a comprehensive legal framework for the prevention of discrimination and the protection and promotion of minority rights, the lack of references to international standards and documents on human rights, minority rights and non-discrimination in the Integration Programme is a gap which should be remedied in the future.[46]

Overall, however, given the existence of strong political opposition, often opposing views on integration, and the lack of dialogue within society on the subject of ethnic policy prior to the public debate over the Framework Document, the authors and many civil society representatives consider the adoption of the Integration Programme as an achievement, even as they acknowledge that it needs to be updated to reflect the changing situation.[47]

2.4 The Programme – Administration/Implementation/Evaluation

The main institutions for administering and funding the Integration Programme are the Society Integration Department (SID) at the Ministry of Justice, and the Society Integration Foundation (SIF). The majority of integration projects being implemented are those which were started before and during its adoption. At the end of 2001, a first group of projects (largely those of State institutions, listed in the A and B project lists) was approved for State funding in a closed process – a fact which drew strong criticism. Two public tenders for State funding were also announced in the first half of 2002 by the SIF, as well as a competition for Phare pilot projects. However, the lack of effective coordination between various authorities and the lack of a clear implementation strategy is likely to hinder successful implementation of the Integration Programme unless these problems are addressed. Minority participation in implementation has also not been sufficient.

The Ministry of Justice bears overall responsibility for implementation while the SID coordinates the activities of various actors (ministries, State institutions, municipalities,

---

[45] *Minority Issues in Latvia*, No. 12, pp. 1–2, <http://racoon.riga.lv/minelres/archive//02172000-19:46:56-14688.html>, (accessed 23 August 2002). Minority organisations also suggested harmonising the Framework Document with international human rights documents. The draft Framework Document included some references but these were excluded in the final version. Summary of the Public Debate, pp. 4–5, <http://www.sfl.lv/seminari/seminari1.htm>, (accessed 23 August 2002) (in Latvian).

[46] Latvia does not possess comprehensive anti-discrimination legislation to comply with the EU Race Equality Directive (Council Directive 2000/43/EC). Latvia has not yet ratified the FCNM or the European Charter for Regional or Minority Languages; nor has it adopted a comprehensive minority law.

[47] OSI Roundtable, Riga, June 2002.

NGOs, international organisations, etc). In addition, the SID elaborates the criteria for evaluating and monitoring the integration policy and process, manages this evaluation (see below), and is responsible for the communications strategy (see Section 2.5).[48]

The SIF manages the allocation of State as well as donor funding.[49] Seven expert SIF commissions evaluate projects submitted in different subject areas. The SIF is funded by the Government as well as by the EU (Phare funding represented over 35 percent of its overall budget in 2002).[50]

A Council supervises the work of the SIF.[51] The composition[52] of this Council has been criticised by many, including minority representatives, for the following reasons:

- Lack of transparency of the selection process for NGO representatives;[53]

- The possibility of political interference in the work of the SIF (several of its members are ministers and some of the NGO representatives also belong to

---

[48] For a full description of the responsibilities of the SID, see Bylaw of the Society Integration Department, 12 December 2000, § 2, para. 2, p. 1, <http://www.integracija.gov.lv/doc_upl/SID_no1.3.piel..doc>, (accessed 23 August 2002). LVL 16,000 (€27,923) was allocated from the 2002 State budget for its functioning. Government Contribution to Social Integration in Latvia, Ministry of Foreign Affairs, 9 August 2002, p. 2, <www.am.gov.lv/en/?id=804>, (accessed 25 September 2002). The exchange rate is calculated at LVL 0.573 (Latvian Lats) = €1.

[49] See the Law on the Society Integration Foundation, 5 July 2001 (Art. 3), at <http://www.integracija.gov.lv/doc_upl/SIF_Likums.doc>, (accessed 23 August 2002).

[50] The total SIF budget in 2002, including project money, consisted of LVL 447,000 (€780,105), of which LVL 282,000 (€492,147) was allocated by the Government, and LVL 165,000 (€287,958) by the EU (Phare 2000). Interview with the Director of the SIF Secretariat, Riga, 15 May 2002.

[51] Decree No. 515 of the Cabinet of Ministers "On the Council of the Society Integration Foundation," 24 October 2001, <http://www.integracija.gov.lv/doc_upl/NEW_SIF_Padome.doc>, (accessed 23 August 2002).

[52] The SIF Council is elected for three years and consists of a representative of the President, five ministers (Education and Science; Culture; Welfare; Justice; Environmental Protection and Regional Development), five municipal representatives and five NGO representatives. Law on the Society Integration Foundation, Art. 9.

[53] Latvian Centre for Human Rights and Ethnic Studies, *Human Rights in Latvia in 2001*, Riga, March 2002, p. 17, <http://www.politika.lv/polit_real/files/lv/LCHRES2001en.pdf>, (accessed 26 September 2002). Some have assumed the existence of a criterion of "loyalty" of NGOs towards State policies for membership. *Minority Issues in Latvia*, No. 35, p. 3, <http://racoon.riga.lv/minelres/archive//09012001-11:21:50-22362.html>, (accessed 23 August 2002).

political parties), and of changes in the ruling coalition which would result in major changes to the Council which could negatively affect its work;[54]

- There are too few representatives of minority NGOs (two out of 16 members).

A Secretariat supports the work of the SIF and its Council.[55] It is also responsible for overseeing expenditures, requesting reports from the implementing authorities and monitoring the implementation of projects supported through the SIF (see below).

Funding

In November 2001, the SIF Council approved funding for 21 of the 60 project proposals included in the Programme's A and B project lists.[56] The approval procedure was strongly criticised by representatives of civil society and minorities as well as by international organisations due to the fact that the SIF commissions of experts were not involved and because the funding decisions were made before rules for open competitions had been prepared.[57] They also criticised the fact that about half of the projects supported[58] concerned social rather than ethnic integration, and did not correspond to the "original concept of integration."[59]

In a first tender announced in January 2002 (deadline end May 2002), LVL 120,000 (€209,424) was to be allocated as follows: 50 percent for projects in the field of ethnic

---

[54] See A. Pabriks, "*Integrācijas fonds krustcelēs*" (The Integration Foundation at a Crossroads), <http://www.politika.lv/index.php?id=102179&lang=lv&print=;>, (accessed 26 September 2002); and also N. Lebedeva, "Who Needs the Great Fiction of Integration?," *Chas*, 26 March 2002 (in Russian). Some observers believe that the ministers' competence in budget matters and political authority are assets. OSI Roundtable, Riga, June 2002.

[55] Law on the Society Integration Foundation, Art. 11(1).

[56] A total of LVL 126,845 (€221,370) was allocated from the 2001 State budget; LVL 20,000 (€34,904) had been earmarked for projects to provide language training for naturalisation applicants.

[57] SIF representatives explained that implementation needed to start in 2001 already and that tenders take a lot of time to organise. Interview with the Deputy Director of the SIF Secretariat, Riga, 28 March 2002.

[58] R. Belousova, "*Par Sabiedrības integrācijas fondu*" (About the Society Integration Foundation), *Latvijas Vēstnesis* (*Official Gazette*), 19 December 2001.

[59] LCHRES, *Human Rights in Latvia in 2001*, p. 17.

integration;[60] 30 percent in the field of social integration, including at the municipal level; and 20 percent in the field of regional integration.[61] Ten information seminars organised by the SIF to explain the application rules were attended by about 600 participants.[62] In June 2002, the SIF approved 64 projects for a total of LVL 96,549 (€168,497).[63]

In July 2002, the SIF announced a second tender (deadline 16 September 2002) for a total of LVL 62,000 (€108,202) from the State budget, with an emphasis on the theme of ethnic integration (nearly 70 percent of the funding). It also announced the first Phare pilot project tender in the field of ethnic integration in the amount of €140,000, including €40,000 of State co-financing. Again, seminars were organised by the SIF in several cities on how to prepare Phare proposals.[64]

The following two main priorities for funding from the State budget for 2003 were defined by the SIF Council in March 2002:

- Latvian language training for naturalisation applicants (LVL 200,000, €349,040);

- State co-financing for Phare-funded projects in 2003 (LVL 320,000, €558,464).

As of August 2002, funding was expected for the second priority while none was forthcoming for the first one.[65]

---

[60] The six themes of ethnic integration projects are: Latvian language training for naturalisation applicants (LVL 12,000, €20,942; funding is also available in the amount of LVL 20,000, €34,904, from a reserve in the 2001 State budget); research on the integration process (LVL 3,000, €5,236); programmes of assistance to NGO projects in the field of ethnic integration (LVL 10,000, €17,452); exchange of pupils and cooperation programmes (LVL 10,000, €17,452); assistance to minority cultural organisations (LVL 15,000, €26,178); and media programmes to promote the consolidation of society (LVL 10,000, €17,452).

[61] Information provided by the Deputy Director of the SIF Secretariat, Riga, 28 March 2002.

[62] *Integration of Society in Latvia: from Plans to Implementation. March–April 2002*, p. 5 <http://www.am.gov.lv/en/?id=2683>, (accessed 23 August 2002).

[63] 390 project proposals were submitted to the SIF. The largest number of them were in the area of social integration and from representatives of the regions. 68 percent of the approved projects will be implemented outside Riga. M. Līdaka, "*Par SIF projektu konkursu*" (About the SIF Project Tender), *Latvijas Vēstnesis*, 28 June 2002, pp. 1, 5.

[64] *Integration of Society in Latvia: From Plans to Implementation, June–July 2002*, Ministry of Foreign Affairs, pp. 2–3, <http://www.am.gov.lv/en/?id=2950>, (accessed 27 August 2002).

[65] Interview with the Director of the SIF Secretariat, Riga, 12 August 2002.

Participation of minorities and NGOs

Few minority NGOs are participating in the implementation of projects under the Integration Programme, although allegedly all of the projects submitted by minority NGOs were included.[66] The majority of projects in the A and B categories are being implemented by State institutions. In February 2000, the Naturalisation Board organised a tender to solicit ideas from civil society. However, these project proposals, including some submitted by minority NGOs (these are the C projects), have not been funded through this tender.

According to some observers, minority NGOs submitted few projects due to insufficient skills in project proposal writing, capacity and experience; a sense of alienation from the State; lack of information; and lack of resources. Another explanation is that project information for inclusion in the A and B categories was gathered primarily from the ministries.[67] Participation continues to be low, even though several minority NGOs (predominantly dealing with culture) participated in the 2002 project tenders.[68] The limited funding – a maximum of LVL 1,000 (€1,745) per project from the SIF – seems to have also been a factor hindering participation.[69]

Monitoring and evaluation

As the mechanisms for administering and funding implementation of the Integration Programme have only recently been established, and in the absence of a monitoring system (in the process of elaboration as of Summer 2002), an assessment of the overall impact of the Integration Programme or the effectiveness of its projects cannot yet be

---

[66] OSI Roundtable, Riga, June 2002. Only one minority NGO – "*Zelta Kamoliņš*" (Golden Ball) (see Section 3.4.5) and a few projects by minority schools were supported by the SIF in November 2001.

[67] Interviews with: the Director of the LCHRES, Riga, 4 April 2002; the Director of the Latvian Association of Teachers of the Russian Language and Literature, Riga, 30 July 2002; the Director of the SID, Riga, 1 August 2002; and the Head of the Information Centre of the Naturalisation Board, Riga, 31 July 2002.

[68] The SIF has pointed out that many project proposals (e.g. 58 percent of projects in the field of ethnic integration) were incomplete or did not comply with the tender's guidelines, showing insufficient skills or experience in project proposal writing, especially among NGOs, including many minority organisations. Interviews with: the Deputy Director of the SIF Secretariat, Riga, 2 August 2002; and the Project Coordinator of the festival "Golden Ball," Riga, 7 August 2002. On the other hand, some minority representatives are concerned about the SIF's insufficient trust in the capacity of NGOs, and of minority NGOs specifically. Interview with a Representative of the Latvian Human Rights Committee, Riga 3 August 2002.

[69] OSI Roundtable, Riga, June 2002. Interview with the Project Coordinator of the festival "Golden Ball," Riga, 7 August 2002.

made. No public reports on expenditures under the Integration Programme are available.[70]

Already, there appears to be a general lack of coordination between different authorities in the field of integration policy and a lack of clearly defined responsibilities for each institution.[71] Civil society and minority representatives have also pointed to the lack of a clear implementation strategy, as well as the lack of clear divisions of responsibilities and expected results.[72] It should also be noted in this context that Latvia's framework for minority-related policy in general is fragmented and decentralised. There is no body specialising in monitoring or combating ethnic/racial discrimination explicitly or dealing with minority issues comprehensively. This might result in additional coordination problems.[73]

In order to improve the situation, the SID is working on the elaboration of a monitoring mechanism which will also serve to define the new priorities of the Integration Programme.[74] This monitoring aims to evaluate integration policy and the integration process in general, rather than implementation of the Programme and projects specifically.[75] There is no formal obligation of the SID to monitor or evaluate specific projects.[76] The SIF in its turn, will monitor the projects funded by the SIF

---

[70] Some of the prior projects incorporated in the Integration Programme were evaluated upon the initiative of the implementing authority or of the funding institution. See e.g. A. Pabriks, *The National Programme for Latvian Language Training. Promotion of the Integration of Society 1996–2000. Impact Report.*

[71] Interview with the Director of the SID, Riga, 14 May 2002.

[72] EU Accession Monitoring Program, *Monitoring the EU Accession Process: Minority Protection*, Open Society Institute, Budapest, September 2001, pp. 302–307, (hereafter, "*Minority Protection 2001*"). Interviews with: the Project Coordinator of the festival "Golden Ball," Riga, 7 August 2002; the Director of the SFL Programme "Changes in Education," Riga, 28 March 2002; and a Representative of the Latvian Human Rights Committee, Riga, 3 August 2002.

[73] OSI Roundtable, Riga, June 2002.

[74] In June 2002, a task force coordinated by the SID and consisting of representatives of ministries, State institutions and municipalities was established with the purpose of coordinating implementation of the Integration Programme and to define new priorities. An expert group recruited in May 2002 is currently elaborating a monitoring system of the integration policy and process. Independent research institutes will be asked to carry out the research on the basis of which the analysis will be made. These activities are funded by the UNDP. The State has not invested in the elaboration of monitoring system. It has been suggested that the SIF could provide additional funding. Interview with the Director of the SID, Riga, 3 August 2002.

[75] Interview with the Director of the SID, Riga, 1 August 2002.

[76] Interview with the Director of the SID, Riga, 1 August 2002.

only.[77] Thus, it will be important to coordinate the various monitoring activities foreseen in order to obtain a comprehensive picture. Complementary independent monitoring would also be advisable.

The priorities of the Integration Programme are to be revised every year, based on the results of the monitoring system.[78] However, the 2003 priorities will have to be defined already by Autumn 2002, before the results of the first round of monitoring are available. It is not clear how the new priorities are to be defined. Also, the impact of the SIF-financed projects (project tenders) on integration will be evaluated in 2004, only then will it be possible to assess impact in each integration area.[79]

2.5 The Programme and the Public

The Framework Document, the Integration Programme and related information materials have been widely distributed at seminars, conferences, and on the websites of various State institutions and NGOs as well as through the Information Centre of the Naturalisation Board. Nevertheless, there has been a lack of publicly available information on implementation, especially concerning on-going activities of the Ministry of Justice, the SIF (except for information about project tenders)[80] and the status of implementation of projects – both prior projects as well as those supported through the SIF. Several steps have been taken recently by the SID to remedy this situation: it is creating a database on institutions and projects in the field of integration.[81] It is also developing a communication strategy with UNDP funding, including a new website launched in August 2002 to provide information on key activities in the field of integration, as well as relevant institutions and research.[82] The aim of the communication strategy is to promote understanding and support for the Programme's objectives and results as well as to encourage participation in implementation.[83]

---

[77] It is planned that monitoring will consist of an assessment of individual projects, financial control, as well an assessment of progress made in specific areas (to be carried out at the end of 2003 for projects started in 2001). OSI Roundtable, Riga, June 2002.

[78] Interview with the Director of the SID, Riga, 14 May 2002.

[79] Interview with the Director of the SIF Secretariat, Riga, 12 August 2002.

[80] The new SIF website (in Latvian, Russian and English) provides information on the 2002 project tenders, <www.lsif.lv>, (accessed 23 August 2002).

[81] Interview with the Director of the SID, Riga, 1 August 2002.

[82] <www.integracija.gov.lv>, in Latvian only as of Summer 2002.

[83] Interview with the Director of the SID, Riga, 8 April 2002.

The domestic media periodically publishes information and opinions about activities of the Integration Programme but comprehensive and analytical articles on the Programme and on integration in general are rare, in both the Latvian- and the Russian-language press.[84]

The public debate and social surveys organised around the draft Framework Document showed that civil society, including minority representatives, generally welcomed the idea of integration, viewing this as "a change in attitudes towards national minorities."[85] Survey data from 2000 ("Towards a Civil Society") showed that Latvian residents in most cases perceived integration as a feeling of belonging to the State and collaboration between the State and individuals, rather than the integration of minorities into Latvian society specifically.[86] Also, the "two-way process" approach of the Integration Programme, i.e. the promotion of the integration of ethnic Latvians as well as of minorities, and of collaboration between different groups, is generally seen as a positive aspect.[87] Indeed, 44 percent of citizens and 56 percent of non-citizens considered a society open to different cultures as the preferable model (against 38 percent of citizens and 13 percent of non-citizens who preferred a single-community society).[88] According to another survey from 1999, the most important issues in the opinion of residents were the resolution of social problems affecting the quality of life, education, corruption, and crime. At the same time, considerably more minority respondents (59 percent) than ethnic Latvians (34 percent), considered the promotion of minority rights as a "very important" task for integration.[89]

---

[84] I. Apine, L. Dribins, A. Jansons, *et al.*, *Etnopolitika Latvijā (Ethnopolicy in Latvia)*, Elpa, Riga, 2001, p. 88.

[85] *More NGOs on integration of the society in Latvia*, 22 April 1999.

[86] The Baltic Institute of Social Sciences and the Naturalisation Board, *Towards a Civil Society, Public Survey 2000/2001*, p. 81, <http://www.politika.lv/polit_real/files/lv/uzpilssab2001.pdf>, (accessed 26 September 2002) (in Latvian), (hereafter, "*Towards a Civil Society 2000/2001*"). According to the survey data, 38 percent of citizens and 46 percent of non-citizens had heard about the Framework Document. Among them, 70 percent of citizens and 63 percent of non-citizens positively evaluated its contents. In general, they (71 percent of citizens and 67 percent of non-citizens) supported the need for such a Programme and accepted the State's role as coordinator of the integration process.

[87] OSI Roundtable, Riga, June 2002.

[88] *Towards a Civil Society 2000/2001*, p. 10.

[89] *Latvijas fakti (Facts of Latvia), Survey of Public opinion. Report of the Research*. Riga, July 1999, p. 90.

A concern expressed by minority representatives is the lack of dialogue between the State and minorities in the integration process.[90] It has also been noted that there is a shortage of persons who could initiate dialogue between ethnic Latvians and minorities, a lack of consensus among State institutions on the concept of integration and an insufficient will of Government officials to popularise the idea of integration.[91]

2.6 The Programme and the EU

The European Commission in its Regular Reports has recommended implementing activities to promote the integration of minorities and has positively evaluated developments in this field, including the adoption of the Integration Programme.[92] It has also welcomed measures to simplify naturalisation procedures. Accordingly, through its Phare Programme, the EU has strongly supported efforts to promote integration since 1996, allocating significant funds to support Latvian language training and naturalisation. This is in line with its assessment that these are key instruments for integration.[93]

Latvian language training for various categories of the population (through the NPLLT) is one main area of EU support.[94] The work of the NPLLT has been positively evaluated, as has been the fact that, in 2001, the Government allocated funding to it for the first time; however, the significant shortage of Latvian language

---

[90] An MP from "For Human Rights in United Latvia" (FHRUL) has noted that: "[t]he Integration Programme should be started with dialogue with the opposition and different organisations representing the rights and interests of minorities in Latvia." A. Elkin, "Integration as the breadwinner of functionaries," *Vesti Sevodnya* (*News Today*), 6 December 2001 (in Russian).

[91] Interview with a Researcher at the Institute of Philosophy and Sociology, Riga, 4 April 2002.

[92] European Commission, *2001 Regular Report on Latvia's Progress Towards Accession*, Brussels, 13 November 2001, p. 24, (hereafter, "*2001 Regular Report*").

[93] See the medium-term priority in Latvia's 1999 Accession Partnership to "pursue integration of non-citizens in particular by extending language training programmes for non-Latvian speakers." DG Enlargement, *Latvia: 1999 Accession Partnership*, <http://europa.eu.int/comm/enlargement/dwn/ap_02_00/en/ap_lv_99.pdf>, (accessed 26 September 2002). Indeed, the 2001 Regular Report states that: "[t]he ongoing efforts to support the integration of non-citizens need to be sustained through the implementation of the comprehensive Society Integration Programme in all its aspects, including activities to encourage naturalisation and the expansion of Latvian language training." *2001 Regular Report*, p. 27.

[94] In 2000, Phare funding represented 16 percent of the NPLLT's overall budget and the EU has annually invested €500,000 in its activities since 1996. A. Pabriks, *The National Programme for Latvian Language Training*, p. 23; see also <http://www.lvavp.lv/eng/frameset.php?PHPSESSID=7eac25821853ca264a5348de81ac4036>, (accessed 26 August 2002).

teachers was noted, as well as the need for more Government funding.[95] The EU has not explicitly evaluated NPLLT and Phare expenditures, mainly due to the difficulty of evaluating the implementation of projects which are in different stages.[96]

Promotion of naturalisation is a second priority area. In 1998, €500,000 was allocated to a project of the Naturalisation Board entitled "Promotion of Integration through Information and Education." Its objectives were to strengthen the Information Centre of the Naturalisation Board and to implement pilot projects.[97]

The EU has not assessed the impact of the Integration Programme on the degree to which minority rights are protected and promoted in Latvia, beyond viewing it as a means of supporting primarily the integration of non-citizens. The European Commission has, however, drawn attention to problems with the transition of minority schools to bilingual education within the context of educational reform, noting the lack of sufficient training for teachers from minority language schools and teaching materials.[98] It has also emphasised the need to maintain the use of minority languages at all minority schools as far as possible. Yet, while the 2001 Regular Report states that "[i]n continuing with the educational reform, it will be important to ensure that the confidence in the process is maintained [...],"[99] it does not assess the level of popular support for this controversial reform.

Phare 2000 funding was allocated to increase the capacity and transparency of the SIF with a view to its becoming the implementing agency of Phare national projects and the administrator of Phare-funded pilot projects.[100] EU experts will provide assistance starting in Autumn 2002 by evaluating the normative acts concerning the SIF and presenting recommendations for improving its funding, evaluation and administrative procedures.[101]

---

[95] *2001 Regular Report*, p. 25.

[96] Information provided by the Delegation of the European Commission to Latvia, Riga, 28 March 2002.

[97] E.g. partial financing of sociological research, conferences, a student contest "Towards a Civil Society." Information provided by the Delegation of the European Commission to Latvia, Riga, 28 March 2002.

[98] The European Commission welcomed the increased allocation of State funds for the reform. *2001 Regular Report*, p. 25.

[99] *2001 Regular Report*, p. 25.

[100] €500,000 was allocated for institutional strengthening and to improve the capacity of the SIF, and €100,000 was allocated for pilot projects. OSI Roundtable, Riga, June 2002.

[101] Standard Summary Project Fiche LE00.07.00, Promotion of Integration of Society in Latvia 2000 (Sector: Social Integration), Ministry of Justice, Ministry of Education and Science, pp. 7–11.

A further €1,283,850 is to be granted to the SIF under Phare 2001 for the implementation in 2003 and 2004 of projects approved through tenders based on EU grant procedures; State co-financing is required (see Section 2.4).[102] It is expected that a further €1,500,000 will be allocated to the SIF under Phare 2002 for 2004 and 2005.[103] The EU Phare programme will support projects in the field of ethnic integration only.[104]

Starting in 2003, the SIF also plans to administer the ACCESS programme, consisting of an additional € one million for NGO activities.[105]

Latvia was deemed to have fulfilled its short-term priorities concerning the 1999 Language Law[106] and Latvian language training "to a considerable extent,"[107] but to have only "partially met" its medium-term priorities (pursing the integration of non-citizens especially by extending Latvian language training) through the adoption of the Integration Programme and the establishment of the SIF.[108] Latvia's Accession Partnership has been revised on the basis of the conclusions of the 2001 Regular Report.[109]

3. THE GOVERNMENT PROGRAMME – IMPLEMENTATION

3.1 Stated Objectives of the Programme

The main goal of the Integration Programme, as stated in its introduction, is to "form a democratic, consolidated civil society, founded on shared basic values. An

---

[102] Standard Summary Project Fiche LE01.01.01, Promotion of Integration of Society in Latvia 2001 (Sector: Political Criteria), Ministry of Justice, pp. 4–8. The overall 2001 Phare Programme consists of an allocation of €31.4 million, of which €2 million is to be allocated to "Priority 1: Political Criteria, including Promotion of Integration of Society in Latvia." *2001 Regular Report*, p. 9.

[103] Interview with the SIF Project Manager, Riga, 2 August 2002.

[104] Interview with the Director of the SIF Secretariat, Riga, 12 August 2002.

[105] Interview with the Director of the SIF Secretariat, Riga, 12 August 2002.

[106] The Law on the State Language entered into force on 1 September 2000. See Section 3.4.2.

[107] *2001 Regular Report*, p. 115.

[108] *2001 Regular Report*, p. 118. It is explained that "[t]here is still a significant shortage of language teachers, and it will be important that the Government's supported for the Latvian Language Training Programme be maintained and increased in the coming years."

[109] Latvia's new Accession Partnership is at <http://europa.eu.int/comm/enlargement/report2001/aplv_en.pdf>, (accessed 26 September 2002).

independent and democratic Latvian state is one of these values."[110] More specific goals are outlined in individual chapters (see below).

3.2 Government Programme and Discrimination

While the Integration Programme does not directly address issues of discrimination against minorities, it often refers to disadvantages experienced by residents of Latvia in general, including minorities, such as problems in the area of social and regional integration (unemployment, poverty, regional differences) and the lack of funding for cultural activities. It also mentions lack of citizenship and proficiency in the Latvian language as well as alienation from the Latvian State and culture. It acknowledges specific disadvantages experienced by minorities, including: obstacles to applying for citizenship, limited contacts between minorities and ethnic Latvians, lack of contact between Latvian-language and minority schools, insufficient means to pay for Latvian lessons, the development of two separate information spaces, and inadequate legislation in the area of minority culture.

Views about discrimination in Latvian society are polarised. There is no shared understanding between State institutions, NGOs and broader society of what constitutes discrimination. This situation prevents a constructive dialogue between ethnic Latvians and minorities, as well as between the State and minorities. Many representatives of State institutions and officials involved in the elaboration and implementation of the Integration Programme do not consider discrimination to be a problem concerning minorities specifically, stressing rather the disadvantages experienced by both ethnic Latvians and minorities (such as access to education, employment issues, discrimination on the basis of gender, etc.)[111] At the same time, minorities, significantly more often then ethnic Latvians, claim to experience discrimination, predominantly on grounds of language or ethnicity.[112]

---

[110] Integration Programme, p. 8.

[111] OSI Roundtable, Riga, June 2002.

[112] According to a 2000 survey, 24 percent of respondents (31 percent of non-ethnic Latvians and 33 percent of non-citizens) had experienced discrimination in the previous three years; 37 percent of non-citizens and 36 percent of non-ethnic Latvians cited language as the grounds of human rights violations; and 43 percent of non-citizens and 40 percent of non-ethnic Latvians mentioned ethnic origin. Baltic Data House, *Cilvēktiesības (Human Rights)*, Unpublished survey commissioned by the NHRO, 2000.

Latvia does not possess comprehensive anti-discrimination legislation to comply with the EU Race Equality Directive.[113] The Constitution contains a general equality clause, as do a number of other laws.[114] Latvia has not ratified Protocol No. 12 to the European Convention on Human Rights and Fundamental Freedoms (ECHR).[115] However, the new Labour Law prohibits direct and indirect discrimination and provides for reversal of the burden of proof in certain cases; in fact, the EU Race Equality Directive is considered complied with only in the field of the new Labour Law.[116] A work group under the Ministry of Welfare has begun work on implementation of the EU Race Equality Directive.[117]

There is a need to raise public awareness of discrimination and of procedures for seeking redress as well as for training of public authorities dealing with the application of legal norms.[118] The need to establish a specialised body to deal with issues of discrimination, including racial and ethnic discrimination, has been stressed by several

---

[113] Council Directive 2000/43/EC of 29 June 2000 implementing the principle of equal treatment between persons irrespective of racial or ethnic origin. The European Commission Against Racism and Intolerance (ECRI) recently noted that "[t]here is no comprehensive body of anti-discrimination legislation covering all fields of life [...] and providing for effective mechanisms of enforcement and redress." Council of Europe, European Commission against Racism and Intolerance. *Second report on Latvia adopted on 14 December 2001 and made public on 23 July 2002*, p. 8, <http://www.coe.int/T/E/Human_Rights/Ecri/1-ECRI/2-Country-by-country_approach/Latvia/Latvia_CBC_2.asp#TopOfPage>, (accessed 26 August 2002), (hereafter, "*2002 ECRI Report*").

[114] The Constitution (*Satversme*) is at <http://www.saeima.lv/Lapas/Satversme_Visa.htm>, (accessed 26 September 2002). Other laws containing anti-discrimination clauses are: the Labour Law, the Education Law, the Criminal Code, the Law "On the Unrestricted Development of National and Ethnic Groups of Latvia and the Rights to Cultural Autonomy," and the Sentence Execution Code. *Minority Protection 2001*, pp. 279–280.

[115] The ECHR was signed in November 2000. Protocol No. 12 broadens the scope of Article 14 on non-discrimination.

[116] The Labour Law (entered into force 1 June 2002) is at <http://www.likumi.lv/doc.php?id=26019>, (accessed 26 August 2002). See also G. Feldhūne and M. Mits, *Legal analysis of national and European anti-discrimination legislation. A comparison of the EU Racial Equality Directive & Protocol No. 12 with anti-discrimination legislation in Latvia*, European Roma Rights Center/Interights/Migration Policy Group, Budapest/London/Brussels, September 2001, p. 25, <http://www.migpolgroup.com/uploadstore/Latvia%20electronic.pdf>, (accessed 26 September 2002).

[117] Information provided by the Director of the LCHRES, Riga, 21 August 2002.

[118] G. Feldhūne and M. Mits, *Legal analysis of national and European anti-discrimination legislation*, p. 28.

experts.[119] The NHRO[120] acknowledges the need for such a body but points to a lack of resources.[121]

There have been no successful court cases concerning discrimination on the basis of language or ethnicity.[122] However, following amendments to the Law on the Constitutional Court, it may also hear individual appeals.[123] A larger number of complaints of discrimination on the grounds of (lack of) citizenship or language can therefore be expected in the near future.[124]

3.2.1 Education

The lack of contact between Latvian- and Russian-language schools has been identified as a major problem in the field of education, encouraging ethnic prejudices and stereotypes.[125] The Integration Programme stresses the need to create a "unified educational system" in order to ensure "the development of Latvian society as a civic society with common values and responsibilities."[126] In particular, it stresses the importance of a "common language" for successful integration and therefore the need for Latvian language training, "especially so that the younger generation is able to use it freely as a means of communication." At the same time, it states the need to preserve the identity of minorities.[127]

---

[119] G. Feldhūne and M. Mits, *Legal analysis of national and European anti-discrimination legislation*, p. 33. ECRI has also stressed the need for a specialised body to supervise the implementation of anti-discrimination legislation, either as a separate entity or within the NHRO. *2002 ECRI Report*, pp. 8–9.

[120] The NHRO is an independent, ombudsman-like institution established in 1995 to promote the observance of human rights. Its competencies include examining complaints regarding discrimination on racial, ethnic and linguistic grounds (although there have been few such complaints); it also analyses the situation in these fields. For more, see *Minority Protection 2001*, pp. 302–303.

[121] NHRO, *Topical Human Rights Issues in Latvia in the Second Quarter of 2002*, pp. 13–14, <http://www.politika.lv/polit_real/files/lv/2002g2cet.pdf>, (accessed 26 August 2002).

[122] See *Minority Protection 2001*, p. 281.

[123] The amendments entered into force on 1 July 2001. See the Law on the Constitutional Court (14 June 1996), Art.17, <http://www.likumi.lv/doc.php?id=63354>, (accessed 26 September 2002).

[124] G. Feldhūne and M. Mits, *Legal analysis of national and European anti-discrimination legislation*, p. 19.

[125] Framework Document, p. 29.

[126] Integration Programme, p. 60.

[127] Integration Programme, p. 60.

The goals of the Integration Programme in the area of education are, *inter alia*:

- The development and implementation of minority education programmes (bilingual education);[128]
- The promotion of collaboration between Latvian and minority schools.[129]

The measures proposed by the Integration Programme in the area of education are viewed as the most controversial by many minority and civil society representatives, as they are based on the 1998 Education Law. While the officially stated aim of the education reform is to promote the integration of minorities and to increase their competitiveness in entering higher education establishments as well as on the labour market through the promotion of Latvian language training,[130] many civil society representatives and minority parents view elements of the reform as discriminatory and as producing disadvantages. Some experts have highlighted a lack of preparation in many schools as well as insufficient State funding, and have recommended that it be implemented only in those schools which are ready.

Most of the projects implemented in this area were those started by the NPLLT and the SFL prior to the adoption of the Integration Programme (mostly with foreign funding) and have registered success. The SIF has also recently approved a series of small projects connected with education. More governmental efforts and resources are needed for the training of teachers, policy monitoring, promotion of information about the education reform and more effective participation of minorities in the further planning and implementation of the reform.

Education reform

The aims of the Integration Programme in the area of education are in line with the 1998 Education Law which proposes the transition of all public secondary schools to

---

[128] The implementation of minority primary education programmes is also referred to by officials as "bilingual education" since two languages of instruction are used. Programme for the Gradual Transition of Secondary Education to the State Language and Increase in the Number of Subjects Taught in the State Language in Primary School Education Programmes until 2005, p. 10.

[129] Other objectives include: the development of a methodology for bilingual education; "intercultural education;" the promotion of cooperation between Latvian-language and minority-language schools; the training of teachers in the social sciences; the development of a civic education programme; ensuring the participation of minorities in the elaboration of education programmes and in the implementation of educational policy, etc. Integration Programme, Chapter on "Education, Language and Culture," pp. 60–72.

[130] Programme for the Gradual Transition of Secondary Education to the State Language and Increase in the Number of Subjects Taught in the State Language in Primary School Education Programmes until 2005, p. 16.

Latvian as the language of instruction and the implementation of education programmes for national minorities (bilingual education) in primary schools. Thus, from 1 September 1999, all State and municipal general educational institutions with languages of instruction other than Latvian had to either start implementing minority education programmes (see below) or to proceed with the transition to education in the State language. On 1 September 2004, all tenth grades[131] of State and municipal general education institutions and first year classes of State and municipal vocational education institutions are to begin teaching in Latvian only.[132]

Bilingual education is not precisely defined in Latvia's normative acts.[133] In Spring 1999, the Ministry of Education and Science introduced four models for minority education programmes for the primary level, defining the proportions of use of Latvian and minority languages (instruction in Latvian only, bilingually, in the minority language only). State-funded minority schools may also elaborate their own model, according to standards developed by the Ministry. Some schools began implementing minority education programmes before September 1999 on a voluntary basis.[134]

Education reform is one of the most controversial issues in the context of integration as well as in the area of minority rights.[135] Views about education reform and bilingual education are split. In general, the majority of residents, including minorities, support the bilingual education approach.[136] Nevertheless, while approximately half of minority

---

[131] Beginning of the secondary level.

[132] Education Law, Transitional Provisions (17 November 1998), Art. 9(3), <http://www.likumi.lv/doc.php?id=50759>, (accessed 26 September 2002), (hereafter, "1998 Education Law"). These provisions will be referred to as "education reform." See also *Minority Protection 2001*, pp. 289–293.

[133] Interview with the Director of the Society Integration Section of the General Education Department, Ministry of Education and Science, Riga, 5 August 2002.

[134] In the 2000/2001 academic year, there were 732 schools with Latvian as the language of instruction, 173 – with Russian as the language of instruction, and 149 – with two languages of instruction (Latvian and Russian). There were also a few Polish, Jewish, Ukrainian, Estonian, Lithuanian and Belarussian schools, as well as Romani language classes in two schools. The number of students being taught in Latvian increased from 66 percent in 1999/2000 to 72.3 percent in 2001/2002, <http://www.am.gov.lv/en/?id=800>, (accessed 26 August 2002). Apart from the growing interest of minority parents in sending their children to Latvian schools, other reasons for a decreasing number of students in Russian-language schools are emigration and the decreasing birth rate of ethnic Russians. *Minority Protection 2001*, p. 291.

[135] In this section dealing with issues of discrimination and equal access to education, the focus will be on Latvian language training and on the quality of education. Issues related to the language of instruction and the promotion of the minority identity will be further discussed in Section 3.4.1 on minority rights in education.

[136] *Towards a Civil Society 2000/2001*, p. 104. According to the survey, 81 percent of citizens and 74 percent of non-citizens support bilingual education.

school students, teachers and principals generally support an equal number of subjects being taught in the mother tongue and in Latvian (as proposed in minority primary education programmes), many respondents (41 percent of students, 37 percent of teachers, 34 percent of principals and 31 percent of parents) prefer education mostly in the minority language.[137] Regarding the transition to Latvian as the language of instruction in 2004 at the secondary level, around half of minority parents, school directors and teachers are opposed, while the other half are in favour.[138]

Despite the considerable amounts invested,[139] experts are concerned that State financial support for minority education reform is insufficient and that the reform has been insufficiently prepared and poorly managed.[140] The lack of preparedness of teachers for bilingual education is a major problem. Although in a 2002 survey minority school teachers evaluated their own readiness for bilingual teaching at the middle or the highest level, insufficient Latvian language skills as well as insufficient training and access to methodology and materials about bilingual education represent serious

---

[137] See Baltic Institute of Social Sciences, Canadian International Development Agency, OSCE, SFL, *Analysis of the Implementation of Bilingual Education*, Riga, 2002, p. 20, <http://www.politika.lv/polit_real/files/lv/bilingv_en.pdf>, (accessed 26 September 2002), (hereafter, "*Analysis of the Implementation of Bilingual Education*"). This survey covered minority school (i.e. with Russian as the language of instruction) teachers at the primary and secondary level, principals, and students in grades 2 to 3, 6 to 7, and their parents. The number of respondents in each survey group varied; survey methodology also differed.

[138] 58 percent of students, 52 percent of teachers, 48 percent of parents and 46 percent of principals "rather don't" or "absolutely don't" support teaching mainly in the Latvian language starting in 2004. *Analysis of the Implementation of Bilingual Education*, p. 20. According to another survey, 86 percent of ethnic Latvian citizens, 55 percent of Russian citizens and 47 percent of non-citizens support the switch to Latvian as the language of instruction in secondary schools; 42 percent of non-citizens are against it. *Towards a Civil Society 2000/2001*, p. 102.

[139] See E. Papule, "State measures in bilingual education: Characterisation of minority education policy," *Bulletin Tagad*, <http://www.lvavp.lv/eng/frameset.php?PHPSESSID=7eac25821853ca264a5348de81ac4036>, (accessed 26 August 2002).

[140] They also noted that more attention was devoted to training bilingual teachers only after the launch of the reform in 2000. E. Vēbers, "Reform of Bilingual Education," in *A Passport to Social Cohesion and Economic Prosperity. Report on Education in Latvia 2000*, SFL, Riga, 2001, pp. 77–87; A. Pabriks, E. Vēbers and R. Āboltiņš, *Atsvešinātības pārvarēšana. Sabiedrības integrācija* (*Overcoming Alienation. Integration of Society*), Nims, Nipo NT, Riga, 2001; B. Lulle. "*Būtiskākās problēmas mazākumtautību izglītības reformas īstenošanā Latvijā*" (Important Problems in the Implementation of Minority Education Reform in Latvia), *Politikas zinātnes jautājumi* (*Issues in Political Science*), University of Latvia, Faculty of Social Sciences, Department of Political Science, Riga, 2002, pp. 205–238; interview with the Director of the SFL Programme "Change in Education," Riga, 22 March 2002.

problems.[141] Some critics also feel that bilingual education is presented in the education reform and in the Integration Programme not as a modern teaching method to improve the quality of education, Latvian language proficiency and the preservation of the minority identity, but simply as the means for transition to Latvian-only education.[142]

Many representatives of minority NGOs, experts, and parents have expressed concern that opportunities and guarantees for primary and secondary education in the minority language are increasingly limited, and that the choices of minority parents and of schools participating in the reform are also limited. While the Latvian language proficiency of minority students is better compared to that of other groups of respondents (e.g. parents, teachers), and is increasing,[143] a significant percentage of principals and teachers are concerned that bilingual education will result in a lower quality of education and knowledge of subjects for students.[144] Teachers are also concerned that the Latvian language skills of students are insufficient for participating in bilingual education. Also, students in Russian-language schools appear to be at a disadvantage in contests conducted in Latvian.[145] At the same time, according to the

---

[141] According to a 2002 survey, more than one third of minority school teachers evaluated their Latvian language skills at the lowest level, and only ten percent at the highest level, even though teachers in public schools are required to speak Latvian at the highest level of proficiency. *Analysis of the Implementation of Bilingual Education*, pp. 22, 34, 19.

[142] Interviews with: the Director of the SFL Programme "Change in Education," Riga, 22 March 2002; and the Director of LASHOR, Riga, 28 March 2002. There is also concern about the interference of ruling parties, often ignoring the quality of education and other social, economic and political aspects of education reform.

[143] In grades 6 and 7, 68 percent can speak Latvian fluently or without major difficulties, 30 percent can discuss simple subjects only, while 2 percent cannot speak at all (as evaluated by students themselves). The majority of principals (86 percent) and teachers (78 percent) stated that bilingual education had resulted in better Latvian language skills among students. *Analysis of the Implementation of Bilingual Education*, pp. 25, 39.

[144] For example, 51 percent of teachers and more than half of minority school principals believe that students' knowledge in specific subject areas decreases as a result of bilingual teaching; 42 percent of teachers and 54 percent of principals concluded that the understanding of issues discussed by teachers decreases; and around one third of teachers and principals were concerned with a decrease in students' attention and interest in subjects. *Analysis of the Implementation of Bilingual Education*, p. 39.

[145] B. Zeļcermans and N. Rogaļeva, "Minority Education Policies in Latvia: Who Determines Them and How?", in *On the Way to Social Cohesion and Welfare Education in Latvia, Report 2000*, SFL, Riga, 2001, pp. 90–91.

Ministry of Education and Science, there has been no decrease in the level of knowledge of students in minority schools.[146]

Thus, though the Ministry of Education and Science claims that the majority of minority secondary schools are prepared for the transition to Latvian in 2004, it is an abiding concern that many are not.[147] There have been some initiatives to determine the level of demand for education in the mother tongue among parents, and to influence State policy accordingly.[148] Experts have also suggested extending the deadline for the transition, stressing the need for the State to invest more resources in the implementation of education reform.[149] It has also been recommended that the switch to Latvian should be made only in schools which are demonstrably ready for it.[150]

The main actors currently providing free in-service training for bilingual teachers and elaborating teaching materials are the NPLLT and the SFL (with foreign funds mostly).[151] Some of the projects supported by the SIF in November 2001 will also be analysed below.

---

[146] Interview with the Director of the Society Integration Section of the General Education Department, Ministry of Education and Science, Riga, 5 August 2002.

[147] The Ministry estimates that 60 percent of minority secondary schools are prepared to teach in Latvian as they already teach in two languages; 10 percent already teach in Latvian; 25 to 35 percent already teach three subjects in Latvian (but it is noted that they still have about three years to prepare). E. Papule, "State Measures in Bilingual Education: Characterisation of Minority Education Policy," *Bulletin Tagad*, <http://www.lvavp.lv/eng/frameset.php?PHPSESSID=7eac25821853ca264a5348de81ac4036>, (accessed 26 August 2002). According to a survey, among the 50 schools investigated, it was estimated that 16 percent were ready for the transition, and that 40 percent could manage with some difficulties, while 44 were not ready. See *Analysis of the Implementation of Bilingual Education*, p. 46.

[148] E.g. the widely-attended conferences "For Education in the Mother Tongue" organised in 2000 and 2001 by LASHOR; a follow-up is planned for September 2002. A letter signed by nearly 6,000 persons was also addressed to the Parliament, Government officials and the OSCE in 2001–2002. Information provided by LASHOR, Riga, 2 August 2002; see also <http://www.lashor.lv>, (accessed 26 August 2002).

[149] E. Vēbers, "Reform of Bilingual Education," pp. 77–87; A. Pabriks, E. Vēbers, and R. Āboltiņš, *Overcoming Alienation. Integration of Society*, pp. 133–147.

[150] *Analysis of the Implementation of Bilingual Education*, p. 8.

[151] Other initiatives include: bilingual education centres in four cities which inform people about bilingual education and integration issues and offer Latvian language and bilingual education courses with the support of the Ministry of Education and Science; a Teacher Training Support Centre; the Riga Teachers' Education Centre; the Multicultural Education Centre at the University of Latvia; school councils; etc.

NPLLT activities

Since 1997, in response to increasing demand, the NPLLT has provided Latvian language courses for teachers (Latvian as a second language – LSL – courses) in order to meet the level of knowledge required for their job. 15,413 teachers had received Latvian language training by 2001. The annual NPLLT evaluation surveys indicate that the LSL course is positively evaluated by participants.[152] Courses on bilingual methodologies were also launched in October 2000 and are planned until 2006; approximately 1,500 teachers have already received such training.[153]

The NPLLT has developed teaching materials in several areas: LSL teaching materials for schools (grades 1 to 9); methodological teaching literature for teachers and different professional groups; and LSL teaching materials for a broader audience. In 2001, the book "Bilingual Education – A Handbook for Teachers" was published.[154] In 2002, slides for the bilingual teaching of history, biology and geography in the seventh and eighth grades were being prepared.[155]

However, the main burden for implementing bilingual education appears to be on teachers themselves. Often, they do not have enough time or technical and material resources to develop their own methodologies and teaching aids, even when they have the knowledge to do so.[156] The weakest point in the training of bilingual teachers is the lack of a unified methodology for bilingual education.[157]

An independent evaluation of the NPLLT's activities concluded that they have played a major role in establishing a dialogue with minorities and in involving

---

[152] See <http://www.lvavp.lv/eng/frameset.php?PHPSESSID=7eac25821853ca264a5348de81ac4036>, (accessed 26 August 2002).

[153] Interview with the NPLLT Project Coordinator for bilingual education, Riga, 28 March 2002.

[154] It is available free of charge to teachers attending training courses on bilingual education; others can buy it. I. Ieviņa and S. Eisaka, "Implementation of Bilingual Education: The Contribution of the NPLLT," *Bulletin Tagad* 2002, <http://www.lvavp.lv/eng/frameset.php?PHPSESSID=7eac25821853ca264a5348de81ac4036>, (accessed 26 August 2002).

[155] Interview with the NPLLT Project Coordinator for bilingual education, Riga, 28 March 2002.

[156] Interview with the NPLLT Project Coordinator for bilingual education, Riga, 28 March 2002.

[157] "Many teachers suppose that we will offer them certain work methods for their classes. But we do not have a united system of methods for bilingual education. We can only offer possible solutions." I. Ieviņa, "A teacher in bilingual education," 2001.

them in bilingual education reform.[158] Still, the NPLLT is perceived by some minority NGOs as a tool for the State's assimilatory policies in the field of education.[159] The future of such initiatives after the NPLLT ceases to exist (in 2006) will have to be ascertained.

Project "Open School" of the SFL

The project "Open school" was started by the SFL in 1999 and was due to last until 2003. Its aim is to support the creation of an educational system that fosters the ethnic integration of society by developing common values and goals, promoting tolerance of diversity, and encouraging cooperation between Latvian and non-Latvian speakers. It consists mainly of the implementation of four models of bilingual education in pilot schools.[160] An evaluation of the project carried out in 2000 concluded that it was positively received by its beneficiaries; recommendations for further improvement were also made.[161]

SIF-supported projects

Several projects supported by the SIF in November 2001 are connected with the transition to instruction in Latvian. Many represent the continuation of projects realised before the adoption of the Integration Programme. The Ministry of Education and Science as well as minority schools are the main implementing authorities.

As an example, LVL 2,160 (€3,770) was allocated to the Ministry of Education and Science and the NPLLT for the project "Involvement of National Minority Teachers and Parents in the Integration Process" which aims to facilitate the understanding of bilingual education reform by teachers and parents. Altogether, eight seminars for parents and teachers were held in the cities of Riga, Daugavpils and Liepāja. These showed that parents had very little information about the

---

[158] A. Pabriks, *The National Programme for Latvian Language Training. Promotion of the Integration of Society 1996–2000*. Impact Report, pp. 15–18.

[159] I. Pimenov, "Who is politicising school reform?," *Bizness & Baltia*, 19 November 2001 (in Russian).

[160] The project involves 20 Russian schools, 17 Latvian schools (with minority children), 14 kindergartens and seven pedagogical universities. Other activities include: conferences and seminars on bilingual education, the development of bilingual education materials, summer camps for teachers, integration camps and cooperation between schools, an information campaign, etc. Information materials prepared by the coordinators of the SFL "Open School" Project; interview with the Project Coordinator, Riga, 25 March 2002.

[161] E. Nadirova and E. M. Stallman, *An Evaluation of Implementation. "Open School" Project. The Soros Foundation – Latvia*. Teachers College, Columbia University, Spring 2000, <http://www.politika.lv/polit_real/files/lv/Open_school.pdf>, (accessed 13 April 2002).

reform and a poor understanding of bilingual education; teachers were better informed. It was stressed that more information about bilingual education was needed.[162] Accordingly, 40 more seminars are planned.[163]

Collaboration between schools

Several activities promoting collaboration between minority and Latvian schools – either between teachers or between students – have been realised, primarily by the NPLLT and the SFL.[164] These aim to promote cross-cultural communication, to increase students' knowledge of other cultures, to increase proficiency in Latvian of students and teachers, to increase their interest in Latvia, and to promote the social participation of students.

NPLLT activities

Since 1998, the NPLLT has been organising informal language training projects such as integration camps, youth clubs, and cooperation between schools.[165] The State contributed for the first time in 2001. About 1,000 students and teachers have benefited from these initiatives. NPLLT experts have evaluated almost all of the projects in progress and have concluded that the integration camps have been useful in promoting increased interaction between different cultures as well as Latvian language practice.[166] However, some criticisms have been expressed regarding the unclear, unrealistic and unmanageable goals of the camps. Independent experts also positively evaluated the camps, noting an increase of both minority and ethnic Latvian children's awareness of each other's cultures and better communication skills; they also concluded that the NPLLT had contributed to increasing the readiness of Latvian schools to collaborate with

---

[162] Interview with the NPLLT Project Coordinator for Bilingual Education, Riga, 28 March 2002.

[163] Interview with the Director of the Society Integration Section of the General Education Department, Ministry of Education and Science, Riga, 5 August 2002.

[164] The SFL also organises integration camps for students and for teachers and is implementing a project to publish a magazine (*Tilts*) through joint efforts of ethnic Latvian and minority children.

[165] In 2001, the NPLLT allocated funding to 14 camps, 12 clubs and nine school collaboration projects. Each camp received LVL 1,700 (€2,967), each youth club – LVL 700 (€1,222), and each school cooperation project – LVL 800 (€1,396) from the State. 80 percent of the funding comes from the NPLLT, the rest from other sources, such as municipalities, parents, etc. The data on the share of State funding in 2001 was not available.

[166] S. Vigule, J. Sniķeris, S. Kucina *et al.*, *Evaluative reports of integration camps*. Evaluation materials prepared by experts of the NPLLT, Riga, 2001.

minority schools.[167] These projects will continue to receive support from the NPLLT in 2002, which has already received Phare funding for the organisation of 15 camps.[168]

SIF-supported projects

The SIF has put an emphasis in the 2002 tender themes on "exchange and collaboration between students" (see Section 2.4). In June 2002, six projects in this area were approved, and additional projects are expected to be approved in the second tender.

Given that the SIF has only recently begun functioning, and given its broad overall objectives and limited funds, its initiatives can be considered as only partly complementary to other measures in the area of education reform. Nevertheless, its activities to date have served to disseminate information about bilingual education and to promote collaboration between schools. Additional activity in this area seems warranted.

From the viewpoint of social integration, it is extremely important that the State promote more effective participation from minorities in the further planning and implementation of education reform, taking into consideration the capacity and demands of schools and parents. There is also a strong need to invest more resources in the training of teachers as well as in policy monitoring.

3.2.2 Employment

The Integration Programme focuses on Latvian language training as a means of promoting employment, since poor language skills are considered an obstacle to finding a job for non-Latvian speakers. Initiatives to promote employment for the whole population were implemented by the Government before the adoption of the Integration Programme. Latvian language training has also been provided by the NPLLT. However, there seems to be a greater demand for Latvian language training than can currently be met due to the shortage of qualified teachers and funds.

---

[167] I. Apine, L. Dribins, A. Jansons, *et al.*, *Etnopolitika Latvijā* (*Ethnopolicy in Latvia*), Elpa, Riga, 2001, pp. 12–13.

[168] Interview with the NPLLT Director, in "*Neformālie latviešu valodas apguves projekti*" (Informal Latvian Language Training Projects), *Izglītība un Kultūra* (*Education and Culture*), 21 December 2001, p. 11.

The Integration Programme states the need to promote employment as one of its objectives in the chapter on "Social and Regional Integration of Society."[169] It identifies insufficient proficiency in the Latvian language and a low level of education as hindering the competitiveness of unemployed non-Latvians (understood as non-ethnic Latvians) in the labour market.[170] It also notes that many people are not able to take advantage of possibilities to learn the Latvian language because of insufficient financial means.[171] Indeed, studies show that Latvian language proficiency is lower among unemployed persons compared to other population groups. Many unemployed persons, especially in the Latgale region and in Riga, do not possess a State language proficiency certificate and their knowledge of Latvian is often weak.[172] This clearly constitutes an obstacle to finding a job, including through the State Employment Service (SES), as in certain cases (job proposals) require that applicants possess such a certificate or a certain level of proficiency in the Latvian language.[173]

The Integration Programme does not address issues of ethnic discrimination in employment and there is also a lack of information about such cases. Some problems with the legal framework have been highlighted. Thus, the new Labour Law does not apply to access to employment in the civil service, where minorities are under-

---

[169] Integration Programme, p. 44.

[170] Integration Programme, p. 48. Only 43 percent of citizens whose native language is not Latvian and 23 percent of non-citizens would be able to perform a job that requires knowledge of Latvian; 30 percent and 28 percent could do so with difficulty only; 22 percent and 38 percent could not at all because they do not know the language. *Towards a Civil Society 2000/2001*, p. 99.

[171] Framework Document, p. 35.

[172] As of October 2001, around 12 percent of the total number of persons registered as unemployed did not possess a document on their Latvian language proficiency. Information provided by the Division of Active Market Measures of the State Employment Service, Riga, 25 October 2001. By self-evaluation, 58 percent of unemployed persons looking for a job and whose native language is not Latvian have the lowest level of Latvian language proficiency, and 9.6 percent do not know Latvian at all. The Baltic Institute of Social Sciences and the NPLLT, *Language. A sociological survey, November 2001 – January 2002*.

[173] See Regulations on the Proficiency Degree in the State Language Required for the Performance of the Professional an Positional Duties and on the Procedure of Language Proficiency Tests (adopted in 2000), § 1, para. 8, at <http://www.riga.lv/minelres/NationalLegislation/Latvia/Latvia_LangRegProficiency_English.htm>, (accessed 26 August 2002). The June 2001 amendments to the Administrative Violations Code stipulate fines for employers who hire persons lacking sufficient Latvian language proficiency.

represented.[174] There are also several questionable restrictions on the employment of non-citizens in the private sector, preventing them from working as legal assistants, heads of private detective agencies,[175] aeroplane pilots, and security guards.[176]

Some survey data suggest that minorities face disadvantages in the job market. For example, according to a 2000 survey, ten percent of ethnic Latvians but 17 percent of persons of other ethnic origins stated that they were unemployed and did not receive benefits.[177] The share of officially registered unemployed ethnic Latvians decreased from 53.7 percent of all unemployed in 1997 to 49.8 percent in 2000; the share of unemployed persons of minority origin has therefore increased.[178] Minorities report experiencing a greater sense of social and economic insecurity than ethnic Latvians.[179]

There is also an imbalance between the share of minorities in the public and private sectors. Minorities are less represented in the public sector and are under-represented in decision-making bodies (see Section 3.4.3).[180] On the other hand, minorities are better represented in private enterprises.[181] Minorities are proportionally represented or even over-represented in some State institutions, e.g. in the police, prison administration and several State enterprises (a legacy of the Soviet period).[182]

The efforts of the Government to develop employment opportunities for the whole population were started before the adoption of the Integration Programme. Initiatives

---

[174] The Civil Service Law does not contain an equality clause, and the Labour Law's anti-discrimination provisions concerning the hiring of civil servants does not apply. State Civil Service Law, 22 September 2000, <http://www.likumi.lv/doc.php?id=10944>, (accessed 23 August 2002); see also *Minority Protection 2001*, pp. 287–288.

[175] Law on Detective Activity (1 November 2001), Art. 4, <http://www.likumi.lv/doc.php?id=26311>, (accessed 1 October 2002).

[176] *Minority Protection 2001*, p. 288. According to Article 3 of the Law on Firearms and the Special Means for Self-defence, only Latvian citizens have a right to obtain firearms, <http://www.likumi.lv/doc.php?id=63056>, (accessed 26 August 2002).

[177] R. Rose, *New Baltic Barometer IV: A Survey Study. Studies in Public Policy*, No. 284, Centre for the Study of Public Policy, University of Strathclyde, Glasgow, 2000, p. 5; see also *Minority Protection 2001*, p. 288.

[178] Central Statistical Bureau of Latvia, *Statistical Yearbook of Latvia*, Riga, 2001, p. 58.

[179] See R. Rose, *New Baltic Barometer IV*, pp. 7, 9, 11, 13.

[180] See A. Pabriks, *Occupational Representation and Ethnic Discrimination in Latvia*, LCHRES, SFL, Nordik Publishing House, Riga, 2002, p. 50.

[181] According to a 2000 survey, 35 percent of ethnic Latvians and 21 percent of minorities were employed in State budgetary institutions, compared to 29 percent and 37 percent respectively in new private businesses. R. Rose, *New Baltic Barometer IV*, p. 5.

[182] A. Pabriks, *Occupational Representation and Ethnic Discrimination in Latvia*, pp. 26–36.

to promote employment through Latvian language training have been implemented by the NPLLT.

NPLLT activities

Since 1997, approximately 30 percent of NPLLT funds for training have been invested in Latvian language training for adults; overall, 42,630 representatives of various professional and social groups attended courses organised by the NPLLT between 1996 and 2001.[183] The NLPTT also produces study materials, audio and video materials, study programmes for the radio, television and Internet, etc. Language training for unemployed persons has been organised by the NPLLT with support from Phare 2000 and Phare 2001. Finally, the NPLLT has cooperated with the SES to support language training for persons who are undergoing professional retraining as well as for young people.

Minorities generally evaluate the NPLLT positively; however, the demand for Latvian language training is much greater than the supply. A shortage of qualified teachers is preventing the expansion of NPLLT activities in this area.[184] Thus, statistics show that the number of unemployed persons who had attended NPLLT activities up to the year 2001 (476 persons)[185] represents only a small share of those interested. Currently, at least 10,000 registered unemployed persons do not have a State language proficiency certificate.[186]

Possible future projects

The Integration Programme mentions the possibility of developing language training for unemployed minorities. The SEC has offered some Latvian language training but its capacity is weak due to limited funding.[187] Some NGOs and municipalities (e.g. Liepāja City Council) have also offered free Latvian language training.

---

[183] <http://www.lvavp.lv/eng/frameset.php?PHPSESSID=7eac25821853ca264a5348de81ac4036>, (accessed 26 August 2002).

[184] Interview with the Director of the NPLLT, Riga, 15 February 2002.

[185] <http://www.lvavp.lv/eng/frameset.php?PHPSESSID=7eac25821853ca264a5348de81ac4036>, (accessed 26 August 2002).

[186] Information provided by the Division of Active Market Measures of the State Employment Service, Riga, 25 October 2001.

[187] In 2001, the SEC submitted the project "Integration of Unemployed Non-Latvians in the Labour Market" to the SIF but it was not approved, mainly due to the large amount of funding required: LVL 70,500 (€123,037). Interview with the Deputy Director of the SIF Secretariat, 28 March 2002.

While demand is likely to remain high,[188] the future of State-supported Latvian language training for adults remains uncertain, especially after 2006 when the work of the NPLLT is due to end. Future projects will largely depend on the Government's priorities. A positive step in this direction was the announcement by the SIF of a project tender for the second half of 2002 to elaborate a model for the organisation of Latvian language training for adults, with a possibility of funding through the SIF.[189] While some experts believe that the way forward is through the expansion of State-funded language training,[190] others think that the best way to promote Latvian language use is by widening language regulation in private sector[191] and other means, for example, by promotion of a positive attitude to Latvian language use[192] and strengthening of the Latvian language environment.[193]

---

[188] Survey data show that 69 percent of respondents whose native language is not Latvian would like to improve their Latvian skills, and 36 percent of minority representatives would like to attend Latvian courses. The Baltic Institute of Social Sciences and the NPLLT, *Language. A sociological survey, November 2001 – January 2002.*

[189] SIF, Ethnic Integration Programme "Latvian Language Training for Adults," Guidelines for Applicants in the Tender, 2002, pp. 5–6, <http://www.lsif.lv/docs/vl_2/ei_latvval.doc>, (accessed 26 August 2002).

[190] A. Pabriks, E. Vēbers, R. Āboltiņš, *Atsvešinātības pārvarēšana. Sabiedrības integrācija* (Overcoming Alienation. The Integration of Society), Riga, 2001, pp. 133–154; I. Apine, L. Dribins, A. Jansons, et al., *Ethnopolicy in Latvia*, p. 38; I. Indāns and V. Kalniņš, *Sabiedrības integrācijas institucionālās politikas analīze (Institutional Policy Analysis of Social Integration)*, Latvian Institute of International Affairs, Riga, 2001.

[191] An attempt by the State Language Centre to broaden its authority to regulate language use in the private sector through the elaboration of amendments to the State Language Law stipulating a new list of professions in local governments and private sector has been unsuccessful due to the intervention by the Minister of Foreign Affairs who argued that this would cause a negative international reaction. LCHRES, *Human Rights in Latvia, 1 January 2002 – 30 June 2002*, p. 3.

[192] For example, the Commission on the State Language established in early 2002 (see Section 3.2) issued a recommendation to officials in the city of Daugavpils (inhabited predominantly by minorities) to consider implementing a campaign to promote Latvian language use; it also recommended moving some governmental institutions to Daugavpils. *Minority Issues in Latvia*, No. 46, 8 March 2002, p. 4, <http://racoon.riga.lv/minelres/archive//03182002-19:44:34-4063.html>, (accessed 30 September 2002).

[193] I. Kuzmina, "*Neliesim ūdeni tukšā mucā*" (Let's not pour water into an empty barrel), *Elections Newspaper*, Appendix to *Lauku Avīze*, No. 8, 13 September 2002, pp. 12–13. Some experts argue that one obstacle to Latvian language use is the fact that many ethnic Latvians speak Russian with minorities.

3.2.3 Housing and other goods and services

There are no provisions concerning equal access to housing or other goods and services in the Integration Programme. Available data do not indicate significant disparities on ethnic grounds in these areas.[194]

3.2.4 Healthcare and other forms of social protection

The Integration Programme refers to measures implemented by the Ministry of Welfare in the field of healthcare and social protection.[195] The SIF has also supported several projects for disadvantaged and disabled groups. However, these do not concern minorities specifically.

3.2.5 The criminal justice system

The Integration Programme does not address the issue of equal access to the criminal justice system. In this context, a provision of the Law on the State Language, according to which State, municipal and judicial institutions are obliged to accept written documents from private persons in Latvian only or with an attached notarised translation is considered by human rights experts to be in contradiction with international human rights standards (ECHR, FCNM) in the case of persons who do not know Latvian and cannot afford to pay for notarised translation (e.g. prisoners and persons under investigation).[196]

---

[194] E.g. A. Aasland, *Ethnicity and Poverty in Latvia*, Fafo Institute for Applied Social Science, <http://ano.deac.lv/html_e/index_09.htm>, (accessed 26 August 2002).

[195] Integration Programme, pp. 44–50.

[196] G. Feldhune and M. Mits, *Legal analysis of national and European anti-discrimination legislation*, p. 39. The NHRO recently recommended establishing a State institution dealing with this type of translation services and also suggested that State and municipal bodies accept documents regarding violations of the law or civil offences, including requests and applications to the courts, in a foreign language if there are objective reasons why the applicant cannot provide a translation. NHRO, *Topical Human Rights Issues in Latvia in the Second Quarter of 2002*, pp. 13–14.

3.3 Protection from Racially Motivated Violence

Racially motivated violence is not an acute problem in Latvia, and the Integration Programme does not directly address the issue of racially motivated violence. It does, however, reject extremism, intolerance and national hatred,[197] and some activities to promote tolerance have received funding.[198] Furthermore, projects of the Integration Programme to promote intercultural communication, such as language camps, collaboration between schools, and cultural activities, are partly aimed also at coping with ethnic stereotypes and intolerance.

There have been no recorded instances of racially motivated crime.[199] Provisions prohibiting incitement and/or propagation of hate speech are included in several laws.[200] However, there appear to be some problems in applying existing legislation. Thus, the formulation of Article 78 of the Criminal Code requires the demonstration of an intent to promote national or racial hatred;[201] this is considered as one reason why very few cases have been proven.[202] Law enforcement authorities have also received little training on issues relating to racism, xenophobia or extremism.[203]

---

[197] Integration Programme, p. 10.

[198] These include projects implemented by the Museum and Documentation Centre "Jews in Latvia" to address issues of anti-Semitism. Support was also received from the SIF in 2001 in the amount of LVL 2,585 (€4,511). Information provided by the Deputy Director of the SIF Secretariat, Riga, 28 March 2002.

[199] N. Muiznieks, *Extremism in Latvia*, LCHRES, Riga, 2002, pp. 10–11, <http://www.policy.lv/index.php?id=102443&lang=en>, (accessed 27 September 2002).

[200] See *Minority Protection 2001*, pp. 300–301.

[201] Criminal Code (17 June 1998), Art. 78(1), <http://www.likumi.lv/doc.php?id=25829>, (accessed 28 August 2002).

[202] This provision is also in contradiction with Article 4 of the International Convention on the Elimination of All Forms of Racial Discrimination (ICERD) to which Latvia is a party. G. Feldhune and M. Mits, *Legal analysis of national and European anti-discrimination legislation*, p. 36. As regards the Criminal Code, ECRI notes that its Article 78 does not contain a provision "explicitly prohibiting acts aimed at degrading the national dignity of a person." ECRI has also expressed concern that, while Article 156 prohibits offending the honour of a person, "this Article does not appear to be suited to cover expressions targeting groups of persons, nor has it ever been tested for offensive behaviour committed on ethnic or national grounds." *2002 ECRI Report*, pp. 7–8.

[203] N. Muiznieks, *Extremism in Latvia*, pp. 10–11.

3.4 Promotion of Minority Rights

The Integration Programme emphasises that integration does not mean either forced assimilation or the limitation of minority rights.[204] It also states the aim to promote the "the right of minorities to cultural autonomy and the assurance of the fulfilment of cultural autonomy."[205] However, the focus is on the right of minorities "to preserve their native language and culture" and "to maintain their ethnic identity," rather than on the need to protect other internationally recognised minority rights, such as the right to use one's mother tongue in various spheres of life, the right to mass media in the minority language, or the right to participation in public life.

Some Government officials and experts have questioned whether the promotion of certain minority rights would contribute to achieving the goals of the Integration Programme – to promote Latvian language use and overall social cohesion. They also stress that the protection of minority rights is not the primary aim of the Integration Programme, and that one should therefore not analyse minority protection based on this document.[206]

Not much progress has occurred in the area of minority rights since 2001. No steps have been taken to ratify the FCNM (signed on 11 May 1995) or to adopt the Law on the Rights of National Minorities (drafted in 2000).[207] Positive developments can, however, be reported regarding the Latvian proficiency requirements in elections (see Section 3.4.3).

3.4.1 Education

As noted above, one of the proposed measures of the Integration Programme in the area of education is the elaboration and implementation of minority educational programmes (in the context of education reform) in order to promote Latvian language learning and the development of a unified educational system (see Section 3.2.1). At the same time, minority education programmes are viewed also as a means of promoting the preservation of identity among minorities and their integration into Latvian society.[208] Yet, while the impact of these programmes on minority identity is uncertain (see below), no projects to specifically protect or promote minority identities in education are proposed in the

---

[204] Integration Programme, p. 88.

[205] A purely declarative Law on Unrestricted Development of National and Ethnic Groups of Latvia and the Right to Cultural Autonomy was adopted on 19 March 1991, *Minority Protection 2001*, pp. 279–280.

[206] OSI Roundtable, Riga, June 2002.

[207] *Minority Protection 2001*, p. 280.

[208] Integration Programme, p. 60.

Integration Programme.[209] There are few State initiatives to promote the minority identity in education or to increase the interest of ethnic Latvian children in minority cultures and history. There is a need for a greater participation of minorities in developing minority education programmes and for more research on the impact of these programmes on the minority identity and mother tongue knowledge. More efforts are also needed to make the education system "intercultural."[210]

The State has supported education in the mother tongue for Russians and seven other minority groups. Still, there is concern among civil society representatives about the lack of guarantees in domestic legislation concerning primary and secondary education in the mother tongue. Education reform based on the 1998 Education Law has been criticised by minorities who want State-funded secondary schools with instruction predominantly in the minority language to be maintained beyond 2004.

The legislative framework guaranteeing opportunities for education in minority languages and minority language teaching is not comprehensive.[211] The 1999 General Education Law allows for primary and general secondary programmes to be combined with "minority education programmes, including teaching minority languages and subjects related to the identity of the minority and the integration of the society of Latvia."[212] However, according to the 1998 Education Law, on 1 September 2004, teaching will be only in the Latvian language in all tenth grades of State and municipal general education institutions and in the first year classes of State and municipal vocational education institutions.[213] According to the same law, a minority language can be used as the language of instruction in private schools and in State and municipal schools which are implementing minority education programmes.[214] However, State funding may only be allocated to private schools where State-accredited education programmes in the State language are being implemented.[215]

---

[209] In 2001, the SIF allocated LVL 1,500 (€2,618) to the project "National Minority Children in Latvian Language Schools" initiated by the Ministry of Education and Science. However, this project does not seek to promote the identity of minority children; rather, its goals are to ascertain the number of minority children studying in Latvian-language schools (in grades 1 to 3), and to develop methodological recommendations for teaching in linguistically heterogeneous classes. SIF materials, Riga, 2002.

[210] Integration Programme, p. 61.

[211] For a more detailed analysis, see *Minority Protection 2001*, pp. 289–290.

[212] General Education Law (11 June 1999), Art. 30(5) and Art. 42(2), <http://www.likumi.lv/doc.php?id=20243>, (accessed 26 August 2002).

[213] 1998 Education Law, Art. 9(3).

[214] 1998 Education Law, Art. 9(2).

[215] 1998 Education Law, Art. 59(2). The Education Law also does not require local governments to establish or maintain minority schools/classes on minority parents' request.

The 1998 Education Law also does not require local governments to establish or maintain minority schools/classes on the request of minority parents.

Surveys and observations show that many minority representatives are concerned that education reform and bilingual education may have a negative impact on the ethnic identity of students as well as their language skills in the mother tongue.[216] There is a lack of research to determine the role of minority education programmes in the preservation and development of the ethnic and cultural identity of minority students.[217]

Again, State-funded minority schools can elaborate their own educational models at the primary level, according to State standards. However, the fact that only the Ministry of Education and Science is authorised to determine the subjects within minority education programmes to be taught in the State language has been criticised.[218] Several (predominantly non-Russian) minority schools have indeed elaborated such models which promote the ethnic identity of students.[219] The Association for the Support of Russian Language Schools in Latvia (LASHOR) stresses the importance of education in the mother tongue for the child's intellectual development and has elaborated an alternative minority education programme for minority primary and secondary schools.[220] Another NGO, the Latvian Association of the Teachers of Russian Language and Literature, has asserted that more attention should be paid to the teaching of Russian as a mother tongue.[221] Many civil society representatives believe that greater and more effective participation of parents, schools

---

[216] According to one study, around one-third of teachers and almost half of school principals think that students' Russian language skills decrease as a result of bilingual teaching; many respondents are also concerned about a possible negative impact of education reform on the development of Russian culture. See *Analysis of the Implementation of Bilingual Education*, p. 56.

[217] Interview with the Director of the Society Integration Section of the General Education Department at the Ministry of Education and Science, Riga, 5 August 2002.

[218] See *Minority Protection 2001*, p. 289.

[219] These are Polish, Jewish, Ukrainian, and Belarussian schools, and, rarely, Russian schools. Interview with the Director of the Society Integration Section of the General Education Department, Ministry of Education and Science, Riga, 5 August 2002.

[220] See the programmes at <www.lashor.lv>, (accessed 27 September 2002).

[221] There is an opinion that the bilingual education models proposed by the Ministry of Education and Science promote the marginalisation of Latvian and minority students because students are not familiar with both the Latvian and the Russian culture. Observations show that students' knowledge of Russian as the mother tongue is insufficient. E. Chuyanova, "There is not enough bravery of the state for the action," *Vesti Sevodnya*, 10 November 2001 (in Russian).

and civil society in general is necessary to design effective minority educational programmes, at both the primary and secondary levels.[222]

A positive step in this direction was the establishment in March 2001 of an Advisory Council on Education Issues at the Ministry of Education and Science. In early 2002, based on consultations with the Council, the Ministry of Education and Science started to elaborate minority education programmes for secondary schools as well. These programmes will define the proportions for use of Latvian and minority languages, and are to be implemented in 2004, once minority schools have switched to Latvian. As of August 2002, information on these programmes was not yet available to the broader public.[223] Three minority NGOs will also organise a public debate on expected changes in the system of secondary education for parents, with the support of the Baltic-American Partnership Programme.[224] Despite the initiation of dialogue, some minority representatives in the Advisory Council are concerned that their participation is rather formal and that predominantly persons who already support the State's education policy were recruited (representatives of State institutions, municipalities and minority schools).[225] There is also a concern that the work of the Advisory Council is not transparent enough.[226]

One of the directions in which further action has been requested is the promotion of "intercultural education" not only for minorities but in the general education system.

---

[222] Interviews with: the Director of the SFL Programme "Changes in Education", Riga, 28 March 2002; and a Researcher at the Institute of Philosophy and Sociology, Riga, 4 April 2002. European Parliament Committee on Foreign Affairs, Human Rights, Common Security and Defence Policy 1999–2004, *Draft Report on the State of Enlargement Negotiations*, p. 13.

[223] A model for a minority secondary education programme is currently being developed by a working group of the Ministry of Education, including 14 minority school directors. The main issue is the proportion of teaching in Latvian and in the minority languages. It was discussed with the directors of minority schools in eight regional conferences in April 2002. At present, it is foreseen that 30 percent of study time could be taught in the minority language (not including the teaching of the minority language). The working group has also recommended that the school environment be bilingual and that it be allowed that explanations be given to students in their native language. Interview with the Director of the Society Integration Section of the General Education Department at the Ministry of Education and Science, Riga, 23 April 2002.

[224] Interview with the Director of LASHOR, Riga, 16 July 2002.

[225] Interviews with: the Director of LASHOR, Riga, 28 March 2002; and the Director of the Latvian Association of the Teachers of Russian Language and Literature, Riga, 30 July 2002.

[226] Observations at the conference "The Switch to a United Education System in Latvia," organised by Liepāja Secondary School No. 8 and the Centre for Social and National Integration on 12 April 2002.

Already around half of students in Latvian schools study Russian as a foreign language.[227] A few initiatives have been supported by the State to increase the awareness and interest of ethnic Latvian children regarding minority cultures and history but more efforts are needed. For example, a textbook on the "History of Ethnic Relations in Latvia" was distributed to all schools; there is no information on how many students use it nor on the opinions of minority representatives.[228] The SFL has recommended implementing bilingual and multicultural education also in Latvian language schools.[229]

3.4.2 Language

The section devoted to "Language" states the goal to "establish a stable society which shares a common official language – the Latvian language – and to ensure opportunities to use the language in the public sphere throughout the country while at the same time supporting minorities in the cultivation of their languages in harmony with the law."[230] The main directions for action are the need to improve legal guarantees for the use of languages and to improve "legislation in the field of language and the right to cultural autonomy of minorities."[231] Yet, apart from these rather vague statements, no concrete implementation mechanisms are proposed.

---

[227] Interview with the Director of the Society Integration Section of the General Education Department, Ministry of Education and Science, Riga, 5 August 2002.

[228] L. Dribins (ed.), *Etnisko attiecību vēsture Latvijā* (*The History of Ethnic Relations in Latvia*), *Methodological Literature for History Teachers*, Riga, Puse Plus, 2000. Interview with the Director of the Society Integration Section of the General Education Department, Ministry of Education and Science, Riga, 5 August 2002.

[229] SFL, *A Passport to Social Cohesion and Economic Prosperity. Report on Education in Latvia*, Executive Summary, Riga, 2001, p. 5.

[230] Integration Programme, p. 73.

[231] The Integration Programme states (p. 73) that: "Legislation should ensure opportunities for use of the state language in the public sphere […] while at the same time guaranteeing the opportunities for minorities to cultivate their language in harmony with the law […]. Legislation on language should help to establish a balance […] between the state and minority languages. If a balance is found, the feeling of insecurity will disappear and mutual distrust will decrease."

Latvian language legislation and recent initiatives aim to strengthen the position of Latvian as the State language.[232] Human rights experts as well as the European Commission have noted the disadvantages derived from the provisions of the 1999 State Language Law for concrete segments of the population. Thus, the European Commission has noted that "[…] the requirement to submit documents to [the] state and municipalities in the state language only or else accompanied by a notarised translation has been reported to pose certain difficulties for some groups of the population […] given the cost of official translations."[233] It has called for a less restrictive application of the State Language Law.[234] The European Commission has also called for revisions to the Administrative Violations Code which imposes fines for violating the State Language Law in various circumstances, for example in the case of "disrespect towards the state language."[235]

The EU has not suggested in its Regular Reports the adoption of provisions to allow for the use of minority languages at the State or local level, although there are currently no such provisions. In practice, however, Russian is often used in contacts with public officials.[236] Some municipalities (e.g. Daugavpils) have hired a translator with their own resources.

Another problem connected with the State Language Law concerns the spelling of personal names and surnames in identification documents which must be done according to the rules of Latvian grammar, while the original spelling in Latin transliteration can be added

---

[232] Article 4 of the Constitution, amended on 15 October 1998, states that "the Latvian language is the State language in the Republic of Latvia." Article 5 of the State Language Law states that any languages used in Latvia other than Latvian with the exception of the Liv language, are considered as foreign languages. For more on Latvian language legislation, see e.g. *Minority Protection 2001*, pp. 283–287; see also Sections 3.2.3 and 3.2.4. A recent initiative has been the establishment of a Commission on the State Language on 16 January 2002, following an initiative of the Latvian President.

[233] *2001 Regular Report*, p. 26. It also states (p. 25) that "[..] the Language Law (of 1999) and the implementing regulations are essentially in conformity with Latvia's international obligations […]. However, some of the provisions are worded in such a way that they could give rise to different interpretations."

[234] *2001 Regular Report*, p. 25.

[235] *2001 Regular Report*, pp. 25–27.

[236] 36 percent of citizens and 42 percent of non-citizens speak Russian only in State institutions. *Towards a Civil Society 2000/2001*, p. 97.

on request.[237] Some experts consider that the "Latvianisation" of personal names and surnames is in contradiction with international human rights standards.[238]

To summarise, there has been a general lack of measures to guarantee the use of minority language use in different fields. The status of minority languages in national legislation is currently under discussion in the context of possible ratification of the FCNM.[239] It will be important to provide more guarantees for the protection and promotion of minority languages in order to achieve the Programme's goals of establishing a balance between the State and minority languages and promoting mutual understanding and cooperation between individuals.

3.4.3 Participation in public life

The approach of the Integration Programme in the chapter on "Civic Participation and Political Integration" is to promote the participation of all inhabitants of Latvia, independently of ethnicity.[240] It is argued that the strengthening of civic participation fosters political integration – understood as "bringing together socio-political values, interests and goals of people."[241] Many of the objectives of this chapter are also relevant for minorities, for example the objectives to increase political integration and the active participation of residents at all levels of the parliamentary process; to promote dialogue between the individual and the State through information; and to promote the development of and participation in NGOs. An important issue related to the participation in public life of minorities is also addressed: the need to promote naturalisation. However, another important area for achieving the general aim of this

---

[237] Individuals may have their name in Latin transliteration added in their passport, but on another page. Decree of the Cabinet of Ministers No. 245, 18 June 2002, Riga, para 5, at <http://www.likumi.lv/doc.php?id=63930>, (accessed 1 October 2002).

[238] See the views of experts at <http://www.pctvl.lv/surnames/index.php?cat=00080&lan=lv>, (accessed 1 October 2002). There are currently two cases connected with the "Latvianisation" of personal names and surnames registered at the European Court of Human Rights. See *Minority Issues in Latvia*, No. 54, 31 August 2002, p. 3, <http://lists.delfi.lv/pipermail/minelres/2002-August/002262.html>, (accessed 30 September 2002.

[239] Ratification would entail amending several laws or making reservations primarily on the use of minority languages in the mass media, in place names, and in contacts with public administration. However, according to an expert, "it is entirely possible that the eighth Saeima will ratify the [FCNM], while making a number of reservations." N. Muiznieks, "Social Integration Issues and the Eighth Saeima," 3 September 2002, <http://www.policy.lv/index.php?id=102473&lang=en>, (accessed 27 September 2002).

[240] Integration Programme, pp. 14–26.

[241] Integration Programme, p. 14.

chapter – promoting the participation of minorities in several State institutions and decision-making bodies – has not been addressed in the framework of the Integration Programme or by other means. The promotion of dialogue between minorities specifically and the State has also not been addressed.

The main actor in the area of projects to support naturalisation has been the Naturalisation Board. While its initiatives have succeeded in stemming the decrease in naturalisation rates, more funding for measures to promote naturalisation, including Latvian language training for naturalisation applicants, are needed as the demand for language training remains high.

There is also a need for additional mechanisms to promote dialogue between minorities and the State and increased participation of minorities in public life. Positive initiatives include State support through the SIF for NGOs as well as for initiatives of municipalities to facilitate the participation of minorities, including non-citizens, in local public affairs. There is a need to ensure that these local initiatives are coordinated with the work of bodies implementing the Integration Programme at the national level.

Promotion of naturalisation

The Integration Programme stresses the need to "promote the prestige of citizenship in order to achieve a positive change in the psychological attitude concerning issues related to Latvia's citizenship and its acquiring through the naturalisation procedure."[242]

The process of naturalisation has been slow.[243] As of 31 December 2001, there were 523,095 non-citizens (22 percent of residents); the monthly average for naturalisation applications in 2001 was 723, down from 891 in 2000, and 1,265 in 1999.[244] However, since late 2001, the number of applications has marginally increased, possibly due to some measures to facilitate naturalisation, such as the reduction of the naturalisation fee,[245] information campaigns and the organisation of language training. In 2001 the measure allowing secondary school students to combine the centralised Latvian examination at graduation with the language examination required for

---

[242] Integration Programme, pp. 15–16.

[243] See the analysis of requirements for and obstacles to naturalisation in: *Minority Protection 2001*, pp. 273–275.

[244] LCHRES, *Human Rights in Latvia in 2001*, p. 17.

[245] On 5 June 2001, the naturalisation fee was reduced from LVL 30 (€52) to LVL 20 (€35). It is lower for certain categories of the population: LVL 10 (€17) – for pensioners, partly disabled persons, and students; LVL 3 (€5) for the unemployed, families with more than three children, and those whose income is under the subsistence level. "Politically repressed" persons, first-category disabled, orphans and recipients of State or municipal social care are exempt.

naturalisation was also introduced.[246] However, significant obstacles remain, including a sense of alienation from the State, lack of information and insufficient Latvian language skills, especially among middle-aged persons and the older generation. At the same time, there have also been delays in the naturalisation process.[247]

The main actor in this area has been the Naturalisation Board. Most of its funding to date has come from international donors. The activities of the Naturalisation Board, which have been included in the Integration Programme, have consisted of promoting information about citizenship as well as Latvian language training for non-citizens.

Information

For example, the project "Promotion of Integration through Information and Education" was implemented in 2000 with Phare 1998 support. In November 2001, a Naturalisation Information Campaign was initiated by the OSCE Mission to Latvia, in cooperation with the Naturalisation Board, the UNDP and international donors. USD 275,000 (€297,556) were invested.[248] The campaign ended in February 2002. According to an independent evaluation, the Information Campaign together with other measures of the Naturalisation Board to promote naturalisation succeeded in reversing the decrease of naturalisation applications, at least temporarily.[249]

Latvian language training

In 2000–2002, the Naturalisation Board, in collaboration with the Latvian Folk School (a non-governmental entity) and foreign donors, organised Latvian language training for naturalisation applicants.[250] Since May 2002, the Latvian

---

[246] LCHRES, *Human Rights in Latvia in 2001*, p. 18.

[247] The process of naturalisation was suspended in February 2002 due to an investigation into alleged bribery within the Naturalisation Board. Some minority observers claimed that this was part of a deliberate attempt to delay naturalisation. After nearly four months, the process was resumed and about 1,800 persons who had passed the naturalisation test were granted citizenship. *Minority Issues in Latvia*, No. 49, 1 May 2002, p. 3, <http://racoon.riga.lv/minelres/archive//05022002-20:49:44-27893.html>, (accessed 26 August 2002).

[248] LCHRES, *Human Rights in Latvia in 2001*, p. 18.

[249] I. Brands Kehris, "Public Awareness and Promotion Campaign for Latvian Citizenship. Evaluation," pp. 6–7, <http://www.politika.lv/polit_real/files/lv/campaign_en.pdf>, (accessed 27 September 2002).

[250] This initiative was launched as a pilot project in January 2000 by the Naturalisation Board, in cooperation with the US-based NGO Freedom House and the Latvian Folk School. The free courses helped 78 percent of the overall number of participants pass the Latvian language exam. Interview with the Director of the Latvian Folk School, Riga, 11 April 2002.

Folk School has been providing such courses with State funding through the SIF. Approximately 3,100 adults have attended courses for naturalisation applicants over three years.[251] The main problems that have been identified by participants during evaluations have been lack of time to attend courses and to study, as well as the lack of an environment in which to use Latvian.[252]

Additional State (SIF) and municipal financial support for the continuation of these courses has been promised;[253] the project was also included in the "B" category and presented to the SIF in November 2001. However, it was not approved, mainly due to its large budget as well as to the opinion that instruction should not be provided by the same organisation that is testing language knowledge, i.e. the Naturalisation Board.[254] In January 2002, therefore, the SIF announced an open competition for language instruction organisations. Altogether LVL 32,000 (€55,846) has been allocated for the instruction of 250 persons without any prior knowledge of Latvian to the level of knowledge required by the Naturalisation Board for passing the naturalisation examination.[255] The competition was won by the Latvian Folk School and courses will take place from May to December 2002 for about 250 persons. However, demand is higher than supply.[256]

The SIF and the Naturalisation Board have prepared a new project for 2002–2006, anticipating an increase in the number of participants from 1,200 in 2001, to 5,000 in 2006.[257] From January 2003, the NPLLT will be the implementing institution.

---

[251] This is the overall number of participants in courses funded by the Naturalisation Board as well as through the SIF from January 2000 to May 2002. The total amount of foreign and State funding has been LVL 215,520 (€376,126).

[252] Summary of questionnaires completed by course attendants, Riga, 2001.

[253] During the project presentation, Prime Minister Andris Bērziņš promised financial assistance through the SIF. Liepāja and Daugavpils municipalities also offered LVL 1,000 (€1,745) each. Interview with the Director of the Latvian Folk School, Riga, 11 April 2002.

[254] Interview with the Deputy Director of the SIF Secretariat, Riga, 28 March 2002.

[255] The SIF Council reserved LVL 20,000 (€34,904) from its 2001 budget and also received LVL 12,000 (€20,942) from the 2002 State budget. SIF papers, Project Competition Guidelines "Latvian language instruction for persons wanting to naturalise," Riga, January 2002.

[256] Interview with the Director of the Latvian Folk School, Riga, 11 April 2002.

[257] Project "Ensuring State Language Training for Persons Wishing to Obtain Latvian Citizenship," SIF working papers.

However, funding has not yet been secured,[258] and sufficient funding from the State is not likely to be forthcoming.[259]

Promotion of dialogue between the individual and the State

The promotion of dialogue between individuals and the State is a priority of the Integration Programme which emphasises the need for better information about the work of State institutions and local authorities, the substance of Government decisions before they are adopted, and political events, *inter alia*.[260] There is no specific focus on the creation of a dialogue with minorities.

At the same time, the lack of a constructive dialogue between minorities and State institutions as well as with political parties representing mostly ethnic Latvians has been identified as an important obstacle to integration. Minority NGOs also point to the difficulty of influencing policies concerning them, especially in the field of education. At the same time, some observers note that minority NGOs do not always have sufficient skills or capacity to influence State policy.[261]

Civil society representatives believe that existing mechanisms to promote dialogue with different ethnic groups at the national level are insufficient.[262] For example, the President's Advisory Council on Nationality has not been convened since 1999 and the Department on National Affairs at the Ministry of Justice was closed in 1999. Since 2000, the Department of National Minority Affairs at the Naturalisation Board has been responsible for dealing with minority culture issues and promoting dialogue; however, its capacity in this field is low due to lack of funds and insufficient staff.[263] Officials as well as minority representatives have also called for improved coordination of minority-related policies at the national level, e.g. through the appointment of a

---

[258] A total of LVL 600,000 (€1,047,120) is needed from the State budget. As the SIF cannot provide such funding, a model for the inclusion of subsidies from different sources of funding as well as from the State budget specifically has been worked out.

[259] The requirement from the 2003 State budget (LVL 200,000, €349,040) was opposed by the Ministry of Defence which argued that it was not a priority. The SIF emphasises that foreign donor funding is also necessary for the implementation of this project. The solicitation of funds from the EU is also being considered. Interview with the Director of the SIF Secretariat, Riga, 12 August 2002.

[260] Integration Programme, pp. 14–15.

[261] Interviews with: the Director of the SID, Riga, 1 August 2002; and the Director of LASHOR, Riga, 28 March 2002.

[262] OSI Roundtable, Riga, June 2002.

[263] Interview with a Senior Expert of the Information Centre of the Naturalisation Board, Riga, 31 July 2002. See also Section 3.4.5.

Minister of Integration and the establishment of a Department on National Minority Affairs at the Ministry of Justice.[264]

Minorities continue to be under-represented in State bodies. According to recent data, only eight percent of employees in ten ministries surveyed were minorities (minorities constitute 23.7 percent of Latvian citizens).[265] Minorities are also insufficiently and unevenly represented in municipal councils and administration,[266] and are under-represented in the judiciary.[267] Yet no measures to promote minority representation in the public sphere and in decision-making bodies have been proposed.

Some minority representatives are concerned with the lack of legal guarantees and other mechanisms to promote minority representation.[268] An expert has noted that "the lack of parity at State and local government institutions promotes an increased distrust in State institutions among less-represented groups," and has recommended monitoring representation and potential discrimination as well as encouraging the involvement of minorities in the work of State institutions and informing potential employers and civil servants about discrimination.[269]

On 9 May 2002, the Saeima (Parliament) abolished the requirement of the highest degree of proficiency in the Latvian language for candidates in parliamentary and municipal elections.[270] These amendments were initiated in light of two important

---

[264] OSI Roundtable, Riga, June 2002.

[265] A. Pabriks, *Occupational Representation and Ethnic Discrimination in Latvia*, pp. 25–26. For example, there are only 5.7 percent of minorities at the Ministry of Education and Science; 14 percent – in the Ministry of Economy; however, the share of minorities at the Ministry of Interior is larger: 28 percent.

[266] According to research data, the share of minority representatives is 12.3 percent in city councils, 6 percent in district councils; 11 percent in municipal administration, and 12 percent in district administration. A. Pabriks, *Occupational Representation and Ethnic Discrimination in Latvia*, pp. 15–24.

[267] Minority judges made up 7.5 percent of all judges in the 35 courts investigated. A. Pabriks, *Occupational Representation and Ethnic Discrimination in Latvia*, p. 26.

[268] *Minority Protection 2001*, pp. 297–300. Interviews with: the Director of the Latvian Association of the Teachers of Russian Language and Literature, Riga, 30 July, 2002; and the Project Coordinator of the festival "Golden Ball," Riga, 7 August 2002.

[269] A. Pabriks, *Occupational Representation and Ethnic Discrimination in Latvia*, pp. 25–26.

[270] These were contained in the Saeima Election Law, and the Election Laws on City Council, District Council and Parish Council Elections. According to the cancelled provisions of these laws, candidates had to submit proof of proficiency in the state language at the third (highest) level in order to be registered. They will now evaluate their proficiency themselves and cannot be excluded on this basis. LCHRES, *Human Rights in Latvia, 1 January 2002 – 30 June 2002*.

decisions by international bodies.[271] However, prior to this measure, on 30 April 2002, several amendments to the Constitution were adopted, strengthening the position of the Latvian language in order to "compensate" for the soon-to-be-enacted amendments to elections laws; it is suggested that the implementation of these amendments may impinge further on the political participation rights of minorities.[272]

Several of the projects incorporated into the Integration Programme seek in some way to promote minority participation and dialogue between individuals and the State by providing information about citizenship, human rights, and State policy, conducting research on integration issues, etc. (e.g. projects by the Naturalisation Board, the NPLLT, the SFL). Given that the mechanisms for dialogue between minorities and the State are insufficient, additional measures to promote the political participation of minorities should be considered.

Support to NGOs

The need to support NGOs and to promote participation in NGOs is one of the Integration Programme's objectives.[273] The chapter on "Culture" also deals with some aspects of support to NGOs, primarily cultural associations. State support for NGOs is evaluated as insufficient at present.[274] However, two of the selected themes for the SIF's

---

[271] See the 25 July 2001 ruling of the UN Human Rights Committee concerning Antonina Ignatane, a candidate to the municipal elections in 1997 whose Latvian language proficiency was re-examined; as a result, she was struck off the electoral lists. The text of the decision is at <http://www.un.org/cases/UNHRC_Ignatane_2001.html>, (accessed 26 August 2002). See also the 9 April 2002 ruling of the European Court of Human Rights regarding Ingrida Podkolzina's rights to free and genuine elections, <http://hudoc.echr.coe.int/Hudoc2doc2/HFJUD/200208/podkolzina%20-%2046726jv.chb4%2009042002f.doc>, (accessed 26 August 2002).

[272] See LCHRES, *Human Rights in Latvia, 1 January 2002 – 30 June 2002*, p. 6. Art. 18 of the Constitution now stipulates that an elected MP must take an oath in Latvian, swearing "to be loyal to Latvia, to strengthen its sovereignty and the Latvian language as the only official language, to defend Latvia as an independent and democratic State." Problems could arise if this provision is interpreted in such a way that minority deputies cannot submit proposals to strengthen the status of minority languages. Art. 21 states that "the working language of the Saeima is the Latvian language." Art. 101 establishes the exclusive right of Latvian citizens to stand for election in local government (this norm will have to be amended when Latvia acceded to the EU to extend voting rights to EU citizens in Latvia; it also places an additional barrier for granting voting rights to non-citizens at the municipal level) and that the working language of local government is Latvian. Art. 104 of the Constitution stipulates the right to receive answers from State and municipal bodies in the State language. It is unclear whether this means that answers can be issued in Latvian only.

[273] Integration Programme, p. 119.

[274] *Minority Protection 2001*, pp. 307–308; OSI Roundtable, Riga, June 2002.

2002 project competitions are connected with supporting NGOs.[275] There is also a theme of assistance to cultural associations of national minorities and for strengthening their role in the development of minority culture, education and languages. The total budget for the project theme in the project tender organised in the first half of 2002 was LVL 15,000 (€26,178), with a maximum of LVL 1,000 (€1,745) per project.[276] As already mentioned, criticism has been expressed by minority representatives who find that the budget for individual NGOs projects is too small.

Initiatives of municipalities in the field of integration

The elaboration and implementation of the Integration Programme has promoted discussions on ethnic issues and initiatives also at the municipal level. The Integration Programme calls for the involvement of local governments and the establishment of social integration councils to "provide opportunities allowing people to participate in social life and to influence decision-making […]."[277]

Municipalities are participating in implementation of the Integration Programme in two main ways:

- A first group of municipalities (typically small ones, e.g. Gulbene[278] and Pededze[279]) is trying to implement the Integration Programme without any revisions, with an emphasis on the involvement of their municipality in SIF project competitions. These municipalities either do not have the necessary resources or do not see the need for their own integration programme.[280] Their priority is to determine which of the integration issues mentioned in the Integration Programme are the most important for them, to develop projects in these areas, and to obtain funding from the SIF.

- A second group of municipalities, due to their specific situation, have worked out their own integration programme or are currently working on one, drawing upon parts of the Integration Programme or asking the SIF for financial assistance to

---

[275] One of them is the programme of financial assistance to NGO projects in the area of ethnic integration, based on the assumption of a decrease in foreign funding for NGOs. The project tender for the first half of 2002 ensured an allocation of LVL 10,000 (€17,452), with a maximum of LVL 1,000 (€1,745) per project. SIF working papers.

[276] SIF working papers.

[277] Integration Programme, p. 123.

[278] M. Ilgaža, "*Integrācijas darba grupa izstrādās četrus projektus*" (The integration work group will work out four projects), *Dzirkstele* (*Spark*), 7 October 2000.

[279] L. Zara, "*Piesaista finasējumu*" (Search for Financing), *Alūksnes ziņas* (*Aluksne News*), 14 March 2002.

[280] Telephone interviews with: a Representative of the Latgale Integration Programme in Rēzekne region and a Representative of Krāslava region, 25 March 2002.

develop a local programme. Big cities and regions dominate in this group (e.g., Latgale region, Zemgale region, Jelgava, Jūrmala, Liepāja, Tukums, Rēzekne, Rēzekne region, Ventspils, Alūksne region, etc.).[281]

Since 1999, integration working groups, councils or committees consisting of representatives from local municipalities, educational institutions, governmental institutions, and NGOs, have also been established in several municipalities.[282] As of May 2002, there were 17 such municipal integration councils or working groups.[283] In 2000, Ventspils became the first city to adopt an integration programme, upon an initiative of the head of the Ventspils City Council and the Mayor, and with local funds.[284] The programme is to be renewed every three years. An Advisory Board on non-citizen affairs, whose members include non-citizens and newly-naturalised citizens, was formed in Spring 2000 and was granted the status of a local government commission. It can therefore delegate members to other local government commissions.[285] It has played an active role in the decision-making process of the municipality. However, a lack of financial and human

---

[281] Sometimes, the integration programme of a municipality is part of the development programme of a bigger city or region (e.g. in Latgale, Zemgale and the city of Rēzekne).

[282] In some regions or cities, there is a special person responsible for the coordination of integration issues.

[283] Information provided by the Information Centre of the Naturalisation Board, Riga, 31 July 2002. The common aims of these municipal integration bodies are: to facilitate and promote implementation of the Integration Programme; to provide information and suggestions to the mass media, NGOs, local government institutions and to cooperate with them; to take part in informational and educational activities; to conduct public opinion research and to analyse data on integration and naturalisation issues. Statutes of the Society Integration Process Coordinating Council in Rēzekne region; Statutes of the Society Integration Committee of Jelgava; Statutes of the Rēzekne City Integration Promotion Committee.

[284] Interview with the Head of the Ventspils Advisory Board on Non-citizen Affairs, Ventspils, 3 August 2002.

[285] UNDP, *Human Development Report 2000/2001*, Riga, 2001, pp. 91–92. The main aim of the Advisory Board is to compensate the lack of voting rights of about one third of all adult inhabitants in Ventspils. The Advisory Board works as a consultative office for Ventspils inhabitants – mostly minorities and non-citizens. It also develops and helps implement projects, e.g. the project "Towards a Civil Society" – special courses for high school students and adults in order to get naturalised; it also helped with the "Golden Ball" and "Ventspils Vainags" festivals – a multiethnic festival which took place in November 2001 and was funded by Ventspils City Council in the amount of LVL 3,085 (€5,384); the SIF will be asked to support it in 2003. Interview with the Head of the Ventspils Advisory Board on Non-citizen Affairs, Ventspils, 3 August 2002.

resources, as well as lack of time and experience in elaborating and administering large projects have constituted obstacles to implementation.[286]

Jelgava and Jūrmala have tried to follow the example of Ventspils by creating non-citizens' advisory councils, but these initiatives are still at an early phase.[287] Liepāja has developed its own integration programme and has established a special fund where minority organisations, *inter alia*, can submit projects.[288]

The SIF has already started to support the elaboration of local integration programmes. One of the themes for the first 2002 SIF project competition was supporting the elaboration of society integration programmes at the municipal level for a total amount of LVL 8,000 (€13,962), or a maximum of LVL 300 to 800 (€524 to 1,396) per project.[289] Ten projects were already approved in June 2002 for a total of LVL 11,748 (including co-funding).

Support for activities at the municipal level should be continued and extended on the basis of an evaluation of achievements and areas in need of improvement. There is a need for greater collaboration between municipal bodies and the bodies responsible for implementing the Integration Programme at the national level.

3.4.4 Media

The existence of two information spaces "corresponding to those people who commonly speak Latvian and those who speak Russian" is an important obstacle to integration and is particularly stressed in the Integration Programme.[290] Ensuring access to information, the creation of a unified information space as well as the use of new information technologies are the main directions for action in the chapter devoted

---

[286] Interview with the Head of the Ventspils Advisory Board on Non-citizen Affairs, Ventspils, 3 August 2002.

[287] A. Šabanovs, "Non-citizens have finally been noticed," *Chas* (*The Hour*), 17 July 2001 (in Russian); J. Novika, "The board on non-citizen affairs: the experience of Ventspils exists only on paper still in Riga," *Chas* (*The Hour*), 13 September 2001 (in Russian).

[288] Telephone interview with the Coordinator of the Liepāja Integration Project, 25 March 2002.

[289] SIF working materials.

[290] Framework Document, p. 46. The problems mentioned include: the fact that a segment of the population is influenced by Russia's media; the sceptical and ironic tone of many materials in several Russian-language newspapers; and often different approaches in Latvian and Russian newspapers, e.g. regarding foreign policy.

to "Information."[291] The need for the State to promote information about minority cultural activities in the Latvian language (as well as about Latvian culture in the Russian language) on national television as well as cultural programmes on television and radio devoted to minorities is also highlighted in the chapter on Culture.[292]

Accordingly, one of the themes for the 2002 SIF project tenders was the promotion of Latvia as a multicultural State.[293] Projects are to be implemented by public relations companies with the aim of promoting collaboration between Latvian- and minority-language media. Two projects have already received support. In July 2002, the SIF also announced a project tender for television programmes on integration issues with the aim to promote public debate.[294]

State support to projects encouraging collaboration between Russian- and Latvian-language media should be continued in order to promote discussions and exchanges of ideas between different segments of the population. Discussion of minority issues on public television should also be encouraged. Finally, existing restrictions on the use of minority languages in private electronic media[295] should be reviewed, as they are

---

[291] Integration Programme, pp. 100–105. It emphasises that "[t]he time devoted to transmissions in Latvian and other languages on the radio should be implemented with flexibility by taking into account the situation with respect to language usage in each particular region." It also calls for the elaboration of regional integration programmes for the mass media; encouraging press services reflecting a variety of viewpoints; dissemination of information about events uniting society; the promotion of patriotic feelings with the assistance of the mass media; the promotion of joint media projects in different languages, etc.

[292] Integration Programme, p. 80.

[293] The overall budget for this theme in the first half of 2002 was LVL 10,000 (€17,452), with a maximum of LVL 5,000 (€8,726) per project. SIF working papers.

[294] The overall budget for this theme from the State budget is LVL 16,000 (€27,923). *Integration of Society in Latvia: From Plans to Implementation, June–July 2002 (26)*, Ministry of Foreign Affairs, p. 2, <http://www.am.gov.lv/en/?id=2950>, (accessed 27 August 2002).

[295] Latvian legislation does not regulate language use in print media. However, according to the Law on Radio and Television, one of the two public radio and television channels must broadcast only in the State language, while the other can allocate up to 20 percent of its airtime to broadcasts in minority languages, Art. 62(2) and (3). No more than 25 percent of the programming of private entities can be in a foreign language, Art. 19(5). The Law on Radio and Television (24 August 1995) is at <http://www.likumi.lv/doc.php?id=36673>, (accessed 26 August 2002); see also Amendments to the Law on Radio and Television (29 October 1998), § 7, at <http://www.likumi.lv/doc.php?id=50688>, (accessed 26 August 2002); see also *Minority Protection 2001*, p. 293.

considered to be in contradiction with international human rights standards.[296]

3.4.5 Culture

The Integration Programme devotes a separate chapter to the issue of culture.[297] The uneven distribution of cultural values, insufficient development of a common information space, and insufficient development of cultural policy in general have also been stressed as significant problems.[298] Although some funding has been allocated to support minority culture, State support in this area is still generally considered insufficient by some experts,[299] and additional support for strengthening the capacity of minority NGOs is necessary. There is a need for a comprehensive strategy towards the promotion of minority culture, including improved legislation on the right of minorities to cultural autonomy.[300] The Integration Programme thus proposes to articulate the content and scope of cultural rights, increase funding for cultural activities, and enhance cultural dialogue, *inter alia*.[301]

To date, there has been no progress in achieving the Programme's aim to "improve legislation on the rights of minorities to cultural autonomy."[302]

Several Government and municipal institutions support minority cultural activities through project tenders or donations. These include: the Ministry of Culture and institutions under its supervision (with State funding) (such as the Cultural Capital Foundation and the National Centre of Folk Art), the Department of National

---

[296] Such as the ECHR, FCNM. See: G. Feldhūne and M. Mits, *Legal analysis of national and European anti-discrimination legislation*, p. 39; L. Raihmans, "*Vai katram sava – televīzija?*" (Should Everybody Have Their Own TV?), *Jaunā Avīze* (*New Newspaper*), 1 February 2002, p. 7.

[297] Integration Programme, pp. 79-99.

[298] Framework Document, pp. 38-39.

[299] I. Apine, L. Dribins, A. Jansons, *et al.*, *Ethnopolicy in Latvia*, pp. 30–31. LVL 14,500 (€25,305) has been distributed annually from the State budget since 1995 for projects of national cultural societies. Funding has also been allocated since 2000 to the Association of National Cultural Societies (consisting of 20 minority associations). LVL 45,000 (€78,534) was allocated in 2002 from the State budget for the Latvian Roma National Culture Society (compared to LVL 15,000, €26,178, in 2001), <http://www.am.gov.lv/en/?id=46&page=804&printer=on>, (accessed 27 September 2002).

[300] "No mechanism was developed to suit the cultural autonomy of the Latvian nation which could widely influence minority cultural life. Non-Latvian participation in culturally related legislation and its implementation has so far been inconsistent." Framework Document, p. 38.

[301] Integration Programme, p. 79.

[302] Integration Programme, p. 79.

Minority Affairs at the Naturalisation Board,[303] as well as minority schools and municipalities. Some NGOs and international organisations (e.g. the SFL) have also supported minority cultural activities. However, the demand for State support for minority cultural activities is increasing and exceeds funding possibilities. In 2001, the Department of National Minority Affairs received funding requests from minority NGOs for a total of LVL 157,277 (€274,480) – eleven times more than the amount of funds earmarked from the State budget and an increase of about 35 percent over the previous year.[304] Reportedly, insufficient skills and experience in writing project proposals and poor Latvian language skills also hinder the participation of minority cultural associations and NGOs in project tenders.[305]

In 2000, the Ministry of Culture elaborated the National Programme "Culture" which states the objectives of supporting the activities of national cultural associations and their collaboration and elaborating a concept for the development of multiculturalism, *inter alia*.[306] According to some minority activists, however, minorities have benefited little from the "Culture" programme until now; for example, no minority cultural centres have received State support.[307] Some observers also claim that minority culture is not a priority for the Ministry of Culture, and that State institutions which have supported some minority cultural activities believe that the SIF should fund these activities.[308]

---

[303] The Department of National Minority Affairs gathers information about minority organisations and collaborates with them; analyses and elaborates minority-related legislation; elaborates and, in collaboration with other State and municipal bodies, implements policies in the sphere of minority integration; identifies the necessary funds for minority organisations; monitors the implementation of domestic and international minority-related legislation, etc. Bylaw of the Department of National Minority Affairs at the Naturalisation Board, Riga, 18 July 2001.

[304] LVL 116,117 (€202,647) had been requested in 2000. *2001 Annual Report*, Department of National Minority Affairs at the Naturalisation Board, p. 8 (in Latvian). See also I. Apine, L. Dribins, A. Jansons, *et al.*, *Ethnopolicy in Latvia*, pp. 30–31.

[305] For example, only five out of the 28 minority cultural associations and NGOs which participated in a seminar funded by the Baltic American Partnership Programme wrote project proposals and received funding; seven did not write any; others wrote applications (not project proposals) for State funding to the Department of National Minority Affairs only. Six organisations have no computer or Internet access. Information provided by the Lecturer of the seminar, Riga, 8 August 2002.

[306] K. Pētersone, National Programme "Culture" 2000–2001, Ministry of Culture, Republic of Latvia (short version), Riga, 2000, p. 28, <http://www.km.gov.lv/UI/ImageBinary.asp?imageid=306>, (accessed 27 September 2002) (in Latvian).

[307] I. Vinnik, Minority Cultural Programmes, Theses for Presentation, 2001.

[308] Interview with the Project Coordinator of the festival "Golden Ball," Riga, 7 August 2002.

Several projects to promote minority cultures and cultural dialogue are listed in the Integration Programme, including projects traditionally implemented by the Ministry of Culture and State institutions under its supervision (see above). A few projects by minority NGOs are also included. However, many of these projects have not been implemented.[309]

Some projects in the area of minority culture were supported by the SIF in November 2001. Also, a priority theme in the 2002 project tenders was support for minority cultural associations (see Section 2.4). A first group of 15 projects of national cultural associations, schools and cultural establishments was approved in June 2002.

Minority Children and Youth Festival "Zelta Kamoliņš" (Golden Ball)

The youth festival "Zelta Kamoliņš" (Golden Ball) is an example of a successful project in the area of minority culture. It has been organised since 1994 with the participation of about 5,000 different national minority children and young people from all over the country.[310] This is one of the few projects by minority NGOs to be included in the Integration Programme and has received SIF support twice.[311] The participants – leaders of cultural groups ("collectives") from schools – tend to positively evaluate the festivals. However, the future of the festival is unclear as neither the Government nor the Ministry of Culture have indicated the intent to fund it; however, some funding was allocated by the SIF in November 2001, and again in June 2002.[312]

4. EVALUATION

Although the Integration Programme targets society as a whole rather than minorities in particular, it nevertheless states the need to protect minority rights and addresses a number of issues of relevance to minorities such as Latvian language training, bilingual education, collaboration between schools, naturalisation, promotion of minority cultures, intercultural dialogue, and access to media.

---

[309] Primarily those submitted by NGOs, either because they not did receive funding through the SIF or other sources, or were not submitted to the SIF project tender.

[310] Until 2001, these festivals were funded by the SFL, municipalities, the Cultural Capital Foundation and the Department of National Minority Affairs.

[311] At the end of 2001, the SIF approved the project for Jelgava (Zemgale region). The budget of the project was LVL 3,532 (€6,164) and was financed solely by the SIF. About 13 associations (290 participants) took part in the festival in Zemgale in 2002. Feedback on the project submitted to the SIF, 5 April 2002.

[312] LVL 989 (€1,726), about 50 percent of the budget. SIF working papers.

Latvian society generally supports the need for integration and for such a programme, although many people, both from the majority and minority communities, consider social integration problems to be more pressing than ethnic integration. Views on how minorities should integrate, however, still tend to differ between ethnic Latvians and minorities; opinions also vary among ethnic Latvians.

Many representatives of minorities are particularly concerned by the lack of a comprehensive legal framework and other policy measures for the protection and promotion of minority rights. This concern is accentuated by the fact that several minority rights claimed by civil society and minorities (such as greater access to education in the mother tongue, mass media, greater promotion of a dialogue between minorities and the State, public participation of minorities, and the promotion of minority languages) are not addressed or are insufficiently addressed in the Integration Programme. The link between integration policy and minority rights should therefore be strengthened in the future, especially in light of the need to ratify and implement the FCNM, but also in the interest of social cohesion and effective minority participation.

The Government should also seek to further develop social dialogue on integration and ethnic policy within the context of implementation of the Integration Programme. The outcome of these debates should be taken into account when revising and reformulating the priorities of the Integration Programme. In addition, ethnic integration should be prioritised within the framework of the Integration Programme in order to minimise overlap with other governmental initiatives to resolve social integration problems. Increased governmental and political support for minority integration and the promotion of minority rights are prerequisites for the success of the Integration Programme in the long term.

In general, protracted delays and low levels of financial support from the State have hindered the rapid adoption and implementation of the Integration Programme. As the mechanisms for administering the Programme and for allocating funds have only recently begun to function, it is too early to draw any conclusions about their efficiency. Yet, already, several potential problem areas related to the activities of the SIF and the SID can be noted:

- There is a lack of coordination between different institutions (State bodies, municipalities and NGOs) and a risk of overlap between the work of the SIF and that of other institutions active in the field of integration of society;

- The implementation of the Integration Programme and the integration process have not yet been evaluated and there is no comprehensive information on the various projects being realised;

- The involvement of minorities in implementation has been low thus far. Minority NGOs are under-represented in the SIF Council, and few projects by minority NGOs have been included in the Programme or have received funding from the SIF thus far;

- Despite the establishment of several websites and newsletters, there is a lack of information available to the broader public concerning activities related to implementation of the Integration Programme, especially concerning on-going activities of the Ministry of Justice, SIF activities (except information about project tenders) and various projects. Analysis of integration issues is rarely on the agenda of most Latvian- and Russian-language mass media;

- The composition of the SIF Council has led to concerns within civil society and experts of political interference;

- The SIF's budget has been too small to achieve the objectives of the Programme. Implementation will depend to a large extent on the SIF's administrative capacity to oversee Phare funds starting in 2003 and increased State funding for integration projects, as well as on the capacity of NGOs to manage Phare funding.

The most significant and effective initiatives to date in the field of integration of minorities have been in the field of Latvian language training and promotion of naturalisation. These were launched before the adoption of the Integration Programme and have been funded mostly by foreign donors, including the EU (with some State contribution). In 2002, with limited funding, the SIF sought to increase the participation of civil society and municipalities and provided training to representatives of municipalities, educational and cultural establishments and NGOs through the organisation of project tenders addressing several topical issues in the field of ethnic integration.

While education reform has improved the Latvian language skills of minority students, many minority representatives and parents remain concerned about its impact on the quality of teaching and assert that many secondary schools are not ready for the transition to Latvian in 2004. Despite recent efforts to improve the situation, many teachers still need Latvian language and bilingual methodology training; there is also a lack of adequate study materials, a lack of public information about the reform, and low levels of support from many minority representatives.

There is still a lack of sufficient activity to address several problems identified in the Integration Programme. For example, initiatives to address unemployment through the promotion of Latvian language training have posted modest success, but demand far outstrips supply. No steps have been taken to improve the legal framework in the sphere of cultural autonomy and to clarify minority rights. Programmes on minority issues in the State media are also needed. There are few State-supported measures either within or beyond the scope of the Integration Programme to promote minority languages.[313]

Taking into consideration the inconsistent implementation of the Integration Programme, the low level of participation of minorities, and limited financial support by the State, it must be concluded that the role of the Integration Programme in improving minority protection and the integration of minorities in Latvia has thus far been limited.

5. Recommendations

To the Government

- Strengthen the mechanisms for dialogue between minorities and the State. Consider, *inter alia*, the establishment of a Department on Minority Affairs at the Ministry of Justice, a Minority Culture Department at the Ministry of Culture, and a Minister for Integration; re-establish the President's Advisory Council; promote effective minority participation in the work of these bodies.

- Review the legal framework in the field of minority rights and discrimination and:
    - Ratify the FCNM and take steps to adapt domestic legislation accordingly, including through the easing of language restrictions in the electronic mass media, guaranteeing the use of minority languages in official contacts, and guaranteeing and expanding opportunities for education in the minority language;
    - Adopt a comprehensive Minority Law;
    - Adopt comprehensive anti-discrimination legislation to comply with the EU Race Equality Directive.

- Support the establishment of a specialised section dealing with discrimination issues at the NHRO.

- Adopt new priorities on the basis of the results of monitoring, with the involvement of civil society and minorities; prioritise ethnic integration issues. Consider the following priorities and possible themes for project tenders:

---

[313] There are no provisions allowing for the use of minority languages in official contacts at the State or local level; minority language use in education is also insufficiently guaranteed in legislation.

- Training and support to NGOs;
- Support for municipal initiatives promoting minority participation and integration;
- Promotion of discussions on integration and minority issues in the media and mutual collaboration between Latvian- and Russian-language media;
- Expansion of Latvian language training for naturalisation applicants and information campaigns to promote naturalisation;
- Promotion of the participation of civil society and minorities in public life, especially in decision-making at the national and municipal levels;
- Promotion of greater representation of minorities in public administration;
- Monitoring and evaluation of the impact of minority education reform, including on the quality of education and on the minority identity, and promotion of public participation in the reform;
- Support for Latvian language training for unemployed and socially-excluded persons;
- Support for projects to promote the minority language, culture and identity;
- Promotion of multicultural awareness, including awareness among ethnic Latvians of minority rights, languages and cultures.

- Increase support for the training of bilingual teachers and the development of materials for bilingual schools.
- Increase the budget of the SIF.
- Review the composition of the SIF Council to ensure a more effective representation of minorities.
- Support the efforts of the SID to coordinate and monitor implementation of the Integration Programme.

To the Society Integration Department

- Improve coordination between institutions implementing projects in the field of integration; develop general guidelines for the work of implementing bodies.
- Make the implementation of the Integration Programme more transparent by implementing a comprehensive communications strategy in both Latvian and Russian, including the publication of reports on implementation for the mass media and the promotion of public discussions concerning its implementation.

- Make the implementation of the Integration Programme more transparent by implementing a comprehensive communications strategy in both Latvian and Russian, including the publication of reports on implementation for the mass media and the promotion of public discussions concerning its implementation.

- Revise the priorities of the Programme, taking into consideration the following:
  - Involvement of civil society, minorities and municipalities in the modification of the priorities and organisation of public discussions;
  - Analysis of the measures implemented by various bodies and their efficiency, including in the field of minority rights;
  - Development of an implementation strategy, including a clear division of responsibilities between various State bodies and NGOs involved.

- In collaboration with other bodies dealing with minority issues and with NGOs, promote the revision and adoption of new minority-related legislation.

To the Society Integration Foundation

- Develop a mechanism for evaluating the results of the projects implemented and draw upon lessons learned when selecting new funding priorities.

- Contribute to making implementation of the Integration Programme more transparent by preparing public reports on SIF expenditures and implemented projects.

To the European Commission

- Conduct a critical analysis of the implementation of the Integration Programme and its impact on the situation of minorities, integrating the opinions of civil society representatives and minorities.

OPEN SOCIETY INSTITUTE 2002

Minority Protection in Lithuania

AN ASSESSMENT OF THE PROGRAMME FOR THE INTEGRATION
OF ROMA INTO LITHUANIAN SOCIETY 2000–2004.

Table of Contents

1. Executive Summary 368
2. The Government Programme –
   Background 372
   2.1   Background to Present Programme 374
   2.2   The Programme – Process 373
   2.3   The Programme – Content 374
   2.4   The Programme – Administration/
         Implementation/Evaluation 376
   2.5   The Programme and the Public 380
   2.6   The Programme and the EU 382
3. The Government Programme –
   Implementation 383
   3.1   Stated Objectives of the Programme 383
   3.2   Government Programme
         and Discrimination 384
         3.2.1   Education 386
         3.2.2   Employment 392
         3.2.3   Housing and other
                 goods and services 395
         3.2.4   Healthcare and other forms
                 of social protection 397
         3.2.5   The criminal justice system 403

3.3 Protection from
Racially Motivated Violence 404
3.4 Promotion of Minority Rights 405
  3.4.1 Education 406
  3.4.2 Language 409
  3.4.3 Participation in public life 409
  3.4.4 Media 411
  3.4.5 Culture 412

4. Evaluation 413

5. Recommendations 414

1. Executive Summary

The Programme for the Integration of Roma into Lithuanian Society 2000–2004 (hereafter, "Integration Programme," or "the Programme")[1] aims to promote Roma integration while protecting and promoting Roma national identity. In its first stage, it focuses mostly on improving the situation of Roma living in the Kirtimai settlement in Vilnius. Additional measures to address the situation of Roma in other cities and regions are to be developed and implemented in a second phase.

The Programme does not reflect a fully comprehensive approach to minority protection; there are few concrete measures either to protect Roma against discrimination or to promote the protection and cultivation of their identity.

Background

The Integration Programme was not preceded by any similar governmental initiative; previously, the Government had undertaken only *ad hoc* efforts to address issues faced by Roma, most often in cooperation with non-governmental organisations.

Administration

Overall responsibility for coordinating Programme implementation is assigned to the Minorities Department. However, the Department does not have the competence to require implementation of Programme tasks from ministries and other State or municipal bodies; as there are no mechanisms for reporting or evaluation, it does not have a detailed overview of project activities or expenditures under the Programme, especially regarding funds allocated by local authorities.[2]

Responsibility for implementing Programme measures is assigned to a variety of State and local actors, in most cases the Minorities Department, Vilnius Municipality and the Ministry of Education and Science.[3] Many of its most important initiatives are

---

[1] Programme for the Integration of Roma into Lithuanian Society 2000–2004, adopted by Government Resolution No. 759 (1 July 2000), in *Valstybės Žinios* (*Government News*), No. 54, 5 July 2000; see also <http://www3.lrs.lt/cgi-bin/getfmt?C1=w&C2=104285>, (accessed 26 September 2002). All citations in this report are from an unofficial English translation prepared for the EU Accession Monitoring Program.

[2] This information was compiled especially for EUMAP, see e.g. Annex A.

[3] Also the Ministry of Social Protection and Labour, the Migration Department (Ministry of Interior), Vilnius Municipality, Vilnius County Administration and the State Commission of the Lithuanian Language.

being implemented by a few key NGOs,[4] yet their formal role in relation to the Programme is unclear, blurring the line between the State and NGO sectors.

Limited funding for implementation was allocated from the 2001 State budget as well as by Vilnius Municipality, Vilnius County, and the State Commission of the Lithuanian Language.[5] International funding and some funding from the Ministry of Education and Science was also made available for Programme measures through NGOs; some Programme measures are to be fulfilled through existing governmental programmes for the general population.

EU Support

The EU has not directly supported implementation of the Integration Programme, though it has provided financial support for NGO initiatives that are complementary to Programme measures; in some cases, these initiatives have in fact been presented as Programme measures. No information assessing expenditures and achievement of EU-funded projects was available for this report.

The 2001 Regular Report highlighted the need to pay more attention to the issue of housing. It also called for more funding for the Integration Programme and for upgrading the capacity of the Minorities Department.[6] It did not draw attention to problems of discrimination or the need for more targeted action in the areas of unemployment, healthcare, and access to social services, nor did it reiterate the 2000 Regular Report's call for more consultation with Roma.[7]

Content and Implementation

There has been little research on the situation of Roma communities, and this posed an important obstacle to the Department's efforts to draft a comprehensive programme.

---

[4] Notably the Lithuanian Children's Fund (LICF) and the Foundation for Educational Change, both of which have received EU as well as other international funding, *inter alia*.

[5] In 2001, a total of LTL 730,605 (€207,135) was allocated for implementation of Programme measures by various governmental bodies (80 percent of the amount originally foreseen for 2001 from all sources). The exchange rate is calculated at LTL 3.5272 (Lithuanian Litas) = € 1.

[6] European Commission, *2001 Regular Report on Lithuania's Progress Towards Accession*, Brussels, 13 November 2001, p. 23, <http://www.europa.eu.int/comm/enlargement/report2001/lt_en.pdf>, (accessed 1 February 2002) (hereafter, "*2001 Regular Report*").

[7] *2000 Regular Report from the Commission on Lithuania's Progress Towards Accession*, Brussels, 8 November 2000, p. 21, <http://www.europa.eu.int/comm/enlargement/report_11_00/pdf/en/lt_en.pdf>, (accessed 15 April 2002) (hereafter, "*2000 Regular Report*").

However, the experience of Roma leaders was not utilised effectively to make up for this deficiency during the process of Programme preparation.

As a result, the Integration Programme insufficiently reflects the concerns of Roma and covers a limited number of areas only – primarily social issues and problems related to education, healthcare and migration, *inter alia*. The Programme also outlines a number of concrete measures to be implemented, and states the aim of protecting Roma identity. At the same time, however, the "linguistic, cultural and ethnic features" of Roma are identified as an obstacle to integration. Moreover, key issues for Roma leaders, such as unemployment and housing, are barely addressed, and there are no measures to combat discrimination or to promote a more positive image of Roma among the majority population.

Measures in the area of minority rights are largely limited to support for cultural activities; no measures have been proposed to support education in Romanes or teacher-training which would allow such classes to be offered in the future. However, there are plans to publish a textbook for studying Romanes, which would set the stage for further progress in this area.

There are no concrete Programme measures to promote a more active participation of Roma in public life, and Roma find it difficult to access either State or international funding sources. Training for Roma community leaders and activists in public administration as well as project management skills could bring multiple benefits, by facilitating the emergence of a group of Roma who would be capable of leading Programme implementation in the long term.

Implementation has centred on the establishment of a Roma Community Centre in Kirtimai Tabor.[8] The Centre has offered a range of educational and cultural activities for Roma residents of the Tabor, including pre-school classes to prepare children for primary school. However, future funding for these activities is uncertain, and there have been few attempts to evaluate the initiatives taken to date with a view to extending and improving upon their results.

Mechanisms have been established to enable Roma participation in the management of the Community Centre. However, Roma community leaders still feel that most Programme measures have been decided upon without their input, and that the Programme does little to place them at the forefront of efforts to improve the situation in their communities. They have consistently and unanimously called for more active participation in designing and implementing Programme measures. In response, the

---

[8] The Minorities Department emphasises that a number of the measures proposed are also intended for Roma in other parts of Lithuania.

Minorities Department has promised to involve Roma more effectively during the second stage of Programme development.

Few measures have been implemented in other areas. Though a vocational training programme for Vilnius Roma was prepared in 2001, there are no plans for implementing it. Some steps have been taken to improve conditions in Kirtimai Tabor, but there has been no progress in addressing the urgent issue of illegal construction and lack of ownership of land in the Tabor.

An initiative to provide health education for Roma is perceived as demeaning and unnecessary by Tabor residents, who point out that poor sanitary conditions are not due to lack of awareness but to lack of basic services and poor living conditions. Measures to facilitate equal access to social protection have been insufficient; many Roma lack personal documents which are necessary for the receipt of various social benefits.

Racially motivated violence is not identified as a problem in the Integration Programme and no official complaints of racially motivated violence have been registered. Police raids continue to be carried out in Kirtimai Tabor without search warrants; police claim that warrants cannot be obtained for houses that are not legally registered – which is the case for most houses in the Tabor.

There have been few governmental measures to communicate Programme goals and initiatives to the broader public, or to encourage commitment to Programme implementation among the relevant authorities. There are no media in the Romani language, and no measures to encourage mainstream media to integrate Romani perspectives more effectively. The Government should increase its efforts to ensure that State institutions, local authorities, and the public at large are informed about the Integration Programme and its aims and goals, to ensure that its measures are well-received.

Conclusion

Though the adoption of the Integration Programme constitutes an important signal of the Government's intention to bring about improvements in the situation of Roma, most State authorities remain unconvinced that it is needed; in the absence of sufficient political will, funding has been minimal, and progress on implementation has been slow. The Minorities Department has faced difficulties in winning cooperation from bodies tasked with responsibilities under the Programme, and there has been little coordination to ensure that the realisation of discrete projects complements and contributes to overarching Programme goals and objectives.

The Programme itself is in need of review and revision to ensure more effective integration of the perspectives and viewpoints of Roma, and to begin the process of developing a comprehensive, long-term strategy that will provide opportunities for Roma throughout Lithuania to take the lead in addressing the issues faced by their communities.

2. The Government Programme – Background

The "Programme for the Integration of Roma into Lithuanian Society 2000–2004" (hereafter, "Integration Programme" or "the Programme") was adopted on 1 July 2000.[9] The Programme was developed by the Department of National Minorities and Lithuanians Living Abroad (hereafter, "Minorities Department") on the basis of a recommendation of the Seimas Committee on Human Rights.[10]

The Integration Programme represents the first governmental attempt to address the situation of Roma in a comprehensive and systematic manner. It appears to have been motivated, at least in part, by the aspiration to address EU concerns about the situation of Roma in Europe.[11]

2.1 Background to Present Programme

Prior to the adoption of the Integration Programme, some *ad hoc* initiatives had been undertaken to address issues faced by the Roma community[12] – principally in Kirtimai "Tabor"[13] in Vilnius – by the Minorities Department, the Ministry of Education and Science (hereafter, "Ministry of Education"), and NGOs.

An NGO project launched in March 2000 can be considered a precursor of the Roma Community Centre which was later supported by the Government under the Programme (see Section 3.2.1).

---

[9] Programme for the Integration of Roma into Lithuanian Society 2000–2004, adopted by Government Resolution No. 759 (1 July 2000), in *Valstybės Žinios* (*Government News*), No. 54, 5 July 2000; see also <http://www3.lrs.lt/cgi-bin/getfmt?C1=w&C2=104285>, (accessed 26 September 2002).

[10] Weekly agenda of the Plenary meetings of the Seimas of the Republic of Lithuania, 14 June 1999, <http://www3.lrs.lt/cgi-bin/preps2?Condition1=82742&Condition2=>, (accessed 16 March 2002).

[11] Integration Programme, Chapter I "Introduction," p. 1.

[12] The size of Lithuania's Roma minority is estimated at about 3,000. See Integration Programme, p. 2; see also EU Accession Monitoring Program, *Monitoring the EU Accession Process: Minority Protection*, Open Society Institute, Budapest, September 2001, p. 342 (hereafter, "*Minority Protection 2001*"). The results of a new population census conducted in 2001 are expected in Autumn 2002. See also Section 3.2.3.

[13] From the Lithuanian word "taboras" referring to a large group of Gypsies. Kirtimai Tabor consists of three sections: the Upper Tabor, the Lower Tabor and the Tabor of Rodunės road; it is located in an industrial area of Vilnius.

2.2 The Programme – Process

In December 1999, the Government acknowledged that special efforts to improve the situation of Roma were necessary, as they "have specific problems which are not experienced by other ethnic minorities;" the Minorities Department and four other ministries were tasked with the preparation by mid-2000 of a programme to promote the integration of Roma.[14]

On 14 March 2000 a draft programme was presented to the Government. In the course of preparation, the Minorities Department consulted broadly with a number of ministries[15] as well as with the Lithuanian Labour Market Training Authority, the Migration Department in the Ministry of Internal Affairs, Vilnius County Administration, Vilnius Municipality and the State Commission of the Lithuanian Language. None of the institutions which interact directly with residents of Kirtimai Tabor were consulted.[16]

Little comprehensive research was available for the purpose of developing the Programme (see Section 2.3) and the Minorities Department did not make up for this deficiency by consulting with Roma representatives and the full range of civil society organisations.[17] Thus, the concerns and perspectives of Roma were not taken into account when establishing priority areas for action and developing measures.[18]

The Roma Community Union "Roma Mission" protested the manner in which the Programme was adopted,[19] and the Minorities Department subsequently announced

---

[14] Government Resolution No. 1497 (28 December 1999) "On the Ratification of Measures for the Implementation of the 1999–2000 Programme of the Government of the Republic of Lithuania," *Valstybės Žinios*, No. 114-3316, 1999, <http://www3.lrs.lt/cgi-bin/preps2?Condition1=93237&Condition2=romų>, (accessed 16 March 2002).

[15] The Ministry of Public Administration Reform and Local Authorities, the Ministry of Education and Science, the Ministry of Social Protection and Labour, and the Ministry of Finance. The Ministry of Health was consulted but did not participate in drafting the Programme. The Ministry of Culture and the Ministry of Economy were not consulted.

[16] E.g. Vilnius School No. 58, Naujininkai Police, Naujininkai Passport Division, Vilnius Municipal Health Division, and the Naujininkai Primary Healthcare Centre.

[17] See also *Minority Protection 2001*, p. 338.

[18] *Minority Protection 2001*, pp. 337–339.

[19] Letter No. 3-02-27 dated 26 June 2000 from A. Kasparavičius, President of Roma Mission, to V. Landsbergis, Seimas Chairman; Letter No. 3-02-39 dated 2 August 2000 from A. Kasparavičius, President of Roma Mission, to the Minorities Department. See also the 21 July 2000 Declaration of Roma NGOs of Lithuania to Prime Minister Kubilius; and the Declaration of the Fifth World Roma Congress to Prime Minister Kubilius and President Adamkus, 26 July 2000 (all on file with EUMAP).

that Roma organisations would be invited to participate in developing measures to be implemented in a second stage.[20]

2.3 The Programme – Content

The Integration Programme aspires to be comprehensive; it aims to encourage integration while protecting Roma ethnic identity. However, it does not address either discrimination or minority rights to a sufficient extent.

The Programme focuses initially on the situation of Roma in Vilnius, on the basis of a judgement that the living conditions there are the worst and on the fact that Vilnius-based organisations had already received funding for a Roma community centre.[21] Activities are to be expanded beyond Vilnius in a second stage.[22]

Roma representatives have suggested that it would have been preferable to address the entire Roma community from the outset.[23] The Government has pointed out that measures to improve the situation of Roma in other parts of the country are to be developed and implemented in a second stage, and that the Programme also contains a number of measures that promote integration for Roma more generally, without distinction to where they live.[24]

The Integration Programme identifies problems in the social sphere as well as in relation to education, healthcare, and migration, and enumerates specific measures to be taken in these areas, as well as to support "preservation of ethnic identity."[25] Though the Programme identifies a number of "other problems" such as "a preconceived hostile attitude towards Roma," poor knowledge of the Roma culture

---

[20] Letter No. 1-01-684 dated 31 July 2000 from the Minorities Department to V. Landsbergis, Seimas Chairman, and A. Kasparavičius, President of Roma Mission, in response to Letter No. 23-6693 dated 18 July 2000 from the Seimas.

[21] Letter No. 1-01-684 dated 31 July 2000.

[22] Integration Programme, Chapter VIII "Stages of Programme Implementation," pp. 6–7.

[23] Interviews with the President of Roma Mission, the Chairman of Romen, the Chairman of Bachtalo Drom, the Representative for Lithuania in the Parliament of the International Romani Union, a member of the Council of Roma Mission and member of the Honorary Court of the International Romani Union, the Chairman of the Gypsy Community Organisation in Lithuania, and the Director of the Kaunas Roma Information Bureau, Kaunas, 28 July 2002.

[24] Letter No. 1-01-684 dated 31 July 2000.

[25] See Implementation Measures of the Programme for the Integration of Roma into Lithuanian Society 2000–2004 (hereafter, "Implementation Measures"), adopted by Government Resolution No. 759 (1 July 2000).

among the majority, and stereotyping in the media,[26] there is no corresponding section in the annex listing specific measures to be implemented to deal with these problems.

Roma assert that the failure to consult with them during the process of preparing the Programme is evident in the language it uses as well as in its content and approach. For example, Roma leaders identify housing and employment as the most pressing issues for their communities. Though the Programme does mention these problems, neither is addressed in detail, but rather in the context of other "social problems," such as lack of personal documents, poverty, and criminality, and no specific remedial measures are proposed.[27] By contrast, the Integration Programme identifies drug-peddling and addiction as "[o]ne of the most painful problems among Roma, especially among those living in Vilnius [...]."[28]

Roma claim that consultation could have helped prevent a number of factual inaccuracies in the Programme. For example, it states that "[Roma] only started to live in a settled manner during the 1970s;"[29] Roma claim that some Roma had settled already prior to World War II, and that many others were forced to settle starting in 1956.[30] Furthermore, the Programme asserts that "most Roma can speak only the Russian language;"[31] according to Roma leaders, the mother tongue of the majority of Lithuanian Roma is Romanes.[32] The Programme often generalises the situation of Roma in referring to the situation of Roma in Kirtimai Tabor, although some authorities acknowledge that the situation in the Tabor is not necessarily replicated elsewhere in the country.[33]

Finally, the absence of input from Roma is also evident in the Programme's perspective and tone. Though the Programme proposes to implement measures to preserve Roma identity, it identifies the "linguistic, cultural and ethnic features" of Roma as obstacles to integration.[34] Though it acknowledges that hostile attitudes towards Roma may

---

[26] Integration Programme, Chapter VII "Other Problems," p. 6.
[27] Integration Programme, Chapter III "Social Problems," pp. 4–5.
[28] Integration Programme, Chapter III "Social Problems," pp. 4, 5.
[29] Integration Programme, Chapter I, "Introduction," p. 1.
[30] On the basis of Resolution No. 552 of the Lithuanian SSR Council of Ministers of 17 November 1956 "On Labour Involvement of Vagabond Gypsies," *Chronological Collection of Laws of the Lithuanian SSR, Decrees of the Supreme Soviet Presidium and Resolutions of the Government*, State Publishing House of Political and Research Literature, Vilnius, 1956, pp. 584–585.
[31] Integration Programme, Chapter IV "Education Problems," p. 5.
[32] Most Roma also speak Russian or Lithuanian as a second language.
[33] Interview with the General Director of the Minorities Department, Vilnius, 30 July 2002.
[34] Integration Programme, Chapter I "Introduction," p. 1.

affect their ability to find employment,[35] it stops short of acknowledging discrimination or stipulating measures to address discriminatory behaviours.

As a result of these shortcomings, the Programme is not well accepted within the Roma community.

2.4 The Programme – Administration/Implementation/Evaluation

The Minorities Department, which bears the principal responsibility for coordinating the Programme, has not been given the necessary competence to do so effectively; the lack of an effective reporting and monitoring mechanism has made it difficult for the Department to compile a detailed overview of the status of Programme projects or expenditures. Funding from the State budget has been in line with projects under the Programme, but appears to be insufficient to achieve full implementation of Programme goals.

The Programme assigns responsibility for implementing its different measures to a variety of State bodies: the Minorities Department, Vilnius Municipality, the Ministry of Education, the Ministry of Social Protection and Labour, the Migration Department (Ministry of Interior), the Head of Vilnius County Administration, the Lithuanian Labour Market Training Authority, and the State Language Commission.[36]

Programme responsibilities are not always clearly defined. In many cases, more than one actor is mentioned without any indication of who bears overall responsibility. Several NGOs are also implementing projects in line with the objectives and measures stipulated in the Programme, with funding from the EU and other sources; though these NGOs are not assigned formal responsibility for measures under the Programme,[37] the Minorities Department appears to consider their activities as part of the governmental effort.[38]

---

[35] Integration Programme, Chapter III "Social Problems," p. 4.

[36] Implementation Measures.

[37] For example, the LICF supports some of the activities of the Roma Community Centre with EU funds; yet, only the Minorities Department and Vilnius Municipality are named in relation to the Centre and its activities. See Implementation Measures. However, the LICF is mentioned as one of the actors involved in overall Programme implementation in the text of the Programme itself. Integration Programme, Chapter IX "Implementation and Coordination of the Programme," p. 7.

[38] Interview with the Deputy Director and the Senior Specialist of the Minorities Department, Vilnius, 20 March 2002.

The Minorities Department bears overall responsibility for coordinating Programme implementation.[39] Accordingly, the Department formed a coordination working group in Autumn 2001. The group has 15 members, 12 of whom are experts appointed by various State institutions and three are NGO representatives – including two from Roma organisations.[40] In practice, the working group has met infrequently and not all members seem to be involved.[41]

Moreover, neither individual working group members nor the Department itself appear to have the capacity to compel effective implementation or reporting. For example, Vilnius Municipality reports not to the Department but to the Ministry of Interior and other ministries;[42] allegedly, cooperation has been difficult.[43] As members are not the heads of their institutions, they have little capacity to influence other divisions within their own institutions.

The Mayor of Vilnius has established a separate working group for coordinating Programme implementation,[44] *inter alia*, at the request of the Minorities Department.[45]

Funding

The Programme states that financing is to be provided "by the national budget [...] non-governmental organisations, and also by international organisations and

---

[39] Integration Programme, Chapter IX "Implementation and Coordination of the Programme," p. 7.

[40] Interview with the Deputy Director and the Senior Specialist of the Minorities Department, Vilnius, 20 March 2002. The Director of the LICF is also a member of the coordination working group.

[41] Two meetings were held in 2001; not all members knew that they were part of the group yet or had participated in one meeting only. Interviews with: the Methodologist/Inspector of the Education Division of Vilnius Municipality, Vilnius, 25 March 2002; the Deputy Director of the Passport Division of the Migration Department, Ministry of Interior, Vilnius, 26 March 2002; and the President of Roma Mission, Kaunas, 29 March 2002.

[42] See Government Resolution of 8 November 2000, <http://www3.lrs.lt/cgi-bin/getfmt?C1=w&C2=159067>, (accessed 10 August 2002); see also the Law on Local Self-Governance (1994, last amended on 30 June 2002), *Valstybės Žinios*, No. 55-1049.

[43] Interview with the Head of the Minorities Division, Minorities Department, Vilnius, 30 July 2002.

[44] Decree No. 492V (16 July 2001) of the Mayor of Vilnius "On the Formation of a Work Group for the Execution of the Programme for the Integration of Roma into Lithuanian Society 2000–2004." As of 18 April 2002, there was no head of the work group.

[45] Letter No. 3-10-206 dated 4 April 2001 from R. Motuzas, General Director of the Minorities Department, to A. Zuokas, Mayor of Vilnius.

foundations."[46] The Ministry of Finance is requested to secure funding for Programme measures as possibilities permit, on the basis of annual budgets presented by various implementing institutions.

The Minorities Department has made it a practice to address various State and local actors during the preparation of the annual budget, reminding them to set aside funds for the implementation of measures under the Programme.[47]

No State funding was allocated for implementation of the Programme in 2000, as it was approved during the second half of the year. In 2001, funding from the State budget was roughly in line with what was planned, though this level of funding is rather low.[48] For 2002, LTL 157,000 (€44,511) has been made available for some of the activities of the Roma Community Centre from various governmental sources,[49] and Vilnius Municipality is also expected to contribute (see Section 3.2.1). No information is available on governmental funding of the Integration Programme in 2002 more generally.

The Minorities Department also funds several initiatives which are not specifically stipulated in the Programme, including the construction of a laundry and shower

---

[46] Integration Programme, Chapter IX "Implementation and Coordination of the Programme," p. 7.

[47] Interview with the Head of the Minorities Division, Minorities Department, Vilnius, 30 July 2002.

[48] In 2001, a total of LTL 730,605 (€207,135) was allocated for Programme measures by various governmental bodies (about 80 percent of the planned budget for 2001). The Minorities Department allocated LTL 601,100 (€170,418) (see Annex A); Vilnius municipality contributed LTL 119,705 (€33,938) for the maintenance of the Roma Community Centre and the installation of water pumps (interview with the First Vice Mayor of Vilnius, Vilnius, 25 March 2002 and information provided by the water utility company "Vilniaus Vandenys" on 18 June 2002); Vilnius County Administration – LTL 4,000 (€1,134) (interview with the Director of the LICF, 28 March 2002 and with the Specialist of the Education Division of Vilnius County Administration, Vilnius, 25 March 2002); the Lithuanian Language Commission – LTL 1,400 (€397) (telephone interview with the Senior Programme Coordinator of the Lithuanian Language Commission, 19 June 2002. LTL 4,400 (€1,247) was also provided by the Ministry of Labour and Social Protection through Vilnius Municipality to pay for meals for children attending the pre-school classes (interview with the Director of the Roma Community Centre, Vilnius, 18 March 2002).

[49] Interview with the Director of the Roma Community Centre, Vilnius, 18 March 2002.

facility in Kirtimai Tabor and the renovation of a building for the use of a Roma NGO in Kaunas.[50]

Roma organisations may apply for funding from the Minorities Department for projects that are carried out under the Programme's component on "Preservation of Ethnic Identity;" these proposals are evaluated together with applications from other minorities, which are also funded by the Department. Five elected members of the Council of National Communities play an advisory role in the process of project selection; the Roma representative on the Council is not among them, although he participates in selecting those five members.

Roma leaders are critical of the fact that few Roma are active participants in Programme implementation; most projects for Roma are not developed or led by Roma. They feel that the absence of Roma participation leads to projects which do not reflect the needs and interests of their communities, and which may do little to change negative perceptions of Roma as the passive beneficiaries of governmental assistance. Roma leaders unanimously call for a more active role in Programme implementation.[51]

Monitoring and evaluation

The Integration Programme lacks a centralised mechanism for monitoring and evaluating implementation of its various components. Some implementing bodies have collected information on their own activities and expenditures, but no public report on overall implementation had been prepared by the Minorities Department as of mid-2002. Information on the results of the various measures taken to date is incomplete, not easily available or not up-to-date.

Moreover, the reports of the various implementing bodies often do not indicate activities for Roma separately, or whether they were implemented within the context of the Integration Programme. For example, a report of the Ministry of Education on activities realised in 2001[52] provides information on the goal of "supporting education

---

[50] LTL 100,000 (€28,351) has been allocated to date, and the Department has committed to fully fund renovation and to contribute to maintenance. Letter No. 3-03-92 from S. Vidtmann, Deputy Director of the Minorities Department, to the Mayor of the City of Kaunas, 15 February 2001.

[51] Interviews with the President of Roma Mission, the Chairman of Romen, the Chairman of Bachtalo Drom, the Representative for Lithuania in the Parliament of the International Romani Union, a member of the Council of Roma Mission and member of the Honorary Court of the International Romani Union, the Chairman of the Gypsy Community Organisation in Lithuania, and the Director of the Kaunas Roma Information Bureau, Kaunas, 28 July 2002.

[52] 2001 Annual Report of the Ministry of Education and Science, at <http://www.smm.lt/Bendr_info/smm_atask_02.doc>, (accessed 26 September 2002).

initiatives through the Foundation for Educational Change," which appears to include measures for which the Ministry is responsible under the Integration Programme, although this is not specified (see Section 3.2.1).

There are no common accounting guidelines for reporting expenditures under the Programme, and executing bodies are not required to submit such information to the Minorities Department. Some actors, such as Vilnius Municipality, do not distinguish in their reports between expenditures under the Programme and other municipal initiatives which may also benefit the Roma minority.[53] The Board of the Roma Community Centre does not prepare any evaluation reports. Executing bodies are not required to submit information to the Minorities Department on how much they have allocated for measures of the Programme. As a result, the Minorities Department does not have an overview of sources of funding for various measures or of Programme expenditures, apart from its own.[54]

2.5 The Programme and the Public

The Integration Programme is little known among the Roma community or the general public and is rarely presented in the media.

The Minorities Department has not developed a coordinated public relations strategy to ensure regular communication of information about Programme goals and activities. Roma leaders claim that the Government has not done enough to express clear support for the Programme.[55]

---

[53] Interview with the First Vice Mayor of Vilnius, Vilnius, 25 March 2002.

[54] This information was gathered by EUMAP by requesting data from different institutions responsible for executing components of the Integration Programme, and from members of the coordination working group of the Minorities Department (see Annex A). Information on funding allocated for 2002 was also requested but had not been received as of 6 August 2002. The Minorities Department reports only about its own expenditures in its Annual Report. See Section 1.2 "Support for the integration of Roma into Lithuanian Society," 2001 Annual Report of the Minorities Department, 26 February 2002, at <http://www3.lrs.lt/cgi-bin/getfmt?C1=w&C2=165800>, (accessed 26 September 2002).

[55] Interviews with the President of Roma Mission, the Chairman of Romen, the Chairman of Bachtalo Drom, the Representative for Lithuania in the Parliament of the International Romani Union, a member of the Council of Roma Mission and member of the Honorary Court of the International Romani Union, the Chairman of the Gypsy Community Organisation in Lithuania, and the Director of the Kaunas Roma Information Bureau, Kaunas, 28 July 2002.

The adoption of the Programme was announced on national television and in the national press.[56] The media has not covered implementation systematically, but a number of articles on the establishment of the Roma Community Centre and its activities have appeared in national dailies. Some presented this initiative and the Roma community in a negative light,[57] while others presented the concerns of the Roma community more sympathetically.[58]

Awareness of the Integration Programme among the Roma community, even among Roma representatives[59] and direct beneficiaries, is very low.[60] Tabor residents appear to be aware of some of the measures taken under the Programme, but not that these form part of a broader governmental programme.

The Minorities Department has taken some steps to disseminate information on the activities of minority NGOs through the publication of a regular newsletter,[61] which

---

[56] G. Vitkus, "*Valdžia ketina keisti čigonų gyvenimą*" (Authorities intend to change the life of Gypsies), *Lietuvos Aidas*, 4 July 2000, p. 9; see also R. Grumadaitė, "*Čigonams – valstybės globa*" (For Gypsies – State care), *Lietuvos Rytas*, 22 June 2000, pp. 1, 2; A. Andriuškevičius, "*Skurdas nutildė čigonų dainas*" (Poverty has silenced Gypsy songs), *Kauno Diena*, 27 June 2000, pp. 1, 4.

[57] One article about the establishment of the Roma Community Centre in Kirtimai Tabor included the following statement: "Already earlier a conclusion was drawn that Gypsies had to be beckoned to school by material offers: free food and clothing, and that is also intended to be done through the establishment of the Gypsy Community Centre." D. Babickas, "*Čigonai – būsimi profesoriai*" (Gypsies – Future Professors), *Sostinė (The Capital)* (Supplement of *Lietuvos Rytas*), 10 March 2001, p. 3. See also: R. Parafinavičius, "*Čigonai nori mokytis*" (Gypsies want to study), *Lietuvos Žinios (Lithuanian News)*, 10 September 2001, p. 5; M. Peleckis, "*Čigonai nori uždaryti jiems pastatytą visuomeninį centrą*" (Gypsies want to close the Community Centre built for them), *Respublika*, 5 October 2001, p. 18.

[58] Some articles quoted Roma leaders on the poor level of collaboration with the Minorities Department and their doubts about the Programme's selected priorities, emphasising the need to implement measures for the entire Roma community of the country. See e.g. A. Andriuškevičius, Poverty has silenced Gypsy songs, pp. 1, 4.

[59] Interviews with: the President of Gypsy Bonfire, Vilnius, 25 March 2002; and the President of Roma Mission, Kaunas, 29 March 2002.

[60] Interviews with residents of Kirtimai Tabor, Vilnius, 18 March 2002.

[61] The quarterly "Informational Newsletter of the National Communities" has a circulation of 200 copies which are distributed to each of the 200 minority organisations.

has featured articles on the Roma Community Centre.[62] However, the newsletter does not appear to be broadly known among Roma leaders.[63]

2.6 The Programme and the EU

The EU has not directly supported implementation of the Integration Programme as the protection of minorities is not considered a priority area for Phare funding in Lithuania.[64] However, some EU funding has been allocated in support of NGO projects to benefit the Roma community, mainly in the area of education and also healthcare; some of these projects support broader Programme objectives.

For example, the Lithuanian Children's Fund (LICF) and the French NGO *"Un Enfant par la Main"* received funding under the 1999 and 2000 Phare LIEN Programmes to support activities for Roma in Kirtimai Tabor, including the establishment of the Roma Community Centre.[65] The Foundation for Educational Change (FEC) received funding under the 1999 European Initiative for Democracy and Human Rights (EIDHR) Programme for a project to mentor Roma pupils.[66]

An assessment of the effectiveness of EU support is difficult to make as no public report is available on project implementation or expenditures. The European Commission Delegation provides information on recipient organisations, but not about specific projects supported or amounts of funding provided; there are no public reports on EU support for Roma projects in Lithuania.[67]

---

[62] See for example, J. Rumša, *"Atidarytas Romų centras"* (The Roma Centre has opened), *Tautinių Bendrijų Informacinis Biuletenis*, (Informational Newsletter of the National Communities) No. 4, July–September 2001, p. 8.

[63] Interviews with: the Chairwoman of Nevo Drom, Vilnius, 18 March 2002; a representative of Lithuania in the International Romani Union, the President of Roma Mission, the Chairman of Romen, a member of the Council of Roma Mission, Vilnius, 20 March 2002; and the President of Gypsy Bonfire, Vilnius, 6 May 2002.

[64] See e.g. the 2001 Accession Partnership at <http://www.europa.eu.int/comm/enlargement/report2001/aplt_en.pdf>, (accessed 26 September 2002).

[65] Interview with the Director of the LICF, Vilnius, 28 March 2002.

[66] See 2001 Annual Report of the Foundation for Educational Change, <http://skf.osf.lt/Ataskait2001.doc>, (accessed 12 August 2002).

[67] Information provided by the Public Relations Administrator of the Information Centre of the Delegation of the European Commission to Lithuania, via e-mail, Vilnius, 25 March 2002.

No Roma NGOs have been recipients of EU funds. Many lack staff with experience in the preparation and administration of project proposals; many lack the funding to retain permanently employed staff at all. Roma representatives also claim that it is difficult to obtain information on available funding and applications procedures. The Delegation would perform an important service if it provided targeted outreach and training support in these areas to Roma organisations in particular, and civil society organisations more generally.

The European Commission has not yet evaluated implementation of the Integration Programme; it has, however, noted the difficult situation of Roma in its 2001 Regular Report, emphasising that "much more attention" should be paid to the issue of housing; it has also called for more State funding as well as for an increase in the capacity of the Minorities Department in order to improve effectiveness of minority programmes generally.[68] While the European Commission had previously called for increased consultation with the Roma community,[69] it did not assess progress on this point; nor did it draw attention to problems of discrimination, or the need for more targeted action in the areas of employment, healthcare and access to social services.

3. THE GOVERNMENT PROGRAMME – IMPLEMENTATION

3.1 Stated Objectives of the Programme

The goals of the Integration Programme are to create the conditions for the integration of Roma into majority society and to provide for the protection and cultivation of Roma ethnic identity "by taking into account the specific conditions of their lives."[70]

To achieve these goals, the Programme proposes to: implement a national policy for Roma integration; take effective measures to promote equal opportunities for Roma and other inhabitants of the country; promote tolerance and a more positive image of Roma through efforts to provide information about Roma culture and history; and

---

[68] European Commission, *2001 Regular Report on Lithuania's Progress Towards Accession*, Brussels, 13 November 2001, p. 23, <http://www.europa.eu.int/comm/enlargement/report2001/lt_en.pdf>, (accessed 1 February 2002) (hereafter, *"2001 Regular Report"*).

[69] *2000 Regular Report from the Commission on Lithuania's Progress Towards Accession*, Brussels, 8 November 2000, p. 21, <http://www.europa.eu.int/comm/enlargement/report_11_00/pdf/en/lt_en.pdf>, (accessed 15 April 2002) (hereafter, *"2000 Regular Report"*).

[70] Integration Programme, Chapter I "Introduction," p. 2.

encourage Roma integration at the national and municipal levels through cooperation with international and non-governmental organisations."[71]

The first stage of the Programme, which is principally designed to benefit Roma in Vilnius, aims to achieve the following:

- Establishment of a "Roma Community Centre;"
- Guidance for school-age children;
- Improvement of social conditions;
- Access to primary healthcare;
- Promotion of cultural activities.[72]

The goals of the second stage are "to prepare and implement measures for improvement in the situation of Roma living in other towns and regions of Lithuania."[73] Implementation of the second stage has not yet begun.

3.2 Government Programme and Discrimination

The Integration Programme recognises the existence of negative societal attitudes toward Roma, noting that "[a] preconceived hostile attitude towards Roma has still not been overcome [...]. Frequently, persons of their ethnicity are regarded as potential criminals."[74] However, no specific measures are proposed to counter these perceptions.

Moreover, the Integration Programme does not acknowledge that negative attitudes may lead to discriminatory behaviour, and thus proposes no specific measures to combat discrimination or to promote equal opportunities. In fact, Roma themselves appear to be held responsible for the slow pace of integration.[75]

Rather, the Programme proposes "to take effective measures to form equal opportunities for Roma *and other inhabitants of the country* to participate in the life of society (emphasis added)."[76] This reflects the concern that positive measures on behalf

---

[71] Integration Programme, Chapter I "Introduction," p. 2.
[72] Integration Programme, Chapter VIII "Stages of Programme Implementation," pp. 6–7.
[73] Integration Programme, Chapter VIII "Stages of Programme Implementation," pp. 6–7.
[74] Integration Programme, Chapter VII "Other Problems," p. 6.
[75] Integration Programme, Chapter I "Introduction," p. 1.
[76] Integration Programme, Chapter I "Introduction," p. 2.

of Roma could provoke a backlash from socially disadvantaged segments of the majority population.[77]

High level Government officials responsible for minority protection deny that Roma face discrimination.[78] The Office of the Seimas Ombudsman has not received any complaints of discrimination from Roma.[79] The Chairman of the Seimas Committee on Human Rights and the General Director of the Minorities Department also state that they have not received any complaints of discrimination on racial or ethnic grounds from Roma.[80]

On the other hand, Roma leaders report that discrimination is an everyday experience, and discriminatory attitudes towards Roma have also been identified by some employees of public institutions and domestic NGOs.[81] They criticise the Programme for its lack of measures to enhance legal protection against discrimination and violations of human rights.[82] In fact, a recent review of Lithuanian legislation in

---

[77] Integration Programme, Chapter VII "Other Problems," p. 6. See also Section 3.2.3.

[78] Telephone interview with the Head of the Seimas Ombudsmen's Office, Vilnius, 12 April 2002; telephone interview with the Senior Specialist of the Minorities Department, Vilnius, 15 April 2002. Also, in 2000, the General Director of the Minorities Department submitted a report at an international meeting on Roma issues where he stated that: "racist persecutions, discrimination or intolerance cases were recorded neither in Soviet period, nor in independent Lithuania." R. Motuzas, General Director, Minorities Department, "Situation of Roma Minority in Lithuania," paper presented at a Roundtable Meeting of the Council of Europe, Tallinn, 24 November 2000, p. 1. See also Section 3.2.2.

[79] Letter No 01-100 dated 22 April 2002 from the Head of the Seimas Ombudsmen's Office to E. Kučinskaitė. The annual reports of the Seimas Ombudsmen do not cover the situation of Roma.

[80] Interviews with: the Chairman of the Seimas Committee on Human Rights, Vilnius, 29 July 2002; and the General Director of the Minorities Department, Vilnius, 30 July 2002.

[81] Interview with the Director of the Centre for Dependency-Related Illnesses, Vilnius, 8 April 2002; see also the Roma Pupils Mentoring Programme of the Foundation for Educational Change, EIDHR, Microprojects Compendium 2000, pp. 4–5.

[82] Interviews with the President of Roma Mission, the Chairman of Romen, the Chairman of Bachtalo Drom, the Representative for Lithuania in the Parliament of the International Romani Union, a member of the Council of Roma Mission and member of the Honorary Court of the International Romani Union, the Chairman of the Gypsy Community Organisation in Lithuania, and the Director of the Kaunas Roma Information Bureau, Kaunas, 28 July 2002.

comparison with the EU Race Equality Directive has concluded that such measures are necessary.[83]

3.2.1 Education

The Programme places a priority on improving access to education for Roma, focusing on the problems of absenteeism, low school attendance, and high drop-out rates.[84] It attributes these problems principally to the "non-traditional way of life of Roma,[85] though poverty, insufficient knowledge of Lithuanian, early marriage for girls, and lack of motivation are also identified as factors. The Programme asserts that "children living in other social environments could achieve better results at school."[86]

A number of Programme measures aim to create a positive learning environment for Roma children at the Community Centre in Kirtimai Tabor. Other measures are intended to help overcome disadvantages in the area of education more generally. Most activities implemented in 2001 and the first half of 2002 have been connected with the Roma Community Centre, and have relied heavily on NGO involvement and external funding. Attendance rates at the Centre's pre-school and Lithuanian language classes have been rather low, and funding for necessary textbooks and other school materials was insufficient.

There have also been initiatives to improve school attendance and performance by establishing separate classes for Roma children at School No. 58 in Vilnius.[87] Roma leaders have expressed ambivalent attitudes towards this initiative; while the measure does appear to have improved attendance levels, some assert that establishing separate classes for Roma is not an appropriate means of doing so.[88]

---

[83] T. Baranovas, *Legal analysis of national and European anti-discrimination legislation. A comparison of the EU Racial Equality Directive & Protocol No. 12 with anti-discrimination legislation in Lithuania,* European Roma Rights Center/Interights/Migration Policy Group, Budapest/London/Brussels, September 2001, <http://www.migpolgroup.com/uploadstore/Lithuania%20electronic.pdf>, (accessed 26 September 2002).

[84] Integration Programme, Chapter IV "Education Problems," p. 5. See also *Minority Protection 2001*, pp. 321–322.

[85] Integration Programme, Chapter IV "Education Problems," p. 5.

[86] Integration Programme, Chapter IV "Education Problems," p. 5.

[87] For more on prior initiatives in the area of education, see *Minority Protection 2001*, pp. 322–323.

[88] Interview with the President of Gypsy Bonfire, Vilnius, 18 March 2002.

The Roma Community Centre

The Minorities Department shares formal responsibility for the establishment of the Roma Community Centre with Vilnius Municipality. In practice, the Centre, which was inaugurated in September 2001,[89] has been constructed and operates as part of a collaborative effort with an NGO.

Most of the planned budget of the Integration Programme for 2001 was related to construction of the Community Centre.[90] It is jointly managed by its four founders: the Minorities Department, Vilnius Municipality, the LICF and the Roma Community Organisation "Gypsy Bonfire," through a Board of nine persons (two from each founding organisation and the Director of the Centre). Five of the Board members are also members of the Minority Department's coordination working group for the Integration Programme.[91]

Roma have been appointed to several positions of responsibility at the Centre: the President of "Gypsy Bonfire" serves as Chairman of the Board and five of the 12 employees of the Centre are of Roma origin, including the Deputy Director (the Deputy President of Gypsy Bonfire). However, representatives of Gypsy Bonfire claim that they have not been sufficiently informed about the Centre's activities and plans,[92] and that the original intention to serve the entire Tabor community has not been achieved.[93]

A "Council of Observers" was established by the Board of the Roma Community Centre in March 2002 in an effort to strengthen Roma participation in Centre activities; it consists of seven Roma representatives

---

[89] The Centre is the property of the Government (Minorities Department), while the land on which it was built was leased by Vilnius Municipality to the LICF free of charge for construction of the Centre with the right to use it for 99 years. The legal status of the Centre is that of a public institution.

[90] Planned construction costs represented nearly 20 percent of the total budget for 2000–2004, and 75 percent of the budget for 2001. LTL 450,000 (€127,580) was allocated by the Government. One-third of overall construction expenses was covered through non-governmental sources, with support from a coalition of Dutch foundations. Information provided by the Director of the LICF, Vilnius, 19 July 2002.

[91] Two representatives of the Minorities Department, the Chairman of Gypsy Bonfire, a methodologist of the Education Division of Vilnius Municipality, and the Director of the LICF.

[92] Interview with the President of Gypsy Bonfire, Vilnius, 13 August 2002.

[93] Most residents of the Upper Tabor participate in the activities of Gypsy Bonfire and of the Roma Community Centre. The Chairman of the Board has also made efforts to involve unofficial Roma leaders and activists from the Lower Tabor in the Centre's activities; the Lower Tabor is also represented on the Board and Council of Observers (see below).

nominated by Gypsy Bonfire. The Council's task is to increase awareness of the Centre's work among the Tabor's Roma community.[94]

Future funding for the Roma Community Centre is uncertain and the Centre is expected to apply for additional project money from external sources to cover its staff salaries and activity costs. Vilnius Municipality earmarked LTL 161,600 (€45,815) to cover salaries in 2002.[95] However, according to the First Vice Mayor, this amount will be provided only if an equivalent amount is received from the State budget.

LTL 157,000 (€44,511) was allocated for education activities under the Programme in 2002;[96] LTL 233,000 (€66,058) had been foreseen. No funds had been allocated by Vilnius Municipality for activities in 2002 as of July 2002.

Pre-school education

An EU-funded educational project for Roma children[97] served as a precursor to the Roma Community Centre. As part of this project, 21 Roma children began attending a pre-school class in September 2000 at School No. 58, a school which is located outside the Tabor, and which uses Russian as the language of instruction.[98] According to the school's principal, those Roma children who

---

[94] The Council of Observers is also supposed to sit in on Board meetings. As of July 2002, it had not yet been able to attend, as the Board had last met in May 2002. The Board meets less frequently than it did in the past.

[95] Summary of the 2001–2004 Programme Objectives, Tasks and Budget, Strategic Action Plan of Vilnius Municipality for 2002–2004, 1 March 2002, <http://www.vilnius.lt/new/vadovybe.php?open=135>, (accessed 22 March 2002).

[96] Interview with the Director of the Roma Community Centre, Vilnius, 18 March 2002.

[97] "Roma Problems: Social Integration," leaflet from an international workshop, Vilnius, 10–11 January 2002, organised by the Project "Kirtimai Roma Community Centre," Un Enfant Par La Main and LICF; supporters: Minorities Department and Vilnius City Municipality; funding: EU (Phare).

[98] This initiative covered only a portion of Vilnius' school-age Roma population. A total of 94 Roma children were studying at School No. 58 during the 2001/2002 school year at various levels in integrated classes as well as in one separate class taught in Lithuanian. All receive free meals. Interview with the Principal of School No. 58, Vilnius, 19 March 2002. Roma children had previously attended this school in integrated classes only: three Roma children attended in 1986/1987; three between 1989 and 1995; nine in 1996/1997; 13 between 1997 and 1999; and 28 in 1999/2000. See Appendices No. 2 and 3 to the presentation of the Principal of School No. 58, "Artistic training is a factor of integration into the culture of the country," Vilnius, 22 January 2001 (unpublished). There are also Roma children attending other schools in Vilnius.

have received pre-school education are more motivated and achieve better results than those who have not.[99]

This project was continued in 2001/2002 at the newly-established Roma Community Centre; in line with the measures outlined in the Integration Programme, two pre-school classes were launched in September 2001; the two teachers of the pre-school classes also organise cultural activities and excursions.[100] Classes are taught primarily in Lithuanian, but a Roma teacher's assistant has also served as an interpreter. According to the Director, the aim is to integrate Roma children from the Tabor into Lithuanian-language elementary classes.[101] The teachers who work at the Centre also attend a Romani language course at Vilnius University.

According to the Director of the Centre, attendance has been a problem. Only 18 of the 26 children enrolled completed pre-school classes in the 2001/2002 school year.[102] Following testing organised by the Municipal Division of Education in Spring 2002, about 50 percent of these children were recommended for elementary school.[103] Thus, only about 35 percent of the children who started the classes will move on to first grade.

While some of the parents interviewed were satisfied with the classes and activities at the Centre, as well as at School No. 58, they emphasised that harsh living conditions, especially in the winter, makes education a secondary concern. Lack of transportation to School No. 58 (and other schools) also makes school attendance difficult.[104] Some parents said they were reluctant to allow their children to go to school unaccompanied, as drug-users are known to frequent the Tabor.[105] Finally, though the children in pre-school classes have been

---

[99] Interview with the Principal of School No. 58, Vilnius, 19 March 2002.

[100] In 2001, the Minorities Department allocated LTL 45,000 (€12,760) for four months of activity; Vilnius Municipality also contributed LTL 40,000 (€11,340). Phare funding helped cover staff costs through March 2002. Main Roma Community Centre 2002 Organisational Plan, Appendix to Minutes of Meeting No. 4, of the Board, 23 January 2002.

[101] Interview with the Director of the Roma Community Centre, Vilnius, 29 July 2002.

[102] Interview with the Director of the Roma Community Centre, Vilnius, 29 July 2002.

[103] Interview with the Director of the Roma Community Centre, Vilnius, 29 July 2002.

[104] Apparently, there is no administrative basis for making the State programme of school transportation for rural children available within Vilnius. During the 2000/2001 school year, the LICF covered transportation costs to the pre-school class at School No. 58.

[105] Interviews with residents of Kirtimai Tabor, Vilnius, 18 March 2002.

learning Lithuanian, most will attend the Russian-language School No. 58;[106] at present their numbers are not enough to form a Lithuanian-language class at the school.[107]

Some parents have requested the establishment of a first grade class at the Centre.[108] However, this option has not been pursued, as the Centre is not equipped to meet schooling requirements; moreover, the aim of the Programme is to integrate Roma children into classes at regular schools.[109]

Lithuanian language classes for adults

The Centre planned to offer Lithuanian language courses to four groups of approximately 45 students; in October 2001, two groups were formed for about 20 students of different ages. EU funding covered the costs of one group (through the LICF), and the Lithuanian Language Commission the other; the Language Commission has provided funding for 2002 as well.[110]

Attendance has also been a problem in regard to these classes. It is not known how many of the students who registered actually completed the classes. The aim of these courses was not clearly defined, which may have contributed to low interest. However, they may have been intended to enhance employment opportunities by improving Lithuanian language skills.[111] Also, the courses have not been linked directly with employment training or counselling, which may be another factor contributing to low motivation.

Other initiatives

In addition, a number of *ad hoc* educational initiatives are identified under the Programme, such as recreational camps, the purchase of textbooks and school

---

[106] Some parents actually prefer their children to attend School No. 58, as their siblings are already enrolled there. Interview with the Director of the Roma Community Centre, Vilnius, 29 July 2002.

[107] A minimum of 20 children is needed to establish a Lithuanian language class according to the 2001 bilingual education project for minority schools of the Ministry of Education and Science.

[108] Interview with the Director of the Roma Community Centre, Vilnius, 18 March 2002.

[109] Minutes of Meeting No. 5 of the Board of the Roma Community Centre, Vilnius, 20 March 2002. Interview with the President of Gypsy Bonfire, Vilnius, 3 August 2002.

[110] Interview with the Director of the Roma Community Centre, Vilnius, 18 March 2002.

[111] Interviews with: the President of Gypsy Bonfire, Vilnius, 25 March 2002; and the Director of the Roma Community Centre, Vilnius, 29 July 2002.

materials,[112] and teacher-training. The Programme also proposed the development of a concept of education for Roma. The Minorities Department also supported the organisation of a Sunday school class for Roma children in Kaunas,[113] as a Roma NGO project complementary to Programme goals.

The FEC implements many activities that are directly or indirectly linked to the Integration Programme, some independently, and some with Government funding. In some cases, governmental bodies appear to consider the FEC's activities as the equivalent of State action to implement the Programme.[114] For example, though the Ministry of Education is assigned responsibility for organising teacher-training courses under the Programme, it has not implemented any measures in this area; however, in 2002 it did provide full funding for a number of workshops for teachers organised by the FEC.[115]

The Programme proposes to develop a "concept of education for the Roma of Lithuania,"[116] though this is not identified as a specific measure to be implemented. As part of an initiative to develop a "Concept of Ethnic Policy of Lithuania," the Minorities Department has established a working group to prepare a "concept of education of ethnic minorities" by the end of 2002, on the basis of which a separate concept for Roma is to be developed; no Roma

---

[112] No Government funding was provided for this purpose in 2001, though the FEC allocated LTL 47,798 (€13,551), and estimates that this provided for about 70 percent of Roma pupils. However, Roma representatives claim that lack of textbooks and school supplies is a persistent problem among Roma communities. According to the Director of the Community Centre, there is a lack of adequate textbooks, methodologies and training materials for the Centre's pre-school classes. Interview with the Director of the Roma Community Centre, Vilnius, 29 July 2002.

[113] This is an initiative of the Roma NGO Nevo Drom. The Sunday school, which offers mathematics, Lithuanian language classes and art classes, is attended by about fifteen Roma teenagers and youth who have not attended any school previously or have dropped out. The Minorities Department provided LTL 2,400 (€680) in 2001 and the same amount in 2002, under Section V of the Implementation Measures "Preservation of Ethnic Identity."

[114] Interview with the Deputy Director and the Senior Specialist of the Minorities Department, Vilnius, 20 March 2002. Also, the Ministry of Education and Science is one of the founders (and funders) of the Foundation for Educational Change (the Open Society Fund–Lithuania/OSFL is the other founder).

[115] The FEC also realised a number of initiatives for teachers in 2001 as part of the "Support for Roma Pupils" programme, with funding from the EU and the OSFL. Information provided by the Director of the FEC, via e-mail, on 10 April 2002, and in an interview in Zubiškės (Jonava district), 28 July 2002.

[116] Integration Programme, Chapter IV "Education Problems," p. 5.

representatives have been directly involved in this working group thus far.[117] In preparing this programme, the experience of pre-school preparatory classes and other educational initiatives should be taken into account. Moreover, a broad range of Roma representatives, parents, and community leaders should be consulted and involved directly in the preparation of specific initiatives to improve the situation for Roma at all levels of education.

In implementation of the new Concept, Government partnership with expert civil society organisations should be encouraged; however, the State should assume primary responsibility for implementation of the Concept and for efforts to improve access to education for Roma more generally.

3.2.2 Employment

A chapter on "Social Problems" identifies lack of education, job qualifications and training as key causes of widespread unemployment among Roma, and points out that many experience difficulties in arranging the necessary documents to set up their own businesses.[118] The Programme states that, in these conditions, Roma are prone to "conditions for illegal work or involvement in criminal activities are formed."[119] However, only one measure has been proposed to address these problems – a vocational training programme; furthermore, while some funding is foreseen for its development, no provision has been made for implementation of the actual programme.[120]

There are no official data on unemployment among Roma,[121] or on the percentage who are not officially registered at the Labour Exchange, which does not keep ethnic

---

[117] The working group consists of two members from the Minorities Department, two experts, and one representative of the Russian minority. Other persons are also being consulted, such as the Coordinator of the Council of National Communities. The Concept will be placed on the website of the Minorities Department once it is ready. Interview with the Head of the Minorities Division, Minorities Department, Vilnius, 30 July 2002.

[118] Integration Programme, Chapter III "Social Problems," p. 4.

[119] Integration Programme, Chapter III "Social Problems," p. 4.

[120] Comments on the Programme for the Integration of Roma into Lithuanian Society 2000–2004 and Its Implementation Measures, Appendix No. 5 to the Letter dated 3 August 2000 from Roma Mission to the Seimas Committee on Human Rights.

[121] However, a Government-sponsored survey conducted in May 2000 indicated that members of ethnic minority groups are at higher risk of unemployment. Government Resolution of 8 May 2001 "On the Confirmation of the Programme for Increased Employment 2001–2004," Point 2.4.1: Formation of a labour market that is accessible to everyone, *Valstybės Žinios*, No. 40-1404, <http://www3.lrs.lt/cgi-bin/getfmt?C1=w&C2=132114>, (accessed 16 March 2002).

statistics. However, as most Roma from the Tabor are registered under one address, it is possible to determine from records at the Labour Exchange that many Roma are not registered.[122] According to the Programme "[e]ven those [...] who are registered at the labour exchange do not get unemployment benefits because usually they have no record of employment."[123] Unemployment benefits are only available for persons who have worked no less than 24 months during the preceding three years,[124] and social support is linked to so-called "public benefit jobs."[125]

While it acknowledges that "[e]ven those [Roma] who do have [a speciality] are unemployed because it is especially difficult for Roma to compete in the labour market due to negative public attitudes towards them,"[126] the Programme does not acknowledge the problem of discrimination in the labour market explicitly.

State officials also maintain that discrimination is not an issue. For example, the Head of the Seimas Committee on Human Rights stated in a recent interview that the problems faced by Roma in the sphere of unemployment are similar to the problems experienced by non-Roma, asserting that many Roma are "unable to work," and that they "need to want to work."[127] The General Director of the Minorities Department acknowledged that the State has done little to provide employment opportunities for Roma, but added that "Roma do not like to work."[128]

---

[122] A total of 122 persons from this address had registered as unemployed since the beginning of 2000 when the electronic database of Vilnius Labour Exchange was started. By the end of April 2002, only 25 were still registered. Only six of the 122 found employment, and only three of those had been trained under programmes offered by the Labour Exchange. Information provided by the Head of the Information System Management Division of Vilnius Labour Exchange, Vilnius, 11 April 2002.

[123] Integration Programme, Chapter III "Social Problems," p. 4.

[124] Government Resolution No. 836 (14 July 2000) "On the Partial Amendment of Resolution No. 441 of 17 April 2000 'On Regulations for the Granting and Payment of Social Welfare Benefits'," *Valstybės Žinios*, No. 58-1736, 19 July 2000, <http://www3.lrs.lt/cgi-bin/preps2?Condition1=105324&Condition2=>, (accessed 18 April 2002). Earlier, an unemployed person had the right to social protection after six months of being registered as unemployed.

[125] An unemployed person acquires the right to six months of support after completing a two-month contract for a public benefit job or for jobs supported by the Employment Fund. This support is cancelled if the person refuses to do these jobs, attends a training course, and/or accepts the work that is proposed. However, labour exchanges offer only a limited number of public benefit job opportunities; Vilnius Labour Exchange was able to propose public benefit jobs for about every ninth registered unemployed person in 2001.

[126] Integration Programme, Chapter III "Social Problems," p. 4.

[127] Interview with the Head of Seimas Committee on Human Rights, Vilnius, 29 July 2002.

[128] Interview with the General Director of the Minorities Department, Vilnius, 30 July 2002.

Occupational Training Programme

The Lithuanian Labour Market Training Authority (LLMTA)[129] was tasked under the Programme with developing a "Programme of Vocational Training and Employment for Vilnius Roma," together with the Ministry of Labour and the Ministry of Education. The budget foreseen for this measure is very small,[130] and no funds have been allocated. The same task is also mentioned in the Programme for Increased Employment 2001–2004, intended for the whole population.[131]

Accordingly, experts of the LLMTA prepared a draft Vocational Training Programme in Autumn 2001, with the following objectives:

- Informing the Vilnius Roma community about the labour market situation and employment opportunities;

- Preparing short-term training programmes for Roma in order to improve their employment opportunities.[132]

In preparing the Vocational Training Programme, LLMTA experts asked Roma representatives to select training interests from a list of professions;[133] they were not asked for their opinions as to what kind of measures would be needed to promote employment. The Vocational Training Programme was submitted on 18 April 2002 to the Ministry of Education and was under review by the Ministry of Labour as of August 2002. It is not clear whether and when it will be implemented. Furthermore, the general Employment Programme explicitly

---

[129] The LLMTA at the Ministry of Social Protection and Labour is a national agency responsible for developing vocational training and job counselling programmes and for coordinating their implementation. For more information about the LLMTA, see <http://www.ldrmt.lt>, (accessed 8 April 2002).

[130] LTL 10,000 (€2,835) for 2001, and the same amount for 2002, to cover, *inter alia*: professional orientation and consultations for Roma, licensed programme expertise, and "adaptation" costs of programmes. LLMTA, Draft Programme for Vocational Training and Employment of Vilnius Roma, 5 October 2001.

[131] Government Resolution of 8 May 2001 "On the Confirmation of the Programme for Increased Employment 2001–2004," Point 2.4.1: Formation of a labour market that is accessible to everyone (hereafter, "Employment Programme, Point 2.4.1"), *Valstybės Žinios*, No. 40-1404, <http://www3.lrs.lt/cgi-bin/getfmt?C1=w&C2=132114>, (accessed 16 March 2002).

[132] LLMTA, Draft Programme for Vocational Training and Employment of Vilnius Roma, p. 2.

[133] Information provided by the Specialist of the Curriculum Division of the LLMTA, Vilnius, 10 April 2002. The selected professions include: tree trimmer and grass mower; motorised loader operator; electric loader operator; cleaner; and nursing assistant, *inter alia*.

rejects the possibility of employing affirmative action measures or quotas[134] and does not clearly link training to employment opportunities.

The general Employment Programme contains other measures aimed at ethnic minorities. For example, the Department of Statistics was asked to prepare an analysis of the employment situation of minorities in 2002, and the Ministry of Labour was asked to develop proposals for improving their employment prospects. No further information on either of these initiatives was available for this report.

Roma representatives have been particularly critical of the Programme for its lack of a strategy to tackle unemployment – an area they consider a priority. Comprehensive measures should be developed in close consultation with Roma communities, clearly linking training to the possibility of employment. Roma should be encouraged to register with the Labour Exchange by providing them with information about how doing so can work to their benefit. Legal assistance and counselling should be made available to Roma entrepreneurs who wish to establish their own businesses.

3.2.3 Housing and other goods and services

Housing

In the chapter on "Social Problems," the Programme identifies housing as "one of the most sensitive problems," highlighting the fact that many Roma have not been able to obtain legal ownership of land or houses in the Tabor, due to lack of personal documents and permanent jobs. The Programme acknowledges that some of the dwellings in Kirtimai Tabor "could meet current requirements and could be legalised,"[135] but it proposes no measures for doing so.

The Second Vice Mayor of Vilnius has emphasised that a generalised housing shortage is affecting the population as a whole, making it difficult to adopt special measures to benefit Roma in particular.[136] Most Roma do not qualify for housing loans, as only families with a steady, legal source of income higher than the minimum wage are eligible. Moreover, according to Roma leaders, many Roma are not aware of application procedures for municipal housing.[137] In practice, then, most Roma living in the Tabor have few practical alternatives for seeking better housing elsewhere.

---

[134] Employment Programme, Point 2.4.1.
[135] Integration Programme, Chapter III "Social Problems," p. 4.
[136] Interview with the Second Vice Mayor of Vilnius, Vilnius, 31 July 2002.
[137] Interview with representatives of Bachtalo Drom and Roma Mission, Kaunas, 28 July 2002.

The Programme does propose to improve living conditions and basic infrastructure in Kirtimai Tabor by ensuring regular garbage removal and providing a water pump as well as a pay telephone booth.[138]

Improving conditions in Kirtimai Tabor

The extremely difficult living conditions at the Tabor[139] have not improved significantly as a result of Programme implementation, although residents admit that some progress has been achieved.[140] In line with Programme measures, Naujininkai district officials arranged for five garbage containers to be installed, and a new water pump was installed (and another repaired) in 2001; Kirtimai now has five working pumps to serve its approximately 500 inhabitants.[141] Costs were covered by the water utility company, the State Energy and City Economy Department and the LICF. The plan to install a public telephone booth was not realised because it was considered too expensive.

According to the Minorities Department, discussions with Vilnius Municipality have been initiated regarding steps to resolve the ownership of Tabor land; by the end of 2002, planning will be completed, on the basis of which plots will be legalised and renovations will take place.[142] The First Vice Mayor of Vilnius stated that legal issues represented a significant barrier to improving conditions in the Tabor, and claimed that the resolution of these issues would require decisions at higher political levels.[143]

---

[138] Section II "Social Issues," Implementation Measures.

[139] Very few houses in the Tabor have proper heating, running water, or indoor plumbing; the water drainage and sewage system is poor to non-existent; streets are not paved, and are littered with used syringes and other refuse.

[140] Interviews with residents of Kirtimai Tabor, Vilnius, 18 March 2002.

[141] According to the preliminary data of the 2001 Census, there were 428 persons living in 72 houses at Kirtimai Tabor. Interview with the Head of the Naujininkai District Office, Vilnius, 19 March 2002. The official number of Roma in Lithuania registered during the 2001 Census of Population and Households was 2,571 persons, <http://www.std.lt/Surasymas/Rezultatai/PDF/Tautybes_e.pdf>, (accessed 26 September 2002).

[142] Interview with the General Director of the Minorities Department, Vilnius, 30 July 2002. The General Director emphasised that lack of funding and low priority of the issue may impede implementation, and expressed the hope that EU structural funds could be allocated for this purpose.

[143] The residents of the Tabor would have little chances of winning a public tender for privatisation of land lots due to the fact that these are in great demand in Vilnius, and are therefore expensive. Interview with the First Vice Mayor of Vilnius, Vilnius, 25 March 2002.

Roma representatives have criticised the lack of measures to resolve the issue of illegal housing and of land ownership, and assert that measures proposed to improve conditions in the Tabor are insufficient.[144] Clearly, political will to improve the situation significantly by removing legal barriers to land ownership and access to affordable municipal housing is necessary – but has been lacking to date.

Other goods and services

The Integration Programme does not deal with the issue of equal access to public goods and services. The delivery of public utilities services to the inhabitants of Kirtimai Tabor is sporadic and uncertain, and depends largely on ongoing mediation by Roma representatives[145] as well as by the Minorities Department. Individual electric meters have been installed in homes and higher amounts are currently being charged to all families to pay off the accumulated debts of the Tabor.[146]

3.2.4 Healthcare and other forms of social protection

Healthcare

The Programme highlights health problems such as tuberculosis and other respiratory and gastrointestinal diseases, as well as a lower life expectancy,[147] which it attributes to "difficult material and household conditions"[148] and insufficient education about hygiene.[149] Residents of the Tabor assert that they experience difficulties accessing certain healthcare services, such as dental care,[150] but there is little official data to provide more detailed information. In fact, the Programme acknowledges that lack of

---

[144] Comments on the Programme for the Integration of Roma into Lithuanian Society 2000–2004 and Its Implementation Measures, Appendix No. 5 to the Letter dated 3 August 2000 from Roma Mission to the Seimas Committee on Human Rights.

[145] See e.g. Letter No. 631-92 dated 15 March 2002 from Rytų Skirstomieji Tinklai Company (the utility distribution network) to J. Tyčina, President of Gypsy Bonfire; see also Letter dated 19 February 2002 from Vilniaus Vandenys (the municipal water utility company) to J. Tyčina, President of Gypsy Bonfire, regarding a contractual arrangement.

[146] As of 10 April 2002, the Tabor's electricity debts totalled LTL 153,088 (€43,402).

[147] Integration Programme, Chapter V "Problems of Healthcare," pp. 5–6.

[148] Integration Programme, Chapter V "Problems of Healthcare," p. 5.

[149] According to the text of the Programme, "a number of Roma do not have the simplest habits of sanitary hygiene." Integration Programme, Chapter V "Problems of Healthcare," p. 6.

[150] Interview with residents of Kirtimai Tabor, 18 March 2002.

data impedes effective implementation of disease-prevention programmes[151] and that Roma face obstacles to access to healthcare services.[152]

Three health-related measures are proposed under the Programme: organising primary and secondary healthcare for Roma without social health insurance; providing training on health and hygiene issues for Roma; and implementing a drug-abuse prevention and treatment programme at the Tabor.[153]

Healthcare for Roma without insurance

This task has not been implemented. According to the Minorities Department, most Tabor inhabitants already receive social welfare benefits or are registered with the Labour Exchange and have social health insurance.[154] However, Exchange statistics suggest that this may not be the case (see Section 3.2.2).

Naujininkai Primary Healthcare Centre (hereafter, "PHC"), which serves the territory of Kirtimai Tabor, did not receive any additional funding under the Integration Programme to provide healthcare services to Roma. Nonetheless, a general practitioner (GP) and a pediatrician were recruited to serve the Tabor community and to carry out an immunisation programme.[155] The Director of the Roma Community Centre proposed that a dispensary should be established at the Centre, but the idea did not win support from the Municipality.[156]

Education on hygiene issues

No Government funds were allocated for this measure. However, as part of its EU-funded project, the LICF provided support for the designated GP and pediatrician from the Naujininkai PHC to engage in supplementary activities, including home visits. In the opinion of some Roma leaders, poor sanitation is due to the lack of basic services and poor living conditions rather than poor hygiene; some also consider this measure demeaning.[157]

---

[151] Integration Programme, Chapter V "Problems of Healthcare," p. 6.

[152] If unemployed persons are not registered at the labour exchange, they are excluded from social welfare support and therefore social security health insurance. Healthcare for children under 18 is free. See also *Minority Protection 2001*, p. 323.

[153] Section III "Health Protection," Implementation Measures.

[154] Interview with the Deputy Director and the Senior Specialist of the Minorities Department, Vilnius, 20 March 2002.

[155] Interview with the Deputy Director of Naujininkai PHC, Vilnius, 19 March 2002.

[156] Interview with the Director of the Roma Community Centre, Vilnius, 18 March 2002.

[157] Interview with the President of Roma Mission and a member of the Council of Roma Mission, Kaunas, 20 March 2002.

Drug prevention and treatment programmes

In June 2001, Vilnius Municipality started a "Blue Bus" programme for AIDS prevention among intravenous drug users; this initiative was continued in 2002. The programme was not implemented as part of the Integration Programme but as an independent initiative of Vilnius Municipality.[158] However, as the bus serves different parts of Vilnius, including the Tabor, it does reach a small number of Roma.[159]

A number of other projects have also targeted drug-users in the Tabor. Prior to the adoption of the Integration Programme, in Autumn 1995, the Vilnius Centre for Dependency-Related Illnesses launched a programme in response to concerns about the danger of HIV infection from intravenous drug use of inhabitants of Kirtimai Tabor who were not using its services. According to the Director of the Centre, Roma who came to use its services were abused and insulted by other drug-users.[160] A GP from the Naujininkai PHC was also recruited for an AIDS prevention programme in which 37 persons of Roma origin participated from 1996 to 1998.[161]

Other initiatives

Preparations are underway for the construction of a "hygiene centre" next to the Roma Community Centre, which is to offer laundry and shower facilities for a

---

[158] Interview with the Head of the Health Division of Vilnius Municipality, Vilnius, 30 July 2002.

[159] A total of 899 people of Vilnius had used this service by the end of its first month in 2001 but only four to six percent of daily visitors were estimated to be Roma by the medical staff. "*Pirmasis 'Mėlynojo autobusiuko' programos mėnuo pranoko jos vykdytojų lūkesčius*" (The first month of the 'Blue Bus' Programme surpassed expectations of executives), website of the Lithuanian Association of Dependency Psychiatry, <http://www.lppa.lt/vnc/autobusiukas2.html>, (accessed 3 April 2002). About 30 Roma from the Tabor, aged 16 to 22, had used the programme's services in 2002 (as of April). Information provided by the Head of the Social Assistance and Prevention Division of the Centre for Dependency-Related Illnesses, Vilnius, 9 April 2002.

[160] The Centre operates under Vilnius County Administration with funding from Vilnius Municipality. Interview with the Director of the Centre for Dependency-Related Illnesses, Vilnius, 9 April 2002.

[161] The GP estimated that this number represented about 70 percent of the Tabor's Roma who were using intravenous drugs. Interview with the Director of the Centre for Dependency-Related Illnesses, Vilnius, 9 April 2002; see also E. Subata and Y. Tsukanov, "The Work of General Practitioners Among Lithuanian Roma in Vilnius: Incorporating Harm Reduction into Primary Medical Practice," *Journal of Drug Issues* 29(4), Fall 1999, pp. 805–806.

small fee. Funding for the centre is to be fully provided by the Minorities Department.[162]

Social protection

As noted above, many Roma are not eligible for unemployment benefits (see Section 3.2.2). In addition, the Integration Programme acknowledges that social welfare allowances (LTL 80 to 90 per month, €23 to 25) are extremely low.[163] Most Tabor residents receive social welfare payments.

Receipt of certain social benefits is contingent upon proof of familial relationship; this causes difficulties for residents of the Tabor, who lack necessary documents such as certificates, etc. Residents have lost social benefits as a result of their inability to prove marriage, parenthood, or registration at the Labour Exchange,[164] *inter alia*. Many residents claim to have lost benefits in the early months of 2002; some believe that this may be a result of surveys conducted by various authorities in the Tabor in Autumn 2001 (see below).[165]

Three Programme measures indirectly address access to social protection: the employment of social workers; a sociological survey; and a measure to put personal documents in order.

Social work

At the request of the Minorities Department, the Deputy Director of the Roma Community Centre works as a social worker for the Tabor on a part-time basis, presumably in fulfilment of the Programme measure "to establish a service of special teachers and social workers and to ensure their activities."[166] The Deputy Director received no special training in social work as preparation for this task; his work consists principally of acting as an intermediary for residents at the

---

[162] Interviews with: the Director of the Roma Community Centre, Vilnius, 18 March 2002; the General Director of the Minorities Department, Vilnius, 30 July 2002.

[163] Integration Programme, Chapter III "Social Problems," p. 4.

[164] Letter No. 10-08-510 from the Director of the Social Support Department of the Ministry of Social Protection and Labour on behalf of the social support divisions, 23 January 2002.

[165] In Autumn 2001, information was collected from Tabor residents by officials from the Naujininkai District of Vilnius, the local police, and the Passport Office, as well as by interviewers conducting a sociological survey. Information collected by the police was also submitted to the Social Welfare Office. Interviews with: residents of Kirtimai Tabor, Vilnius, 18 March 2002; and the Chief Commissioner of the Naujininkai Police Division, Vilnius, 19 March 2002.

[166] Section I "Education," Implementation Measures.

municipal Social Welfare Office, the Passport Division and other institutions. There are no other social workers working in the Tabor.[167]

Sociological study

In line with the Programme,[168] the Minorities Department commissioned a sociological study from the Institute of Labour and Social Research on the situation of Roma living in the Tabors. 151 heads of families were interviewed for the survey in September 2001; they were asked questions on a broad range of issues, including family size and structure, birthplace, nationality, employment, sources and structure of income, school attendance, viewpoints on education, knowledge of Lithuanian, media used, participation in community work, frequency of use of medical services, and perceived level of integration in Lithuanian society.[169] The results of the study and recommendations were published[170] and presented at an international workshop.[171]

Although it is clear that lack of information about Roma communities presents an obstacle to the development of more effective public policies in a wide range of areas, Roma leaders have expressed concern about the aims of the study,[172] and about the way in which it was carried out. According to residents, interviewers were accompanied by a police officer or an employee of Naujininkai District; in some cases, in order to ensure the accuracy of the information,

---

[167] The LICF (Phare Lien) project funded the employment of a student of the Pedagogical University as a social worker for the Tabor from March 2001 until March 2002, although information on the results of his work was not available for this study. Interview with the Director of the LICF, Vilnius, 28 March 2002.

[168] Section II "Social Issues," Implementation Measures.

[169] Results showed that a household consisted of five to six persons on average; that housing of 62 percent of families consisted of one room, and housing of 30 percent of families – of two rooms. 76 percent said that conditions of life were bad in the Tabor. Institute of Labour and Social Research, "Sociological Study of Roma living in Vilnius City Tabors: Report of the Second Stage of Research," Vilnius, 2001 (on file with EUMAP).

[170] "Vilniaus romai" (Roma of Vilnius), Žmogaus Teisių Žinios (Human Rights News), No. 6, 2002, p. 7.

[171] "Roma Problems: Social Integration," Vilnius, 11 January 2002.

[172] Interviews with the President of Roma Mission, the Chairman of Romen, the Chairman of Bachtalo Drom, the Representative for Lithuania in the Parliament of the International Romani Union, a member of the Council of Roma Mission and member of the Honorary Court of the International Romani Union, the Chairman of the Gypsy Community Organisation in Lithuania, and the Director of the Kaunas Roma Information Bureau, Kaunas, 28 July 2002.

residents were visited by these interviewing "teams" again.[173] Some residents reportedly felt that their right to privacy had not been respected and that they were not sufficiently informed as to the purposes for which the information collected is intended to be utilised.

The study made a number of recommendations, including: continued support for the Roma Community Centre's activities to promote employment, with the involvement of experts on Roma culture as well as Roma themselves; the proposal of public benefit jobs by the Vilnius Labour Exchange; and additional research by students of social work on attitudes towards existing programmes among Tabor residents as well as on the Labour Exchange's capacity to offer them appropriate employment opportunities.[174]

Regularisation of personal documents

The Programme proposes to facilitate the process of obtaining personal documents for those Roma who are legal residents only,[175] referring particularly to those who arrived from the Kaliningrad region, and still have old Soviet passports.[176] No information on implementation was available for this report.[177]

The Chapter on "Migration Problems" asserts that these Roma "do not care about acquiring citizenship of the Republic of Lithuania or permits for permanent residence in Lithuania. For this reason, some Roma cannot make use of the social guarantees provided by the State of Lithuania."[178] At the same time, some Roma claim that they have not been able to obtain their documents due to language barriers or illiteracy.[179]

According to data from the Passport Division, as of 10 May 2002, of the 554 persons living on the territory of the Tabor, 242 were citizens of Lithuania; 82 were non-Lithuanian citizens with permanent residence, of whom 57 had no citizenship (stateless persons);[180] 14 were persons without documents and who

---

[173] Interview with residents of Kirtimai Tabor, Vilnius, 18 March 2002.

[174] Roma of Vilnius, *Žmogaus Teisių Žinios*, No. 6, 2002, p. 7.

[175] The Migration Department is listed as responsible for this measure for which LTL 500 (€142) is foreseen annually over 2001–2004. See Implementation Measures.

[176] Integration Programme, Chapter VI "Migration Problems," p. 6.

[177] Interview with the Deputy Director of the Passport Division of the Migration Department, Ministry of Interior, Vilnius, 26 March 2002.

[178] Integration Programme, Chapter VI "Migration Problems," p. 6.

[179] Interview with the Chairman of the Gypsy Community Organisation, Kaunas, 17 March 2002.

[180] These stateless persons have permission to live in Lithuania and have travel documents; they have a right to apply for social support, but cannot participate in elections.

had not yet applied.[181] The remaining 216 persons were reportedly not of full legal age and were therefore not required to have their own passport.

The number of Roma without personal documents is believed to be higher. According to Gypsy Bonfire, in 1996 about 250 persons from the Tabor did not have documents, and Roma without documents from other parts of the country have moved into the Tabor since then.[182] Some have difficulties documenting long-term residence – a requirement for obtaining a residence permit or a passport.[183]

3.2.5 The criminal justice system

A recent study concluded that, "[a]ccess to justice remains a problem, especially for vulnerable groups [...]. The Roma remain the most vulnerable ethnic community in Lithuania."[184] The Seimas Ombudsman has pointed to the existence of general problems such as violations of laws and ethics, bureaucracy, violence towards prisoners, overcrowded cells and lack of medical services.[185] The Chief Commissioner of the Naujininkai Police Division denies that Roma experience particular problems in the criminal justice system.[186]

While the Integration Programme does not explicitly discuss the issue of equal access to the criminal justice system, it does propose to raise awareness of possibilities for legal recourse among Roma and to offer legal assistance.[187] In line with this proposal, the

---

[181] Interview with the Chief Commissioner of the Third Police Commissariat of Vilnius, Vilnius, 30 July 2002.

[182] Interview with the President of Gypsy Bonfire, Vilnius, 25 March 2002.

[183] "Roma Denied Documents and Rights in Lithuania," *Roma Rights*, No. 1, 2002, pp. 126–127.

[184] T. Baranovas, *Legal analysis of national and European anti-discrimination legislation*, p. 7.

[185] See *2000 Annual Report of the Seimas Ombudsmen's Office*, Vilnius, 2001, at <http://www3.lrs.lt/owa-bin/owarepl/inter/owa/U0038428.doc>, (accessed 20 August 2002), and *the 2001 Annual Report of the Seimas Ombudsmen's Office*, Vilnius, 2002, at <http://www3.lrs.lt/owa-bin/owarepl/inter/owa/U0070562.doc>, (accessed 20 August 2002).

[186] Interview with the Chief Commissioner of the Naujininkai Police Division, Vilnius, 19 March 2002.

[187] Section IV "Migration Problems," measure #17, Implementation Measures. The Law on Guaranteed Legal Assistance, which entered into force in 2001, ensures equal access to legal information, consultations, defence, and representation during court proceedings. See also T. Baranovas, *Legal analysis of national and European anti-discrimination legislation*, p. 20.

Minorities Department organised two workshops on legal issues.[188] The first, in Autumn 2001, focused on passport issues which were discussed together with the Chief Commissioner of the Third Police Commissariat of Vilnius who is responsible for Kirtimai Tabor. At a second, Roma representatives met with police to discuss the problem of police searches in the Tabor (see below).

3.3 Protection from Racially Motivated Violence

Racially motivated violence is not identified as a problem in the Integration Programme. No statistics on racially motivated violence against Roma are available. According to the Chief Commissioner of the Third Police Commissariat of Vilnius, there has been no case of racially motivated violence during the past two years.[189]

No claims have been brought under the Lithuanian Criminal Code.[190] Individuals can also apply to the Seimas Committee on Human Rights but there are no known cases of any Roma having filed such a complaint.

Complaints of police abuse have also been reported, mainly in connection with the police raids which are carried out at the Tabor.[191] The police frequently search houses without warrants, claiming that warrants cannot be obtained to search unregistered houses;[192] moreover, as most residents are registered under a single address, if police officers obtain a warrant for that address, they can effectively search any house in the Tabor. Police authorities view raids as a preventive measure, as they believe that "90 percent of the Tabor inhabitants sell drugs."[193] Some efforts have begun to encourage discussion of this problem to bring about improvements in relations between the police and the Roma community, but no concrete measures have been proposed or taken to regularise procedures for policing the Tabor. Legal registration of home ownership would be an important first step.

---

[188] LTL 4,000 to 5,000 (€1,134 to 1,418) is foreseen per year. Implementation Measures. The Minorities Department allocated LTL 2,000 (€567) for the two workshops.

[189] Interview with the Chief Commissioner of the Third Police Commissariat of Vilnius, Vilnius, 30 July 2002.

[190] Under the Criminal Code, Article 72(1), racially motivated actions that have "serious consequences" are punishable by up to ten years' imprisonment.

[191] Interviews with residents of Kirtimai Tabor and the President of Gypsy Bonfire, Vilnius, 18 March 2002; see also *Minority Protection 2001*, pp. 327–328.

[192] Interviews with residents of Kirtimai Tabor, Vilnius, 18 March 2002.

[193] Interview with the Chief Commissioner of the Third Police Commissariat of Vilnius, Vilnius, 30 July 2002.

3.4 Promotion of Minority Rights

The Programme aims "to promote mutual tolerance and confidence [and] to acquaint society with Roma culture and history" as a way of promoting a more positive image of Roma among the public.[194]

Six Programme measures support these aims,[195] mostly through support for the cultural and educational activities of Roma organisations. Two other proposed measures – the preparation of a publication and a film on Roma history and culture – target the majority population.[196] A textbook for studying Romanes is under preparation.

Roma representatives are critical of the fact that they have been assigned only a limited role in implementation of this part of the Programme. At the same time, they feel that the Programme's approach, by which Roma are primarily the recipients of support for cultural activities rather than active agents in efforts to improve their situation, only reinforces existing stereotypes.

Roma leaders are agreed on the need to protect Roma identity and culture, and support measures to expand opportunities to learn Romanes at school and to provide more information about Romani culture and history to the majority society.[197] However, they claim that Roma cultural associations lack the means to undertake such projects on their own.[198]

---

[194] Integration Programme, Chapter I "Introduction," p. 2.

[195] Section V "Preservation of Ethnic Identity," Implementation Measures. A total of LTL 23,000 (€6,521) (2.5 percent of the overall budget for 2001) was planned for these measures in 2001.

[196] Measure #22: to issue a publication on Roma history and culture, and measure # 23: to create a film about Roma history and culture. LTL 50,000 (€14,176) is foreseen for each.

[197] Interview with the President of Roma Mission and Representative on the Council of National Communities, Kaunas, 28 July 2002.

[198] Interviews with the President of Roma Mission, the Chairman of Romen, the Chairman of Bachtalo Drom, the Representative for Lithuania in the Parliament of the International Romani Union, a member of the Council of Roma Mission and member of the Honorary Court of the International Romani Union, the Chairman of the Gypsy Community Organisation in Lithuania, and the Director of the Kaunas Roma Information Bureau, Kaunas, 28 July 2002.

A new Minority Law is due to be adopted by the end of 2002.[199] Some measures for the protection of minority rights are also expected as part of a new National Action Plan for the Protection and Support of Human Rights, which is being prepared by the Seimas Committee on Human Rights with the support of the United Nations Development Programme (UNDP).[200] Roma organisations claim that though they are aware this plan is under development, they have not been consulted further.

3.4.1 Education

The Integration Programme does not propose to organise education in Romanes,[201] nor does it seek to assess the demand for such classes among Roma parents and the Roma community as a whole. However, it does propose to prepare a textbook for studying Romanes.

Roma leaders attach great importance to the use of Romanes in pre-school education establishments and, where possible, also at schools.[202] Some Vilnius Roma organisations have expressed concern that children attending pre-school classes at the Roma Community Centre might lose their command of Romanes, as they receive

---

[199] Interview with the Chairman of the Seimas Committee on Human Rights, Vilnius, 29 July 2002. The current Minority Law dates back to 1989 and was last revised in 1991; the Constitution (Art. 37, Art. 45) also provides basic minority rights guarantees. See *Minority Protection 2001*, pp. 320, 328–329; see also *Report Submitted by Lithuania Pursuant to Article 25, Paragraph 5, of the Framework Convention for the Protection of National Minorities*, received on 31 October 2001, <http://www.humanrights.coe.int/Minorities/Eng/FrameworkConvention/StateReports/2001/lithuania/Lithuania.htm>, (accessed 6 April 2002).

[200] The first two stages, which included data gathering and analysis of the situation, were completed in May 2002. The Plan is currently being prepared for approval by the Seimas (deadline not indicated). See the text of the background document (in English) at <http://www3.lrs.lt/pls/inter/w3_viewer.ViewDoc?p_int_tekst_id=10162&p_int_tv_id=844>, (accessed 21 July 2002).

[201] There is no network of State-funded schools in the Romani language. See *Minority Protection 2001*, pp. 330–331.

[202] Interview with the President of Gypsy Bonfire and the Chairwoman of Nevo Drom, Vilnius, 29 July 2002.

instruction principally in Lithuanian;[203] at present, opportunities for these children to be taught Romanes are limited to a once-weekly class.[204]

There is reportedly little or no information about Roma culture and history in the textbooks used in mainstream schools,[205] and no specific measures are proposed to remedy this deficiency.[206] However, the Ministry of Education has adopted new regulations regarding the preparation of textbooks, and reportedly more information on the Roma minority may be included in new textbooks. Roma representatives should be consulting during the preparation process.

The Programme's proposed measure to prepare a publication on the Roma culture and history in 2002 has been postponed; according to the Minorities Department, this was due to a lack of qualified staff.[207] It is not clear whether the proposed publication is intended for use in schools.

Romanes textbook

A textbook for studying Romanes is under preparation, in consultation with a Romani language expert, and is scheduled for publication in 2002. The Ministry of Education, which is responsible for this measure under the Programme, formed a

---

[203] However, the teacher's assistant employed at the Centre speaks Romanes, and reportedly provides translation assistance to the children as necessary.

[204] In the 2001/2002 school year, a lecturer of Romani from Panevėžys (the Chairwoman of Nevo Drom) came to Vilnius once a week to teach the pre-school groups at the Roma Community Centre with support from Phare LIEN funds. Since March 2002, as the Phare LIEN project has ended, her salary is fully covered by the OSFL. It is expected that these classes will be continued in the 2002/2003 school year. The Chairwoman of Nevo Drom also teaches a Romani language course at Vilnius University.

[205] A study was conducted to investigate how minorities are presented in textbooks. The findings were presented in March 2001 at a workshop organised by the FEC. See T. Tamošiūnas, *"Ar europietiški mūsų vadovėliai: multikultūrinis požiūris?"* (Are Our Textbooks European: A Multicultural Approach?), cited in the 2001 Annual Report of the FEC, p. 17.

[206] It is not clear whether a proposed publication on the Roma culture and history (measure #22) is intended for use in schools and, furthermore, the Ministry of Education and Science is not listed as responsible for this task.

[207] Interview with the Deputy Director and the Senior Specialist of the Minorities Department, Vilnius, 20 March 2002. In 2001, the FEC published a book on Roma: *Lietuvos Čigonai: Tarp Praeities ir Dabarties* (*Lithuanian Gypsies: Between Past and Present*), V. Toleikis (ed.), Garnelis, Vilnius, 2001. However, this initiative was not funded by either the Ministry of Education and Science or the Minorities Department.

working group to facilitate preparations, with participation from the LICF as well as a Romani language expert. However, no funds had been allocated as of July 2002.[208]

According to a specialist of the Ministry, the book could be used at schools with high concentrations of Roma students.[209] However, many Roma students either attend integrated classes or do not attend school at all. There are few teachers qualified to present classes in Romanes.[210] Once the textbook has been finalised, the working group should be tasked with developing a comprehensive strategy to promote its use, including training for teachers and possibilities for organising study groups at mainstream schools; these efforts should be supported by the Ministry of Education.

Other initiatives of the Ministry of Education

On 16 January 2002, the Ministry of Education approved new regulations for minority education.[211] A working group on Polish minority education has prepared a draft plan of measures, and working groups for other minorities are also planned. It is unclear whether a separate such group will be formed on minority education for Roma; according to one expert, this will probably be covered through the Integration Programme.[212] As Roma leaders have expressed interest in mother tongue education, a working group should be established for Roma as for other minorities.

There is also an Expert Commission on the Mother Tongue of Ethnic Minorities consisting of nine members, which was established at the Ministry of Education on 29 February 2000. At present, there are no Roma sitting on this Commission.

---

[208] Interview with the Chairwoman of Nevo Drom, Vilnius, 29 July 2002.

[209] Interview with the Specialist of the Division of Basic and Secondary Education of the Ministry of Education and Science (also a member of the work group of the Minorities Department for the Integration Programme), Vilnius, 10 April 2002.

[210] Interview with the Specialist of the Division of Basic and Secondary Education of the Ministry of Education and Science, Vilnius, 10 April 2002.

[211] Resolution of the Ministry of Education and Science of 16 January 2002 "On Regulations on the Education of Ethnic Minorities," *Valstybes Žinios*, No. 9-337, 2002, <http://www3.lrs.lt/cgi-bin/getfmt?C1=w&C2=159045>, (accessed 12 August 2002).

[212] Interview with the Director of the Department of General Education, Ministry of Education and Science, Vilnius, 12 August 2002.

3.4.2 Language

The Integration Programme does not propose specific measures to promote the public use of Romanes.[213] Although Romanes is widely spoken among Lithuanian Roma, it is believed that there are no public officials of Roma origin, and the use of Romanes in official communications has not been raised as an issue. Translators are not available in the court system, but opinions are mixed among Roma leaders as to the degree to which this constitutes a problem, and there has been no research on the issue.

The new Minority Law is expected to address issues related to the use of minority languages in the private and public spheres.[214]

3.4.3 Participation in public life

The Integration Programme proposes to "take effective measures to form equal opportunities for Roma and other inhabitants of the country to participate in the life of the society,"[215] and for Roma women in particular. Roma representatives have called for a greater role in developing and implementing governmental policy towards Roma, including in implementation of the Integration Programme.

There is no Roma representative in the Seimas;[216] no Roma are known to be employed in Government bodies, public administration bodies, the criminal justice system, or the police. The Government has attempted to provide a mechanism for structured input from minority groups through the Council of National Communities,[217] which includes one seat for a Roma representative.[218]

---

[213] Lithuanian is the sole State language (Constitution, Art. 14; see also the Law on the State Language, adopted on 31 January 1995); however, according to the Minority Law, minority languages may be used in addition to Lithuanian in "offices and organisations located in areas serving substantial numbers of a minority with a different language." Minority Law, Art. 4 (as amended on 29 January 1990).

[214] As of August 2002, Lithuania had not signed the European Charter for Regional or Minority Languages.

[215] Integration Programme, Chapter I "Introduction," p. 2.

[216] Members of all ethnic groups have equal rights to propose candidates and participate in elections but lack of citizenship or difficulties with documents prevent participation in political life. See *Minority Protection 2001*, pp. 332–333.

[217] An advisory body to the Minorities Department established in 1995 in which 18 ethnic groups are now represented; the Roma community is represented since 1997.

[218] Minorities of under 10,000 members can elect one representative to the Council.

There have been some difficulties in the process of identifying a single person to represent the entire Roma community. The selection of the first Council representative in 1997 was apparently based at least partly on residence in Vilnius.[219] After Roma leaders called for improved exchange of information between the Council and the Roma community, a new representative, the President of Roma Mission, was selected in 2000. Council work is carried out on a volunteer basis; transport and other representational expenses are not compensated (for any minority group). The current representative claims that his advisory capacity has not resulted in sufficient consultation on a partnership basis with the Government.[220] Mechanisms should be explored to provide opportunities for input for a broader range of representatives of the Roma community, from different geographical regions.

As communications with public administration officials can be difficult, individual Roma often look to their community leaders for assistance in resolving a host of issues that are properly the responsibility of the State. At the same time, Roma leaders claim that many governmental and non-governmental bodies ask them to provide information, mediation, or project preparatory work – often on a volunteer basis. Given the demands placed upon them, Roma community leaders should be supported with as much training and support as possible; to the extent possible, Roma should be recruited for paid positions in public administration.

Participation of Roma women

The Integration Programme draws attention to low levels of public participation by Roma women,[221] and recommends the Minorities Department to develop activities to promote greater involvement. No information was available for this report on implementation of this measure. The first Roma women's NGO, the Roma Women and Youth Community Organisation, was formed in late 2001 and registered in 2002; however, it has received no governmental support to date.[222]

---

[219] When two Roma representatives (one from the city of Panevėžys, the other from Kaunas) went to the selection meeting, they were strongly advised to select a representative from Vilnius, as meetings would be organised there. Interview with the President of Roma Mission, Kaunas, 12 April 2002.

[220] Interview with the President of Roma Mission, Kaunas, 12 April 2002.

[221] Integration Programme, Chapter VII "Other Problems," p. 6.

[222] Interview with the Chairwoman of the Roma Women and Youth Community Organisation, Vilnius, 29 July 2002.

3.4.4 Media

The Integration Programme identifies stereotyping in the media as a matter of concern,[223] but presents no concrete measures to promote tolerance or a more positive image of Roma in the media. According to Roma leaders, this is a significant shortcoming, as media articles tend to reinforce negative attitudes towards Roma.[224] Articles often present Roma as crime suspects; when a Rom is arrested, his or her ethnicity is stressed.[225]

There are also instances in which reporters present the opinions of Roma,[226] but there has been no systematic attempt to encourage them to do so on a more consistent basis, or to provide mainstream newspapers with Romani perspectives on current issues on a more regular basis. There are no television or radio programmes especially devoted to the Roma minority, and no broadcasts or newspapers in Romanes.[227] Roma organisations have expressed interest in establishing a periodical but have emphasised their lack of training and experience in this area.

Roma press agencies established in the Czech Republic, Hungary and Slovakia could provide a useful example of how more positive reporting – and thus a more positive image of Roma communities – could be promoted. These agencies have provided

---

[223] "A preconceived hostile attitude towards Roma has still not been overcome in Lithuania. Frequently, persons of their ethnicity are regarded as potential criminals. The media has not been successful in dissociating itself from certain stereotypes." Integration Programme, Chapter VII "Other Problems," p. 6.

[224] See e.g. K. Griškevičius, "*Policijos operacija čigonų tabore sukėlė sumaištį*" (Police Operations Caused Chaos at the Gypsy Tabor), *Valstiečių Laikraštis* (*News of the Rural Population*), 13 March 2002, p. 13; "Gypsies look for asylum in Finland," *Respublika*, 16 August 2001, p. 2; E. Utyra, "*Vilniaus čigonų taboras išvažiuoja į Rusiją*" (The Tabor of Vilnius Gypsies emigrates to Russia), *Lietuvos Žinios*, 13 May 2002.

[225] See e.g. V. Trainys, "*Pakaunėje čigonai nepamiršta savo tradicinio amato*" (Gypsies do not forget their traditional craft), *Laikinoji Sostinė* (*Provisional Capital*), 9 February 2001, p. 4; A. Dumalakas, "*Sostinėje siautėja nesugaunamas čigonas*" (A Gypsy that can't be caught goes on a rampage in the capital), *Sostinė* (Supplement of *Lietuvos Rytas*), 10 March 2001, p. 8; A. Kuzmickas, "*Garsiame narkotikų prekybos 'taške' šeimininkavo čigonės*" (Gypsy women ran the well-known 'point' of drug sales), *Lietuvos Žinios*, 9 November 2001, p. 6; N. Mitkevičienė, "*Čigono gaujos galas*" (End of a Gypsy Gang), *Valstiečių Laikraštis* (*News of the Rural Population*), 3 January 2002, p. 13.

[226] E.g. S. Pocius, "*Skurdo nualinti čigonai palieka miestą*" (Gypsies, worn out by poverty, leave the city), *Laikinoji Sostinė*, 10 March 2001, pp. 1–2.

[227] The Minority Law guarantees all minorities the right "to have newspapers and other publications and information in one's native language" (Art. 2). As part of a new programme on State Television on Sunday mornings which presents a different minority each time for about ten minutes, the initiatives of the LICF for the Roma were presented.

training to Roma journalists, who prepare regular news reporting for publication in mainstream newspapers on Roma issues. In the absence of such initiatives, the public receives little direct information regarding Roma communities or the activities of Roma organisations to counter prevailing stereotypes.[228]

3.4.5 Culture

The Programme allocates a small amount of funding for the organisation of cultural projects by Roma organisations.[229] Cultural activities are also organised at the Roma Community Centre. EU funding has supported classes on dance, visual arts and music.

Before the adoption of the Integration Programme, Roma NGOs could apply for support to the Minorities Department under the "Programme of Social and Cultural Integration of Ethnic Minorities;"[230] the Integration Programme itself is partially funded through this Programme.[231] The Minorities Department has also provided some funding to allow Roma organisations to participate in international events.[232] Finally, Roma NGOs can also apply for funding to the Ministry of Culture as part of its programme of support to NGOs.

Though these programmes are important for preservation of ethnic identity *within* the Roma community, little information is available about the extent to which they promote awareness of minority identity and culture *beyond* this community, within society as a whole.

---

[228] According to a 2000 survey, 47.4 percent of respondents had not heard about the activities of Roma organisations. The main sources of information about Roma mentioned were: television and radio broadcasting (29.2 percent), daily newspapers (20.8 percent), and friends and acquaintances (15.3 percent); only 7.6 percent stated that they had received most of their information about Roma from Roma themselves. See I. Čepulkauskaitė-Žilionienė, "*Kam patinka čigonai?*" (Who likes Gypsies?), *Penki kontinentai Online*, 4 January 2001, pp. 2–3, <http://www.online.5ci.lt/Article.asp?Lang=L&ArtcleID=2032>, (accessed 1 January 2002).

[229] A total of LTL 20,000 (€5,670) was allocated to support cultural and educational projects and Roma amateur arts in 2001, out of an overall budget of LTL 23,000 (€6,521) for activities for Section V of the Implementation Measures, "Preservation of Ethnic Identity."

[230] Under this Programme, the Minorities Department provides support to 18 minorities, including the Roma. The Programme consists largely of supporting the activities proposed by minority NGOs; no separate Programme text or description/evaluation of activities supported is available. No information is available on the amount of funding allocated to Roma NGOs. Telephone interview with an official from the Minorities Department, 24 July 2002.

[231] Interview with the General Director of the Minorities Department, Vilnius, 30 July 2002.

[232] See e.g. Letter No. 3-01-532 dated 15 October 2001 from S. Vidtmann, Deputy Director of the Minorities Department, to the President of Roma Mission.

4. EVALUATION

The Integration Programme represents a clear sign of the Government's positive intention to address some of the difficult issues faced by the Roma minority. There are a number of important ways in which its content and implementation can be improved upon.

Lack of data and research on Roma communities presented a significant difficulty to those who drafted the Integration Programme. The drafters did not engage in consultations with Roma representatives, though this might have helped compensate for this deficiency. Engaging in such consultations during the preparation of stage two of the Programme will allow for expansion to other areas of Lithuania as well as necessary modifications to content and approach. In order to demonstrate its commitment to the Programme, the Government should begin these consultations as soon as possible.

Additional research among Roma communities to better articulate the problems and issues they confront could enhance these efforts; at the same time, the mistrust engendered by a sociological survey conducted without adequately informing the Roma community of its aims and goals clearly demonstrates that such research should only be conducted in close partnership with Roma community leaders.

Review of the content of the Programme in consultation with Roma representatives is likely to result in the elaboration of concrete measures to address issues in several areas that it does not currently address sufficiently, such as employment, housing and social protection. Integration of Romani perspectives would also entail greater acknowledgement of the reality of discrimination against Roma, and the development of measures to raise awareness among public officials of their duty not to discriminate in the provision of public goods and service, as well as among Roma communities of their right to file complaints. Additional measures in this area are also required to bring Lithuanian legislation into compliance with the EU Race Equality Directive.

At present, Programme measures to protect and promote minority identity have been limited to support for Roma NGOs. Additional measures are needed to enhance opportunities to study Romanes, promote broader and more effective participation in public life for Roma, and encourage a more positive presentation of Roma communities in the mainstream media.

Programme implementation has been hampered by poor coordination and limitations on the Minorities Department's ability to influence other key actors. Responsibilities are not clearly distributed among the national, county and municipal levels. Levels of funding from the State budget have proven insufficient to meet Programme goals; moreover, in many cases, the sources of funding and financial obligations of implementing authorities are not clearly spelled out in the Programme.

Implementation has depended to a great extent on EU and non-governmental funding; indeed many Programme initiatives are being carried out principally by NGOs. This causes confusion as to which initiatives constitute measures of the Programme, and blurring of responsibility between State and non-State actors. The Government should clearly and unequivocally assume overall responsibility for Programme implementation.

There has been no systematic effort to evaluate or assess progress on Programme implementation to date, and no provision has been made to ensure regular reporting from implementing bodies. The coordinating working group established by the Minorities Department should be tasked with regular review and evaluation of the individual projects implemented under the Programme, with a view towards ensuring that experiences and lessons-learned are utilised to modify existing projects as necessary as well as to develop proposals for new projects. The working group should solicit broad and active participation from a broad range of Roma community representatives and activists.

Most importantly, the Roma community feels that the Programme conforms to stereotype by placing them in the role of passive recipients of Government assistance, and have called for a more active role in implementation. Some efforts have been made to encourage active Roma involvement in the management of the Roma Community Centre. These efforts should be expanded and complemented by practical training in project development and management, to enable Roma leaders to articulate clear proposals on behalf of their communities, and to take the lead in project implementation.

5. RECOMMENDATIONS

To the Government

- Open consultations with a broad range of Roma representatives and activists to review the Integration Programme and begin preparations for stage two, with a focus on filling existing gaps in content and approach.

- Define the managerial and financial responsibilities of State institutions in Programme implementation and evaluation, drawing a clear distinction between the roles and responsibilities of the Government and those of NGOs.

- Enhance the capacity of the Minorities Department to coordinate Programme implementation by providing it with high-level political support and sufficient staffing, training, and financial resources; provide appropriate training and resources to local bodies tasked with responsibilities under the Programme.

- Provide for the establishment of a mechanism to monitor Programme implementation; to review its content and approach on a regular basis in light of project experience; to issue public implementation reports; and to make recommendations for improvements.

- Ensure enhanced opportunities for Roma to participate fully in all aspects of Programme implementation and assessment; provide training in project development, budgeting and management to community leaders and activists to enable them to take a leadership role.

- Take measures to ensure full compliance with the EU Race Equality Directive; conduct training courses for public administration officials and court personnel on their obligation to ensure provision of public goods and services without discrimination on racial or ethnic grounds.

- Conduct monitoring in various areas and propose effective remedies if discrimination is ascertained; provide training to raise awareness of opportunities for legal recourse within the Roma community.

- Consider the adoption of positive measures to enhance capacity among Roma leaders to take on paid employment within the public administration of municipalities and State services in areas in which large numbers of Roma reside.

- Integrate human and minority rights and multiculturalism into the university curricula for public administration, social work, healthcare workers, teachers, and judges, *inter alia*.

- Develop comprehensive measures to address large-scale unemployment among Roma, combining language training with employment counselling and training in job skills; training courses should reflect both the interests and needs of local communities and actual job opportunities.

- Consider establishing a minority press centre to provide training to minority representatives, including Roma, and to ensure the preparation of news and broadcast material that more effectively integrate the perspectives and views of minorities.

- Provide for the early resolution of housing and land ownership; facilitate access to citizenship, legal residency, and other personal documents for Roma who do not possess them, as a means of facilitating access to public housing, unemployment benefits, and other social services.

ANNEX A – IMPLEMENTATION MEASURES – 2001

Programme for the Integration of Roma into Lithuanian Society 2000–2004

Areas	Executing Bodies	Planned expenses (000) LTL	Amount allocated by the Minorities Department (000) LTL	Funding recipient and title of project/expenses, if funding was allocated by the Department of National Minorities and Lithuanians Living Abroad
I. Education				
1. To establish a Roma Community Centre:	Department of National Minorities and Lithuanians Living Abroad with Vilnius Municipality		0.1	The Roma Community Centre was established 1 August 2001 (Bylaws drafted, officially registered, and name patented).
1.1. To support construction of the Community Centre building		450	450	The Roma Community Centre was built (with two-thirds funding from the Government).
1.2. To provide basic facilities and other goods		100	100	Main office furnishings were acquired (desks, tables, chairs, bookcases, boards, etc.).
1.3. To ensure maintenance of the building		26	15	Sum allocated for Centre maintenance, 1 August 2001 to 31 December 2001.
2. To support the activities of the Roma Community Centre:	Department of National Minorities and Lithuanians Living Abroad with Vilnius Municipality			
2.1. To establish pre-school learning groups and ensure their activities		35		Two pre-school learning (development) groups established for which two teachers teach 26 pupils (2001/2002 school year).
2.2. To organise additional learning activities for children		35		Visual arts, music, and dance circles are organised; the position is for one, but three persons job share.
2.3. To establish a service of special teachers and social workers and to ensure its activities		30		Half of the workspace was designated for social work in 2001; one employee is of Roma ethnicity.
3. To organise education of Roma (children and adults).	Department of National Minorities and Lithuanians Living Abroad with Vilnius Municipality	18		Computer courses were organised jointly with the LICF.
4. To organise free meals for Roma children attending pre-school groups.	Ministry of Social Protection and Labour with Vilnius Municipality	31		*(Note: The Ministry of Labour and Social Protection allocated funds for this purpose through Vilnius Municipality. Source: Interview with the Director of the Roma Community Centre, Vilnius, 18 March 2002.)*
5. To organise State language courses for adult Roma.	Department of National Minorities and Lithuanians Living Abroad, State Lithuanian Language Commission under the Seimas	12		Courses were organised from 1 September 2001 to 31 December 2001 with funds provided by the State Commission of the Lithuanian Language. *(Note: another class was also organised by the LICF with Phare LIEN funding. See Section 3.2.1.)*

Measure	Responsible	Col3	Col4	Notes
6. To organise summer recreation for Roma children.	Head of Vilnius County Administration	25		*(Note: Summer camps were organised by the FEC with international funding. The LICF also organised one camp with partial support from Vilnius County Administration, as part of its programme of support to NGOs. See Section 3.2.1.)*
7. To provide textbooks and other training materials for Roma children, both at the Centre and those attending general education schools.	Ministry of Education and Science, and the Department of National Minorities and Lithuanians Living Abroad	30		The Minorities Department purchased exercise books. However, this measure is essentially realised by the Ministry of Education and Science through the FEC.
8. To prepare individual training programmes for Roma children.	Ministry of Education and Science	5		No information available.
9. To organise professional advancement courses and seminars for teachers who work with Roma children	Ministry of Education and Science	10		*(Note: The FEC organised workshops for teachers with international funding. See Section 3.2.1.)*
II. Social Issues				
10. To develop a vocational training and employment programme for Roma of Vilnius.	Ministry of Social Protection and Labour, Lithuanian Labour Market Training Authority, Ministry of Education and Science	5		*(Note: the Programme was developed by the LLMTA as planned, even though no funding was allocated. See Section 3.2.2.)*
11. To perform a sociological study of Roma living in the Vilnius Tabors.	Department of National Minorities and Lithuanians Living Abroad	5	15	Study completed.
12. To improve living conditions for Roma living in Tabors (ensure regular garbage removal; provide a water supply pump and a pay telephone booth).	Department of National Minorities and Lithuanians Living Abroad with Vilnius Municipality	20		A measure of Vilnius Municipality.
III. Health Protection				
13. To organise primary and secondary healthcare for Roma without social health insurance.	Department of National Minorities and Lithuanians Living Abroad with Vilnius Municipality	20		A measure of Vilnius Municipality.
14. To organise education for Roma on sanitary and hygiene issues	Head of Vilnius County Administration	1		*(Note: This measure was realised by the LICF.)*
15. To carry out drug-abuse prevention and treatment programmes at the Tabors.	Head of Vilnius County Administration with Vilnius Municipality	25		
IV. Migration				
16. To put in order personal documents for Roma legally residing in Lithuania.	Migration Department at the Ministry of Interior	0.5		

17. To organise legal education for Roma and provide counselling on legal issues.	Department of National Minorities and Lithuanians Living Abroad	4	2	Two workshops were organised.
V. Preservation of Ethnic Identity				
18. To support Roma public organisation projects for cultural and educational activities.	Department of National Minorities and Lithuanians Living Abroad with Vilnius Municipality	15	*14*	Nine cultural and educational projects accomplished.
19. To support Roma amateur arts.	Department of National Minorities and Lithuanians Living Abroad with Vilnius Municipality	5	*5*	One international Roma festival organised by Gypsy Bonfire.
20. To initiate public activities by Roma women.	Department of National Minorities and Lithuanians Living Abroad	3		Public organisation for Roma women established.
21. To prepare a Romani language textbook	Department of National Minorities and Lithuanians Living Abroad with Vilnius Municipality		n.a. (measure to be implemented starting in 2002)	
22. To issue a publication on Roma history and culture	Department of National Minorities and Lithuanians Living Abroad with Vilnius Municipality		n.a. (measure to be implemented starting in 2002)	
23. To create a film about Roma history and culture	Department of National Minorities and Lithuanians Living Abroad with Vilnius Municipality		n.a. (measure to be implemented starting in 2004)	
TOTAL		910.5 (€ 258,137)	*601.1* (*€ 170,418*)	

Source: Unless otherwise indicated, the Department of National Minorities and Lithuanians Living Abroad, information provided via e-mail, on 17 April 2002, compiled for the EU Accession Monitoring Program. The table provides information on actual expenses for different components of the Integration Programme, as well as the title headings of projects/expense categories when funding was provided directly by the Minorities Department (noted in bold italic font). A column is also inserted indicating the budget as foreseen in the Annex to the Integration Programme on Implementation Measures. No funding was allocated for implementation of the Programme in 2000 and the Minorities Department had not provided any information about financing and projects for 2002 as of 6 August 2002.

Minority Protection in Poland

PILOT GOVERNMENT PROGRAMME FOR THE ROMA COMMUNITY
IN THE MAŁOPOLSKA PROVINCE FOR THE YEARS 2001–2003.

Table of Contents

1. Executive Summary 422

2. The Government Programme –
   Background 426
   2.1 Background to Present Programme 426
   2.2 The Programme – Process 426
   2.3 The Programme – Content 428
   2.4 The Programme – Administration/
       Implementation/Evaluation 431
   2.5 The Programme and the Public 438
   2.6 The Programme and the EU 440

3. The Government Programme –
   Implementation 441
   3.1 Stated Objectives of the Programme 441
   3.2 Government Programme
       and Discrimination 442
       3.2.1 Education 445
       3.2.2 Employment 453
       3.2.3 Housing and other goods
             and services 454
       3.2.4 Healthcare and other forms
             of social protection 456
       3.2.5 The criminal justice system 458

    3.3 Protection from Racially
        Motivated Violence 458
    3.4 Promotion of Minority Rights 460
        3.4.1 Education 462
        3.4.2 Language 463
        3.4.3 Participation in public life 464
        3.4.4 Media 466
        3.4.5 Culture 467

4. Evaluation 469

5. Recommendations 472

1. Executive Summary

In March 2001, Poland launched the Pilot Government Programme for the Roma Community in the Małopolska Province for the Years 2001–2003 (hereafter, the "Programme").[1] The Programme focuses on the southern region of the country where the conditions of Roma have been described as "particularly difficult,"[2] but is intended to be expanded to other areas.

This is the first comprehensive policy of the Government for Roma, and it represents a welcome advance. The most serious impediment to implementation to date has been the Government's failure to adequately fund the Programme; thus, the majority of the measures proposed have not yet been implemented and only a portion of the projects relating to education were funded. Without sufficient funding, the policy improvements that the Programme could represent will remain mere aspirations.

Even if fully implemented, however, the Programme would still require significant improvement. While its substantive provisions generally reflect the concerns of the Roma community, the problem areas it identifies are narrowly defined or not addressed at all, such as discrimination, even though Roma representatives have identified this as a problem, especially at the local level; no concrete measures are proposed to promote minority rights. Underlying the concerns of Roma is the assumption, evident in the Programme, that Roma are particularly responsible for their own plight, and that broader patterns of social discrimination on the part of the majority are perhaps less relevant to any reform effort.

Background

The initiative to launch the Programme stems from the Government's awareness of the "particularly difficult situation" of the Roma community in Małopolska Province but also from its acknowledgement that local authorities cannot deal with the scale of the problems experienced by Roma on their own. A very positive aspect has been the significant effort of the Government to consult with local Roma leaders to determine the Programme's priorities. Thus, its substantive provisions generally reflect the concerns of those who were consulted.

---

[1] Ministry of Internal Affairs, *Pilotażowy program rządowy na rzecz społeczności romskiej w województwie małopolskim na lata 2001–2003* (Pilot Government Programme for the Roma Community in the Małopolska Province for the Years 2001–2003), Warsaw, February 2001, <www.mswia.gov.pl/index1_s.html>, (accessed 26 July 2002) (citations in this report are from the official English translation), (hereafter, the "Programme"). The Programme covers the region inhabited by Roma of the Bergitka group and by the "Polish Roma."

[2] Programme, p. 3.

Administration

The Programme is formally coordinated by the Minister of Internal Affairs, while day-to-day administration and implementation is overseen by the Division of National Minorities within the Ministry, in close cooperation with the Task Force for National Minorities.[3] An important role is also played by the Małopolska Province Plenipotentiary for National Minorities in facilitating cooperation at the local level.

The main actors are commune councils and municipalities in Małopolska Province.[4] A few NGOs, including one Roma organisation, are also involved. Each year, local government units can submit project proposals to implement tasks for which they are listed as responsible in the Programme; they are required to contribute about 20 percent of the budget.

It is difficult to assess the mechanisms for Programme administration and evaluation due to the limited scale of implementation thus far, while the centralised mechanism for monitoring implementation is not sufficiently linked to compliance mechanisms. This might prove problematic, especially with respect to local governments whose cooperation is essential to successful implementation. However, the Division of National Minorities can exert some leverage on local bodies implementing tasks as information on project realisation and expenditures over the previous year must also be provided when they apply to realise new projects in 2003.

Stronger mechanisms for ensuring systematic participation by Roma are also necessary, especially at the local level.

EU Support

The Roma minority is not a priority for EU funding and the EU has not provided direct funding to activities of the Programme. It has, however, supported a project in Małopolska Province whose aim is to train Roma assistants for local schools, through the 1999 ACCESS Programme.

The European Commission took note of the Programme in its 2001 Regular Report, qualifying it as "a first step by the government to combat the precarious situation of

---

[3] The Task Force for National Minorities consists of representatives of the relevant ministries and other Government bodies; neither minorities nor local government representatives are represented.

[4] The Province (*województwo*) is a regional administrative unit controlled by the central Government. The next level is the District (*powiat*). This is followed by the Commune or County (*gmina*) which is a unit of local government, and the Municipality (*miasto*).

the Roma minority in Polish society [...]," but considered that it was too early to evaluate its implementation.[5]

Content and Implementation

The Programme proposes over 200 tasks to be carried out between 1 March 2001 and 31 December 2003 in seven issue areas: education; combating unemployment; health; living conditions; security; culture; and "knowledge in and about the Roma community."[6] Despite this impressive scope of activity, some important issues – such as discrimination and minority rights – are either not included or given an unnecessarily narrow scope.

A principal shortcoming is that the Programme does not identify discriminatory practices, and does not establish any mechanisms to monitor discrimination and intolerance, even though Roma leaders have identified discrimination as a problem. This gap is in apparent contradiction with the primary goal of the Programme "to achieve full participation of Roma [...] and to mitigate the disparities between this group and the rest of the society."[7] In fact, it attributes a large share of responsibility for their difficult situation to the Roma themselves. More generally, Poland also lacks comprehensive anti-discrimination legislation as well as a specialised body to promote equal treatment and to address racial or ethnic discrimination.

The education component aims to improve school attendance and completion rates of primary school but no measures are proposed to support access to secondary and university-level education. The section on "Combating Unemployment" proposes skills upgrading and some retraining but no comprehensive vocational training or support for establishing small businesses. The issue of equal access to public services is not discussed at all. Similarly, while the significant health problems faced by Roma are mentioned, access to health care is not addressed; nor is the question of whether Roma are treated equally by the criminal justice system.

While the Programme proposes to prevent crimes committed on ethnic grounds and to recruit Roma into the police, it does little to improve protection from such crimes or to raise awareness of existing channels for making complaints. At the same time, it asserts that Roma are reluctant to cooperate with the police and refers to the types of crimes Roma commit – despite the fact that no official data on the ethnicity of perpetrators is supposed to be kept – which tends to suggest an attitude that disregards the continuing salience of, and indeed to some degree partakes in, discriminatory attitudes towards Roma in the majority population.

---

[5] European Commission, *2001 Regular Report on Poland's Progress Towards Accession,* Brussels, 13 November 2001, p. 24 (hereafter, *"2001 Regular Report"*).

[6] Programme: Timetable for Realisation and Financing, Warsaw, February 2001.

[7] Programme, p. 7.

The Programme proposes measures to promote Roma culture and devotes a separate section to raising the awareness within the majority population about Roma issues. However, no concrete measures are proposed to promote other minority rights such as effective participation in public life, access of Roma to public media, or promotion of the use of the Romani language in the public sphere. Government officials have stated that the Programme is not necessarily intended to protect Roma rights, as these are already protected by the Constitution. This seems an unnecessarily narrow reading of the Programme's proper mandate, and one that, again, suggests an insufficient commitment to truly thorough-going reform.

The major practical obstacle to implementation in 2001 was the withholding of funds by the Government from the special purpose reserve that was to cover the most substantial share of the planned budget. The Ministry of Education was able to provide some funding for some tasks in the area of education;[8] no other component was implemented, with the exception of those funded exclusively from local sources. It is expected that, in 2002, tasks will also be implemented in other areas.[9]

The reaction of beneficiaries and the press to initiatives in the area of education has been generally positive. While recognising progress in this area, Roma leaders also emphasise the need to also fight unemployment and improve living conditions.

Conclusion

The Programme is without doubt a positive development; however, some important issues are not covered. Lack of funding remains the most significant practical impediment. By limiting implementation to the field of education, the Programme loses its most visible asset – its comprehensive approach. It is essential that measures be implemented also in other areas if significant results are to be obtained.

At the same time, those tasks which have been carried out have registered success. Initiatives in the area of education, such as Roma teacher's assistants and remedial classes, have had a positive impact on school attendance and performance. This also suggests that the Programme's attribution of a large share of the blame for low school attendance to Roma parents may require reassessment.

---

[8] The Ministry of Education provided PLN 500,000 (€131,579); this represented only nine percent of the overall planned Government funds for 2001 (not including local sources) and 28 percent of the planned Government funds for the education component in 2001.

[9] For 2002, the total amount of funding foreseen is about PLN three million (€789,474), including PLN two million (€526,316) from the special purpose reserve and PLN 600,000 (€157,895) from the Ministry of Education. Information provided by the Head of the Division of National Minorities, Ministry of Internal Affairs, Warsaw, 8 August 2002.

Opposition or delays at the local level present a potentially serious obstacle. Roma organisations and beneficiaries should also be involved more systematically in implementation, monitoring and evaluation. More efforts are also needed to inform local communities about the Programme's goals, ongoing activities and funding.

Preparations seem to have begun for a national programme covering the whole Roma population of Poland. It is essential that this new programme be more comprehensive, and that it address discrimination and positive minority rights. Systematic and structural solutions should be developed to respond to the problems identified, including measures for positive action in order to remedy the under-representation of Roma in various walks of life and to ensure their effective participation in society and its governance. The Programme and its nation-wide successor represent an opportunity for Polish society, not only to adopt comprehensive policies of reform, but to engage in a needed debate on the relationship of the majority and minority populations it contains.

2. The Government Programme – Background

2.1 Background to Present Programme

The Pilot Government Programme for the Roma Community in the Małopolska Province for the Years 2001–2003 (hereafter, the "Programme") is the first comprehensive governmental policy aiming to improve the situation of a national or ethnic minority in Poland. The recently created Division of National Minorities is responsible for coordinating this complex programme.[10]

2.2 The Programme – Process

The idea for the Programme originated with a project of the European Institute for Democracy in 1999–2000 that included establishing a few local Roma plenipotentiaries.[11]

---

[10] Interview with an official of the Division of National Minorities, Warsaw, 22 March 2002.

[11] This was later mentioned as a task of the Programme. See Section 3.4.3; see also EU Accession Monitoring Program, *Monitoring the EU Accession Process: Minority Protection*, Open Society Institute, Budapest, September 2001, pp. 377–378 (hereafter, "*Minority Protection 2001*").

The Programme[12] was adopted by a Resolution of the Council of Ministers in February 2001.[13] The need to take action in response to the difficult situation of the Roma in Małopolska Province and the inability of local governments to cope with the situation had been highlighted during a session of the Inter-Sector Task Force for National Minorities[14] in March 2000.[15] The Programme was developed between June and September 2000 by the Ministry of Internal Affairs and Administration (hereafter, the "Ministry of Internal Affairs"), in consultation with the relevant units of local government, Roma organisations and NGOs, following a study visit by the Division of National Minorities to Małopolska Province.[16] It was also reviewed by relevant ministries to check compliance with domestic and international legislation.[17]

The Programme declares that "the involvement of the Roma community in the development and implementation of the Programme is a key precondition of its success."[18] Indeed, special efforts were made to consult Roma organisations as well as

---

[12] Ministry of Internal Affairs, *Pilotażowy program rządowy na rzecz społeczności romskiej w województwie małopolskim na lata 2001–2003* (Pilot Government Programme for the Roma Community in the Małopolska Province for the Years 2001–2003), Warsaw, February 2001, <www.mswia.gov.pl/index1_s.html>, (accessed 26 July 2002) (citations in this report are from the official English translation) (hereafter, the "Programme"). The Programme covers the region inhabited by Roma of the Bergitka group and by the "Polish Roma."

[13] Resolution of the Council of Ministers of 13 February 2001 concerning the adoption of the multi-annual "Pilot Government Programme for the Roma Community in the Małopolska Province for the Years 2001–2003."

[14] Since May 2002 known as the "Task Force for National Minorities." The Task Force consists of representatives of relevant ministries and other State bodies at the national level; there are no formal representatives of Roma organisations or local governments. See *Minority Protection 2001*, pp. 374–375 (where this body is referred to as the "Interdepartmental Group for National Minorities").

[15] Programme, p. 6.

[16] Programme, p. 6. These consultations were held as a follow-up to the project of the European Institute for Democracy.

[17] Interview with the Head of the Division of National Minorities, Warsaw, 22 March 2002.

[18] Programme, p. 6.

other NGOs during the drafting process:[19] the Division of National Minorities defined Programme priorities by asking Roma leaders what was needed;[20] discussions were also held with Roma organisations prior to the start of Programme implementation.[21]

The priorities of the Programme generally reflect the concerns of those Roma organisations that were consulted, although certain suggestions were not incorporated.[22]

No consultations were held with the EU during the development of the Programme;[23] it was not discussed in any public fora during its elaboration.

2.3 The Programme – Content

The Programme is intended for areas inhabited by Roma of the Bergitka Group and by the "Polish Roma" (or "Polska Roma" which are part of a larger group known as the

---

[19] Interview with the Head of the Division of National Minorities, Warsaw, 22 March 2002. One Roma leader confirmed that "Government representatives, in particular the Head of the Division of National Minorities personally, together with the representatives of the Ministry of Culture and the Ministry of Education, consulted Roma organisations, especially the Association of the Roma in Nowy Sącz Region and the Social and Cultural Association of the Roma in Poland." Interview with the leader of the Association of the Roma in Nowy Sącz Region, Laskowa Górna, 27 March 2002. Another Roma leader stated that the components of the Programme corresponded exactly to the issues that had for a long time been highlighted by the Roma community. Interview with the leader of the Social and Cultural Association of the Roma in Poland, Tarnów, 3 April 2002. The leader of a third organisation confirmed being consulted, even though his association was not involved in implementation of the Programme as it is based in Cracow. Interview with the leader of the Association of the Roma in Cracow, Cracow/Nowa Huta, 5 April 2002.

[20] Interview with the Head of the Division of National Minorities, Warsaw, 22 March 2002.

[21] However, not all Roma organisations in Małopolska Province were involved. According to the leader of another Cracow-based organisation, "I became acquainted with the Programme thanks to kindness of the Małopolska Province Plenipotentiary for National Minorities in 2001 [...] Before that, not only had I not been consulted, but our Association had not been informed that such a programme was already in force." Written comments of the leader of the Association of Roma Women, Cracow, 26 July 2002.

[22] See, e.g., written comments of the leader of the Association of Roma Women, Cracow, 26 July 2002.

[23] According to one official, it would not have been appropriate to consult the EU as this is an internal matter. Comments by the Head of the Division of National Minorities, Warsaw, 8 August 2002.

"Carpathian Roma"), the largest of four traditional Roma groups residing in Poland,[24] in the south of the country. The areas the Programme covers are: Limanowa, Nowy Sącz, Nowy Targ and Tatry districts, inhabited by the Bergitka Roma, and Tarnów, inhabited by the Polish Roma.

The Programme is designed as a pilot initiative, to be implemented in Małopolska Province from 1 March 2001 until 31 December 2003; it is to be extended to other parts of the country based upon the results and experience gained from its implementation. The Government explains its decision to focus initially on Małopolska Province by the fact that the Roma community there is in a "particularly difficult situation."[25]

The Programme begins with a general description of the situation of the Roma communities in Małopolska Province, followed by the justification for the initiative, its objectives, and a set of general measures in the following issue areas:

- Education
- Combating Unemployment
- Health
- Living Conditions
- Security
- Culture
- Knowledge in and about the Roma Community

Attached to the Programme is a "Timetable for Realisation and Financing"[26] which lists concrete activities in each of these areas, followed by the institutions responsible

---

[24] The other two Roma groups in Poland are the Vlach and the Sinti. The size of the Roma population living in Małopolska Province is estimated at 3,000 to 3,500 – between seven and 10 percent of the overall estimated Roma population of Poland. There are no official statistics on the size of the Roma or of other ethnic or national minorities living in Poland; thus, available data refer to estimates by experts. The census held in Poland in May and June 2002 included, for the first time since before World War II, a question on *narodowość* ("nationality" or ethnic origin) and language spoken "most frequently at home." Census results are expected in Autumn 2002.

[25] Programme, p. 3.

[26] Ministry of Internal Affairs, *Pilotażowy program rządowy na rzecz społeczności romskiej w województwie małopolskim na lata 2001–2003: Harmonogram wykonania i finansowania zadań* (Pilot Government Programme for the Roma Community in the Małopolska Province for the Years 2001–2003: Timetable for Realisation and Financing), Warsaw, February 2001, <www.mswia.gov.pl>, (accessed 26 July 2002). This document was prepared by the Division of National Minorities together with the Task Force.

for realisation (usually the relevant unit of local government), sources of financing, and the budget for 2001–2003.

While the key problems faced by Roma are acknowledged, responsibility for their difficult situation is placed to a significant extent on the Roma community itself. Thus, the Programme asserts that

> [t]he key problems of the Roma community are related to the low level of education of its members [...]. Roma do not attach due importance to schooling, considering education to be of little benefit [...]. The financial situation of Roma families is exceptionally difficult due to the high rate of unemployment, the fact that families have many children, and alcoholism [which is] a common problem. Simultaneously, the community is characterised by a demanding attitude and feeble efforts undertaken to change the life situation of its own members.[27]

At the same time, the Programme acknowledges that local governments have been unable to cope with the difficult situation of Roma in Małopolska Province on their own, and notes a need for the central Government to intervene.[28]

Despite the Programme's impressive scope of activity, many topics are narrowly defined and some important issues are left unaddressed. A principal shortcoming is that, despite the Programme's objective to achieve the full participation of Roma and to mitigate disparities between Roma and the majority society,[29] the problem of discrimination is not addressed. Rather, it is assumed that it is sufficient to introduce measures to create equal opportunities in those areas in which Roma face particular difficulties.[30] As explained by a Government official, "the Programme concerns a weaker minority group which needs to be provided with such conditions that will lead to equal opportunities."[31]

Minority rights are likewise not addressed in any comprehensive fashion. The Programme confirms the status of Roma as a national and ethnic minority entitled to full protection and assistance from the State.[32] It proposes measures in the area of

---

[27] Programme, p. 3.

[28] "The difficult situation of the Roma community in the Małopolska Province and the inability of local governments to cope with it were the factors underlying the decision about the involvement of government administration in solving the problems which have emerged [...]." Programme, p. 6.

[29] Programme, p. 7.

[30] "It is particularly important to achieve equal levels of development in areas such as education, employment, health, hygiene, accommodation conditions, skills for functioning in a civil society." Programme, p. 7.

[31] Interview with the Head of the Division of National Minorities, Warsaw, 22 March 2002.

[32] Programme, p. 4.

culture, and also seeks to promote awareness of Roma identity and culture among the majority population. However, it does not propose measures to promote other minority rights such as effective participation in public life or promotion of the use of the minority language in the public sphere. Government officials emphasise that the Programme is not necessarily intended to protect Roma rights as these are protected by the Constitution.[33]

Some of the areas that the Programme does address are too narrowly defined. Concerning education, for example, the focus is on improving completion rates of primary education but secondary education or access to higher education are not covered.[34] Other important issues left out include: ensuring access to public institutions, including State-owned media (as professional staff); vocational training; monitoring of discrimination and intolerance; and promoting awareness of existing channels for submitting complaints regarding racially motivated crime.

There are no other initiatives apart from this Programme that aim to protect the Roma minority (or minorities in general) as such. However, some initiatives of the Ministries of Education and Culture outside the scope of the Programme also benefit Roma and other minority groups.[35]

2.4 The Programme – Administration/Implementation/Evaluation

Mechanisms for programme administration, monitoring and evaluation seem to be operating but, due to the limited scale of implementation thus far, it is difficult to assess their overall effectiveness. A centralised mechanism for monitoring the implementation of the Programme is in place, but is not sufficiently linked to compliance mechanisms; this might prove problematic with respect to local governments whose cooperation is essential to successful implementation. Stronger mechanisms for ensuring systematic participation by Roma representatives are also needed, especially at the local level.

The Minister of Internal Affairs bears overall responsibility for coordinating implementation of the Programme;[36] the Ministry's Division of National Minorities

---

[33] Interview with an official from the Division of National Minorities, Warsaw, 22 March 2002. See Section 3.4.

[34] There are no Government scholarships to encourage Roma to apply to universities. *Minority Protection 2001*, p. 355.

[35] See Section 3.4.5.

[36] Programme, p. 8.

administers and monitors implementation at the national level,[37] and cooperates with the Task Force for National Minorities[38] concerning implementation and problems that emerge.[39] The Division also maintains regular contact with local institutions as well as with Roma representatives. The Plenipotentiary for National Minorities plays an important role in facilitating cooperation between local governments and Roma communities.[40]

Local actors play a key role in implementation as the Programme's projects are mostly supposed to be implemented by commune councils and municipalities in Małopolska Province (except for Cracow/Kraków, which is not covered by the Programme).[41] Every year, local government institutions can submit project proposals to the Division of National Minorities concerning tasks for which they are responsible according to the Timetable for Realisation and Financing. Only twelve of the 228 tasks proposed in the Timetable under the responsibility of institutions other than these local government authorities; at present, only a small number of Roma and other NGOs are expected to be able to participate in implementing projects.[42] Roma leaders have called for greater Roma participation in implementation.[43]

---

[37] The Division of National Minorities was established in January 2000.

[38] The Task Force for National Minorities consists of representatives of ministries and other government bodies. Neither minorities nor local governments are represented. *Minority Protection 2001*, p. 375, footnote 139.

[39] Interview with the Head of the Division of National Minorities, Warsaw, 22 March 2002.

[40] OSI Roundtable, Warsaw, July 2002. *Explanatory note: OSI held a roundtable meeting in Poland in July 2002 to invite critique of the present report in draft form. Experts present included representatives of the Government, Roma representatives and non-governmental organisations.* The Małopolska Province Plenipotentiary for National Minorities, appointed by the Governor of the Province, is not of Roma origin. There are, however, several plenipotentiaries of Roma origin who also assist with implementation (see Section 3.4.3).

[41] Cracow will be covered when the Programme is expanded. OSI Roundtable, Warsaw, July 2002.

[42] Governmental agencies include: the Małopolska Provincial Police, the National Police, representatives of the Catholic Church, NGOs, the Małopolska Department of Education, the local unit of the Health Service in Nowy Sącz. The Catholic Church and various NGOs are also mentioned. Only one Roma organisation, the Association of the Roma in Nowy Sącz Region, is listed as responsible for implementing tasks (five in total). Timetable for Realisation and Financing, pp. 20-21. A number of NGOs are also mentioned as being "involved in implementing the Programme" as they are realising projects which are considered to fall within its general scheme. Programme, p. 8.

[43] According to one leader: "The Roma should not play their role as beneficiaries only, but also as decision-makers. They should have real influence on their life and Roma organisations should really implement the Programme." Written comments of the Chair of the Association of the Roma in Nowy Sącz Region, Laskowa Górna, 27 August 2002.

Funding

The Programme is to be financed from various sources, the most substantial of which is a special purpose reserve within the State budget.[44] Normally, these resources are to be released at the request of the Minister of Internal Affairs, and transferred via the Małopolska Provincial Governor to local government units in the Province.[45] In general, about 80 percent is to come from the State budget, and 20 percent from predominantly local actors.[46]

The budget of the Programme is as follows (all sources combined):[47]

Areas	2001	2002	2003	Total
1. Education	PLN 2,093,659 (€550,963)	PLN 2,332,144 (€613,722)	PLN 2,301,972 (€605,782)	PLN 6,727,775 (€1,770,467)
2. Combating Unemployment	PLN 530,689 (€139,655)	PLN 893,749 (€235,197)	PLN 771,760 (€203,095)	PLN 2,196,198 (€577,947)
3. Health	PLN 232,340 (€61,142)	PLN 128,693 (€33,867)	PLN 107,621 (€28,321)	PLN 468,654 (€123,330)
4. Living Conditions	PLN 3,397,953 (€894,198)	PLN 4,853,590 (€1,277,261)	PLN 4,258,661 (€1,120,700)	PLN 12,510,204 (€3,292,159)
5. Security	PLN 252,942 (€66,564)	PLN 249,074 (€65,546)	PLN 255,212 (€67,161)	PLN 757,228 (€199,271)
6. Culture	PLN 326,800 (€86,000)	PLN 365,124 (€96,085)	PLN 318,663 (€83,859)	PLN 1,010,587 (€265,944)
7. Knowledge in and about the Roma Community	PLN 200,220 (€52,689)	PLN 232,820 (€61,268)	PLN 170,220 (€44,795)	PLN 603,260 (€158,753)
Total	PLN 7,034,603 (€1,851,211)	PLN 9,055,194 (€2,382,946)	PLN 8,184,109 (€2,153,713)	PLN 24,273,906 (€6,387,870)

Note: The exchange rate is calculated at PLN 3.8 (Polish złoty) = € 1.

---

[44] Other sources of funding foreseen include: the Ministries of Education and Culture, local departments of education, local units of the Health Service, the Labour Office, the Labour Fund, the Małopolska Provincial Office, the police, commune councils and municipalities, the Foundation for Supporting the Countryside, and Polish Television. Grants from international governmental and non-governmental sources are also foreseen. Programme, p. 8.

[45] Programme, pp. 24–25.

[46] Local governments often rely on NGOs and foundations to help fund-raise for specific projects. For example, the British Know How Fund helped commune councils and municipalities raise funds for the project of Roma assistants. Information provided by the Małopolska Province Plenipotentiary for National Minorities, via e-mail, Małopolska Provincial Office, 8 May 2002.

[47] See the Timetable for Realisation and Financing.

Every year, the Government announces the overall amount available for the realisation of projects planned in the Timetable for Realisation and Financing.[48] The Division of National Minorities proposes the actual allocation to specific components of the Programme.

In practice, the amount actually allocated by the Government differs greatly from the funds foreseen in the Programme's budget. Thus, in 2001, the Government announced that funds to be allocated from the State budget would amount to PLN 1,500,000 (€394,737). However, due to a crisis of public finances, funds from the special purpose reserve were withheld; no money was allocated from this source for implementation of the Programme in 2001. Although the Ministry of Education provided PLN 500,000 (€131,579) for the realisation of tasks related to education,[49] this represented only nine percent of the overall funds which the Government planned to allocate in 2001 (PLN 5,664,613, €1,490,688), and only 28 percent of planned Government funds for the education component for 2001 (PLN 1,755,677, €462,020).[50]

For 2002, a total of PLN 3,000,000 (€789,474) is foreseen: PLN 2,000,000 (€526,316) has already been transferred from the special purpose reserve to the Małopolska Provincial Office for further distribution; PLN 600,000 (€157,895) is soon to be allocated by the Ministry of Education; and PLN 400,000 (€105,263) is expected from local sources.[51] Again, this is much less than what had been foreseen.[52] Moreover, the funding provided by the Ministry of Education is earmarked for tasks in the area of education only, while the amount allocated from the special purpose reserve is available for tasks in all areas (including education).[53]

---

[48] Plans for Government financing of the Programme are modified every year according to the Budget Act which indicates the amount of public finances to be spent. Information provided by the Małopolska Province Plenipotentiary for National Minorities, via e-mail, on 2 August 2002.

[49] According to the Head of the Division of National Minorities, this testifies to the good will and responsibility of officers working in the Ministry of Education. Interview with the Head of the Division of National Minorities, Warsaw, 22 March 2002.

[50] These are figures for planned contribution by the Government, not including local sources, based on the Timetable for Realisation and Financing.

[51] Information provided by the Head of the Division of National Minorities, Ministry of Internal Affairs, Warsaw, 8 August 2002.

[52] A total of PLN 9,055,194 (€2,382,946) (all sources combined) had been foreseen in the Timetable for Realisation and Financing for 2002, of which PLN 1,950,842 (€513,379) was to be allocated from the special purpose reserve to tasks in the area of education alone. Thus, the budget for 2003, all sources combined, is one third of the original amount planned for that year.

[53] Comments provided by the Head of the Division of National Minorities, Warsaw, 8 August 2002.

Local actors can initiate requests for funding by presenting project proposals[54] along with a detailed budget and timeline for implementation.[55] Project proposals are first evaluated by the Małopolska Provincial Office, which transmits them, together with a written opinion, to the Division of National Minorities, which in turn also evaluates them; the final decision about approval is made by the Minister of Internal Affairs.[56]

Roma organisations are not directly involved in the funding approval process, although they are consulted and may also submit projects for funding. One Roma organisation expressed concerns that Roma have no influence on the use of Programme funds placed at the disposal of local governments.[57] Reportedly, some local governments have been unwilling to propose projects for their Roma communities.[58]

Monitoring and evaluation

The Małopolska Provincial Office is responsible for monitoring implementation of the Programme. Institutions responsible for implementing tasks of the Programme and all institutions that have received funding must report annually on the realisation of activities and expenditures to the Division of National Minorities via the Małopolska Provincial Office.

The Division of National Minorities determines whether the Programme is performed according to plan. Neither the Division nor the Government can require compliance

---

[54] Application forms for project proposals are available on the website of the Ministry of Internal Affairs at <www.mswia.gov.pl>, (accessed 26 July 2002).

[55] Information provided by the Małopolska Province Plenipotentiary for National Minorities, via e-mail, on 2 August 2002.

[56] Information provided by the Małopolska Province Plenipotentiary for National Minorities, via e-mail, on 2 August 2002; written comments of the Head of the Division of National Minorities, Warsaw, 8 August 2002.

[57] "Even though the funds [...] should serve to improve the situation of the Roma in Małopolska, we have no influence on how they are spent nor even the possibility to check the effectiveness of the use of these funds." Written comments of the leader of the Association of Roma Women, Cracow, 26 July 2002.

[58] "Some commune offices and municipalities ignore realisation of the Programme. For instance, Limanowa commune did not prepare any projects to improve the extremely difficult situation of the Roma in the Koszary settlement." Written comments of the Chair of the Association of the Roma from Nowy Sącz Region, Laskowa Górna, 27 August 2002. According to another Roma leader, "one of the biggest failures of the Programme is that decisions which are important for the Roma are left to the local administration." Written comments of the Chair of the Association of the Roma in Nowy Sącz Region, Laskowa Górna, 27 August 2002. OSI Roundtable, Warsaw, July 2002.

from the local bodies involved in implementation.[59] However, the Division may exert some leverage: the new application forms introduced in 2002 include sections on realisation and expenditures over the previous year; the fact that annual reporting has become a pre-condition for renewed funding is seen as a means of monitoring Programme implementation.[60]

Monitoring also includes on-site visits by officials of the Division of National Minorities to see whether funding is being used appropriately.[61] The implementation of projects under the Programme is also discussed in sessions of the Task Force for National Minorities in Warsaw.[62]

A separate monitoring mechanism has been established for the education component, involving the Local Department of Education in Cracow which reports directly to the Małopolska Provincial Office.[63] In February 2002, an interim evaluation report focussing on the activities undertaken in the first half of the 2001/2002 school year was prepared by the Local Department of Education, together with the Division of Health and Social Policy (Małopolska Provincial Office);[64] this report has been sent to the Division of National Minorities but has not been made public. A more detailed report is due after the end of the school year, following a new round of evaluation.[65] Implementation of the education component is also discussed in the Sub-Section on the Education of National Minorities within the Task Force for National Minorities.[66]

As no other components were implemented in 2001, no assessment can be made yet regarding the effectiveness of general monitoring and evaluation mechanisms.

---

[59] Municipalities, communes and district administration are not under the direct authority of the central Government.

[60] OSI Roundtable, Warsaw, July 2002.

[61] OSI Roundtable, Warsaw, July 2002.

[62] The Task Force used to meet monthly; however, since May 2002, it only meets irregularly. Interview with officials of the Division of National Minorities, Warsaw, 22 March 2002.

[63] Interview with officials from the Division of National Minorities, Warsaw, 22 March 2002.

[64] Małopolska Provincial Office, Division of Health and Social Policy, *Analiza i ocena realizowanych zadań, ujętych w Pilotażowym Programie Rządowym na Rzecz Społeczności Romskiej w Województwie Małopolskim, w zakresie edukacji, za okres VII–XII 2001 r.* (Analysis and Evaluation of Task Performance in Accordance with the Pilot Government Programme for the Roma Community in the Małopolska Province, concerning education, during the period July to December 2001), Cracow, 2 February 2002, (hereafter, "Education Report").

[65] OSI Roundtable, Warsaw, July 2002. As of July 2002, no such report was available.

[66] Protocols of the Task Force for National Minorities, <www.mswia.gov>, (accessed 26 July 2002).

Opinions vary as to whether the Programme can be modified.[67] According to one official, even if it emerges that a particular task is difficult to realise or has become irrelevant, it cannot be discontinued or replaced, for example the specialist courses for adults.[68]

Preparations for a programme for Roma in the whole of Poland have begun through preliminary consultations with Roma leaders.[69] It is not clear how the results of implementation of the Programme will be used in designing the national programme.

There are no formal mechanisms for collaboration between governmental and non-governmental bodies.[70] There is also a lack of systematic consultations between governmental bodies and Roma representatives on assessing implementation, especially at the local level.

Some local Roma organisations are involved in implementation and evaluation of the Programme. For example, the Association of the Roma in Nowy Sącz Region assisted with the evaluation of the education component by organising the distribution of questionnaires to Roma parents and school directors. The Plenipotentiary for the Roma Community in Nowy Sącz also assists with implementation.[71]

However, some Roma representatives have criticised the level of cooperation with local officials,[72] and the fact that there are no Roma members in the Task Force for National

---

[67] OSI Roundtable, Warsaw, July 2002.

[68] See Section 3.2.1.

[69] OSI Roundtable, Warsaw, July 2002; see also "Polish Government Works on Program for Roma," RFE/RL *Newsline*, 2 August 2002.

[70] NGOs implementing projects for Roma tend to cooperate with local government units rather than with the central Government.

[71] A representative of the Association of the Roma in Nowy Sącz Region was appointed by the Division of National Minorities as Plenipotentiary for the Roma Community in Nowy Sącz Region in 2000; the Division of National Minorities defined his competencies and duties and also covers his salary. Information provided by the Małopolska Province Plenipotentiary for National Minorities, Małopolska Provincial Office, via e-mail, 8 May 2002. Two other Plenipotentiaries, also of Roma origin, have been appointed by the Division of National Minorities to facilitate cooperation with local officials as well as implementation of the Programme (see Section 3.4.3).

[72] "The Roma community has problems in contacts with local administration officials. It may be due to the result of the low level of education of the Roma, but unfortunately it leads to the marginalisation and pauperisation of Roma society." Written comments of the Chair of the Association of the Roma in Nowy Sącz Region, Laskowa Górna, 27 August 2002. "We would welcome it if local officials had such contacts with us as the Minister [of Internal Affairs] does." Interview with the leader of the Social and Cultural Association of the Roma in Poland, Tarnów, 3 April 2002.

Minorities;[73] representatives of Roma organisations (and local governments) attend Task Force meetings on an *ad hoc* basis only.[74] Suggestions have been made to involve Roma in regularly monitoring Programme implementation and to systematically communicate with Roma communities to identify their needs,[75] for example through a permanent consultative body of Roma at the local level to improve cooperation with local authorities, or a sub-team of Roma representatives for more formal consultations at the national level.[76]

2.5 The Programme and the Public

No official public campaign was carried out following the adoption of the Programme and there have been no systematic efforts to explain why it is needed or to promote its goals. However, officials of the Division of National Minorities visited the Nowy Sącz region to inform local communities about the Programme. Meetings with local government officials and Roma representatives to which the media was invited were also organised.[77] Efforts were also made to publicise the Programme through local media.[78]

Media coverage of the Programme is based mainly on informal contacts between Government officials and journalists.[79] In most cases, the media has positively described its launch, which was reported mostly in the regional media or in regional supplements to the national press. For example, articles published by regional supplements of *Gazeta Wyborcza* tended to cover the adoption of the Programme in a positive light and informed readers

---

[73] The fact that many Roma are not informed about the specific activities of the Programme has also been criticised. The need for Roma to be able to participate in a dialogue with institutions responsible for implementation at the local level has been especially emphasised. OSI Roundtable, Warsaw, July 2002.

[74] OSI Roundtable, Warsaw, July 2002.

[75] Interview with J.C., a local Roma leader, Limanowa, 28 March 2002; interview with a representative of the Association of the Roma in Nowy Sącz Region, Laskowa, 27 March 2002.

[76] OSI Roundtable, Warsaw, July 2002.

[77] Written comments of the Head of the Division of National Minorities, Warsaw, 8 August 2002.

[78] OSI Roundtable, Warsaw, July 2002.

[79] Interview with the Head of the Division of National Minorities, Warsaw, 22 March 2002.

about the difficult situation of Roma, devoting a large number of articles to the question of education. *Rzeczpospolita*, a national daily, also focused on this issue.[80]

Critical assessments in the media tend to focus on its limited implementation. For instance, a local newspaper, *Echo Tarnowa*, strongly criticised the lack of funding for the Programme in 2001, as well as the fact that no measures concerning housing were implemented, suggesting that local governments should have participated in financing the Programme.[81] An article in the regional *Dziennik Polski* criticised the fact that Cracow was not included in the Programme, arguing that Roma there live in very difficult conditions, over 90 percent of them being unemployed.[82] According to some experts, however, media coverage has also had a negative effect.[83]

Interviews conducted among Roma communities benefiting under the Programme suggest that Roma are familiar with it.[84] However, some Roma representatives note that a large number of Roma in the region still lack information about the Programme and

---

[80] According to a press review conducted for the purpose of this report, in 2000 there were four articles, in 2001 – three articles, and in 2002 – three articles, in the national daily *Rzeczpospolita* describing the education situation of Roma children. There were also articles on unemployment: "Surveys conducted last year among the Roma in Świętokrzyska Province showed that only one out of 66 persons has a profession […]. Unemployed Roma also rarely use social aid for the unemployed." See "*Szansa dla Roma*" (An opportunity for a Rom), *Gazeta w Kielcach*, a regional supplement of *Gazeta Wyborcza*, 26 July 2001, p. 4.

[81] "*Wozy nie pojadą taborami*" (Wagons will not budge in trains/caravans), *Echo Tarnowa*, 7 November 2001, p. 3.

[82] "*Są zbyt zaradni!*" (They are too smart!), *Dziennik Polski*, 2001.

[83] The Director of the Ethnographic Museum in Tarnów points out that "the enthusiasm of journalists and the great interest in the [Małopolska] Programme was harmful both for the Programme and for the Roma community. The press quoted the amount of Government funding to be attributed for the realisation of particular tasks, which was interpreted by most Roma in Tarnów as an amount to be divided among individuals […]." Interview with the Director of the Ethnographic Museum in Tarnów, Tarnów, 20 March 2002; see also: "*Miliony dla Romów*" (Millions for the Roma), *Gazeta w Krakowie* (regional supplement of *Gazeta Wyborcza*), 27 March 2001, p. 5.

[84] Ten interviews were conducted amongst the Roma community for the purpose of this report in the following villages and towns: Krośnica, Maszkowice, Laskowa, Ochotnica Górna, Limanowa and Nowy Targ. Eight out of ten persons confirmed knowing about the Programme, while two stated that they knew more or less about the Programme but lacked further information.

funding allocated to projects.[85] The text of the Programme is available on the website of the Ministry of Internal Affairs. However, it has been noted that not everyone – and especially not inhabitants of Roma settlements – can afford Internet access.[86]

2.6 The Programme and the EU

The Programme declares that the "Roma problem" in Poland, "though acute, is of much less intensity than in some other countries of Central and Eastern Europe. Consequently, the European Union's interest and its readiness to provide measurable and tangible assistance in solving problems in Poland is relatively low."[87] Nonetheless, EU grants are considered a potential source of funding.[88]

Protection of the Roma minority is not a priority area for EU funding.[89] The EU has accordingly not provided direct funding to the Programme,[90] although it has provided some financing through the 1999 Phare ACCESS Programme (€44,860) to an important initiative to train Roma assistants for schools in Małopolska Province.[91]

---

[85] OSI Roundtable, Warsaw, July 2002. According to one Roma leader: "[m]ost of the persons I visited in Roma settlements in 2001 did not know anything about the [Małopolska] Programme. I have appealed to representatives of the local government to disseminate information about the Programme […]. I proposed to provide such information through television so that the Roma can get acquainted with the entire complexity of the Programme, but no such television programme was produced." According to the same person, it is also hard to obtain information on the funding allocated to projects. Written comments of the leader of the Association of Roma Women, Cracow, 26 July 2002.

[86] OSI Roundtable, Warsaw, July 2002.

[87] Programme, p. 6.

[88] According to the European Commission Delegation, the Government has not requested any Phare support for the Programme. Information provided by an Official of the Delegation of the European Commission to Poland, Warsaw, 25 April 2002.

[89] The protection of Roma is not listed as a priority in Poland's Accession Partnership. See the latest Accession Partnership, revised in 2001, based on the conclusions of the European Commission, *2001 Regular Report on Poland's Progress Towards Accession*, Brussels, 13 November 2001, <http://europa.eu.int/comm/enlargement/report2001/appl_en.pdf>, (accessed 19 September 2002) (hereafter, *"2001 Regular Report"*).

[90] Information provided by an Official of the Delegation of the European Commission to Poland, Warsaw, 25 April 2002.

[91] This project is being implemented by the Małopolska Association of Education since January 2002. Information provided by an Official of the Delegation of the European Commission to Poland, Warsaw, 4 September 2002.

Another project funded under the 1999 ACCESS Programme, while not specifically targeting the Roma community, also served it. Under the project "Mobile Citizens Assistance and Referral Services" (€142,000), a sub-project, implemented by the Polish-Roma Integration Association from July 2001 to September 2002, aimed to create a mobile outreach information system for Roma in Małopolska Province.

The European Commission noted the adoption of the Programme in its 2001 Regular Report, considering it a "first step by the government to combat the precarious situation of the Roma minority in Polish society[.]"[92] It considered that it was too early to assess results of implementation.[93] Monitoring reports are available from the European Commission Delegation in Warsaw upon request; however, no final evaluation reports are available yet for these projects.[94]

3. The Government Programme – Implementation

3.1 Stated Objectives of the Programme

The main objective of the Programme is "to achieve full participation of Roma who live in [Małopolska Province] in the life of a civil society and to mitigate the disparities between this group and the rest of the society;" it is also stated that "[i]t is particularly important to achieve equal levels of development in areas such as education, employment, health, hygiene, accommodation conditions, skills for functioning in a civil society."[95] Furthermore, the Programme is intended as a set of long-term solutions to the problems faced by Roma rather than "quick-fix" measures.[96]

---

[92] *2001 Regular Report*, p. 24.

[93] Information provided by an Official of the Delegation of the European Commission to Poland, Warsaw, 25 April 2002.

[94] A third project under ACCESS 1999 (€142,000) addresses Roma issues in Northeast Poland as part of a project to support disadvantaged groups in border regions and is being implemented from August 2001 to October 2002. Information provided by an Official of the Delegation of the European Commission to Poland, Warsaw, 4 September 2002.

[95] Programme, p. 7.

[96] "The Programme is not designed to offer *ad hoc* assistance in a difficult situation which the Roma community has found itself in, but to develop mechanisms which would make it possible to achieve the above-mentioned objectives […]. Its minimum duration should range between one and two decades. The three-year period as laid down in the law is clearly not long enough to achieve the strategic objectives of the Programme defined in Chapter III." Programme, p. 7.

3.2 Government Programme and Discrimination

The Programme does not identify discrimination as a problem.[97] Rather, it refers to the difficult situation of Roma, recognising that the Roma community – and the Bergitka Roma in particular – suffered most during the period of systemic transformation.[98] Among other causes of this situation, the Programme mentions the influence of "far-reaching historical and social determinants as well as many errors committed during the Polish People's Republic period."[99] While it stresses the importance of achieving equal levels of development for Roma in various areas, it neither frames these objectives as issues of discrimination nor proposes concrete measures to achieve them.

Outside the framework of the Programme, basic anti-discrimination provisions are contained in the Constitution,[100] the Labour Code,[101] and the Law on the Protection of Personal Data.[102] The Law on National and Ethnic Minorities, currently being examined by the Sejm (Lower Chamber of Parliament), will reportedly also contain anti-discrimination provisions.[103]

---

[97] It notes, however, that international organisations have identified discrimination against Roma in Poland as a problem, quoting for example a report by the European Commission Against Racism and Intolerance: "Prejudices against the Roma/Gypsy community persist in society and certainly lead to discrimination in everyday life [...]. It is reported that the Roma community is generally excluded from the Polish communities alongside which it lives and that conflicts on the local level occur, although they are seldom acknowledged to be on ethnic grounds [...]. Some sources have also indicated that Roma/Gypsy communities face discrimination on the part of local authorities in the provision of services [...]." Council of Europe, European Commission Against Racism and Intolerance (ECRI), *Second Report on Poland*, adopted on 10 December 1999, CRI (2000) 34, in Programme, p. 5, (hereafter, "CRI (2000)").

[98] The reasons presented by the authors of the Programme as to why the Roma community has been negatively affected by the effects of transformation are "the low level of education of its members" and its so-called "cultural specificity." Programme, p. 7.

[99] Programme, p. 3.

[100] The Constitution, Art. 32, establishes the general principle of equality and non-discrimination, without specifically prohibiting discrimination on racial, ethnic or other grounds; Art. 60 provides the right of equal access to public services; Art. 53 guarantees freedom of faith and religion. Constitution of the Republic of Poland, *Official Gazette*, No. 78, item 483, 2 April 1997.

[101] The Labour Code, Art. 11(3), states that "any form of discrimination in labour relations, in particular on the grounds of [...] race, nationality, belief [...] cannot be admitted."

[102] The Law on the Protection of Personal Data, Art. 27, forbids the use of data on racial or ethnic origin. At the same time, it prevents the gathering of data on discrimination on the basis of racial or ethnic background. Law on the Protection of Personal Data, *Official Gazette*, No. 133, item 883, 29 August 1997; see also *Minority Protection 2001*, p. 351.

[103] OSI Roundtable, Warsaw, July 2002.

However, numerous provisions of the EU Race Equality Directive[104] are not yet incorporated into Polish law, which does not include any definition of direct or indirect discrimination based on national or ethnic origin; nor are there provisions for the reversal of the burden of proof in cases where direct or indirect discrimination is claimed.[105] Poland has not signed Protocol No. 12 to the European Convention on Human Rights and Fundamental Freedoms (ECHR). At present, no legislative changes have been proposed, even though Poland lacks comprehensive anti-discrimination legislation as well as a specialised body to promote equal treatment and to address racial or ethnic discrimination.[106]

There are no official statistics to prove or disprove the existence of discriminatory practices against Roma, and no cases of discrimination against Roma on ethnic or racial grounds have been proven.[107] Moreover, Government officials have evinced a lack of belief that discrimination might be a problem; also, according to one expert, Roma are not discriminated against in the cultural sphere but are rather privileged compared to other groups; nor does he believe that are they discriminated against in the sphere of legislation or governmental policy.[108] The Ministry of Internal Affairs considers discrimination against national and ethnic minorities to be within its competence;[109] at the same time, it maintains that investigations into this issue could be wrongly interpreted – alleging, for example, that "the presence of an official from the Ministry in a court hearing could be perceived as pressure on the independence of

---

[104] Council Directive 2000/43/EC of 29 June 2000 implementing the principle of equal treatment between persons irrespective of race or ethnic origin.

[105] See P. Filipek, *Legal analysis of national and European anti-discrimination legislation. A comparison of the EU Racial Equality Directive & Protocol No. 12 with anti-discrimination legislation in Poland,* European Roma Rights Center/Interights/Migration Policy Group, Budapest/London/Brussels, September 2001, pp. 10–11, 25, <http://www.migpolgroup.com/uploadstore/Poland%20electronic.pdf>, (accessed 26 September 2002); see also *2000 Regular Report by the Commission on Poland's Progress Towards Accession,* Brussels, 8 November 2000, pp. 56–57 (hereafter, *"2000 Regular Report"*).

[106] See P. Filipek, *Legal analysis of national and European anti-discrimination legislation;* see also CRI (2000); *Minority Protection 2001,* pp. 350–351.

[107] The Office of the Commissioner for Citizens' Rights (Ombudsman) has competence regarding minority rights. In 1998, it established a department for the protection of minority rights that employs a "Senior Specialist for the rights of aliens and national and ethnic minorities." Reportedly, the majority of minority rights complaints received originated with Roma. *Minority Protection 2001,* pp. 372–373.

[108] Interview with the Director of the Ethnographic Museum in Tarnów, Tarnów, 20 March 2002.

[109] OSI Roundtable, Warsaw, July 2002.

courts[.]"[110] There have been no governmental measures outside the Programme to promote full and effective equality (such as through affirmative action) for the Roma or other minorities.

Roma leaders have themselves identified discrimination as a problem,[111] citing problems of institutional discrimination by public officials, especially the police and local commune councils and municipalities, treatment as second-class citizens by the State administration, discrimination in the workplace, and exclusion from the rest of society;[112] discrimination against Roma women[113] and children[114] in particular has also been reported.

Discrimination against Roma, especially in education, housing and employment, is sometimes described in the Polish press.[115] Reports by international NGOs also point

---

[110] According to another official, "We have received a few complaints which could eventually serve as evidence of discrimination against the Roma, but the [Ministry of Internal Affairs] is not a division of complaints and cannot do much with that [...]." Interview with officials of the Division of National Minorities, Warsaw, 22 March 2002. For a comprehensive discussion of judicial independence in Poland's courts, see EU Accession Monitoring Program, *Monitoring the EU Accession Process: Judicial Independence,* Open Society Institute, Budapest, October 2001; id., *Monitoring the EU Accession Process: Judicial Capacity,* Open Society Institute, Budapest, November 2002, both available at <www.eumap.org>.

[111] Officials claim that the Roma representatives consulted during the preparation of the Programme did not highlight the issue of discrimination as a top priority. OSI Roundtable, Warsaw, July 2002.

[112] Interviews with: the leader of the Social and Cultural Association of the Roma in Poland, Tarnów, 3 April 2002; the leader of the Association of the Roma in Nowy Sącz Region, Laskowa Górna, 27 March 2002; and the leader of the Association of the Roma in Cracow, Cracow/Nowa Huta, 5 April 2002.

[113] A recent survey conducted by a Roma organisation amongst young Roma women in one village in Małopolska Province showed that they need encouragement and equal treatment by schoolmates and teachers in order to make progress in education. They also complained about discrimination. Written comments of the leader of the Association of Roma Women, Cracow, 26 July 2002.

[114] See *Minority Protection 2001,* p. 352.

[115] See for example in the national daily *Rzeczpospolita:* "*Czarny brat, czarna siostra*" (A black brother, a black sister), 14 March 2000; "*Katastrofa edukacyjna*" (An educational catastrophe), 8 September 2001; "*Prawa mają równe, szanse – nie*" (They have equal rights but no chances), 13 March 2002; "*Niektóre dzieci są całkiem białe"* (Some children are totally white), 23 March 2002; and in another national daily *Nowy Dziennik:* "*Cygańska dola"* (Gypsy fate), 24 August 2001; in the regional daily *Gazeta Krakowska:* "*Romowie jadą na odsiecz"* (The Roma go for succour), 17 February 1999; "*To jawny rasizm"* (It's obvious racism), 25 April 1998; in the monthly *Rrom p-o drom:* "*Pieniądze albo życie"* (Your money or your life), July/August 2000; in *Gazeta Lubuska,* a regional supplement *of Gazeta Wyborcza:* "*U nas dole i niedole*" (Our fate and bad fate), pp. 15–16, July 2000.

to discrimination and inequalities in certain areas.[116] ECRI has called for establishing a system of monitoring and evaluating discrimination and racism against minority groups, especially the Roma community.[117]

3.2.1 Education

Education support is considered the Programme's priority because it is seen as a key to improving conditions in other areas.[118] The hiring of Roma teacher's assistants and introduction of remedial classes have had a positive impact on school attendance and educational success of Roma children; they have also been positively received by parents and school directors; this also suggests that attributing the blame for low school attendance to Roma parents may require reassessment.

The Programme identifies the main problem as the "low level of education of Roma children which is related to internal community practices,"[119] as well as to other factors such as poor knowledge of Polish, low levels of parental education, lack of pre-school preparation, and poverty. There is no mention of possible discrimination or disadvantages experienced by Roma children in the Polish educational system.

The Programme's main objectives are

> to raise the level of education among Roma through increasing the completion rate [for primary education], improving school attendance and learning achievements of Roma children and young people, and facilitating further study in post-primary schools for Roma young people [sic].[120]

The Programme clearly prefers an integrated rather than segregated education model, due to problems encountered with "Roma classes[.]"[121] Reportedly, the practice of

---

[116] P. Filipek, *Legal analysis of national and European anti-discrimination legislation*, p. 15; see also CRI (2000), p. 11, 12, 17.

[117] CRI (2000) 34, p. 4.

[118] Programme, p. 10.

[119] "Roma children do not attend school regularly or at all; this is because their parents underestimate the role of education at a later stage of life and treat school as a repressive institution and as a threat to the Roma identity." Programme, p. 9.

[120] Programme, p. 10.

[121] Programme, p. 9. Separate "Roma classes" were set up starting in 1991 as an experiment by a Catholic priest in order to address low literacy and high drop-out rates among Roma children. However, the quality of education of these classes tended to be very low. Roma representatives have advocated ending the practice of establishing such classes. For more on segregated classes and other issues in the area of education, see *Minority Protection 2001*, pp. 352–355.

setting up such classes has been discontinued in Małopolska Province and they are now organised only for older children and youths because of the practical difficulty of teaching older children who have completed only one year of primary education together with younger children.[122]

Education projects constitute the largest group of projects to be implemented: between 2001 and 2003; 102 sub-projects are proposed in fifteen local administration units.[123] They include:

- Employing Roma assistants (in 15 schools);[124]
- Providing financial support for education in "zero classes" (pre-school education) and ensuring the possibility of extending education at the pre-school level;
- Introducing compensatory classes;[125]
- Providing financial support for purchasing textbooks, teaching aids and supplies;
- Hiring supporting teachers and organising special interest clubs and courses;
- Providing financial support for extra school meals;
- Providing financial support for children to attend nursery schools;
- Enabling Roma children to take part in summer and winter camps;
- Organising psychological and pedagogical support and setting up "therapeutic rooms" (both for children and their parents);
- Providing financial support for teachers helping Roma children;
- Organising educational activities for adults;
- Organising vocational courses for young people and adults;
- Introducing additional lessons in Polish;
- Providing financial support for transporting children to schools;

---

[122] OSI Roundtable, Warsaw, July 2002.

[123] These are the cities of Limanowa, Nowy Targ, Nowy Sącz, Szczawnica and Tarnów, and the communes of Bukowina Tatrzańska, Czarny Dunajec, Grybów, Jabłonka, Krościenko nad Dunajcem, Limanowa, Łącko, Nowy Targ, Ochotnica Dolna and Szaflary. Timetable for Realisation and Financing, pp. 1–10; see also Programme, p. 11.

[124] These are teacher's assistants of Roma origin. The Association of the Roma in Nowy Sącz Region is listed as responsible for implementing this task, together with the Małopolska Department of Education. Timetable for Realisation and Financing, p. 1.

[125] These are remedial classes including Polish language classes but not exclusively.

- Providing financial support for insuring pupils against accidents;
- Organising summer integration-oriented leisure activities in "Gypsy camps" for Roma and Polish children.[126]

Roma representatives have pointed to the fact that the Programme does not propose any measures to encourage Roma to attend secondary schools and universities.[127] Government officials stress the need to address primary education first and expect that access to secondary and tertiary education, as well as courses to help applicants prepare for exams, will be dealt with later.[128]

The following expenditures are foreseen in the field of education:[129]

	2001	2002	2003	Total
Total estimated budget	PLN 2,093,659 (€550,963)	PLN 2,332,144 (€613,722)	PLN 2,301,972 (€605,782)	PLN 6,727,775 (€1,770,467)
Amount to be covered from local sources[130]	PLN 337,982 (€88,943)	PLN 381,302 (€100,343)	PLN 487,590 (€128,313)	PLN 1,206,874 (€317,598)

---

[126] Timetable for Realisation and Financing, pp. 1–10; Programme, p. 11.
[127] Interview with the leader of the Association of the Roma in Nowy Sącz Region, Laskowa Górna, 27 March 2002; OSI Roundtable, Warsaw, July 2002.
[128] OSI Roundtable, Warsaw, July 2002.
[129] Timetable for Realisation and Financing, p. 10.
[130] Local sources of funding include local administration units, county labour offices, and the police.

Due to the withholding of the State budget's special purpose reserve, only PLN 500,000 (€131,579) provided by the Ministry of Education were available in 2001.[131] This amount was allocated to fifty projects (out of the 102 planned) in thirteen local administrative units.[132]

As the Government announced that less funding would be available than planned, local governments applied for fewer projects, although some funding was also provided by local governments themselves.[133] Project proposals submitted for areas other than education were not funded. One justification advanced for funding only education

---

[131] PLN 1,755,677 (€462,020) should have been allocated from the special purpose reserve in 2001 for tasks in the area of education alone.

[132]

Administrative units receiving funding in 2001	Number of projects approved	Funding from Ministry of Education PLN (€)
Association of Roma in Nowy Sącz Region (placement of Roma assistants)	1	0/NA
Bukowina Tatrzańska commune	4	PLN 45,000 (€11,842)
Czarny Dunajec commune	4	PLN 50,000 (€13,158)
Krościenko nad Dunajcem commune	3	PLN 12,000 (€3,158)
Limanowa commune	4	PLN 6,180 (€1,626)
Łącko commune	6	PLN 55,000 (€14,474)
Nowy Targ commune	3	PLN 4,100 (€1,079)
Ochotnica Dolna commune	4	PLN 30,000 (€7,895)
Szaflary commune	3	PLN 7,600 (€2,000)
Grybów commune	0/NA	0/NA
Jablonka commune	0/NA	0/NA
Limanowa city	5	PLN 35,000 (€9,211)
Nowy Sącz city	5	PLN 128,000 (€33,684)
Nowy Targ city	4	PLN 30,000 (€7,895)
Szczawnica city	1	PLN 7,120 (€1,874)
Tarnów city	4	PLN 90,000 (€23,684)
Total (estimate)	50	PLN 500,000 (€131,579)

Source: Małopolska Provincial Office, Division of Health and Social Policy, Analysis and Evaluation of Task Performance in Accordance with the Pilot Government Programme for the Roma Community in the Małopolska Province, (Cracow, 2 February 2002), covering the period July to December 2001.

[133] For e.g., the city of Tarnów contributed PLN 18,767 (€4,939), mainly for the purchase of school kits. Written comments of an official from Tarnów municipal office, 29 July 2002. No overview of the contributions of local governments is available yet for 2001.

projects is that raising the currently low levels of education will lead to improvements in all other areas.[134]

The following is a summary of the education-related tasks realised under the Programme in 2001:[135]

- *Roma assistants* were employed in four communes and four municipalities.

- *Supporting teachers* were also employed (to assist Roma children and teach compensatory classes but also, in some cases, to conduct special interest clubs) in three communes and two municipalities.

- *Compensatory classes* were organised in seven communes and four municipalities (though not exclusively for Roma).

- *"Zero classes"* were organised in one commune and two municipalities.

- *"Special interest clubs"* (dance, music, handicrafts, art, etc.) were set up in two communes and three municipalities (though not exclusively for Roma).

- *Textbooks and school kits* were distributed to Roma children in seven communes and four municipalities.

- *Teaching aids* (for compensatory classes) were purchased for schools in three communes and two municipalities.

- *Excursions* were organised in two communes; a *summer camp* for Roma children and a *workshop camp for Roma youth* were organised in one municipality.

- *Workshops for supporting teachers* were organised in one municipality.

- A *nursery school* was established in one commune.

- Eight pupils commuting from one commune received bus tickets, insurance and extra meals.

---

[134] OSI Roundtable, Warsaw, July 2002.

[135] The data presented below are drawn from the following sources: Małopolska Provincial Office, *Education Report*; and also *Ankieta dla dyrektora szkoły* (Questionnaire for school directors) – these were distributed to the directors of the schools covered by the Programme by the Association of the Roma in Nowy Sącz Region in February/March 2002, for use by the Division of National Minorities; ten interviews were also conducted in March 2002 for the purpose of this report with representatives of the Roma community in the following villages and towns: Krośnica, Maszkowice, Laskowa, Ochotnica Górna, Limanowa and Nowy Targ.

- A course (totalling 100 hours on reading, writing, mathematics, natural science, computer skills and "preparing for family life") was organised for Roma parents in one commune.

Most of these projects were coordinated by local administration units, in cooperation with the local departments of education and the Ministry of Education. Roma participation in project coordination was confined to informal consultations.

Overall, most of the activities that received funding were implemented successfully, although some of the planned activities were not realised,[136] and a few others were implemented with some delay.[137] Preliminary data[138] suggests that about 520 Roma pupils and 40 adults benefited from the above-mentioned initiatives.[139]

The joint evaluation of sub-projects prepared by the local Department of Education in Cracow and the Małopolska Provincial Office, based upon questionnaires distributed to Roma parents and school directors by the Association of the Roma in Nowy Sącz Region,[140] noted an increase in school attendance and an improvement in the performance of pupils.[141] This appeared to be due to the involvement of Roma assistants in primary schools who have been credited by school directors with improving

---

[136] Such as, for example the educational courses for adults in Bukowina Tatrzańska commune. In Krościenko nad Dunajcem commune, no Roma assistant was employed (because the person proposed by the commune was not accepted by the local Roma community) and no "zero classes" were set up. In Limanowa commune, planned activities such as compensatory classes, the purchase of textbooks and school kits for Roma children, etc., were not implemented because Limanowa commune argued that there were no Roma attending schools on its territory. However, members of the Roma community do inhabit Limanowa commune and Roma pupils attend primary school No. 4 in the city of Limanowa. Małopolska Provincial Office, *Education Report*, p. 3.

[137] In Tarnów municipality, some textbooks and school kits were purchased in November rather than in September 2001. A local Roma leader from Krośnica also pointed out that the commune took a long time to solve problems related to purchasing textbooks and school kits for Roma pupils. Interview with a local Roma leader, Krośnica, 28 March 2002.

[138] A full evaluation of the education component is expected after the end of the 2001/2002 school year. Małopolska Provincial Office, *Education Report*.

[139] These estimates were compiled on the basis of information concerning the number of beneficiaries from tasks implemented by individual units of local government. Małopolska Provincial Office, *Education Report*.

[140] See Questionnaires for Roma parents, distributed by the Association of the Roma in Nowy Sącz Region in February/March 2002, for use by the Division of National Minorities.

[141] Małopolska Provincial Office, *Education Report*, pp. 6–7.

communication between the school, pupils and their parents.[142] The joint evaluation also found that the purchase of textbooks and school kits for Roma children has had a positive impact on their results at school.[143] There have also been reports that the Programme has contributed to decreasing prejudice towards Roma children in schools.[144]

The overall reaction of Roma parents and the Roma community has also been positive – although it is sometimes difficult to separate their evaluation of the educational projects from criticism that other components of the Programme were not implemented in 2001. Thus, Roma parents are generally satisfied with Roma assistants and compensatory classes;[145] most Roma leaders also positively evaluated these initiatives.[146]

Some failures were also pointed out in the joint evaluation. The attendance of children was low in some cases, while the courses planned for adult Roma were not held; one Government official suggested that the topic of these courses may not have been of sufficient interest for the community.[147]

Roma leaders also identified some shortcomings, such as the lack of financial support for extra meals in schools[148] and delays in providing textbooks after the beginning of the school year.[149] Some parents mentioned the need for additional compensatory

---

[142] Małopolska Provincial Office, *Education Report*. The same opinions are expressed by school directors; see Questionnaires for school directors, distributed by the Association of the Roma in Nowy Sącz Region for use by the Division of National Minorities, February/March 2002.

[143] Małopolska Provincial Office, *Education Report*, pp. 6–7.

[144] Interviews with: M. C., a Roma man, 28 March 2002, Limanowa; and W. S., a local Roma leader, Ochotnica Górna, 28 March 2002.

[145] See Questionnaires for Roma parents.

[146] Ten interviews were conducted with representatives of the Roma community in the following villages and towns: Krośnica, Maszkowice, Laskowa, Ochotnica Górna, Limanowa, Nowy Targ in March 2002 for the purpose of this report.

[147] "There are also tasks which could not be performed. These include, in particular, adult education. The lack of performance of such a task stems from the lack of the interest among the Roma society to participate in education courses." Letter dated 9 January 2002 of the Małopolska Province Plenipotentiary for National Minorities, Division of Health and Social Policy, Małopolska Provincial Office, to the Secretary of the Inter-Sector Task Force for National Minorities, p. 2 (on file with EUMAP). OSI Roundtable, Warsaw, July 2002. However, allegedly, one Roma leader had asked about the possibility of covering the costs of education fees at the secondary level, computer courses, driving courses, and foreign language courses "but the executors of the Programme do not take into account that the Roma themselves know what they want to learn; instead, they propose their own offers." Written comments of the leader of the Association of Roma Women, Cracow, 26 July 2002.

[148] Interview with a representative of the Association of the Roma in Nowy Sącz Region, Laskowa, 27 March 2002.

[149] OSI Roundtable, Warsaw, July 2002.

classes,[150] while others called for music and arts clubs to be established. A recommendation was also made for teachers working with Roma children to display more understanding and sensitivity.[151]

Roma leaders as well as local inhabitants also had critical remarks concerning the limited implementation of the Programme, stating that education initiatives were not sufficient, and that employment, housing and living conditions were the biggest problems confronting the Roma community.[152] The need for better health care was also mentioned.[153]

The Małopolska Province Plenipotentiary for National Minorities concluded that the Programme should be continued, with the education section as a priority, and that the quality of sub-project implementation should be monitored more closely.[154] It is not known exactly how much will be made available for education projects in 2002. At least PLN 600,000 (€157,895) is expected to be allocated by the Ministry of Education,[155] and it is expected that the educational component will continue to receive Government funding until it is fully implemented.[156]

One general remark is warranted regarding the Programme's approach to the issue of education, which assumes that the low school attendance of Roma children stems from the attitude of parents towards education.[157] However, interviews with Roma parents have shown that they perceive the education of their children to be important or very

---

[150] Małopolska Province Office, *Education Report*, p. 7.

[151] Questionnaires for Roma parents. Teachers from schools attended by Roma children are now reportedly being trained on the Roma culture and customs. OSI Roundtable, Warsaw, July 2002.

[152] Interview with local Roma leaders in Maszkowice, Limanowa and Ochotnica Górna, 28 March 2002. "We are very satisfied with the new possibilities in education. But as concerns housing, we did not get any help. Also, unemployment is a big problem; almost everyone is unemployed." Interview with L. S., a Roma man, Ochotnica Górna, 28 March 2002.

[153] Interviews with local Roma leaders in Krośnica, Limanowa, and Maszkowice, 28 March 2002. Interviews with: M.C., a Roma man, 28 March 2002, Limanowa; and E. G., a Roma woman, Nowy Targ, 27 March 2002.

[154] Małopolska Provincial Office, *Education Report*, p. 7.

[155] This represents about 30 percent of the planned amount of funding from central sources. The PLN two million allocated from the special purpose reserve is also intended to cover tasks in the area of education, though not exclusively. Contributions from local sources are also expected.

[156] OSI Roundtable, Warsaw, July 2002.

[157] "[...] parents underestimate the role of education at a later stage of life and treat school as a repressive institution and as a threat to Roma identity." Programme, p. 9.

important.[158] Roma children attend school more frequently when accompanied by Roma assistants with whom they feel comfortable. Thus, blaming Roma parents for the low school attendance of their children does not seem to provide an optimal diagnosis of this problem's cause and may ultimately affect the impact of the Programme in the area of education.

3.2.2 Employment

The "Combating Unemployment" section of the Programme proposes to address the extremely high levels of unemployment among Roma in Małopolska region by:[159]

- Creating subsidised jobs in traditional Roma occupations;
- Providing retraining courses;
- Promoting an active approach towards job seeking;
- Creating public works and companies willing to employ low-skilled workers.[160]

Important issues not covered by this section of the Programme include: monitoring of racial or ethnic discrimination at the workplace,[161] access to public jobs,[162] and vocational training, including training on how to establish small private enterprises; however, some retraining is proposed.

---

[158] Interviews conducted in March 2002 for the purpose of this report with representatives of the Roma community in the following villages and towns: Krośnica, Maszkowice, Laskowa, Ochotnica Górna, Limanowa, Nowy Targ; see also Questionnaires for Roma parents.

[159] Even though unemployment among Roma is not statistically monitored, numerous sources acknowledge high rates of Roma unemployment. Estimates by Roma leaders put unemployment at 90 percent in Cracow and Tarnów, and at 99 percent in Nowy Sącz. *Minority Protection 2001*, p. 361.

[160] Programme, pp. 11–13.

[161] Representatives of the Roma community confirm the existence of problems in this area: "I had many difficulties to get a job until I was employed as a Roma assistant," M.C. explained in an interview on 3 March 2002 in Limanowa. "Now everyone is unemployed and there is no chance to find a job," S.L., a Roma man from Ochotnica Górna, stated in an interview on 28 March 2002. Disadvantages experienced by Roma on the labour market are seen by ECRI as frequently attributable to direct discrimination and prejudice as well as to discrimination in other areas, such as in access to education and social inequality. CRI (2000) 34, para. 38.

[162] Given the high unemployment rates among Roma and the general lack of higher education, it can be assumed that Roma representation in the sphere of public employment is equally low. *Minority Protection 2001*, pp. 369–370.

No tasks were implemented in 2001 or in the first half of 2002 due to lack of funding. Because funding has reportedly been allocated for tasks in all areas in 2002, it is expected that some tasks will be implemented in the area of employment in (the second half of) 2002.[163]

Government officials also expect results in the area of employment as a result of activities to improve education levels, due to the belief that the greatest cause of unemployment is lack of education.[164] However, it has also been argued that better education will not guarantee jobs for the Roma and that it is an overstatement to assume education will solve all the problems.[165] The need to discuss what jobs can be made available for the Roma, based upon a needs assessment in a regional context, has also been highlighted;[166] one Roma leader pointed out that the Programme would be better accepted by the local community if it created job opportunities in general and not only for Roma.[167]

3.2.3 Housing and other goods and services

Housing

The Programme notes that the premises inhabited by Roma in Małopolska Province need repairs, that apartments are overcrowded, and that existing housing often does not meet regulations or lacks construction licenses. Roma representatives, too, have repeatedly identified sub-standard housing and living conditions among the biggest problems the Roma community has to cope with.[168] The section on "Living conditions" aims to "improve Roma's living conditions, and accommodation conditions in particular."[169] Specific measures proposed include:

- Repairing existing apartments and buildings;
- Settling outstanding disputes about ownership of land;

---

[163] Written comments of the Head of the Division of National Minorities, Warsaw, 8 August 2002.

[164] OSI Roundtable, Warsaw, July 2002.

[165] OSI Roundtable, Warsaw, July 2002.

[166] OSI Roundtable, Warsaw, July 2002.

[167] Written comments of the leader of the Association of Roma Women, Cracow, July 2002.

[168] "We did not receive any aid for housing, we live in very difficult conditions." Interview with S.L., a Roma man from Ochotnica Górna, 28 March 2002. "The most important thing is to provide us with water supply." Interview with C.W., a local Roma leader from Krośnica, 28 March 2002. See also *Minority Protection 2001*, pp. 357–358.

[169] Programme, p. 15.

- Building low-cost or subsidised apartments;
- Allocating land for construction sites and arranging construction activities (drawing up technical documentation, purchasing construction materials, providing engineering supervision);
- Providing installations for electricity and water supply and connecting Roma settlements to water supply and sewage systems; etc.[170]

It might be worth to add in this context that some Roma representatives call on the Government/local governments to use the services of Roma companies and firms employing Roma workers to carry out constructions and installations.[171]

The Programme does not recognise or address discrimination in access to housing, which Roma leaders allege is a serious problem.[172]

No tasks of the "Living Conditions" component were implemented in 2001 due to withholding of Government funding. The municipality of Tarnów spent PLN 10,625 (€2,796) to renovate flats in 2001; however, this initiative did not target the Roma community specifically.[173] Because funding has reportedly been allocated for tasks in all areas in 2002, it is expected that some tasks will be implemented in this area later in 2002.[174]

---

[170] Programme, pp. 14–15. It is worth noting that some activities planned under this section are in fact part of general commune investments, e.g. connecting Roma settlements to water supply and sewage systems, etc. Some other tasks are aimed at achieving "the financial situation which would make it easier for them to benefit from other areas of the Programme, e.g. Education." Programme, p. 15. These tasks, e.g. special allocations for the purchase of clothing, fuel and medicine, will be briefly analysed together with the issue of social protection in Section 3.2.4.

[171] Written comments of the Chair of the Association of the Roma from Nowy Sącz Region, Laskowa Górna, 27 August 2002.

[172] Allegedly, racial discrimination in access to housing and segregatory practices are a problem. The Association of Roma Women has noted that some practices of local governments could lead to the "cleansing" of Roma from neighbourhoods, citing the resistance of local governments to deal with settling the question of land ownership or to assign grounds for building houses. Also, in the town of Bochnia (which is in Małopolska Province but is not taking part in the Programme), local officials have offered to build social flats if Roma move from the centre to the outskirts of the town. Written comments of the leader of the Association of Roma Women, Cracow, 26 July 2002; see also *Minority Protection 2001*, p. 357.

[173] Written comments of an Official from Tarnów municipality, 29 July 2002.

[174] Written comments of the Head of the Division of National Minorities, Warsaw, 8 August 2002.

Other goods and services

The Programme does not address the issue of equal access of Roma to goods and services.[175] According to the Head of the Division of National Minorities, no reports of such discrimination have been received recently.[176]

3.2.4 Healthcare and other forms of social protection

Healthcare

The Programme notes that the health conditions of Roma living in the foothill areas of Małopolska Province as "extremely poor" and found that "[t]hey suffer from diseases such as viral hepatitis B, asthma, pneumonia, bronchitis, tuberculosis, anaemia, mental handicaps and hyperthyroidism."[177] It also states that serious health problems result from "disastrous living conditions: no water supply and sewage system, no heat insulation in buildings and their appalling technical condition, lack of money for fuel, poor diet, limited access to healthcare services, and no tradition to monitor pregnancy among Roma women [...]."[178]

The "Health" section of the Programme aims to improve health conditions by facilitating access to healthcare services for Roma and by improving hygiene practices, with special attention paid to children and young people. The measures proposed are mostly hygiene-related, including:

- Employing community nurses of Roma origin;
- Promoting vaccination;
- Carrying out summary examinations, and increasing the frequency of medical examinations for Roma women;
- Subsidising medicine;
- Promoting improvement in hygiene.[179]

---

[175] It has been reported that Roma are frequently denied access to public accommodations and are refused credit by some businesses. *Minority Protection 2001*, pp. 359–360.

[176] Written comments of the Head of the Division of National Minorities, Warsaw, 8 August 2002.

[177] Programme, p. 13 (citing report by J. Beesley, Westminster for Democracy, November 1999).

[178] Programme, p. 13.

[179] Programme, pp. 13–14.

The Programme does not consider the possibility of discrimination in access to healthcare services.[180]

This component was likewise not implemented in 2001 due to the withholding of Government funding. Because funding has reportedly been allocated for tasks in all areas in 2002, it is expected that some tasks will be implemented in the area of health in (the second half of) 2002.[181]

Social protection

Social protection is not addressed as a separate issue in the Programme but only indirectly in the section on "Living Conditions," where it is noted that "the overwhelming majority" of the Roma [...] in Małopolska province [are] social welfare clientele" and that "social welfare benefits have so far been granted in the form of cash allowances, which enhances the already strong demanding attitude among Roma."[182] The issue of whether special institutions for providing social assistance to the Roma should be created was raised with the Minister of Internal Affairs.[183]

In general, then, the Programme and the posture of relevant Government officials suggest that the problem is entirely one of socio-economic opportunity and access, rather than allowing the possibility that discrimination plays a role in limiting Roma's level of social protection. The Programme does call for special social welfare programmes that take into account the "specificity" of Roma,[184] yet given the language employed – such as the description of Roma's "demanding attitude"[185] – it is not clear

---

[180] This approach reflects the Government's view that the problem is not one of limited access but that of the failure of Roma to use existing services. OSI Roundtable, Warsaw, July 2002. Roma suffer from inadequate access to healthcare providers, services and insurance; this results in increased vulnerability to diseases and illnesses. Poor living conditions also negatively affect the health situation of Roma. *Minority Protection 2001*, p. 356.

[181] Comments provided by the Head of the Division of National Minorities, Warsaw, 8 August 2002. There are plans, for example, to train a Roma woman to work as a nurse in the city of Limanowa. OSI Roundtable, Warsaw, July 2002.

[182] Programme, p. 14.

[183] The Minister of Internal Affairs was quoted as saying that "[t]his is a community which demands the same aid as settlements of unemployed or poor people. All such communities need our assistance, and it does not matter whether they are Poles or Roma." E. Cichocka, Interview with Krzysztof Janik, Minister of Internal Affairs, in "*Mniejszości się nas boją*" (Minorities are afraid of us), *Gazeta Wyborcza*, 8 March 2002, p. 18.

[184] "Roma are a special group of social welfare beneficiaries due to their specific culture. Therefore, standard measures aiming to stimulate their psychosocial activity fail to bring desirable outcomes. Roma should be covered by special social welfare schemes which take into account their specificity." Programme, p. 14.

[185] Programme, p. 3.

that specificity represents a fully good-faith effort to make meaningful and responsive accommodations.

Measures related to social protection include:

- Granting social benefits;
- Mobilising the Roma community in order to ensure its psychological and social independence through social work and guidance;
- Granting specific-purpose and periodical allowances for the purchase of clothes, medicines, fuel;
- Improving the skills of social workers.[186]

None of these measures were implemented in 2001 due to lack of funding.

3.2.5 The criminal justice system

Equal access to the criminal justice system is not addressed in the Programme. Due to the limited research available as to whether Roma are discriminated against in the criminal justice system, it would be useful to further investigate this question.

3.3 Protection from Racially Motivated Violence

Racially motivated violence is one of the biggest problems faced by the Roma community in Poland; both international NGOs and Roma representatives have also identified racially motivated violence as a serious problem.[187] However, official acknowledgement of and response to this problem has been insufficient. According to one Roma representative, "even in cases of serious attacks, Roma do not mention the names of perpetrators to the police because they are afraid and they fear for their own and their children's safety."[188] Officials of the Division of National Minorities acknowledge that the statistical data gathered by the police do not show racially

---

[186] Programme, p. 15.

[187] See *Minority Protection 2001*, pp. 362–364.

[188] Interviews with: the leader of the Social and Cultural Association of the Roma in Poland, Tarnów, 3 April 2002; the leader of the Association of the Roma in Cracow/Nowa Huta, 5 April 2002; and the leader of the Association of the Roma in Nowy Sącz Region, Laskowa Górna, 27 March 2002.

motivated violence against Roma as a problem because there is no indication of the ethnicity or race of victims.[189]

There are no special governmental programmes to combat racially motivated violence. Racially motivated violence is prohibited by the Penal Code,[190] although there are no disciplinary regulations concerning racially motivated abuse by law enforcement personnel. Hate speech is prohibited by the Polish Constitution[191] and the Penal Code.[192] Since 2000, the Division of National Minorities has requested regular reports from Police Headquarters in Warsaw on racially motivated crime in Poland; since 2001, monthly reports must be prepared.

The Programme acknowledges the problem of racially motivated violence, but little is proposed to improve protection against racially motivated crime or to raise awareness of channels for complaint. While the Programme recognises that Roma are the minority most exposed to racist attacks in Poland,[193] it also states that, according to General Police Headquarters, Roma are not frequent victims of crimes, and that police react rapidly when crimes are committed against Roma.[194] The Programme does not deal directly with police abuse, stating rather that Roma have not submitted official complaints about the conduct of police officers.[195] Roma are depicted as being responsible to a certain degree for the fact that racially motivated crimes are rarely investigated. The Programme asserts that Roma are reluctant to cooperate with the police,[196] and refers to the types of crimes Roma commit, despite the fact that no official data on the ethnicity of perpetrators are supposed to be kept[197] – which tends to suggest an attitude that disregards the continuing salience of, and indeed to some degree partakes in, discriminatory attitudes towards Roma in the majority population.

---

[189] Interview with officials of the Division of National Minorities, Warsaw, 22 March 2002.

[190] Penal Code, Art. 119, *Official Gazette,* No. 88, item 553, 6 June 1997.

[191] Constitution of the Republic of Poland (Art. 13), *Official Gazette,* No. 78, item 483, 2 April 1997.

[192] Penal Code (Arts. 256, 257 and 119), *Official Gazette,* No. 88, item 553, 6 June 1997.

[193] Programme, p. 15.

[194] Programme, p. 15.

[195] Programme, p. 15.

[196] "Some Roma communities complain that the Police are sluggish in reacting to racist attacks, they do not however, submit official complaints about the conduct of individual officers. An important factor which makes it more difficult to detect perpetrators is the reluctance among Roma themselves to cooperate with the Police." Programme, pp. 15–16.

[197] "Even though the Police does not keep any detailed registers of crime perpetrators or victims with respect to their ethnic origin, the experience gathered shows that offences or crimes most often committed by Roma are thefts, thefts with burglary, and robberies." Programme, p. 16.

The Programme seeks to "improve security by enhancing the sensitivity of the Police to racist crimes and taking action to change the conviction that such acts are not socially harmful."[198] Another stated objective is "to help Roma see the necessity for cooperation with the Police in combating crime and to build greater confidence in law enforcement agencies."[199] Specific measures proposed in Programme include:

- Training police officers working in areas inhabited by Roma;[200]
- Preventing crimes committed on ethnic grounds and ensuring rapid reactions to such crimes; providing support for the victims;
- Patrolling areas inhabited by Roma;
- Recruiting persons of Roma origin in the police;
- Ensuring cooperation and exchange of information between the Police and representatives of the Roma community;
- Changing the attitude of Roma so that they see the necessity of cooperating with the Police in order to punish perpetrators of crimes against Roma, etc.[201]

No task from this component was implemented in 2001 with central Government funding. However, the prevention department of the Cracow Police implemented a few initiatives to facilitate cooperation between the police and Roma. One Roma woman is being trained as a police officer in the city of Nowy Sącz; a number of Roma are also due to be trained in Tarnów.[202] While, according to one Government official, the increased presence of Roma police officers should lead to an improvement in the situation, some Roma representatives have expressed doubts that the hiring of Roma will result in improved protection from racially motivated violence.[203]

3.4 Promotion of Minority Rights

Minority rights are likewise not addressed in any comprehensive fashion. The Programme states that the Roma community is treated as a national and ethnic minority, and as such is entitled to receive full protection and assistance from the State in accordance with

---

[198] Programme, p. 16.
[199] Programme, p. 16.
[200] Timetable for Realisation and Financing, p. 21.
[201] Programme, pp. 16–17.
[202] OSI Roundtable, Warsaw, July 2002.
[203] OSI Roundtable, Warsaw, July 2002.

international agreements and with national legislation, including the Constitution.[204] A Law on National and Ethnic Minorities has been in preparation since 1998.[205]

The Programme emphasises that Roma must be enabled to preserve their own cultural distinctness and that preserving the "positive elements of the Roma culture may help this community to find its place in the [sic] contemporary Poland."[206] Thus, it proposes to protect and promote the Roma identity and culture by supporting initiatives in the fields of education and culture.

A separate section is devoted to increasing awareness within the majority population about the Roma community as well as the Roma community's own awareness about the changes taking place in Poland. The Programme identifies the problem that "[…] Polish society has too little knowledge about the situation of Roma […]". It also notes that relations between Roma and non-Roma in Poland are largely based on stereotypes.[207]

Measures proposed include:

- Promoting publications about Roma;
- Organising a Polish-Roma camp with an integration programme;
- Broadcasting regular programmes about Roma in local and national media.[208]

---

[204] Programme, pp. 16–17, 4. The 1997 Polish Constitution contains a provision ensuring citizens belonging to ethnic and national minorities the right to "maintain and develop their own language, customs, traditions and culture." (Art. 35). Provisions concerning national minorities are dispersed in Polish legislation, including the Electoral Law to the Sejm of the Republic of Poland and the Senate of the Republic of Poland (12 April 2001), the Act on Radio and Television Broadcasting (29 December 1992), and provisions guaranteeing education in the mother tongue (See Section 3.4.1). Poland finally submitted its report on implementation of the Framework Convention for the Protection of National Minorities (FCNM) (entered into force 1 April 2001) on 10 July 2002; see Report submitted by Poland Pursuant to Article 25, Paragraph 1, of the Framework Convention for the Protection of National Minorities, at <http://www.humanrights.coe.int/minorities/Eng/FrameworkConvention/StateReports/2002/Poland%20state%20report.doc>, (accessed 14 October 2002); see also the "shadow report" by S. Łodziński, *The Protection of National Minorities in Poland*, Helsinki Foundation for Human Rights, Warsaw, September 1999, <http://www.minelres.lv/reports/poland/poland_NGO.htm>, (accessed 26 August 2002).

[205] A draft Law on National and Ethnic Minorities was developed by the Sejm Committee on National and Ethnic Minorities and submitted to the Sejm in 1998. *Minority Protection 2001*, p. 365.

[206] Programme, p. 7.

[207] Programme, p. 18; see Sections 3.4.3 and 3.4.4 for more on projects planned in this area.

[208] Programme, p. 19.

However, none of these measures has received funding from the Government yet. More seriously, no measures are proposed to promote other, core minority rights, such as effective participation in public life or support for minority language media.

Government officials have emphasised that the Programme is not necessarily intended to protect Roma rights as these are protected by the Constitution.[209] Such an attitude, together with the lack of any comprehensive measures addressing minority rights, constitutes an unnecessarily narrow reading of the Programme's proper mandate, and one that – when considered in the context of the seemingly moribund deliberations on the draft Law on National and Ethnic Minorities – suggests an insufficient commitment to truly thorough-going reform.

3.4.1 Education

The Programme's education section does not include any measures to promote the teaching of the Romani language or its use in the educational system. State-funded instruction of, or in, the Romani language is theoretically possible according to Polish legislation which provides for education in the mother tongue,[210] but it is not available on the territory covered by the Programme. There are no textbooks in the Romani language; textbooks for other national minorities are systematically published and financed by the Ministry of Education.[211]

While it is generally accepted that the Romani language is a fundamental component of Roma identity and that Roma, in general, want to preserve their specific language and culture, there is a need to assess the level of demand for instruction of, and in, the

---

[209] Interview with an official from the Division of National Minorities, Warsaw, 22 March 2002.

[210] See Act on the Educational System (7 September 1991), Art. 13, *Official Gazette* 96.67.329, item 425, the Regulation of the Minister of National Education of 24 March 1992 on the organisation of the education system enabling students who belong to national minorities to sustain the feeling of national, ethnic and linguistic identity (*Official Gazette*, No. 34, item 150), and the Regulation of the Minister of National Education (21 March 2001, as later amended), on the rules of grading, classifying and promoting of students and learners and of conducting exams and tests in state schools (*Official Gazette*, No. 29, item 323). These measures provide for instruction in the mother tongue at the primary level if the child's parents so wish. A minimum of seven pupils is needed to constitute a State-funded class with a minority language as the language of instruction.

[211] In 2002, for instance, it plans to publish three textbooks for the Belarussian minority, three textbooks for the Slovak minority, and five textbooks for the Ukrainian minority. Minutes of the Fifth Session of the Education Sub-section of the Inter-Sector Task Force, 4 October 2001, pp. 5–6.

Romani language.²¹² The Roma community should be informed that a right to be taught in their mother tongue exists, and the option of education in the mother tongue should be offered.²¹³

The Programme deals briefly with the need to train teachers and to include information on the Roma culture in mainstream schools. Thus, it states that supporting teachers working with Roma children "should have access to literature on Gypsy issues as well as to assistance of intercultural methodologists […]."²¹⁴ Reportedly, some teachers are being trained in such matters.²¹⁵ However, there are no plans to produce new textbooks with information on Roma history and culture for use in Polish schools.²¹⁶

The Programme also proposes to organise "classes devoted to Roma culture and traditions" and "education and integration classes for children and young people to promote tolerance and to support Roma's adaptation in a new environment."²¹⁷ No measures to this effect were included in the Timetable for Realisation and Financing, suggesting that they play a rather marginal role.

The section on "Knowledge in and about the Roma Community" does not propose any measures in the area of education.

3.4.2 Language

The Programme makes no provision for promoting the use of the Romani language on public signs or in communication with public authorities.

Polish is the official language (Constitution, Art. 27). Language issues are regulated, *inter alia*, by the Act on the Polish Language (7 October 1999).²¹⁸ The right of speakers of foreign languages to be provided with a translation in courts is also guaranteed.²¹⁹ In practice, Romanes is hardly ever used in official contacts.

---

[212] OSI Roundtable, Warsaw, July 2002.
[213] OSI Roundtable, Warsaw, July 2002.
[214] Programme, p. 10.
[215] OSI Roundtable, Warsaw, July 2002.
[216] OSI Roundtable, Warsaw, July 2002.
[217] Programme, p. 11.
[218] *Official Gazette,* No. 90, item 999, 7 October 1999.
[219] See the Code of Administrative Procedure (14 June 1960), Art. 69; the Code of Criminal Procedure (6 June 1997), Art. 72; and the Code of Civil Procedure (17 November 1964), Art. 265.

The draft Law on National and Ethnic Minorities contains a section on the use of minority languages and would grant, *inter alia*, the right to freely use one's mother tongue in private and public affairs; the right to use one's name as it is spelled and pronounced in a minority language; and the right to display in the minority language information of a private nature visible to the public.[220] Poland has not signed the European Charter for Regional or Minority Languages.

3.4.3 Participation in public life

The Programme's objectives include that of achieving the full participation of Roma in the life of civil society.[221] However, no concrete means of promoting the participation of Roma in public life are proposed.

One of the problems identified in the section on "Knowledge in and About the Roma Community" is that "[…] Roma […] can hardly find their way in the contemporary realities of a civic society."[222] The isolation of the Bergitka Roma in particular is noted, as is the fact that "[…] living in social isolation which have been imposed on and chosen by them, Roma are distrustful and contemptuous of 'outsiders' […]".[223] The Programme thus proposes a series of tasks to raise the awareness of Roma of the changes taking place in Poland, as a complement to other tasks proposed in the same section to promote the tolerance and openness of the majority population towards Roma. None of these have been implemented yet. However, efforts to consult Roma representatives when drafting the Programme can be considered as a first positive step to promote the participation of minorities in policies affecting them.

There are no formal mechanisms to enable or ensure the participation of Roma in decision-making bodies at the local, regional and national levels. However, the leaders of the Roma community are regularly consulted by central and local Government officials.[224]

---

[220] S. Łodziński, *The Protection of National Minorities in Poland*, Article 4.

[221] Programme, p. 7.

[222] Programme, p. 18.

[223] Programme, p. 18.

[224] Interviews with: the leader of the Association of the Roma in Nowy Sącz Region, Laskowa Górna, 27 March 2002; the leader of the Social and Cultural Association of the Roma in Poland, Tarnów, 3 April 2002; and the leader of the Association of the Roma in Cracow, Cracow/Nowa Huta, 5 April 2002.

Participation in elections is provided for by the Act on Electoral Law to the Sejm of the Republic of Poland and the Senate of the Republic of Poland (12 April 2001);[225] the Roma minority, however, has not yet benefited from this regulation as Roma have not yet formed their own election committee.

Measures proposed in the Programme include establishing posts of local plenipotentiary for the Roma community and organising a "mobile Citizen Consultancy Centre[.]"[226] This component of the Programme was not implemented in 2001 due to the withholding of Government funding. However, three plenipotentiaries of Roma origin were appointed in 2000–2001.[227]

The Programme proposes no measures to directly increase the share of Roma in particular areas of public life. Certain proposed activities relating to health and security might lead to an increase in the share of Roma in public work places (such as activities to recruit persons of Roma origin for the police forces and as community nurses);[228] it is doubtful, however, that they will have a significant impact on the overall representation of Roma in these areas. Furthermore, Roma's generally low levels of secondary education present an obstacle to hiring for various positions.[229]

---

[225] *Official Gazette*, No. 46, item 499; Art. 134 exempts election committees of registered organisations of national minorities from the requirement that they obtain at least five percent of the total number of votes validly cast nation-wide in order to be considered in the process of allocating seats between constituency lists of candidates for MPs. See also S. Łodziński, "The Protection of National Minorities in Poland: Law and Practice after 1989," in *Law and Practice of Central European Countries in the Field of National Minorities Protection After 1989*, edited by Jerzy Kranz, Centre for International Relations, Warsaw, 1998; A. Szmyt, "Representation-Election-Democracy," in *The Principles of Basic Institutions of the System of Government in Poland*, Sejm Publishing Office, Warsaw, 1999, pp. 119–133.

[226] Programme, p. 19.

[227] A Plenipotentiary for the Roma Community in Nowy Sącz was appointed in 2000; the second plenipotentiary represents the Roma of Limanowa district. Both plenipotentiaries were appointed in consultation with the Roma community and local governments but are paid by the Ministry of Internal Affairs. A third plenipotentiary, from Tarnów, has recently resigned.

[228] Programme, p. 7. There are no official data on the number of Roma employed in the civil service, police, or judicial system.

[229] It has been noted that, in legal terms, there is equal access but that the lack of secondary education makes it difficult to employ Roma as nurses, police officers, etc. OSI Roundtable, Warsaw, July 2002.

3.4.4 Media

The Programme does not contain a separate section on the media to support the development of Romani-language media or programmes prepared by Roma themselves.[230] However, it recognises the importance of the media in the process of improving the image of Roma in Polish society and includes several projects to broadcast programmes about the Roma in the local and national media, such as:

- A regular television programme devoted to the Roma community;[231]
- Education through the media;[232]
- Cyclic broadcasting in local media.[233]

Media-related projects proposed in the Programme were not implemented in 2001 due to the withholding of Government funds. There have nevertheless been some initiatives in the field of media. Since February 2002, the third channel of Polish Television has broadcast "*Klimaty Etniczne*" (Ethnic Climates), devoted to national and ethnic minorities, including irregular broadcasts of reports in the Romani language.[234]

Starting in September 2002, the Cracow branch of Polish Television plans to broadcast short, monthly reports in the Romani language which will be produced in cooperation with young Roma journalists. The news reports will be presented within the framework of the programme "*U siebie*" (At home) (a programme devoted minorities which has been broadcast since 1991, including regular broadcasts concerning the Roma). These reports are to be partially subsidised by funds from the Programme for 2002.[235]

---

[230] The Romani language can be heard only very rarely on Polish State Television. For example, it can be heard very rarely in the programme "*Sami o sobie*" (About ourselves) produced by the regional branch of Polish Television in Białystok (Eastern Poland). There are no radio broadcasts in the Romani language. See also *Minority Protection 2001*, pp. 370–371.

[231] Timetable for Realisation and Financing, "Culture," p. 21.

[232] Timetable for Realisation and Financing, "Knowledge in and about the Roma Community," p. 23.

[233] This is a broadcast which is repeated at certain intervals within a particular television or radio programme. Timetable for Realisation and Financing, Knowledge in and About the Roma Community," p. 24.

[234] Information provided by the Editor of "*Klimaty Etniczne*," Polish Television, Warsaw, July 2002.

[235] OSI Roundtable, Warsaw, July 2002.

The Division of National Minority Cultures in the Ministry of Culture supports two periodicals for the Roma community, although funding has been decreasing.[236]

3.4.5 Culture

The Programme aims to preserve and support the Roma culture through activities designed to present this culture to wide circles of society; it also seeks to promote tolerance and openness towards other cultures among Roma and other communities.[237] According to the Ministry of Culture's Department of National Minority Cultures, Roma cultural initiatives ought to play a small role given the community's difficult socio-economic situation.[238] On the other hand, Roma leaders emphasise the importance of protecting and promoting their culture and identity amongst the majority society.[239]

The Programme proposes to:

- Provide support for existing musical bands and for establishing new bands;
- Organise reviews of Roma artistic works;
- Provide support for a regular television programme devoted to the Roma community;
- Support young people in developing their artistic talents;
- Prepare historical documentation covering the history of Roma in Małopolska;
- Finance publications;
- Establish a House of Roma Culture in Tarnów;
- Support an International Memory Camp of the Roma;
- Provide support for cultural and sporting events organised by the Roma community.[240]

---

[236] These are: *Rrom p-o drom* (a monthly in both the Romani and Polish languages), and *Pheniben-Dialog* (a quarterly in Polish mainly). See *Minority Protection 2001*, p. 371.

[237] Programme, p. 18.

[238] "A big Roma festival does not have any meaning for the poor Roma, because they do not have the financial means to come to see it." *The Roma in 2000 and 2001*, internal document of the Department of National Minority Cultures, Ministry of Culture, 22 March 2002.

[239] One Roma leader noted that "by maintaining our culture, we can show ourselves to the majority from a positive aspect." Interview with the leader of the Association of the Roma in Nowy Sącz Region, Laskowa Górna, 27 March 2002. Another Roma leader suggested opening a "World Centre of Promotion and Protection of the Roma Culture" in Tarnów, but there were no funds. Interview with the leader of the Social and Cultural Association of the Roma in Poland, Tarnów, 3 April 2002.

[240] Programme, p. 18.

According to one expert, the Programme planned for cultural projects on a scale beyond what was realistic.[241]

Since no Government funds were appointed specifically to initiatives outlined in the "Culture" section of the Programme in 2001, the only cultural initiatives of Roma funded by the Government were those supported by the Department of National Minority Cultures, as well as small projects foreseen under the Programme but exclusively supported by local government units.[242]

Projects supported by the Ministry of Culture

While the Department of National Minority Cultures does not participate directly in the Programme, the cultural projects it administers in fact support the objectives of the Programme.[243] The total amount of funds allocated to Roma cultural activities by the Ministry of Culture increased to PLN 569,100 (€149,763) in 2001, compared with PLN 391,000 (€102,895) in 2000; all of these projects were proposed by the Roma community and, in most cases, Roma organisations also implemented them.[244]

Projects of local government units

The city of Tarnów supported some Programme projects in the area of culture with its own resources, financing the modernisation of an exhibition of the Ethnographic Museum in Tarnów and publishing booklets for Roma children.[245] However, a planned House of Roma Culture was not established due to lack of funding. In Tarnów, projects have also been proposed for 2002 (including a festival for Roma children and youth); it is not clear yet whether Government funding will be forthcoming.[246]

---

[241] The expert also noted that Roma associations have limited capacity to realise projects proposed under the Programme. Interview with the Director of the Ethnographic Museum in Tarnów, Tarnów, 20 March 2002.

[242] Interview with an official of the Department of National Minority Cultures, Ministry of Culture, Warsaw, 22 March 2002.

[243] Interview with the Director of the Ethnographic Museum in Tarnów, Tarnów, 20 March 2002.

[244] "The proposals should come from the minority itself, otherwise we would not finance them." *The Roma in 2000 and 2001*, internal document of the Department of National Minority Cultures, Ministry of Culture, Warsaw, 22 March 2002.

[245] "We did not receive any money from the Government, but the amount of money planned to be allocated to the Roma community from the municipal budget was used for this purpose." Interview with the Head of the Division of Culture, Tarnów municipal office, Tarnów, 20 March 2002.

[246] Interview with the Head of the Division of Culture, Tarnów municipal office, Tarnów, 20 March 2002.

4. Evaluation

The Programme is the first comprehensive governmental initiative to improve the situation of a minority group in Poland. It is intended as a long-term effort, with education emphasised as key in achieving progress in other areas.

Although a welcome initiative, the Programme seems to incorporate social attitudes and assumptions that limit its potential for positive change. Although for the most part its substantive provisions reflect the priorities of the Roma community, it fails to recognise the seriousness of indirect social discrimination, assuming rather that formal guarantees of equal access will be sufficient. Moreover, it makes reference on several occasions to the Roma's supposed own large share of responsibility for the difficult situation which "they have found themselves in" as well as to their supposedly "demanding attitude."[247] These omissions and postures suggest an incomplete commitment to reform, not only in economic and legal terms, but in the broader social context that meaningful improvement in the situation of the Roma will require. The problems of Roma in Poland are not merely economic or social; they are inextricably tied up in issues of identity recognition, community relations, and embedded discriminatory attitudes; the Programme does not confront or contemplate this reality.

More in-depth research into the marginalisation of Roma due to complex social practices is urgently needed, as the successful implementation of the Programme depends to a great extent on the assumptions upon which it operates. Monitoring of racial or ethnic discrimination and intolerance towards Roma is also needed. While this would not in itself improve the situation of Roma, it would make it easier to understand and identify the most serious problems.[248] Positive action is also needed to rectify the under-representation of Roma in various spheres; here, too, monitoring is necessary to identify the nature and severity of the problem in specific fields.

Criticism is also warranted by limitations on the scope of the Programme's activities. Without doubt, limited funds were a constraining factor on the selection of priorities. It should be noted, nevertheless, that some areas have been defined in an unnecessarily narrow fashion, while others – such as discrimination and positive minority rights – have been left out. This will limit the effectiveness of the Government's efforts in the long run.

As a practical matter, the withholding of the special purpose reserve was the most significant obstacle to implementation of the Programme in 2001. Only a limited number of tasks were therefore realised in the first year. Although the Ministry of

---

[247] Programme, pp. 7, 3.
[248] See e.g. European Parliament, *EU Anti-Discrimination Policy: From Equal Opportunities Between Women and Men to Combating Racism,* Public Liberties Series, LIBE 102 EN, 02, Brussels, 1998.

Education's parallel funding efforts did allow core education projects to proceed, those funds were not nearly sufficient to make up the shortfall.

Furthermore, by confining implementation to education, the Programme has sacrificed the benefit from one of its most valuable aspects – its comprehensive approach.[249] The education projects that have been realised in 2001 have been very successful – notably the programmes for Roma teacher's assistants and compensatory classes – and have been widely welcomed by Roma parents, leaders and school directors. At the same time, there has been a great sense of disappointment that other critical areas, such as unemployment, housing and healthcare, were neglected.[250]

Mechanisms for Programme administration, monitoring and evaluation seem to be operating, although the limited scale of implementation thus far makes it difficult to assess their effectiveness. Representatives of the Roma community have noted that successful communication with Government officials at the central level is not always matched at the local level. It might therefore be desirable to improve the coordination of the Programme between these two levels as well as to strengthen monitoring of projects, including local contributions, so that they are fully realised and according to schedule. Incentives to encourage the participation of local governments should also be considered.

Local Roma communities were consulted in a process of designing the Programme and enthusiastically welcomed its launch. They have also been involved in implementation, monitoring and evaluation, albeit to a limited degree. Later, however, significant criticism was raised due to the limited scale of implementation and the withholding of Government funds. It is therefore essential that the Programme be realised according to plan in 2002 and beyond in order to boost its credibility in the eyes of the local Roma communities.[251]

There is also a strong need to establish a body for the systematic participation of Roma representatives, especially at the local level. As one Roma representative has pointed

---

[249] "If someone has no work, no place to live, what use does he have from a book his child has received?" Interview with a representative of the Social and Cultural Association of the Roma in Poland, Tarnów, 3 April 2002.

[250] According to a local Roma leader, results would have been more visible had the tasks proposed in other fields been implemented simultaneously. He was also very concerned by the lack of funds, claiming that 2002 would be even worse in this respect than 2001. Interview with a representative of the Social and Cultural Association of the Roma in Poland, Tarnów, 3 April 2002.

[251] Here, a comment on the need for well-defined Government policy concerning the Roma in Poland should be noted: "In the past, effectiveness was measured by the amount of funds earmarked for the Roma. We hope now that the Programme will bring a well-defined policy of the state vis-à-vis Roma, which will incorporate a sustainable approach. OSI Roundtable, Warsaw, July 2002.

out, "[t]he Małopolska Programme should be implemented with the full participation of the Roma community, not only through consultation, but also in decision-making. It is also important to improve the mechanism for distributing funds so that they reach the Roma community and respond to its needs, without having to rely on the preferences and evaluation of local administration."[252]

Both national and regional media generally support the idea of the Programme, although they have occasionally criticised the inadequacy of the funding. However, media reports about the money to be allocated under the Programme resulted in hostile reactions in some local majority communities. Isolated efforts to explain the need for the measures of the Programme to the majority have yielded very positive results, highlighting the importance of promoting the Programme and its goals to the local communities; in this connection, more efforts are also needed to provide information about ongoing and planned activities as well as the funding allocated.

In conclusion, while the Government has demonstrated its willingness to begin addressing the problems of the Roma community in Małopolska Province, there is still much to be done to move beyond a phase of good intentions and towards full and meaningful implementation that creates the conditions for real change. Adequate funding is needed to ensure that the Programme can be implemented in its intended scope, and it is essential that measures be implemented also in areas other than education if significant results are to be obtained. Roma organisations and beneficiaries should be involved more systematically in the implementation, monitoring and evaluation of the Programme. As preparations seem to have begun for a programme covering the whole Roma population of Poland, it is essential that this new programme be more comprehensive, embracing systematic and structural solutions, including measures for positive action to remedy the under-representation of Roma in various walks of life and to meet the objective of ensuring the effective participation of Roma in society and its governance. The Programme and its nation-wide successor represent an opportunity for Polish society, not only to adopt comprehensive policies of reform, but to engage in a needed debate on the relationship of the majority and minority populations it contains.

---

[252] Written comments of the Chair of the Association of the Roma in Nowy Sącz Region, Laskowa Górna, 27 August 2002.

5. Recommendations

To the Government

- Acknowledge that the ultimate success of the Programme and similar reform efforts will require commitment to change, not only in economic or social policy, but in the broader social context in which those policies are embedded. Recognise the continuing salience of deeply held social attitudes in limiting the participation and flourishing of the Roma communities.

- Review the content, scope, and underlying premises of the Programme to ensure that it incorporates approaches consistent with a genuine and thorough-going commitment to confront discriminatory and exclusionary social attitudes.

- Develop a more balanced and appropriate assessment of the problems faced by Roma, relying on in-depth empirical research.

- Ensure that implementation of the Programme is comprehensive, rather than restricted to a single field such as education.

- Expand the scope of the Programme to those areas the current Programme fails to address, including:

  - monitoring of racial or ethnic discrimination and xenophobia against Roma;

  - educating the society at large not only about Roma culture but also about forms of cultural dominance and discrimination;

  - instituting measures to rectify the presumed under-representation of Roma among school teachers, local government officials, nurses, police, etc;

  - supporting the access of Roma to public institutions, including public media;

  - supporting the access of Roma to higher and university-level education;

  - introducing courses on Roma culture and history in school curricula;

  - instituting vocational guidance and training, including support for establishing small private enterprises;

  - establishing effective systems for preventing racially motivated violence.

- Develop systematic and structural solutions for the problems confronting the Roma (such as capacity building and the development of institutional mechanisms) rather than simply providing them with goods.

- Strengthen coordination and cooperation between the national Government and local governing units in order to improve implementation.

- Incorporate stronger incentives for local actors involved in realising projects so that a greater number participate in implementation of the Programme.

- Design Programme mechanisms that ensure an even greater involvement of Roma organisations and beneficiaries in implementation and evaluation.

- Local and central government units responsible for Programme implementation should also seek to better inform their local constituencies, both Roma and non-Roma, about the rationale and provisions of the Programme, so as to increase public understanding and support for individual projects.

Minority Protection in Romania

AN ASSESSMENT OF THE STRATEGY OF THE GOVERNMENT
OF ROMANIA FOR IMPROVING THE CONDITION OF ROMA.

Table of Contents

1. Executive Summary 478

2. The Government Programme –
   Background 482
   2.1   Background to Present Programme 482
   2.2   The Programme – Process 482
   2.3   The Programme – Content 484
   2.4   The Programme – Administration/
         Implementation/Evaluation 485
         Central Government bodies 486
         County – Prefecture bodies 489
         Local bodies 490
         Participation from civil society 491
   2.5   The Programme and the Public 493
   2.6   The Programme and the EU 494

3. The Government Programme –
   Implementation 497
   3.1   Stated Objectives of the Programme 497
   3.2   The Government Programme
         and Discrimination 498
         3.2.1   Education 501
         3.2.2   Employment 503
         3.2.3   Housing and
                 other goods and services 506
         3.2.4   Healthcare and other forms
                 of social protection 509
                 Social benefits 511
         3.2.5   The criminal justice system 513

3.3	Protection from Racially Motivated Violence		513
3.4	Promotion of Minority Rights		515
	3.4.1	Language	516
	3.4.2	Education	517
	3.4.3	Participation in public life	518
	3.4.4	Media	520
	3.4.5	Culture	522

4. Evaluation 523

5. Recommendations 524

1. EXECUTIVE SUMMARY

The Romanian Government's approach to improving the situation of Roma is set forth in the "Strategy of the Government of Romania for Improving the Roma Condition" (hereafter, the "Government Strategy"), adopted in April 2001.

The Government Strategy sets forth a detailed programme to address the situation of the Roma, incorporating measures at the central, provincial, and local government levels. It is notable for its forthright approach to combating discrimination, and in the extent to which it provides for Roma representation at the different levels of Government. With the appointment of the National Council for Combating Discrimination in July 2002, its structural measures have largely been implemented. However, measures that would tangibly improve conditions in Roma communities have not yet been realised. The number of projects the Government has carried out to implement the practical provisions of the Strategy remains very low; Phare funding has been the primary source of support, as no State budget resources were allocated directly to Strategy implementation in 2002.

Collaboration between the Government and NGOs, as well as cooperation among NGOs themselves, has dissipated since the Strategy was adopted, partially due to concerns that the Government has chosen to work almost exclusively with a single politically active organisation rather than consulting with a broader range of Roma representatives and experts. The fundamental problems of low levels of formal education, high unemployment, and racially motivated violence have not been sufficiently addressed by the Strategy to date.

Background

The "Strategy for the Improvement of the Roma Condition" is the first governmental initiative to take a comprehensive approach to addressing the problems facing the Roma minority. A project to develop a programme addressing the situation of Roma was first undertaken in 1998, with Phare support. During this phase, considerable consultations were held with Roma organisations, in particular the coalition of NGOs known as the Working Group of Roma Associations. Shortly before the end of its mandate in December 2000, the Government approved a memorandum on a strategic framework. The new Government took up the issue in March 2001, and acting on the orders of the Prime Minister, quickly developed and published the present Strategy in May 2001.[1]

---

[1] Government Decision Number 430/Aprilie/2001, 25 April 2001, published in the Official Gazette number 252, 16 May 2001.

Administration

The Joint Committee for Monitoring and Implementation is responsible for organisation, coordination, and monitoring of Strategy implementation; it is comprised of State Secretaries representing the ministries responsible for implementing the Strategy and leaders of Roma NGOs. As of July 2002 the Joint Committee had met only six times, in most cases with the participation of lower-level staff delegated by the State Secretaries of each ministry.[2] The National Office for Roma, under the Ministry of Public Information's Department for Inter-Ethnic Relations, is the executive body of the Joint Committee.[3]

Each ministry involved in implementing the Strategy is also to form its own Commission on Roma; 16 have nominally been established to date, but many are inactive.[4] The level of funding for projects is left to the discretion of the individual ministries, as the Strategy does not provide for any centralised accounting or budget oversight mechanism. There are no mechanisms for sanctioning ministries that fail to accomplish the activities assigned to them under the Strategy.

The Strategy also gives substantial responsibilities to local authorities. Bureaux for Roma have been established in each county; each Bureau has at least on Roma staff member. Roma experts are to be appointed within mayors' offices as well, although financial constraints have limited implementation of this measure to date. These structural measures constitute an important aspect of the Strategy: increasing Roma participation in decision-making. However, realisation of these measures has been uneven and concerns that the appointment process has been politicised have prevented those appointed from fulfilling the active role envisioned by the Strategy.

EU support

Phare funding has been essential to the Government Strategy, from the EU's support for the drafting process in 1998 to the implementation of pilot projects testing the

---

[2] Ministry of Public Information, "Report on the Status of Implementation of the Strategy for Improvement of the Condition of Roma – April 2002," p. 2, (hereafter, "Ministry of Public Information, *Report on the Status of Implementation*"). See <http://www.publicinfo.ro/ENGLEZA.html>, (accessed 28 September 2002).

[3] Order of the Ministry of Public Information no. 259/02; see also, Government Strategy, Chapter VIII, point 1.

[4] OSI Round Table, Bucharest, June 2002. *Explanatory note: the Open Society Institute held a roundtable meeting in Bucharest in June 2002 to invite critique of a draft version of this report. Experts present included representatives of the Government, Roma groups, and non-governmental organisations.*

Strategy principles in 2001 and beyond.[5] Although some organisations have expressed dissatisfaction with the rigidity of Phare application procedures, EU support has made possible many projects addressing the needs of the Roma community. The EU's policy of funding projects under the Strategy directly supports the recommendations of its Regular Reports, in which the Commission has praised the Government for adopting the Strategy, but has noted that its measures must be comprehensively implemented, with special attention to eliminating discrimination.

Programme content and implementation

The Government Strategy sets out broad directives in its chapter on Lines of Action, and details 123 more specific activities and projects in the Master Plan of Action. These activities address both prevention of discrimination and promotion of minority rights and are quite comprehensive. However, the programme fails to explicitly address racially motivated violence, and in particular police brutality, which both domestic and international observers have identified as a serious problem.

Measures to prevent discrimination were enhanced by the adoption of Law 48/2002 on the elimination of all forms of discrimination. The Law provides for a National Council to Combat Discrimination, which was appointed only at the end of July 2002 and does not include any Roma members. Successful results in the fight against discrimination have been achieved in the education sphere, where Government-mandated affirmative action measures have increased the number of Roma university students and graduates. Measures to improve access to healthcare through the introduction of community mediators have also shown promise. However, the overall implementation of substantive anti-discrimination projects remains very low, corresponding to the level of resources the Government has allocated. Projects selected under the EU's Phare Partnership Fund for Roma, particularly in the employment sphere, have shown promise, and civil society programmes have also played an important role in addressing inequalities in several spheres.

The Government's promotion of minority rights has again been most effective in the sphere of education, where opportunities for Romani language education have been expanded considerably in the past several years. Efforts to increase Roma representation in all levels of Government have not met expectations, as the offices created have not been adequately integrated into existing structures or delegated responsibilities that would make the appointments meaningful. Moreover, the Government's partnership with a single Roma organisation, the Roma Social Democrat Party, has raised concerns about the marginalisation and exclusion of other organisations.

---

[5] See R.W. Murray, *Testing the Strategy*, Mede European Consultancy, October 2001. See <http://www.rroma.ro/download/testing_strategy.pdf>, (accessed 2 October 2002).

Conclusions

The Government Strategy represents an important step towards greater inclusion of Roma in all spheres of Romanian society. Roma organisations contributed to drafting the programme and mechanisms for their continuous input are incorporated into its provisions The Strategy addresses most spheres where problems have been identified by domestic and international monitors, with the exception of racially motivated violence and violence against Roma by law enforcement officials.

Nevertheless, the test of the Strategy's efficacy can only come through meaningful implementation, which remains at a very low level more than a year after the programme's adoption. The Government allocated few resources for Strategy implementation in 2002; those projects that have been undertaken have almost exclusively been funded through the Phare Partnership Fund for Roma, which is not administered by the Government directly. The coordinating bodies created by the Strategy meet irregularly and with few results.

One of the most important aspects of the Strategy is the degree to which it provides for Roma participation at all levels of Government. In particular, these measures call for the establishment of local structures, with Roma representation, to implement the Strategy and ensure it meets the needs of individual Roma communities. These measures have the potential to institutionalise Roma representation in local governance, to create a powerful network of Roma civil servants and to capitalise on the increasing number of Roma university graduates. However, many of these offices have not yet been able to exert significant influence on decision-making processes, as their activities and responsibilities in relation to other governing bodies remain to be defined.

Moreover, local experts on Roma affairs have mainly been appointed based on the proposals made by the Roma Social Democrat Party, without regard to standard hiring procedures or taking into consideration proposals from other representatives of Roma civil society. A single political organisation has thus come to be accepted as the sole representative body for the highly diverse Roma population, failing to take into account the expertise and experience developed within other Roma non-governmental organisations. Roma activists have also blamed the Government's selective interaction with civil society for exacerbating divisions rather than facilitation cooperation within the Roma NGO community.

Where adequate human and financial resources have been committed to addressing the situation of Roma, Romania has demonstrated impressive results through its Government Strategy. Sustained efforts must be complemented by the allocation of sufficient resources to ensure full implementation that meets the Strategy's goals.

2. The Government Programme – Background

2.1 Background to Present Programme

The programme "Strategy for the Improvement of the Roma Condition" is the first governmental initiative to take a comprehensive approach to the Roma minority. Earlier efforts to address Roma issues included the Department of Inter-Ethnic Relations' RAXI programme, which was designed to support local initiatives against racism and xenophobia, and the Counterparty Fund, which implemented local projects for disadvantaged minorities, including Roma. These programmes were never formally evaluated, and there is little information available regarding the degree to which they were successful in meeting the needs of the Roma community.

2.2 The Programme – Process

The "Strategy of the Government of Romania for Improving the Roma Condition" (hereafter "Government Strategy") was adopted as Government Decision Number 430/Aprilie/2001, published on 16 May 2001.[6]

The idea of developing a wide-ranging programme to address the situation of Roma was first considered some three years before the Government Strategy was adopted. In 1998, the Government tasked the National Office for Roma within the Department for the Protection of National Minorities (hereafter, DPMN) with developing a strategic framework. This project received support from a 1998 Phare programme, which provided for the elaboration of a "white paper" outlining a future strategy for improving the situation of Roma.[7]

In order to ensure structured participation and input from the Roma community, the DPNM signed a partnership protocol in March 2000 with the Working Group of Roma Associations, consisting of the most active Roma NGOs in the country at that time.[8] The Working Group issued several documents, including a "General Policy Recommendation" on the implementation of the Government programme for improving the situation of Roma. Concurrently, an Inter-Ministerial Sub-Commission for Roma was established to assist in identifying strategies in relevant spheres and to

---

[6] Official Gazette number 252, 16 May 2001.

[7] The National Office for Roma was responsible for implementing Phare RO 9803.01, Improvement of the Situation of Roma, with a €2 million total budget.

[8] See EU Accession Monitoring Program, *Monitoring the EU Accession Process: Minority Protection*, Open Society Institute, Budapest, 2001, p. 245, (hereafter, *Minority Protection 2001*) Available at <www.eumap.org>, (accessed 3 October 2002).

coordinate their implementation as part of a future national strategy. However, beyond the formation of these groups and an inconclusive series of meetings, little progress towards a programme document was made in the course of 2000.[9]

In its last session before the hand-over to the newly elected authorities in December 2000, the Government approved a memorandum entitled "Strategic Framework of the Romanian Government for Improving of the Condition of Roma." Nevertheless, there was widespread disappointment in the Roma community that the political will to adopt a formal programme still had not materialised.

Some members of the Working Group of Roma Associations considered that the adoption of the Strategic Framework memorandum in December 2000 had fulfilled the Working Group's mandate, although the body was not officially dissolved.[10] A new body was therefore organised to constitute an official Government partner in the implementation of a future Strategy. In February 2001, the Federation Framework Convention of Roma (hereafter, FFCR) was established as an association of five Roma NGOs,[11] which submitted a general policy recommendation to the Prime Minister's office shortly thereafter.[12]

All five organisations in the FFCR were based in Bucharest, causing concern among some of the former members of the Working Group that the representation was geographically unbalanced and that the leading Roma organisations from Bucharest did not support a unified Roma civil society movement.[13]

At the end of March 2001, the Prime Minister asked the Ministry of Public information to prepare a strategy to address the situation of the Roma within a very short time frame. The Ministry appointed a team headed by a State Secretary; with the support of the National Office for Roma, this team began to compile information on

---

[9] See *Minority Protection 2001*, p. 103; Information from MEDE Consultants, Bucharest, 31 October 2000. The 2000 Regular Report observed, "work on [the national] strategy has been delayed and preparations are still at an early stage. The newly appointed Inter-ministerial Sub-Committee for Roma has met during the reporting period but proved unable to produce any substantial results. [...] The Accession Partnership's short-term priorities still need to be met (elaborating a national Roma strategy and providing adequate financial support to minority programmes." 2000 Regular Report, pp. 24–25.

[10] Telephone interview with Dan Oprescu, National Office for Roma, 8 May 2002.

[11] Consisting of the Roma Social Democrat Party (*Partida Romilor* in Romanian, RSDP), Romani CRISS, *Aven Amentza*, the Community Development Agency "Together" and the SATRA/ASTRA Association of Anti-Racist Roma Students.

[12] Unpublished Recommendation, submitted to the Prime Minister's Office on 8 February 2001.

[13] Interview with Ötvös Géza, member of the Working Group of Roma Associations, president of Wassdas Foundation in Cluj Napoca, 7 April 2002, Cluj Napoca.

the subject, based on the previous efforts of the Working Group of Roma Associations, the "Strategic Framework" memorandum, and additional consultations with Roma and NGO representatives. The Ministry's Strategy was approved by the Government on 25 April 2001, and was generally accepted by Roma community leaders as a positive development.

According to a State Secretary within the Ministry of Public Information, a number of the principles presented by the Working Group of Roma Associations were incorporated into the Government Strategy.[14] These included the focus on eliminating discrimination and on partnership with Roma associations, the recommendation to establish ministerial commissions on Roma, and a mechanism for allocating funding for the implementation of programmes.

2.3 The Programme – Content

The Government Strategy provides for measures in ten sectors or areas, with detailed goals under each heading, an action plan, and a time frame for each action specified. The ten sectors are:

- Community Development and Public Administration
- Housing
- Social Security
- Healthcare
- Economics
- Justice and Public Order
- Child Welfare
- Education
- Culture and Denominations
- Communication and Civic Participation[15]

---

[14] OSI Round Table, June 2002. *Explanatory note: the Open Society Institute held a roundtable meeting in Bucharest in June 2002 to invite critique of a draft version of this report. Experts present included representatives of the Government, Roma groups, and non-governmental organisations.*

[15] See the "Strategy for Improving the Roma Condition," Government Decision No. 420/Aprilie/2001, Chapter VII, Sector Fields, available at <http://www.rroma.ro>, (accessed 30 October 2002), (hereafter, "Government Strategy").

The text of the Strategy sets forth its guiding principles in some detail. These include:

- The consensus principle, by which the Strategy is defined as "a joint effort of the Government and the representative organisations of the Roma community;"
- The social utility principle, which calls for measures to respond to the specific needs of the Roma community;
- The principle of "sectoral distribution," by which tasks are assigned to various bodies according to their respective sectors or spheres of competence;
- The decentralisation principle, by which specific responsibilities are assigned to public institutions at the local level;
- The principle of identity differentiation, which provides that measures should enable Roma to enhance and protect their distinct minority identity; and
- The equality principle, which states that measures to protect Roma should not put other groups at a disadvantage.[16]

The Government Strategy is complemented by existing legislation, including the Romanian Constitution, which guarantees equal rights for all Romanian citizens and the right to identity of individuals belonging to national minorities.[17] Of particular importance is Law 48/2002, (formerly Government Ordinance 137/2000) on the elimination of all forms of discrimination, which brings Romania closer to compliance with the EU Race Equality Directive.

2.4 The Programme – Administration/Implementation/Evaluation

Particular attention has been given to establishing structural mechanisms for implementing the Government Strategy. Coordinating bodies are provided for at the Government, ministry, and county levels, with Roma representation in each. These structures have in most cases been established, but with disappointing results as they so far lack authority and are not well integrated with existing structures. Coordination meetings are infrequent, and attendance appears to be a low priority for the participating representatives. Consequently, Roma communities have seen few concrete results from the Strategy, with implementation falling behind schedule in many areas. Roma organisations have made several efforts to press for increasing the pace of implementation, but have not been successful in uniting to advocate for their common interests.

---

[16] Government Strategy, Chapter I.
[17] See Romanian Constitution, 1991, Articles 4, 16 and 6.

Central Government bodies

The Ministry of Public Information is the principal governmental body responsible for the elaboration and implementation of the Government Strategy in the field of public information and inter-ethnic relations.[18] The Ministry's Department for Inter-Ethnic Relations is responsible for minority issues in general, including Roma issues.

A specialised structure within the Department, the National Office for Roma, is directly responsible for coordinating implementation of the Strategy together with local public bodies. The National Office for Roma has a staff of six, headed by a Sub-State Secretary. Previously, the Department for the Protection of National Minorities had been responsible for Government policy regarding Roma; the Department for Inter-Ethnic Relations took over its competencies with the formation of a new Government in 2000. This shift effectively diminished the status of minority issues, by transferring responsibility from the level of a department led by a minister to a department within a ministry, run by a Sub-State Secretary.

The Joint Committee for Monitoring and Implementation, the main structure responsible for the implementation of the Strategy, was established in July 2001.[19] It is comprised of State Secretaries representing the relevant Government ministries and leaders of Roma NGOs. The Committee is in charge of organisation, planning, coordination and management of implementation of the Government Strategy. The National Office for Roma is the executive body of the Joint Committee.[20]

As of June 2002 the Joint Committee had met only six times in the ten months since its establishment, in most cases with the participation of staff delegated by the State Secretaries of each ministry.[21] An Alternative Report on the programme's implementation drafted by the Aven Amentza Roma Centre for Public Policies (hereafter, "Alternative Report") characterises the Joint Committee as an unsuccessful copy of the earlier Inter-ministerial Sub-commission for Roma. Although the Joint Committee is required to meet monthly,

---

[18] Romanian Government Decision no. 13/4 January 2001 regarding the Organisation and Functioning of the Ministry of Public Information, published in Romanian Official Monitor no. 16/10 January 2001.

[19] Order of the Ministry of Public Information no. 259/02; see also, Government Strategy, Chapter VIII, point 1.

[20] Government Strategy, Chapter VIII.

[21] Ministry of Public Information, "Report on the Status of Implementation of the Strategy for Improvement of the Condition of Roma – April 2002," p. 2. See <http://www.publicinfo.ro/ENGLEZA.html>, (accessed 3 October 2002). The document was completed with information from ministries and MEDE European Consultancy, the company that administered the Phare Programme for Improvement of the Situation of Roma and prepared by the Ministry of Public Information, (hereafter, Ministry of Public Information, "Report on the Status of Implementation").

the Alternative Report suggests that it ceased to do so because of its limited access to information and differences among members' decision-making authority and expertise.[22] There are Roma representatives in the Joint Committee, but they are appear to enjoy little authority and no resources have been placed at their disposal to facilitate their work.[23]

Under the Joint Committee are individual Ministerial Commissions on Roma. To date 16 such Commissions have been formed to oversee implementation of Strategy activities within each ministry's competence.[24] Each of these Commissions is headed by a State Secretary, and comprised of a member of the Joint Committee and three to four additional members, one of whom is to be a Rom nominated by Roma NGOs. The "Alternative Report" alleges that the Ministerial Commissions also fail to meet regularly, and that they are "semi-secret."[25] Roma experts have been nominated by the FFCR. However, apparently due to a lack of clear internal regulations, the Roma members have not been not consulted or invited to all the meetings of the Joint Committee or the Ministerial Commissions.[26] Both the low priority of Roma issues and organisational adjustments to the new Commissions' structure within the ministries may have contributed to their weakness to date.

Oversight and reporting on Strategy expenditures is regulated by general Government regulations on accountability. Additional measures are usually specified by international donors such as the EU or the UNDP, and are provided for in individual project contracts. The Strategy does not provide for any centralised accounting or budget oversight mechanism; the level of funding for projects is left to the discretion of the individual ministries. As noted by the Advisory Committee on the Framework Convention for the Protection of National Minorities (hereafter, FCNM), "the different ministries vary considerably in their commitment to take effective action to

---

[22] "Implementation of GD 430/2001 'Strategy for Improvement of the Situation of Roma,' Alternative Report," *Aven Amentza* magazine no. 19–20, April–May 2002.

[23] Nicolae Păun – President of RSDP and M.P., Vasile Ionescu – President of Roma Centre for Public Policies Aven Amentza and expert of the Ministry of Culture and Denominations, Delia Grigore – President of ASTRA/SATRA, Costel Bercuș – Executive Director of Romani CRISS, Mariea Ionescu – Expert in the National Office for Roma.

[24] Commissions have been formed in the Ministries of Public Information; Public Administration; Small and Medium-Sized Enterprises; Industries and Resources; Public Transport and Housing; Agriculture; Labour and Social Solidarity; Health and Family; Youth and Sports; Justice; Culture and Denominations; Education and Research; Foreign Affairs; Internal Affairs; National Defence; and in the National Authority on Child Welfare.

[25] "Implementation of GD 430/2001 'Strategy for Improvement of the Situation of Roma,' Alternative Report," *Aven Amentza* magazine no. 19–20, April–May 2002.

[26] Both Costel Bercuș and Vasile Ionescu reported that they were not officially invited to any of the Committee meetings, telephone interviews, 25 April 2002.

improve the situation of the Roma."[27] The Committee goes on to recommend that the Government should "take special care to ensure the plan is fully and consistently implemented by all the bodies concerned, given that the National Office for Roma has only very limited resources and competencies."[28]

Indeed, the current level of Government funding for the Strategy is very low. At the request of the National Office for Roma, the technical assistance company, MEDE European Consultancy, estimated that the level of funding required to implement the Strategy as it was drafted is approximately €105 million, of which the Government should contribute 31 percent, and the remaining 69 percent could be funded from extra-budgetary resources.[29] Yet in the preparation of the 2002 State budget, no funding was allocated directly to Strategy implementation, although some measures outside the Strategy's framework are expected to benefit many Roma.[30]

It is expected that the 2003 budget will include some allocations for Strategy implementation.[31] The Government Strategy also provides for the creation of a public interest foundation for Roma affairs, to attract extra-budgetary funds from within the country as well as abroad to be used in implementing the Strategy. At the end of 2001, the Resource Centre for Roma Communities (RCRC) signed an agreement with the Ministry of Public Finance – Central Finance and Contracts Unit for administration of the Phare 2000 Civil Society Fourth Roma component.

Chapter IX of the Strategy, the "Master Plan of Measures for Applying the Strategy," sets forth 123 projects and activities in some detail. In many cases, deadlines are specified for projects' completion, and the responsible ministry or ministries are also indicated. Nevertheless, these deadlines often have not been met. A lack of specificity in assigning tasks allows ministries to shift responsibility for carrying out a given activity between different departments or agencies within the ministry, and to delay the release of resources allocated for implementation. After some delays due to difficulties collecting information from the ministries, the Joint Committee's report on Strategy implementation to date was made public in April 2002.[32] While the sections on institutions, public administration, and education are well elaborated and detailed in this first evaluation, other sections report little progress and can only reiterate the provisions of the Strategy itself. Nevertheless, the Government has demonstrated a

---

[27] Advisory Committee on the FCNM, *Opinion on Romania*, Strasbourg, 2001, para. 25.

[28] Advisory Committee on the FCNM, *Opinion on Romania* 2001, para. 25.

[29] Estimate completed by MEDE European Consultancy after consultation with each ministry involved in the implementation of the Strategy, 2001.

[30] Including social security measures, addressed in Section 3.2.4, below.

[31] Interview with Mariea Ionescu, National Office for Roma, Bucharest, 15 March 2002.

[32] Ministry of Public Information, *Report on the Status of Implementation*, p. 4.

commitment to assessing itself in regard to Strategy implementation, which will be increasingly important as the pace of implementation improves.

The executive body of the Joint Committee of Implementation and Monitoring, the National Office for Roma, has only limited power to advance implementation of the Strategy. Because the Strategy was adopted as a Government decision, it does not have the character of a law and therefore does not provide for sanctions if competent bodies fail to accomplish the activities provided for. As the head of Government, only the Prime Minister could compel greater adherence to the Strategy and require ministries to carry out their respective obligations. Representatives of the RSDP have requested the Prime Minister's involvement to re-activate the process, and he is expected to address Strategy implementation as part of his regular teleconferences with prefects (county level Government representatives).

Some of the measures called for under the Government Strategy will also be on the agenda of the "National Plan for Local Development of Roma Communities," which the Strategy names as one of the organisational measures to be taken under its auspices.[33] These measures mainly concern improvements to infrastructure and rehabilitation of housing, job creation, and health. A Phare project to design the plan is in preparation with the National Office for Roma, and should be realised in 2003 with a proposed budget of €6 million, of which the Government should contribute €1.25 million. The project is designed to strengthen institutions at the local and county levels, aimed at establishing equitable and sustainable partnerships of Roma communities and the public administration.

County – Prefecture bodies

County bureaux for Roma have been established within the prefects' offices, under the Ministry of Public Administration's Ministerial Commission on Roma. The County Bureaux were created to evaluate the situation of Roma at the local level, and to coordinate realisation of local development programmes under the Government Strategy. Each Bureau has a staff of three to four, at least one of whom is to be a Rom. Hiring Bureau staff is the responsibility of the prefecture. In most cases, those hired as Roma experts have a university degree, and were nominated to their post by the Roma Social Democrat Party (RSDP).[34] By May 2002, the last county to select a Roma

---

[33] Government Strategy, Chapter XI, Master Plan of Measures for Applying the Strategy of Improving Roma's Condition, Point 20.

[34] Ivan Gheorghe, Sub-State Secretary, Ministry of Public Information, Statement in the Seminar regarding the Improvement of the Situation of Roma in Romania, 2-3 November 2001, "…Out of these, 30 have graduate degrees and are not politically involved. … Twelve have high-school level studies, and, among them, some are older persons coming from the activist sphere."

expert had made an appointment and established its Bureau for Roma. Generally, staff of the County Bureaux report that their tasks mainly involve handling requests for public support documents, unemployment certification, and housing, identity and property documents.[35]

Experts with the County Bureaux indicate that they have adequate resources at their disposal, although several have noted that a car or other means of transport would facilitate their work in Roma communities.[36] The Ministry of Public Administration covers the salaries and associated administrative costs of the Roma experts hired for County Bureaux for Roma, and the Ministry of Public Information has contributed computers and printers to each of the 42 offices through a contract with the "Together" Community Development Agency Bucharest.

The County Bureaux for Roma are expected to convene mixed working groups at the county level, including representatives of the Bureau, NGO representatives, and Roma community leaders. Out of 42 counties, fewer than 15 had managed to set up working groups as of Summer 2002.[37] At the initiative of the "Together" Community Development Agency, a project funded through the Phare Access 2000 programme will support the creation of another ten working groups.[38] Even those that have been formed have failed to achieve concrete results: according to one County Bureau representative, the local working group does not function properly because the County Bureau has no authority or influence over the institutions represented, such as county labour offices and health centres.[39]

Local bodies

According to the Government Strategy, positions for local experts on Roma are to be created within mayors' offices, answering to the mayor and the County Bureau for Roma.[40] Implementation of this measure has only recently begun, as no additional

---

[35] Interviews with Roma experts from County Office for Roma: Viorica Gotu in Galaţi County, Corina Copeţi from Hunedoara County, Turcata Nicolae from Mureş county, Elena Dumitraşcu from Suceava County, July–August 2002.

[36] Interview with Viorica Gotu, Roma expert, County Office for Roma, Galaţi, 1 August 2002; interview with Turcata Nicolae, Roma expert, County Office for Roma Tîrgu Mureş, 14 August 2002.

[37] 13 groups are mentioned in the "Implementation of GD 430/2001 'Strategy for Improvement of the Situation of Roma,' Alternative Report," *Aven Amentza* magazine no. 19–20, April–May 2002.

[38] Interview with Gelu Duminică, Director of Community Development Agency "Together," 5 April 2002; the project is funded by Phare ACCESS 2000 micro-projects component.

[39] Interview with Viorica Gotu, Roma expert, County Office for Roma, Galaţi, 1 August 2002.

[40] Government Strategy, Chapter VIII, point 4.

funding has been allocated and most localities do not have the resources to create a new post. A total of 399 local experts on Roma had been officially nominated as of April 2002.[41] However, not all of these experts are Roma, and in many cases, officials in existing positions were designated as the "Roma expert," and related tasks were simply added to their existing responsibilities as resources for hiring additional staff were not available. A representative from a County Bureau for Roma noted that, "these civil servants do not have any knowledge and motivation to work for solving Roma problems; it is just another responsibility for them."[42]

Participation from civil society

Roma involvement in both the development and implementation of the Government Strategy has been extensive, but has become politicised and even counter-productive in some cases.[43] Since the Strategy's adoption, NGO representatives have registered their dissatisfaction over delays in implementation, especially regarding anti-discrimination provisions.[44] NGOs have also expressed concerns about the objectivity of the Joint Committee, and the allegedly political criteria used to select personnel for Roma-related projects.[45] Many complaints have related to the appointment of Roma experts within the local governments. Some representatives of Roma NGOs have stated that the Government has a different vision regarding the implementation of the Strategy than their own, and have called for more effective collaboration with civil society in its implementation.[46]

Ministry of Public Information officials consider their collaboration with Roma civil society organisations to be constructive, and have underlined that they consider this cooperation indispensable, as where public institutions fail, NGOs may have greater

---

[41] Ministry of Public Information, *Report on the Status of Implementation*, p. 5.

[42] Interview with Viorica Gotu, Roma expert, County Office for Roma, Galați, 1 August 2002.

[43] Statement of Vasile Ionescu, Conference on the Improvement of the Condition of Roma in Romania, organised by United Nations Agencies in Romania and the Romanian Government, 2-3 November 2001.

[44] See Report of the seminar organised by the UN and the Romanian Government regarding the improvement of the Roma Condition in Romania, 2–3 November 2001 Bucarest, (hereafter, "November 2001 Seminar Bucharest"); statement of Costel Bercuș, Executive Director of Romani CRISS.

[45] Statement of Vasile Ionescu, President of the Aven Amentza-Roma Centre for Public Policies at the November 2001 Seminar Bucharest.

[46] Statement of Vasile Ionescu, President of the Aven Amentza-Roma Centre for Public Policies at the November 2001 Seminar Bucharest.

success.[47] However, the Government's main partner, the RSDP, has been unable to mobilise existing Roma resources at the local level. In an effort to improve the effectiveness of Strategy implementation, the RSDP formed a new body, "Cartel RO 430" to liase with the Government.[48] However, the body has produced few visible results, and some Roma activists have remarked that it exists only on paper.[49]

The membership of each representative body is generally drawn from the same group of Roma leaders, sometimes resulting in confusion over the continued relevance of any one body. This has paradoxically limited Roma organisations' ability to identify common issues for advocacy or to articulate a joint approach to Strategy implementation. In an interview, the Sub-State Secretary of the Ministry of Public Information declared that the FFCR, created during the same year and with the same objective as Cartel RO 430 "does not exist any more" because all the members moved to the Cartel and "the Framework Convention of Roma was absorbed." The President of the FFCR added that, "the Federation Framework Convention of Roma has a protocol signed with the Government regarding implementation. However, most of the members of the [FFCR's] Permanent Committee are also members of the Joint Committee for Implementation and Monitoring and a resignation of these members will mean a blockage of the Strategy."[50]

In June 2002, the RSDP and the Social Democrat Party signed an agreement, the "Collaboration and Political Partnership Protocol," which focuses on cooperation between the Social Democrat Party (SDP) and the RSDP in the promotion and monitoring of the implementation of the Government Strategy. The Protocol calls for establishing a new "State Department for Roma problems," and promotion of Roma issues at the international level. There is also a more explicitly political dimension to the agreement, relating to the promotion of Roma representatives in positions within State institutions, consultations at the Parliamentary level, RSDP endorsement for the SDP's candidates, and collaboration at the county and local level.[51] However, RSDP representatives have since expressed dissatisfaction with the SDP's commitment to the

---

[47] Remarks of the Ministry of Public Information State Secretary Dan Jurcan, at the launch of the "Fund for Improvement of the Situation of Roma" the fourth component of the Phare Civil Society Development 2000 program.

[48] DIVERS Bulletin No. 44, 8 November 2001: Interview with the Sub-State Secretary Ivan Gheorghe, "Cartel RO 430 will have the role of 'contributing to the effectiveness of the implementation of the Strategy for Improvement of the Condition of Roma' and will be the sole organisation that will support the Government in implementation."

[49] Interview with Toader Burtea, president of Roma Free Democratic Association Sașa Petrosani, 12 April 2002, Cluj Napoca.

[50] DIVERS Bulletin, Year I, no. 44, 8 November 2001.

[51] Available at <http://www.psd.ro/documente/protocol-psd-partida-romi.pdf>, (accessed 2 October 2002).

Protocol,[52] and have even indicated that the RSDP will sign an agreement with the far-right Greater Romania Party if Strategy implementation does not improve.[53]

2.5 The Programme and the Public

There has been little effort to present the Government Strategy to the public at large. Government resources allocated to public awareness of Strategy projects and objectives have been minimal, although one component of the Strategy is the improvement of communication and civic participation. In 2001 and 2002, Government representatives gave presentations on Strategy implementation at various national and international meetings, including the OSCE Conference in September 2001, the United Nations Agencies Roma conference in November 2001, and the Braşov Conference on Implementation at the Local Level of the Strategy for Improvement of the Condition of Roma, also in November 2001.

Romanian media has frequently relied upon negative stereotypes in its reporting on Roma issues, and although some positive references to the Government Strategy have appeared, negative representations persist. The independent Roma Press Agency regularly reports on general Roma issues, and the implementation of Strategy projects is often featured.[54] (See Section 3.4.4)

Greater efforts are needed to build public support for the Strategy. The general public has received the Strategy as a necessary measure, particularly in view of the EU accession process, but confidence that the programme will achieve its objectives seems to be low.[55] The Government Strategy was welcomed by Roma civil society organisations and by Roma political leaders, who have particularly emphasised the importance of political will at both the highest State and local government levels; it is understood that implementation will hinge on the level of commitment from State authorities.[56]

---

[52] Ethnic Minority Briefs No. 20, 26 August 2002.
[53] See RFE/RL *Newsline*, 15 August, "Romanian Romany Leader Threatens to Back Extremist Party."
[54] The Roma Press Agency produces an English-language digest at <http://groups.yahoo.com/group/roma_news_en>, (accessed 25 October 2002).
[55] Interview with Mariea Ionescu, National Office for Roma, 15 March 2002, Bucharest.
[56] OSI Round Table, Bucharest, June 2002.

2.6 The Programme and the EU

Phare and other EU funding has been essential to the Government Strategy, from its support for the drafting phase in 1998 to the implementation of projects testing the Strategy principles in 2001 and beyond.[57] Although some organisations have expressed dissatisfaction with the rigidity of Phare application procedures, EU support has made possible many projects addressing the needs of the Roma community. The EU's policy of funding projects under the Strategy directly supports the recommendations of its Regular Reports, in which the Commission has praised the Government for adopting the Strategy, but has also noted that its measures must be comprehensively implemented, with special attention to eliminating discrimination.

The Government Strategy was drafted with the support of a 1998 Phare programme.[58] A Dutch company, MEDE European Consultancy, was selected as the Contracting Authority in partnership with the British Minority Rights Group. The "Improvement of the Condition of Roma" project had two objectives: to assist the Government in the development of a White Paper/Strategy to contribute to the elimination of all forms of discrimination against Roma. The project also provided for the establishment of a "Partnership Fund for Roma" which would distribute €900,000 in project grants.

Implementation of the two components was delayed by some two years, in part due to difficulties in consolidating support within the political establishment, and in building a partnership between the Government and the Roma Social Democrat Party. Elections in 2000 also slowed the pace of implementation.

The first component, the White Paper, was fulfilled through the adoption of the Government Strategy in April 2001, while the second component, the "Partnership Fund for Roma" was established in January 2001 with the following objectives:

- To test ministerial strategies by supporting initiatives between (local) government organisations and the Roma community.

- To build the capacity of existing Roma NGOs and to stimulate the development of new Roma organisations in areas where none are operating

---

[57] See R.W. Murray, *Testing the Strategy*, Mede European Consultancy, October 2001, (hereafter, "*Testing the Strategy*"). See <http://www.rroma.ro/download/testing_strategy.pdf>, (accessed 2 October 2002).

[58] RO 9803.01, "Improvement of the Condition of Roma in Romania" programme, with a total budget of €2 million.

- To identify and support sustainable partnerships and innovative projects between Roma communities and local public authorities.[59]

Of 334 applications received, 40 projects, covering most strategy sectors, were selected and have been implemented in the course of 2001–2002.

The selection process was governed by the applicable procedures under Phare guidelines.[60] An Evaluation Committee and team of assessors were chosen, to include representatives with experience in the area and a reputation for impartiality and confidentiality. The names of the Evaluation Committee members and Assessors are not made public,[61] but in 2001 one of the Committee members was a Rom, while in 2002 there are two Roma representatives in a team of three. Their assessments form the basis of the Evaluation Committee's recommendations for funding, which are reviewed by the EU Delegation with special regard to the procedural and financial aspects of the process. The Contracting Authority (previously MEDE European Consultancy, presently the Central Finance and Contracting Unit of the Ministry of Public Finance) then makes the final decision on the list of projects to be funded.

Some applicants have expressed concern that the Phare process is not sufficiently transparent, and its lack of flexibility can be especially burdensome for smaller organisations seeking lower levels of support. The same procedures apply, regardless of a project's size, subject matter, or the level of funding requested.

In recent years, most projects for Roma that have been funded by the European Union or other international donors have been implemented on an *ad hoc* basis, and have mainly addressed social and economic problems. As no formal Government programme existed prior to 2001, there was no structure within which to integrate these various initiatives. An interim evaluation of projects supported under the Partnership Fund observed that, "projects were designed and implemented based on local needs and solutions that were identified in particular communities, they were not designed to test specific government measures, and they were not projects commissioned by [the] central

---

[59] Guidelines for Applicants, Partnership Fund for Roma, officially launched on 26 January 2001. See also the official web site of European Union Delegation in Romania, <http://www.infoeuropa.ro/start.php>, (accessed 3 October 2002).

[60] See <http://europa.eu.int/comm/europeaid/tender/gestion/pg/e_en.htm>, (accessed 3 October 2002).

[61] *Practical Guide to EC external aid contract procedures*, p. 158. "The entire procedure, from the drawing-up of the Call for Proposals to the selection of successful applicants, is confidential. The Evaluation Committee's decisions are collective and its deliberations must remain secret. The committee members are bound to secrecy."

[G]overnment."⁶² The Partnership Fund for Roma has nevertheless been the most consistent source of European Union funding for Roma in Romania.

Through the Phare Lien and Phare Democracy Programmes, between 1995 and 1999, approximately €200,000 was distributed as grants for 26 projects related to Roma issues; of these only ten projects were directly implemented by Roma organisations, while the rest were carried out by other NGOs or by public institutions. In 2002–2003, as part of the Phare Civil Society Development 2000 Programme,⁶³ one component was devoted to Roma issues. The component, the "Fund for Improvement of the Situation of Roma" has a total budget of €927,500, which will be distributed in the form of grants to 29 projects.⁶⁴

Under the 2001 Phare programme, a database and a publication were compiled under the title, "Projects for Roma in Romania, 1990–2000;" these were intended as a tool for Government institutions, donors, and NGOs for the development and implementation of future policies.⁶⁵ The large number of implemented projects listed in this index is disproportionate to the results achieved, and it is debatable whether all the projects were in fact focused on Roma or disadvantaged populations more generally.

In the 1999 Regular Report, released prior to the adoption of the Strategy, the European Commission was strongly critical of the Government's level of commitment to addressing the problems faced by the Roma community.⁶⁶ By contrast, the 2001 Regular Report praised the adoption of the Government Strategy, which had been a priority in the 1999 Accession Partnership (since revised),⁶⁷ referring to it as a "comprehensive and high quality document that was elaborated together with Roma organisations and has been welcomed by them."⁶⁸ Decentralisation and the involvement of local level institutions are singled out as important features of the

---

⁶² *Testing the Strategy*, p. 1.

⁶³ Phare RO 0004.02 Civil Society Development 2000, with a total budget of € four million.

⁶⁴ The list of the 29 projects is available at <http://www.romacenter.ro/documente/PR%20ROMA%20RO%20castigatori.doc>, (accessed 2 October 2002).

⁶⁵ *Projects for Roma in Romania, 1990–2000*, edited by Viorel Anăstăsoaie and Daniela Tarnovski.

⁶⁶ Commission of the European Communities, *2000 Regular Report from the Commission on Romania's Progress Towards Accession*, Brussels, 2000, p. 23.

⁶⁷ Commission of the European Communities, *2001 Regular Report on Romania's Progress Towards Accession*, Brussels, November 2001, p. 29, (hereafter, "EU Regular Report 2001").

⁶⁸ EU Regular Report 2001, p. 29.

Strategy;[69] Partnership Fund support has accordingly been allocated almost exclusively to local initiatives.[70]

The Regular Report emphasises that Roma NGOs will have to play an active role in the implementation of the Strategy, while observing that the lack of unity between Roma organisations could pose an obstacle.[71] Civil society organisations have pointed out that this perspective fails to take account of the diverse community their organisations represent, and does not examine the ways in which Government policy has contributed to tension and friction within the NGO sector.[72]

3. The Government Programme – Implementation

3.1 Stated Objectives of the Programme

The Government Strategy addresses a broad range of issues affecting the Roma minority, addressing the prevention of discrimination, setting forth measures to redress present inequalities, and supporting the promotion of minority identity. The general objectives of the Strategy are the following:

- Delegating political objectives and responsibilities concerning the Roma that are currently assumed by the Government to the central and local public authorities in the implementation of measures to improve the condition of the Roma;

- Supporting the formation and promotion of an intellectual and economic elite within Roma communities, to facilitate the application of social integration and modernisation policies;

- Counteracting the stereotypes and prejudices held by some civil servants in public institutions;

- Encouraging change in public opinion concerning Roma, on the basis of principles of tolerance and social solidarity;

- Stimulating Roma participation in the economic, social, educational, cultural and political spheres, based on their involvement in various assistance and community development projects;

---

[69] EU Regular Report 2001, p. 29.
[70] See generally, *Testing the Strategy*.
[71] EU Regular Report 2001, p. 29.
[72] OSI Round Table, Bucharest, June 2002.

- Preventing institutional and social discrimination against Roma in access to social services;

- Ensuring conditions for Roma to have equal opportunities to attain a decent standard of life.[73]

3.2 The Government Programme and Discrimination

The Government Strategy identifies the elimination of discrimination as one of the most important factors in improving the condition of the Roma. The opening statement of the Strategy acknowledges that "in the course of history, Roma were objects of slavery and discrimination, phenomena that have left deep marks on the collective memory and have led to the social limitations of the Roma."[74] Throughout the text, the Strategy accordingly sets out specific measures to address inequalities, and to prevent future incidences of discrimination. These measures include:

- Establishing the National Council for Combating Discrimination and including Roma representatives in this structure;

- Monitoring the application of Emergency Ordinance No. 137/2000 (now Law 48/2002) and sanctioning civil servants who commit discriminatory acts;[75]

- Creating programmes to prevent and combat discrimination against institutionalised Roma children and other groups of children in need;[76]

- Establishing a programme for fighting discrimination in the media;

- Drafting programmes to provide information about combating discrimination in employment;

- Calling attention to cases of public or private discrimination against Roma through the media;

- Developing and implementing programmes to support the development of Roma civil society, in order to facilitate their efforts to prevent and combat discrimination.[77]

---

[73] Government Strategy, Chapter III.
[74] Government Strategy, Chapter I.
[75] Government Strategy, Chapter VII Section A, Point 6.
[76] Government Strategy, Chapter VII Section G, Point 2.
[77] Government Strategy, Chapter VII, Section J, Points 2,3,6,8.

Local activists and the international community welcomed the much-delayed entry into force of Law 48/2002 as a comprehensive and potentially powerful tool against discrimination.[78] The Law includes a broad definition of discrimination on grounds of ethnicity, race, and sex, and stipulates equality in economic activity, employment; access to legal, administrative and public health services; access to other goods, services, and facilities; access to education; and the right to personal dignity.[79] The law provides for a monitoring and enforcement body, the National Council for Combating Discrimination (NCCD).

However, the Law does not meet the standards prescribed by the EU Race Equality Directive, which are intended to represent minimal protection against discrimination.[80] Law 48/2002 fails to adequately define indirect discrimination, referring only to "active" and "passive" discrimination.[81] There are also no provisions regarding harassment or intimidation, and the standard of evidence is not adequately defined explicitly to allow the introduction of statistical evidence. The Law does not provide for reversal of the burden of proof in discrimination claims, although the NCCD could do so in defining its own procedures.

The NCCD is administratively subordinated to the Government General Secretariat, although it is designed to be an independent body. It has six members and one president holding the rank of Secretary of State.[82] After a significant delay, the NCCD was established by a decision of the Prime Minister on 31 July 2002. It members were appointed based on proposals from the relevant ministries,[83] and its President is a former director in the Governmental Law Harmonisation Directorate.[84] Disappointingly, no Roma member was appointed, as had been anticipated.[85] Although there were several

---

[78] See, e.g. EU Regular Report 2001, p. 29.

[79] See Government Ordinance 137/2000, Chapters I, II, II, IV, V. English text available at <http://www.minelres.lv/NationalLegislation/Romania/Romania_antidiscrim_English.htm>, (accessed 2 October 2002).

[80] See *Minority Protection 2001*, p. 394.

[81] See Government Ordinance 137/2000, Art. 2 (2).

[82] Government Decision on Organisation and Functioning of the National Board on Fighting Discrimination, Art. 4.

[83] Prime Minister Decision No. 139/31 July 2002, regarding the nomination of the members of the National Council for Combating Discrimination. Proposals were received from the Ministries of Public Information, Labour and Social Solidarity, Justice, Health and Family, Public Administration, Education and Research and Interior.

[84] See Divers – Romania Ethnic Diversity Briefs, No. 18, 12 August.

[85] Government Decision on Organisation and Functioning of the National Board on Fighting Discrimination, Article 5(5): "When appointing the Directory College members, the presence of the persons belonging to the national minorities or to the disabled categories shall also be taken into consideration."

proposals from the SDRP, there was no consultation with representative Roma NGOs, which could offer significant experience and trained staff in the field of combating discrimination.[86] The NCCD will have a budget of approximately ROL 3 billion (Romanian Lei, approximately €280,000[87]) in 2002, and should ultimately have a staff of 50.

Despite the adoption of the anti-discrimination Law as a provisional ordinance in 2000, no sanction for discrimination against Roma was imposed under this legislation for more than a year. During this period, the courts rejected some claims of discrimination on the grounds that the NCCD (which had not yet been appointed) is the only body that can rule on discrimination, although in fact regular courts are still required to hear claims raised under other legislation.[88] It is therefore crucial that the Government provide training for judicial and legal professionals on the new legislation; this is clearly necessary to ensure its effective implementation.

The NGO community has actively pursued the development of anti-discrimination law and practice. Civil society groups contributed to elaborating the text of Ordinance 137, and have already taken test cases through the courts, in order to begin building authoritative interpretation of the Law's provisions. Recently, the manager of a Bucharest football club was fined ROL 1.5 million (less than €50) for failing to prevent supporters from unveiling a banner with racist overtones and shouting remarks directed at the Roma fans of the opposing team.[89] Though the fine was small, the significance of the ruling is great; this is reportedly the first time that a penalty of this kind has been imposed.

NGOs have supported information campaigns against discrimination: the RCRC carried out a Phare-supported information campaign on anti-discrimination legislation in 2001 with young Roma activists. The programme, "Defend Your Rights!" was funded by the European Union within the European Initiative for Democracy and Human Rights, and its purpose was to present the Ordinance 137/2000 to 40 Roma communities in Cluj, Bucharest, Iași, Timișoara, Craiova, Bacău, Mureș, and Sibiu. As a result of the campaign, approximately 4,000 Roma community members learned of the existence of this legislation, and at least 200 Roma know the contents of the ordinance in detail and understand the role of the NCCD and other institutions defending human rights.

---

[86] Interview with Mariea Ionescu, National Office for Roma, 23 August 2002, Constanța.

[87] The exchange is calculated at ROL 32,093 to €1.

[88] Ordinance 137/2000, Chapter V, Art. 20 (3). See also, Romani CRISS, Annual Report 2001, Human Rights Department, *CRISS vs. Angely*.

[89] See RFE/RL *Newsline*, 21 March 2002, "First Fine Imposed in Romania for Racism Display."

3.2.1 Education

Education is a high priority under the Strategy, in a context in which the level of formal education and professional qualification of the Roma population is generally low. Impressive results have been achieved in higher education through affirmative action measures to ensure places for Roma at most universities. The Government Strategy does not address discrimination within the school system directly, but sets more modest goals such as compiling better statistics and preparing studies and reports on means of improving levels of school attendance among Roma schoolchildren.

Encouraging school attendance and decreasing the drop out rate are priority areas in the Government Strategy.[90] To this end, The Ministry of Education and Research has received Phare funding in 2002 for the programme "Access to education of disadvantaged groups, with a special focus on Roma." The programme has total funding of €7 million and the EC Delegation is currently in the process of selecting the technical assistance company. The Ministry will contribute €1.33 million to this programme, which is to be implemented in between 2002 and 2004. On 10 September 2002, the grants component was officially launched, opening the process for applications from County School Inspectorates in partnership with County Councils or NGOs with experience in the field of education or the protection of minorities.[91]

The Institute for Educational Sciences, the Ministry of Education and Research and UNICEF Romania have also elaborated a strategy for stimulating the participation of Roma children and youths in the educational system, which is currently awaiting approval by the Ministry of Education and Research.[92]

The Strategy calls for analysis of the possibility of organising secondary and vocational school institutions for Roma in the spheres of arts and trades, vocational education, and professional reorientation.[93] A collaborative project between the Ministry of Education and the Education 2000+ Centre has completed preliminary research into this possibility,[94] but the Government has not yet initiated any projects on the basis of project findings.

---

[90] Government Strategy, Chapter VII, Section H, Paragraph 1.

[91] EC Delegation Press Release, launching the "Access to education for disadvantaged groups, with special focus on Roma," Bucharest, 10 September 2002. The value of grants given is between €200,000 and €500,000 per project; the applicant must contribute with at least 10 percent of the total value of the project. A total of €4 million is to be allocated through this component.

[92] Ministry of Public Information, *Report on the Status of Implementation*, p. 14.

[93] Government Strategy, Chapter VII, Section H, Paragraph 2.

[94] Funding was provided by the Dutch government's MATRA programme. The Education 2000+ Centre is member of the Soros Open Network Romania, based in Bucharest.

Training programmes for school mediators and intercultural programmes for teachers are also planned under the Strategy.[95] The Government has not taken any steps towards implementing this point, although 11 mediators are currently active in schools through the project "A Second Chance," implemented by the Education 2000+ Centre.

To facilitate access to higher education for Roma, the Strategy provides for reinforcement of the existing incentives and support to Roma university and college students.[96] In the majority of universities, places for Roma students are already set aside based on affirmative action measures previously mandated by the Ministry of Education and Research.[97] Supplementary measures have been enacted by the University of Cluj Napoca, the University of Constanța, and the National School for Administrative and Political Sciences, which have allocated seats for Roma candidates beyond the level required by the Ministry of Education.[98] Between 150 to 200 Roma students have begun their university education annually since 1998, and it is estimated that approximately 800 Roma students are now registered in university studies, with both State-funded and private support.[99] Non-governmental organisations have also offered scholarships since 1987.[100]

The Strategy further provides for drafting and implementing programmes to encourage Roma parents to participate in school and extra-curricular educational activities.[101] For example, it obliges school administrations to organise remedial courses for Roma at all educational levels,[102] and allows the possibility for individuals or organisations to

---

[95] Government Strategy, Chapter VII, Section H, Paragraph 3.

[96] Government Strategy, Chapter VII, Section H, Paragraph 8.

[97] Order no. 3577/15 April 1998, Order no. 5083/26 November 1999, Order no. 3294/01 March 2000, Order no. 4542/18 September 2000, are normative acts of the Ministry of Education and Research (formerly the Ministry of National Education).

[98] L. Murvai, ed., *Minorities and Education in Romania*. School year 2000/2001, Editura Studium, Cluj Napoca, 2001, p. 64–65.

[99] L. Murvai, ed., *Minorities and Education in Romania*. School year 2000/2001, Editura Studium, Cluj Napoca p. 64. "... 150–200 distinct places were given annually for Roma candidates at the entrance examinations at different faculties and colleges at the University of Bucharest, Cluj-Napoca, Iași, Timișoara, Brașov, Sibiu, Constanța, Oradea, Suceava and the National School of Political and Administrative Studies of Bucharest."

[100] Approximately 100 Roma students from Romania received scholarships through the Open Society Institute's Roma Memorial University Scholarship Program in 2001. The Open Society Foundation Romania, between 1987 and 1999; the RCRC between 2000–2001, and the Open Society Institute Budapest in 2001 have offered university scholarships for Roma students.

[101] Government Strategy, Chapter VII, Section H, Paragraph 6.

[102] Government Strategy, Chapter VII, Section H, Paragraph 9.

suggest new initiatives. However, there is no indication that the Government has taken steps to implement any of these measures.

As a means of encouraging the employment of Roma experts in public administration, the Strategy encourages Roma students to apply to institutions that train civil servants and the staff for public institutions, such as social work and public administration, as well as medical faculties, military academies, schools for officers and non-commissioned officers for police departments, and the Ministry of National Defence.[103] With the exception of initiatives to increase Roma applications for the Bucharest police force (see Section 3.3.), little appears to have been accomplished to achieve this objective.

3.2.2 Employment

The Strategy addresses inequalities in the sphere of employment primarily through economic development. The Master Plan of Action provides for the elaboration of measures to encourage entrepreneurial activity, but these have not been developed. In contrast, training and employment projects funded by the Phare Partnership Fund for Roma have been implemented and suggest that such activities can be both sustainable and productive.

The Strategy provides for measures to improve the practice and revival of traditional Roma handicrafts; it also calls for the development and implementation of specific financing programmes for income-generating activities and small businesses for Roma families and communities, especially Roma women.[104] Of particular note is a provision offering financial incentives for entrepreneurs who hire Roma;[105] however, according to a Memorandum of Understanding signed between the Government of Romania and the IMF, any existing fiscal incentives will be cut in order to ensure equal opportunities for investors.[106] The Strategy calls for "fighting against any forms of discrimination in hiring the Roma," without specifying how this will be accomplished or elaborating specific means of doing so.[107]

The Strategy also foresees support for agricultural activities, in connection with the land ownership process; support for small and medium enterprises (SMEs) owned by Roma through a soft credit system; and greater inclusion of Roma communities in

---

[103] Government Strategy, Chapter VII, Section H, Paragraph 10.
[104] Government Strategy, Chapter VII, Section E.
[105] Government Strategy, Chapter VII, Section E.
[106] Ministry of Public Information, *Report on the Status of Implementation*, p. 14.
[107] Government Strategy, Chapter VII, Section E.

regional development projects.[108] The Master Plan of Measures for applying the Strategy calls for the presentation of a set of measures for the partial financing of entrepreneurial activities and small businesses for Roma families and communities, in cooperation with Roma leaders and NGOs.[109] The Ministry of Public Information's 2002 *Report on the Status of Implementation of the Strategy for Improvement of the Roma Condition* (hereafter, "Report on the Status of Implementation") notes that Roma leaders have proposed a project offering partial funding to workshops in Roma communities; the Ministry of Small and Medium Enterprises and Cooperatives approved a similar project, but a source of funding has not been identified (the project cost has been estimated at €700,000).[110]

Few of the Government's objectives in the sphere of employment have been achieved to date; of the 232 Roma who graduated from professional qualification courses in 2001, only 71 (31 percent) found a permanent job.[111] Nevertheless, in 2002 a further 243 Roma are expected to take part in professional qualification courses based on a separate National Employment Programme.

Projects under the Partnership Fund for Roma

In comparison, several civil society pilot initiatives are functioning successfully. Under the Partnership Fund for Roma, there are a number of projects promoting professional qualification and employment. As pilot projects, most are localised and being implemented on a small scale, drawing on local resources and expertise. A high level of collaboration between Roma associations and local authorities is a common feature of most successful projects. The Government must begin to assume responsibility for utilising the experience gained through these projects in developing larger-scale initiatives, and in identifying and addressing systemic obstacles to employment among Roma.

The following projects were included in an internal evaluation of Partnership Fund initiatives:

The "Amare Phrala" Association in Cluj Napoca, in partnership with the Cluj Napoca "Spiru Haret" Vocational School, trained 83 young Roma, who studied for qualifications in more than 14 trades or specialisations such as auto mechanics, sewing, computer operation, bartending, and hairdressing. After the six-month course, almost all of those enrolled passed their qualification exams and received a diploma. 15 of the trainees found employment, and four who were previously employed received a pay increase afterwards. The project was implemented between September 2001 and

---

[108] Government Strategy, Chapter VII, Section E.
[109] Government Strategy, Chapter XI, Point 55.
[110] Ministry of Public Information, *Report on the Status of Implementation*, p. 14.
[111] Ministry of Public Information, *Report on the Status of Implementation*, p. 10.

March 2002, and it is seen as an example of good practice as a result of the positive collaboration it engendered between the Roma association and the school. The project was recommended as having high potential for replication in other areas.[112]

In Jimbolia, the Mayor's Office offered vocational training over three months to 34 people, in partnership with a local group of Roma. Twenty-one Roma men received training in bricklaying and 13 Roma women in sewing, and all the participants graduated from the training course. A success factor in this project was the excellent collaboration between the town hall and the Roma group, as well as the commitment of the Roma leader, himself a successful young businessman, to develop projects for his community. The town hall has expressed interest in developing an ongoing partnership with the Roma community for the development of further projects.[113]

In Baia Mare, the "Friendship" Roma Association, in partnership with Maramureş county, the Satulung Mayor's Office, and the Transylvania Business Centre, initiated a brick-production project that will employ 25 Roma. The project is intended to develop existing brick-making activities by doubling production and modernising the process. In spite of difficulties operating in the winter, the project team managed to accomplish its objectives. According to the Partnership Fund's evaluation, the level of collaboration between the Roma Association and its partners was very good. If the brick factory becomes profitable, this project will provide an example of best practice in the economic sphere.[114]

In Resiţa, the local Inspectorate for Environmental Protection, worked with the Caraş-Severin county Alliance for Roma Unity and four village mayors' offices, to establish an "Ecological Guardians Corps." 50 Roma were selected from the four villages and trained in environment, legislation, hygiene, and employment issues. At the end of the course, they were to be evaluated, and 20 participants were to receive offers of permanent positions, with the remaining 30 eligible for seasonal contracts. However, the project assessment found there were significant differences in the way the Alliance and the Inspectorate understood the project goals. The Roma saw the project as a source of direct assistance to participants, while the Inspectorate prioritised the interests of the municipality, considering the training aspect a secondary concern.[115]

---

[112] Resource Center for Roma Communities, field monitoring fiche of the project, "Vocational Training and Assistance for Socio-Professional Integration," (PFRO 130), Cluj Napoca, 2002.

[113] Viorel Anăstăsoaie, MEDE consultant, Evaluation Fiche, "Rroma Access: A Concrete Step for the Improvement of the Social Condition of the Roma Community from Jimbolia Town" (PFRO 329), Cluj Napoca, 2002.

[114] MEDE Evaluation Fiche, "The Friendship Brickwork" (PFRO 178), Cluj Napoca, 2002.

[115] MEDE Evaluation Fiche, "The Establishment of the Ecological Guardians Corps in rural area of upper Timiş, Caraş-Severin county" (PFRO 322), Cluj Napoca, 2002.

Consequently, the Roma participants were dissatisfied with their role, and the official assessment also concluded the level of Roma participation should have been greater.[116]

In Movileni, the Roma Community from Romania, in association with the mayor's office of Movileni Commune, sought to employ 40 Roma in a workshop that would produce tar-paper for roofing. After facing some difficulties in implementation, especially due to the lack of participation from the mayor's office, the project was completed with positive results at the end of March 2002. The Roma community ultimately reached an agreement with the mayor's office to use the building and site free of charge for two years.[117] The MEDE evaluation noted that the prospects for a profitable business seem favourable.[118]

Explicitly discriminatory job vacancy notices in mainstream newspapers have long been identified as a problem.[119] Two legal complaints against these advertisements filed by Romani CRISS in 2001 based on Law 148/2000 were rejected because it was considered that "these public ads are not under the provisions of the Law 148/2000 regarding publication."[120] In April 2002, however, the daily newspaper *România Liberă* was sanctioned for publishing discriminatory job vacancy advertisements based on ethnic grounds. This is the first such case in which sanctions have been applied by the Bucharest Municipality inspectors on the basis of Law 148/2000.[121]

3.2.3 Housing and other goods and services

The Government Strategy proposes a variety of measures to resolve problems related to the right of ownership, and to rehabilitate housing and the environment in areas inhabited by Roma.[122] However, most provisions call for the elaboration of further strategies and do not set out concrete projects. The Strategy notes that financial support must be provided to ensure minimum living conditions including electricity,

---

[116] MEDE Evaluation Fiche, "The Establishment of the Ecological Guardians Corps in rural area of upper Timiș, Caraș-Severin county" (PFRO 322), Cluj Napoca, 2002.

[117] MEDE Evaluation Fiche, "A Better Life" (PFRO301), Cluj Napoca, 2002.

[118] MEDE Evaluation Fiche, "A Better Life" (PFRO301), Cluj Napoca, 2002.

[119] See, e.g. Advisory Committee on the FCNM, *2001 Opinion on Romania*, para. 38, *Minority Protection 2001*, p. 406.

[120] See Annual Report 2001 Romani CRISS, Human Rights Department Romani CRISS – official answer from Bucharest Municipality and Romanian Ombudsmen in *CRISS vs. Anuntul Telefonic* and *CRISS vs. Anuntul de la A la Z*.

[121] See *România Liberă* case in Interim Report – Human Rights Department of Romani CRISS, 2002.

[122] Government Strategy, Chapter VII, Section B.

drinking water, sewer systems, gas, and sanitation services. The Strategy calls for the direct involvement of Roma representatives in the implementation of programmes for building and restoring accommodations.

The Strategy objective to develop a national strategy to resolve Roma property rights issues within four years has not yet been realised.[123] The Report on the Status of Implementation indicates that the Ministry of Public Administration has elaborated proposals for projects to legalise housing and connect utilities in areas inhabited by Roma.[124] This general national programme is planned for ten years in total, with "urgent" measures to address the needs of Roma in particular in its first four years.[125] The protocol signed in June 2002 by the Social Democrat Party and the Roma Social Democrat Party also calls for a national housing strategy to be elaborated.

At the local level, the Strategy calls for Mayors' Offices and Prefects to identify local needs for the rehabilitation of Roma housing, and for the development of a national plan addressing these needs.[126] Although the deadline specified in the Master Plan is 1 March 2002, little had been accomplished by Summer 2002; the Report on the Status of Implementation only mentions plans for a "National programme for rehabilitation of houses and environment, including areas inhabited by Roma."[127] It is expected that the County Bureaux for Roma will assist in collecting the local data, while discussions for drafting the national plan are the responsibility of the Ministry of Public Works, Transportation, and Housing.[128] Several of the housing measures called for in the Government Strategy will be addressed in the "National Plan for Local Development of Roma Communities."

Apart from Government initiatives, one relevant pilot project financed under the Partnership Fund for Roma for social housing demonstrates productive collaboration between civil society and local government. The project, implemented by the Roma County Association "O del Amentza" in partnership with the Mayor's Office in Turdaş (Hunedoara county) took the initiative to repair the apartments of 176 Roma living in three buildings. The Roma association was responsible for coordination of the entire project, including the selection of the construction company, supervision of the work, and reporting. The Mayor's Office was responsible for acquiring authorisations for water and gas installation, evaluation of the quality of the construction, and ensuring that these apartments would be sold to the Roma families at a minimum price

---

[123] Government Strategy, Chapter XI, Point 24.
[124] Ministry of Public Information, *Report on the Status of Implementation*, p. 9.
[125] Ministry of Public Information, *Report on the Status of Implementation*, p. 9.
[126] Government Strategy, Chapter XI, Point 25.
[127] Ministry of Public Information, *Report on the Status of Implementation*, p. 7.
[128] Government Strategy, Chapter XI, Point 25.

agreed on with the buildings' owner. Although resources were limited and more construction work was needed than had been expected, the project went well, with the participation of 80 Roma.

The evaluation completed as part of the Phare Partnership Fund for Roma concluded that, "The beneficiary families are very satisfied since they have seen a real improvement in terms of their quality of living; they have running water and gas for heating and cooking."[129] Previously, the residents had shared a single pump and had no sewage system. Moreover, the purchase price of the flats was relatively low.[130] However, the evaluation also noted that the majority community perceived the improvements as unjustified assistance for Roma.[131] There is also concern that the beneficiaries do not have sufficient income to continue paying utility costs and risk having the services cut off.[132]

Although discrimination in the housing sphere is not explicitly addressed in the Strategy, Roma representatives and civil society organisations identify housing discrimination as a serious issue affecting their community. For example, human rights organisations such Liga Pro Europa Tîrgu Mureş and Romani CRISS Bucharest have extensively documented the situation in Piatra Neamţ in which the Mayor's Office planned to construct a new neighbourhood near the city in 2001, and to move the Roma residents out of two existing buildings into that neighbourhood, ultimately creating a Roma ghetto outside the city.[133] The case was widely publicised both by the local and national media,[134] and, after intervention from the Government and Roma NGOs, the plans were not pursued further.

In other areas as well, local authorities appear determined to evict Roma from city neighbourhoods to the margins of towns and cities. Daily newspapers have chronicled

---

[129] MEDE Evaluation Fiche, "Improvement of the Living Conditions of Roma Community from Turdaş through renovation of their Houses" (PFRO 240), Cluj Napoca, 2002, (hereafter, "MEDE Evaluation Fiche on Turdaş Renovation Project").

[130] MEDE Evaluation Fiche on Turdaş Renovation Project.

[131] MEDE Evaluation Fiche on Turdaş Renovation Project.

[132] MEDE Evaluation Fiche on Turdaş Renovation Project.

[133] See Romani CRISS Documentation Report on the Piatra Neamţ case, on file with Romani CRISS, Bucharest.

[134] See press articles published in the newspapers: *Cotidianul* (10 October 2001), *Monitorul de Bucureşti* (10 October 2001), *Adevărul* (11 October 2001), *Jurnalul Naţional* (11 October 2001), *Azi* (12 October 2001), *Curierul Naţional* (16 October 2001), *Ultima Oră* (16 October 2001)

this trend.[135] The Anti-Discrimination Law 48/2002 contains provisions against discrimination in housing, but these have never been tested before civil courts. Before the NCCD was formed in July 2002, no other body was empowered take action against such policies. With the NCCD in place, court actions can be expected.

In 2001, Roma university students reported frequent discrimination in access to public facilities such as bars, restaurants, or discotheques. Romani CRISS, together with ROMANITIN, the Iaşi Roma Students Association, has filed two legal complaints which are pending before the local court in Iaşi. Romani CRISS has two additional such cases on appeal.[136] NGOs continue to monitor cases of discrimination in 2002, and their petitions have prevailed in several instances.[137] Following a complaint lodged by CRISS, the Local Office for Customer Protection in Rădăuți issued a ruling against and imposed sanctions on the owner of a restaurant who had prohibited entry to Roma, although based on Law 12/1990, rather than 148/2000.[138]

3.2.4 Healthcare and other forms of social protection

In the healthcare sector, the Government Strategy focuses on the need to improve access to public medical services for Roma,[139] and on training for Roma healthcare workers, nurses and physicians to work within Roma communities. Here, as elsewhere in the Strategy's Master Plan, provisions call for drafting concepts or programmes to address the problems identified, and therefore set out relatively few measures to resolve issues directly. The Strategy provides for identifying measures to prompt greater numbers of Roma to register with family doctors.[140] It also provides for the elaboration

---

[135] Newspapers have generally presented the situation of eviction in most of the cases around Bucharest and also the intention of several Mayors to remove Roma from the cities at the margins. In regard to municipalities from Barlad:see daily *Adevărul* 1 March 2001, Piatra Neamţ, in all dailies from Romania around 9–12 October 2001, Deva and Baia Mare, dailies in articles from 11 October 2001.

[136] See Annual Report 2001 Romani CRISS: *CRISS vs ARTENIS SRL and CRISS vs. COMPACT IMPEX SRL.*

[137] See Interim Report 2002, Romani CRISS-Roma Center for Social Intervention and Studies.

[138] See *Rădăuţi* case in Interim Report –Human Rights Department of Romani CRISS , 2002.

[139] Many Roma are excluded from the health insurance system, due to their inability to pay mandatory contributions, their lack of identity documents and other administrative barriers. See, e.g. I. Zoon, *On the Margins: Roma and Public Services in Romania, Bulgaria, and Macedonia*, New York, 2001, pp. 80–81.

[140] Government Strategy, Chapter VII, Section D.

of projects to improve healthcare information programmes and contraceptive education and family planning for Roma women.[141]

There are specific provisions to increase the number of healthcare workers active in Roma communities[142] and the number of Romani medical staff by setting aside places for Roma students in State medical universities.[143]

The Health and Family Ministry been exceptionally active in supporting Roma issues, both before and since the Strategy was adopted, due in part to the appointment of a Counsellor in the Ministry of Health in August 2000; the Counsellor has proven to be an effective focal point for Roma health issues. The Ministerial Commission for Roma in the Health Ministry was also among the first established.[144] Although implementation of the Strategy has been at its most efficient in the health field, its Ministerial Commission for Roma has met only twice since it was formed, suggesting that the Commission structure may not be the most effective means of focusing attention on Roma issues.[145]

A particularly promising initiative under the Strategy involves the introduction of health mediators into local Roma communities. The mediator is to act as a representative of the community, facilitating communication with medical staff as a means of improving access to medical services for Roma. Mediators are also expected to provide information to the Roma community regarding their rights and responsibilities. The position of health mediator is now listed as an official profession in the Classification of Occupations in Romania,[146] and the Ministry of Health and Family, in partnership with Romani CRISS, is implementing a programme to train Roma health mediators. As of October 2002, 166 health mediator positions have been created in 34 counties; these mediators will receive training from Romani CRISS with funding previously allocated by the Ministry.

---

[141] Government Strategy, Chapter VII, Section D.

[142] Government Strategy, Chapter XI, Point 44.

[143] For the academic year 2002-2003, according to the Order of Ministry of Education and Research no. 3693/15.05.2002, seven seats are allocated to Roma candidates at the University of Medicine and Pharmacy in Cluj Napoca.

[144] Order of Minister of Health and Family No. 283/11.05.2001.

[145] Interview with Mariana Buceanu, Roma member of the Ministry of Health and Familiy Ministerial Commission, Iași, 29 August 2002. Mariana Buceanu is also coordinator of the Romani CRISS programme for development of the Health Mediators.

[146] In the Classification of Occupations in Romania, the health mediator is listed at the Base Group "Workers in service for the population," code 513902.

A similar project was initiated under the Partnership Fund for Roma. In Alexandria, 50 Roma health mediators took part in training to improve access to health services,[147] and a handbook was published in both Romanian and Romani.

The Strategy calls for additional research on the health situation of Roma. However, there has been no Government action on this point, although some research has been initiated by private organisations.[148]

The Partnership Fund for Roma, has also funded a project to facilitate the access of Roma from Zabrauți and Stefăneștii de Jos to quality family planning and reproductive healthcare.[149] Three Roma women were selected in each community to disseminate information, raise awareness, and assist other Roma with health issues in general, and more specifically on family planning and sex education. The project included training for sex education teachers. In these two locations, 55 identification documents and ten birth certificates were also issued. Although the first priority of the project was health education, many Roma participants valued it more for the fact that it offered them an employment opportunity.

In Cluj Napoca, the Association for the Emancipation of Roma Women, in partnership with the Director of the Public Health Service for Health Promotion and the Cluj branch of SECS, implemented a project to improve access to information about family planning for Roma women in Cluj county. SECS trained 23 women from six Roma communities as family planning counsellors. The counsellors advise women on available resources at family-planning consulting centres, and have assisted in the dissemination of Romani-language flyers containing information on contraceptives and family planning. Contraceptives were also distributed free-of-charge, together with instructions for usage.

Social benefits

Increasing welfare allowances for large families without any means of support who meet established criteria is a governmental priority outside the framework of the

---

[147] Training was organised by the Christiana Philanthropic Medical and Christian Association, in partnership with the "Voice of the Roma" Cultural Association, the Brinceni mayor's office, and the Ministry of Health.

[148] Research carried out over the past four years by the Bucharest Research Institute for Quality of Life contains some information on the health situation of Roma. The Open Society Institute New York, in collaboration with Centre for Services and Health Policies also initiated a large-scale study on the health situation of Romanian Roma in April 2002.

[149] The project was implemented by the Society for Contraceptive and Sexual Education (SECS), in partnership with the RSDP from the Fifth District of Bucharest (Stefăneștii de Jos branch), the Local Council of the Fifth District of Bucharest, and the Mayoralty of Stefăneștii de Jos commune.

Strategy.[150] The Status of Implementation Report observes that Roma children and families are among the beneficiaries of social security through the monthly State allowance for children; the supplementary allowance for families with children;[151] the minimum guaranteed income allowance, and the National Solidarity Fund.[152] These allowances are universal, however, and not targeted specifically at Roma families. Moreover, as Roma families tend to be large, they are disproportionately affected by a four-child limit on benefits.[153]

The Government Strategy sets out objectives of providing subsidies to non-governmental organisations providing social services programmes, measures already in place at the time of adoption of the Strategy.[154] One proposed Strategy initiative is to increase financial incentives for enterprises that hire persons from families with many children and without any means of support;[155] such affirmative action measures have proven difficult to put into practice, however.

In the past, Roma have reported discrimination in the distribution of social benefits, alleging that some social service employees discriminatorily apply restrictive conditions and procedures exclusively to Roma to disqualify them from receiving benefits.[156] The FCNM Advisory Committee's 2001 Opinion on Romania suggests that the Government should examine the possibility of issuing guidelines for local authorities to implement the Social Aid Act 67/1995, which would reduce concerns of arbitrary decision-making at the local level.[157] In response, the Government indicated that in addition to amending the Act to ensure the funds necessary to implement the

---

[150] Law no. 416/2001 on minimum guaranteed income. A large proportion of the beneficiaries are Roma.

[151] The supplementary allocation, according to Law no. 119/1997, is ROL 50,000 for families with two children, ROL 100,000 for families with three children and ROL 125,000 for families with four or more children.

[152] Ministry of Public Information, *Report on the Status of Implementation*, p. 5.

[153] See I. Zoon, *On the Margins*, p. 33.

[154] According to the Ordinance 26/2000, the NGOs can receive the status of a "public utility," which allows them to receive funding from the State for programmes related to social services. No NGO has received such funds so far. According to Law 34/1998 regarding State funds allocated for associations and foundations that are engaged in social work, Roma NGOs may also propose such initiatives.

[155] Government Strategy, Chapter IX, Point 38.

[156] I. Zoon, *On the Margins*, p. 33.

[157] Advisory Committee on the FCNM, *Opinion on Romania 2001*, para. 29.

guaranteed minimum income Act, Roma inspectors will be appointed to in county offices to assist in serving clients.[158] To date, no action on this point has been reported.

The widespread lack of identity documents among the Roma community has also been an obstacle for accessing certain forms of social protection. The Government Strategy provides for urgent measures to draft an action plan for issuing identity cards and marital status documents to all entitled Roma.[159] In spite of a 15 November 2001 deadline, only small-scale initiatives have been undertaken.[160]

However, civil society organisations have initiated projects in cooperation with the police, and as a result some 3,400 identity cards were issued between 2000 and 2001.[161] In a project implemented under the Phare Partnership Fund for Roma, the Mayor's Office in Giarmata, Timiş county, in partnership with the Association of Gypsy Women "For Our Children" in Timişoara are helping Roma to acquire identity cards, property papers and jobs. Through this project, 280 household were recorded in the agricultural register of the commune, and 25 Roma obtained identity papers and birth certificates. The national census conducted in March 2002 is also expected to lead to further activities to assist Roma in obtaining official documents and registration.

3.2.5 The criminal justice system

This sphere is addressed in the Government Strategy's section on Justice and Public Order. Under this heading, the Strategy identifies as priorities the elimination of the discriminatory effects of regulations in force and improvements to the current legal system.[162] However, there are few projects, if any, specifically addressing discrimination in the criminal justice system. (See also Section 3.3.).

3.3 Protection from Racially Motivated Violence

There is no mention of racially motivated violence in the Government Strategy; the issue is given cursory mention in Section F on Justice and Public Order, where the

---

[158] Comments of the Government of Romania on the Opinion of the Advisory Committee on the Implementation of the FCNM, 2001, comments on para. 29.

[159] Government Strategy, Chapter XI, Point 30.

[160] Ministry of Public Information, *Report on the Status of Implementation*, pp. 7, 8.

[161] Interview with Adrian Vasile, Romani CRISS, 9 September 2002, Bucharest. Romani CRISS has also implemented a project called "Equal chances for Roma children without identity documents," funded by OSI Budapest.

[162] Government Strategy, Chapter VII, Section F.

Ministry of the Interior is called upon to begin "identifying, preventing and solving conflicts likely to generate family, community or interethnic violence." [163] This lack of specificity is a serious omission in a sphere where problems have been highlighted by both domestic and international observers for the past decade.[164] Clear objectives related to combating intolerance and particularly addressing police brutality would serve to meet the Strategy's own goals of changing public opinion and eliminating discrimination.[165]

The Strategy proposes to develop information programmes for Roma leaders, the executive boards of public institutions, and NGOs to facilitate efforts to address cases of discrimination, in line with Law 48/2002. Other objectives are connected to initiating programmes of legal education and delinquency prevention together with members of the Roma communities, and hiring citizens of Roma origin to work in law enforcement services and the police force.

However, very little has been done to implement these objectives. In March 2002, interviews were conducted with 50 Roma applicants for positions in the Bucharest police force. On the basis of an agreement signed between the Ministry of the Interior and the RSDP, ten Roma police officers are to be employed in each district of the capital. According to media reports, the Roma Party agreed to propose new candidates if those already identified happen to fail the examinations. [166]

In Cluj Napoca, the Ethnocultural Diversity Resource Centre, in cooperation with the institute for Research and Prevention of Criminality and the National School for Police sub-officers "Vasile Lascar," implemented a project for conflict prevention within multicultural communities. The project consists of 14 training sessions for police staff that are working in multicultural communities. Each session is designed for 25 participants; to date a total of 350 police officers from 26 counties have taken part. Meetings have also been organised in different areas, in which the participants – including police officers, civil servants, local authorities, and representatives of minorities – analysed problems and sought to build consensus around solutions. The project started in 2000; beginning in 2002 it will receive additional funding from the

---

[163] Government Strategy, Chapter VII, Section F.

[164] In many documented incidents of police violence against Roma, applicable legal provisions are not applied, basic investigations are not carried out, and cases seldom resolved. See European Roma Rights Center, *State of Impunity*, Budapest, 2001. The book was translated in Romanian and 2,000 copies distributed to relevant organisations, including police. Available at <http://www.errc.org>, (accessed 2 October 2002). See also, Romani CRISS Human Rights Department, Annual Report 2001.

[165] Government Strategy, Chapter III, Points 3 and 4.

[166] Network BlitzRoma News, March 4-8, 2002, available at <http://groups.yahoo.com/group/roma_news_en>, (accessed 3 October 2002).

Phare European Initiative for Democracy and Human Rights. As a result of collaboration between the Ethnocultural Diversity Resource Center and the Institute for Prevention of Criminality within the Ministry of the Interior more police with knowledge of a minority language have been hired to work in areas where minorities constitute more than 20 percent of the population.[167]

In the absence of Government activity in this area, civil society organisations have taken steps to document violence against Roma and to develop conflict resolution mechanisms to discourage racially motivated violence. Romani CRISS has been especially active in this respect. Recently, following a violent confrontation between Roma and non-Roma in Scorteni (Bacău county), Romani CRISS with the support of the local authorities in Bacău and the NGO Rom Star Bacău, organised a roundtable to gather representatives of the local government, local and county police, representatives of RSDP from Bacău and Scorteni, the Scorteni mayor's office, and County counsellors to analyse the causes of community violence, as well as to identify concrete solutions to decrease tension in the area. Participants concluded an agreement, emphasising that partnership between the local authorities and Roma organisations is key to the prevention of future conflicts, as is the active involvement of the relevant local authorities in confronting and taking steps to diffuse inter-ethnic conflict. Implementation of this agreement should be monitored, as it could form a model for other conflict resolution projects. However, without the participation of experienced mediators, such partnerships are not likely to materialise.

In some areas, the RSDP has also initiated a custom of signing protocols with local police stations, agreeing to work to prevent violent situations and to exchange information.[168] However, these agreements have been rather formal in nature; most Roma are unaware they exist, and the Party rarely acts as a mediator between the police and the Roma community in practice.

3.4 Promotion of Minority Rights

The Strategy states the Government's commitment to cultural diversity, and to the fight against forms of extremism that promote intolerance and ethnic hatred. The Government's efforts to promote minority rights have been most visible in the sphere of education, where the availability of Roma language education has expanded considerably in the past several years. Efforts to increase Roma representation in all

---

[167] Interview with Gábor Ádám, Program Coordinator, Ethocultural Diversity Resource Center in Cluj Napoca, 9 September 2002.

[168] See Romanian Ethnic Minority Briefs, No. 25, 30 September 2002, "Parthenrship [sic] Between Roma Representatives – Romanian Gendarmerie."

levels of Government have not met expectations, as the offices created have not been adequately integrated into existing structures or assigned responsibilities that would make the appointments meaningful. Moreover, the Government's reliance on a single organisation to represent Roma, the Roma Social Democrat Party, has given rise to concerns that other organisations have been effectively excluded.

The Government Strategy provides for programmes to "reinvigorate and assert the Roma ethnic identity,"[169] especially in the spheres of culture, language, religion, education, training, and public life.[170] The responsible coordinating structure is the National Office for Roma.

3.4.1 Language

The Government Strategy makes no mention of measures to promote the use of Romani with public authorities. However, such measures are contained in other legislation. According to the Romanian Constitution, judicial procedure shall be conducted in Romanian, with an exception for national minorities, who have the right to an interpreter. In criminal cases, an interpreter must be provided free of charge.[171] The Law on Public Administration permits the use of minority languages in public administration in areas where a minority makes up 20 percent of the population.[172] A Government Decision[173] provides that bilingual signs shall be put up in areas where a minority population comprises 20 percent or more of the total population. However, there has been no initiative from local governments or Roma groups to put up signs in Romani, and indeed there has been little demand for such rights from the Roma community generally.

The recent census may help to build support for realising these rights among Roma, as it registered an increase in the Roma population. The initial data shows that 535,250 citizens identified themselves as Roma, approximately 135,000 more than in 1992

---

[169] Government Strategy, Chapter VII, Section I.

[170] Government Strategy, Chapter VII, Section I.

[171] Romanian Constitution, Article 127.

[172] Law 215/2001 on Public Administration, Official Gazette 204 of 23 April 2001, Articles 40 (7) and 51.

[173] Government Decision no. 1206/2001 on the approval of the right of citizens belonging to a national minority to use the mother tongue in local public administration under the Law of Public Administration no 215/2001.

census.[174] Moreover, interest in and knowledge of the Romani language has received a significant boost from Strategy initiatives in the education sphere.

3.4.2 Education

Point 95 in the Master Plan for applying the Strategy calls for the introduction of optional Roma history and language classes in educational institutions. The Ministry of Education had already established the option for Roma language and history classes in primary and secondary schools in 1999,[175] and this measure has been implemented in some schools, where pupils study Romani for three to four hours per week. Classes in Romani can be established upon parental request, and if the teacher of the class does not speak the language it is possible to hire someone who does; the required teaching qualifications may be waived if necessary.[176] In the sixth and seventh grades, parents may also request an hour per week of "history and traditions of the Roma."[177]

The Ministry of Education and Research has supported increasing the number of Romani-language teachers: with funding from a broad spectrum of donors,[178] between 1999-2001 the Ministry organised summer schools with approximately 50 participants per year for study of Romani. Most of the participants are now involved in teaching Romanes at the local level, or work as School Inspectors for Roma within the County Inspectorates. As a result of these efforts, the process of teaching Romani has greatly expanded. In 1992-1993 only 368 Roma children studied Romani, while at present it is being studied by 200 Roma and non-Roma teachers and approximately 11,000

---

[174] Efforts to encourage Roma to identify themselves as such were carried out. There was considerable controversy around accusations that Roma were identifying themselves as Hungarians to obtain rights in Hungary under the Status Law. See Network BlitzRoma News, 28 February, "Roma People Advised to Declare Their Ethnic Identity." See also, RFE/RL *Newsline*, 22 March, "Cluj Mayor Claims Foul Play In Romanian Census."

[175] Order of the Ministry of National Education (now Ministry of Education and Research) no. 3533/31.03.1999 regarding the study of mother tongue language by the students belonging to national minorities who attend Romanian language schools.

[176] Order of the Ministry of National Education no. 3533/31.03.1999, Article VII.2, "In case of limited number or non-existence of qualified teachers for Romani language, Roma having at least a high-school degree will teach the classes. In special situations, the classes may be held by Roma graduates of high-schools without a Bachelors degree or by graduates of a minimum of 10 classes…"

[177] Telephone interview with Gheorghe Sarau, 19 August, 2002.

[178] Summer-school funding is provided by the Department for Protection of National Minorities, Open Society Foundation Romania, Education 2000+ Centre, Resource Centre for Roma Communities, Embassy of Great Britain, Romani CRISS, and the Ministry of Education and Research.

children.[179] In 2001, Romani teachers formed a professional association, "Ketanes," in order to support the professional training of teachers.

The Strategy also includes a commitment to support NGOs offering extracurricular correspondence courses for teachers of Romani.[180] To date, 50 Roma teachers have received long-distance training, at a personal cost of approximately €300 per year, as no State funding has been made available. For students enrolled in 2001, independent scholarships were available from various sources.[181] Even with these efforts, the demand for studying Romani continues to exceed the number of qualified teachers.[182]

The introduction of teaching modules for specialists in the public administration, social work, health, police, and education are also foreseen in the Strategy, in order to ensure a better understanding of the Roma social, economic, and cultural situation.[183] However, no specific activity related to this point was included in the Master Plan, and no activities have been funded.

3.4.3 Participation in public life

The Strategy explicitly aims to improve levels of Roma participation in political and administrative structures, particularly at the local level. The "Communication and civil participation" component of the Government Strategy aims to promote Roma leaders' participation in the political decision-making process, and includes specific provisions to enhance Roma participation in public life. It also aims to support the development of Roma civil society groups. The Master Plan outlines plans to organise monthly meetings between mayors and Roma leaders,[184] and to specify the conditions for recruitment and promotion of civil servants as a form of affirmative action.[185] Roma are represented in the

---

[179] See Ministry of Education and Research web site, <http://www.edu.ro/scurt.htm>, (accessed 2 October 2002), "A Short History of Romani Language Teaching."

[180] Government Strategy, Chapter IX, Point 88.

[181] Scholarships are available through the Roma Memorial University Scholarship Program of the Open Society Institute Budapest, the Centre for Education 2000+, and Resource Centre for Roma Communities.

[182] Roma News, March 18-22 2002, "Not enough Romani speaking teachers".

[183] Government Strategy, Chapter VII, Section H.

[184] Government Strategy, Chapter XI, Point 17.

[185] Government Strategy, Chapter XI, Point 23.

National Minorities Council and in the Chamber of Deputies by the RSDP.[186] It is estimated that ROL 130 billion (approximately €4 million) is allocated annually for ethnic minority organisations.[187] Of this, the Roma Social Democratic Party received approximately ROL 18 billion (approximately €500,000) in 2002.[188]

An uneasy collaboration has developed between the representatives of Roma NGOs active in the field and many County Bureaux for Roma, exacerbating existing weaknesses in cooperation among local institutions. A lack of clear responsibilities and chain of command for local Roma experts has constituted an impediment to Strategy implementation. While the main implementing agency is the National Office for Roma, the Ministry of Public Administration hires the local Roma experts to work under the Prefect's office. Thus, it is not always clear into which organisational structure the local experts fit.

As part of the Strategy's structural framework, special positions for Roma have been created at the local level in the mayors' offices (See Section 2.4.). The appointment process has come under particular criticism for exacerbating existing political tensions within the Roma community. For example, five local Roma NGOs in Aninoasa submitted a complaint to the local mayor's office regarding the nomination of the local Roma expert by the RSDP.[189] The letter cites the Strategy's consensus principle, which calls for Strategy initiatives to be a joint effort of the Government and representative organisations of the Roma community – meaning all organisations and not only the RSDP.

According to administrative procedure, when a civil servant is to be hired, a competition should be organised and specific professional criteria fulfilled by the candidates. However, a letter to the mayor's office signed by the County Prefect, stated the following:

> In order to achieve and implement the measures stated in the Strategy for Improvement of the Condition of Roma, […] according to the Law of the State Budget for year 2002, you will nominate one person as local expert on Roma issues.

---

[186] The National Minorities Council was established by Government Decision No. 589, 21 June, 2001, published in the Official Gazette No. 365 on 6 July, 2001. The Council includes representatives of all ethnic minorities living in Romania. The RSDP holds a seat in Parliament through a provision that sets aside one seat for each ethnic minority group that fails to reach the 5% electoral threshold. See *Minority Protection 2001*, pp. 415–416.

[187] Ministry of Public Information, see <http://www.publicinfo.ro>, (accessed 3 October 2002).

[188] Interview with Mariea Ionescu, National Office for Roma, 15 March 2002, Bucharest.

[189] Complaint registered with the Aninoasa mayor's office, no. 274/07.02.2002, on a disagreement over the nomination of a local expert for Roma after consultation with the RSDP only; the letter's authors propose that the job should be filled only after a competition.

> The nomination of the person will be made by the mayor of the locality [...] with the consultation of the County Bureau for Roma and the local branch of the RSDP.
>
> It is recommended that the person who will be nominated as local expert for Roma to belong to the Roma community and be member of the RSDP. The RSDP – Hunedoara County Branch – recommends that Mr. A.I.A be nominated for this position...[190]

The letter illustrates the common failure to respect relevant hiring procedures in appointing Roma representatives, and to the widespread perception that the RSDP leaders prioritise party loyalty over professional qualifications, resulting in the politicisation of Strategy implementation. In this context, communication between the RSDP and other local NGOs, already strained, has almost ceased. Meanwhile, there is no shortage of qualified candidates: there are approximately 600 Roma university students and graduates, as well as many potential candidates with extensive experience working within civil society organisations.

3.4.4 Media

Media are addressed in the "culture and denominations" and "communication and civic involvement" sections of the Government Strategy. The Strategy proposes supporting the development of national cultural and information channels for Roma, including television programmes, radio broadcasts, and publications. The Strategy also provides for the elaboration of programmes for fighting discrimination in the media, and elaborating information campaigns on health and employment issues.

At present, one Roma-oriented television programme airs on a weekly basis on national television, together with the other programmes designed for national minorities. Under the Strategy, the Ministry of Public Information is responsible for initiating a programme to fight discrimination in the media, but no action has been taken to implement this measure, although the deadline was set for November 2001.[191]

Through monitoring projects, NGOs have identified the need to improve the perception and representation of Roma in the mainstream media and have disseminated news

---

[190] Official letter from the Hunedoara County Prefect, registration no. 310/16.01.2002.
[191] Government Strategy, Chapter IX, Point 110.

related to Roma issues.[192] A report issued by the Academia Cațavencu Media Monitoring Agency lists the stereotypes of Roma extracted from five national newspapers: out of 14 stereotypes identified in an analysis of 335 articles, 10 are considered negative.[193]

A number of media initiatives have been implemented with Phare or other EU funding. While these are not connected directly to Strategy implementation, they nonetheless support general Strategy objectives. Under the Partnership Fund for Roma, a Roma News Agency was established as the result of a partnership between the Media Monitoring Agency Department within the Academia Cațavencu, Romani Criss, the National Press Agency *Rompres* and the Centre for Independent Journalism.[194] The Roma News Agency functions as part of the Romani CRISS office and has been extremely active since its launch in September 2001; approximately 800 news items have been produced and disseminated.[195] The Roma News Agency will ultimately become an independent organisation, according to its statute.

The News Agency also organised training for journalists: 11 Roma trainees were selected for three months of training in media, news agency, State institutions, English, computer skills, and television production. The team took the initiative to produce and distribute a video clip regarding the issue of Roma self-identification for the 2002 Census.

The Centre for Independent Journalism published a guide for best practices in journalism, focusing on anti-discrimination, funded by the Phare programme for Improvement of the Situation of Roma.[196]

---

[192] The Aven Amentza Public Policies Roma Centre in Bucharest monitors the presentation of Roma issues in media, and produces the *Inforrom* bulletin, which is widely distributed through its daily e-mail. In Cluj Napoca, "Amari Emisiunea," a monthly television programme designed for Roma communities in ten counties in Transylvania, is broadcast with support from the Resource Center for Roma Communities.

[193] Media Monitoring Agency – Academia Cațavencu, "Roma population reflected in the Romanian media," Media Monitoring Report, January–August 2001.

[194] The Center for Independent Journalism is an international NGO founded by the Independent Journalism Foundation based in New York. It has branches in four regional capitals: Budapest, Bucharest, Bratislava and Prague, working with local journalists to encourage independent, impartial, diverse, and ethical reporting.

[195] Of these 800 articles, 30 percent were disseminated by the Romanian State Press Agency Rompress, and ten percent were published in newspapers.

[196] Phare RO 9803.01, Improvement of the Situation of Roma.

3.4.5 Culture

Section I of the Government Strategy addresses "Culture and Denominations," calling for measures in the artistic, economic, and media spheres to enable Roma to develop and express their cultural identity. Again, many of the measures provided in the Master Plan of Action are preliminary: preparing plans for cultural festivals, feasibility studies for a Roma theatre, and other research.[197] While some of these studies may have been carried out, the effect on Roma communities has so far been limited.

The Phare-funded analysis of projects for Roma communities implemented during 1990–2000 mentions that "the fields of activity of Roma NGOs are reflecting the main areas of interest for the Roma community," and that almost 50 percent of NGO projects have a cultural component;[198] this may also reflect the priorities of the funding and donor agencies on which local NGOs depend. However, some Roma activists perceive activities to promote Romani culture and identity as an important tool for the integration of Roma into the larger community, while preserving their distinctive traditions and language.[199] Phare funding has also provided support for the efforts of some Roma NGOS to raise awareness of Roma identity by organising education in local history for young Roma.[200]

The Ministry of Culture and Denomination, in collaboration with the Aven Amentza Roma Center for Public Policies, organised a "Caravan for intercultural education and revitalisation of cultural heritage" in Winter 2002.[201] The caravan visited all 41 counties in an effort to establish the basis for harmonising local minority policies, encouraging dialogue and exchange between local Roma communities and local authorities, and attracting funding for cultural and other initiatives.[202]

---

[197] Government Strategy, Chapter IX, points 100–108.

[198] Projects for Roma in Romania, 1990–2000, published by Ethnocultural Diversity Resource Center Cluj Napoca, under the Phare project for Improvement of the Situation of Roma (RO 9803.01), "A quantitative analysis of the projects for Roma" chapter, page 65.

[199] Interview with Ötvös Géza, President of Wassdas Foundation, Cluj Napoca, April 2002.

[200] Projects for Roma in Romania, 1990-2000, published by Ethnocultural Diversity Resource Center Cluj Napoca, under the Phare project for Improvement of the Situation of Roma (RO 9803.01), page 184.

[201] Ministry of Public Information, *Report on the Status of Implementation*, pp. 22–23.

[202] Round-tables were organised in all counties except three in which the collaboration of the local authorities was minimal, between 20 February – 16 March 2002.

4. EVALUATION

The Government Strategy represents an important step towards achieving greater inclusion of Roma in all spheres of Romanian society. The Government consulted with Roma organisations throughout the process of drafting the Strategy and during its implementation, and it reflects many of the needs and concerns they have articulated. However, it does not address serious concerns relating to racially motivated violence by private and public actors, which has been widely documented by domestic and international human rights observers. Still, the Roma community generally approves of the content of the Strategy.

Though the Strategy is comprehensive in scope and sets out more than 120 actions or projects to be undertaken, it does not provide detailed plans and fails to specify concrete activities. Implementation of the Strategy remains at a very low level more than a year after its adoption. Even where the Master Plan for applying the Strategy calls for assessment or preparation of more detailed plans, in many cases nothing had been achieved by the specified deadline. The Government has allocated little or no resources for Strategy implementation; those projects that have been undertaken have been funded almost exclusively through the Phare Partnership Fund for Roma, which is not administered by the Government directly. Initiatives taken by civil society organisations greatly outpace Government-sponsored projects, and although many NGO programmes do receive some State or local government support, there is no existing mechanism to incorporate experiences and lessons learned into Government policy.

One of the most important strengths of the Strategy is the degree to which it provides for Roma participation at all levels of Government. In particular, it calls for the establishment of local structures, with Roma representation, to implement the Strategy and ensure it meets the needs of individual Roma communities. To this end, County Bureaux for Roma have been established, and Roma experts have been appointed in Mayors' Offices at the local level. These measures have the potential to institutionalise Roma representation in local governance, and to create a powerful network of Roma civil servants.

In practice, several problems have emerged during the process of establishing this network First, a single political organisation (the Roma Social Democrat Party) has been accorded the right to appoint Roma experts, without regard to standard practice for the recruitment and hiring of civil servants. This practice fails to tap into the extreme diversity of the Roma political and non-governmental spheres. It has also tended to result in politicised appointments based on party loyalty, rather than the recruitment of qualified university graduates and professionals.

Second, the failure to appoint qualified and committed civil servants, in the County Bureaux for Roma as elsewhere, can quickly lead to the de-legitimisation of the

Strategy as a whole. There is no shortage of well-educated Roma professionals: affirmative action measures taken in the past few years by the Ministry of Education have resulted in approximately 800 young Roma studying in different universities and faculties, who could bring important skills and training to local government.

Finally, according to some Romani activists, the Government's reliance on a single political organisation to represent the Roma community has had the effect of fragmenting the Roma NGO community. According to one representative, the Federation Framework Convention of Roma has ceased virtually all its activities due to the "politicisation of the Strategy and of the fact that the Government treated the partnership with the Roma civil society differently" and "associated unilaterally and preferentially, without taking into consideration the degree of expertise, with a sole [representative] of civil society… violating the principles of the Strategy…"[203]

5. Recommendations

In the interest of achieving full and effective implementation of the Strategic Framework for the Improvement of the Situation of Roma, the Romanian Government should:

- Re-analyse the text and make the adjustments to the Strategy and the Master Plan so as to reflect the latest developments and applicable regulations as well as new input, especially from NGOs implementing projects complementing Strategy objectives.

- Consider adoption of the text as a law, to make its provisions enforceable.

- Re-estimate the cost of implementation and allocate Strategy funds under the State budget for 2003–2004. Collaborate with European Union institutions and other donors to ensure international funding for Roma is directed towards Strategy implementation.

- Task the State Secretary responsible for the Department for Inter-ethnic Relations with leading the Joint Committee for Monitoring and Implementation. Increase the frequency of meetings of the Joint Committee and ensure the participation of its members.

---

[203] "Implementation of GD 430/2001 Strategy for Improvement of the Situation of Roma, Alternative Report," *Aven Amentza* magazine No. 19–20, April–May 2002.

- Strengthen the capacity of the National Office for Roma by enlarging the number of trained and committed Roma professionals, university students or graduates on its staff.

- Mobilise the Ministerial Commissions on Roma in each ministry; establish and enforce specific deadlines and targets including those for reporting on whether and how commitments have been met.

- State clear-cut responsibilities for project implementation at the local level for Prefects, County Councils and Local Councils and allocate necessary resources.

- Re-analyse the anti-discrimination legislation to bring it into compliance with the European Union Race Directive.

- Ensure the independence of the National Council for Combating Discrimination; ensure that the selection of staff members is transparent and make available resources for its operation.

- Provide training for lawyers, attorneys and judges regarding the new anti-discrimination legislation, including professionals from the Roma community.

- Continue to carry out measures to raise public awareness, particularly among minority communities of discrimination and possibilities for recourse.

- Undertake measures to hire Roma professionals as civil servants, while ensuring that selection is based on fair competition and professional merits, not political affiliation.

- Work with a broad range of Roma civil society representatives to foster constructive dialogue and reduce frictions that hinder effective cooperation within the Roma community as well as between the Roma and non-Roma population.

- Ensure the participation of Roma civil society representatives in the decision-making processes of institutions responsible for implementing various strategy objectives and programmes.

Recommendations for Roma organisations

- Actively seek the implementation of Strategy measures: re-activate the consultation structures of the Roma associations. Wherever possible, issue common opinions, press releases, and articles for the media and the general public.

- Ensure open communications between Roma communities and those responsible for Strategy implementation at the local and national level.

- Offer support to the local Experts for Roma within the County Bureaux for Roma through local working groups.

- Increase participation in public debates and develop clear and consistent reporting and reactions to negative events regarding the situation of Roma.

- Make use of the NCCD, once it is functioning, to file complaints of discrimination.

- Help identify and train future Roma civil society activists and politicians.

- Make use of the human resources existing at the local level, including Roma university students, young NGO activists, local community leaders.

Recommendations to international organisations and international donors

- Increasingly make funding contingent on proportional contributions by the Government.

- Promote assessment and evaluation of Strategy implementation by supporting the preparation of domestic monitoring reports and critiques, and organise seminars and conferences at which such reports can be discussed.

- Facilitate the incorporation of projects implemented with international support into Government-administered programmes.

Minority Protection in Slovakia

AN ASSESSMENT OF THE STRATEGY FOR THE SOLUTION OF THE PROBLEMS
OF THE ROMA NATIONAL MINORITY AND THE SET OF MEASURES
FOR ITS IMPLEMENTATION – STAGES I AND II.

Table of Contents

1. Executive Summary 530

2. The Government Programme – Background 535
   2.1 Background to Present Programme 535
   2.2 The Programme – Process 536
   2.3 The Programme – Content 537
   2.4 The Programme – Administration/ Implementation/Evaluation 540
   2.5 The Programme and the Public 548
   2.6 The Programme and the EU 549

3. The Government Programme – Implementation 553
   3.1 Stated Objectives of the Programme 553
   3.2 Government Programme and Discrimination 553
        3.2.1 Education 555
        3.2.2 Employment 560
        3.2.3 Housing and other goods and services 563
        3.2.4 Healthcare and other forms of social protection 568
        3.2.5 The criminal justice system 570

    3.3　Protection from Racially
         Motivated Violence 571
    3.4　Promotion of Minority Rights 575
         3.4.1　Education 576
         3.4.2　Language 578
         3.4.3　Participation in public life 579
         3.4.4　Media 581
         3.4.5　Culture 582

4. Evaluation 583

5. Recommendations 586

1. Executive Summary

The Slovak Government's current policy towards its Roma minority is based upon a two-stage Strategy adopted in 1999–2000 (hereafter, "Strategy for Roma").[1] To enhance implementation, the former Government[2] adopted a set of "Priorities" in April 2002.

The Strategy, which is complemented by an Action Plan to combat discrimination, racism and intolerance, aims to set forth a comprehensive set of measures to address the problems faced by Roma. Although review and revision of the Strategy is in progress, the present version reflects insufficient research and planning, and implementation has consisted principally of short-term projects in a few priority areas; these projects do not yet add up to a coherent long-term policy. Funding from the State budget has also been insufficient. Moreover, Strategy implementation has offered few opportunities to Roma to participate as decision-makers and managers in developing solutions to the problems their communities face. Still, several promising NGO initiatives are now in the pilot phase, and, with greater State support, may offer opportunities for both further refinement of the Strategy and more direct participation from the Roma community.

Recent steps to improve the institutional framework for administering, coordinating and communicating policies and projects to improve the situation for Roma should be reinforced. In particular, the Office of the Plenipotentiary should be accorded additional political backing, manifested through the allocation of additional human and financial resources as well as statements of support from public officials at the highest levels.

Background

Previous governmental policies towards Roma had characterised their situation as a purely social problem, of "citizens requiring special care," with discrimination and the protection of Roma identity and culture receiving less attention. In implementation, these policies often suffered from lack of funding and weak institutional capacity.

---

[1] Strategy of the Government of the Slovak Republic for the Solution of the Problems of the Roma National Minority and the Set of Measures for Its Implementation – Stage I, adopted by Government Resolution No. 821 (27 September 1999); and Elaboration of the Government Strategy for Addressing Problems of the Romani National Minority into a Package of Concrete Measures for the Year 2000 – Stage II, adopted by Government Resolution No. 294 (3 May 2000).

[2] Parliamentary elections were held on 20–21 September 2002. For final results and the composition of the new Government, see "Slovak Party Leaders Meet with President," RFE/RL *Newsline*, 24 September 2002.

The Government elected in 1998 declared the integration of Roma as one of its main priorities and elaborated a two-stage strategy in 1999–2000. Government officials engaged in consultation with Roma representatives, civil society, and domestic as well as international experts during the drafting process, although some Roma representatives feel that the impact of their input on the final content was minimal.

Administration

Overall responsibility for implementing the Strategy is borne by the Deputy Prime Minister for Human Rights, Minorities and Regional Development (hereafter, "Deputy Prime Minister"), with support from the Section for Human Rights and Minorities (Office of the Government) as well as the Plenipotentiary for Roma Communities.

The Government has taken several steps to reinforce administrative capacity to implement and coordinate the Strategy, including through the establishment of an Inter-Ministerial Commission for Roma Community Affairs (IMC), chaired by the Plenipotentiary, and by strengthening and expanding the capacity of the Plenipotentiary.[3] However, the ability of the Deputy Prime Minister and the Plenipotentiary to secure sufficient funding and compel effective implementation from the ministries and other State bodies tasked with responsibilities under the Strategy is still limited.

While the Government has produced several general reports on the Strategy, there is no mechanism for evaluating the impact or effectiveness of implementation systematically, and with structured input from civil society. The Plenipotentiary recently proposed a review of governmental efforts to improve conditions in Roma settlements.

Roma representatives are engaged with the Strategy mainly in an advisory capacity; many have called for greater involvement in project implementation and evaluation. There are no Roma in positions of responsibility within governmental bodies responsible for implementing components of the Strategy, with the notable exception of the Plenipotentiary. Generally speaking, NGO participation in implementing components of the Strategy and Phare-funded projects has been low.

---

[3] A new, third, Statute of the Plenipotentiary has been proposed which would enhance her competence to coordinate and evaluate implementation of the Strategy by placing her under the direct responsibility of the Prime Minister rather than the Deputy Prime Minister; if adopted, the new Statute would also strengthen the Plenipotentiary's position under the Law on Competencies and the Law on Public Service. The proposed Statute is at <http://www.vlada.gov.sk/orgovanova/dokumenty/novy_statut.doc>, (accessed 22 October 2002); see also Government Resolution No. 1069 (18 September 2002).

EU Support

The EU has provided significant financial support for projects to improve the situation of Roma, primarily to Government initiatives to improve access to education, ameliorate living conditions in segregated Roma settlements, and promote tolerance towards Roma and other minorities. Civil society organisations have called for greater transparency in procedures for allocating and evaluating expenditure of Phare (and governmental) funding. Roma representatives have criticised the fact that Roma NGOs have not been sufficiently involved in the implementation of Phare-funded projects.

The European Commission has welcomed the adoption of the Strategy, but has repeatedly called for further efforts to eliminate the "gap between good policy formulation and its implementation," and for improved efforts to fight discrimination.[4]

Content and Implementation

The Strategy for Roma – Stage I outlines a series of general measures to be implemented in the areas of: human rights, minority rights and support for NGOs; training and education; language and culture; employment; housing; health; social services; and regional development. Stage II lists more specific tasks (with the exception of the last area). In many cases, implementation either has not started or is still in progress and there has been little evaluation of results to date.

A set of priority areas for action were identified in 2002,[5] mainly in the areas of education, housing, and raising public awareness of Strategy initiatives and Roma issues. Specifically, the 2002 Priorities propose to support a comprehensive programme to improve conditions in Roma settlements and to train social workers for jobs in Roma communities.

The Strategy's formal recognition of discrimination in the past is not matched by concrete measures to identify and sanction discriminatory acts in the present. An Action Plan to combat discrimination, racism, and intolerance[6] is intended to fill this gap in the Strategy; the 2002–2003 follow-up Action Plan contains a separate section devoted to Roma, including a proposal to address discriminatory practices by local public administration in the area of social assistance. However, efforts in this area continue to be hampered in the absence of comprehensive anti-discrimination legislation.

---

[4] See European Commission, *2000 and 2001 Reports on Slovakia's Progress Towards Accession*, available at <http://www.europa.eu.int/comm/enlargement/slovakia/index.htm>, (accessed 30 September 2002).

[5] Priorities of the Government of the Slovak Republic with regard to Roma Communities for 2002, adopted by Government Resolution No. 357 (10 April 2001).

[6] Action Plan for the Prevention of All Forms of Discrimination, Racism, Xenophobia, Anti-Semitism and Other Forms of Intolerance for the Period 2000–2001.

Insufficient legislation has posed a major obstacle to the implementation of measures in the area of education, such as the organisation of pre-school preparatory classes and the employment of Roma teacher's assistants. The expansion of these programmes – which have been successful in the pilot phase – will require additional State support. The Plenipotentiary has criticised the Ministry of Education for its failure to develop a systematic, long-term strategy for improving access to education for Roma, an area which is universally acknowledged to be key to improving the situation for Roma more broadly.

Many Roma lack educational qualifications and job training, and unemployment rates among Roma communities approach 100 percent in some regions. The Strategy has supported mainly short-term measures, such as "public benefit jobs," which are not likely to stimulate initiative or offer additional job qualifications to Roma job-seekers. Moreover, even these measures have met with opposition from regional and local public administrations. Outside the scope of the Strategy, the National Labour Office has initiated several programmes that offer training, job counselling, and small grants to Roma entrepreneurs; though implementation is still at an early stage, these programmes are promising, as they engage Roma as active participants in enhancing their own employability.

Segregation and extremely poor living conditions pose a pressing existential problem for many Roma, particularly those living in segregated settlements. The 2002 Priorities aim to improve the infrastructure in these communities as a matter of urgency; efforts are under preparation. Many settlements are illegally-constructed, impeding infrastructural improvements and the extension of basic municipal services and utilities, and the Strategy has not addressed this issue. Central government bodies appear incapable of overcoming resistance to settlement improvement initiatives from local authorities and residents. However, the Plenipotentiary's recent initiative to train social workers to work as mediators between Roma communities and local public administration may bring about improvements in this area.

The Strategy proposes few measures to address serious healthcare issues arising from poor living conditions and limited access to healthcare. No measures have been proposed to respond to serious allegations of discrimination in access to healthcare and other public goods and services.

Additional research and monitoring is necessary to determine the extent of discrimination against Roma in the criminal justice system, which some international and domestic observers have identified as a serious problem. Information of this kind would greatly facilitate State efforts to ensure that Roma (as well as non-Roma) are treated fairly by law enforcement officers and the police as well as judges and prosecutors, and would complement existing Strategy initiatives to provide human rights training to these officials.

Enhanced legislation to identify and prosecute racially motivated violence has not been accompanied by sufficient training or other awareness-raising activities. Meanwhile, ongoing incidents involving police violence or intimidation of Roma tend to reinforce reluctance among Roma communities to bring complaints of racially motivated violence to the police; visible governmental efforts to improve policing in Roma communities is necessary.

The Plenipotentiary has established a Language Commission to produce a revised codification of Romanes for use in textbooks and other teaching materials; as codification would greatly facilitate efforts to support the use of Romanes in schools and in public life, the work of the Commission should receive full State support. Otherwise, efforts to promote tolerance and multiculturalism among teachers and in schools have been limited.

The Strategy identifies the need to involve Roma directly in efforts to address problems faced by their communities. However, it fails to propose concrete means of achieving such involvement; very few Roma are employed as civil servants or on governmental bodies for directing and coordinating Strategy implementation, and there are no projects to train or recruit Roma into such positions at present; some efforts have been made to recruit Roma in the police force.

Conclusion

The Strategy for Roma sets out a relatively comprehensive set of policy measures to address issues faced by Roma. During implementation, a number of gaps have become apparent, which should be addressed as part of a regular process of Strategy revision and updating.

First, there is a need for greater research and planning to ground Strategy initiatives more solidly in response to an accurate and detailed picture of the most important issues and problems. Second, there is a need for this information to be integrated, together with the experience gained from the implementation of pilot projects, to develop more coherent, longer-term strategies in key areas, as well as an overall policy concept; the Plenipotentiary must be granted the capacity and the authority to play this crucial coordinating role. Third, comprehensive anti-discrimination legislation is a necessary first step to undertaking necessary measures to combat discriminatory acts by private individuals as well as by State officials; the adoption of such legislation will need to be complemented by broader training for representatives of public administration as well as civil society, to ensure that it is effective in practice. Finally, the Government must demonstrate clear and unequivocal support for Strategy objectives and initiatives, to send a message to public officials at all levels as well as the broader public that implementation is to be taken seriously.

2. The Government Programme – Background

2.1 Background to Present Programme

In the years following 1989, a series of policy documents concerning Roma were adopted, most of which treated the "Roma issue" as a social problem, to be addressed through social assistance programmes.[7] This approach – which was developed largely without participation from Roma representatives – neglected the ethnic dimension of the issues faced by Roma.

Representatives of civil society welcomed these incipient efforts, but highlighted the obstacles to effective implementation raised by the lack of a comprehensive strategy with concrete measures, weak institutional capacity, a failure to assign responsibility for implementation, and the lack of financial resources.[8] Implementation of these programmes was also hampered by the constantly changing political environment as well as a lack of public support.

---

[7] See Principles of Government Policy Regarding the Roma, adopted by Government Resolution No. 153 (April 1991); Concept of an Approach to Citizens Requiring Special Care, adopted by Government Resolution No. 310 (30 April 1996), at <http://www.vlada.gov.sk/uznesenia/1996/0430/uz_0310_1996.html>, (accessed 16 May 2002); and Conceptional Plans Regarding Solving Problems of the Roma, adopted by Government Resolution No. 796 (November 1997). The position of "Plenipotentiary for the Solution of the Problems of Citizens Requiring Special Assistance" was also created at the Ministry for Labour, Social Affairs and Family, reflecting the social assistance approach toward the Roma as a socially-handicapped group. Interview with the Head of the Parliamentary Committee for Human Rights, Bratislava, 14 March 2002.

[8] For more, see M. Vašečka, *Country Report on Minority Practices in Pre-EU Accession Slovakia*, Bratislava, 2001, p. 14, <http://www.ivo.sk/subory/country_report_mr.pdf>, (accessed 26 April 2002); see also M. Vašečka, "Roma," in *Slovakia 1998–1999. A Global Report on the State of Society*, G. Mesežnikov and M. Ivantyšyn (eds.), Institute for Public Affairs, Bratislava, 1999, pp. 759–760; M. Vašečka, "The Romanies in Slovakia," in *National Human Development Report Slovakia 1998*, L. Vagač (ed.), United Nations Development Programme (UNDP), Bratislava, 1999; and UNDP, *Towards Diversity with a Human Face*, Roma Regional Human Development Report 2002 (draft), April 2002.

2.2 The Programme – Process

The Government elected in 1998 identified the integration of Roma as one of its priorities, as part of a general effort to improve the situation of minorities.[9] The Deputy Prime Minister for Human Rights, Minorities and Regional Development, Pál Csáky (hereafter, "Deputy Prime Minister"), was accordingly tasked with elaborating a Strategy, which was drafted by the newly-appointed Plenipotentiary for Addressing the Issues of Roma.[10] In a significant departure from previous practice, the Government opened consultations with Roma representatives as well as experts from civil society during the process of developing the Strategy.[11]

The Strategy was adopted in two stages. First, in September 1999, the "Strategy for the Solution of the Problems of the Roma National Minority and the Set of Measures for Its Implementation" (hereafter, "Strategy for Roma – Stage I") was adopted.[12] Relevant ministries and heads of regional and district State administration were then asked to submit concrete measures to implement the objectives outlined in the priority areas; these were integrated into the Strategy, as the "Elaboration of the Government Strategy for Addressing Problems of the Romani National Minority into a Package of Concrete Measures for the Year 2000" (hereafter, "Strategy for Roma – Stage II"), in May 2000.[13]

---

[9] See *Programme Declarations of the Government of the Slovak Republic*, Section IV.1 "Democratic legal state," 19 November 1998, <http://www.vlada.gov.sk/VLADA/VLADA_1998/PROG_VYHL/pvv98_en.rtf>, (accessed 24 April 2002).

[10] See Government Resolution No. 127 (10 February 1999) on the Creation of the Office of the Plenipotentiary for Addressing the Issues of Roma. Vincent Danihel, a Roma lawyer, was appointed in March 1999. See also EU Accession Monitoring Program, *Monitoring the EU Accession Process: Minority Protection*, Open Society Institute, Budapest, September 2001, pp. 479–480 (hereafter, *"Minority Protection 2001"*).

[11] Working meetings were organised; the Plenipotentiary's Advisory Board was also consulted. See Strategy for Roma – Stage I, pp. 13–14; see also the "List of Respondents," pp. 25–26. The draft was also debated by the Council on National Minorities and Ethnic Groups. See Section 2.4.

[12] Strategy of the Government of the Slovak Republic for the Solution of the Problems of the Roma National Minority and the Set of Measures for Its Implementation – Stage I, adopted by Government Resolution No. 821 (27 September 1999), <http://www.government.gov.sk/INFOSERVIS/DOKUMENTY/ROMSTRAT/en_romstrategia.shtml>, (accessed 16 May 2002) (official English translation).

[13] Elaboration of the Government Strategy for Addressing Problems of the Romani National Minority into a Package of Concrete Measures for the Year 2000 – Stage II, adopted by Government Resolution No. 294 (3 May 2000), <http://www.vlada.gov.sk/csaky/strategia_II_eng.doc>, (accessed 16 May 2002) (official English translation).

In an effort to improve implementation in the time remaining before the September 2002 elections, the Plenipotentiary[14] selected a number of priority areas.[15] The "Priorities with regard to Roma Communities" adopted in April 2002[16] were discussed within the renewed Advisory Board of the Plenipotentiary, consisting of Roma representatives and other civil society experts; they were also sent out to Roma organisations for comments.[17]

The opportunity to provide direct input to the Government has been welcomed by Roma representatives. However, some feel that their ability to influence the content of the Strategy has been insufficient in practice.[18] Other critics have pointed out that greater preparation, research and in-depth consultation with experts during the Strategy preparation process would have been desirable.[19]

2.3 The Programme – Content

The Strategy for Roma reflects a fairly comprehensive approach; it presents an overview of the problems faced by Roma and proposes solutions in a number of critical areas: employment, housing, health, social sector and education. It also proposes to strengthen efforts in the areas of human rights, minority rights, cooperation with NGOs, and regional development.[20]

---

[14] A new Plenipotentiary, Klára Orgovánová, was appointed on 1 July 2001.

[15] Evaluation of the Activities of the Government of the Slovak Republic in the Area of the Resolution of the Problems of the Roma Communities for the Year 2001, 27 February 2002, p. 2, <http://www.ial.sk/appl/material.nsf/0/B3A021C510C0CFE5C1256B670045211D?OpenDocument>, (accessed 16 May 2002) (in Slovak) (hereafter, "Evaluation of Roma Activities 2001").

[16] Priorities of the Government of the Slovak Republic with regard to Roma Communities for 2002, adopted by Government Resolution No. 357 (10 April 2002), <http://www.vlada.gov.sk/orgovanova/dokumenty/priority_vlady_2002_en.doc>, (accessed 30 September 2002) (official English translation).

[17] Interview with the Plenipotentiary for Roma Communities, Bratislava, 8 May 2002.

[18] Interviews with: the Director of the Good Roma Kesaj Village Foundation, Košice, 22 March 2002; the Chairman of the Association of Young Roma, Starý Smokovec, 23 March 2002; and the Chairman and the Deputy Chairman of the Council of NGOs of Roma Communities, Bratislava, 10 July 2002.

[19] See the interview with Anna Jurová, an expert on Roma issues, in February 2001 (sic), in "Society is still not in a position to resolve the Romany issues," Roma Press Agency, 18 July 2002, p. 7, <http://www.rpa.sk/clanok.aspx?o=zc&n=119&l=en>, (accessed 26 September 2002).

[20] Strategy for Roma – Stage I, p. 15.

Stage I presents the main issues and assigns a set of general tasks to be fulfilled by the relevant bodies in seven areas:

- Human Rights, Rights of Persons Belonging to National Minorities, and NGOs
- Education and Training
- Language and Culture
- Employment
- Housing
- Social Sector
- Health
- Regional Development

The Strategy for Roma – Stage II lists concrete tasks to be implemented in these areas (with the exception of the last area).

The Strategy for Roma acknowledges the discrimination and disadvantages faced by Roma in the past and calls for measures to prevent discrimination by public authorities.[21] It states the need to reassess the situation with regard to protection against racially motivated violence, and proposes a few measures in this area. However, it fails to identify discriminatory practices underlying many of the problems currently faced by Roma. More specifically, the Strategy has been criticised for failing to identify and offer solutions to discriminatory practices in accessing social services and benefits, and for not proposing remedies to violations of basic civil rights.[22]

However, to enhance its efforts in the area of non-discrimination and racism, the Government adopted a complementary "Action Plan for the Prevention of All Forms of Discrimination, Racism, Xenophobia, Anti-Semitism and Other Forms of Intolerance for the Period 2000–2001" (hereafter, "Action Plan 2000–2001").[23] The Action Plan 2000–2001 aimed to improve the general framework for combating

---

[21] Strategy for Roma – Stage I, pp. 15, 16.

[22] I. Zoon, *On the Margins. Access of Roma to Public Services in Slovakia,* Open Society Institute, New York, 2001, p. 3.

[23] Action Plan for the Prevention of All Forms of Discrimination, Racism, Xenophobia, Anti-Semitism and Other Forms of Intolerance for the Period 2000–2001, approved by Government Resolution No. 283 (3 May 2000), <http://www.vlada.gov.sk/csaky/akcny_plan-en.doc>, (accessed 16 May 2002). The Action Plan was prepared by the Deputy Prime Minister for the International Year against Racism and Discrimination (2001).

discrimination, racism and intolerance through a public awareness campaign, human rights education and improving awareness of legal remedies; it was not aimed at Roma in particular. It proposed a broad range of measures for tolerance education in schools and training for professional groups (police, judges, prosecutors, prison and court guards, army, healthcare and social workers, and social officers in district and regional administration).[24]

The follow-up Action Plan 2002–2003[25] is more thorough and proposes special measures to address intolerance against Roma, to be implemented by relevant ministries in cooperation with the Plenipotentiary. Among its tasks, it includes measures to address discriminatory practices by regional and district State administration in the area of social assistance.[26]

Although the Strategy for Roma stresses the importance of implementing legal guarantees in the areas of human and minority rights,[27] and recognises the importance of measures to protect and preserve Roma language and culture,[28] it proposes few concrete initiatives to this effect.

The Strategy for Roma has been criticised by experts for failing to clearly define its objectives.[29] The 2002 Priorities, on the other hand, clearly establish directions for action. Some observers have asserted that the Strategy and 2002 Priorities continue to reflect a principally socio-economic approach.[30] In fact, the Priorities identify housing but also education and influencing public opinion as among the most acute problems to be addressed;[31] the most significant initiatives are two programmes which aim to

---

[24] See Action Plan 2000–2001, pp. 10–11.

[25] The Action Plan 2002–2003 was adopted by Government Resolution No. 207 (6 March 2002), <http://www.vlada.gov.sk/csaky/akcny_plan_02_03_en.doc>, (accessed 16 May 2002).

[26] Action Plan 2002–2003, Section 6.

[27] Strategy for Roma – Stage I, p. 16.

[28] Strategy for Roma – Stage I, pp. 18–19.

[29] *2000 Regular Report from the Commission on Slovakia's Progress Towards Accession*, 8 November 2000, p. 21, at <http://europa.eu.int/comm/enlargement/report_11_00/pdf/en/sk_en.pdf>, (accessed 26 September 2002) (hereafter, "*2000 Regular Report*"). See also written comments provided by a Researcher at the Institute for Public Opinion, Bratislava, 5 July 2002.

[30] See the interview with Anna Jurová, in "Society is still not in a position to resolve the Romany issues," p. 7.

[31] The 2002 Priorities cover the following issues: (1) Education; (2) Support for the Construction of Municipal Rental Flats and Public Utilities; (3) Influencing Public Opinion; (4) Establishment of a "House of the Roma" in Bratislava; and (5) Research.

improve conditions in the Roma settlements and to train social workers.[32] While the need to make efficient use of existing resources is understandable, the exclusive focus on Roma settlements has drawn criticism from some Roma representatives, who assert that this approach fails to reflect the diversity of Roma communities.[33] The 2002 Priorities are considered complementary to the Strategy; at the same time, they are intended to serve as the foundation for long-term action.[34]

Finally, in addition to the tasks ensuing from the Strategy for Roma and the Action Plans, various ministries and other governmental bodies have undertaken initiatives which can also have a positive impact on the situation of the Roma.[35] However, despite several steps taken by the Government after 1998 to improve the legal framework for the protection and promotion of minority rights, a number of issues in this area remain unresolved; most notably, efforts to draft comprehensive anti-discrimination legislation are presently on hold.[36]

2.4 The Programme – Administration/Implementation/Evaluation

The Government has made several attempts to enhance administrative capacity to implement and coordinate the Strategy, including through the establishment of an Inter-Ministerial Commission for Roma Community Affairs (IMC) and the allocation of additional support for the Plenipotentiary for Roma Communities. However, substantive participation in implementation from key ministries has been low, and there is no mechanism for requiring their more active involvement. Funding from the State budget has been insufficient – an additional indication that political will to

---

[32] See "Comprehensive Development Programme for Roma Settlements," at <http://www.government.gov.sk/orgovanova/dokumenty/rozvojovy_program_romskych_osad_en.doc>, (accessed 26 September 2002), and "Social Field Workers – A Pilot Programme," <http://www.government.gov.sk/orgovanova/dokumenty/program_socialnych_terennych_prac_en.doc>, (accessed 26 September 2002); both proposed programmes are annexed to the 2002 Priorities.

[33] Interview with a Representative of the Roma Press Agency, Košice, 17 July 2002.

[34] 2002 Priorities, p. 1.

[35] E.g. a programme of the Ministry of Justice to provide adult education in prisons. OSI Roundtable, Bratislava, June 2002. *Explanatory Note: OSI held a roundtable meeting in Slovakia in June 2002 to invite critique of the present report in draft form. Experts present included representatives of the Government, the Commission Delegation, representatives of the Roma community and non-governmental organisations.* The National Labour Office has also realised measures to support employment for Roma, see Section 3.2.2.

[36] See Sections 3.2 and 3.4.

support effective implementation is missing. There are no mechanisms for evaluating the effectiveness of activities under implementation, though monitoring of efforts to improve conditions in Roma settlements will be initiated.

At present, Roma representatives participate in Strategy implementation in an advisory capacity, and many have called for broader dialogue and greater opportunities for participation at decision-making and project management levels. Recent efforts to improve communication with NGOs are welcome, although there is still significant room for improvement.

Overall responsibility for implementation of the Strategy for Roma is borne by the Deputy Prime Minister, who is assisted by the Section for Human Rights and Minorities (Office of the Government).[37] The Plenipotentiary is entrusted with drafting, coordinating and implementing concrete projects for Roma in line with the Strategy, as well as with collecting information on implementation.[38] The position of Deputy Prime Minister, Plenipotentiary, and the Section for Human Rights and Minorities are all based on the elected Government's programme declarations rather than law,[39] rendering their positions rather precarious.

The Deputy Prime Minister organised an audit, with support from the World Bank, in order to evaluate the capacity and activities of the Plenipotentiary and a number of improvements in Strategy coordination and implementation were initiated as a result.[40] A new Plenipotentiary was appointed in July 2001,[41] and her mandate later

---

[37] Government Resolution No. 821/1999, Task B.1, p. 2.

[38] Government Resolution No. 821/1999, Tasks B.8-B.13, p. 3.

[39] For example, the position of the Plenipotentiary, unlike the Plenipotentiary on Data Protection, is not covered by the Law on Competencies (Law No. 575/2001, as amended in Law No. 143/2002); and the staff of the Section for Human Rights and Minorities is not covered under the Law on Public Service (Law No. 312/2001, entered into force 1 April 2002). Interview with the Director of the Section for Human Rights and Minorities, Office of the Government, Bratislava, 15 April 2002.

[40] Interview with an Official of the Section for Human Rights and Minorities, Bratislava, 17 March 2002.

[41] The new Plenipotentiary, Klára Orgovánová, was selected in a tender monitored by the Council of Europe and the EU. Evaluation of Roma Activities 2001, pp. 1–2.

strengthened.[42] In addition to an Office in Bratislava,[43] the Plenipotentiary also has a Regional Office with three full-time employees in Prešov (Eastern Slovakia), where more than two-thirds of Slovak Roma live. The Prešov Office monitors implementation of the Plenipotentiary's two priority programmes to improve conditions in settlements[44] and to train field social workers;[45] it also provides informal consultation services to Roma individuals on a broad range of topics.[46]

The IMC was established with the general aim of strengthening cooperation among the ministries involved in Strategy implementation, monitoring the fulfilment of tasks, and evaluating the effectiveness of expenditures on Roma projects.[47] However, the IMC consists exclusively of representatives of the relevant ministries,[48] and has met

---

[42] The Plenipotentiary is given responsibility for proposing, coordinating and monitoring activities aimed at improving the situation for Roma communities. See Statute of the Plenipotentiary for Roma Communities, adopted by Government Resolution No. 886 (19 September 2001), Art. 1(2) and Art. 3, <http://www.vlada.gov.sk/orgovanova/statut.html>, (accessed 24 April 2002); see also Information on the Strengthening of the Office of the Plenipotentiary for the Solution of the Problems of the Roma Minority through a Grant of the World Bank, 23 January 2002, <http://www.ial.sk/appl/material.nsf/0/B22D2D7F3D4799C7C1256B41003655E6?OpenDocument>, (accessed 26 September 2002).

[43] The Secretariat of the Plenipotentiary is placed under the Office of the Prime Minister, but its work is supervised by the Deputy Prime Minister. It has no separate budget line; its budget is belongs under that of the Office of the Prime Minister, though on occasion the Deputy Prime Minister has taken decisions on budgetary issues related to the Plenipotentiary's Secretariat. It employs 11 persons.

[44] Comprehensive Development Programme for Roma Settlements, see Section 3.2.3.

[45] Social Field Workers – A Pilot Programme, see Section 3.2.4.

[46] The Secretary is of Roma origin. The Staff's competence is rather general; concerning legal issues, for example, it must consult with the legal expert in the Bratislava Secretariat. Interview with the staff of the Prešov Office of the Plenipotentiary, 11 July 2002.

[47] For the Statute of the IMC, see <http://www.government.gov.sk/orgovanova/dokumenty/statut_medzirezort_komisie.doc>, (accessed 16 May 2002).

[48] The IMC consists of a Chairperson (the Plenipotentiary) and 13 representatives from the relevant ministries, at the level of State secretary, section directors or unit directors. The Statute does not provide for Roma or civil society representation; however, the IMC currently includes two Roma members. The full list of IMC members is at <http://www.government.gov.sk/orgovanova/dokumenty/clenovia_medzirez_komisie.doc>, (accessed 16 May 2002). The IMC also has the mandate to cooperate with NGOs, including Roma NGOs.

infrequently.[49] The Plenipotentiary, as chair of the IMC, has no competence to require activity or reporting from individual ministries, and may make proposals to the Government only through the Deputy Prime Minister.[50] A low level of participation from some ministries, such as the Ministry of Education, has been noted.[51]

Stage I of the Strategy assigned few concrete tasks;[52] however, 282 additional tasks were set forth in Stage II. These are to be realised primarily by ministries, Government agencies at the national level, regional and district level public administration bodies, and several local governments.[53] Most of these tasks were formulated by these bodies themselves and coordination has proven difficult.[54] Specific tasks were also assigned by the Government in support of the measures proposed in the 2002 Priorities.[55]

In addition to the above-mentioned institutions, there are specialised sections responsible for minority policy within certain ministries, such as the Section of Minority Culture (Ministry of Culture) and the Department of Minority Education (Ministry of Education). Allegedly, very few Roma are employed at these and other relevant ministries. There is also the Council for National Minorities and Ethnic Groups – an advisory body on minority policy; however, its role in Strategy implementation has been limited.[56]

---

[49] The first meeting of the IMC was held on 17 December 2001. According to its Statute (Art. 8), it should meet at least once every three months but, as of end September 2002, no further meetings had been held.

[50] Statute of the Plenipotentiary, Art. 5.

[51] OSI Roundtable, Bratislava, June 2002.

[52] See "Set of Measures for Implementation – Stage I," Strategy for Roma – Stage I, Part 1, pp. 8-12; tasks are also assigned by Government Resolution No. 821/1999 (by which the Strategy for Roma – Stage I was adopted). Part 2 consists of an Explanatory Report, followed by the text of the Strategy itself.

[53] A non-binding recommendation is made for several municipalities to cooperate in the implementation of certain tasks. See e.g. Government Resolution No. 364 (25 April 2001), <http://www.ial.sk/appl/material.nsf/0/74382D6F8D293FC8C1256A410024A7E4/$FILE/Zdroj.html>, (accessed 26 September 2002).

[54] 2002 Priorities, p. 1.

[55] See Government Resolution No. 357 (10 April 2002), by which the 2002 Priorities and the two annexed programmes were adopted, which assigns specific tasks to various State actors (ministries, regional State administration as well as the Plenipotentiary and the Deputy Prime Minister) based on the directions for action outlined in the 2002 Priorities.

[56] Fourteen minority associations, including two Roma organisations, nominate members to the Council for National Minorities and Ethnic Groups, which is chaired by the Deputy Prime Minister.

Funding and reporting on expenditures

There are three main sources of State funding for the realisation of tasks under the Strategy: the General Treasury Reserve; funding from individual ministries; and Phare co-funding.

First, the Office of the Plenipotentiary is allocated a certain amount of funding for the implementation of projects from a special reserve of the General Treasury on the basis of a request from the Deputy Prime Minister. This request is based on project proposals received from various ministries and other governmental bodies. Under the September 2001 Statute, the Plenipotentiary is jointly responsible for the distribution of financial resources from the General Treasury.[57]

Increasing amounts of State funding have been allocated to regional and district governments for projects to address the needs of Roma; from SKK 15 million (€359,540) in 1999,[58] funding increased to SKK 30 million (€719,080) in 2001, most of which was allocated to the priority area of improving housing and infrastructure in Roma settlements.[59] However, demand clearly exceeds available resources,[60] and the funding necessary to realise many of the tasks outlined in the Strategy has not been secured.[61] In 2002, no funds were earmarked for the implementation of special programmes for Roma from the State budget; the Plenipotentiary therefore proposed an allocation of SKK 50 million (€1,198,466) from the General Treasury for priority

---

[57] Statute of the Plenipotentiary, Art. 3.

[58] Information of the Government of the Slovak Republic on the Status of Implementation of the Problems of the Roma National Minority for the Period November 1998 to May 2000, adopted on 17 May 2000, p. 5, <http://www.government.gov.sk/csaky/rom_p_stav_1998-2000.html>, (accessed 16 May 2002). The exchange rate is calculated at SKK 41.72 (Slovak Koruna) = €1.

[59] In 2001, the breakdown of funding for 90 projects was as follows: 62 percent was allocated to projects to improve the infrastructure of Roma settlements and to reconstruct primary schools; 23.3 percent to projects in the area of culture; 8.3 percent to employment projects; 3.7 percent to education and training projects; and 2.7 percent to projects in the field of social issues and healthcare. Evaluation of Roma Activities 2001, p. 13. See also a breakdown of grants for 2001 by topic at <http://www.vlada.gov.sk/orgovanova/dokumenty/sumar_projekty_2001.doc>, (accessed 26 September 2002).

[60] Already as of 15 February 2001, the database of the Secretariat of the Plenipotentiary showed 517 project proposals totalling SKK 1.1 billion (€26,366,251). Evaluation of Roma Activities 2001, p. 13.

[61] Interviews with: the Head of the Parliamentary Committee for Human Rights, Bratislava, 11 April 2002; and a Representative of the Roma Press Agency, Košice, 17 July 2002.

projects;[62] a total of SKK 22,374,860 (€536,310) had been allocated as of October 2002.[63] The Plenipotentiary has called for funding to be increased.[64]

Second, funds may be allocated by individual ministries, either for the purpose of projects specifically for Roma or other projects which also include the Roma.[65] Individual ministries report to the Ministry of Finance and the National Audit Office on their expenditures.

By entrusting individual ministries and heads of State administration at the district level with the responsibility to allocate their own budgetary resources, the Government has sought to decentralise authority and involve public administration authorities at all levels in Strategy implementation; it has also hoped in this way to encourage cooperation at the local level between local governments, the Roma community and NGOs.[66] However, both the incentive and the means to implement projects to benefit Roma have often been lacking;[67] civil society representatives have reported a reluctance of many municipal and regional authorities to cooperate on Strategy implementation.[68] This may be due in part to the fact that – though accorded responsibilities under the Strategy – regional and district State authorities have not been provided with additional resources sufficient to fulfil these responsibilities.

---

[62] "Proposal for the Structure of the General Treasury Administration Chapter – Social and Cultural Needs of the Roma Community and the Reserve for Projects Addressing Roma Community Problems in 2002," 2002 Priorities, pp. 6–7.

[63] SKK 3,023,130 (€72,462) was allocated from the General Treasury by Government Resolution No. 358 (10 April 2002); SKK 3,180,000 (€76,222) by Government Resolution No. 459 (9 May 2002); SKK 5,669,500 (€135,894) by Government Resolution No. 627 (12 June 2002); SKK 4,063,000 (€97,387) by Government Resolution No. 789 (17 July 2002); and SKK 6,439,230 (€154,344) by Government Resolution No. 884 (21 August 2002). The Resolutions are at <http://www.vlada.gov.sk/orgovanova/zoz_uznesenia.html>, (accessed 23 October 2002).

[64] 2002 Priorities, p. 1; see also "*Orgovánová: Spolupráca s rómskym etnikom bola pozitívna*" (Orgovánová: Cooperation with the Roma Ethnic Minority has been positive), *SME Online*, 5 September 2002, <http://www.sme.sk/clanok.asp?rub=online_zdom&cl=652680>, (accessed 26 September 2002).

[65] More than SKK 165 million (€3,954,938) from the budget of regional State administration and ministries was secured for regional and departmental programmes under Stage II. Strategy for Roma – Stage II, p. 2.

[66] Strategy for Roma – Stage I, pp. 13–14.

[67] Interview with the Director of the Good Roma Kesaj Village Foundation, Košice, 22 March 2002.

[68] G. Adam, Member of the Council for National Minorities, "The Activities of Non-Governmental Organisations to Address the Problems of the Romany Ethnic Minority," presentation at the conference "Slovakia and the Roma: Partnership and Participation," Bratislava, 2 May 2002, p. 2.

Finally, projects to support Strategy implementation may be funded through Phare programmes, to which the Government has allocated increasing amounts of co-financing.[69] These expenditures are monitored by the Central Financial and Contract Unit of the Office of the Government.

Monitoring and evaluation

Through the IMC, the Plenipotentiary annually compiles information on Strategy implementation, based on information from ministries and regional authorities; however, there is no mechanism to require implementing authorities to submit information on their efforts to fulfil their tasks under the Strategy.[70] The Deputy Prime Minister has produced two public reports based on this information.[71] While mostly descriptive, these reports have offered some level of evaluation as well. For example, the 2001 report noted that lack of effective coordination had led to dispersion of efforts and resources.[72]

The Plenipotentiary recently pointed out that cooperation with local mayors has been insufficient and has called for increased governmental involvement in Strategy implementation.[73]

The Plenipotentiary has emphasised the importance of evaluating the effectiveness of efforts and has therefore proposed to conduct project monitoring, a sociographic survey of Roma settlements, and to prepare an analysis of governmental policies from 1948 to 1989.[74]

---

[69] Under Phare 2000, for example, €309,000 was allocated by the Government as project co-financing; under Phare 2001, Government co-financing totalled €9,075,000. See Overview of the Projects Phare under the Auspices of the Deputy Prime Minister for Human Rights, Minorities and Regional Development, 22 August 2002, <http://www.government.gov.sk/csaky/phare_summary_en.doc>, (accessed 26 September 2002), (hereafter, "Overview of Phare Projects").

[70] Government Resolution No. 821/1999, Task B. 10; see also Statute of the IMC, Arts. 3(2) and 3(3).

[71] Information of the Government of the Slovak Republic on the Status of Implementation of the Problems of the Roma National Minority for the Period November 1998 to May 2000; and Evaluation of Roma Activities 2001.

[72] Evaluation of Roma Activities 2001, pp. 1–2.

[73] "Orgovánová: Cooperation with the Roma Ethnic Minority has been positive," *SME Online*, 5 September 2002.

[74] See the chapter on "Research," 2002 Priorities, pp. 5-6. SKK 870,000 (€20,853) has been allocated for the survey and analysis of governmental policies by Government Resolution No. 884 (21 August 2002), <http://www.vlada.gov.sk/orgovanova/dokumenty/uznesenie_884_2002.rtf>, (accessed 23 October 2002); project monitoring was not specifically mentioned.

NGO and Roma participation

Roma representatives have pointed out that few Strategy measures have been implemented at the local level and they attribute this to persistent negative attitudes toward Roma within local public administrations and lack of funding. They claim that this lack of activity contrasts sharply with Government statements that improving the situation for Roma is a priority.[75] According to some Roma representatives, local efforts to build an effective programme on a flawed and inefficient Strategy structure stand little chance of success.[76]

Roma representatives have been especially critical of the low degree of participation from Roma NGOs in implementing components of the Strategy and Phare-funded projects,[77] and of the fact that non-Roma NGOs appear to have received much of the funding for projects to benefit Roma.[78] In fact, NGO participation has been low in general; although NGOs can also apply for grants through the Office of the Plenipotentiary, most of the funding for Strategy implementation has been allocated to State actors (primarily ministries and regional offices).

Roma and civil society representatives have participated in Strategy implementation and evaluation primarily in an advisory capacity, especially through the Advisory Board of the Plenipotentiary. Most members of this Advisory Board[79] are Roma. However, according to one Board member, there have been few consultations regarding implementation of the 2002 Priorities.[80] With the notable exception of the Plenipotentiary, there are no Roma directly responsible for implementing components of the Strategy or for coordinating implementation within the various relevant governmental bodies.[81] There are no positions reserved for Roma or civil society

---

[75] Interviews with: the Director of the Good Roma Kesaj Village Foundation, Košice, 22 March 2002; and a Representative of the Association of Young Roma, Starý Smokovec, 23 March 2002.

[76] Interviews with: the Director of the Good Roma Kesaj Village Foundation, Košice, 22 March 2002; and the Head of Lunik IX Public Administration, 23 March 2002.

[77] Interviews with: the Chairman and the Deputy Chairman of the Council of NGOs of Roma Communities, Bratislava, 10 July 2002; a Representative of the Association of Young Roma, Starý Smokovec, 23 March 2002; and a Representative of the Roma Press Agency, Košice, 17 July 2002.

[78] J. Červeňák, "*Vznikne na Slovensku rómsky tretí mimovládny sektor?*" (Will a Roma Non-governmental Third Sector emerge?), *Romano Nevo L'il*, No. 392–399, 1999.

[79] For the composition of the Advisory Board of the Plenipotentiary, see <http://www.vlada.gov.sk/orgovanova/zoznam_cl_porad_zbor_orgov.html>, (accessed 16 May 2002).

[80] Interview with the Chairman and the Deputy Chairman of the Council of NGOs of Roma Communities, Bratislava, 10 July 2002.

[81] Interview with the Chairman and the Deputy Chairman of the Council of NGOs of Roma Communities, Bratislava, 10 July 2002.

representatives in the IMC. The Plenipotentiary has appointed a Coordinator for Cooperation with NGOs. Still, many Roma representatives assert that there is a need for more concerted governmental efforts to develop cooperation with a broad cross-section of the Roma community.[82]

Implementation of the Action Plan

The Deputy Prime Minister, together with the Section for Human Rights and Minorities, is responsible for implementation of the Action Plan. The Coordination Committee responsible for the Action Plan 2000–2001[83] has been replaced by an inter-sectoral group, consisting of representatives of ministries involved in implementing the Action Plan 2002–2003. As with the Coordination Committee, there are no Roma or civil society representatives in this group, apart from the Plenipotentiary. The Plenipotentiary has been tasked with coordinating the specific activities for the Roma under the Action Plan 2002–2003.[84] An evaluation of the Action Plan 2000–2001 concluded that it had registered some success, but emphasised the need for continued efforts to ensure full implementation.[85] Several NGOs are implementing projects under the Action Plan.[86] However, civil society representatives have criticised the low level of funding made available for implementation and the lack of a coherent, long-term communications strategy to combat racism and intolerance (see Section 3.4.4).

2.5 The Programme and the Public

The Strategy points out that care must be taken to ensure that special measures to improve the situation for Roma do not provoke negative reactions from local communities which are also suffering from economic hardship.[87] Some efforts have

---

[82] Interviews with: the Chairman and the Deputy Chairman of the Council of NGOs of Roma Communities, Bratislava, 10 July 2002; the Director of the NGO "Projekt Schola," Košice, 11 July 2002; and the Director of the Good Roma Kesaj Village Foundation, Košice, 11 July 2002.

[83] Evaluation of the Action Plan for the Prevention of All Forms of Discrimination, Racism, Xenophobia, Anti-Semitism and Other Forms of Intolerance for the Period 2000–2001 (hereafter, "Evaluation of Action Plan 2000–2001"), 8 January 2002, p. 1, <http://www.vlada.gov.sk/csaky/akcny_plan_2000-2001.html>, (accessed 16 May 2002) (in Slovak).

[84] Section 6 "Implementation of activities aimed at dealing with the problems of Roma communities in the Slovak Republic," Action Plan 2002–2003.

[85] Evaluation of Action Plan 2000–2001.

[86] E.g. the NGO People Against Racism received State support for a tolerance campaign. See Section 3.2.

[87] Strategy for Roma – Stage I, p. 15.

been made to present Strategy objectives and activities to the public through the media and conferences. The Plenipotentiary has also made attempts to involve NGOs, including Roma NGOs, in the implementation process.

The Plenipotentiary has appointed a Coordinator for Contacts with the Public and the Media to improve communications regarding the Strategy.[88] The Prešov Office also distributes information on the Strategy but has no specialised public relations staff.[89] Among other communications initiatives undertaken by the Plenipotentiary, such as the establishment of a website,[90] the Plenipotentiary has organised two information campaigns to disseminate information about the situation of Roma and about the Strategy; one was launched in Autumn 2001 with funding from the World Bank; the other on 8 April 2002 (International Roma Day).

The first formal public presentation on the Government's Strategy for Roma and achievements was organised in May 2002 by the Deputy Prime Minister.[91] The event consisted of a series of official reports on the 2002 Priorities and proposed projects as well as on Phare-funded projects. However, there was no opportunity for public discussion.

2.6 The Programme and the EU

The EU has provided considerable financial support for projects to improve the situation of the Roma through the Phare National Programme, allocating a total of €16,050,000 between 1998 and 2001.[92] Phare funding has supported projects in some of the priority areas identified by the Government, notably education, improvement of the situation in Roma settlements, and efforts to promote tolerance towards minorities.

---

[88] Evaluation of Roma Activities 2001, p. 2.

[89] Interview with the staff of the Prešov Office of the Plenipotentiary, 11 July 2002.

[90] <http://www.vlada.gov.sk/orgovanova/> and <http://www.vlada.gov.sk/romovia/>, (accessed 16 May 2002). Some Roma representatives have pointed out that the website must be complemented by other communications efforts, as few Roma living in Eastern Slovakia have access to the Internet.

[91] The Conference "Slovakia and the Roma: Partnership and Participation" (Bratislava, 2 May 2002) was a high-profile event where the EU Commissioner for Enlargement Günter Verheugen, *inter alia*, was invited to make a statement.

[92] In 2001 alone, € ten million was allocated, not including funding from the Phare Civil Society Development Programmes (€78,170 in total), nor other Phare funding. For a full list of Phare-funded projects in Slovakia as of May 2002, see DG Enlargement Information Unit, *EU Support for Roma Communities in Central and Eastern Europe*, May 2002, pp. 28–29, <http://europa.eu.int/comm/enlargement/docs/pdf/brochure_roma_may2002.pdf>, (accessed 22 August 2002); see also Overview of Phare Projects.

The European Commission noted the adoption of the Strategy favourably, but has repeatedly called for improved implementation. In 2001 the Commission also highlighted the need for improved efforts to fight widespread discrimination.[93] Subsequent Phare funding has been matched to these findings, supporting tolerance training, and efforts to further elaborate the Strategy as well as to improve implementation capacity,[94] *inter alia*.

There have been problems with financial administration and reporting of Phare funds. Due to suspicion of fraud as well as irregularities in reporting,[95] funds were frozen in July 2001, resulting in a serious disruption in project implementation.[96] An investigation by Phare's control unit (OMAS) did not find any irregularities in the management of Phare funds by the Section for Human Rights and Minorities.[97] However, it noted a need to improve the capacity of the Department of Project Coordination within the Section for Human Rights and Minorities, which is

---

[93] European Commission, *2001 Regular Report on Slovakia's Progress Towards Accession*, 13 November 2001, p. 24, <http://www.europa.eu.int/comm/enlargement/report2001/sk_en.pdf>, (accessed 26 September 2002) (hereafter, "*2001 Regular Report*").

[94] Efforts in this last area are being supported through a Twinning Project with France "Improvement of the Situation of the Roma in the Slovak Republic" (Phare 2000 allocation of €550,000), from January 2002 to December 2003. See <http://www.vlada.gov.sk/romovia/twinning/index_en.php3>, (accessed 30 September 2002). The Twinning Project also aims to develop short and medium-term strategies in the areas of education, employment, housing and health.

[95] New reporting guidelines in 2001 for Phare funds meant that more administrative capacity and better coordination between the various units involved in managing the funds were required. This led to irregularities in reporting. Written comments of the Director of the CSDF, Bratislava, 26 July 2002.

[96] Many organisations which were already involved in implementation or which had been selected found themselves without any resources. Interview with a Representative of the Sándor Márai Foundation, Dunajská Streda, 16 March 2002.

[97] OMAS Consortium, Middle Unit, *Interim Evaluation of the European Union Phare Programme, Country: Slovak Republic*, Interim Evaluation Report No. R/SR/JHA/01041, 25 September 2001 (hereafter, "2001 OMAS Report"). OMAS reviewed the Phare 1998, 1999 and 2000 Programmes, through September 2001. The report was not made public but copies may be obtained from the Department of Project Coordination. Information provided by the Director of the Department of Project Coordination, Section for Human Rights and Minorities, Bratislava, 9 May 2002.

responsible for administering Phare projects for minorities.[98] Phare funding was released in September 2002, once suspicions had been dispelled.[99]

The OMAS Report also found that effective evaluation of Phare expenditures is hampered in general by broad definitions of project objectives and poorly-elaborated indicators of achievement.[100] Despite the numerous problems identified, implementation of the Phare projects was generally evaluated as "satisfactory" by OMAS,[101] as well as by the Government.[102] While OMAS did not find any irregularities in the organisation of Phare tenders,[103] Roma representatives and civil society experts have asserted that there is a lack of transparency in project selection.[104] Future reports on the effectiveness of Phare funding for Roma should move beyond an assessment of formal compliance with procedures to incorporate critiques from civil society organisations, particularly Roma organisations.

Both OMAS and Roma representatives have highlighted the lack of sustainability of Phare-funded projects as a major source of concern. To address this issue, OMAS recommended that the Government guarantee continuity within the Department of Project Coordination[105] and noted that more active involvement from the Roma community would also boost sustainability.[106]

---

[98] 2001 OMAS Report, p. 2.

[99] Ten percent of the funds (€ five million) had been withheld. They were released on 25 September 2002, after Slovakia's Supreme Audit Office concluded that there had been no misuse and that police, working jointly with a team from the European Commission's European Anti-Fraud Office (OLAF), reached the same conclusion. "EU Releases Frozen Phare Funds to Slovakia," RFE/RL *Newsline*, 26 September 2002.

[100] 2001 OMAS Report, p. 10.

[101] 2001 OMAS Report, p. III. This overall positive evaluation of Phare-funded projects was made despite the fact that, under the Spiš project (Phare 1998 Pilot Project "Improvement of the Situation of the Roma in the Spiš Region"), for example, the reconstruction of a kindergarten in the town of Markušovce was not realised by the firm from Banská Bystrica which won the tender, so the funding (€49,000) had to be returned to Phare in Brussels. Interview with the Director of the Department of Project Coordination, Section for Human Rights and Minorities, Bratislava, 9 May 2002. The 2001 OMAS Report does, however, mention problems with the construction of the kindergarten. 2001 OMAS Report, pp. 2–3.

[102] Overview of Phare Projects, p. 1; see also the presentation by the Director of the Department of Project Coordination, Section for Human Rights and Minorities, at the conference "Slovakia and the Roma: Partnership and Participation," Bratislava, 2 May 2002.

[103] 2001 OMAS Report, p. III.

[104] NGOs are selected in a closed tender upon invitation by the Government.

[105] 2001 OMAS Report, p. 20.

[106] To improve sustainability of the Spiš project, for example, it suggested that local authorities support the kindergarten and community centre buildings. 2001 OMAS Report, p. III; see also pp. 17–18.

Roma have also asserted that they should be more involved in decisions regarding the allocation and use of Phare funding to benefit Roma communities, and in implementing Phare projects.[107]

According to an EU representative, the bureaucratic requirements of preparing and administering a Phare proposal make it difficult for medium and small NGOs, including most Roma NGOs, to participate in Phare tenders.[108] Mechanisms should be developed to make funding more accessible to NGOs, especially Roma NGOs, including by offering training on Phare grants procedures and participation in tender commissions.[109] This would also make funding more available to NGOs beyond Bratislava, who have tended to be excluded from EU funding to date.[110]

NGOs (including Roma NGOs)[111] have received Phare funding through the Civil Society Development Foundation (CSDF), and the CSDF has made it a practice to offer practical assistance in project preparation. However, OMAS identified a need for improvement in monitoring and reporting on these grants; its recommendations have been taken into account by the CSDF since May 2002.[112]

---

[107] Interview with the Chairman and the Deputy Chairman of the Council of NGOs of Roma Communities, Bratislava, 10 July 2002.

[108] Interview with an Official of the Delegation of the European Commission to Slovakia, Bratislava, 10 July 2002.

[109] Roma representatives are included on steering committees for monitoring implementation of Phare projects. Interview with the Director of the Department of Project Coordination, Section for Human Rights and Minorities, Bratislava, 9 May 2002.

[110] G. Adam, "The Activities of Non-Governmental Organisations to Address the Problems of the Romany Ethnic Minority," p. 2.

[111] In 2001, €1,465,00 was allocated to minority projects; while most of the funding was allocated to projects for Roma (26 projects), the exact share of Roma NGOs which received funding is not known. 2001 OMAS Report, pp. 3–5, 12; see also list of projects in Annex 6. See also the website of the CSDF (*Nadácia pre podporu občianskych aktivít*–NPOA) at <www.changenet.sk/npoa>, (accessed 26 August 2002).

[112] 2001 OMAS Report, p. III. The recommendations included the introduction of changes to the management of financial reports, processing guidelines and internal reporting mechanisms. According to the CSDF, the recommended changes were introduced at the end of May 2002. Written comments of the Director of the CSDF, Bratislava, 26 July 2002.

3. The Government Programme – Implementation

3.1 Stated Objectives of the Programme

The aim of the Government Strategy, as set forth in the Stage I document, is to "creat[e] conditions for Roma national minority problem resolution in areas where the situation is critical – unemployment, housing, health status, social sector and the school system, or where there are grounds for improvement – human rights, rights of persons belonging to national minorities, cooperation with NGOs and regional development."[113] Stage II of the Strategy focuses on implementation of these objectives through concrete measures.

The 2002 Priorities document also proposes measures to be implemented in a reduced set of priority areas for action; no new objectives are defined.

3.2 Government Programme and Discrimination

The Strategy acknowledges that Roma have experienced discrimination in the past and aims to prevent future discrimination by public administration authorities.[114] At the same time, it appears to assign at least partial responsibility for this to Roma themselves: "[s]ome aspects of life of a certain part of this minority cause social distance in the majority society, which is then unjustly applied to the whole minority."[115]

The Strategy outlines several measures to fight discriminatory practices by providing human rights training (with special attention to the Roma minority) to members of professional groups such as the police, prison guards and court officials, and local authorities.[116] Human rights training for professional groups and public awareness-raising activities were proposed in the context of the Action Plan 2000–2001 and its follow-up as well. Those activities which have been implemented – such as an anti-racism campaign organised by the NGO "People Against Racism" – report successful

---

[113] Strategy for Roma – Stage I, p. 15.
[114] Strategy for Roma – Stage I, pp. 15, 16.
[115] Strategy for Roma – Stage I, p. 15.
[116] Government Resolution 821/1999, Tasks B.15 (Minister of Justice), B.16 (Minister of Interior); see also Strategy for Roma – Stage II, pp. 6–8.

results,[117] despite relatively low levels of funding.[118] (For more on implementation of the Action Plans, see Sections 3.2.5 and 3.3.)

The Strategy also recommended research and monitoring on discrimination and that consideration be given to making amendments to legislation and to the system for social protection if necessary (see Section 3.2.4).[119] Subsequent Government research has concluded that existing legislation does not comply with the EU Race Equality Directive,[120] but efforts to adopt comprehensive anti-discrimination legislation have stalled.[121]

There is no specialised body to monitor and investigate discrimination. The Ministry of Labour, Social Affairs and Family (hereafter, "Ministry of Labour") took some steps

---

[117] According to a survey realised after phase one of the campaign, it reached 44 percent of Slovak residents, 67 percent of which evaluated it positively. Evaluation of Action Plan 2000–2001, p. 12.

[118] SKK 499,100 (€11,963) was allocated in total for two campaigns and the creation of a website, <www.racism.sk>. Information provided by an Official of the Section for Human Rights and Minorities, Bratislava, 12 June 2002. See also Evaluation of Action Plan 2000–2001, p. 12.

[119] See Government Resolution 821/1999, Task B. 14, p. 4; see also Strategy for Roma – Stage II, p. 5; see also Government Resolution 821/1999, Recommendation C.1, p. 5.

[120] Council Directive 2000/43/EC of 29 June 2000 implementing the principle of equal treatment between persons irrespective of racial or ethnic origin. Interview with an Official of the Section for Human Rights and Minorities, Bratislava, 17 March 2002. For a comprehensive review of Slovak legislation compared to the Directive, see Ján Hrubala, *Legal analysis of national and European anti-discrimination legislation. A comparison of the EU Racial Equality Directive & Protocol No. 12 with anti-discrimination legislation in Slovakia*, European Roma Rights Center/Interights/Minority Policy Group, Budapest/London/Brussels, September 2001, at <http://www.migpolgroup.com/uploadstore/Slovakia%20electronic.pdf>, (accessed 22 October 2002); see also *Minority Protection 2001*, pp. 440–442.

[121] This is not a specific task of the Strategy or the Action Plan. See, however, the Action Plan 2002–2003, Section 8, where efforts to draft legislation on equal treatment and an "Equal Treatment Centre" are mentioned. The Section for Human Rights developed a proposal in cooperation with NGOs and international organisations, which was adopted by the Government in May 2002; however it was not considered prior to the September 2002 elections. Memorandum on Anti-Discrimination Legislation, Centre for Legal Analysis/Kalligram Foundation, July 2002, <http://www.cla.sk/projects/project.php?melyik=anti_discrimination&nyelv=en&direkturl= anti_discrimination/cla_analysis/anti_discrimination_memo_july_02.htm>, (accessed 22 October 2002). The draft legislation comprised of two statutes: an Act on Equal Treatment, <http://www.ial.sk/appl/material.nsf/0/AF1121D2FA91FE33C1256B6D003E92C4?Open Document>, (accessed 26 September 2002), and a proposal to establish a Centre for Equal Treatment, at <http://www.ial.sk/appl/material.nsf/0/9982E11807844812C1256B6D003F73EF?OpenD ocument>, (accessed 26 September 2002).

toward establishing such a body, but this initiative, too, is on hold until after the September 2002 elections.

The appointment of a Parliamentary Commissioner for Human Rights (Ombudsman) in March 2002[122] offers one avenue for dissemination of information about discrimination and receipt of complaints.[123]

In the meantime, awareness of existing channels for submitting complaints is low, and there has been little practical governmental assistance for the preparation, filing and pursuit of discrimination claims.[124]

3.2.1 Education

Education has been identified by the Government as a priority area for action.[125] In the Strategy, the fact that many Roma do not complete basic education is attributed not to discrimination, but to the "rigid school system," low attendance at kindergarten, and language problems, and thus measures have sought to address these issues in particular. Though most measures are still in the pilot phase, several initiatives, such as the organisation of pre-school preparatory classes (or so-called "zero classes") and the employment of Roma teacher's assistants, have achieved promising results.

The Strategy sets forth the principal goal of "creat[ing] conditions for changing the education system so that Romani children can be as successful as the others,"[126] which it aims to achieve by adopting "fast solutions to the most critical issues."[127] The

---

[122] The Law on the Parliamentary Commissioner was adopted on 4 December 2001. After an unsuccessful first attempt in February 2002, Parliament elected Pavol Kandráč – the candidate of the opposition Movement for a Democratic Slovakia (HZDS) of former Prime Minister Mečiar – on 19 March 2002. Two of the governing coalition parties allegedly voted for this candidate. See "Slovak Government Disunity Marks Ombudsman Vote," *Transitions Online*, 19–25 March 2002.

[123] However, there have been delays in setting up his office. Interview with the Head of the Parliamentary Committee for Human Rights, Bratislava, 11 April 2002.

[124] US Department of State, *Country Reports on Human Rights Practices – 2001, Slovak Republic*, Section 5, <http://www.state.gov/g/drl/rls/hrrpt/2001/eur/8338.htm>, (accessed 30 September 2002).

[125] Strategy for Roma – Stage I, p. 17; 2002 Priorities.

[126] Strategy for Roma – Stage II, p. 10.

[127] Strategy for Roma – Stage I, p. 17.

Ministry of Education is assigned the task of elaborating mid- and long-term concepts for education[128] for Roma at all levels of education except the tertiary level.

Regional and district authorities have been tasked with drafting plans for the education of Roma children in their areas.[129] The Ministry is still working on a Concept for the Education and Instruction of Roma Children as part of broader efforts to develop a long-term concept for education more generally, to cover the next 15 to 20 years (also known as the "Millennium Project");[130] as the Concept has not yet been completed, no funding has yet been requested or set aside for its implementation.[131]

Another task of the Ministry of Education was to conduct "sectoral research on the situation of the Romany child and pupil in the school education and training system with the aim of determining the reasons for difficulties experienced by Roma children in the field of education.[132] Since 2000, the Methodological Centre in Prešov has been implementing this initiative on the basis of which pilot kindergartens and elementary schools with a high concentration of Roma children have been selected for participation in Phare projects.[133]

Concrete activities are focussed on the pre-school and primary levels, and consist largely of expanding existing pilot initiatives to establish pre-school preparatory classes

---

[128] Strategy for Roma – Stage I, pp. 8, 9; see also Strategy for Roma – Stage II, p. 10.

[129] Strategy for Roma – Stage I, p. 9.

[130] Government Resolution 821/1999, Task B.17, p. 4. The Strategy for Roma – Stage II (p. 10) tasked the Ministry of Education with completing the concept.

[131] Evaluation of Roma Activities 2001, p. 7. The Ministry was tasked by the Government with completing the Concept by 15 June 2002. See Government Resolution No. 357 (10 April 2002), Task B.1. See also 2002 Priorities, p. 2. However, the Ministry's efforts to develop its concept are supported by the Twinning Project with France, which is assisting the Government in fleshing out the Strategy for Roma more broadly. In the area of education more specifically, early indications are that the Concept will include pre-school education, the integration of Roma children in primary schools, and the increase in the number of Roma students in secondary schools and universities. See the Report on Education from the opening seminar held in Bratislava on 13–14 June 2002, p. 2, <http://www.vlada.gov.sk/romovia/twinning/dokumenty/education.doc>, (accessed 30 September 2002).

[132] See Government Resolution 821/1999, Task B.18, p. 5; see also Strategy for Roma – Stage I, p. 18.

[133] László Szigeti, State Secretary at the Ministry of Education, "The Education Development Programme for the Roma," presentation at the conference "Slovakia and the Roma: Partnership and Participation," Bratislava, 2 May 2002.

and to train and employ Roma teacher's assistants,[134] as well as to introduce improved Romanes-language curricula. All of these measures are intended to help improve school attendance and educational achievement among Roma children. While the Strategy mentions that few Roma reach secondary schools and universities,[135] it does not propose measures to address this problem directly.[136]

Roma teacher's assistants

In 2001, in line with the Strategy for Roma, the Ministry of Education commissioned the Wide Open School Foundation to design a programme to support the training and employment of Roma teacher's assistants.[137]

In parallel, a project of the National Labour Office aims to train and hire Roma teacher's assistants in cooperation with a Roma NGO, the Association of Young Roma (see Section 3.2.2), as part of a creative solution to hire the assistants under the National Employment Action Plan rather than through the Ministry of Education, as this was not possible under existing legislation (see below); again, training is being provided by the Wide Open School Foundation.

This initiative has received favourable evaluations in its pilot phase.[138] Teacher's assistants have helped facilitate communications between children and teachers and also between teachers and parents; through Roma assistants, many parents have reportedly become more involved in their children's education. According to some observers, Roma assistants have not always been accorded a sufficient role in class, which does not provide a good model for Roma children.[139] With

---

[134] The Ministry is also tasked with continuing to support the Education Centre at the Secondary School of Romani Arts in Košice. Strategy for Roma – Stage I, pp. 8, 9; see also Strategy for Roma – Stage II, p. 10.

[135] Strategy for Roma – Stage I, p. 18.

[136] However, a sub-project of the Phare 1999 "Minority Tolerance Programme" aims to increase the share of minorities in high schools and universities (with a special focus on Roma). See Overview of Phare Projects, p. 2.

[137] The budget for training assistants was estimated at €160,000; a further €170,000 was estimated for teaching equipment for the university departments, methodological centres and ten pilot elementary schools involved. 2001 OMAS Report, p. 9; see also Information on Projects related to the Roma Issue with a Focus on the Educational Process (draft), No. 857/2001, Ministry of Education, Bratislava, 5 September 2001, p. 4 (on file with EUMAP).

[138] *Poverty and Welfare of Roma in the Slovak Republic,* World Bank, Foundation SPACE, INEKO, The Open Society Institute, Bratislava, 2002, p. 57, <http://www.worldbank.sk/Data/povertyinslovak.pdf>, (accessed 30 September 2002). Interview with the Director of Projekt Schola, Košice, 11 July 2002.

[139] Interview with the Director of Projekt Schola, Košice, 11 July 2002.

proper legal and financial support, as well as more extensive evaluation of results to identify and address issues such as these, the programme can be expected to achieve positive results.

Pre-school preparatory classes

Pre-school preparatory classes for Roma children (also referred to as "zero classes") are intended to help Roma children prepare for the first grade of elementary school (and thus to improve performance and reduce drop-out rates). Zero classes were first launched in Košice in the 1992/1993 school year as a pilot project;[140] to date, 85 zero classes have been introduced in 61 elementary schools, with a total of 1,057 participants.[141]

Zero classes have also been welcomed as a remedy to the lack of pre-school education in some areas,[142] and have posted positive results in improving attendance and performance.[143] However, some observers have suggested that, in order to be truly effective, the zero classes should be integrated into a more comprehensive governmental strategy; in this view, plans to introduce six months compulsory pre-school education is a step in the right direction but is not sufficient to address inequalities in the educational system as a whole.[144] Others have noted that zero classes have been implemented without sufficient methodological and training support to teachers.[145]

The expansion of these two initiatives has been impeded by legal obstacles. For example, the employment of Roma teacher's assistants had been found to violate the equality principle and existing legislation did not permit the implementation of positive measures. In 2001, the position of pedagogical assistant was established by the Ministry of Education, but assistants can be employed through the Ministry only after

---

[140] Concept of Education and Instruction of Roma Children and Pupils, p. 12 (on file with EUMAP).

[141] These initiatives have also been supported under the Phare 2000 Programme "Improvement of the Situation of the Roma in the Slovak Republic and Society." See 2001 OMAS Report, p. 9; see also Evaluation of Roma Activities 2001, p. 9.

[142] Interview with the Director of Projekt Schola, Košice, 11 July 2002.

[143] See *Poverty and Welfare of Roma in the Slovak Republic,* p. 56.

[144] Written comments of a Representative of the NGO "Spolu do budoucnosti," 15 July 2002.

[145] Interview with the Director of Projekt Schola, Košice, 11 July 2002.

an amendment to the Law on Public Service was passed in Summer 2002.[146] Similar legal obstacles prevented the systematic establishment of pre-school classes.

Roma representatives criticise the fact that the Strategy does not recognise discrimination as a factor contributing to poor school performance and high drop-out rates among Roma children, and thus stipulates no measures to combat discriminatory phenomena such as segregation and the disproportionate placement of Roma children in special schools for the mentally and physically handicapped.[147] The majority of Roma children from settlements attend special schools.[148]

The Strategy does recognise that graduates of special schools are disadvantaged in the job market, and calls for the establishment of "flexible equalising basic school classes" with fewer pupils, as well as for educational psychological counselling centres.[149] It also recognises the need for a multicultural and tolerant school environment,[150] and for further research.[151] With assistance from Phare, the Ministry of Education is re-evaluating existing school entrance tests for children from disadvantaged backgrounds, with an eye to reducing the number of Roma children being placed in special schools. A similar initiative will receive support under the new Phare 2001 project.[152]

A recent governmental evaluation acknowledged that most Strategy measures in the area of education are still at the pilot stage and have been realised by NGOs, and that Phare support has been key.[153] The fact that the Ministry of Education has not taken

---

[146] Written comments of an Official from the Delegation of the European Commission to Slovakia, Bratislava 15 July 2002. See *"EK: SR musí novelizovať školský zákon aj kvôli Rómom"* (European Commission: The Slovak Republic must amend the Law on Schools because of the Roma), *SME Online,* 20 June 2002; see also *"Peniaze na rómskych asistentov dostaneme"* (We will get the funding for Roma assistants), SITA (Slovak News Agency), 20 June 2002. See Law No. 408 (27 June 2002) amending Law No. 313/2001 on Public Service, <http://www.vlada.gov.sk/orgovanova/dokumenty/novela_skolskeho_zakona.pdf>, (accessed 23 October 2002).

[147] Interview with the Director of Projekt Schola, Košice, 18 April 2002; see also *Minority Protection 2001,* pp. 442–447.

[148] See UNDP, *Towards Diversity with a Human Face,* Roma Regional Human Development Report 2002 (draft), April 2002, pp. 40–42; see also Roma Rights Center, *Human Rights Report on the Situation of Roma in Eastern Slovakia 2000–2001,* Košice, pp. 37–45.

[149] Strategy for Roma – Stage I, p. 18.

[150] Strategy for Roma – Stage I, p. 17.

[151] Strategy for Roma – Stage II, p. 11.

[152] Written comments of an Official from the Delegation of the European Commission to Slovakia, Bratislava 15 July 2002.

[153] Evaluation of Roma Activities 2001, p. 7.

any real steps to implement the Strategy for Roma in the field of education has also been criticised.[154]

Many observers have emphasised that the scale and the importance of the problems facing Roma in the area of education demand the implementation of a well-planned, consistent, comprehensive and sustained strategy. This strategy should:

- Cover all levels of education, including access to universities;

- Integrate the experience gained during the implementation of pilot projects by civil society organisations;

- Complement measures to improve school attendance and performance with measures to address the problem of segregation and ensure that additional measures proposed do not reinforce existing patterns of segregation;

- Build in mechanisms to ensure that assignment of competencies in the area of education to regional and local public administration does not create obstacles to implementation.

3.2.2 Employment

The Strategy for Roma – Stage I recognises the problem of extremely high levels of unemployment among Roma, which is estimated at nearly 100 percent in some areas of Eastern Slovakia.[155] However, it does not set forth a comprehensive approach to address this problem. While it notes the need to create incentives for Roma job-seekers, few concrete initiatives have been implemented under the Strategy in this area.

The Strategy attributes high unemployment to: low skills, poor health, low morale, and discriminatory attitudes.[156] It does not address discrimination against Roma in the

---

[154] 2002 Priorities, p. 2; see also Evaluation of Roma Activities 2001, p. 7.

[155] See Evaluation of Roma Activities 2001, p. 8; see also Strategy for Roma – Stage II, p. 24; and also *Poverty and Welfare of Roma in the Slovak Republic*, pp. 14, 27–30.

[156] Strategy for Roma – Stage I, pp. 19–20.

labour market,[157] though there are many indications that this is a serious problem;[158] many young educated Roma claim that they have almost no chance of finding a job.[159]

Measures proposed under the Strategy include:

- Provision of "public benefit jobs;"
- Educational initiatives to benefit the unemployed (mainly young Roma);
- Improvement of the general economic situation through regional policies;
- Re-assessment of the possibility of granting incentives for employers who hire Roma;
- Job counselling for Roma entrepreneurs to promote private business development.

The 2002 Priorities do not include any measures in the field of employment, apart from the programme to train field social workers, whose competencies will include dealing with employment issues (see Section 3.2.4).

The Ministry of Agriculture as well as several regional governments are tasked under the Strategy with creating public benefit jobs (mostly in unskilled labour) for the long-term unemployed. However, only the Nitra region has allocated funding for implementation (SKK 120,000, or €2,876). Reportedly, a number of local governments actively oppose the initiative. The regional government for Bratislava has supported job counselling for Roma entrepreneurs.[160]

A "Public Benefit Works" programme, complementary to public benefit jobs programmes under the Strategy, was initiated in 2000 by the Ministry of Labour. In 2001, the National Labour Office (NLO) spent SKK 1.4 billion (€33,557,047) to create or preserve 48,000 jobs.[161] The Government has recommended that a further SKK 2,874,000 (€68,888) be allocated by the NLO to district offices in 2002 for such

---

[157] The Ministry of Labour is tasked under the Strategy with conducting research on discrimination, in cooperation with the Ministry of Interior. However, no funding has been allocated for this task.

[158] M. Vašečka, "Roma," in: *Slovakia 1998–1999. A Global Report on the State of Society*, p. 180; see also Good Roma Kesaj Village Foundation, *The White Book 2000*, Košice, 2000.

[159] Interview with a Representative of the Association of Young Roma, Bratislava, 23 March 2002.

[160] SKK 160,000 (€3,835) was allocated for this purpose.

[161] Edit Bauer, State Secretary of the Ministry of Labour, "Social Programme for Roma," presentation at the conference "Slovakia and Roma: Partnership and Cooperation," Bratislava, 2 May 2002, p. 3.

jobs.[162] However, this programme is not targeted at Roma specifically and local municipalities may decide not to hire Roma candidates.[163]

According to critics, public benefits jobs are ineffective in creating work incentives or addressing long-term unemployment: they generally last only three months, allow few opportunities for participants to develop work skills, and offer salaries that are not much higher than social assistance benefits.[164] One observer has noted that public benefits jobs programmes actually increase the incentive for Roma to remain on social assistance.[165]

Some of the most promising initiatives to improve employment prospects for Roma are being implemented by the NLO, outside the scope of the Strategy.

Initiatives of the National Labour Office

The NLO has recently begun to implement a number of programmes aimed at addressing unemployment among Roma, allocating significant resources for this purpose from its own budget.[166] The NLO is implementing three types of programmes for the Roma: (1) training for Roma teacher's assistants; (2) off-the-job employment training; and (3) employment counselling. It also seeks to locate jobs for Roma who have completed training programmes. For example, in 2001 the NLO helped arrange for the employment of 116 trained Roma teacher's assistants.[167] Off-the-job training and personal counselling reportedly provided assistance to 699 persons.[168]

In 2002, the NLO approved a twelve-month project to provide training to an additional 237 Roma assistants, in cooperation with the Association of Young Roma, as part of the National Employment Action Plan. The assistants will first

---

[162] Government Resolution No. 884 (21 August 2002), Recommendation C.1.

[163] See e.g. A. Koptová and S. Schmidt, *The Truth about Roma?*, Good Roma Kesaj Village Foundation, Košice, 2001, pp. 66–70.

[164] For more on the Public Benefit Works Programme, see *Poverty and Welfare of Roma in the Slovak Republic*, pp. 30–31; see also I. Radičová, "*Rómovia = problém*" (Roma = Problem), *Sociológia*, No. 5, 2001, pp. 436–437.

[165] According to the newly-amended Law on Social Assistance (entered into force 1 July 2000), persons who have not worked for more than two years have their social assistance cut; however, public benefits jobs count as employment for these purposes. Written comments of a Representative of the Association of Roma and Roma Advisor, Banská Bystrica, 7 July 2002.

[166] NLO initiatives do not form part of the Strategy for Roma. Interview with a Representative of the NLO, Bratislava, 10 May 2002.

[167] Total funding provided by the NLO: SKK 24 million (€575,264).

[168] Total funding provided by the NLO for these programmes: SKK 8,060,356 (€193,201).

receive training from the Wide Open School Foundation and will then be employed in seven regions (see also Section 3.2.1).[169]

The NLO has undertaken a number of other initiatives as well, including the provision of concrete assistance and training to Roma who wish to set up small businesses. Persons who prepare an adequate business plan can apply for small NLO grants of up to SKK 200,000 (€4,794). Projects to provide job training and counselling to unemployed Roma have been implemented in Prešov (Eastern Slovakia)[170] and in Banská Bystrica.[171]

While it is too early to assess the impact of these initiatives on unemployment rates among Roma communities, they reflect a clear tendency to promote active participation from Roma and Roma organisations in addressing the issue. These pilot projects should be examined carefully as the process of developing a comprehensive strategy to reduce unemployment moves forward.[172]

3.2.3 Housing and other goods and services

Housing

The Strategy for Roma – Stage I identifies improvement of the housing conditions for Roma living in settlements as one of the most important issues to be addressed.[173] It asserts that, as "Roma settlements will never disappear, it is important to change the quality of living standards [...]."[174] The Strategy also proposes to implement projects to support "the comprehensive re-socialisation of the Romany community living in [...] settlements, which in addition to the housing issue include also education and

---

[169] The project "Roma Assistant 2002–2003" is to receive nearly SKK 25 million (€599,233) from the NLO. Information distributed at the press conference of the Association of Young Roma, Bratislava, 10 July 2002 (on file with EUMAP).

[170] Seventeen training sessions for approximately 270 persons were organised for a total amount of SKK three million (€71,908). Interview with a Representative of the NLO, Bratislava, 10 May 2002.

[171] The NLO has allocated SKK seven million (€167,785) for the project. Interview with a Representative of the NLO, Bratislava, 10 May 2002.

[172] This would be particularly useful in the context of the Phare 2000 Twinning Project, which aims to improve the Government's Strategy for Roma with regard to employment, *inter alia*.

[173] Strategy for Roma – Stage I, p. 20. The population of Roma settlements has grown dramatically as Roma move back to them due to the lack of affordable housing; according to estimates by local authorities, the number of Roma living in settlements grew from 14,988 in 1988 to 123,034 in 1997. *Poverty and Welfare of Roma in the Slovak Republic*, pp. 2–3, 11.

[174] Evaluation of Roma Activities 2001.

training, employment, counselling, etc."[175] The importance of active involvement in these efforts and in the development of comprehensive, long-term policy solutions by members of the Roma community is emphasised.[176]

Most concrete efforts to implement Strategy objectives in the area of housing are still in the pilot phase. To date, most effort has been focused on urgent measures to construct affordable social housing and to improve the infrastructure in segregated settlements.

The Strategy does not address certain key issues. For example, no measures have been proposed to facilitate the acquisition of legal title to the land on which Roma settlements are built; at the moment, most settlements are illegal. Nor does the Strategy outline efforts to address discrimination in housing, which some experts claim has had an impact on the increasing segregation of Roma in settlements.[177] Polls generally indicate that the overwhelming majority of the population supports the segregation of Roma communities,[178] and active opposition to housing initiatives has presented a serious obstacle to the effective use of EU[179] and State funding initiatives in this area.

Social housing programme

In April 2001, the Government approved a programme to support the construction of low-income social housing and to improve the infrastructure

---

[175] Strategy for Roma – Stage I, p. 21.

[176] Strategy for Roma – Stage I, p. 21.

[177] Ina Zoon, *On the Margins*, pp. 80–83. There have been numerous reports regarding the adoption of discriminatory housing regulations and policies to exclude Roma by blocking the construction of flats, refusing permanent residence documents to Roma, etc. See *Minority Protection 2001*, pp. 451–456; Roma Rights Center, *Human Rights Report on the Situation of Roma in Eastern Slovakia 2000–2001*, pp. 6–8; and *White Book 2000*.

[178] However, some sources indicate that public opinion has softened. According to a poll carried out in 2001, 66 percent of the population would not want to have a Roma neighbour, compared to 86 percent in a 1999 poll. The poll also indicated that persons under the age of 30 are more tolerant towards Roma than older persons. US Department of State, *Country Reports on Human Rights Practices – 2001, Slovak Republic*, Section 5.

[179] Information from Klára Orgovánová, quoted by O. Štefucová, *Kampaň pre zblíženie rómskej a nerómskej komunity na Slovensku* (The campaign to reduce the gap between the Roma and non-Roma communities in Slovakia), 5 April 2002, Radio Free Europe, <http://www.slobodka.org/programs/dompolitika/2002/04/20020405075116a.sp>, (accessed 23 October 2002).

(public utilities) in Roma settlements.[180] Municipalities have been eligible to receive loans from the State Housing Development Fund at advantageous rates, as well as subsidies from the Ministry of Construction and Regional Development to cover up to 80 percent of the purchase price of a low-income social housing unit (flat/block of flats) in Roma settlements; the remaining 20 percent is to be covered by an in-kind contribution (generally of labour) from those who will occupy the housing units. The flats will be owned by local governments. The Office of the Plenipotentiary and the Ministry of Construction and Regional Development organised a series of seminars for 350 mayors to explain the new scheme. In the district of Stará Tehelná (Prešov), for example, 88 flats were completed (out of 176 planned) in October 2001, and allocated primarily to Roma families.[181] In the village of Rudňany 51 new flats are being built in 2002.[182]

However, as of April 2002, only five local authorities had applied for subsidies to build municipal rental flats, and only 15 had requested subsidies for the construction of public utilities.[183] According to the Plenipotentiary, the principal reason for the low rate of participation is that local governments lack necessary human and financial resources to administer projects; as a consequence, the Plenipotentiary has requested special funding to assist municipalities in project preparation and implementation;[184] funding to this has effect has been allocated.[185]

---

[180] Government Resolution No. 335 (11 April 2001). See the task of the Ministry of Construction and Regional Development to propose a programme for the construction of rental blocks of flats for individuals with low incomes, "among whom Romani citizens can also be included." Strategy for Roma – Stage II, p. 29; see also 2002 Priorities, pp. 3–4; and Evaluation of Roma Activities 2001, pp. 8–10.

[181] The municipality also contributed. Evaluation of Roma Activities 2001, p. 9.

[182] Information on the Implementation of Housing Policy for Roma for the Least Developed Roma Communities.

[183] 2002 Priorities, pp. 3–4. In 2001, subsidies amounting SKK 19,225,000 (€460,810) were allocated to implementation of this programme. *Informácia o realizácii bytovej politiky Rómov s najviac zaostalých rómskych komunít* (Information on the Implementation of Housing Policy for Roma for the Least Developed Roma Communities), 27 February 2002, p. 1, <http://www.ial.sk/appl/material.nsf/0/098A7666D0792F52C1256B6700457AAD?OpenDocument>, (accessed 23 October 2002).

[184] 2002 Priorities, p. 4.

[185] See e.g. Government Resolution No. 627 (12 June 2002) which allocated SKK 5,669,500 (€135,894) from the General Treasury Reserve to Banská Bystrica, Košice and Prešov Regional Offices to support the preparation of project documentation by local districts and municipalities.

According to some observers, the Government favours social housing initiatives because they are "easy to sell to the media and Roma communities as well."[186] In many cases, however, local governments and communities have opposed them.[187] For example, in Hunčovce (Eastern Slovakia), the local council rejected the mayor's proposal to construct social housing for Roma, even though State funding had already been allocated.[188] In Dobšina, a petition organised by the Real Slovak National Party (PSNS) was signed by local inhabitants (including Roma) to protest against plans to build flats for Roma.[189]

There have been a number of other obstacles to effective implementation as well, including lack of construction permits and lack of land suitable for construction. A major obstacle to these projects is presented by the fact that legal ownership of the land on which most settlements are built has not been established; often, the local government cannot (or will not) implement infrastructural improvements until this question is addressed.[190]

As social housing units may be constructed in a location determined by the municipality, the programme also opens the possibility that new segregated settlements could be created, or existing patterns of segregation reinforced.[191] The OMAS Report suggested that consideration should also be given to programmes to relocate Roma to majority communities rather than investing considerable amounts to improve the infrastructure in segregated settlements.[192] Still, there are plans to expand activities in this area with Phare 2001 and Government funding.[193]

---

[186] Interview with a Representative of the Sándor Márai Foundation, Dunajská Streda, 16 March 2002.

[187] Information on the Implementation of Housing Policy for Roma for the Least Developed Roma Communities, p. 1.

[188] Interview with the Head of the Parliamentary Committee for Human Rights, Bratislava, 11 April 2002.

[189] See "Fears of Fears," Roma Press Agency, 26 July 2002.

[190] *Poverty and Welfare of Roma in the Slovak Republic*, p. vii.

[191] Evaluation of Roma Activities 2001, p. 9.

[192] 2001 OMAS Report, p. IV.

[193] The project "Infrastructure Support for Roma Settlements" was prepared by the Department of Project Coordination, in close cooperation with the new Plenipotentiary. Phare has allocated €8,300,000 while governmental co-financing amounts to €8,400,000.

Despite considerable funding allocated to district and municipal offices through tax incentives, little improvement in settlement conditions can be observed.[194] According to some observers, the key factor is political will: where local authorities have the will to make improvements, progress has been achieved; however, in many places mayors hesitate to make improvements out of the fear that if conditions improve in a given settlement, more Roma will come to settle there.[195]

Programme to improve conditions in Roma settlements

Under the 2002 Priorities, a Comprehensive Development Programme for Roma Settlements is proposed, in line with the Strategy.[196] The programme aims to address housing issues; improve infrastructure in settlements; provide support for education and employment; and support local businesses and field social workers, drawing upon the experience of past projects. The importance of partnership between local Roma and non-Roma communities is emphasised. SKK 210,000 (€5,034) has been allocated[197] for the preparation of a list of villages to participate in the pilot phase of the programme.

Considerable Government support has been allocated to the Phare 2001 project "Infrastructure Support for Roma Settlements," though this project is still in the tender phase.[198]

There is an urgent need for a mechanism to oversee and evaluate the utilisation of funding allocated for infrastructure improvement initiatives, particularly in light of the fact that funding allocations are set to increase. It will also be necessary to ensure more effective cooperation and coordination between central and local authorities in developing and implementing housing policies.

---

[194] "*Na podielových daniach mali Spišiaci za Rómov stovku miliónov korún*" (The Spiš region collected one hundred million crowns for Roma through distributional taxes), Roma Press Agency, 25 June 2002.

[195] Interview with the Director of the Good Roma Kesaj Village Foundation, Košice, 11 July 2002.

[196] The Strategy emphasises the importance of supporting the links between housing policy, job creation, protection of the environment, preservation of cultural heritage, etc., when addressing conditions in Roma settlements. Strategy for Roma – Stage I, p. 21. See also the Comprehensive Development Programme for Roma Settlements.

[197] Government Resolution No. 884 (21 August 2002).

[198] Phare allocation of €8,300,000, Government allocation of €8,400,000.

Other goods and services

Despite continuing reports of discrimination against Roma in access to public goods and services,[199] the Strategy does not propose steps to address the issue. The Slovak Trade Inspection has not proven effective in uncovering or addressing discriminatory practices in this area.[200]

3.2.4 Healthcare and other forms of social protection

Healthcare

The Strategy acknowledges that there has been no systematic research on the healthcare issues faced by Roma communities, despite abundant anecdotal evidence of extremely poor health conditions in settlements, in particular.[201] However, it does not propose strategic research or analysis; nor does it address issues of discrimination in access to healthcare, a problem which has been highlighted by NGOs and Roma leaders.[202]

The Strategy stipulates several tasks to the Ministry of Health,[203] and the Ministry has allocated funding for the implementation of projects to provide health education in schools (SKK 250,000, €5,992) and among Roma children (SKK 750,000, €17,977). An initiative to teach Roma about marriage and family planning received SKK 500,000 (€11,985). Finally, SKK 800,000 (€19,175) funding was provided to regional and district offices for vaccinations programmes and to test drinking-water supplies.[204]

---

[199] M. Vašečka, "Rómovia" (The Roma), in *Slovensko 2000. Súhrnná správa o stave spoločnosti* (Slovakia 2000. A Global Report on the State of Society), G. Mesežnikov and M. Kollár (eds.), Institute for Public Affairs, Bratislava, 2000, p. 180; see also *White Book 2000*; and Roma Rights Center, *Human Rights Report on the Situation of Roma in Eastern Slovakia 2000–2001*.

[200] In the first half of 2001, the Slovak Trade Inspection carried out 11,397 checks and found that 7,350 violations had occurred (64,50 percent). However, the report did not mention any cases of discrimination. Slovak Trade Inspection Report, 2001, <http://www.soi.sk/kcinnost/zoznam/vysledkyprvypolrok.htm>, (accessed 26 September 2002).

[201] See e.g. Strategy for Roma – Stage I, p. 22; Evaluation of Roma Activities 2001, p. 12; *Poverty and Welfare of Roma in the Slovak Republic*, p. vii, p. 40; Roma Rights Center, *Human Rights Report on the Situation of Roma in Eastern Slovakia 2000–2001*, p. 8.

[202] See *Poverty and Welfare of Roma in the Slovak Republic*, p. 40; see also *Minority Protection 2001*, pp. 447–450.

[203] Strategy for Roma – Stage I, pp. 22–23; Strategy for Roma – Stage II, pp. 39–41.

[204] Strategy for Roma – Stage II, p. 39–40.

The 2002 Priorities do not set forth any specific healthcare initiatives, although efforts to improve the infrastructure in Roma settlements are expected to have a positive impact on healthcare in those communities as well.

The Ministry of Health has not initiated any additional programmes under the Strategy.[205] However, under the Action Plan, it is tasked with introducing anti-discrimination training into the curricula for training healthcare workers.[206] No information was available on the degree to which this task has been implemented, and with what results.

Social protection

The Strategy notes that the transition to a market economy has had a significant impact on the most vulnerable segments of the population, including Roma. The principal measures proposed include training for social workers to work within Roma communities and the employment of Roma Advisors in district and regional offices (see Section 3.4.3).[207]

Stage I of the Strategy proposed research on social exclusion and possible modifications to the social protection system.[208] The Action Plan 2002–2003 proposes monitoring of administration of social assistance by regional and district public administrations to prevent discriminatory practices, though not with respect to Roma specifically.[209] It also proposes anti-discrimination training for relevant public officials also at the district and regional levels.[210]

"Field social workers"

The position of "field social worker" was first established in 1996/1997.[211] Under the Strategy, a number of steps were taken to facilitate the work of social workers employed in regions where Roma live. First, their job descriptions were adjusted to allow them to focus on fieldwork within communities rather than on administrative tasks connected to the distribution of unemployment and social

---

[205] Information provided by the Spokesperson of the Ministry of Health, Bratislava, 20 May 2002.
[206] Government Resolution No. 207/2002, Task 2.20, p. 3.
[207] Strategy for Roma – Stage II, p. 35.
[208] Government Resolution 821/1999, Task B. 19 (of the Ministry of Labour, Social Affairs and Family), p. 5.
[209] Action Plan 2002–2003, Parts 6.2.2 and 6.2.3.
[210] Government Resolution No. 207/2002, Task 2.5, p. 1.
[211] Government Resolutions No. 310/1996 and 796/1997.

benefits.[212] Second, in the 2000/2001 school year, a new programme to train social workers for work especially with Roma communities was launched at the Department of Romani Studies of the Pedagogical Faculty in Nitra, including mandatory Romani language classes; however, the programme has now been streamlined and students can specialise in work with Roma communities only in the fourth year; the Romani language classes have become optional.[213]

Under the 2002 Priorities, social workers are receiving special training to help them better address the needs of Roma communities, and to facilitate communications between settlements and the municipal administrations and communities to which they are linked.[214] These field social workers provide assistance on a range of issues, including healthcare and employment. The selection and training process, which began in July 2002, is being carried out by an NGO, in cooperation with the Prešov Office of the Plenipotentiary. Twenty newly-trained field social workers, approximately half of whom are Roma, are expected to start work in Autumn 2002.[215]

3.2.5 The criminal justice system

The Strategy and the Action Plan stipulate systematic and regular human rights and tolerance training for judges and candidate judges, prosecutors and prosecutor trainees, and prison officials.[216] According to a governmental report, several seminars on related

---

[212] Their job description was also changed so that they could address not the problems of "citizens requiring special assistance" but rather the problems of the Roma. Government Resolution No. 821/1999, Task B.6, p. 3.

[213] Interview with a Professor at the Pedagogical Faculty of Constantine the Philosopher University in Nitra, Bratislava, 10 July 2002.

[214] Social Field Workers Programme – A Pilot Programme.

[215] Interview with the staff of the Prešov Office of the Plenipotentiary, 11 July 2002. Funding has been allocated by the Government for their training and remuneration until the end of 2002 for a total amount of SKK 1,106,690 (€26,527). See Government Resolution No. 884 (21 August 2002).

[216] See Strategy for Roma – Stage II, p. 8; see also Government Resolution 283/2000 (Action Plan 2000–2001), Task C.10 of the Ministry of Justice, and Task D.1 of the Prosecutor General, pp. 4, 5. The Action Plan 2002–2003 proposes to step up systemic and regular training for these various professional categories.

topics were organised in 2000 and 2001 by the Ministry of Justice[217] and the Office of the General Prosecutor.[218]

Some international organisations and Roma representatives have asserted that Slovak Roma face discriminatory treatment in the criminal justice system,[219] including more frequent and longer periods of pre-trial detention. However, delays in court procedures are a general problem;[220] there is no official Government data to either confirm or disprove allegations that Roma suffer from particularly harsh treatment. Additional research and monitoring is necessary to determine whether and to what extent discrimination is a problem in this area; in any case, the *perception* of disparate treatment among Roma should be addressed, as widespread distrust and suspicion of law enforcement officials and institutions among Roma communities will limit the effectiveness of any anti-discrimination legislation that might be adopted.

3.3 Protection from Racially Motivated Violence

The Strategy identifies racially motivated violent crime against Roma as a problem, noting that most offences are not reported.[221] The Strategy introduces a number of measures to address violence by private individuals as well as law enforcement officials, and steps have been taken to facilitate recognition of racial motivation in law and in practice. However, additional measures are required to reduce distrust for law enforcement agencies among Roma communities; unless this is done, improved legislation will remain under-utilised.

Violence by private individuals

The Strategy tasks the Ministry of Interior with monitoring localities where tension and conflict have been noted, especially with regard to skinhead attacks on Roma, and

---

[217] Evaluation of Action Plan 2000–2001, p. 4.

[218] Written comments of the Office of the General Prosecutor, Bratislava, 30 July 2002.

[219] See e.g. Implementing Roma Rights in Europe: Written Submission by the European Roma Rights Center to the Parliamentary Assembly of the Council of Europe, 4 March 2002, pp. 15–16, at <http://errc.org/publications/legal/PACE_March_4_2002.doc>, (accessed 26 September 2002).

[220] The European Court on Human Rights receives the highest number of complaints per million inhabitants from Slovakia; most of these pertain to court delays. "Human Rights Court Receives Highest Number of Complaints from Slovakia," RFE/RL *Newsline*, 11 July 2002. See also *Monitoring the EU Accession Process: Judicial Capacity*, Open Society Institute, Budapest, 2002, available at: <http://www.eumap.org>.

[221] Strategy for Roma – Stage I, p. 15. In 2001, 40 racially motivated crimes were registered by the police, of which 23 were resolved. Evaluation of Roma Activities 2001, p. 6.

with taking appropriate action as necessary.[222] The Action Plan 2002–2003 adds that the Ministry should act to secure the adoption and implementation of measures designed to prevent and prosecute neo-Nazi acts and racial violence.[223]

The Ministries of Interior and Justice were to collaborate in enacting necessary changes to the legal system "in cases of yet non-punishable racially-motivated crimes;"[224] accordingly, an amendment to the Criminal Code was adopted to sanction hate speech on the Internet.[225] The earlier introduction of enhanced sentencing for crimes committed with a racial motivation significantly strengthened the legislative framework in this area.[226]

According to Government statistics, the number of persons convicted of racially motivated crimes in the period 1996–2001 has been decreasing.[227] However, NGO reports suggest that the incidence of such crimes has not decreased. This may indicate low awareness of new legislation, or reluctance to utilise it. On 31 August 2001, a court in Žilina sentenced three men who had participated in the widely-publicised fatal attack against A. Balažová to three to five years' imprisonment; however, their crimes were not recognised as racially motivated.[228] Police were also criticised for failing to establish a racial motivation in a February 2002 attack against Roma residents in the village of Gánovce (near Poprad).[229]

The Action Plan calls for special attention to the application of legislation against racism and intolerance; in response, the Office of the General Prosecutor has organised

---

[222] Strategy for Roma – Stage II, pp. 5–6.

[223] Government Resolution No. 207/2002, Task 2.19, p. 3.

[224] Strategy for Roma – Stage II, Task 3, p. 6.

[225] Amendment to the Criminal Code, adopted on 19 June 2002. Written comments of the Ministry of Justice, Bratislava, 15 July 2002.

[226] Written comments of the Section for Foreign Relations and Human Rights, Ministry of Justice, Bratislava, 16 July 2001. See also *Minority Protection 2001*, p. 463.

[227] In 2001, there were seven convictions, compared to 13 in 2000, 11 in 1999, 23 in 1998, 68 in 1997, and 50 in 1996. Information provided by the Ministry of Justice, Bratislava, 15 July 2002.

[228] "*Útok na Balážovcov: súd rasový motív neuznal*" (The Attack on the Balážovs: The court did not recognise a racial motive), *SME*, 30 August 2001. However, a fourth defendant was convicted of racially motivated manslaughter in March 2001. See *Minority Protection 2001*, pp. 463–464.

[229] "Facts about Gánovce," Roma Press Agency, 20 June 2002.

human rights training for prosecutors, with a special focus on combating racially motivated crime.[230]

The Ministry of Interior has prepared a report on extremist organisations,[231] according to which 3,400 right wing extremists are currently active in Slovakia.[232]

The Strategy also required the Ministry of Interior to discontinue the practice of registering the ethnic origin of those convicted of crimes, as this had been observed to stir animosity against Roma when published in the media.[233] However, there have been reports that such data has been posted on the website of the Ministry of Justice.[234]

An informal Commission for Racially Motivated Crime was established at the Ministry of Interior. The Commission includes experts from the Presidium of the police force as well as NGO representatives among its members.[235] Its principal aim is to investigate allegations of racially motivated crime, but it also deals with prevention.[236] According to NGOs, the Commission had met only infrequently until recently.[237]

Several NGOs have taken independent action to raise awareness of existing legislation and to provide legal assistance to those wishing to bring charges. Notably, the NGO "People Against Racism" has launched an anonymous hotline for victims of racially motivated attacks.[238] Between May 2001 and May 2002, the line received 170 calls,

---

[230] Written comments of the Office of the General Prosecutor, Bratislava, 30 July 2002; see also Evaluation of Action Plan 2000–2001, pp. 9–10.

[231] Ministry of the Interior, *Annual Report on the State and Development of Extremism on the Territory of the Slovak Republic*, Bratislava, April 2002, <http://www.minv.sk/en/index.htm>, (accessed 23 October 2002).

[232] Human rights NGOs have generally welcomed this report, though they have noted that it was mainly descriptive, failing to cover the activities of neo-nazi and skinhead organisations in sufficient detail. Press Statement of People Against Racism, 11 April 2002.

[233] See Strategy for Roma – Stage II, Task 5, p. 6.

[234] See e.g. the 2001 Statistical Yearbook of the Ministry of Justice, <www.justice.gov.sk>, (accessed 21 October 2002). See also "Slovak Romany Organisations Say Justice Ministry Violating Law," RFE/RL *Newsline*, 19 September 2002.

[235] These NGOs are: People against Racism, the Citizen and Democracy Foundation, the Open Society Foundation–Slovakia, and ZEBRA (Association of Africa-Slovak Families). The Commission deals with prevention and also training of the police. Evaluation of Action Plan 2000–2002, p. 8.

[236] "*Rezort vnútra prizval k spoluprácii MVO*" (The Ministry of Interior has called for cooperation with NGOs), *Changenet News*, 18 February 2002, <www.changenet.sk>, (accessed 26 September 2002).

[237] Written comments of a Representative of People Against Racism, Bratislava, 17 June 2002.

[238] See "Hotline Against Racism Introduced in Slovakia," RFE/RL *Newsline*, 27 September 2001.

and offered legal assistance in 30 cases; however the hotline has not received any governmental support.[239]

Violence by police

The Strategy reports that the police have been taking more energetic measures against skinheads since 1998,[240] but civil society representatives assert that police action to prevent racially motivated crime remains rare.[241] Domestic NGOs have sought to attract media coverage of racist attacks as a means of exerting pressure on police forces to investigate cases.

In 2001, there were 4,156 complaints against the police, out of which 2,742 were investigated and 20 percent were found admissible.[242] Allegations of abuse of power by the police constitute the most common complaint; 69 such cases were reported in 2000.[243] Complainants also frequently allege inappropriate behaviour or tolerance of racist or neo-nazi groups by policemen.[244] However, Roma in particular are often afraid to bring charges against policemen, for fear that they will find themselves the target of counter charges.[245]

Regarding the highly publicised Sendrei case, in which a Romani man was beaten to death in police custody, three policemen and the mayor of the village of Magnezitovce were charged with assault on 9 July 2001. On 8 October 2002, the remaining four police officers were charged.[246] Following this case, the Minister of Interior announced

---

[239] Information provided by a Representative of People Against Racism, Bratislava, 15 May 2002; written comments of a Representative of People Against Racism, Bratislava, 17 June 2002.

[240] Strategy for Roma – Stage I, p. 15.

[241] See *"Policajt a zákon: kto znamená viac?"* (The Police and the Law: which is more important?) *Národná obroda*, 10 July 2001; see also the interview with the President of People Against Racism, Radio Twist, news at 6, 25 February 2002; and also *Romano Nevo L'il*, No. 526–532, 2002, p. 12.

[242] See "Policajní šéfovia čelia trestným oznámeniam" (Police chiefs have to face criminal charges), *SME*, 27 April 2002, p. 2.

[243] *"Policajt a zákon: kto znamená viac?"* (The Police and the Law: which one is more important?) *Národná obroda*, 10 July 2001.

[244] Written comments of the Office of the General Prosecutor, Bratislava, 30 July 2002.

[245] See, e.g. "Romany Leader Says Community Lives in Fear of Slovak Police," RFE/RL *Newsline*, 18 April 2001.

[246] "Slovak Police Charged Over Rom's Torture, Death While in Custody," RFE/RL *Newsline*, 9 October 2001.

that all police would undergo training on the use of force, and that only graduates of special police schools would be accepted as police candidates.[247]

These initiatives are in line with tasks assigned under the Strategy, requiring the Ministry to introduce new courses on human rights and communications (with special emphasis on the Roma minority) at police academies.[248] The Action Plans also propose police training,[249] as well as additional logistical support and equipment for police units dealing with racially motivated crime;[250] little information is available on implementation.

In fact, the Ministry of Interior has adopted a police training concept and has provided training on the identification of racially motivated crime.[251] For example, an 18-month project was implemented in cooperation with the Dutch police, providing training on policing in minority communities. The project also promoted the employment of minority policemen.[252] At present, an estimated 20 Roma are employed within the national police force, and 50 within municipal police departments.[253] However, some have expressed scepticism about the degree to which these initiatives form part of a broader policy to recruit Roma.[254] Indeed, some Government officials maintain that a systematic policy to recruit and hire Roma policemen would violate the principle of equality.[255]

The Commission for the Solution of the Problem of Racially Motivated Violence at the Ministry of Interior also deals with training of police (see above).

3.4 Promotion of Minority Rights

The former Government placed the promotion and protection of minority rights among its priorities,[256] and logged some progress in strengthening the legal framework. Though there is no comprehensive minority law, Slovakia has ratified both the

---

[247] "Slovak Police to be Re-trained in Use of Force," RFE/RL *Newsline*, 13 July 2001.
[248] Strategy for Roma – Stage II, Tasks 8 and 9, pp. 5–6.
[249] Government Resolutions No. 283/2000, Task C. 16, p. 5; No. 207/2002, Task 2.15, p. 3.
[250] Government Resolution No. 207/2002, Tasks 2.17, 2.18, p. 3.
[251] Evaluation of Action Plan 2000–2001, p. 7.
[252] Evaluation of Action Plan 2000–2001, p. 8.
[253] Interview with the Chairman of the Commission for the Solution of the Problem of Racially Motivated Violence, Ministry of Interior, Bratislava, 25 August 2002.
[254] Press Release of People Against Racism, 29 May 2002.
[255] Written comments of the Office of the General Prosecutor, Bratislava, 30 July 2002.
[256] Strategy for Roma – Stage I, p. 12; see also Programme Declarations of the Slovak Government.

Framework Convention for the Protection of National Minorities (FCNM) and the European Charter for Regional or Minority Languages (ECRML).[257]

Further, the Strategy states that "Roma [...] represent a specific national minority" and acknowledges that the degree to which they enjoy access to minority rights in practice is still insufficient.[258]

3.4.1 Education

The Constitution guarantees members of national minorities the right to education in their mother tongue;[259] however, education legislation does not extend this right to Roma unequivocally,[260] which the Council of NGOs of Roma Communities has challenged before the Constitutional Court.[261] The case is pending.

The Strategy acknowledges that State efforts to support minority education for Roma have been insufficient, and states that, depending on the need and interest of the Roma community, it will promote Romanes as a supplementary language of instruction. It proposes to do this through the implementation of pilot initiatives such as the employment of Roma assistants;[262] it does not propose to establish schools or classes providing Romani language education, though it (as well as the 2002 Priorities) plan to

---

[257] In the May 2001 census, 89,920 persons declared themselves to be Roma (1.7 percent of the population, compared to 83,988 or 1.4 percent in 1991). At the same time, 99,448 persons declared Romanes to be their mother tongue. See the 2001 Census results, at <http://www.statistics.sk/webdata/slov/scitanie/namj.htm>, (accessed 26 September 2002). The Government estimates the actual size of the Roma population to be between 360,000 and 400,000. Evaluation of Roma Activities 2001, p. 1. Unofficial estimates place the Roma population closer to 500,000.

[258] Strategy for Roma – Stage I, p. 15.

[259] Constitution of the Slovak Republic, adopted on 3 September 1992, Art. 34(2a), at <http://www.concourt.sk>, (accessed 26 September 2002).

[260] The Law on Primary and Secondary Schools (350/1994), which enables ethnic minorities to exercise this right, is extended to all minorities, but though Act 29/1984 on the Network of Primary and Secondary Schools explicitly guarantees education in the mother tongue to the Czech, Hungarian, German, Polish and Ukrainian/Ruthenian minorities, it does not mention the Roma.

[261] See "*Právo na vzdelanie v materinskom jazyku si Rómovia uplatňujú na Ústavnom súde*" (Roma are claiming the right to education in the mother tongue at the Constitutional Court), *SME Online*, 9 February 2002, <http://www.sme.sk/clanok.asp?cl=234179>, (accessed 26 September 2002).

[262] Strategy for Roma – Stage I, p. 18.

continue and expand support to the Secondary School of Arts in Košice.[263] Specialised secondary schools to improve the quality of education in and about Roma language and culture are also under consideration in Banská Bystrica and Košice.[264] Finally, the Government has promised support for a programme in Roma culture for first-grade teachers at the University of Nitra.[265]

At present, few Roma enjoy access to education in Romanes.[266] According to some experts, providing the option of Romanes-language education could improve education levels in Roma communities.[267] Roma representatives emphasise that even if State-supported education in Romanes is not feasible at present, children should be able to use their mother tongue at school without feeling ashamed; the development of a strong network of Roma assistants and the introduction of language courses in Romanes in schools would be an important first step.[268]

The Strategy also aims to ensure multicultural education for all students and recognises the need to promote tolerance by providing information about Roma culture and history in schools, *inter alia*.[269] However, there have been relatively few programmes in support of these goals; Roma history and culture are not yet part of the regular curricula of elementary and secondary schools. The Ministry of Education has added a one-hour course on discrimination in the general curriculum; Roma activists claim that this is insufficient to counter widespread discriminatory attitudes.[270] The Ministry has

---

[263] Strategy for Roma – Stage I, p. 8; 2002 Priorities, p. 3.

[264] Interview with the Director of the Good Roma Kesaj Village Foundation, Košice, 22 March 2002.

[265] *"Univerzita Konštantína Filozofa sa dostala po Nitre a Spiši aj do Lučenca"* (After Nitra and Spiš, the University of Constantine the Philosopher is coming to Lučenec), Roma Press Agency, 18 July 2002.

[266] In addition to the Secondary School of Arts in Košice, Romanes is also used at the Romani Culture Department at Nitra University as well as at the Research and Advisory Centre in Spišská Nová Ves, by Roma assistants, and as a supporting language in nursery schools and pre-school preparatory classes with a high concentration of Roma pupils. Interview with a Professor at the Pedagogical Faculty of Constantine the Philosopher University in Nitra, Bratislava, 22 July 2002. See *Report submitted by the Slovak Republic pursuant to Article 25, Paragraph 1, of the Framework Convention for the Protection of National Minorities*, Article 14, at <http://www.riga.lv/minelres/reports/slovakia/Article_14.htm>, (accessed 26 September 2002).

[267] Interview with the Head of the Parliamentary Committee for Human Rights, Bratislava, 11 April 2002.

[268] Interviews with: the Director of the Good Roma Kesaj Village Foundation, Košice, 22 March 2002; the Director of Projekt Schola, Košice, 11 July 2002; and a Representative of the Roma Press Agency, Košice, 17 July 2002.

[269] Strategy for Roma – Stage I, p. 17.

[270] OSI Roundtable, Bratislava, June 2002.

also supported a number of workshops, essay contests and other activities to raise awareness of discrimination among schoolchildren, and has supported the preparation and publication of a new book on Roma history by an expert of the State Pedagogical Institute.[271] The book, which is to be used in elementary schools, is scheduled for publication in 2002; information on the degree to which Roma experts participated in the preparation of the book was not available for this report.

Some Phare projects include components promoting or supporting the Roma identity or education in Romanes. For example, the Phare 1999 programme proposes the establishment of a Roma education, information, documentation and advisory centre; Phare 2000 aims to support Roma identity through pre-school education, elementary education, "zero classes," and training for teachers working with Roma, *inter alia*.[272] There has been little evaluation of the efficacy of these programmes to date, as they are still either under preparation or being implemented. Results should be scrutinised carefully, with participation from Roma experts, to determine which elements could be incorporated into developing governmental policies to improve minority education for Roma.

3.4.2 Language

Though a significant number of Roma speak Romanes as their mother-tongue,[273] the Strategy makes no provision to support its use in public life. It has been claimed that the lack of a codified form of Romanes constitutes an obstacle to minority language rights for Roma.[274]

The Office of the Plenipotentiary has established a Language Commission to examine and revise (as necessary) the codification of the Romani language; the last codification effort took place in 1971. It has already recommended the publication of a Slovak–Romani Vocabulary and a Romanes grammar book. As the Commission's work is essential to

---

[271] The Ministry of Education allocated SKK 500,000 (€11,985) for its publication.

[272] See also Section 3.2.1.

[273] The Government estimates that as many as 80 percent of Roma use the Romani language in everyday life. Evaluation of Roma Activities 2001, p. 8.

[274] Most existing research on Romanes was issued in a Romani-Czech version, since codification efforts took place under the former Czechoslovakia, and most experts were based in the present Czech Republic. According to the "Information on State of Preparation of Romany Language Recodification," the Eastern Slovakian Romani dialect (which is used as a colloquial language by about 80 percent of Roma in Slovakia) should serve as the basis for the orthography of the Romani language. Information on the State of Preparation of Romani Language Recodification, 23 January 2002, <http://www.ial.sk/appl/material.nsf/0/2D1A8F8DBD52AED2C1256B410035F905?OpenDocument>, (accessed 26 September 2002).

ensuring that Roma enjoy access to minority language rights in practice, human and financial resources should be allocated to support its work as a matter of priority.

There is little awareness of language rights among Roma communities.[275] Only eight Roma settlements meet the 20 percent threshold set by the Minority Language Law;[276] furthermore, the use of minority languages in contacts with regional authorities is covered neither by the Minority Law nor by the ECRML.[277] Moreover, very few Roma are employed in State administration. Thus, opportunities for using the Romani language in public life are likely to remain minimal in the immediate future,[278] and a long-term strategy and policy is necessary.

3.4.3 Participation in Public Life

The Strategy for Roma emphasises the need for provide opportunities for Roma to participate in resolving their own problems;[279] however, it fails to propose concrete means to promote their participation. The Advisory Committee on the FCNM has asserted that "shortcomings that remain as concerns the effective participation of the Roma in social and economic life and the negative impact that these shortcomings have on the social and economic living-conditions of this minority in general and of Roma women in particular."[280]

---

[275] The ECRML grants Romanes the official status of a "regional or minority language." Alleged contradictions between the Charter and domestic legislation could represent an obstacle to effective implementation of the ECRML. Information provided by the Center for Legal Analyses/Kalligram Foundation, Bratislava, 15 July 2002.

[276] Act 184/1999 On the Use of Languages of National Minorities, adopted on 10 July 1999.

[277] Information provided by the Section for Human Rights and Minorities, Bratislava, 10 October 2002.

[278] See Advisory Committee on the Framework Convention for the Protection of National Minorities, Opinion on Slovakia, adopted on 22 September 2000, Art. 10, para. 36, <http://www.humanrights.coe.int/minorities/Eng/FrameworkConvention/AdvisoryCommittee/Opinions/Slovakia.htm>, (accessed 26 September 2002); see also *2001 Regular Report*, pp. 23–24.

[279] Strategy for Roma – Stage I, p. 23.

[280] Opinion on Slovakia, Art. 15, para. 47.

There are no Roma in the Parliament[281] or in positions of responsibility within the Government, including within bodies responsible for implementing policies concerning the Roma, with the notable exception of the Plenipotentiary for Roma Communities. Participation in local political life is higher,[282] and several Roma parties and candidates hope to win representation at the local elections in December 2002.

The Strategy established the position of "Roma Advisor" at the level of regional State administration.[283] However, no additional funding was allocated, and these responsibilities were taken up by existing staff, who received no additional training. Moreover, it is not explicitly stated that these positions should be occupied by Roma, and it is up to each office to decide whether they want to hire a Roma Advisor or not. To date, only three Advisors have been established at the regional level. A position of district advisor was also established following lobbying by several Roma NGOs.[284] According to NGO sources,[285] only two are of Roma origin (one regional Advisor and one district Advisor).

The 2002 Priorities propose the establishment of a bilingual (English-Slovak) secondary school to train future civil servants, to include a course in Roma studies.[286] This measure and other positive measures of this kind should receive support, as they will increase the number of qualified and trained Roma employed in the civil service over time, which would in turn greatly facilitate communications between State administrations and Roma communities.

Roma participate in an advisory capacity in the Plenipotentiary's Advisory Board, the Council for National Minorities, and the Advisory Commission which allocates funding from the Ministry of Culture. The Ministry of Interior has also established a special advisory position for Roma issues. Roma members of the IMC represent the ministries which delegated them rather than the Roma community *per se*. Although

---

[281] Two Roma parties qualified to take part in the 2001 Parliamentary elections; several mainstream political parties also presented Roma candidates. However, none managed to obtain a seat in the new Parliament. See K. Magdolenová, "Analysis: Roma and the 2002 Elections in Slovakia," Roma Press Agency, 7 October 2002, <http://www.rpa.sk/clanok.aspx?o=zc&n=320&l=en>, (accessed 23 October 2002).

[282] See *Minority Protection 2001*, p. 474; see also, M. Vašečka, "Roma," in *Slovakia 1998–1999. A Global Report on the State of Society*, p. 764.

[283] See Government Resolution No. 821/1999, Task B.7 (to be covered by existing staff of regional offices), p. 3; see also Strategy for Roma – Stage II, Regional Offices, Task 1, p. 35.

[284] Interview with the Advisor for Roma Issues in Spišská Nová Ves, 3 April 2002.

[285] Interview with the Chairman and the Deputy Chairman of the Council of NGOs of Roma Communities, Bratislava, 10 July 2002.

[286] 2002 Priorities, p. 3.

there are no official data, it is widely believed that Roma are severely under-represented in the civil service, the criminal justice system, and the police, *inter alia*.

Increasing numbers of Roma are participating in the development and implementation of policy towards Roma through NGOs. The Strategy recognises the importance of this development, and promises support to NGO activities.[287] Considering the acknowledged necessity for cooperation with the civil society sector if the Strategy is to be implemented in full, there is a need for more effective mechanisms to facilitate the solicitation and processing of NGO input in the course of regular Strategy review and updating.

3.4.4 Media

The Strategy sets forth the objective of supporting projects for and about the Roma in the mass media[288] as well as the creation of Roma editorial boards in State-owned media.[289] However, according to some Roma professionals it gives too little attention to fostering Roma and Romani-language media.[290]

Accordingly, the Plenipotentiary signed an agreement on cooperation on an anti-discrimination campaign with the Director of Slovak public television in March 2002.[291] There is currently a 30-minute Romanes-language programme for the Roma minority, which is broadcast within the national Hungarian programme as well as on the regional public television station in Prešov, which is also preparing an additional weekly regional television programme.

The 2002 Priorities aim to address negative majority opinions about Roma through mass media campaigns, several of which have already been implemented. For example, from October 2001 to April 2002, the Plenipotentiary implemented a campaign entitled "We are all Citizens of the Slovak Republic," targeting journalists, State administration officials, and local governments as well as the broader public, in an effort to overcome negative stereotypes about Roma.[292] As part of this campaign, a second campaign, entitled "*Čačipen*" ("truth" in Romanes), was launched on 8 April

---

[287] Strategy for Roma – Stage I, p. 16; Strategy for Roma – Stage II, p. 5.

[288] Strategy for Roma – Stage II, p. 20.

[289] Strategy for Roma – Stage I, p. 19.

[290] Interview with a Representative of Jekhetane and *Romano Nevo L'il*, Bratislava, 10 July 2002.

[291] Interview with the Plenipotentiary for Roma Communities, Bratislava, 8 May 2002.

[292] See 2002 Priorities, p. 4. The campaign received support from the World Bank.

2002 (International Roma Day).[293] It covered many activities throughout the country with the aim to narrow the distance between Roma and non-Roma. The Action Plan 2002–2003 has recommended sustained follow-up to these campaigns, but it is not clear whether State support is forthcoming. Civil society representatives have criticised the lack of a sustained governmental strategy to promote tolerance in the media.[294] Clear and visible governmental support – both financial and political – will also be essential to the success of campaigns of this nature.

The Strategy tasks the Ministry of Culture with supporting the publication of Roma journals and newspapers,[295] and in 2002, SKK 1,650,000 (€39,549) was allocated for this purpose. Civil society representatives assert the need for a longer-term strategy to support minority media; at present, funding is allocated on an annual basis, impeding effective long-term planning.[296] Roma print media can not survive without State support.[297]

On 15 April 2002, the first independent Roma Press Agency opened in Košice, on the basis of successful models in Hungary and the Czech Republic. It provides regular feature stories on issues of importance to the Roma community – often written by Roma journalists – to mainstream newspapers and periodicals. In this way, the Agency aims actively to promote a more positive image of the Roma community in the mass media.[298]

3.4.5 Culture

The Strategy for Roma states the need to "positively encourage the development of Roma culture by adopting a mechanism of regular and early subsidy from the State

---

[293] See Klára Orgovánová, in O. Štefucová, "*Kampaň pre zblíženie rómskej a nerómskej kommunity na Slovensku,*" Radio Free Europe, 5 April 2002.

[294] Written Comments of a Representative of People Against Racism, Bratislava, 17 June 2002.

[295] Strategy for Roma – Stage I, p. 9.

[296] Interview with a Representative of Jekhetane and *Romano Nevo L'il*, Bratislava, 10 July 2002.

[297] There is at present one weekly – *Romano Nevo L'il* (published in Romanes and in Slovak), one monthly for Roma youth (*Ternipen*), and one bi-monthly for children (*Štarprajtanoro*).

[298] See "Slovakia's First Romany Press Agency Opens," RFE/RL *Newsline,* 16 April 2002. The RPA's website is at <http://www.rpa.sk>, (accessed 26 September 2002).

budget [...]."²⁹⁹ Initiatives singled out to receive State support include the Romathan theatre ensemble in Košice³⁰⁰ and a "House of the Roma" in Bratislava.³⁰¹

In line with the objectives of the Strategy, the Ministry of Culture provides support for the cultural activities of many Roma NGOs. In 2001, SKK 5,799,000 (€138,998) was allocated for Roma projects; an additional SKK 500,000 (€11,985) was allocated for research (to non-Roma organisations); in 2002, SKK 7,353,000 (€176,246) was allocated for projects of Roma organisations.³⁰² An evaluation of the extent to which these activities attract interest from the majority community as well would help determine whether they foster appreciation for Roma culture within society as a whole.

4. EVALUATION

The adoption of the Strategy was an important indication of the Government's intention to address issues faced by the Roma community, as part of its broader efforts to improve minority protection. Implementation is still at an early stage, but already a number of areas for improvement can be identified.

The Strategy aims to address complex problems in a wide range of areas, including education, employment, housing, social services, and healthcare. At the same time, it extends recognition to the Roma language and culture and recognises the need to promote their development. Yet, while comprehensive in scope, the Strategy does not deal with the various issues identified in depth. Given the complexity and scope of problems in each of these areas, the Strategy will need to be reviewed and revised, with an eye to developing a series of "sub-strategies" in each of these areas, on the basis of extensive research, substantial and substantive participation from Roma communities, and allocation of necessary human and financial resources.

As an example, though it recognises discrimination, the Strategy does not go deep enough; it does not identify the specific discriminatory practices experienced by Roma in many areas of life, nor does it outline specific remedies. Efforts to adopt anti-

---

[299] Strategy for Roma – Stage I, p. 19.

[300] In 2002, the theatre received SKK 6,850,000 (€164,190); an additional SKK 1.5 million (€35,954) was allocated for reconstruction. Telephone interview with the General Director of the Section for Minority Culture, Ministry of Culture, Bratislava, 24 October 2002.

[301] 2002 Priorities, p. 4. However, as of July 2002, no project proposal had been presented to the Government.

[302] Telephone interview with the General Director of the Section for Minority Culture, Ministry of Culture, Bratislava, 24 October 2002.

discrimination legislation have not yet won the necessary political support. Given low levels of awareness of existing legislation and deep-seeded mistrust for State institutions, including law enforcement officials, among Roma communities, the adoption of such legislation will need to be complemented by implementing guidelines, training, and awareness-raising activities. This could be achieved through intensive training programmes on the new legislation for public officials and civil society representatives and the continuation of existing efforts to improve awareness of human rights norms among law enforcement and court officials.

The 2002 Priorities represent a positive initiative to clarify Strategy goals and deepen the level of engagement in certain specific areas. Addressing poor living conditions in Roma settlements will bring about an immediate and tangible improvement in the quality of life for many Roma. However, a parallel, long-term policy should be elaborated to address the more deeply-rooted problem of segregation; it may not be cost-effective to create new infrastructure in isolated Roma settlements if the long-term goal is to promote integration into affordable and decent housing within majority communities.[303] Civil society representatives have also pointed out that an exclusive focus on Roma living in settlements is reminiscent of earlier policies that treated the "Roma issue" as a purely social problem.

Administration

Effective Strategy implementation requires active involvement from a broad range of State actors at all levels. Accordingly, the current system of administration and management is rather decentralised, and most of the concrete measures listed on the Strategy – Stage II were proposed by ministries or regional and local public administration. However, it would be advisable to balance receptivity to the needs of local communities against the need for overall policy coherence and consistency – which can best be provided by clearly-articulated governmental policies.

At the central level, the Deputy Prime Minister holds political responsibility for Strategy implementation, while the Plenipotentiary is in charge of administration, coordination and monitoring. However, neither can compel ministries to fulfill their tasks under the Strategy and their ability to offer incentives is also weak; the amount of State funding at the disposal of the Deputy Prime Minister and the Plenipotentiary is far below the level of demand. Again, ministries and other State bodies participate at their discretion, and according to their ability (and will) to allocate additional funding from their own budgets. In ministries and local public administrations which themselves lack funding, administrative capacity and staff skilled in project management, Strategy implementation has suffered. The emergence of political and

---

[303] 2001 OMAS Report, p. IV.

popular opposition to certain Strategy initiatives has emerged as a significant obstacle to implementation in some areas.

Some of these obstacles can be addressed through clear and unequivocal expressions of support for Strategy goals and objectives from officials at the highest levels. State bodies which are convinced of the political necessity and wisdom of taking visible steps to demonstrate that they are making efforts to fulfil the Strategy will find the resources to do so. In many cases, creativity and political will are more important than funding; by the same token, increasing funding without ensuring political support and receptivity is not likely to produce positive results.

In addition to improved administration and coordination, there is a need to develop monitoring and evaluation mechanisms to facilitate regular and systematic review and updating of the Strategy. Proposed project monitoring and research on activities to improve conditions in Roma settlements constitute a positive step in this direction.

Minority participation and representation

The creation of advisory bodies to solicit input on policy development and implementation from Roma representatives has created new opportunities for Roma to articulate the needs of their communities *vis-à-vis* the Government.

However, while the Strategy for Roma emphasises the need for Roma to take "co-responsibility for their destiny,"[304] it fails to specify mechanisms for involvement of this nature; as Roma do not share full responsibility for Strategy development and management; they are not able to shoulder responsibility for its implementation either. Where project management capacity is lacking, efforts should be focusing on providing the necessary training to place Roma representatives in positions of leadership in the preparation and administration of governmental programmes to fulfil the Strategy. Where necessary qualifications are lacking, efforts should be focused – as has been recommended by the Plenipotentiary – on providing educational and training opportunities for Roma who would like to take up careers in the civil service.

Greater involvement *from* the Roma community is key to the long-term success of the Strategy *for* Roma. Engaging Roma as equal partners in the process of developing and implementing solutions to the issues faced by their communities is necessary for the achievement of broader Strategy aims to cultivate leadership, responsibility, and initiative among Roma communities.

---

[304] Strategy for Roma – Stage I, p. 16.

5. Recommendations

To the Government

- Send strong, clear and consistent messages to ministries and other bodies tasked with responsibilities under the Strategy that these responsibilities are to be taken seriously.

- Equip Strategy coordination bodies with authority to require reporting (including financial reporting) on tasks under the Strategy; to review and evaluate implementation efforts; and to offer recommendations for improvement.

- Further enhance the capacity of the Plenipotentiary to oversee the development and implementation of consistent, coherent and long-term policies in each of the areas outlined under the Strategy; consider establishing the position of Plenipotentiary in law, to ensure continuity in Strategy implementation over time.

- Support in-depth research and analysis in problem areas, as a necessary step toward developing more effective, targeted policies and programmes.

- Provide training to develop project management, administration, and budgeting skills within individual ministries as well as among local public administrations.

- Develop specific mechanisms to promote increased Roma participation in Strategy implementation and assessment, including through training in policy-making and project management.

- Adopt comprehensive anti-discrimination legislation in line with the EU Race Equality and Employment Directives.

- Adopt guidelines and training for public officials and social workers on the implementation of anti-discrimination provisions, with a view to increasing institutional capacity to ensure equal access to public goods and services in practice.

- Develop training programmes to prepare Roma for employment in public administration and other areas, and develop policies to encourage employment of the graduates of these programmes as civil servants.

- Revise the Strategy to incorporate measures to settle ownership of the land on which Roma settlements are located; consider the development of a policy to promote integration into majority communities rather than reinforcement of existing patterns of segregation.

- Complement measures to improve access to education for Roma through pre-school preparation and extra classroom assistance with efforts to recognise and cultivate Romani language and culture, particularly in areas where many Romani children study.
- Develop specific programmes to support Roma media and training for Roma journalists as a crucial means of promoting enhanced appreciation for Roma culture within the broader community.

OPEN SOCIETY INSTITUTE 2002

Minority Protection in Slovenia

AN ASSESSMENT OF THE PROGRAMME OF MEASURES
FOR HELPING ROMA IN THE REPUBLIC OF SLOVENIA
AND EQUAL EMPLOYMENT OPPORTUNITIES FOR ROMA
– A JOINT CHALLENGE.

Table of Contents

1. Executive Summary 592
2. The Government Programmes –
   Background 594
   - 2.1 Background to Present Programme 595
   - 2.2 The Programme – Process 595
     - 2.2.1 The 1995 Programme 595
     - 2.2.2 The Employment Programme 596
   - 2.3 The Programme – Content 598
     - 2.3.1 1995 Programme 598
     - 2.3.2 Employment Programme 599
     - 2.3.3 Social Inclusion Programme 600
   - 2.4 The Programme – Administration/
     Implementation/Evaluation 600
     - 2.4.1 The 1995 Programme 601
     - 2.4.2 The Employment Programme 603
   - 2.5 The Programme and the Public 604
   - 2.6 The Programme and the EU 605
3. The Government Programme –
   Implementation 606
   - 3.1 Stated Objectives of the Programme 606
     - 3.1.1 The 1995 Programme 606
     - 3.1.2 The Employment Programme 606

3.2		Government Programme and Discrimination	607
	3.2.1	Education	609
	3.2.2	Employment	615
	3.2.3	Housing and other goods and services	618
	3.2.4	Healthcare and other forms of social protection	621
	3.2.5	The criminal justice system	623
3.3		Protection from Racially Motivated Violence	624
3.4		Promotion of Minority Rights	624
	3.4.1	Education	625
	3.4.2	Language	626
	3.4.3	Participation in public life	627
	3.4.4	Media	629
	3.4.5	Culture	630
4.		Evaluation	631
5.		Recommendations	633

1. Executive Summary

Slovenia has adopted two programmes specifically addressing the situation of the Roma. The first and more general programme was promulgated in 1995, the "Programme of Measures for Helping Roma in the Republic of Slovenia" (hereafter, the "1995 Programme"). In May 2000, the Government adopted a more specific programme entitled "Equal Employment Opportunities for Roma – a joint challenge" (hereafter, the "Employment Programme"), which concluded in 2001.

The two programmes, together with more general measures such as the Programme on the Fight Against Poverty and Social Exclusion (hereafter, "Social Inclusion Programme"), address all major spheres of social life, including education, employment, housing, and healthcare. Local authorities implement projects under the auspices of the programmes, with ministries allocating funding through a tender system. There are few mechanisms to coordinate activities under these programmes around a coherent national strategy, and the involvement of Roma themselves in planning and implementing projects has been minimal. Consequently, results have been uneven, with some projects faltering after only a short period, while others have successfully incorporated participants' feedback and have even expanded into new areas. A more coordinated approach, centred around projects that foster initiative from Roma communities and reduce their reliance on Government aid, could be more effective in addressing the critical issues Roma face.

Administration

The Government Office for Nationalities coordinates implementation of the 1995 Programme; individual ministries carry out activities under the Programme by funding local projects generally selected by tender. The Employment Programme was coordinated and implemented by the Ministry of Labour, Family and Social Affairs in collaboration with the Employment Service. However, local bodies are primarily responsible for formulating and carrying out the actual projects, often with minimal coordination from central authorities. Government level evaluations appear to offer little guidance to local authorities for improving existing projects or developing future initiatives. Moreover, a lack of funding has forced the conclusion of many projects despite continuing demand from local Roma communities.

EU Support

The European Union has allocated accession funding to a number of Roma-related projects since 1996.[1] The Employment Programme mentions that it is partly Phare-

---

[1] DG Enlargement Information Unit, *EU Support for Roma Communities in Central and Eastern Europe*, May 2002, p. 30.

financed.[2] However, the most recent Accession Partnership priorities, which generally form the basis for Phare funding areas, do not mention any issues related to minorities.[3] No Phare national programme funds appear to have targeted Roma; smaller projects, such as legal counselling for refugees and parents' education have been supported through the Phare Democracy Programmes.[4]

Content and Implementation

Discrimination is not explicitly addressed in either of the Government programmes, although some measures recognise the need to ensure equal opportunities in spheres such as education and healthcare. Measures to improve access to education for Roma communities have been among the most successful initiatives, many working closely with participants to ensure that projects reflect their needs. While the Employment Programme's text calls for a greater contribution from Roma, its more innovative component of creating public-private partnership cooperatives failed to materialise when there was no response to the project tender. Instead, public works programmes have constitute the primary source of employment under the programmes, with demand exceeding availability in spite of low salaries and lack of opportunity to gain marketable skills.

Although the protection of Roma culture is a priority for many Roma civil society organisations, this dimension of minority policy is not greatly elaborated in any of the Roma Government programmes. The inclusion of "socialisation" elements in many projects developed for Roma suggests that some aspects of Roma culture are still viewed as being at odds with majority society. The Social Inclusion Programme emphasises the importance of reducing factors alienating underprivileged groups, but its provisions do not extend to spheres such as public participation or language rights for the Roma. Government policy thus reflects Slovenia's reluctance to come to terms with multiculturalism when it comes to Roma.

Conclusions

The major success of the 1995 Programme is its existence. The Programme is the first to recognise the need for State involvement in addressing the problems confronting Roma. Since the Programme was developed, many projects have been funded under its umbrella, and local initiatives have started in many municipalities. The Employment Programme developed the themes of the 1995 Programme, but went farther

---

[2] Equal Employment Opportunities for Roma, p. 6.
[3] European Commission, DG Enlargement, *Slovenia: Accession Partnership*, 2001.
[4] DG Enlargement Information Unit, *EU Support for Roma Communities in Central and Eastern Europe*, May 2002, p. 30.

conceptually in recognising the importance of including Roma as active participants, not merely recipients.

Both programmes lack sections on racial violence, discrimination, and minority rights in general. Problems with access to healthcare are also not addressed to the extent necessary. Neither of the programmes addresses the situation and legal rights of the many "non-autochthonous" Roma without citizenship.

The decentralised approach of both programmes has proven to be an effective means to address the varied and distinct problems Roma face in different regions. However, as most of the programming decisions lie with local authorities, their discrete programmes fail to coalesce around a coherent Government policy to address problems in a systematic and comprehensive manner. Consultation with Roma organisations and representatives would facilitate the identification of both specific regional issues and common issues confronting Roma throughout the country. Projects where such consultations have taken place appear to be more successful and durable than those elaborated by local authorities alone. Poorly targeted initiatives offer few obvious benefits to the target group and fail to encourage a long-term shift away from dependence on social welfare or other forms of State support. There are especially few projects designed to increase women's capacity to enter the workforce, as most of the public works projects established involve unskilled labour – jobs usually undertaken by men.

Progress could be more effectively achieved if the many diverse approaches, both successful and less so, were drawn together to construct a more cohesive strategy. The importance of local decision-making should be balanced against the need for the expertise, capacity, and authority of a Government-level body. This would help to ensure that efforts are not misdirected, and expectations are fulfilled.

2. The Government Programmes – Background

Slovenia has adopted two specific programmes designed to address the situation of the Roma minority. The first and more general plan was launched in 1995, the "Programme of Measures for Helping Roma in the Republic of Slovenia" (hereafter, the "1995 Programme"). In May 2000, the Government adopted the special programme entitled "Equal Employment Opportunities for Roma – a joint challenge" (hereafter, the "Employment Programme"). The National Programme on the Fight Against Poverty and Social Exclusion (hereafter, the "Social Inclusion Programme), adopted in February 2000, also includes measures that are intended to benefit the Roma minority, among other disadvantaged social groups.

2.1 Background to Present Programme

The 1995 Programme represents the first effort to draft a Government strategy addressing the needs of the Roma minority, which is granted special status under Article 65 of the Slovene Constitution.[5] Prior to 1995, the only measures in place were scattered legal provisions defining Roma as a vulnerable population group within the Law on Social Protection, the Law on Education, and the Law on Local Communities, *inter alia*.[6] Generally, past Government policy towards Roma was directed towards assimilation.[7]

2.2 The Programme – Process

2.2.1 The 1995 Programme

The 1995 Programme was introduced as a joint initiative of seven ministries, the Government Office for Nationalities of the Republic of Slovenia (hereafter, "Office for Nationalities"), and the governmental body for local government reform. In 1995 the Office for Nationalities, in cooperation with the Roma association "Romani Union," began preparing a report on the situation of the Roma.[8] At the same time, the Government Commission for Roma Questions asked ministries to prepare reports on the current situation of Roma in their respective spheres. The final report drafted by the Office for Nationalities, presented to the Government in April 1995, focused on the poor living conditions of the Roma, and the problems of poverty and underdevelopment. Observing that many Roma are "autochthonous," or indigenous inhabitants of the country, the report recommended that State action was necessary to address the inequalities of their situation.[9]

In response, the Government then passed a decision to draft a strategy addressing the situation, and various ministries were called upon to prepare a programme of measures

---

[5] The Constitution of Slovenia, Article 65 on the Status and Special Rights of Gypsy Communities in Slovenia provides that "the status and special rights of Gypsy communities living in Slovenia shall be such as are determined by statute."

[6] *Informacija o položaju Romov v RS*, EPA 1102, *Poročevalec DZ RS*, (Information on the Situation of Roma in the Republic of Slovenia, Official Gazette of the Parliament of Slovenia), No. 18, p. 56.

[7] Interview with Vera Klopčič, Institute for Ethnic Studies, Ljubljana, 13 March 2002.

[8] The full title of the report was "Information on the situation of Roma in the Republic of Slovenia" No. 019-06/95, 24 January 1995.

[9] Programme of Measures for Helping Roma in the Republic of Slovenia, p. 1, (hereafter, "1995 Programme").

to improve living conditions for Roma, and to secure their cultural and linguistic identity.[10] The Government document was sent to Parliament, which then discussed the programme's priorities and terms. The approach finally adopted incorporates a system of separate legal provisions, rather than a single unitary law for the protection of the Roma minority, although the latter approach was favoured by Roma groups. In practice, just seven laws address Roma rights directly, while the Hungarian and Italian minorities are addressed in 37 provisions.[11]

The 1995 Programme suggests that although the State and local authorities have made efforts to improve the situation of the Roma, the processes of integration and socialisation are too slow.[12] It asserts that responsibility cannot be delegated to local communities alone, but that the State must provide professional and financial support.[13] In the process of preparing the 1995 Programme, the Government solicited the input of local employment offices, especially those in Maribor and Velenje. Although the Programme was drafted in line with European standards, there were no formal consultations with the European Union or other international bodies.

The Roma NGO "Romani Union," which was established in 1991 (and later joined the larger Association of Roma of Slovenia), first proposed that the Government should enact a separate law to regulate Roma rights. Although unsuccessful in arguing for a unitary law, the Association was able to initiate discussions that ultimately led to the promulgation of the 1995 Programme. During this process the Government frequently met and negotiated with Roma representatives.

2.2.2 The Employment Programme

In 2000, the Ministry for Labour, Family, and Social Affairs developed the Employment Programme, after the Alliance of Roma of Slovenia submitted a draft strategy of their own in 1997.[14]

---

[10] 1995 Programme, p. 1.

[11] P. Winkler, *Pregled predpisov o posebnih pravicah Romov v RS. V: Poti za izboljšanje položaja Romov v srednij in Vzhodni Evropi.* (Overview of Regulations About Special Rights of Roma in Slovenia), Council of Europe, Ljubljana 1999, pp. 31–33.

[12] 1995 Programme, p. 1.

[13] 1995 Programme, p. 1.

[14] Open Society Institute EU Accession Monitoring Program, *Monitoring the EU Accession Process: Minority Protection*, Budapest 2001, p. 510, available at <http://www.eumap.org>, (accessed 3 October 2002), (hereafter, "*Minority Protection 2001*").

The Government programme was based on a research project, "Roma and Unemployment in Pomurje," carried out by the Employment Service of the Republic of Slovenia (hereafter, ESS) in June 1995.[15] The Ministry initially convened a group of experts to analyse the employment situation of Roma. The analysis took into account the demographic and social situation in the period from 1994 to 1995, which showed that within the sample of 1,396 Roma families only 13 percent had members who had secured paid employment.[16] Based on the data assembled, the analysis concluded that despite occasional educational and employment campaigns, employment among Roma was increasing only slowly, partly due to low levels of education. Moreover, the analysis indicated that many Roma depended upon State benefits as their primary source of income, and had found only illegal employment. Despite the availability of subsidies to encourage employers to take on Roma employees, there was still a strong reluctance to do so – a symptom of the general tension and lack of understanding between Roma and the rest of the population.[17] The Ministry also took into account studies suggesting that the ways in which Roma support themselves contribute to negative perceptions held by majority society, and engender mistrust, conflicts, and the isolation of the Roma population.[18] However, Roma representatives expressed concern that there was no attempt to consult with the Roma community in preparing the programme.[19]

The strategy developed on the basis of these conclusions was more focused than the 1995 Programme, but only provided for short-term measures. Projects initiated under the Employment Programme began in 2000, and the programme was concluded in 2001.

In order to extend efforts to reduce unemployment among Roma, in 2001 the Ministry for Labour, Family and Social Affairs financed a research project on the "development of models for educating and training Roma aimed at providing increased regular employment." This research was then elaborated into a project with the same

---

[15] The research project provided the first up-to-date information on the number of unemployed Roma in one region of Slovenia. The research determined that 78 percent of Roma had not finished primary education, 12 percent had finished primary school, and only three percent of Roma had more then a primary education. Institute for Employment of the Republic of Slovenia, June 1995, unpublished internal document.

[16] Equal Employment Opportunities for Roma, p. 2. The programme estimated that the majority of families in the study (74 percent) survived with the help of State benefits including child benefits and cash assistance, 41 percent of families had members who worked irregularly, 25 percent of families had occasional or seasonal jobs, 13 percent of families received support from private charitable sources, and six percent of families engaged in "socially unacceptable ways of making a living."

[17] Equal Employment Opportunities for Roma, p. 5.

[18] Equal Employment Opportunities for Roma, p. 3.

[19] See *Minority Protection 2001*, p. 510.

title.[20] The project is part of a broader international project under the Stability Pact for South Eastern Europe, "Roma in the processes of European integration/comparison of models for educating Roma in Slovenia, Austria and Croatia," which is expected to run for three years on an experimental basis.

The project will analyse different models of Roma employment strategies from other countries to identify best practices and formulate potential projects for improving the situation in Slovenia. The National Employment Office and its local branches cooperated in designing the Programme, as they have practical experience with Roma employment. Roma themselves have thus far only been encouraged to propose projects for inclusion.

2.3 The Programme – Content

2.3.1 1995 Programme

The Programme identifies ten broad areas as priorities, including education, healthcare, social benefits, and employment.

There is no explicit mention of anti-discrimination measures in the 1995 Programme. The promotion of minority rights is not addressed directly either, but certain projects incorporate elements to enhance public participation and support minority media.[21] The Programme assumes that the integration and "socialisation" of Roma is necessary, and cannot be achieved without the help of the State. Its perspective characterises the Roma population as "underdeveloped," poor, and socially and economically threatened. Accordingly, its provisions generally target the Roma as passive recipients of State support, with the exception of a measure to help Roma organise themselves and to increase their inclusion within local community organs.[22] The 1995 Programme is essentially decentralised, giving local governments the possibility to initiate Roma-oriented projects and programmes of their own.[23]

While no formal mechanism was established for Roma groups to contribute to drafting the 1995 Programme, their involvement at the local level has been possible. An elected Roma representative in Murska Sobota reported that he had actively collaborated with the municipal authorities in planning local projects since 1999 and is satisfied with the

---

[20] Project leader: Vera Klopčič, Institute for Ethnic Studies.
[21] 1995 Programme, Measure 10, p. 6.
[22] 1995 Programme, p. 6.
[23] 1995 Programme, pp. 1–6.

level of cooperation.[24] Overall, however, Roma programmes receive a lower level of Government support than do projects for the two national minorities, Hungarians and Italians.[25]

2.3.2 Employment Programme

The assessment drafted by the Ministry for Labour, Family, and Social Affairs expert group emphasised four main areas for improving the employment situation for Roma:

- Preparation for employment, including training;
- Facilitating self-employment, through Roma cooperatives and integration companies;
- Public works programmes;
- Subsidised employment.

The aim of the programme was to enable social and labour integration through training for independent work, thereby increasing the proportion of Roma in regular employment. The target group of the programme was unemployed Roma seeking work through the Employment Service of Slovenia (hereafter, ESS) in the Prekmurje and Dolenjska regions, where there are large Roma communities.[26] The Programme also sought to address other important issues for the Roma community, such as education and housing, through training and the development of public work projects in those areas. (See Section 3.2.2)

Prevention of discrimination was not identified as an objective in the Employment Programme, although the text noted that a lack of understanding between Roma and the rest of the population is a problem in some areas.[27] In contrast with the somewhat paternalistic approach of the 1995 Programme, the Employment Programme took the view that the Roma should "contribute through their work and other activities, in accordance with their abilities, to the wider community."[28] The Employment Programme was also

---

[24] Interview with Darko Rudaš, Roma Counsellor in Murska Sobota, 14 April 2002.

[25] Poročevalec DZ RS (Official Gazette of Parliament), Ljubljana 28. 2. 2002, Year XXVIII, Nr. 20: *Predlog zaključnega računa proračuna RS za leto 2000* (Proposal for a financial report for state budget for 2000). The total budget of the Governmental Office for Nationalities in the year 2000 was SIT 253.2 million.

[26] Prekmurje is in the eastern region of the country near Hungary and centred in the town of Murska Sobota, while Dolenjska is on the border with Croatia. The main city is Novo Mesto.

[27] Equal Employment Opportunities for Roma, p. 2.

[28] Equal Employment Opportunities for Roma, p. 1.

based on more thorough research and provides for more specific measures than does the more general 1995 Programme.

As an extension of the Employment Programme's objectives, the "Development of models for educating and training Roma aimed at providing increased regular employment" is planned as a three-year project to offer specific proposals for the experimental implementation of selected projects for education, vocational training and employment of Roma each year. Members of the Roma community are also expected to cooperate in the procedures of proposing and selecting specific models.

2.3.3 Social Inclusion Programme

Although the Social Inclusion Programme does not focus on the Roma population, it designates the Roma as one of the underprivileged, socially excluded groups of beneficiaries. In the Programme's proposals for measures, Roma are specifically addressed in the section on employment, which calls for the integration of Roma into the labour market through cooperative schemes.[29] Other measures, such as those in the education, health, and housing sectors are likely to include Roma in their target groups.

2.4 The Programme: Administration/Implementation/Evaluation

The Employment Programme was coordinated and implemented by the Ministry of Labour, Family and Social Affairs with collaboration of the Employment Service. The 1995 Programme is implemented by the relevant ministries and coordinated by the Office for Nationalities. However, local bodies are primarily responsible for formulating and carrying out the actual projects, often with minimal coordination from the central authorities. Little appears to have been done at the Government level to evaluate the success of the individual projects, or to offer guidance for future initiatives. Moreover, a lack of funding has forced the conclusion of many projects despite continuing demand from local Roma communities.

---

[29] Government of the Republic of Slovenia, National Programme on the Fight Against Poverty and Social Exclusion, Ljubljana, 2000, p. 64 (hereafter, "Social Inclusion Programme").

2.4.1 The 1995 Programme

The Programme is a general responsibility of the Government, with each of the ten priority areas assigned to one of the ministries under the 1995 Programme as follows:

- Improving living conditions: Ministry for the Environment and Planning
- Education: Ministry of Education, Science and Sport
- Employment: Ministry of Labour, Family and Social Affairs; Ministry of Economics
- Family issues: Ministry of Labour, Family, and Social Affairs
- Social welfare: Ministry of Labour, Family, and Social Affairs
- Healthcare: Ministry of Health
- Crime prevention: Ministry of the Interior
- Cultural development: Ministry of Culture
- Media: Office for Nationalities
- Public participation: State Body for the Reform of Local Communities; Office for Nationalities.

At the local level, a number of government bodies and services are responsible for implementing the 1995 Programme, including municipal authorities, employment offices, centres for social work, public health centres, cultural organisations, schools, and media outlets.[30]

Each ministry determines the allocation for Roma programmes within its respective annual budget. The Parliament then confirms the ministries' proposals. Funds are disbursed through one of two ways. NGOs may develop their own projects and apply directly to the ministries for support; the ministries also publish tenders for specific programmes, and select projects on the basis of standard administrative procedures.

Local officials have reported that notification of tender procedures is not always adequate. Municipal authorities in Trebnje indicated in March 2002 that they were not aware of a public tender that had been issued by the Ministry of Economics in January that year.[31] Moreover, as tenders generally do not specify under which Government programme

---

[30] 1995 Programme.

[31] Official Gazette of the Republic of Slovenia, No. 6, 2002: *Javni razpis za sofinanciranje projektov osnovne komunalne infrastrukture na območjih, kjer živi romska etnična skupina* (Public tender for co-financing projects for basic communal infrastructure in regions where the Roma ethnic group lives).

funding is available, funding is not specifically earmarked for Roma projects. Consequently, local bodies submit applications for projects addressing Roma concerns without consulting with Roma representatives. According to one local official, "if a local institution thinks a Roma project could go under the section 'Adults with Special Needs,' they try and apply for funding that might be useful for the Roma community."[32]

To date, no ministry has taken steps to ensure that funding is reserved specifically for Roma programmes and projects through the public tender system, which has been a source of concern. The Slovenian ombudsman for the protection of human rights suggested that a specific fund for the improvement of the situation of Roma minority would help to ensure consistent and focused funding.[33] Municipal officials have also suggested that the Office for Nationalities should have more control over funding decisions than individual ministries, which are not as well informed about the situation of Roma. According to the municipal representative responsible for Roma issues in Trebnje, "the Office for Nationalities should have funds for Roma at its disposal, since they know the situation of Roma best,"[34] and should be responsible for allocating those funds to the local authorities.[35]

One official has suggested amending Article 26 of the Law on Financing Local Municipalities, thereby authorising the Government to require local authorities to allocate more money for the improvement of Roma situation, as is legally required for the Italian and Hungarian minorities.[36] In 2000, the Office for Nationalities allocated SIT 1.27 million (Slovenian Tolars, approximately €5,590[37]) for Roma organisations and SIT 3.75 million (approximately €16,500) for financing Roma radio programmes. In comparison, the Italian national minority – comprising a comparable percentage of the population[38] – was allocated SIT 34 million (approximately €149,600) in the same

---

[32] Interview with Meto Gašperič, Developmental Education Centre, Novo Mesto, 20 June 2002.

[33] *Večer*, "We adopt, Europe takes note," 10 July 2002.

[34] *Dolenjski list*, 4 April 2002; interview with Dušan Mežnaršič, Trebnje, 30 March 2002.

[35] Interview with Dušan Meznaršič, Trebnje, 30 March, 2002.

[36] Telephone interview with the advisor to the Director of the Office for Nationalities, 11 March 2002.

[37] The exchange is calculated at SIT 227.291 = €1.

[38] According to 1991 census figures, ethnic Italians comprise 0.16 percent of the population, Hungarians 0.43 percent, and autochthonous Roma 0.12 percent. See *Minority Protection 2001*, p. 529.

year.[39] To compensate for the lower levels of central funding, the Office for Nationalities has appealed for municipalities to allocate more money to Roma.[40]

Each of the ministries or offices responsible for implementing aspects of the 1995 Programme is required to produce reports on its activities for the Government; however, these reports are not made public, and apparently are not shared with the local authorities implementing projects under the Programme's auspices. NGOs generally must submit interim and final reports on projects that they implement as part of their funding agreement. Locally, municipalities prepare project implementation reports in most cases. Local programmes implemented by the Roma Union are initially assessed by its internal Organisation Assembly, and then are forwarded to the Government Committee for Roma. These reports are public and generally made available through the media.

2.4.2 The Employment Programme

Overall coordination of the Employment Programme was the responsibility of the Ministry of Labour, Family and Social Affairs. Within the Ministry, the Employment Service of Slovenia (ESS) managed some aspects of implementation. In addition, a Roma Employment Coordination Group of the ESS was formed to specifically oversee and direct the Programme. The Coordination Group is comprised of members representing the Ministry of Labour, the Office for Nationalities, the ESS coordinator for people with barriers to employment, and a representative of a Roma organisation.[41] The Coordination Group has posted information about the Programme on several web sites.

General reporting obligations

The Ministry of Labour, Family and Social Affairs and other participating ministries are also obliged to report annually to the Governmental Commission for the Protection of the Roma Ethnic Community.[42] This is a coordinating body consisting of representatives of different ministries and governmental bodies, representatives of five municipalities with larger Roma populations, and the representatives of the

---

[39] The total sum for radio and television programmes for all national minorities in the year 2000 was SIT 134.26 million (approximately €590,700). *Poročevalec DZ RS* (Parliamentary gazette), Ljubljana, 28 February 2002, Vol. XXVIII, No. 20, p. 35.

[40] Telephone interview with the advisor to the Director of the Office for Nationalities, 11 March 2002.

[41] Equal Employment Opportunities for Roma, p. 5.

[42] Interview with Danica Ošlaj, Ministry of Labour, Family and Social Affairs, Ljubljana, 1 July 2002.

Romani Union. The Commission was established in 1997 with three major responsibilities: to develop activities for the improvement of the situation of Roma; to make recommendations to the ministries; and to ensure efficient cooperation between municipalities and State bodies. The Commission is also responsible for producing an annual evaluation of the situation of Roma and any general measures that have been undertaken in this regard. On the basis of this evaluation, the Office for Nationalities prepares and publishes an annual report on the situation of Roma.

While the Commission is only authorised to make recommendations, these have been quite effective in practice. As a result of the Commission's intervention, a large number of Roma settlements have been legalised since 1997, and an initiative has been taken to provide for the election of one Roma councillor in every local municipality where Roma constitute more than two percent of the population. (see Section 3.4.3)

2.5 The Programme and the Public

Generally, awareness of the programmes is quite low. The 1995 Programme was presented to the public in the Roma-oriented newspaper *Romano Them* only after it had been adopted. A summary was presented also at the First Roma Conference in 1997 and thereafter in a workshop discussion. It was also published in the *Gazette Poročevalec* (Parliamentary gazette). Otherwise, there has been no activity to present the Programme to the wider public. Roma representatives – the intended beneficiaries – have criticised the lack of initiatives to inform their communities about the Programmes, and in many cases individual Roma are unaware of the existence of any Government-supported projects.[43] Making the Government's existing reports more widely available could provide an opportunity for broader evaluation of the Programme and its constituent projects. A special governmental committee for Roma questions, which is presently chaired by the former ombudsman, is competent to respond to Roma-related questions from the public, but this committee does not undertake promotional measures.

After its adoption in May 2000, the Employment Programme was presented to the public at an event in Murska Sobota in which many Roma representatives, media, and politicians took part. One of the Government representatives observed that there were no Roma women at the event, and the Ministry of Labour, Family and Social Affairs

---

[43] Interview with Darko Rudaš, 14 April 2002; Interviews in Dolga Vas, 19 April 2002.

thereafter agreed to take special care to ensure their participation.[44] Nevertheless, no programmes targeting Roma women specifically have been implemented to date.

A discussion of the programme "Development of models for educating and training Roma aimed at providing increased regular employment" was held at a roundtable and workshop prepared by the Council of Europe in Novo Mesto from 3 to 5 October 2001. Examples of good practises were presented, and experiences from Slovenia and other countries such as Sweden and Romania compared. The roundtable also took note of significant questions and suggestions for the future. Participants included staff of the local Employment Services and Centres for Social Work, representatives of the Association of Roma of Slovenia, local representatives of Roma from Dolenjska, employers from the region, a representative of the Office for National Minorities, representatives of the Institute for Ethnic Questions, and experts from Sweden and Romania.[45] The event was covered in the local newspaper.[46]

2.6 The Programme and the EU

The European Union has allocated accession funding to several Roma-related projects since 1997.[47] The Employment Programme was partly Phare-financed.[48] However, the most recent Accession Partnership priorities, which generally form the basis for Phare funding areas, do not mention any issues related to minorities.[49] No Phare national programme funds appear to have targeted Roma; smaller projects, such as legal counselling for refugees and parental education have been supported through the Phare Democracy Programmes.[50]

The 2001 Regular Report takes note of the Employment Programme, but observes that "there is still a need for policies promoting Roma socio-economic integration, especially in the areas of employment and health. Sustained efforts are also required in the area of education."[51]

---

[44] Interview with Vesna Miletić, Ministry of Labour, Family and Social Affairs, Ljubljana, 4 July 2002.

[45] Institute for Ethnic Studies, Thesis and documents *(Razprave in gradivo)*, No. 38/39, pp. 309, 2001.

[46] *Dolenjski list,* 3 October 2001.

[47] See *Minority Protection 2001*, p. 495.

[48] Equal Employment Opportunities for Roma, p. 6.

[49] European Commission, DG Enlargement, *Slovenia: Accession Partnership*, 2001.

[50] DG Enlargement Information Unit, *EU Support for Roma Communities in Central and Eastern Europe,* May 2002, p. 30.

[51] European Commission, *2001 Regular Report on Slovenia's Progress Towards Accession,* p. 21.

3. The Government Programme: Implementation

3.1 Stated Objectives of the Programme

3.1.1 The 1995 Programme

The ten priority areas of the 1995 Programme are the following:

- Improvements to the living conditions of Roma
- Socialisation and education of Roma children
- Improving the employment situation for Roma
- Protection of the family
- Social welfare
- Healthcare
- Crime prevention among the Roma population
- The cultural development of the Roma community
- Information for Roma through the media
- Helping Roma to self-organise and support for their interaction with local authorities.

3.1.2 The Employment Programme

The Employment Programme planned the elaboration of special employment projects (cooperatives and "integration companies"[52]) and the establishment of a support structure for enhancing the integration of Roma in the labour market.[53] This was to be accomplished through:

- Increasing work abilities and employment opportunities for Roma;
- Enabling Roma to acquire practical skills and work experience through "learning by doing" programmes;

---

[52] Cooperatives and integration companies were planned as public-private partnerships in which Roma would be able to gain skills and experience with the State subsidising their salaries; however, no such projects have been carried out.

[53] Equal Opportunities for Roma, p. 5.

- Including Roma in public works or subsidised forms of employment;
- Establishing cooperatives or integration companies;
- Setting up local municipal project groups composed of Roma, non-Roma, experts, and representatives of local communities;
- Providing counselling and assistance on self-employment, cooperatives and related themes.

The need to improve Roma living conditions was also addressed, based on the observation that the majority of Roma live in separate or outlying settlements, which in many cases fail to provide even the most basic necessities such as running water, electricity, and sewage systems.[54]

3.2 Government Programme and Discrimination

Discrimination is not addressed in the Government programmes, although some measures recognise the need to ensure equal opportunities in spheres such as education and healthcare. Projects to improve access to education for Roma communities by working closely with participants to ensure that the programmes reflect their needs have been among the most successful. While the Employment Programme's text calls for a greater contribution from Roma, its more innovative component of creating cooperative enterprises failed to materialise when there was no response to the project tender. Instead, public works programmes have been the primary source of employment under the programmes, with demand exceeding the number of places in spite of the low salaries and lack of opportunity to gain marketable skills.

The prevention of discrimination is not generally a priority, which is reflected in the Government programmes' priorities as well. A Government representative has noted that the Employment Programme addressed the effects of discrimination through the creation of equal opportunities, and that programmes cannot explicitly include anti-discriminatory measures as such provisions must be promulgated through legislation.[55] In fact, however, the 1995 Programme includes a priority area based on discriminatory assumptions: the prevention of criminality in the Roma community.[56] Under this heading, the Programme provides for increasing "preventative actions" in the primarily

---

[54] Equal Employment Opportunities for Roma, p. 4. See also, *Minority Protection 2001*, pp. 506–509.

[55] Interview with Vesna Miletić, Advisor to the Minister of Labour, Family and Social Affairs, 4 July 2002.

[56] 1995 Programme, Point 7.

Roma areas of Novo Mesto and Murska Sobota, through measures such as better police training and enhanced visibility of law-enforcement in these areas, all intended to decrease the number of criminal acts perpetrated by Roma.[57]

The anti-discrimination legislative framework is well designed, but has been criticised for the fact that it excludes certain minority groups, particularly the "non-autochthonous" Roma.[58] Generally, there are very few cases of discrimination reported. The Office of the human rights ombudsman is competent to investigate complaints of discrimination, and to propose remedies upon finding a violation.[59] Recently, the human rights ombudsman visited the Hudeje Roma settlement in Trebnje after Roma representatives demanded his intervention because of unemployment and the poor conditions within the settlement. The visit prompted the ombudsman to call for greater State involvement in resolving the situation for Roma more generally.[60]

According to a representative from Semič municipality, local politicians deliberately do not prioritise Roma programmes because the local non-Roma inhabitants would react very negatively.[61] A commonly-held view is that Roma must do more to improve their own situation; acknowledging that discrimination is a factor in preventing the integration of the Roma has not been commonly accepted even among professionals working with Roma.[62]

Although there has been no systematic research on the issue, Roma representatives across Slovenia all identify discrimination as a problem and report that police violence against Roma is widespread.[63] The European Commission has noted that there have been some cases of discrimination against Roma.[64]

---

[57] 1995 Programme, Point 7.

[58] Slovenian law distinguishes between "autochthonous" and "non-autochthonous" Roma, the latter having fewer rights guaranteed. See *Minority Protection 2001*, p. 496. For an analysis of Slovene anti-discrimination law, see generally V. Klopčič, *Legal Analysis of national and European anti-discrimination legislation: Slovenia*, Brussels, 2001.

[59] See *Minority Protection 2001*, p. 522.

[60] Out of 200 persons only one is employed, and only one-fifth of all flats have water. *Dolenjski list*, "*Ombudcman: nujen odločnejši nastop države do Romov*" (Ombudsman: stronger involvement of the State towards Roma is needed), 4 July 2002.

[61] Interview with Sonja Ličen Tesari, Semič, 30 March 2002.

[62] OSI Roundtable, Črnomelj, July 2002. *Explanatory Note: The Open Society Institute held a roundtable meeting in Slovenia in June 2002 to invite critique of the present report in draft form. Experts present included representatives of the Government, municipalities, Roma representatives, and non-governmental organisations.*

[63] Interviews with Roma individuals in Prekmurje, 20–24 May 2002, 4–8 June 2002.

[64] European Commission, *2001 Regular Report on Slovenia's Progress Towards Accession*, p. 21.

3.2.1 Education

As in many other countries in the region, Roma children in Slovenia are disproportionately placed in special schools or education programmes for the mentally handicapped.[65] Roma children in the Leskovec primary school are segregated from other children in a cottage near the school, reportedly because the school does not have money to enlarge the existing building.[66] The Government has supported various initiatives to improve access to education for Roma children, such as covering transport costs and providing meals, and community leaders report a gradual increase in the general level of education.[67]

The Employment Programme also has an educational component, entitled "Programme 5000," which provides for adult education from the primary level to special professional training. This is the only existing programme that offers a formal certificate to adults for primary education or special professional training.

The Ministry of Education, Science and Sport has supported individual educational projects together with municipal educational centres. Projects also receive funding from different ministries at a level determined annually.

Roma socialisation, improvement of the quality of life and education in general

Under the Phare Programme adopted in December 1999, a project for "socialisation of Roma, the improvement of the quality of life and education in general" was approved for a three-year period in Bela Krajina.[68]

The Institute for Education and Culture (hereafter, ZIK) Črnomelj, a municipal body, was invited to collaborate with the Italian NGO Nuova Frontiera on the project. The ZIK applied for funding together with the Association of the Public Universities, as support was conditioned on partnership with an NGO. The project was initially elaborated in 1997 under the title "Increasing the Education of Young Unemployed People," and was not directed at the Roma population. However, when there was little interest in the programme as it was first conceived, with Phare's approval the ZIK modified its approach to target the Roma community, although at this point there had been no consultation with Roma representatives.

---

[65] See *Minority Protection 2001*, p. 502.
[66] Interviews with Roma individuals in Krško area, 20–24 May 2002, 4–8 June 2002.
[67] See *Minority Protection 2001*, p. 502.
[68] Interview with Nada Žagar, Director of ZIK, Črnomelj, 12 March 2002.

When the project began, the project managers made efforts to adapt their plan to suit the Roma beneficiaries and incorporate their suggestions. The project offers vocational training for builders, carpenters and other construction workers, as well as home economics and cooking courses.

Although combating discrimination is not a stated objective of the project, it does aim to moderate educational inequalities. The Director of the ZIK summarised the project's goals as being "not about protection of minorities, only about raising the quality of life and living conditions. Roma in Bela Krajina are at such a low level in this regard, that this should be a priority." She added that "Roma were encouraged to self-organise and one of the results of the programme was three new Roma associations in Bela Krajina."[69]

The EU provided substantial support to the project. Its total budget was estimated at €115,660, of which Phare contributed €92,480, and the Ministry of Education, Science and Sport covered the difference. The European Commission (EC) sent a monitor to observe the project in progress for a week in October 2000, and the ZIK produced complete content and financial reports every three months during the course of the project. The project managers received beneficiary questionnaires from the EC, but because of literacy problems among the participants, their opinions were collected through interviews.

The project has received significant coverage in the media: promotions and presentations appeared in local newspapers, on television and local radio stations. In February 2001, Črnomelj held an International Roma conference with the participation of Roma representatives and Roma experts from Romania, Italy, and Bulgaria. In March 2001, the programme was presented at an Education Festival in Celje.

The Director of the ZIK reported that the project has been very successful and that it continues to address the community's needs. She considered the participation of local partners in the Centre for Social Work, educational institutions, local authorities, and Roma themselves as a positive accomplishment. "Our goal was achieved in this regard, it is up to us now to continue and raise funds from other sources."[70] At the end of the Phare funding period, various ministries allocated funds for the project to be continued.

The role of the family in the integration of Roma children
The Institute for Education and Culture in Črnomelj (ZIK) also initiated an integration programme in elementary schools in Bela Krajina, which began in

---

[69] Interview with Nada Žagar, Director of ZIK, Črnomelj, 12 March 2002.
[70] Interview with Nada Žagar, Director of ZIK, Črnomelj, 12 March 2002.

September 2001 after the ZIK applied for a public tender from the Ministry of Labour, Family and Social Affairs.[71] The programme concluded at the end of June 2002.

Local educators, teachers and social workers working with Roma identified the need for such a programme, which was organised in cooperation with elementary schools in the municipalities of Metlika, Črnomelj, and Semič. In September 2001, while developing their project proposal, the ZIK organised a meeting to identify the needs of Roma in the region, involving four Roma representatives, representatives of the Centres for Social Work in Metlika and Črnomelj and the Novo Mesto Branch employment office.

At the beginning of the project, school-counselling services identified 19 families for involvement in the project, which targets children who have attended classes irregularly or have learning difficulties. Social workers conducted interviews with these families and all but one agreed to participate. 37 children took part in the programme.

Four workshops for Roma parents and individual interviews and counselling were organised in October 2001. The workshop themes addressed the situation of Roma pupils in school, improving communication with public institutions, the position of Roma in adult education, and the role of Roma women in families. There was also training for teachers and school counsellors involved in the programme.

Those who were involved in the programme support its continuance,[72] which has helped to forge a stronger relationship between the ZIK and the Roma community. As a result of this programme, three of the parents have entered an elementary school for adults run by ZIK (in 2002, 30 Roma enrolled overall).[73] The main criticisms noted in an interim report were a lack of time and lack of continuity.[74] Following the model from this project, and in cooperation with Ministry of Health, health promotion was suggested as an additional topic for a future programme.[75] The total costs for the programme were SIT 885,680 (approximately €3,900), which was provided by Črnomelj, Metlika, and Semič municipalities, the Ministry of Labour, Family and Social affairs, and the ZIK.[76]

---

[71] Interview with Nada Babič Ivanuš, programme coordinator, Črnomelj, 12 March 2002.

[72] Interview with Nada Babič Ivanuš , programme coordinator, Črnomelj, 12 March 2002.

[73] Interview with Nada Žagar, Director of ZIK, Črnomelj, 12 March 2002.

[74] Interview with Nada Babič Ivanuš, programme coordinator, Črnomelj, 12 March 2002.

[75] Interview with Nada Babič Ivanuš, programme coordinator, Črnomelj, 12 March 2002.

[76] Expenditures included SIT 58,160 (approximately €255) intended directly to cover beneficiaries' costs, and SIT 87,247 (approximately €384) for material costs. Other costs included salaries, travel costs and *per diem* for programme lecturers and executors.

Pre-school Socialisation of Roma children

A programme for introducing Roma children to the school environment was organised by the primary schools in Metlika and Semič, with financing by the Ministry of Education, Science and Sport under a public works scheme. Regarding this programme, one teacher from Metlika noted that "those Roma children who attended kindergarten are easier to work with when they enter school. The rest sometimes don't even know what a doorknob is, or have never seen running water. These children take more time to teach."[77] Within the public works scheme, schools employ workers who prepare children for class in the morning, occasionally participate in classes to offer individual assistance, accompany children on day trips, and accompany them home, and offer guidance on hygiene issues if necessary.[78]

In Semič, the programme "Socialisation of Roma in Sovinek settlement" operated in the 2000-2001 school year. As part of a public works scheme in cooperation with the Črnomelj Centre for Social Work and the Ministry for Labour, Family and Social affairs, two workers were employed through the scheme to help Roma children in school and at home. The two workers were not Roma, and the municipality experienced difficulties finding people willing to accept the positions. Ultimately, the project proved too expensive for the municipality, and the programme was eliminated after one year.

A similar programme "Group work with Roma children and young people" operates at the Leskovec primary school near Krško, where a social worker and a public worker organise interaction games and workshops with schoolchildren once a week. The programme is carried out during regular school time.[79]

Adult Education Programmes

Since January 2001, the Society of Allies for a Soft Landing *(Društvo zaveznikov mehkega pristanka)* has organised a programme entitled "Work with Roma" in Krško. In addition to many smaller projects, the organisation carried out two education projects as part of the Employment Programme's "Programme 5000," which has also organised primary education for adults in Črnomelj, Trebnje, Novo Mesto and Murska Sobota. The Krško project was also supported by the Employment Service, the Organisation for Promotion of Preventative and Voluntary Work and the Krško Centre for Social Work.

In Krško, 22 illiterate Roma were enrolled in primary education at the Krško Public University for one year. The members of the Society of Allies for a Soft Landing

---

[77] Interview with Milena Hočevar, assistant principal, Metlika Primary school, 11 March 2002.

[78] Interview with Milena Hočevar, assistant principal, Metlika Primary school, 11 March 2002.

[79] Interview with Marina Novak Rabzelj, Krško Centre for Social Work, 7 June 2002.

assisted the participants with individual tutoring in their homes, and group education at the Leskovec primary school. Eighteen participants completed the programme, and six completed an equivalent of six years of primary school. In November 2001, 15 Roma enrolled in primary education through the same project.[80]

The Novo Mesto Developmental Educational Centre also organised primary education for Roma adults in the 2001-2002 school year. Also as part of "Programme 5000," the project was financed by the Ministry of Education, Science and Sport, with travel expenses and scholarships underwritten by the Novo Mesto Employment Service. The programme was carried out in Bršljin, Šmihel and Šentjernej, with a total enrolment of 70 Roma between 15 and 20 years old. The programme is intended for those who have not completed their primary education, but reportedly the Employment Service sends all unemployed Roma into the educational programme.[81]

The programme has been adapted to meet the needs of Roma, as it is organised between October and April to accommodate the season for gathering herbs and mushrooms. During this period participants can finish two classes of primary school.[82]

Trebnje Literacy Programme

The Centre for Education and Culture (hereafter, CIK) has organised a Roma literacy programme in Trebnje municipality since 1992,[83] offering elementary school-level education for adults.[84] The principal participants are illiterate Roma. Soon after the programme started, it was moved from the CIK to a private apartment in Hudeje (a Roma settlement) where it operated for five years. However, when problems arose with renting the apartment, the programme returned to the CIK facility.

The programme was initiated by the Trebnje Centre for Social Work, which shares a building with the CIK. In its first year, the Trebnje Literacy Programme was entirely financed by the municipality. In 1993, the CIK successfully applied for a public tender from the Ministry for Education, and received additional financial support from the

---

[80] Interview with Marina Novak Rabzelj, social worker, Krško Centre for Social Work, 7 June 2002; Report of the programme "Equal Opportunities," Employment Service of the Republic of Slovenia, 6 December 2001.

[81] Interview with Meta Gašperič, creator of the programmes at the Developmental Educational Centre Novo Mesto, 20 June 2002.

[82] Interview with Polde Jevšček, social worker, Novo Mesto Centre for Social Work, 26 April 2002.

[83] *Dolenjski list*, "*Iz obrobja gozda v šolske klopi*," (Coming from the edges of the forest to the school tables), 4 February 2000.

[84] Interview with Darinka Tomplak, Director of Trebnje CIK, 30 March 2002.

Ministry of Labour, Family and Social Affairs. After 1995, the Literacy Programme was incorporated into the 1995 Programme.[85]

Funding currently is provided by both local and State-level sources. The Ministry of Education, Science and Sport covers salaries, the Ministry for Labour, Family and Social Affairs provides tuition for the beneficiaries, and Trebnje municipality covers material costs, rent, and costs for those participants not listed as officially unemployed. In its first year the programme lasted for four months, and eventually developed into a year-round programme.

In the ten years of its existence, the programme has become well recognised and accepted within the Roma community. Currently, it operates for three hours a day, six days a week. In the first year the project had 19 pupils, with the highest attendance in 1999-2000. To date, eight participants have completed the primary school programme, and nine are expected to finish in 2002. One of the former participants now attends vocational school.

The CIK has made a number of adjustments to respond to participants' needs and improve the programme's effectiveness. The Roma community was not involved with the preparation of the programme, and the CIK ascribes some initial difficulties in part to this omission. For example, after encountering initial resistance from participants who feared they would "lose their Roma identity," the CIK began to offer its classes within a Roma settlement, rather than the Centre for Social Work. A number of other modifications have been introduced over time. Participants now work together in small groups divided by age. Groups were initially formed according to the level of previous knowledge, but these groups were too large and the work had to be better tailored to individual needs.[86] Because there has been some friction between Roma from different settlements, the CIK staff has also divided classes along these lines. Language was also an obstacle: the participants' poor knowledge of Slovene often led to misunderstandings. When the first groups returned from the summer break, they had forgotten most of what they had learned, and thereafter the breaks were made shorter.

The programme has become more successful and effective over time as a result of these changes. Some participants have even completed two classes in a single term, and many are thinking about further education. Overall, only 25 percent of the participants have been women.

Similar programmes have been initiated by the CIK in Zagradec and in Grosuplje.

---

[85] Interview with Darinka Tomplak, Director of Trebnje CIK, 3 June 2002.
[86] Interview with Darinka Tomplak, Director of Trebnje CIK, 30 March 2002.

Adult Programmes in Novo Mesto

Since 1999 the Novo Mesto Developmental Education Centre has been organising shorter programmes for adult Roma, with funding from the Ministry of Education, Science and Sport. These included the "School for life," which aimed to help Roma women make use of the facilities they already have at home. Other projects included traffic rule refresher courses, instruction on nursing babies and children, sewing and cooking classes, and courses on the collection and use of local herbs. It is not clear whether this programme was developed in response to the Roma community's interest or in consultation with Roma representatives. A similar programme was carried out in the Roma kindergarten in Novo Mesto, where one of the staff who speaks Romanes led a cooking workshop.

3.2.2 Employment

Measures to improve access to the labour market are included in both the 1995 Programme and the Employment Programme. Decreasing unemployment is also a priority in the Social Inclusion Programme, although its provisions are applicable to all marginalised groups, not only Roma. Discrimination is not explicitly addressed as a factor contributing to high unemployment in the Government programmes, although Roma report discrimination particularly in hiring.[87] While partnerships between local government bodies and private enterprise were originally planned under the Employment Programme as a means of creating longer-term employment prospects, a lack of interest from private businesses and a lack of funds from local governments have limited implementation. Instead, the Government programmes have invested heavily in public works projects. Despite the fact that these programmes offer poorly paid and irregular employment, interest remains high, and demand continues to outstrip the number of positions available.[88]

The Social Inclusion Programme provides for the elaboration of specific policies to focus on employing Roma; the Government's official evaluation report, however, does not detail any such programme for the year 2001.[89] The report does details a number of programmes and policies targeting unemployment generally, but none appear to

---

[87] Some Roma have reported that social welfare staff have suggested they change their names so that prospective employers would not know that they were Roma. OSI Roundtable, Črnomelj, July 2002.

[88] OSI Roundtable, Črnomelj, July 2002.

[89] Ministry of Labour, Family and Social Affairs, *Implementing the Social Inclusion Strategy with Report on the Realisation of the Programme on the Fight Against Poverty and Social Exclusion*, Ljubljana, April 2002, pp. 48–54 (hereafter, "Social Inclusion Implementation Report").

have components directly targeting the needs of the Roma community.[90] The Employment Programme focused on programmes helping to develop professionalism and job-seeking skills, personal growth programmes, professional education and training programmes, and "Programme 5000." (See Section 3.2.1)

The Employment Programme set out more concrete and specific objectives for improving the employment situation for Roma than the 1995 Programme. SIT 70 million (approximately €307,975) was initially allocated for the programme, but when the response was greater than anticipated – 200 participants were expected, and 418 ultimately took part – funding was increased to approximately SIT 118 million (approximately €519,160).[91]

The Employment Programme provided for the establishment of Roma "cooperatives" (partnerships with local governments and businesses) with the assistance of Employment Service experts, but these have not materialised. Although this concept was developed in order to make use of skills such as collecting, processing, and selling mushrooms and medicinal herbs, processing other raw materials, construction, and landscaping, no businesses applied for the tender to set up a cooperative.[92] SIT 2.5 million (approximately €11,000) had been set aside for this purpose in the year 2000, to establish non-profit corporations and provide training for participants and managers, but this funding was reallocated to other projects when the tender failed to attract any offers.

Cooperatives could become an important form of employment for Roma and a way of actively engaging whole communities. This form of enterprise is adaptable to suit different needs, and would allow for a greater degree of individual initiative and autonomy. It is unclear whether further funding will be set aside for this project, or if there are any attempts to revise the project terms to attract bids on a new tender. As an alternative to existing public works schemes, these programmes could offer improved opportunities for Roma to develop marketable skills and find longer-term prospects for employment.

Other subsidised employment projects planned under the Employment Programme also failed to materialise. These projects were to utilise existing "integration companies" to provide occupational training and employment for the unemployed, particularly Roma, in activities selected on the basis of the needs and interests of the community, rather than by the market. The resulting enterprises were to function as non-profit organisations, using any proceeds to expand services or improve working conditions, but the project was never implemented.

---

[90] See generally, Social Inclusion Implementation Report.
[91] Ministry of Labour, Family and Social Affairs, No. 017-002/95, 19 April 2002.
[92] Ministry of Labour, Family and Social Affairs, No. 017-002/95, 19 April 2002.

Some municipalities such as Novo Mesto and Murska Sobota hired Roma under general public works schemes. During 2000, there were nine public works programmes in Novo Mesto municipality, in which 57 Roma participated:

- Improvements to Roma settlements in the Črnomelj local community;
- Development of infrastructure in Roma neighbourhoods in Metlika;
- "Roma for Roma" in Metlika and Trebnje (see Section 3.3.3);
- Construction of individual houses and work on a settlement in Brezje;
- Preventative programmes in the field of social welfare;
- Helping Roma children in the Šmihel primary school;
- Local street construction in the Semič community;
- Promotion of the local environment.

In 2001, the municipality included 55 unemployed Roma in public works programmes. New projects included:

- Revitalisation of local orchards;
- Archaeological work on the Kapiteljska Njiva (Dolenjski Museum, Novo Mesto);
- Work with the Miran Jarc Library in Novo Mesto);
- "Roma for Roma" in Šentjernej (see Section 3.3.3);
- Communal work in Roma settlements.

Despite these efforts, there are fewer Roma employed in Novo Mesto than there were ten years ago. In 1992, just after Slovenia became independent, 50 to 60 Roma were employed in the municipality, but in 1998 between eight and ten Roma were engaged in registered, paid employment.[93]

Between 1991 and 2001 a private enterprise in Novo Mesto, in cooperation with the national Employment Service, organised employment programmes and skills training for both Roma and non-Roma long-term unemployed in a project called "Mint of Knowledge."[94] However, the programme was discontinued due to lack of funds.[95]

---

[93] *Poročilo o reševanju romske problematike v mestni občini Novo mesto* (Report on solving Roma problems in the local municipality Novo Mesto), 7 April 1998.

[94] Interviews with Dora Zagorc, councillor to the director, and Borut Hrovatin, psychologist, Papilot enterprise, Ljubljana, 3 July 2002.

[95] OSI Roundtable, Črnomelj, July 2002.

In Metlika municipality, there are 124 Roma above the age of 15; of these only 17 have permanent employment, including one who runs his own business. Seven work for the municipality in Metlika as cleaners or gardeners. The municipal Workers Union is not active in the area of Roma rights protection, and hostile attitudes are prevalent; one representative asked, "Why would [the Union work to increase Roma employment]? They live better than we do!"[96] Social service staff report that there are no chances for new jobs in the area. The unemployed live on social assistance, and collect mushrooms and herbs in season to earn some additional money. Even these traditional activities have been constrained by new regulations on the protection of wild mushrooms,[97] and there is no agreement to permit collection of herbs across the nearby border with Croatia.

These public works projects, while consistently in demand among Roma, fail to offer a real incentive to move away from dependency on State support. A social worker from Bela Krajina stated that "the law on social protection is very generous, and does not encourage Roma to search for employment […] Roma would rather sit at home in the shade for SIT 25,000 a month than work for [SIT] 40,000 a month."[98] Roma themselves agree that incentives are low, adding that: "[public workers receive] too little money for the hard work they have to do. And those Roma who have regular jobs laugh at others, [saying] that they wouldn't work for such a salary."[99] Moreover, wages can be garnished if an individual owes money to the State, while social benefits are not subject to such deductions.[100] Further public works projects are described in the next Section.

3.2.3 Housing and other goods and services

Discrimination in housing has not been identified as a problem by Roma communities, but it is clear that many Roma live in segregated, poor conditions.[101] Some local projects organised to improve the housing situation for Roma are already financed under the Employment Programme. The Social Inclusion Programme also details a number of measures expected to benefit Roma, among other vulnerable groups. The National Housing Fund offers loans to municipalities to encourage construction of

---

[96] Interview with S. Č, administrator with the municipality, 11 March 2002.
[97] Official Gazette, št. 38/94.
[98] Interview with X, anonymity requested, 13 November 2001.
[99] Interview with Sonja Ličen Tesari, representative of Semič municipality, 18 March 2002.
[100] OSI Roundtable, Črnomelj, July 2002.
[101] See *Minority Protection 2001*, pp. 506–509; 535–541.

social housing and acquisition of land for this purpose. However, available funding has been lower than anticipated.[102]

Examples of local housing projects undertaken as public works include:

Programme for the improvement of public roads in Semič

The programme was implemented between 1996 and 2001 as a public works project, and employed local Roma men for light manual labour such as cutting trees and gardening. The National Employment Office coordinated the project. The costs for year-round implementation of the project in 2000 comprised monthly expenses of SIT 270,000 (approximately €1,190) in transport and material costs, and SIT 60,000 (approximately €264) for paycheque bonuses covered by the municipality. Salaries were covered by National Employment Office, and the project was executed by the Novo Mesto road company. In the year 2001 there were only five Roma applicants: three of these dropped out on account of the poor salary, and one was employed for a single day. The positions were left vacant thereafter. The local authorities subsequently closed down the programme, although there are plans to try to reestablish it.

Local programme for Roma in Šentjernej

In 2001 the programme "Roma for Roma" was initiated in Šentjernej municipality. In cooperation with a private company, the local Employment Office organised work for nine Roma in a clean-up and maintenance programme around the Roma neighbourhood.[103] The local official responsible for the programme noted that the poor condition of the neighbourhood had prompted interest in initiating the project;[104] Roma also cleaned garbage in the municipality, built fences, and worked on the sewage system. In 2001, the municipality also spent SIT 2 million (approximately €8,800) to improve the street to the settlement.

The National Employment Office and the municipality shared the material cost of SIT 1 million (approximately €4,400) in 2001. A municipal official indicated that funding had not been requested to continue the project for a second year, as it was viewed as a failure in the municipality: "Last year's [2001] goals were not achieved – when the project was finished there were again loads of garbage in the settlement. They haven't learned anything."[105]

---

[102] Social Inclusion Implementation Report, p. 70.

[103] Interview with Janez Hrovat, municipal official responsible for public works, Šentjernej, 25 March 2002.

[104] *Dolenjski list*, 1 April 2001

[105] Interview with Janez Hrovat, municipal official responsible for public works, Šentjernej, 25 March 2002.

House Construction in Novo Mesto

Novo Mesto municipality is assisting six to eight Roma in constructing their own houses through public work schemes, with a view towards promoting the acquisition of skills they can then use to find other employment. The municipality also took steps to legalise the Brezje settlement. The municipality is currently managing the project and will provide SIT 2.5–2.7 million (approximately €10,970 to €11,850) for the material to construct the houses and the infrastructure.[106]

Public works scheme "Roma for Roma" in Metlika

This programme has offered employment to Roma in light manual labour such as gardening, cleaning, and maintenance for three years. The work usually lasts for eight months of the year, from morning until mid-afternoon. Salaries are funded from the Ministry for Labour, Family and Social Affairs; otherwise, the municipality receives no State support for Roma projects.[107] In 2002 only 14 Roma enrolled in the programme because of a decrease in funding from the Ministry.[108]

According to municipal officials, the programme was initiated due to the fact that the Roma settlements in the area are neglected and poorly maintained. The programme emphasises the "importance for Roma to learn how to keep their homes and settlements in order."[109]

Roma residents generally agree with the project objectives.[110] While many of the participants are satisfied with the possibility to earn money, they pointed out that after taxes their salary is the same as unemployment benefits.[111] Those involved in the programme do not receive social welfare. However, some Roma involved maintain that their efforts were misused and they were given tasks outside the scope of improving Roma neighbourhoods: "they sent us to work and we had to do also things that weren't in the plan. It looked like the municipality was making up its mind each time. So they sent us ten kilometres away to

---

[106] *Dolenjski list*, "Interview with Mojca Novak, director of the communal administration of the local municipality Novo Mesto," 24 January 2002.

[107] Salaries for Roma workers comprised SIT10.4 million, and SIT 2.7 million went to salaries for mentors and supervisors. The total cost of salaries in 2001 was approximately SIT 14 million (approximately €3,182). Interview with Jože Nemanič, Metlika, 19 February 2002.

[108] OSI Roundtable, Črnomelj, July 2002.

[109] Interview with Jože Nemanič, representative of Metlika municipality, published in *Dolenjski list*, 8 March 2001.

[110] Interviews with Roma in the Boriha settlement, Metlika, 17 February 2002.

[111] Interview with Jože Nemanič, Metlika, 19 February 2002.

another community to clean an old castle, [and] we cleaned roads for other non-Roma communities as well ... we didn't think this was fair."[112]

Improvements to the Boriha neighbourhood

The municipality of Metlika prepared a plan to improve conditions in the Boriha settlement two years ago. The project proposed to legalise the housing situation of the Roma, and to acquire other necessary permits, upgrade sewage infrastructure, connect all houses to the electricity grid, and draw up two different plans to improve housing. All the houses in Boriha lack the necessary permits, although all settlements but one do have water and electricity at present. According to one resident, "only when our children began to get sick, did they give us a water connection."[113] Previously, the Roma had to collect water from the river that is two kilometres away.

However, the municipality cannot legalise its Roma settlements without the Ministry's permission. The municipality sent the project documents to the Ministry of the Environment for approval in 2000, but had not received a response as of July 2002.[114]

Legalisation of the Sovinek settlement, Semič Municipality

Nine Roma families live in Semič municipality, of which only five have houses and the remaining four live in containers. The municipality applied for funds to legalise the settlement and received SIT one million (approximately €4,400) from the Ministry of the Environment for that purpose in 1995. The municipality subsequently allocated land to every family, built a road to the settlement, and provided access to water. In 2002, the municipality applied for Government funds to improve the settlement's infrastructure and connect it to the electricity grid.

3.2.4 Healthcare and other forms of social protection

The 1995 Programme provides that the Ministry of Health shall develop projects to promote preventative healthcare for Roma communities. Additionally, the Programme calls upon the Ministry to reconsider the plan to develop a registry of the specific health needs of the Roma community, and to encourage Roma to enter the health professions.[115] The Social Inclusion Programme also has provisions related to improving

---

[112] Interview with Matjaž Hudorovec, who participates in the programme every year, Metlika, 21 April 2002.
[113] Interview with Sonja Hudorovac from Boriha, 18 January 2002.
[114] OSI Roundtable, Črnomelj, July 2002.
[115] 1995 Programme, Section 6, p. 5.

healthcare for underprivileged groups, including the Roma, and an implementation report indicates that the 2000 National Healthcare Programme "Health for All" includes the elimination of discrimination and improving access to healthcare among its priorities.[116]

The relatively high number of Roma with uncertain status affects their access to healthcare.[117] Social benefits are contingent upon Slovenian residency or citizenship; the difficulty of acquiring official status has been well documented.[118] No action has been taken to follow up the commitments outlined in the 1995 Programme at the national level.

At the municipal level, a number of projects have been carried out to increase access to healthcare and promote healthy lifestyles. In 1998, the Centre for Social Work in Novo Mesto organised an educational programme known as "Minimal Hygienic Standards in Roma Families," which was financed by the Ministry of Labour, Family and Social Affairs. The programme was managed by an instructor in the Novo Mesto Roma kindergarten, who also speaks Romanes. She visited Roma families in their homes on a weekly basis, to provide instruction on hygiene and the use of various cleaning products. The Centre for Social Work opened an account in the one of the local supermarkets for the participants to shop for supplies with the instructor.

Research has shown that Roma, in particular women and children, have higher rates of diseases such as tuberculosis, asthma, diabetes, and anaemia than the general population.[119] To address the problems highlighted by this research, an imaginative project was instituted at the request of the Roma community in Črnomelj, and ran from 2000 to 2001 under the direction of the ZIK. The course "cooking for a large family" brought together eight Roma women from two different settlements for a free 30-hour workshop in Autumn-Winter 2001. The programme's organisers considered it a success in part because it took place outside segregated Roma settlements, and women from different areas had the opportunity to work together.[120] The content was

---

[116] *Social Inclusion Implementation Report*, p. 69.

[117] See *Minority Protection 2001*, p. 505.

[118] See, e.g. International Helsinki Federation, *Annual Report 1998*, 1999, available at <http://www.ihf-hr.org/reports/ar98/ar98slv.htm>, (accessed 3 September 2002); United States State Department, *1998 Human Rights Report*, available at <http://www.state.gov/www/global/human_rights/1998_hrp_report/slovenia.html>, (accessed 3 September 2002).

[119] *Jana*, 12 February 2002, p. 5; Report of the Outpatient Clinic Črnomelj to the Ministry of Health, 16 November 2001.

[120] Interview with Nada Žagar, Director of ZIK, Črnomelj, 12 March 2002.

designed according to the needs of participants, and was a continuation of a programme that took place from 2000 to 2001 in Roma settlements.

In September 2000 the first Women's Forum was created as part of the Association of Roma of the RS. It has 40 members, and aims to promote of women's rights. The Forum has drawn attention to certain women's health issues, such as breast cancer, in addition to its other activities.

No other concrete measures appear to have been implemented in these spheres. A governmental representative from the Ministry of Health recently reported that there are some general healthcare initiatives underway, but there are no specific programmes for Roma.[121]

3.2.5 The criminal justice system

Possible inequalities in the criminal justice system are not addressed in the 1995 Programme or the Employment Programme. No projects have been identified to support additional research or otherwise address discrimination in this sphere. The Social Inclusion Programme recognises the importance of legal aid for indigent defendants, but does not elaborate a strategy beyond the existing guarantees of legal representation and advice.[122]

As mentioned above, the 1995 Programme introduces a measure to authorise increased police activity, which has discriminatory overtones in itself, as it is based on an assumption that a high rate of criminality is prevalent among Roma.

There are reports of discrimination within the penal system. In the Koper prison, Roma have been placed in high-security, closed facilities regardless of whether their conviction merits such severe measures. Social workers and other professionals claim that because Roma are from the lowest classes of society, it is appropriate to confine them to closed wards.[123] Prison officials in Novo Mesto have had Roma inmates sent to other prisons around the country, to reduce the proportion of Roma in the Novo Mesto facility.[124]

---

[121] Telephone interview with Ciril Klanjšček, Ministry of Health, 3 June 2002.
[122] Social Inclusion Implementation Report, p. 76.
[123] Jure Vest, *Slovenske Novice*, 21 September 2002, p. 11.
[124] Jure Vest, *Slovenske Novice*, 21 September 2002, p. 11.

3.3 Protection from Racially Motivated Violence

Local officials in some municipalities acknowledge that instances of racism and racial hatred occur; one official from Trebnje stated that: "No one wants to have [Roma] in their community."[125] Some Roma organisations also identify racially motivated violence as a problem, noting that such incidents less frequently reported in Prekmurje than in the Dolenjska region, where Roma are not allowed to enter some local pubs. However, reports of actual attacks on Roma are few; there has never been a conviction under the Criminal Code's provision against incitement to hatred, and there are no additional provisions or sanctions for racially motivated crime.[126]

Prejudice may be a factor in the lack of attention to racially motivated violence. Rather then focusing on attacks against minorities, official attention has focused on the allegedly violent tendencies of the Roma population. Mayors of three municipalities in the Bela Krajina region reported disturbing levels of violence and criminality among Roma, and requested a greater police presence within Roma settlements or nearby.[127] The negative attitudes expressed by professionals working within local communities also gives cause for concern. One social worker stated: "For Roma it is best that they work with garbage – who else will? They live in garbage anyway."[128] Recent studies suggest that a substantial majority of the Slovenian population as well as some prominent right-wing politicians manifest negative attitudes towards Roma and reject any kind of affirmative action.[129]

3.4 Promotion of Minority Rights

Although the protection of Roma culture is a priority for many Roma civil society organisations, this dimension of minority policy is not greatly elaborated in any of the Government programmes. The inclusion of "socialisation" elements in many projects developed for Roma suggests that some aspects of Roma culture are still viewed as being at odds with majority society. The Social Inclusion Programme emphasises the importance of reducing factors alienating underprivileged groups, but its provisions do not extend to spheres such as public participation or language rights for the Roma.

---

[125] Interview with Dušan Mežnaršič, Trebnje, 30 March 2002.
[126] See *Minority Protection 2001*, p. 512.
[127] *Dolenjski list*, 14. March 2002.
[128] Interview with Y, anonymity requested, 13 November 2001.
[129] Darja Zaviršek, *Ali res hočemo živeti v demokratični družbi?* (Do We Really Want to Live in a Democratic Society?) *Večer*, 31 August 2002, p. 42.

Government policy thus reflects Slovenia's reluctance to come to terms with multiculturalism when it comes to Roma.

Under the 1995 Programme, the Ministry of Culture is responsible for the "development of the cultural integrity of the Roma community."[130] There is no other explicit mention of the promotion of minority rights in the 1995 Programme, and few projects include components that relate to this aspect of minority policy. The Employment Programme cites "the preservation of ethnic identity and progress within it"[131] as a basic premise for the measures provided, although in the sphere of employment there is relatively little scope for expansion of this principle.

There are currently 20 Roma organisations in Slovenia, all of which implicitly or explicitly demand the protection and promotion of their culture and identity. There has been significant growth in Roma civil society since 1991, when the first Roma association, Romani Union, was established. At present there are 15 organisation that participate in Romani Union, most of which have been established since 2000, and many initiated by the president of Romani Union.

3.4.1 Education

Roma minority education is not provided for in the 1995 Programme or in any other Government policy; programmes directed at Roma generally focus on preparing children for mainstream Slovene-language education. Efforts to build interest in mother-tongue education among the Roma community have not met with much support, and available materials on the culture and traditions of Roma for general education purposes have not been included in mainstream curricula.

Within the curricula of mainstream primary schools there is almost no information about Roma, except in a textbook for the seventh grade which features a short text with a photograph of a Roma group.[132] There are some newly published books in Slovene that promote Roma culture, such as the book "Just stay, the Roma are coming!" published in 2001.[133] The title is drawn from a traditional children's game, "Let's run, the Gypsies are coming!" (*Bežimo, tecimo, Cigani gredo!*). The book was written by a Rom from Kosovo, who gives a positive description of the Roma community and its history, customs and current situation. The book also includes some Roma fairy tales, poems and prose.[134] In

---

[130] 1995 Programme, Section 8, p. 5.
[131] Employment Programme, Section 1, p. 2.
[132] See *Minority Protection 2001*, p. 517.
[133] T. I. Brizani, *Le ostanite, Romi gredo!* (Just Stay, the Roma are Coming!), Klagenfurt, 2001.
[134] *Dolenjski list*, 29 March 2001.

1999 a book of poems by Jelenka Kovačič was published in Romanes and Slovenian with the title "Think of me!" *(Domislin pe pu mande – Pomisli name!)*. However, none of these materials have been incorporated into the school curricula.

Kindergartens for Roma children have been established in several municipalities. For example, in the Roma settlement of Brezje in Novo Mesto, the "Pikapolonica" kindergarten for Roma children was established within the Roma community for children who speak only the Roma language.[135] There are six instructors and support staff, one of whom speaks Romanes. The instructors teach the children Slovene, and prepare them for entry into primary school Since 1995 the instructors have received training, emphasising respect for the children as individuals.[136]

Novo Mesto municipality reconstructed and renovated the entire kindergarten facility for Roma in Žabjak. The kindergarten received SIT 1 million (approximately €4,400) in municipal funds out of which SIT 400,000 (approximately €1,760) was used for reconstruction. Presently the kindergarten has 20 pupils and six staff.

The NGO sector has also enhanced the role of these kindergartens. For example, the Organisation for the Promotion of Voluntary Work from Novo Mesto has organised creative workshops in Pikapolonica as part of the project "Roma – Who am I."[137] The group organises discussion groups about different aspects of Roma society and culture to help children improve their Slovene language skills.[138]

3.4.2 Language

The vast majority of public officials and professionals who deal with Roma do not speak Romanes, which is considered a serious problem especially within health institutions, centres for social work and during judicial proceedings. In 2002 the Ministry of Education financed a 70-hour programme of instruction in Romanes for teachers, which was carried out in cooperation with the president of the Romani Union.

The Romani Union also organised and led a two-year project of Romanes instruction in 1999 and 2000, with two-hour lessons every Saturday in Murska Sobota. Most of the participants were younger Roma from various settlements around Prekmurje. Those who took a final exam received certificates.

---

[135] A similar kindergarten has been established in Prekmurje, Murska Sobota municipality.

[136] Interview with Tatjana Vonta, Director of the Research Centre for Education who also runs the Step by Step programme, 25 April 2002.

[137] Financed by the Open Society Institute.

[138] Interview with Andreja Šurla, of the Organisation for the promotion of voluntary work, Novo Mesto, 26 April 2002.

ZIK Črnomelj reports that it will apply for funding from the Ministry of Education to support the organisation of Romanes-language training for primary school teachers.

3.4.3 Participation in public life

While the 1995 Programme provides for measures "helping Roma to self-organise and support for their involvement into the local authorities,"[139] there has been very little activity to implement these objectives. The large number of Roma who lack citizenship or residency status presents an ongoing obstacle to full participation.[140] Moreover, in the 2002 national census only Slovenians, Italians and Hungarians were identified as possible ethnic identities; the Roma population could either choose to identify themselves as one of these groups or as "other."

Still, Roma participation in policy-making has increased since the 1995 Programme was enacted. For example, although there are no formal mechanisms for ensuring Roma participation in policy-making processes, the Ministry of Culture has made it a practice to consult with Roma representatives on the development of projects and invites Roma participation in Ministry meetings that address Roma cultural issues. Staff of the Ministry for Culture also have offered their support and consultation to Roma groups.[141]

While the Hungarian and Italian minorities are guaranteed representation at the local and national levels, Roma are entitled to representation only at the local level and only in those areas where there are "autochthonous" Roma. The Law on Local Autonomy that would provide for Roma representation in a greater number of municipalities had not been fully implemented as of Spring 2002. To date, only Murska Sobota has a Roma representative in the local council.

A recent Constitutional Court ruling determined that the relevant provision in the Law on Local Autonomy must be implemented in other parts of the country.[142] The president of the Romani Union advocated the election of Roma councillors in municipalities with Roma inhabitants as early as 1993; the Office for Nationalities recently suggested that in the local elections in Autumn 2002, 20 municipalities may

---

[139] 1995 Programme, section 10, p. 6.

[140] See *Minority Protection 2001*, pp. 517–518.

[141] E-mail communication with Suzana Čurin Radovič, member of governmental committee for Roma issues, State Secretary of the Ministry of Culture, 17 June 2002.

[142] V. Klopčič, *Legal Analysis of national and European anti-discrimination legislation: Slovenia*, Brussels, 2001, p. 32.

select a Roma councillor.[143] It has been observed that the poor level of communication between Roma communities and the various local government bodies could be greatly improved through a Roma councillor's good offices;[144] however, the level of authority and activity of these posts will only become clear after elections.

Following the Court's ruling earlier in the year, as of 1 September 2002 all 20 local municipalities with a large Roma population were expected to have changed their regulations in order to pave the way for the election of a Roma representative within the municipal council. However, at the end of August, six local municipalities (Beltinci, Grosuplje, Krško, Semič, Šentjernej and Trebnje) publicly refused to change their regulations and claimed that this kind of affirmative action is discriminatory against the Slovene majority. Some local representatives expressed the belief that Roma do not possess sufficient experience or education to be local councillors.[145] There were also claims that new regulations would give more privileges to Roma than to ethnic Slovenes, and local and national politicians have suggested that Roma are not an autochthonous ethnic group and thus not entitled to special recognition. Local representatives have also questioned why the State has not provided for Roma representation in Parliament if such representation is considered necessary at the municipal level.

Officials in Grosuplje municipality in the Dolenjska region addressed an official complaint to the Constitutional Court, demanding an investigation as to whether such affirmative action is constitutional. The strong reaction against this form of positive discrimination is ongoing: as of the time of writing, the Court had determined that those local communities that have already prepared new regulations should hold elections for a Roma councillor, and those that have not yet changed their regulations must still do so, although no deadline has been announced.

Training Roma to become councillors

The private company Papilot carried out a two-month project "Programme for training Roma councillors," on the suggestion of the Association of Roma in February 2002. The programme was carried out for five hours twice a week in Novo Mesto and Murska Sobota, with financing from the municipalities and additional support from the Association of Roma. Not every municipality was willing to support the

---

[143] J. Taškar, DELO, *"Tudi v Romi v svetih občin,"* (Also Roma in municipal councils), 4 March 2002.

[144] OSI Roundtable, Črnomelj, July 2002.

[145] *Dolenjski list*, 29 August 2002, p. 16; Daily *Večer*, 31 August 2002, p. 41.

programme;[146] Grosuplje municipality, for example, did not take part as no Roma wanted to participate.[147]

The programme had 13 components giving participants training in networking skills, how the State system functions, legislation, basic computer skills, English language, and about the role and the work of Roma organisations. The target participants are the current presidents of Roma organisations. The programme was discussion on a local radio broadcast, in which Roma participants expressed a highly positive opinion of the programme.

3.4.4 Media

There are no measures for media development in either the 1995 Programme or the Employment Programme. However, the State does provide limited funding to minority media outlets, including radio programmes for Roma.

An NGO, the Peace Institute, has developed a project to provide training for Roma journalists in reporting techniques and communication skills. The concept was suggested by Roma representatives, who approached Murski Val radio to suggest broader Roma involvement in the production of materials, including the development of programming in Romanes, for an existing Roma-oriented programme. The manager of this programme observed that in response to the EU's focus on improving minority rights, the importance of Roma journalists and media specialists will increase in the future.[148] Enhancing the participation of Roma in the production of media programming could be an effective means to present Roma culture to the general public, potentially challenging negative perceptions of Roma and promoting multiculturalism.

The Journal *Romano Them* receives governmental support from the Ministry of Culture and from the Office for Nationalities, also finances the previously mentioned radio programme on Murski Val radio ("The Roma Sixties") and a television programme ("Roma Views") on TV Murska Sobota. There is also a weekly one-hour radio programme about Roma on the radio programme "Studio D."

---

[146] Interview with Dora Zagorc, Papilot, 3 July 2002.
[147] Telephone interview with Marko Podvršnik, director of the local municipal administration, 8 July 2002.
[148] Telephone interview with Brankica Petkovič, Peace Institute, 22 April 2002.

3.4.5 Culture

Although one component of the 1995 Programme involves the development of Roma culture, the majority of projects in this sphere have been initiated by NGOs and Roma organisations.

The ZIK in Črnomelj, in partnership with the municipality, organised a "week of life-long learning" in October 2001, with the title "Get to know each-other – education and culture of Roma in Bela Krajina." The aim of the event was to present the Roma culture to non-Roma, and emphasise the importance of life-long learning for integration; one day focused on the role of Roma women in particular.

Krško municipality, together with the Society of Allies for a Soft Landing, has organised discussions with young people about Roma traditions, of the importance of maintaining the Roma culture, and challenges facing Roma communities.

Under their programme "Equal Opportunities," the Society of Allies for a Soft Landing also carried out a programme called "a Gypsy pot" in Kerinov Grm, in which approximately 150 Roma took part. The aim of the project was for non-Roma to learn about Roma cuisine, and to emphasise the importance of good nutrition.

The ZIK Črnomelj is currently preparing a number of projects for funding, including artistic and cultural productions and other means of increasing communication and understanding between Roma and non-Roma communities.

In Kamenci, Črenšovci municipality, the first Roma museum is in the process of being established.

However, there have been reports of discrimination in the cultural sphere. Recently, a Roma organisation wanted to take part at a cultural event organised by a municipality with a large Roma community.[149] The Roma organisation applied in April 2002 to perform in an ethnic dance festival. Two weeks before the event was supposed to take place, the organisation was notified that they had been rejected by the local authorities, on the basis that the whole programme had already been set before their official application was received. The organisation was allowed to perform after repeated requests to the organisers, but the president of the Roma organisation expressed the opinion that "the only reason we were rejected was that we are Gypsies."[150] Another member of the community commented: "does it mean that we Roma do not have our culture? What is culture then?"[151]

---

[149] Interview with the president of the Roma organisation S.K., 28 May 2002.
[150] Interview with the president of the Roma organisation S.K., 28 May 2002.
[151] Interview with a member of the local Roma community, 30 May 2002.

4. EVALUATION

The major success of the 1995 Programme is its existence. It is the first Government strategy to adopt a more comprehensive approach to Roma issues, and to recognise the need for State involvement in addressing these issues. Since the Programme was developed, many projects have been funded under its umbrella, and local initiatives have been launched in many municipalities.

The Employment Programme developed the themes of the 1995 Programme, but went farther in recognising the importance of including Roma as active participants, not merely recipients. The Employment Programme also recognised that Roma remain physically segregated from the rest of the society and are seen as people with different values and mentality, but attributed this to "the result of different sets of living standards and moral values followed by the Roma [...] and [their] lack of integration." The tendency to view Roma values as inherently inferior undermines the respect for cultural differences that is a foundation of multicultural society.

Both programmes lack sections on racial violence, discrimination, and minority rights in general. Problems with access to healthcare are also not addressed to the extent necessary. Neither of the Roma programmes, nor the Social Inclusion Programme, addresses the situation of "non-autochthonous" Roma without citizenship rights.

The decentralised approach of both programmes has proven to be an effective means to address the varied and distinct problems Roma face throughout Slovenia. However, there are several serious drawbacks to a system that devolves most of the programming decisions to local authorities.

With no central oversight, there is no comprehensive system of evaluation. This hampers the transfer of knowledge, both of successful projects and best practices, and of problems encountered in implementation. The tender system controlled by the individual ministries and driven by the annual budget process also fails to create incentives for longer-term projects. Where problems with implementation are encountered, the entire project may be abandoned rather than examining the cause of projects' weaknesses and making adjustments as needed. Disbursing funding through an expert body could be more conducive to building institutional knowledge and modifying under-performing programmes to increase efficacy.

Such problems could also be reduced if greater emphasis was placed on consultations with Roma organisations and representatives. Projects where such consultation has taken place appear more successful and durable than those elaborated by local authorities alone, who may be more focused on meeting the needs of the municipality than the needs of the Roma community. Poorly targeted projects offer few obvious benefits to the target group and fail to encourage a long-term shift away from dependence on social welfare or other forms of State support. There are especially few projects designed to increase women's capacity to enter the workforce, as most of the public works projects established are directed at men.

Municipal bodies, such as the Institute for Education and Culture and local centres for social welfare have initiated valuable and productive projects to assist Roma, in many cases in partnership with local authorities. However, some officials still hold discriminatory attitudes, undermining good working relations with Roma groups in those municipalities. More efforts are needed to educate authorities, particularly those working in areas with substantial Roma populations, to reduce prejudice and improve understanding of Roma needs and issues. Tolerance promotion programmes focusing on the Roma should also target the general public.

Much has already been done to address the problems confronting Roma communities in Slovenia. Further progress could be more effectively achieved if the many diverse approaches, both successful and less so, are drawn together to construct a more cohesive strategy. The importance of local decision-making should be balanced against the need for the expertise, capacity, and authority of a Government-level body. This would help to ensure that efforts are not misdirected, and expectations are fulfilled.

5. Recommendations

- A Government level-body should be authorised to oversee implementation of the Government programmes for Roma, to coordinate funding, evaluation, and reporting activities at the State level.

- The Parliament should allocate a set sum of money to Roma programmes in the annual budget, as is the case for the Italian and Hungarian minorities.

- A dedicated body, rather than individual ministries, should oversee the tender procedures for projects to implement the Government programmes.

- Ministries or other bodies offering funding should clearly indicate which tenders are issued for projects under the Government programmes for Roma.

- A single law should be elaborated to specify the rights of the Roma minority.

- Roma should have the option to declare their ethnic identity on the census.

- Training should be available for public officials working with Roma to increase awareness of the specific needs and concerns of the Roma community.

- Roma public participation should be enhanced through support to the election and training of councillors in relevant municipalities.